ALFONSO
LOPEZ

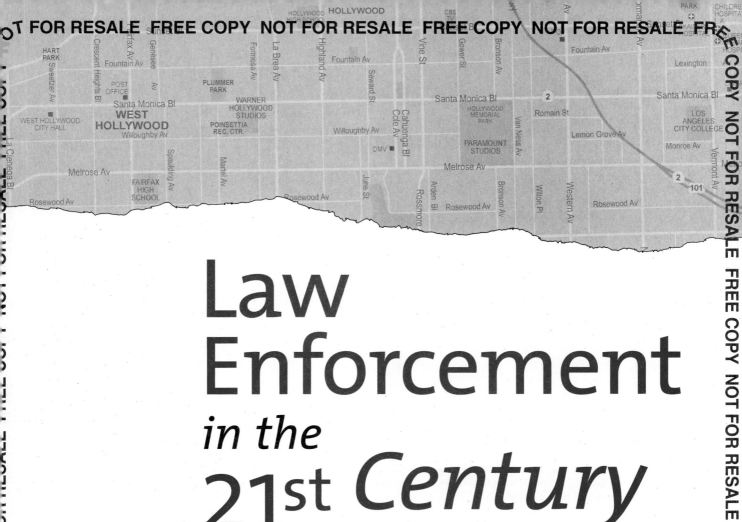

Law Enforcement
in the
21st *Century*

Heath B. Grant
John Jay College of Criminal Justice

Karen J. Terry
John Jay College of Criminal Justice

PEARSON

Boston　New York　San Francisco

Mexico City　Montreal　Toronto　London　Madrid　Munich　Paris

Hong Kong　Singapore　Tokyo　Cape Town　Sydney

Series Editor: *Jennifer Jacobson*
Editorial Assistant: *Emma Christensen*
Marketing Manager: *Krista Groshong*
Editorial Production Administrator: *Anna Socrates*
Editorial–Production Service: *Martha White Tenney*
Composition and Prepress Buyer: *Linda Cox*
Manufacturing Buyer: *JoAnne Sweeney*
Cover Administrator: *Linda Knowles*
Interior Design: *Carol Somberg*
Photo Research: *Katharine S. Cook*
Electronic Composition: *Modern Graphics, Inc.*

For related titles and support materials, visit our online catalog at www.ablongman.com.

Between the time Web site information is gathered and then published, it is not unusual for some sites to have closed. Also, the transcription of URLs can result in unintended typographical errors. The publisher would appreciate notification where these errors occur so that they may be corrected in subsequent editions.

Library of Congress Cataloging-in-Publication Data

Grant, Heath.
    Law enforcement in the 21st century/ Heath Grant, Karen Terry.
      p. cm.
    Includes bibliographical references and index.
    ISBN 0-205-33633-7
    1. Police—United States. 2. Law enforcement—United States.   I. Title: Law enforcement in the twenty-first century. II. Terry, Karen J. III. Title.

HV8139.G72 2004
363.2′0973—dc22

2004041489

ISBN: 0-205-33633-7

Printed in the United States of America
10 9 8 7 6 5 4 3 2 1   VHP   09 08 07 06 05 04

Photo credits appear on p. 439, which constitutes an extension of the copyright page.

Brief CONTENTS

CONTENTS

PART ONE

LAW ENFORCEMENT AND THE CRIMINAL JUSTICE SYSTEM

Chapter 1
Law Enforcement in a Democratic Society   2

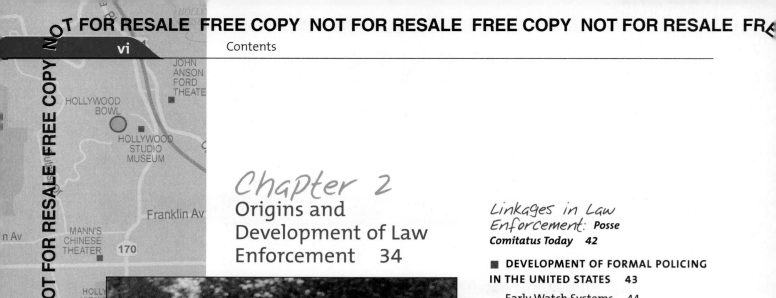

Chapter 3
Traditional Policing and Police Professionalization 58

Chapter 4
Law Enforcement and the Law 80

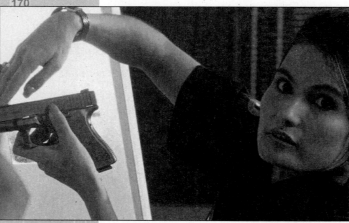

PART TWO

LAW ENFORCEMENT ORGANIZATIONS AND OPERATIONS

Chapter 5
Policing Functions and Units 108

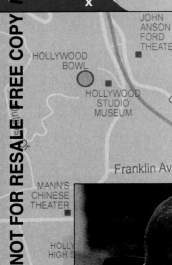

Chapter 6
Patrol and Traffic   140

Chapter 7
Search and Seizure, Arrest, and Interrogation 166

Chapter 8
Investigation
and Evidence
Collection   190

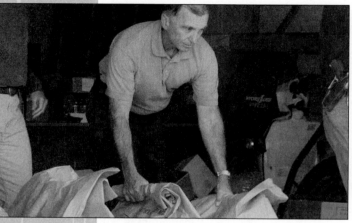

PART THREE

POLICE CONDUCT

Chapter 9
Police Discretion and Behavior 212

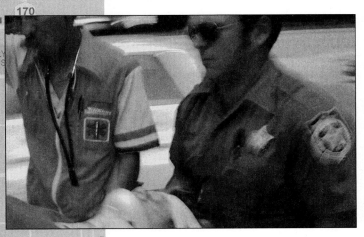

Chapter 10
Policing Multicultural Communities   240

Chapter 11
Policing the Police   262

PART FOUR

THE 21st CENTURY LAW ENFORCEMENT OFFICER

Chapter 12
Community Policing and Problem Solving 288

Chapter 13
Advances in Policing— New Technologies for Crime Analysis   322

Linkages IN LAW ENFORCEMENT FEATURES

PREFACE

Law Enforcement in the 21st Century is the first book to examine the "linkage blindness" in the criminal justice system—the lack of connection between theories of policing and what actually happens in police departments. The text makes linkages between theory and police practice through problem-solving and crime mapping applications.

At the time the authors conceived of *Law Enforcement in the 21st Century*, the intention was to present a fresh, new approach to presenting introductory law enforcement material in a way that could be both practical for the future law enforcement officer and intellectually rewarding for the reader entering a whole new field of study. To meet these two important needs, the text provides a comprehensive overview of research and practice. In response to many challenges facing law enforcement in a post-911 world, all material is presented within the context of several important themes:

- The need for information-sharing across law enforcement and other criminal justice agencies is a core theme from the first to the last chapter of the text.

- The text focuses on linkages between law enforcement strategies and the causes of crime.

- The impact of terrorism on the field is woven throughout the chapters, including areas such as major re-organization efforts currently underway in government, constitutional implications of the war on terror, and technology developments.

- The text constantly seeks to engage the reader in critically thinking around the role of law enforcement within these changed global contexts, and the extent to which public security interests themselves should and/or do outweigh the personal liberties we also value so strongly as a society.

Developmental Presentation of the Course Material

Rather than the standard presentation of the material, this text is organized in a developmental framework.

- Part I introduces readers to law enforcement's place within the criminal justice system, the origins of policing as a profession, and traditional models of policing.

- Part II covers core aspects of police work, such as organizational structure and units, field operations, and investigations.

- Part III discusses major challenges in policing, including discussions of corruption and use of force, discretion, and multicultural policing.

- Part IV includes an expansive overview of community policing and important new technological applications that are currently transforming the nature of law enforcement. The authors then look ahead to proactive strategy development in a practical way with specific case examples, as well as theoretical insights, woven throughout.

Thematic Pedagogy

The authors recognize the importance of making the material clear for the reader. Each chapter begins with a **Chapter Outline** that provides an overview of what is to come. **Chapter Objectives** lay out the specific goals for each chapter, and an **Introduction** grabs readers' attention.

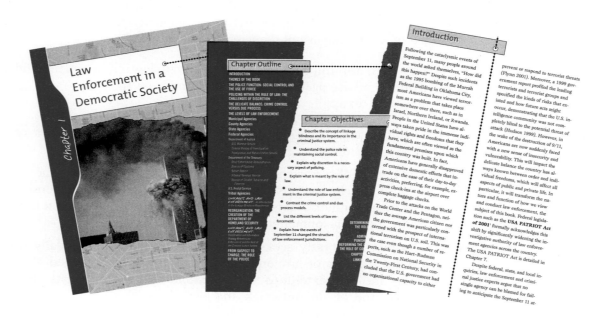

Practical applications and case examples are used to introduce new material and make abstract concepts understandable. The book's **Linkages in Law Enforcement** text boxes highlight the book's central themes of inter- and intra-agency sharing, balancing public safety and individual interests, and proactive strategy developments. Practical applications related to the war on terrorism are emphasized in the linkage boxes. These practical and concrete exercises in every chapter challenge the reader to relate current material to earlier concepts, reinforcing the text's developmental emphasis.

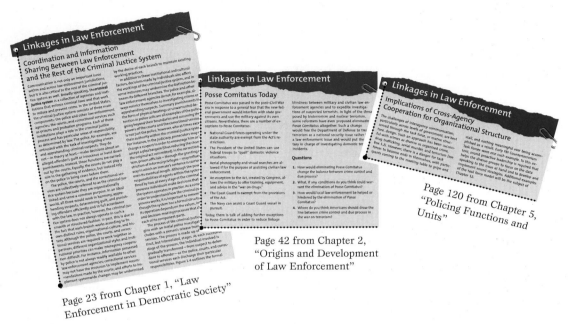

Page 23 from Chapter 1, "Law Enforcement in Democratic Society"

Page 42 from Chapter 2, "Origins and Development of Law Enforcement"

Page 120 from Chapter 5, "Policing Functions and Units"

At the end of each chapter, a **Chapter Summary** provides a recap of the key points. A list of **Key Terms** follows that includes the page reference where the terms was introduced and defined.

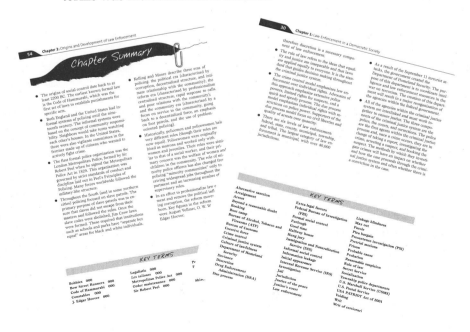

Linking the Dots exercises at the end of each chapter challenge the reader to relate current material to earlier concepts. These exercises provide yet another opportunity for readers to build their knowledge and to make connections.

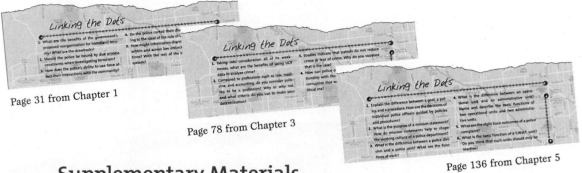

Page 31 from Chapter 1

Page 78 from Chapter 3

Page 136 from Chapter 5

Supplementary Materials

Instructor's Resource Manual and Test Bank

This invaluable instructor resource includes the following tools for each chapter: the chapter-opening and chapter-ending pedagogy from the text for quick and easy reference; instructional ideas and aids; lecture launches and discussion topics; sample syllabi; handouts, and activities.

TestGen EQ Computerized Test Bank

This computerized version of the test bank is available with Tamarack's easy-to-use TestGen software, which lets you prepare tests for printing as well for network and online testing. Full editing capability for Windows and Macintosh is available.

PowerPoint Lecture Presentations

With approximately 15-25 slides per chapter, these PowerPoint lecture presentations help guide your lectures.

Companion Web Site

An online study guide available for free at www.ablongman.com/grant1e offers students quizzing opportunities.

GIS and Crime Mapping Software

Available with *Law Enforcement in the 21st Century,* this crime mapping software in a Windows-friendly format allows researchers and analysts to provide visual representations of any data format (i.e. crimes, demographics, etc.) that can be married to a spatial data format. For example, one could look at a visual representation of all registered sex offenders in an area, by all child day care centers, schools, parks etc. Such discussions are woven into the text, and are especially relevant to Chapter 12. Visit www.ablongman.com/grant1e for more information on how to make this software available for your students or contact your Publisher's Representative.

ACKNOWLEDGMENTS

We would like to thank each of the reviewers of this text who helped us shape its development to meet our goal of providing a fresh way to present introductory law enforcement material that accounts for the many significant changes to the field over the past few years. These include James W. Billings, Jr., University of Southern Colorado; Robert Lee Edwards, Independent Judicial Commission-Bosnia; Harold A. Frossard, Moraine Valley Community College; Jack Gillen, Florida Southern College; Robert E. Grubb, Marshall University; William E. Kelly, Auburn University; Harvey Kushner, Long Island University; William E. Lanning, Guilford Technical Community College; Deborah L. Laufersweiler-Dwyer, University of Arkansas, Little Rock; Sharon Redhawk Love, The Penn State University; Robert W. McKenna, Roger Williams University; Susan V. Pons, Guilford Technical Community College; Chester L. Quarles, University of Mississippi; Jo Ann M. Scott, Ohio Northern University; Ivan Y. Sun, Old Dominion University; Devere Woods, Indiana State University; Kevin C. Woods, Becker College; and Jihong Zhao, University of Nebraska at Omaha.

The authors would like to thank our colleagues in the Department of Law, Police Science, and Criminal Justice Administration at John Jay College of Criminal Justice who were always available to bounce around ideas, or offer valuable insights and information. In particular, two professors in the department deserve special mention. Dorothy Schultz was invaluable to this effort from its outset, dedicating her time to reviewing and offering needed changes to our original draft proposal. Throughout the writing process, Bob Panzarella also requires special mention as the source of information ranging from important historical details needing inclusion to suggestions for innovative application of standard materials. Dennis Kenney and John Kleinig also played an important support role to the authors that helped to make the difficult process of writing an introductory text a rewarding journey. Heath Grant would also like to thank David Sheppard for the mentorship early in his career that helped to shape future directions and perspectives that can be found throughout this text.

No major effort can be undertaken without the support of family and friends, and to this end the authors would like to thank the following individuals (in no particular order): Lisa Goold, Lorna Davidson, Venezia Michalsen, Rene Goodstein, Mark Bernard, Roy Godson, and Steve Perreault.

We also would like to thank our former chair, Robert McCrie, for his support when this project began, and current chair, Maki Haberfeld, for always being someone on whom we can rely. Finally, this effort began with the collaboration of Benjamin Goold, and we would like to acknowledge our appreciation of his assistance, friendship, and significant contributions to the writing of Chapters 5, 9, and 10, as well as his great efforts in copyediting early drafts of this work.

Chapter 1

Law Enforcement in a Democratic Society

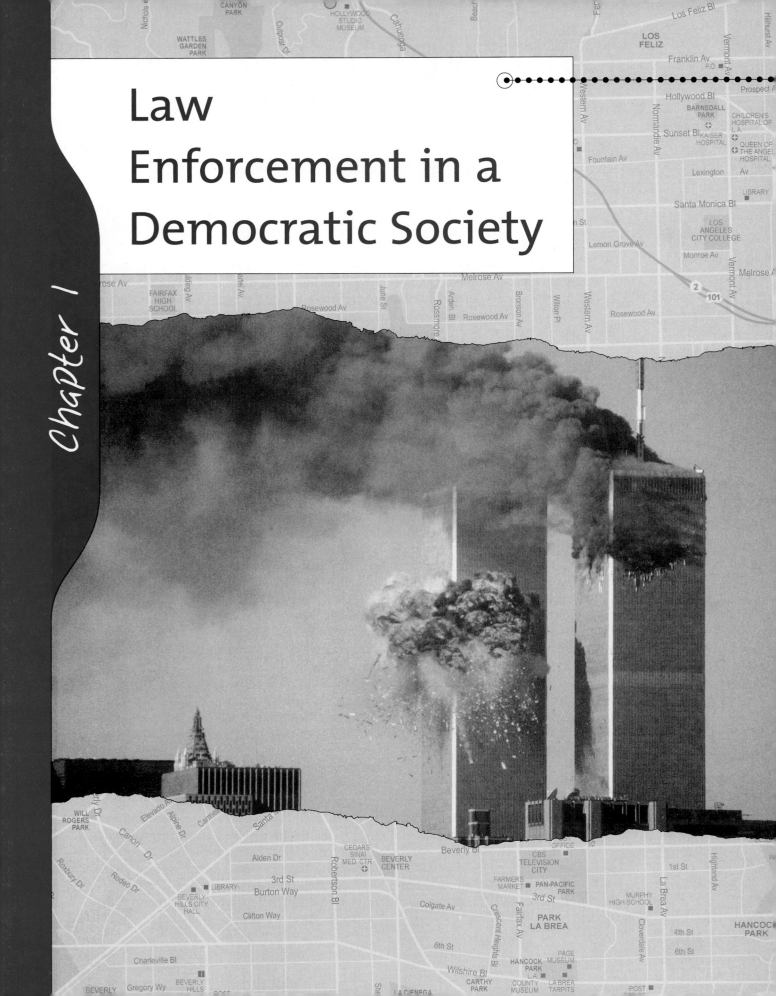

Chapter Outline

Chapter Objectives

● Describe the concept of linkage blindness and its importance in the criminal justice system.

● Understand the police role in maintaining social control.

● Explain why discretion is a necessary aspect of policing.

● Explain what is meant by the rule of law.

● Understand the role of law enforcement in the criminal justice system.

● Contrast the crime control and due process models.

● List the different levels of law enforcement.

● Explain how the events of September 11 changed the structure of law enforcement jurisdictions.

Introduction

Following the cataclysmic events of September 11, many people around the world asked themselves, "How did this happen?" Despite such incidents as the 1995 bombing of the Murrah Federal Building in Oklahoma City, most Americans have viewed terrorism as a problem that takes place somewhere over there, such as in Israel, Northern Ireland, or Rwanda. People in the United States have always taken pride in the immense individual rights and freedoms that they have, which are often viewed as the fundamental premises upon which this country was built. In fact, Americans have generally disapproved of extensive domestic efforts that intrude on the ease of their day-to-day activities, preferring, for example, express check-ins at the airport over complete baggage checks.

Prior to the attacks on the World Trade Center and the Pentagon, neither the average American citizen nor the government was particularly concerned with the prospect of international terrorism on U.S. soil. This was the case even though a number of reports, such as the Hart–Rudman Commission on National Security in the Twenty-First Century, had concluded that the U.S. government had no organizational capacity to either prevent or respond to terrorist threats (Flynn 2001).

Moreover, a 1999 government report profiled the leading terrorists and terrorist groups and specified the kinds of risks that existed and how future acts might occur, demonstrating that the U.S. intelligence community was not completely blind to the potential threat of attack (Hudson 1999). However, in the wake of the destruction of 9/11, Americans are now suddenly faced with a new sense of insecurity and vulnerability. This will impact the delicate balance the country has always known between order and individual freedoms, which will affect all aspects of public and private life. In particular, it will transform the nature and function of how we view and conduct law enforcement, the subject of this book. Federal legislation such as the **USA PATRIOT Act of 2001**[1] formally acknowledges this shift by significantly widening the investigative authority of law enforcement agencies across the country. The USA PATRIOT Act is detailed in Chapter 7. (An abridged version is found in Appendix C.)

Despite federal, state, and local inquiries, law enforcement and criminal justice experts argue that no single agency can be blamed for failing to anticipate the September 11 attacks. Given the complexity of both the intelligence and law enforcement communities and their many overlapping jurisdictions, it was inevitable that key information would slip through the cracks between agencies. The inability to analyze and link critical information across agencies (or even within an agency) is referred to as **linkage blindness**, which will be a major theme in this book. Flynn (2001) provides a useful illustration of this critical law enforcement problem, referring to the arrival of a hypothetical ship carrying questionable cargo and a crew on an intelligence watch list for potential terrorist ties:

The Coast Guard would be likely to know about the scheduled arrival of a tanker carrying hazardous cargo. The Customs Service might have some advance cargo manifest information. The INS might or might not know much about the crew, depending on the kinds of visas the sailors are holding and the timeliness with which the shipping crew faxed the crew list. None of the frontline inspectors in these agencies, meanwhile, are likely to have access to national security intelligence from the Federal Bureau of Investigation or the Central Intelligence Agency. (p. 190)

Because of the elusive nature of terrorism and the apparent ease with which a terrorist can slip through the country's borders, there is a movement for law enforcement investigative authority to shift from federal to local agencies. The attacks on September 11 proved that even with a threat of transnational origins, the frontline responders to an attack are the local law enforcement and fire departments. Thus, terrorism is not simply within the domain of the federal government and the military. What has been exposed is the need to build adequate mechanisms of information sharing across levels of government in an area that is traditionally rife with issues of territoriality and rivalry. This need has led to the formation of the Department of Homeland Security, representing the largest government reorganization in over fifty years.

Themes of the Book

Many myths and stereotypes surround policing, such as the ever-prevalent image of law enforcement officers as crime-fighters engaging in a "war on crime" (Bitner 1980). However, the average officer rarely makes a felony arrest, and most do not ever fire their firearms during the course of their career. However, by definition, the term **law enforcement** suggests that central to the role of the police is the function of enforcing the existing legislation or rules of society. This rather simplistic view of law enforcement ignores the tremendous complexities in agencies, missions, and functions across different levels of government (federal, state, and local) or jurisdiction in the United States. More importantly, such a definition fails to take into account the evolving nature of policing as a strategy (Kelling and Moore 1989). This book explores the changing dynamics and nature of policing within its larger contexts. Although the terms are used interchangeably on occasion, the emphasis on *law enforcement* as opposed to *policing* reflects the larger scope and focus of this book.

A central theme of this text is the linkages across law enforcement jurisdictions and the struggle to develop a coordinated approach to information-sharing and strategy development in the face of any crime, including terrorism. Additionally, the text explains the connections between law enforcement and the rest of the criminal justice system. Moreover, the importance of information sharing and collaboration across the criminal justice system agencies (and thus the relevance of linkage blindness in this context as well) are also woven throughout relevant chapters of the text. New technologies to combat linkage blindness are highlighted in Chapter 13.

Another theme of this text is the changing nature of policing throughout its history, highlighting the movement from reactive to proactive management models. A major philosophical and practical shift in the field of law enforcement came when Herman Goldstein pioneered problem-oriented policing (Goldstein 1979). Law enforcement agencies continue to use the principle of problem solving today with community-oriented policing approaches that attempt to address quality of life concerns. These central elements of problem solving and proactive policing relate underlying causes to strategy, yet another theme revisited throughout the text.

This book is divided into four sections. The first section of the book lays out the framework of the law enforcement field for the reader, establishing common definitions and tracing the origins and developments of the field up to the end of the professionalization movement.

The second section of the book presents the more traditional functions and operations of law enforcement (i.e., structure and operations) in a way that prepares the reader

Although not a new issue, the necessity of communication across all levels of law enforcement (federal, state, and local) became all too apparent following the tragic events of 9/11. Coordination and collaboration with respect to homeland security needs to occur both before and immediately after a terrorist attack. Recognition of this fact has led to the formation of the Department of Homeland Security.

to understand evolving policing models and demands. The legal underpinnings of police work briefly introduced in the first section will be expanded here, with particular attention to the challenges to precedents evident in terrorism-related legislation, such as the USA PATRIOT Act of 2001.

The third section of the text examines challenges to policing, such as the role of discretion and the demands of policing minority communities. Special attention is paid here to changing demographics, as well as the impacts of a post–September 11 world.

The reader is thus exposed to the major issues, challenges, and functions of policing in a developmental manner. The final section challenges readers to analyze future directions and trends in law enforcement.

Throughout the text, interactive boxes aptly named Linkages and Law Enforcement will challenge readers to relate concepts and issues being learned in a current chapter to earlier material or current events, thereby encouraging the developmental learning approach of the book. One of the major themes examined by Linkages and Law Enforcement is the challenges of balancing public safety with individual freedoms or due process.

The Police Function: Social Control and the Use of Force

Most of us are relatively familiar with the general operations of the three major components of the criminal justice process—police, courts, and corrections—as well as the important roles of federal and state governments in creating and modifying laws through the legislative process. What we are often unable to answer, however, is what it is about these institutions that enables them to function as agents of social control. How are they able to achieve order in society?

Informal social control refers to the influences of parents, families, peers, and the community in training individuals about the norms, rules, and customs of a locality in an attempt to compel conformity (this process is also called **socialization**). Informal social control occurs when the influential party reacts to **deviance**, or violations of social rules. Deviance can refer to a range of actions; from something minor such as dyeing one's hair all the way up to acts of murder and rape (see Figure 1.1). Once an act of deviance occurs in which a law is broken, as in the case of murder, it is the responsibility of

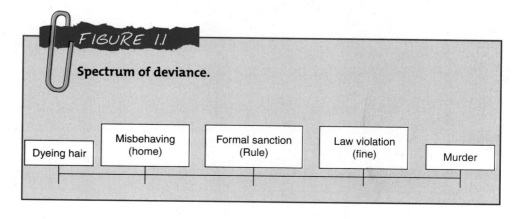

FIGURE 1.1

Spectrum of deviance.

| Dyeing hair | Misbehaving (home) | Formal sanction (Rule) | Law violation (fine) | Murder |

formal social control agents, such as law enforcement officers, to enforce its violation.

Many criminal justice practitioners and scholars have argued that the use of force is the principal way in which order is achieved in society. "Institutions of law and government maintain order and control deviant behavior primarily through force, through the forcible apprehension and incarceration of others" (Eisenhower 1970, p. 6). Law enforcement is generally at the forefront of our minds when it comes to the application of force and apprehension.

According to Manning (1977), policing literally means "controlling, monitoring, tracking, and altering, if required, public conduct" (p. 27). Given the many competing expectations of the police, Klockars (1985) has argued that the meaning of police can be found in what they are supposed to do, rather than on what exactly is done in a given situation. An officer writing traffic citations is still a police officer, as is an officer speaking at a community meeting. To Klockars (1985), the core of policing is identified by its relation to the potential use of force.

But in the examples just given (i.e., traffic citation, community meeting), force is not an element of the policing function. How then can **coercive force** be the defining feature of policing? Bittner's (1970) classic work on policing argues that it is the fact that police are authorized to use force in a number of social situations in response to a variety of social problems that forms the basis of our interactions with police.

Returning to our examples, although a citizen may be equally capable of writing traffic citations, only a police officer will be able to force an individual to be compliant if necessary, such as if a vehicle's operator fails to pull over.

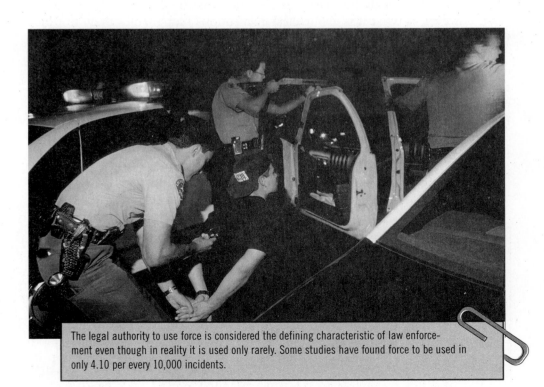

The legal authority to use force is considered the defining characteristic of law enforcement even though in reality it is used only rarely. Some studies have found force to be used in only 4.10 per every 10,000 incidents.

Similarly, community residents often involve the police in community meetings that discuss even minor quality of life issues (i.e., noise disturbances, littering, etc.), because the police will ultimately be able to resort to force if all other options of problem resolution are unsuccessful.

However, although the importance of force in defining the process of policing is clear, policing alone cannot achieve the public order to which police are often held accountable. Because the police cannot possibly be omnipresent, enforcing all deviations from the law, there must also be both a commitment and willingness on the part of the majority of citizens to respect the laws and institutions of society. Without this **culture of lawfulness**, law enforcement would be inundated and unable to carry out its functions effectively (Godson 2000). To achieve this, the average citizen must recognize the legitimacy of the law and its enforcement as an effective means of controlling the behavior of all members of society, from the richest government official to the poorest laborer. Much of this respect will come from the degree to which the government operates within the rule of law and the extent to which decisions are not arbitrarily made at the hands of its officials or enforcers, a topic we turn to now.

Policing Within the Rule of Law: The Challenges of Discretion

Agents at every level of the criminal justice system have a significant level of individual **discretion**, but this is particularly true of law enforcement officers. Agents are said to have discretion when they have the freedom to make decisions—legal or otherwise—based on their own judgment and are not simply bound by formal, inflexible rules. It was in the 1950s, when the American Bar Foundation (ABF) conducted the first field observations of police work, that the central role of discretion in law enforcement was first "discovered" (Walker 1992). Many studies have since validated the significance of discretion in the criminal justice system, but at no point has it ever been officially "recognized" with legislation acknowledging its functional role in police decision making.

Matters such as arrest and charge are, for example, subject to varying degrees of police discretion, as are issues relating to the collection and presentation of evidence. There is no "official" training on how to use discretion, but merely legal factors to guide its use in some instances. For the most part, this discretion exists to ensure that agents within the criminal justice system are free to respond to the particular circumstances and challenges presented by each new case and each new crime. Because each offense is different, flexibility is needed to ensure that justice prevails. Moreover, there is no possible way for an officer to enforce every violation that he or she encounters, making discretion a practical and necessary reality in law enforcement.

In many instances, however, the decisions of individual police officers are not transparent or open to scrutiny. The police are not monitored twenty-four hours a day or required to justify themselves every time they stop someone on the street or in their car. As a consequence, there is a danger that agents within the criminal justice system may make decisions that are not in full accordance with the law or that infringe on the rights of suspects, offenders, or prisoners.

How can we be sure then that two individuals who committed the same crime would not be treated differently because they were caught by different officers or because of **extra-legal factors** (those outside of the legal parameters of an offense) such as differences in skin color or socioeconomic status? It is because of the perception of inequality in law enforcement that discretion can play a divisive role in the community. Discretion can be the result of numerous community, organizational, and individual influences outside of the formal legal codes, a subject to which we will return in Chapter 9.

Although there is no simple way to ensure that discretion is exercised fairly in each and every case, decisions made by individuals within the criminal justice system are meant to be governed by a set of ideals known as the **rule of law**. Developed over many years through case law, statutes, and scholarly writings, the rule of law can be simply stated as follows (National Strategy Information Center 1999):

- All people in society have the opportunity to participate in establishing the law;

- The rules apply equally to everyone; and

- The rules protect individuals as well as society.

Historically, the rule of law was developed in an effort to constrain kings and rulers who regarded themselves as above the law, and at its heart is a commitment to the fundamental idea that equality before the law and justice are inseparable. Regardless of their position or responsibilities, all agents within the criminal justice system are bound by the rule of law, and they are required to exercise their discretion according to the limits it prescribes. Of course, in practice, not every decision meets the high standards required by the rule of law. Much of its significance, however, derives from its status as an *ideal*; it is a standard that guides individuals and agencies within the system, and which—in theory at least—binds them together through a shared commitment to justice and the law.

The Delicate Balance: Crime Control Versus Due Process

Although the "delicate balance" between public safety and individual freedoms has always been a struggle for law enforcement, these issues are particularly salient in the post–September 11 climate. During a lecture immediately following the September 11 attacks, U.S. Supreme Court Justice Sandra Day O'Connor remarked that, "We're likely to experience more restrictions on our personal freedom than has ever been the case in this country" (Greenhouse 2001, B5). Despite protestations otherwise by Attorney General John Ashcroft that "We'll not be driven to abandon our freedoms by those who would seek to destroy them," some individuals are afraid of the potential "slippery slope" of giving expansive powers to law enforcement (Hentoff 2001).

One of the most influential frameworks for explaining the differing views and values of justice has been the crime control/due process model first expounded upon by the sociologist Herbert Packer in the mid-1960s. According to Packer (1968), agents within the criminal justice system can be broadly divided into two camps depending on the strength of their support for either strong law enforcement or protection of civil liberties. For those who see the criminal justice system in terms of **crime control,** the overriding aim is to ensure that suspects are processed as quickly and efficiently as possible. Typically, advocates of this approach emphasize the importance of attempting to distinguish between the innocent and the guilty at the precharge stage. Though the adversarial system is formally based on the assumption that an individual is innocent until proven guilty, advocates of the crime control model assume that once a suspect has been formally charged, he or she can be processed on the basis of an informal "presumption of guilt." Guilty pleas are preferred to lengthy hearings and trials, and informal methods of disposal are preferred over legalistic procedures. Perhaps unsurprisingly, the police and other law enforcement agencies are the most vocal supporters of a crime control approach to criminal justice. Extensive police powers, limited rights for suspects, and greater emphasis on pretrial processes are all seen as vital to the effective functioning of the system. The danger lies in the extent to which this favoring of crime control undermines the rule of law, and thus potentially the legitimacy of law enforcement and the criminal justice system in society (Skolnick 1994).

In contrast, supporters of a **due process** approach argue that the criminal justice system must strive to protect the rights of the innocent and ensure that only the guilty are punished. Although recognizing that the primary aim of the system is to reduce and prevent crime, adherents to the due process model maintain that safeguards are necessary to protect individual rights and to ensure that the number of wrongful convictions is kept to a minimum. "Better that ten guilty men go free than one innocent man be punished" is an idea that is central to the due process approach. Advocates of this model favor considerable restrictions on policing, are suspicious of informal processes, and view the criminal trial as the most reliable method of determining guilt. With the due process model, the civil rights and liberties of citizens outweigh the information needs of law enforcement. Key features of both models are summarized in Table 1.1.

Historically, there has been considerable tension between these two different approaches to crime and the criminal justice process. During the 1960s, the Civil Rights movement helped to increase public awareness of individual rights and placed considerable pressure on the criminal justice system to expand basic due process protections. Responding to the mood of the times, the Supreme Court under Justice Warren—in cases such as *Escobedo v. Illinois* (1964),[2] *Miranda v. Arizona* (1966),[3] and *Terry v. Ohio* (1968)[4]—moved to restrict the powers of the police and emphasized the need for the criminal justice system to recognize and protect the rights of suspects. Due process concerns were also addressed in the landmark case of *Gideon v. Wainwright* (1963),[5] which extended the right to counsel to indigent individuals who would otherwise have been unable to exercise their Sixth Amendment rights.

As crime rates began to rise through the 1970s and 1980s, however, there was a gradual but significant shift towards an emphasis on crime control. Although the largest increase in crime was for the possession and sale of drugs, the rate of serious violent crime—including murder, rape, and robbery—also increased dramatically during this period. In the eyes of many policy makers and

TABLE 1.1

Key Features of the Crime Control and Due Process Models

Crime Control Model	Due Process Model
• Suppression of crime is the overriding aim of the criminal justice system.	• Justice and fairness are the overriding aims of the criminal justice system.
• Cases need to be disposed of quickly and efficiently, even if this means ignoring the rights of suspects.	• Cases need to be dealt with according to formal procedures that protect the rights of suspects.
• Emphasis is on pretrial processes and guilty pleas.	• Emphasis is on the trial process and the determination of legal guilt.
• Authority of the criminal justice system derives from the legislature.	• Authority of the criminal justice system derives from the judiciary.

the general public, the criminal justice system was clearly failing. Proponents of the crime control model argued that the rise in crime was the direct result of an overemphasis on suspects' rights and called for increased police powers and an easing of due process restrictions on law enforcement agencies.

Throughout the 1990s, the crime control model continued to dominate policy making in the United States. Mandatory sentencing for repeat offenders, zero-tolerance policing, and the gradual lowering of the age of criminal responsibility for juveniles all grew out of a desire to make the criminal justice system more efficient and effective. At the same time that these new policies were being promoted, however, several high-profile incidents of police brutality,[6] police corruption,[7] and racial profiling[8] helped to remind the public of the need for due process protections and respect for civil liberties.

At the beginning of the twenty-first century, crime control values still prevail, yet there is a continuing tension between the two models first identified by Packer in the 1960s. In light of the past fifty years of criminal justice history, as well as the United States' newfound war on terrorism, there can be little doubt that the struggle between advocates of crime control and due process will continue to shape the development of criminal justice policy throughout the coming century.

The Levels of Law Enforcement

The current system of law enforcement in the United States is as complex as it is varied, in many ways reflecting the tensions between the crime control and due process models, as well as an overriding fear of too much power being placed in the hands of a centralized, federal law enforcement entity. Representing the largest segment of the criminal justice system with over one million employees in 1996 (Reaves and Goldberg 1998), contemporary law enforcement agencies operate on a variety of levels within local, state, and federal **jurisdictions**, or areas of responsibility. Although the boundaries across these levels would appear to be straightforward in that each enforces the laws of their respective level, in practice the boundaries are often more of a gray tint than a black and white tone. There is no direct order of authority with respect to these jurisdictions. For example, in most cases, federal law enforcement cannot exert authority over local matters unless requested to do so by local authorities. Each level of law enforcement has its own jurisdiction. These difficulties are, of course, further fueled by the territorial nature of many law enforcement agencies.

Municipal Agencies

The United States had 13,524 municipal police jurisdictions in 1999 (Bureau of Justice Statistics 2001), varying in size from large city departments [e.g., New York City Police Department with 39,099 officers in 1999 (Bureau of Justice Statistics 2000)] to local departments of one or two officers (the majority). In 1999, there were 487 municipal police departments with more than 100 or more full-time sworn personnel, but of these, only 51 (10.5 percent) had 1,000 or more full-time sworn personnel that included 500 or more officers responding to calls for service (Bureau of Justice Statistics 2000). Thus, despite the images we are used to in the media of the nature of policing, most departments have a small number of officers who have jurisdiction over largely rural or suburban landscapes.

Municipal police departments unquestionably represent the greatest number of law enforcement officers in the United States and will thus be the primary focus of this text. In 1999, large municipal police departments (those with at least 100 officers) employed 306,560 full-time employees, compared with 30,751 in county departments, 136,616 in sheriff's departments, and 85,442 in state law enforcement agencies (Bureau of Justice Statistics 2000).

Large local law enforcement agencies are more often responsible for investigating serious violent and property crimes in their jurisdiction, compared with half of state agencies (Bureau of Justice Statistics 2000). Local agencies are also more likely to handle fingerprint processing (81 percent); however, state agencies often provide needed support for crime lab services and ballistic testing (Bureau of Justice Statistics 2000).

The city government is usually responsible for appointing a police chief, who is responsible for running the department with general law enforcement authority within the city's boundaries. Most police chiefs are appointed at the discretion of the mayor or city manager and lack contract provisions that protect them from unjustified termination. As a result, the average tenure of most police chiefs is only three to six years (Swanson et al. 2001).

Although similar in nature to municipal police departments, **township police departments** can vary greatly in their level of law enforcement powers and authority. Well-developed townships often operate with responsibilities close to that of municipal police departments. The United States has approximately 19,000 township police departments (Bureau of Justice Statistics 2000).

County Agencies

Although the primary agency at the county level is the sheriff's office, with 3,070 sheriff's departments across the country (Bureau of Justice Statistics 2003), in some jurisdictions this office has been dissolved into a county police force that functions much the same as the municipal police. County police departments usually surface in areas where the workload is too large for the sheriff's department. The local contexts greatly influence the nature and scope of responsibilities for the sheriff's departments. In some jurisdictions, the sheriff's office is entirely law-enforcement focused, with no other responsibilities, whereas in others, its principle responsibilities involve carrying out court orders and summonses or operating the county jail. The majority of sheriff's departments involve some combination of all three responsibilities (Brown 1979). In large cities with populations of over one million, the sheriff's office often only serves correctional functions. In contrast, those serving very small populations generally are the chief law enforcement agents of that jurisdiction (Senna and Siegel 2001).

In all but two states, sheriffs are elected to their positions for two- to four-year terms. Because the sheriff is elected, the office has a greater degree of freedom from local city officials than that of the police chief, who is appointed by a mayor or city manager. However, because it is an elected term, additional forms of accountability and scrutiny can transform the dynamics of the role.

In some jurisdictions, there are courts at the county level that maintain limited jurisdiction as described by statute over civil matters, such as the performance of marriages and trials for minor criminal offenses. Referred to as **justice's courts**, they are under the responsibility of **justices of the peace**, or magistrates of lesser rank than in the higher courts. It should be noted, however, that the trend has been to dissolve the justice's courts and transfer their power to other municipal courts of limited jurisdiction (Nolan and Nolan-Haley 1990).

State Agencies

Many states have police agencies in addition to agencies within specific municipalities, townships, or counties. The first state to establish a police agency was Texas in 1835, with the creation of the Texas Rangers. Massachusetts implemented a state police agency shortly thereafter in 1865, which is often credited as being the first modern state law enforcement agency. The state agency in Pennsylvania is credited with being a model agency for other states, and was viewed as the archetype of modern policing when it was created in 1905.

The power of most state agencies includes the ability to arrest an individual for an offense committed in the presence of the officer, as well as the ability to execute a search warrant. In addition to the state police, some states have established a highway patrol with jurisdiction over all traffic laws on interstate roads. These patrols have the authority to enforce all traffic laws as well as to investigate traffic accidents on highways and freeways. The only state without a state law enforcement agency today is Hawaii.

Federal Agencies

The first federal agency to be established by the U.S. government was the U.S. Marshal Service, which was founded in 1789. Since that time, the U.S. government has created nine additional government departments (with the addition of the Department of Homeland Security discussed below) with twenty-one agencies to deal with issues of law enforcement. Additionally, several of these nine departments contain dozens of smaller offices and bureaus. It is important to note that federal agencies only have the power to enforce federal laws and mandates. The Attorney General, for example, cannot simply call a governor to dictate a certain policy to the state's police unless there has been a constitutional violation of some kind. The Tenth Amendment of the Constitution gives local law enforcement agencies power over local matters. The two federal departments that are most involved in law enforcement are the Department of Justice and the Department of the Treasury, and are the focus of discussion here. However, other federal departments (i.e., the Food and Drug Administration) also have certain law enforcement functions within their mandates.

Department of Justice   The Department of Justice (DOJ) was established in June 1870 and is headed by the Attorney General (AG) of the United States. The current AG is John Ashcroft. The AG is appointed by the president and represents the United States government in legal matters. The AG is also responsible for supervising and directing the administration and operation of the offices, boards, divisions, and bureaus that make up the DOJ, as well as assisting the president, the president's cabinet, and the heads of the executive departments and agencies of the government in legal matters.

The DOJ is the federal agency responsible for conducting and coordinating investigations, both those by the DOJ as well as those by other departments. The DOJ consists of thirty-eight agencies, some of which are listed below. The primary responsibilities of the agency are to enforce federal laws; ensure healthy competition among businesses; safeguard the consumer; enforce drug, immigration, and naturalization laws; and protect citizens through effective law enforcement (U.S. Department of Justice 2001).

U.S. Marshal Service   The passage of the Judiciary Act by Congress in 1789 generated the first formal law enforcement agency under the federal government, the office of the U.S. Marshal. The current organization of the **U.S. Marshal Service (USMS)** was set forth in 1969, which standardized procedures for the U.S. Marshals and provided them with specific regulations on professionalism and duties. The USMS has a variety of duties, including the execution of warrants for the federal courts and the handling of federal suspects and prisoners (e.g., transporting suspects, arresting fugitives, etc.).

Federal Bureau of Investigation   The **Federal Bureau of Investigation (FBI)** is the main investigative agency of the federal government. It currently consists of over 10,000 agents. The agency was created in 1908, and by 1909 it was named the Bureau of Investigation, with its present name designated by Congress in 1935. The primary responsibility of the FBI is to investigate violations of federal criminal law and to assist local agencies in investigations. The FBI has jurisdiction over particular offenses, such as kidnapping, auto theft, organized crime, civil rights violations, and internal security (espionage), and it has the authority to locate and apprehend fugitives who have violated specified federal laws.

Another key responsibility of the FBI is to conduct investigations on terrorism, both domestic and international. As such, it is the responsibility of the FBI to identify supporters of terrorists in the United States and abroad and to design, develop, and implement counterterrorism initiatives. This includes terrorist intrusions through both physical and cyber attacks.

In addition to its investigative responsibilities, the FBI also has responsibility for publishing the *Uniform Crime Report (UCR)* (the annual crime statistics, discussed in Chapter 3) and the *Law Enforcement Bulletin*. It is also responsible for conducting personnel investigations (background checks) for those applying for employment within the DOJ and other government agencies as requested.

The FBI has developed training programs for law enforcement personnel at the local, state, federal, and international levels in order to assist others in the development of new approaches and law enforcement techniques. Several departments within the FBI, such as the FBI Crime Lab, aid local investigators with criminal investigations and provide technical assistance in response to disasters.

Immigration and Naturalization Service   The Bureau of Immigration was first established in 1891 within the Treasury Department, but by 1903 it was transferred to the Department of Commerce and Labor. In 1906, it was renamed the **Immigration and Naturalization Service (INS)**. In 1940, the bureau was transferred to the Department of Justice.

The primary responsibility of the INS was to determine the admissibility of persons seeking entry into the country, to ensure that travelers from other countries had appropriate documentation upon entry into the United States, and to control the status of aliens in the country during their stay. The INS was also responsible for accepting and processing applications from those petitioning for naturalization or citizenship. The INS worked to both control and reprimand those who are in the country illegally, as well as to prevent future acts of illegal entry. One method by which they controlled those already in the country illegally involved the application of sanctions to employers who knowingly hire aliens not authorized to work in the United States.

The INS kept detailed records on any person who came into the country and went through the naturalization process, including the names and addresses of witnesses. It maintained a list of all individuals entering the United States from a foreign country either by plane or boat. One aspect of this work was the maintenance of border controls, the most important ones being those situated along the borders of Mexico and Canada. Border control agents tried to prevent illegal aliens from entering into the country. INS agents were also situated at international airport terminals where they checked the passports and visas of all those arriving into the United States from abroad.

As we discuss below, with the government's creation of the Department of Homeland Security, the functions of the INS were split up and transferred to this new Federal agency. The four functions of this new agency include the U.S. Citizenship and Immigration Service, Bureau of Customs and Border Protection, Bureau of Immigration and Customs Enforcement, and the Office of Immigration Statistics.

Department of the Treasury   The Department of the Treasury has traditionally had several important law enforcement functions, some of which will now be transferred to the newly created Department of Homeland Security. Until recently, the Drug Enforcement Agency (DEA), Internal Revenue Service (IRS), U.S. Customs, and the Secret Service were all Treasury Department agencies.

Drug Enforcement Administration   In an attempt to control the supply of dangerous drugs, the Harrison Narcotic Act was passed in 1917. At the time, it was established as a branch of tax law, and as such its enforcement fell to the Department of the Treasury. In 1930, the Treasury Department created the Bureau of Narcotics, which was reorganized in 1968 to become the Bureau of Narcotics and Dangerous Drugs under the DOJ.

The **Drug Enforcement Administration (DEA)** as we know it today was created in 1973 with the merging of the Bureau of Narcotics and Dangerous Drugs, the Office for Drug Abuse Law Enforcement, the Office of National Narcotics Intelligence, some U.S. Customs officials, and the Narcotics Advance Research Management Team. The DEA, which is responsible for investigating both domestic and international drug violators and traffickers, uses both control and prevention techniques to stop the flow of drugs from their point of manufacture to their eventual distribution and sale.

The primary responsibility of the DEA is to investigate and prepare evidence for the prosecution of major violators of controlled substances laws both domestically and internationally. It is also involved in the collection and analysis of information regarding drug use and trafficking and is responsible for developing strategic plans aimed at eliminating such activities. It has the authority to use nonenforcement methods of drug elimination, such as crop eradication, and it also has the authority to seize assets that are in any way related to drug trafficking.

Bureau of Customs   The **Bureau of Customs** was created in response to the need for revenue shortly after the United States declared independence from Britain (the fledgling country was nearly bankrupt!). The bureau was established after the passage of the Tariff Act of 1789, which authorized the collection of duties on imported goods. The primary duty of Customs is to ensure that all imports and exports comply with U.S. laws and regulations. It collects and protects revenues from duties and tariffs, guards against smuggling, and investigates smuggling activities. It has the authority to interdict and seize illegal contraband. In addition, it is responsible for detecting and apprehending any person who circumvents Customs and related laws, and it also protects intellectual property rights. Today, Customs also helps approximately 40 other agencies enforce laws, particularly quality of life provisions that relate to the environment.

Secret Service   Although the **Secret Service** was originally established to suppress counterfeit currency, by 1901 its duties were modified to include protecting the president, the vice president, and the families of each. Congress believed that this was necessary in light of the assassination of President William McKinley. By 1902, the Secret Service assumed full-time responsibility for protection of the president. Presidents who were elected into office prior to January 1, 1997 receive lifetime protection from the Secret Service; however, those elected after this time will receive Secret Service protection for ten years.

Internal Revenue Service   The **Internal Revenue Service (IRS)** is the largest agency within the Treasury Department. Its roots date back to 1862 when President Abraham Lincoln and Congress decided to enact an income tax to pay for expenses related to the Civil War. Though the income tax was ruled unconstitutional ten years later, Congress once again enacted an income tax in 1913 after the states ratified the Sixteenth Amendment. The mission of the IRS is to regulate compliance with tax laws and to investigate tax evasion and fraud.

The IRS has many divisions, including Appeals, Chief Counsel, Communications and Liaison, and Criminal Investigation. Though most people associate criminal investigations with the FBI, the IRS' Criminal Investigation division is responsible for, among other things, enforcing tax laws and identifying individuals and organizations that launder money. The IRS is the primary agency responsible for enforcing the Racketeer Influenced and Corrupt Organizations (RICO) statutes. In fact, it was the IRS that was responsible for investigating and convicting organized crime gangster Al Capone.

U.S. Bureau of Alcohol, Tobacco and Firearms The **U.S. Bureau of Alcohol, Tobacco and Firearms (ATF)** is primarily concerned with the licensing, investigation, and control over its three components as well as explosives. However, it was originally established as a tax-collecting agency, which is why it is located in the Treasury Department rather than the DOJ. The ATF employs many forensic experts as well as law enforcement experts, including chemists, document analysts, latent print specialists, and firearms and toolmark examiners who are trained in forensic skills relating to arson, explosives, and criminal-evidence examination. The ATF works closely with the FBI in federal investigations that require the expertise of both agencies. A recent case that came to the attention of the public was the involvement of the two agencies with David Koresh's Branch Davidian cult in Waco, Texas. It was the ATF that was originally called to the Koresh compound, beginning the standoff that led to the death of seventy-one individuals.

The FBI/ATF stand-off at Waco, Texas, raised important challenges to the use of force in crisis situations, in addition to posing challenges for interagency collaboration.

U.S. Postal Service   In the past, the average person reading this text might have questioned why the **U.S. Postal Service** would be included in a listing of federal law enforcement agencies. However, following the series of anthrax attacks in the United States in the fall of 2001, most would now appreciate the significance of law enforcement activities related to postal service functions. Approximately 2,200 Postal Inspectors stationed throughout the United States are responsible for the enforcement of over 200 federal laws affecting the U.S. mail system (U.S. Postal Service 2002).

Postal Inspectors are fully designated law enforcement officers in that they can carry firearms, make arrests, and serve federal search warrants and subpoenas (U.S. Postal Service 2002). The Inspection Service also maintains five forensic crime laboratories stationed throughout the United States to carry out its investigative functions. Some examples of laws under U.S. Postal Service enforcement jurisdiction include those relating to:

- Assaults or robberies of Postal Service employees
- Bombs sent through the mail
- Child pornography distribution
- Controlled substance distribution
- Money order crimes
- Theft of mail

Tribal Agencies

Today, 556 tribal entities in thirty-one states are recognized by the Bureau of Indian Affairs (BIA) as Native American tribes. More tribes are located in the Southwest than any other area of the United States, and the largest of these is the Navajo Nation in Arizona. Native American tribes are unique in that they are self-governed and are considered sovereign nations, though they must abide by federal regulations. Tribal agencies face many problems that are either more extreme or unique to tribal entities. For instance, Native Americans have a higher rate of unemployment, a lower level of educational achievement, and a higher rate of suicide than non-Native Americans. The crime rate among Native Americans is also very high, particularly with regards to substance abuse. Because most tribes live in remote areas and are small in number, they are often required to enforce the law on their own relatives. All of these issues create challenges for tribal police agencies.

The goal of law enforcement services for Native American tribes is to provide quality investigative and police services and technical expertise that is specifically designed for Native American tribes. Law enforcement programs operated by tribal governments receive assistance from the BIA's law enforcement program. The BIA wants to create a system for training criminal investigators that is specific to the needs of the tribal entities. The BIA also wants to develop an internal tracking process to monitor the efficiency of police responses to incidents on tribal lands. Few monitoring systems exist that assess the quality and rate of completion of investigations at this time. Similarly, no programs currently monitor the maintenance of professional and cooperative working relationships between tribal officers and federal prosecutors or other law enforcement agencies.

There are training programs for tribal law enforcement personnel, such as the Indian Police Academy in Artesia, New Mexico. Such programs are designed to teach Native American police recruits and other law enforcement personnel the basics of policing, investigative techniques, and justice administration principles.

The interrelationship between federal, state, and local law enforcement, as well as the information flow between them, is presented in Figure 1.2.

FIGURE 1.2

Information flow among agencies. Although communication existed across levels of government, it was often strained by bureaucracy and issues of territoriality. Regular sharing of information existed on some multi-agency task forces, but it was often strained or limited. Linkage blindness thus occurs where information that could benefit multiple agencies slips through the cracks. In a sense, better communication could mean ensuring that all the "pieces of the puzzle" are put together with respect to a given investigation or particular threat. Mechanisms for vertical communication are often particularly challenging. But even across one level (horizontal), given the many agencies working on problems of overlapping jurisdiction, information slippage can occur.

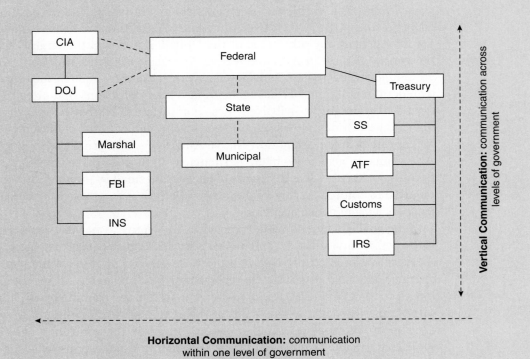

Vertical Communication: communication across levels of government

Horizontal Communication: communication within one level of government

Reorganization: The Creation of the Department of Homeland Security

On July 26, 2002, the House of Representatives approved the creation of a **Department of Homeland Security** in the largest government reorganization in fifty years (Firestone 2002). In an effort to better coordinate its intelligence and law enforcement resources in the war against terrorism, the U.S. government is attempting to eliminate many of the problems of linkage blindness by moving twenty-two formerly disparate domestic agencies into one department.

The restructuring (see Figure 1.3) included the transfer of the Coast Guard, Customs Service, Border Patrol, Federal Emergency Management Agency, Secret Service, Transportation Security Administration, and border inspection component of the Animal and Plant Health Inspection Service to the new department (Firestone 2002).[9] After much discussion, it was determined that the processing functions of the INS would remain in the DOJ despite the transfer of Border Patrol to the new agency.

Although there was even consideration given to folding the FBI and CIA under the Department of Homeland Security umbrella, this idea was rejected

Linkages in Law Enforcement

An Introduction to the Linkage-Blindness Phenomenon

One of the consequences of having a complex and interlocking system of laws and law enforcement institutions is the problem known as *linkage blindness,* discussed earlier in this chapter. When different institutions operate within overlapping areas of specialization and jurisdiction, they inevitably duplicate information among themselves and become interested in the same individuals, organizations, and problems. For example, a suspect wanted by the FBI for drug offenses may also be the subject of a local police investigation for an entirely different offense. Because these two institutions may not readily share information, it is possible that evidence held by the FBI and crucial to the particulars of the police investigation is never made available to officers at the local level and vice versa.

Linkage blindness arises, in part, from the failure of different institutions to recognize areas of mutual interest (Egger 1990)—they are in effect blind to the important connections between them. One of the key challenges for law enforcement agencies in the United States in the twenty-first century is to find ways to overcome this problem and to make the best use of all available information in their efforts to reduce and prevent crime. As described earlier, linkage blindness was identified as a problem following the terrorist attacks on the United States on September 11, 2001. Part 4 of this text will provide information on technological advances and strategies designed to address the problem of linkage blindness.

FIGURE 1.3

Changes implemented through the new Department of Homeland Security. The simple schema of the Homeland Security reorganization highlights the recent attempts to stop linkage blindness from occurring. By housing related agencies, such as Border Patrol, FEMA, and Customs under one department, it is hoped that information sharing across jurisdictions will occur more efficiently. Moreover, a color-coded threat warning system has been developed to keep state and local jurisdictions attuned to changing threat levels. Efforts need to ensure regular communication between local jurisdictions and changing federal intelligence.

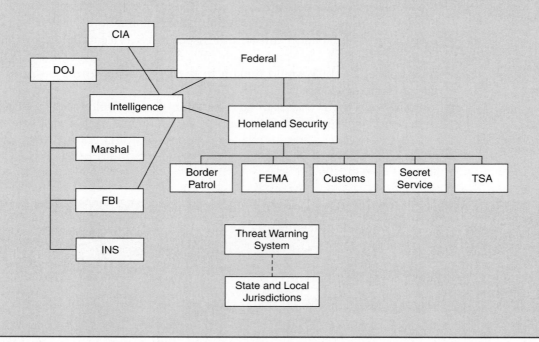

in favor of the establishment of an intelligence analysis division within the new agency that would receive intelligence reports from the CIA and the FBI that were related to terrorist threats (Firestone 2002). The current Senate bill proposes to take this a step further by allowing the Department of Homeland Security to receive even raw intelligence from the CIA and FBI.

Within the FBI itself there has been a significant shifting of focus and responsibilities post–September 11. The FBI is transferring much of its responsibility for bank robbery investigations back to local law enforcement to free up more resources for counterterrorism activities. Future plans to organize coordination and information sharing between the Department of Homeland Security and local law enforcement in an effort to prevent **information leakage** will also be a significant priority for years to come. Information leakage occurs when important intelligence or information that could be prevented by better coordination within or across law enforcement jurisdictions "slips through the cracks."

Linkages in Law Enforcement

Coordination and Information Sharing Between Law Enforcement and the Rest of the Criminal Justice System

Communication is not only an important issue within and across law enforcement jurisdictions, but it is also critical to the rest of the criminal justice system as well. Broadly speaking, the **criminal justice system** is a collection of agencies and institutions that enforce criminal laws and that work to reduce and prevent crime. In the United States, the criminal justice system consists of three main components: the police and other law enforcement agencies; the courts; and correctional services such as prisons and probation programs. Each of these institutions plays a role in the criminal justice process and has particular areas of responsibility as determined by law. The police, for example, are entrusted with the task of investigating crimes and apprehending criminal suspects. They do not—in theory at least—make decisions about an alleged offender's guilt or innocence or hand down punishments. Instead, these functions are carried out by the courts. Equally, the courts do not play a role in the gathering of evidence, but instead rely on the police to bring cases before them.

The police, the courts, and the correctional services are collectively referred to as the criminal justice system because they are organizationally linked and serve a common purpose. In an ideal world, all three would work in harmony, apprehending suspects, determining guilt, and punishing offenders efficiently and in full accordance with the law. In practice, however, the criminal justice system does not always operate in such a smooth or structured fashion. In part, this is due to the fact that each branch works according to its own distinct rules, organizational culture, and history. Although the police, the courts, and correctional services are required to work together as partners, different organizational styles and institutional priorities can make interagency cooperation difficult. For instance, information possessed by police is not always readily available to other law enforcement agencies; correctional services may not have the resources to implement recommendations made by the courts; and efforts to implement systemwide changes may be undermined by the desire of each branch to maintain existing working practices.

In addition to these institutional and cultural factors, decisions made by individuals also affect the workings of the criminal justice system, and in some instances may undermine the distinction between its different branches. The police and other law enforcement agencies do not, for example, always restrict themselves to investigating crimes or apprehending suspects. Summary punishments in the form of physical beatings or unwarranted detention in police cells are all examples of the police going beyond their boundaries and assuming the powers of the courts and the correctional services. It is not just the police, however, who at times exceed their authority within the criminal justice system. For instance, in the judiciary, prosecutors may overcharge a suspect in order to encourage him or her to accept a plea bargain (thus reducing the charge to the original act committed). In the correctional system, prison officials—through the granting or restriction of informal privileges—may influence the way in which an inmate's sentence is carried out or even its eventual length. Although the powers and responsibilities of agents within the system are defined by law, at every stage of the criminal justice process individuals make decisions that affect how the system operates *in practice*. As a consequence, in order to understand how the criminal justice process works, it is important to remember that although the system has a formal structure, much of its operation depends on the values, informal rules, and decision-making processes that characterize each of its component parts.

The process of the criminal justice system begins with an initial police investigation and concludes with a person's release from correctional services. The process is made up of a series of distinct, but interrelated, stages. At each successive stage of the process, the individual involved is gradually transformed—from suspect to defendant to offender—as the police, courts, and correctional services each discharge their particular responsibilities. Figure 1.4 outlines the formal

FIGURE 1.4

The criminal justice process

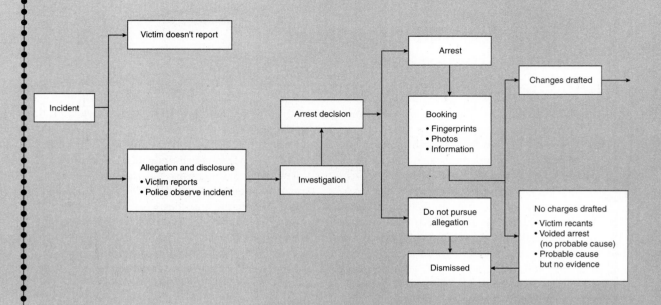

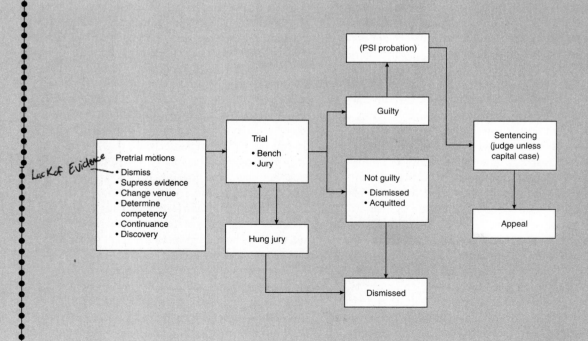

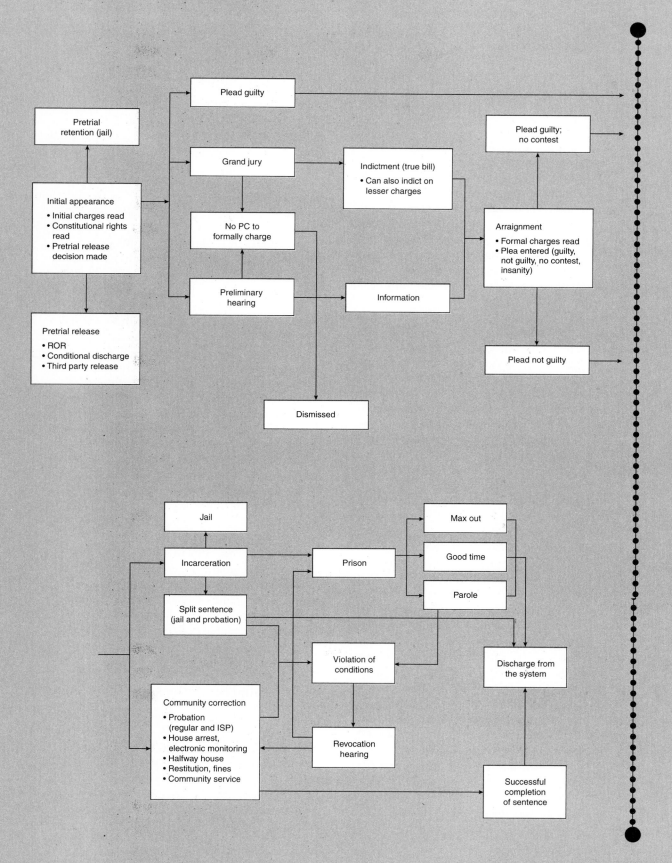

path of a typical state's criminal justice process. In addition to demonstrating the flow of cases through the system, the chart highlights relevant issues facing law enforcement at each stage.

From Suspect to Charge: The Role of the Police

The police are responsible for investigating crimes, apprehending and arresting suspects, taking suspects into custody, and charging them. Once a crime has been committed, it generally comes to the attention of the police in one of two ways: (1) either a member of the public reports it or (2) the police themselves observe it. Although the police undertake regular patrols and carry out various forms of surveillance, most of their information about crime in the community comes from the public. As a result, despite the fact that police officers occupy a unique position in society, they rely heavily on the support and cooperation of the public.

When a crime is observed directly by the police, they can immediately **arrest** those they believe to be responsible and take them into custody for questioning. In those instances when a crime is reported by a member of the public, however, depending on plausibility of the report and the seriousness of the alleged offense, the police can choose either to simply record the report or begin a criminal investigation. The purpose of a criminal investigation is to identify those responsible for the commission of a crime and to gather evidence that proves their guilt. In most cases, once the police have identified a likely suspect, they can either ask the suspect to come to the police station in order to answer questions or, when the suspect is unwilling to cooperate or is believed to be dangerous, arrest the suspect and hold him or her in custody while a case against the suspect is prepared.

Because the police only possess limited powers of arrest, in certain situations they must obtain a warrant of arrest from a magistrate or a judge. In such circumstances, it is necessary for the police to demonstrate that they have **probable cause**. Probable cause exists when the police have evidence that will convince a reasonable person that a crime has been committed and that the person they intend to arrest is responsible for that crime. In principle, the requirement of probable cause serves to restrict the power of the police and to ensure that they do not abuse their powers of arrest.

In practice, however, the need for probable cause does not always prevent the police from using arrest as a means of exercising authority over individuals and controlling suspect populations.

Once a suspect has been arrested, he or she is taken into police custody, booked, and interrogated. **Booking** refers to the process of recording a suspect's entry into detention after an arrest. At that time, the police record the suspect's personal details (name, birth date, address, etc.) and take his or her photograph and fingerprints. The suspect is also required to sign a form stating that his or her constitutional rights have been read and that they are understood.

Prior and subsequent to arrest, the police are responsible for conducting an **investigation** to gather evidence about the crime and the suspect. This is one of the most important steps in the criminal justice process, because evidence gathered at this time is used throughout the pretrial and adjudication phases. During an investigation, the police are often required to conduct a search, and strict constitutional standards must be adhered to when performing a search (these standards are discussed in detail in Chapter 7). There are different types of searches, the least intrusive of which is a stop and frisk, in which the police can pat down an individual if there is **reasonable suspicion** that the person is in possession of a weapon or is carrying drugs. Reasonable suspicion is a lower legal standard than probable cause, which is required for any full-scale search of persons, their residence, their automobile, or their personal possessions.

The Fourth Amendment is perhaps the most important safeguard of individual rights against police powers because it protects individuals from illegal searches and seizures. Several landmark cases have established safeguards for individual rights by limiting the powers of the police at this stage of the criminal justice process. These safeguards are detailed in both Chapters 4 and 7.

Determining Guilt: The Role of the Courts

Once the suspect has been booked and informal charges have been laid out, the police are required to bring the suspect before a court for an **initial appearance**. In order to ensure that the police do not hold suspects in custody without due cause, a suspect's initial appearance must take place within twenty-four hours of arrest or the police risk being held liable for false imprisonment. During the initial appearance, the defendant is informed of his or her rights by the judge and formal charges are considered. At this stage, the individual ceases to be a suspect and becomes a defendant. In addition, at the initial appearance, an attorney is assigned to an indigent defendant, if desired or needed, and a pretrial release decision is made. When deciding whether to release the defendant on bail or remand him or her into custody, the judge will typically consider such factors as the nature and seriousness of the crime, the likelihood that the defendant will voluntarily return for trial, and the safety of the general community.

Concerns over insignificant bail amounts can seriously affect the level of confidence in the police and a corresponding willingness to report crimes to the police in some high-crime neighborhoods. For example, during one of the author's tours of a high-gang-density housing project in Knoxville, Tennessee, many residents informed him that they would not report gang members or gang activity because "they are just going to get right back out again." The fear for personal safety even when formal charges have been laid against an offender can severely hamper the criminal justice process given the importance of victim testimony in the successful resolution of many cases (Grant 1996).

After the initial appearance, formal charges are then filed against the defendant. At this time, the case is given to the prosecutor, who in most jurisdictions is the District Attorney (DA). The prosecutor has the discretion to determine whether there is probable cause to formally charge the defendant and, if so, what the charges are going to be. Policing practices and enforcement standards can be greatly impacted by a prosecutor's enforcement policies. If a department feels that certain types of violations are consistently not pursued, they will very likely divert their enforcement resources to other areas (Swanson et al. 2001).

If the prosecutor decides to proceed against the defendant, the case will be brought before either the grand jury or the bench (in a preliminary hearing) to determine whether there are grounds for a trial. Whether there is a preliminary hearing or the case is brought before the grand jury depends on the jurisdiction and the crime committed, although both produce the same result: a formal charge against the defendant and committal for trial. As Swanson et al. (2001) point out, relations between the prosecutor and police can be severely weakened whenever the prosecutor's office chooses to formally charge a local law enforcement officer.

During the preliminary hearing, the defendant has the option of attending the preliminary hearing with counsel or the defendant may waive the hearing and allow it to continue in his or her absence.[10] Unlike the grand jury, the preliminary hearing is open to the public and the press, and the defendant can object to the infusion of hearsay evidence. When both a grand jury and a preliminary hearing are available, the prosecutor has the discretion to decide which is more appropriate for that particular case. Generally, more serious offenses are brought before the grand jury, whereas misdemeanors and less serious felonies tend to be brought before the bench in a preliminary hearing. In some jurisdictions, a preliminary hearing takes place prior to the grand jury proceeding.

The testimony of the investigating police officer is often crucial at this stage of the process, requiring the presence of the officer or even the subpoena of his or her field notes in some cases. The importance of strong field notes will be apparent to the officer the first time he or she is on the stand and required to remember specifics rather than simply generalities (Adams 2001).

Once there is a formal charge, the defendant enters the first stage of the adjudication process, the **arraignment**. At this stage, the formal charges against the defendant are read and the defendant enters a plea.

During the **pretrial motions**, the judge can decide to suppress evidence if, for instance, he or she finds that it was not gathered legally or is not directly relevant to the case. This decision can lead to frustration on the part of an individual officer or an entire department. This is particularly true in cases when the suppression of evidence could damage the entire case and when the evidence is suppressed because of what is perceived to be an unjustifiable technicality. As with the case of the prosecutor discussed earlier, if judges make it clear that the courts are **voiding** certain categories of arrest continually, decisions may be made to no longer enforce those specific types of offenses.

If the defendant elects to have a jury trial—which is available for more serious crimes that carry a potential sentence of six months or more of imprisonment—then the selection of jurors must also occur prior to the trial.[11] For defendants who do not choose to exercise their Sixth Amendment right to a trial by jury, there is a bench trial, the outcome of which is decided by a judge.

At the trial, it is the responsibility of the prosecutor to prove **beyond a reasonable doubt** that the defendant committed the crime in question, otherwise the defendant must be acquitted. If the prosecution can prove the case, then the accused is found guilty and the case moves on to the sentencing phase of the adjudication process. Occasionally, juries cannot come to a unanimous or a majority decision, in which case a **hung jury** is declared. In such circumstances, the prosecutor has the discretion to retry the case or dismiss it. Because trials are costly and time-consuming, the majority of cases that result in a hung jury are dropped.

It is important to note that although the trial is the cornerstone of the criminal justice system, the majority of criminal cases never actually come to trial. Instead, approximately 90 percent of cases are resolved through the process of plea bargaining at the arraignment stage of the process. **Plea bargains**, which are arranged between the prosecutor, defense attorney, the defendant, and the judge, are negotiations of guilty pleas in exchange for reduced charges or lenient sentences.

Historically, the police have been strongly opposed to the system of plea bargaining. Having spent time and valuable resources apprehending the suspects and collecting evidence against them, the police often feel that the process of plea bargaining devalues their work and provides offenders with an opportunity to "escape justice." Indeed, the plea bargaining system is one of the key sources of tension between the police and the courts within the criminal justice system. Despite these problems and concerns, because it provides a mechanism for disposing of cases quickly and efficiently, plea bargaining remains a vital part of the criminal justice process.

Offenders who plead guilty or are found guilty at trial continue on to the sentencing phase of the adjudication process. Before making a determination of an appropriate sentence for the offender, a **presentence investigation (PSI)** is conducted by the office of probation to investigate the background of the offender, which helps the judge to determine what type of sentence is appropriate within legislated parameters.

Although the corrections stage of the criminal justice process begins after sentencing, sentencing does not necessarily mark the end of the adjudication stage. The offender can appeal either the decision of the trial court or the conditions of custody by filing a **writ**, a formal document requesting an appeal. If the decision is appealed, the facts of the case are not retried, but the legal procedures and decisions from arrest through the trial are reviewed by the appellate court. Although each state has a different appellate court system, most states have an intermediate appellate court and a "court of last resort." The highest appellate court for any case, on a state or federal basis, is the U.S. Supreme Court. Offenders can appeal to have their case reviewed by the Supreme Court by filing a **writ of certiorari**; however, the Court is very selective about the cases it reviews. Generally, only cases that raise serious constitutional or human rights issues are reviewed at this level.

Administering Punishment and Reforming the Offender: The Role of Corrections

Once a defendant has been found guilty, a wide variety of sentencing options are available to the court: the death penalty, prison, jail, split sentences, **boot camp**, probation, residential centers (**halfway houses, furloughs**), house arrest, electronic monitoring, community service, fines, and restitution. Typically, the most significant decision made by the judge during the sentencing process is whether to hand down a community sentence (usually probation) or a sentence of imprisonment. Some offenses require mandatory prison sentences; the Rockefeller drug laws in New York require that any person convicted of selling two ounces of a narcotic or in possession of four ounces of a narcotic receive a minimum prison sentence of fifteen years to life (Lindesmith Center 1999). Nonetheless, in the vast majority of cases the judge has discretion as to the type of sentence and its length.

Offenders can be incarcerated or given a community sentence irrespective of whether they commit a felony or a misdemeanor. If incarcerated for a misdemeanor, the offender will be sentenced to a year or less in jail. **Jail** is a local county or city institution for the temporary detention of persons who are waiting for indictment, arraignment, trial, or sentencing or for those serving short-term sentences for misdemeanors. Offenders incarcerated for felonies will be sentenced to **prison**, which is a state or federal correctional facility that houses offenders serving sentences of a year or more.

There are three main ways in which offenders can be released from prison. They can serve their entire sentence in prison, or **max out**, at which time the state is required to release them. Offenders who abide by the prison rules and receive only positive reports from correctional services are entitled to be released prior to their maximum sentence with **good time**. Offenders in most states may also be released early with **parole**, which allows for supervision by a field agent once the offender is living in the community for the remainder of the sentence. Some states have abolished parole, whereas others have abolished parole for violent offenders and **recidivist**, or repeat, offenders, typically on the grounds that parole undermines the judicial stage of the criminal justice process and leads to inconsistency in the administration of punishment.

Alternative sanctions, also called subincarcerative sanctions or community corrections, are those sentences in which the offender serves part or the entire sentence in the community (i.e., **probation**, intensive supervision probation, house arrest and electronic monitoring, or community service). All of these forms of alternative sanctions are cost-effective. They also help to reduce the problem of prison overcrowding and have similar rates of recidivism as prisons. Some, such as intensive supervision probation (ISP), result in even lower rates of recidivism. However, there are problems that need to be addressed. As technology such as electronic monitoring becomes more sophisticated, so do the offenders who are supervised in such a way.

In order for community corrections to be effective, the various criminal justice agencies must cooperate. The recent successes of police-probation partnerships in Boston (Berren and Winship 1999) and Baton Rouge, Louisiana (Sheppard et al. 2000), demonstrate how increased information-sharing and collaboration between law enforcement and corrections can lead to reductions in recidivism through a combination of increased surveillance and a greater understanding of the needs of the probationer, and thus an ability to place him or her into needed services. Chapter 12 details the nature and successes of the Baton Rouge partnership and other police/corrections collaborative models. The partnership model can be applied to problems as diverse as those of sex offender management and registration. The importance of increased communication related to sex offender registration will be detailed in the final section of the text.

Chapter Summary

- The concept of linkage blindness is central to this text. Linkage blindness refers to a lack of communication between different agencies or even within agencies. The terrorist attacks of September 11 have been argued to be the result of linkage blindness, because various law enforcement agencies or divisions of agencies may have had information on the terrorists but did not share the information with the correct sources.

- The primary duty of the police is to maintain social control within the community. What distinguishes the police from other individuals is their ability to use coercive force if necessary to control a situation.

- Discretion, which is the freedom of an individual to make a decision based on his or her personal judgment, is a necessary aspect of policing. Though police officers must respond to situations within the parameter of the law, they should have the freedom to make a decision based on the circumstances of a particular case. Also, it would be impossible for an officer to respond to every violation of the law, and

- therefore discretion is a necessary component of law enforcement.

- The rule of law refers to the ideas that equality and justice are inseparable and that laws are applied equally to everyone. It is the standard that guides decision making throughout the criminal justice system.

- The crime control model emphasizes law enforcement over individual rights. Advocates of this approach emphasize extensive police powers, limited rights for suspects, and a quick and speedy process. The due process model emphasizes individual rights with restrictions on police power. Supporters of the due process model focus on civil liberties and quality of arrests over quantity.

- There are six levels of law enforcement: federal, state, county, municipal, township, and tribal. The largest category of law enforcement is municipal, with over 13,000 jurisdictions.

- As a result of the September 11 terrorist attacks, the government created the Department of Homeland Security. The purpose of this department is to coordinate intelligence and law enforcement resources in the war on terrorism. The creation of this department involved a major reorganization of the agencies within the federal government.

- All of the agencies within the criminal justice system are interlinked and must work together to ensure justice. The three components of the criminal justice system are the police, the courts, and corrections. The police are the first agents within the criminal justice process and, once a crime occurs, they are in charge of taking a report, investigating the crime, arresting a suspect, and booking the suspect. The methods by which they investigate crimes will have an impact on whether and how the case proceeds through the criminal justice system and often whether there is a conviction in the case.

KEY TERMS

Alternative sanction 29
Arraignment 27
Arrest 26
Beyond a reasonable doubt 28
Booking 26
Boot camp 28
Bureau of Customs 17
Coercive force 8
Crime control 11
Criminal justice system 23
Culture of lawfulness 9
Department of Homeland
  Security 21
Deviance 7
Discretion 9
Drug Enforcement
  Administration (DEA) 17
Due process 11
Extra-legal factors 10
Federal Bureau of Investigation
  (FBI) 15
Formal social control 8
Furlough 28

Good time 29
Halfway house 28
Horizontal communication 20
Hung jury 28
Immigration and Naturalization
  Service (INS) 16
Informal social control 7
Information leakage 22
Initial appearance 26
Internal Revenue Service
  (IRS) 17
Investigation 26
Jail 28
Jurisdiction 12
Justice of the peace 14
Justice's court 14
Law enforcement 6
Linkage blindness 5
Max out 29
Parole 29
Plea bargain 28
Presentence investigation
  (PSI) 28

Pretrial motions 27
Prison 29
Probable cause 26
Probation 29
Reasonable suspicion 26
Recidivist 29
Rule of law 10
Secret Service 17
Socialization 7
Township police
  departments 13
U.S. Bureau of Alcohol, Tobacco
  and Firearms (ATF) 18
U.S. Marshal Service
  (USMS) 15
U.S. Postal Service 19
USA PATRIOT Act of 2001 4
Vertical communication 20
Voiding 27
Writ 28
Writ of certiorari 28

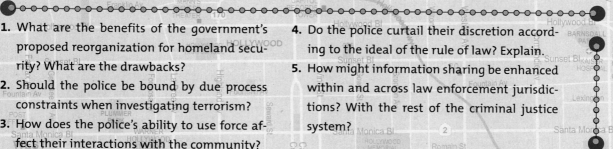

Linking the Dots

1. What are the benefits of the government's proposed reorganization for homeland security? What are the drawbacks?
2. Should the police be bound by due process constraints when investigating terrorism?
3. How does the police's ability to use force affect their interactions with the community?
4. Do the police curtail their discretion according to the ideal of the rule of law? Explain.
5. How might information sharing be enhanced within and across law enforcement jurisdictions? With the rest of the criminal justice system?

REFERENCES

Adams, T. 2001. *Police Field Operations,* 5th ed. Upper Saddle River, NJ: Prentice Hall.

Berren, J., and C. Winship. 1999. "Lessons Learned from Boston's Police-Community Collaboration." *Federal Probation* 63 (2): 25–32.

Bittner, E. 1980. *The Functions of the Police in Modern Society.* Cambridge, MA: Olgeschlager, Gunn, and Hain.

Brown, L. 1979. "The Role of the Sheriff." In *The Future of Policing,* edited by A. Cohn, 227–247. Beverly Hills: Sage.

Bureau of Justice Statistics. 1997. *Sheriffs Departments, 1997.* Washington, D.C.: Bureau of Justice Statistics.

Bureau of Justice Statistics. 2000. *Law Enforcement Management and Administrative Statistics: Data for Individual State and Local Agencies with 100 or More Officers.* Washington, D.C.: Bureau of Justice Statistics.

Bureau of Justice Statistics. 2001. *Local Police Departments, 1999.* Washington D.C.: Bureau of Justice Statistics.

Bureau of Justic Statistics. 2003. *Law Enforcement Statistics.* Available at http://www.ojp.usdoj.gov/bjs/lawenf.htm.

Egger, S. A. 1990. *Serial Murder: An Elusive Phenomenon.* Westport, CT: Praeger.

Eisenhower, M. 1970. *The Rule of Law—An Alternative to Violence: A Report to the National Commission on the Causes and Prevention of Violence.* Nashville, TN: Aurora Publishers.

Firestone, D. 2002. "Traces of Terror: the Reorganization." *New York Times,* July 26, A1.

Flynn, S. 2001. "The Unguarded Homeland: A Study in Malign Neglect." In *How Did This Happen: Terrorism and the New War,* edited by J. Hodge and G. Rose, 183–197. New York: Public Affairs Press.

Godson, R. 2000. Guide to Developing a Culture of Lawfulness. Paper prepared for the Symposium on the Role of Civil Society in Countering Organized Crime: Global Implications of the Palermo, Sicily, Renaissance, December 2000 at Palermo, Italy.

Goldstein, H. 1979. "Improving Policing: a Problem-Oriented Approach." *Crime and Delinquency* 25 (2): 236–258.

Grant, H. 1996. Unpublished video documentary of a gang needs assessment in Knoxville, Tennessee.

Greenhouse, L. 2001. "A Nation Challenged: The Supreme Court; in New York Visit, O'Connor Foresees Limits on Freedom." *New York Times,* September 29, B5.

Hentoff, N. 2001. "Has the U.S. Attorney Read the Constitution." *Jewish World Review,* November 19, 2001. Available at http://www.restoringamerica.org/archive/constitution/has_ashcroft_read.html.

Hudson, R. 1999. *Who Becomes a Terrorist and Why: The 1999 Government Report on Profiling Terrorists.* Guilford, CT: Lyons Press.

Kelling, G., and M. Moore. 1989. *The Evolving Strategy of Policing.* Vol. 4 of *Perspectives on Policing.* Washington, D.C.: Government Printing Office.

Klockars, C. 1985. *The Idea of the Police.* Beverly Hills, CA: Sage.

Lindesmith Center, Drug Policy Foundation. 1999. "The Rockefeller Drug Laws and the Second Felony Offender Law." Available at www.Lindesmith.org/focal8/html.

Manning, P. 1977. *Police Work: the Social Organization of Policing,* 2d ed. Prospect Heights, IL: Waveland.

National Strategy Information Center. 1999. *School-Based Education to Counter Crime and Corruption.* Washington, D.C.: National Strategy Information Center.

Nolan, J., and J. Nolan-Haley. 1990. *Black's Law Dictionary,* 6th ed. St. Paul, MN: West Publishing.

Packer, H. 1968. *The Limits of the Criminal Sanction.* Stanford, CA: Stanford University Press.

Reaves, B. A., and A. L. Goldberg. 1998. *Census of State and Local Police Departments, 1996.* Washington, D.C.: U.S. Government Printing Office.

Senna, J., and L. Siegel. 2001. *Essentials of Criminal Justice.* Belmont, CA: Wadsworth.

Sheppard, D., H. Grant., W. Rowe, and N. Jacobs. 2000. "Fighting Gun Crime." *OJJDP Bulletin in Brief.* Washington, D.C.: U.S. Government Printing Office.

Skolnick, J. 1994. *Justice Without Trial: Law Enforcement in a Democratic Society,* 3d ed. New York: Macmillan College Publishing.

Swanson, C., L. Territo, and R. Taylor. 2001. *Police Administration: Structures, Processes, and Behavior.* 5th ed. Upper Saddle River, NJ: Prentice Hall.

U.S. Department of Justice. 2001.

U.S. Postal Service. 2002. Available at http://www.consumer.gov/postalinspectors/aboutus.htm.

Walker, S. 1992. "Origins of the Contemporary Criminal Justice Paradigm: the American Bar Foundation Survey, 1953–1969." *Justice Quarterly* 9 (1): 47–76.

NOTES

1. Uniting and Strengthening America by Providing Appropriate Tools Required to Intercept and Obstruct Terrorism Act (Public Law 107-56).
2. *Escobedo v. Illinois,* 378 U.S. 478 (1964).
3. *Miranda v. Arizona,* 384 U.S. 436 (1966).
4. *Terry v. Ohio,* 392 U.S. 1 (1968).
5. *Gideon v. Wainwright,* 372 U.S. 335 (1963).
6. The case of Rodney King is an example of this. This incident involved the beating of a black man by four white officers after a car chase. It would not have come to the attention of the public had a citizen not been videotaping the incident.
7. An example of this is the Rampart CRASH scandal in the Los Angeles Police Department, which involved a number of officers involved in criminal misconduct, including working off-duty for Death Row Records, robbing banks, stealing cocaine, falsifying testimony, and beating suspects. At the height of the scandal, two officers shot, framed, and testified against a known gang member, leaving him paralyzed.
8. An example of this is the investigation of the New Jersey State Troopers, which was sparked by an incident in 1998 when two state troopers stopped a van of African American men on the New Jersey Turnpike. During the stop, the van began rolling backwards. The state troopers thought that the driver was trying to run them over, so they began shooting the passengers. Three of the men were wounded. This incident led to a full investigation of state troopers in New Jersey, and an investigation found that the troopers regularly practiced racial profiling in their stops.
9. For a full list of the organizations that are restructured, see the Web site for the Department of Homeland Security at www.dhs.gov/dhspublic/display?theme = 13.
10. *Coleman v. Alabama,* 389 U.S. 22 (1967).
11. In most jurisdictions, defendants charged with serious offenses can choose between a jury trial and a bench trial, though some states require that all defendants who can receive six months or more imprisonment are subject to a jury trial.

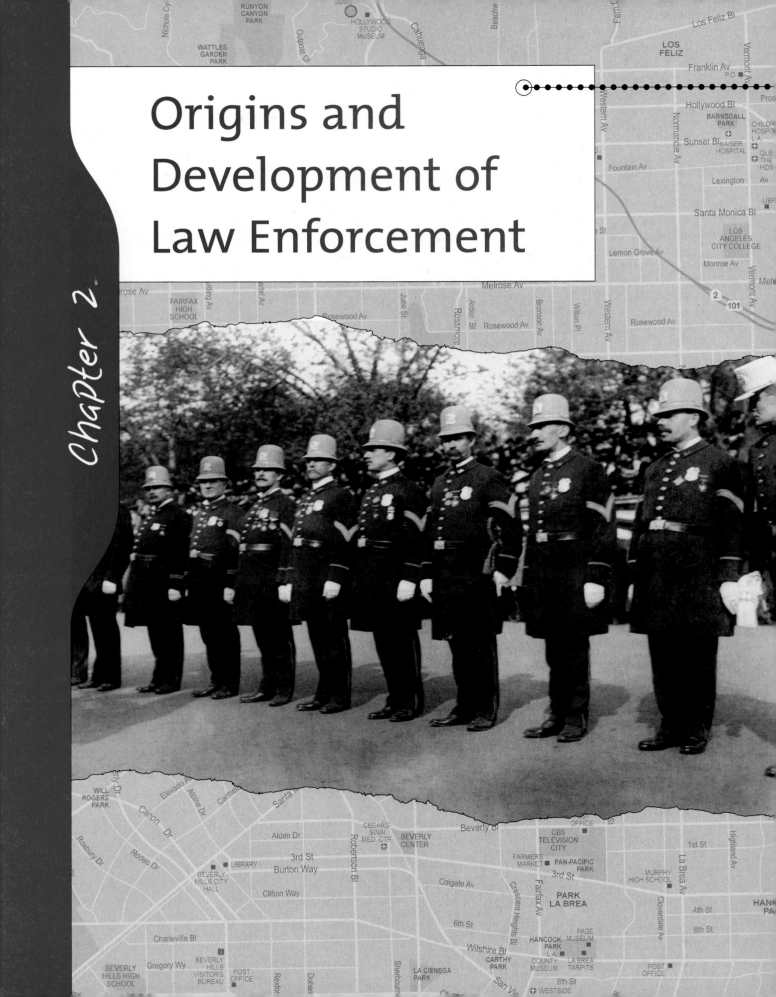

Chapter 2

Origins and Development of Law Enforcement

Chapter Outline

Chapter Objectives

● Discuss key elements of The Reform Era, including its origin, types of reforms, and those responsible for implementing the reforms.

● Explain the origins and meaning of social control.

● Trace the development of informal policing in England and the United States.

● Analyze the development of and impact of the London Metropolitan Police on modern policing.

● Explain regional differences in the development of law enforcement, such as slave patrols and Jim Crow laws.

● Identify Kelling and Moore's eras of policing and describe key events in the Political Era.

● Describe the early role of women and minorities in policing.

Introduction

Happily for English liberty, there has never existed in this country any police force at the disposal of the central government, powerful enough to coerce the nation at large. Our national police have always been of the people and for the people [London 1901] (Lee 1901, quoted in Reiner 1994, p. 61).

After the classical precipitating incident of a fatal fight between a black civilian and a white policeman, rampaging crowds moved up and down Eighth and Ninth avenues beating Negros. Policemen swarmed over the area, cracking the heads of Negroes and doing nothing to restrain the Irish mob. That the Negroes were bitter is hardly surprising seeing that the police not only did not protect them, did not arrest any of the whites involved, but also indulged in gratuitous clubbing [New York City 1901] (quoted in Silver, 1984).

These two quotes, both made the same year in London and New York, highlight the importance of political and cultural contexts in the development of law enforcement. Although New York City set out to replicate the English model of policing, the realities of implementation were far different. Political challenges, including the United States' recent history of slavery, played a significant role in the development and character of its early policing systems.

This chapter examines how formal systems of policing have developed through the centuries. Although any society governed by law must at some point address the question of how best to enforce those laws, the idea that law enforcement should be the responsibility of a permanent professional police force is a modern one.

Up until the last two hundred years, most societies relied on individual citizens and communities to ensure that the law was upheld and criminals apprehended. With the arrival of the Industrial Revolution and rising levels of poverty, crime, and public disorder, however, governments in Europe and elsewhere were forced to develop new and more effective ways of enforcing the law and maintaining order. First in Britain and then the United States, law enforcement eventually passed out of the hands of the ordinary citizen and became the direct responsibility of professional law enforcers: the police.

This chapter traces the historical development of law enforcement and the emergence of the modern professional police force and examines how the idea of "policing" has changed from ancient times to the present. Despite the fact that the modern police officer faces challenges that are very different from those that confronted local sheriffs in feudal England or the Bow Street Runners in eighteenth-century London, much contemporary thinking about law enforcement is rooted in traditions that have changed little over time. Understanding how different societies have throughout history sought to combat crime and enforce the law is an important step towards understanding many of the key issues that now face police forces in the twenty-first century.

Early Origins of Social Control

Any society, if it wishes to survive, needs to develop some system of ensuring that the norms and values of that society are upheld and that members of the community can live free from harm. Prior to the emergence of formal governments and states, early societies were regulated by systems of informal rules and traditions, which dictated how members of the society should behave and how conflicts should be resolved. In prehistoric societies, these rules were extremely basic and sought to ensure that everyone worked together for the survival of the group. Acts such as stealing and murder were prohibited because they created division and distrust and led to conflicts that could threaten the welfare of the community as a whole. Within these early societies, justice was typically an individual matter. The victim of a wrong was responsible for punishing the alleged wrongdoer. Punishment, usually based on the simple notion of an "eye for an eye" (*lex talionis*), was meted out by the victim or the victim's family, with the result that justice was frequently swift, bloody, and final.

As societies became more complex and systems of law emerged, however, these informal methods of social control gave way to more organized systems of law enforcement. In addition to setting out the law to be followed by all citizens, some of the original systems of law also prescribed specific penalties for particular types of wrongs. One of the earliest known systems, the **Code of Hammurabi** (2200 BC), originated in the kingdom of Babylon in Mesopotamia (the geographic area that is now Iraq). Although with this system individuals remained responsible for ensuring that the law was followed, under the Code of Hammurabi, they were not permitted to impose their own punishments. The Code of Hammurabi made the enforcement of law more consistent and established a clear relationship between the type of crime committed and the punishment that could be expected.

Centuries later, the city fathers of Rome established an early system of military policing by assigning responsibility for protecting the Emperor's palace and patrolling the city to the Praetorian Guard and the Urban Cohort. It is the Emperor Augustus, however, who is most frequently credited with establishing the first civilian police force, known as the *vigiles,* shortly before the birth of Christ. Drawn from the general citizenry of Rome, the *vigiles* were originally intended to serve as firefighters, but soon took on the role of law enforcers as well. Unlike the Praetorian Guard or the Urban Cohort, the *vigiles* were given general powers to keep the peace and to investigate crime. They patrolled the streets of Rome dressed in ordinary clothes, keeping a watch over the general public. Renowned for their ruthlessness and for handing down severe punishments, the *vigiles* soon became despised by the people and were regarded by many as no better than state-sponsored spies and informants. Although the system of *vigiles* eventually came to an end with the fall of Rome, the word **vigilante**—a person who takes the law into his or her own hands—finds its origin in this early form of policing. These informal styles of law enforcement soon found their way into England, which was under Roman rule during the time of Augustus, and similar systems were established in place of more traditional, tribal forms of social control.

It should be noted that throughout the ancient world, there was considerable resistance to the idea of organized enforcement of laws. In Egypt, where soldiers and temple officials were responsible for enforcing the law, these early enforcement officers of the aristocracy were seen by many as simple servants of the Pharaoh and other members of the ruling elite, concerned only with protecting the property of the wealthy. In Greece, the philosopher Aristotle (384–322 BC) maintained that the existence of a permanent police force was contrary to the very idea of democracy, arguing that the people should be directly responsible for enforcing their own laws. Interestingly, this same argument was raised again some two thousand years later in England by those concerned about plans for the establishment of the first modern police force. While many centuries may have passed since the time of the ancient Greeks and Romans, the people of London nevertheless found themselves confronted with the question of who should be responsible for enforcing the law: the police or the people themselves.

Development of Formal Policing in England

The Roman emperor Augustus is frequently credited with establishing the first civilian police force, know as *vigiles*. Although, under Roman occupation, this early model of policing would reach England, it would collapse with the progression of the Dark Ages.

Following the fall of Rome approximately 1,600 years ago and end of the Roman occupation of Britain, traditional forms of law enforcement based on individual and tribal justice reemerged throughout England. As in ancient times, each community adhered to its own rules and punishments, leaving law enforcement in the hands of the individual. As the Dark Ages progressed, powerful landholders and rulers began to assert themselves and establish a hold over large areas of the country. Victims and their families, however, remained responsible for pursuing and punishing perpetrators within their communities. As a consequence, there was little consistency in the way in which justice and punishment were administered, and there was no organized system of policing. Punishments during this time were typically severe and frequently resulted in the death of the offender. In some cases, where the truth of the accusation was disputed, the accused was given the opportunity to prove his or her innocence by undergoing some form of predetermined ordeal or trial. Ironically, the process of proving one's innocence could often be as painful as the punishment that accompanied a finding of guilt.

From Tithings to Posse Comitatus

Towards the end of the Dark Ages, the gradual merging of Roman, Germanic, and Anglo-Saxon traditions and the emergence of the monarchy gave rise to the general acceptance of two ideas that were to provide the basis for a more unified and consistent approach to law enforcement. The first of these was the concept of the "King's Peace," which held that any crime against an individual was also a crime against the king. This meant that the crown could claim to have a legitimate interest in the enforcement of the law, even if no offence had been directly committed against the king or his agents.

The second idea was the notion that all of the king's subjects were also his property. Accordingly, anyone who caused harm to any citizen was potentially liable to pay compensation to the crown. These two ideas provided the basis for the legal principle that a criminal act represented a crime against the state as well as the individual, and that the state had a direct interest in ensuring that the laws were upheld and enforced. This principle remains at the heart of criminal law in both England and the United States and provides the basic justification for the existence of the police in both countries. Although the law continued to be enforced according to local tradition, the end of the Dark Ages opened the way for a more centralized approach to the problem of law enforcement.

By the middle of the ninth century, the majority of the English population lived in established towns and cities, each with its own system of rules and organization. During the reign of Alfred the Great (849–899 AD), however, a new system of social organization was imposed. In an effort to make the collection of taxes and the maintenance of the King's Peace easier, Alfred divided England into regions known as **shires.** Each shire, which was similar to the American county, consisted of geographical units known as "hundreds," so named because each contained 100 families. Each of the hundreds was composed of ten **tithings**, and a tithing consisted of ten families. Under this new arrangement, every citizen was tied to a particular tithe and was jointly responsible with all other members of his or her group for the payment of taxes and the maintenance of order (Stead 1985). As a result, a crime committed by one person was held to be a crime committed by his or her entire community, with the punishment to be borne by the group as a whole. In essence, Alfred's aim was to make communities self-regulating when it came to the payment of taxes and the enforcement of law. **Shire reeves**, the precursor to the modern-day sheriff, were the leaders of the shires and were appointed by the king. They were given the task of ensuring that law and order were maintained throughout their region. Drawing on the assistance of locally elected **constables**, shire reeves frequently organized villagers and other members of the community into **posses** that would track down and apprehend offenders.

Although by modern standards the system of policing established by Alfred the Great might appear to be crude, the introduction of shire reeves and local constables revolutionized the way in which laws were enforced throughout medieval England. In the space of a few decades, the administration of justice was taken out of the hands of individuals and made the responsibility of particular communities and their appointed leaders. Law enforcement ceased to be a private matter and became associated with the king and his agents.

Some three centuries later, this system was formalized by the Statute of Winchester (1285), which increased the power of the constables and made them responsible for organizing local watchers. In addition, under the statute, all men between the ages of fifteen and sixty were required to bear arms in defense of the crown and the King's Peace and to assist their local constable in the pursuit of offenders. Failure to heed the constable's call for help—known as the **hue and cry**—was a punishable offense under the new law, and anyone who did not help to apprehend criminals risked being tried with them as associates. It was also around this time that the first justices of the peace began to emerge, who acted as judges and presided over local trials. Typically country gentlemen and members of the aristocracy, these justices were central to the administration of justice throughout the shires, and, like the constables, were also entrusted with the task of keeping the King's Peace.

This system of justices and constables was to change little over the next 400 years. Although criminal law expanded considerably during this time, law enforcement remained the responsibility of local officials answerable to the king. By the eighteenth century, however, the system had begun to fail. In many regions, justices and constables had become corrupt and unaccountable, frequently using their considerable powers to enhance their own positions and wealth. More importantly, the steady process of industrialization and urbanization had also made local peacekeeping more and more difficult. As the population grew, informal methods of policing based on collective responsibility and local ties became unwieldy and ineffective. Lawlessness and disorder became more widespread, with many members of the upper class employing guards to protect them and their property from attack. Faced with the possibility of anarchy, it became clear that something had to be done.

After various efforts failed to rejuvenate the existing system of constables, the government eventually granted the London magistrate Henry Fielding permission to found a group of organized law enforcement agents. Known as the **Bow Street Runners**, these men were given the task of apprehending criminals and recovering stolen goods within London and were paid, in part, from city funds. Because they also had the duty to solve crimes, the Runners were essentially the first paid detectives (Howe 1965). Because they failed to stem the rising tide of crime in the city, they were eventually disbanded some years later. However, the Runners did enjoy a limited degree of success. Many individuals were impressed by their organization and effectiveness, and they had the reputation of being incorruptible and determined (Howe 1965). Soon the idea of maintaining a permanent salaried police force began to gain wider acceptance.

Another driving force behind the push for the foundation of a professional police force was the public outrage following the **Peterloo massacre of 1819,** in which a political protest turned riotous after the military was brought in to break it up. This incident left eleven dead and hundreds injured, as well as a lingering fear in the minds of many of the dangers of relying on the military to handle public-order situations. In the United States, the **Posse Comitatus Act** (18 U.S. Code, Section 1385) was signed in 1878 to separate military functions from local law enforcement. The original intent of this act was to prohibit the use of federal troops in the policing of state elections; however, in effect, the act also prohibits the military from serving as a domestic police force. The act bans the Army, Navy, Air Force, and Marines from participating in arrests, evidence search and seizure, or any other conventional policing activity on U.S. soil.

The Formal System of Policing

Early developments in policing are traced in Table 2.1. Although by the early 1800s London had over 450 paid police officers working throughout the city, there was still no centrally organized system of law enforcement. In 1828, however, the Home Secretary **Sir Robert Peel** established what was to be later

Linkages in Law Enforcement

Posse Comitatus Today

Posse Comitatus was passed in the post–Civil War era in response to a general fear that the new federal government would interfere with state governments and use the military against its own citizens. Nevertheless, there are a number of exceptions to Posse Comitatus:

- National Guard forces operating under the state authority are exempt from the Act's restrictions.

- The President of the United States can use federal troops to "quell" domestic violence situations.

- Aerial photography and visual searches are allowed if for the purpose of assisting civilian law enforcement.

- An exception to the Act, created by Congress, allows the military to offer training, equipment, and advice in the "war on drugs."

- The Coast Guard is exempt from the provisions of the Act.

- The Navy can assist a Coast Guard vessel in pursuit.

Today, there is talk of adding further exceptions to Posse Comitatus in order to reduce linkage blindness between military and civilian law enforcement agencies and to expedite investigations of suspected terrorists. In light of the threat posed by bioterrorism and nuclear terrorism, some reformers have even proposed eliminating Posse Comitatus altogether. Such a change would free the Department of Defense to treat terrorism as a national security issue rather than a law enforcement issue and would put the military in charge of investigating domestic terrorist incidents. The Posse Comitatus Act is found in Appendix B.

Questions

1. How would eliminating Posse Comitatus change the balance between crime control and due process?

2. What, if any, conditions do you think could warrant the elimination of Posse Comitatus?

3. How would local law enforcement be helped or hindered by the elimination of Posse Comitatus?

4. Where do you think Americans should draw the line between crime control and due process in the war on terrorism?

called the London Metropolitan Police. Having served in Ireland for many years and successfully organized the Royal Irish Constabulary, Peel was keen to reform the way in which the law was enforced in England and to create a new police force for the city of London. Parliament was initially resistant to Peel's ideas, largely because they feared the introduction of a military-style force along French lines. They eventually passed the London **Metropolitan Police Act** in 1829, providing funds for the establishment of a 1,000-officer force governed by strict standards of conduct and discipline.

Initially under the command of two magistrates (who later became known as commissioners), this new Metropolitan force differed markedly from previous efforts at law enforcement in England. Most important, the officers were organized along military lines and made subject to clear chains of command and rules of conduct. In order to encourage accountability and professionalism within the force, the police were also required to wear uniforms, making them easily identifiable in public, and to carry badges that showed their identification number. In addition, these officers were direct employees of the state, as opposed to being private citizens charged by law to assist in the apprehension of

TABLE 2.1

Key Dates in the History of Law Enforcement

2200 BC	Code of Hammurabi standardizes laws and punishments in Babylon.
1340 BC	Nile River Police established in Egypt.
510 BC	Romans establish the Praetorian Guard and Urban Cohort.
27 BC	Roman system of *vigiles* instituted by Emperor Augustus.
400–800	Law enforcement in England is based on traditional notions of individual justice and punishment.
899	System of shires, hundreds, and tithes is established by Alfred the Great.
1285	Statute of Winchester establishes the watch-and-ward system in England.
1326	Justices of the peace first appointed by the king in England.
1748	Founding of the Bow Street Runners in London.
1829	Creation of the London Metropolitan Police.

offenders. In these respects, Peel's Metropolitan Police were the first modern police force. Indeed, many forces around the world continue to be organized around the same basic rules and principles contained in Peel's **Principles of Policing** (reproduced in Table 2.2).

Initially, British citizens did not embrace the development of a formal governmental police force. They feared that the police would be a pawn of the government and act as an occupying army in their towns. However, the sentiment towards the police changed in 1833 with the riots in Cold Bath Fields. One riot resulted in the violent death of Police Constable Culley, and at trial, a jury returned a verdict of justifiable homicide for his killer.[1] After a newspaper account published the story of the widow of this officer, the citizens began to show public support for the police and their efforts to stem crime in the city.

After witnessing the effectiveness of the London Metropolitan Police, several other professional forces throughout England were established along similar lines by 1856. As the recruitment and training methods developed by Peel spread, interest in crime prevention grew and the idea of local "policemen"—called **bobbies** after their founder—as the central law enforcement figures in the community gained wide acceptance.[2]

Development of Formal Policing in the United States

During the early years of colonization, law enforcement in America developed along English lines. Towns and villages appointed constables and sheriffs with powers very similar to their English counterparts. Additionally, they organized watch systems that were an adaptation of those that had existed for centuries in

TABLE 2.2

Sir Robert Peel's Principles of Policing (1829)

1. The police must be stable, efficient and organized along military lines.

2. The police must be under governmental control.

3. The absence of crime will best prove the efficiency of the police.

4. The distribution of crime news is essential.

5. The deployment of police strength both by time and area is essential.

6. No quality is more indispensable to a policeman than a perfect command of temper; a quiet determined manner has more effect than violent action.

7. Good appearance commands respect.

8. The securing and training of proper persons is at the root of efficiency.

9. Public security demands that every police officer be given a number.

10. Police headquarters should be centrally located and easily accessible to the people.

11. Policemen should be hired on a probationary basis.

12. Police records are necessary to the correct distribution of police strength.

England. As time went on, and as English policing became increasingly centralized, the development of English policing began to deviate from the pattern that was being established in the United States. In the colonies, following law enforcement traditions brought with them from Europe, citizens were responsible for helping to maintain the peace, and although laws were passed requiring the public to help officials in the apprehension of criminals in larger towns such as Boston and Philadelphia, victims of crime could not always rely on the authorities or the community to bring criminals to justice.

Early Watch Systems

As in England, the first system of policing in the United States was an informal one where individuals within a community protected each other. This informal system consisted of numerous positions, including a justice of the peace, a sheriff, constables, and a night watch. The role of the sheriff was strictly confined to law enforcement and the apprehension of criminals, and he performed duties such as serving warrants and subpoenas and maintaining the local jails. Although initially the sheriff was an appointed position, over time it evolved into an elected one. The sheriff's responsibilities eventually expanded beyond solely law enforcement to include collecting taxes and monitoring the system of cattle branding. Although the main duty of the sheriff continued to be law enforcement oriented, it was a reactive role without any general crime prevention functions.

As the population in cities began to grow, it became increasingly difficult for sheriffs and local marshals (similar to the English constables) to maintain order.

As with their predecessors in England, the early U.S. experiments with watch systems involved members of the community patrolling neighborhoods. In addition to a general lack of efficiency, watch systems were particularly illequipped to handle riot situations.

Consequently, cities such as New York, Boston, and Philadelphia began to experiment with **watch systems**. These watches, which consisted of volunteer citizens, were based on the idea of community responsibility. Members of the community were required by local law enforcement officers to undertake patrols of their neighborhood under the guidance of local marshals or constables. The purpose of these patrols was to watch for signs of criminal activity, though the powers of the watchmen were limited only to arrest and the holding of individuals suspected of wrongdoing.

Although watchmen occasionally averted criminal acts, the watch system was fraught with problems. Night watchmen were unpopular, largely as a result of their lack of enthusiasm, lack of competency, and frequent state of drunkenness. Their weaknesses were most apparent in situations of large-scale disorder, such as riots. By the mid-1840s, most large cities came to regard the night watch system as inefficient and more harmful than beneficial. As a result, this informal system of night watchmen drawn from the community evolved into a system whereby the patrols were undertaken by full-time, paid watchmen. The changeover between volunteer and paid watchmen was gradual, and for many years in some cities (e.g., Philadelphia during the 1830s) the two systems coexisted in a hybrid structure of paid day watchmen and volunteer night watchmen.

Cities were not the only areas experiencing difficulties with law enforcement during the colonial era. Outside of the major towns and cities, lawlessness was often widespread. Vast distances and the absence of communal ties in the frontier made it difficult for individual sheriffs to impose their authority on citizens. As a result, vigilantism was common. In many jurisdictions, **vigilante committees**, made up of area residents wishing to actively fight crime, would take on all law enforcement duties, from pursuing offenders to trying them and punishing them. Individual landholders often employed these vigilantes to protect them, and in many cases the threat of violence was the only effective deterrent to potential offenders.

Slave Patrols and the Jim Crow Laws

While cities in the North developed a night watch system, law enforcement in the South tended to focus on the control and discipline of slaves. **Slave patrols** were first established in the South during the mid-1740s, with officers being given broad powers to punish slaves who committed offenses or refused to submit to their masters. The slave patrols at this time were coordinated by property owners who, individually, had difficulty controlling the slave population and ensuring that they did not defy their masters. Like the night watch system, slave patrols were based on a form of citizen obligation whereby members of a community would watch over all other citizens' slaves to ensure their obedience. Although informal initially, slave patrols evolved into an organized system with a chain of command and organizational structure (Wood 1984). In fact, they are generally considered to be the precursor to modern police forces in the United States despite their extremely narrow and clearly racist focus (Williams and Murphy 1990). By 1837, South Carolina, which had instituted particularly infamous slave codes, had one of the largest police forces in the country, with over 100 officers on slave patrol (Conser and Russell 2000).

Slaves in most states were deemed incapable of exercising the rights of ordinary citizens. Often mounted on horseback and carrying whips, the slave patrols enforced laws that prohibited literacy and commerce amongst slaves. The slave patrols also made sure that slaves were not in possession of weapons or ammunition and had the power to search "Negro houses" to ensure that such laws were not being violated. Even though slaves were not considered full citizens, they were capable of being held criminally responsible for their "crimes," particularly actions such as being away from their masters without carrying passes.

When the slave codes were abolished after the Civil War, a number of states, mainly in the South, adopted "Black Codes" that set out the responsibilities of newly freed slaves through a complex system of laws and judicial conventions. Although the passing of the Civil Rights Act in 1866 helped to improve the position of blacks, many states in the 1880s enacted **Jim Crow laws**. These codes, examples of which are shown in Table 2.3, enforced segregation between whites

Considered the precursor to modern police forces in the United States, slave patrols emerged in the South out of a fear of possible slave insurrection. Slave patrols enforced slave codes prohibiting such things as literacy, commerce, or the possession of weapons by slaves.

and blacks in schools, parks, restrooms, public transportation, sports teams, and most other public facilities. Interracial marriage was prohibited, and employers were required to have separate facilities for their white and black workers. Some states even required separate facilities for whites and blacks in prisons and mental hospitals. The Supreme Court deemed segregation constitutional in 1896 by setting out a "separate but equal" doctrine in *Plessy v. Ferguson*.[3]

Because the police were required to enforce the Jim Crow laws, the black community came to view the police essentially as agents of an oppressive legal system that treated them as second-class citizens. Much of the tension between the police and minority communities that ensued throughout the early twentieth century resulted from the police's enforcement first of the slave codes and subsequently the Jim Crow laws. Even after such codes were abolished, many in the black community viewed the police as "slave patrols in disguise," with police behavior towards minorities still derisive. The relationship between the police and minority communities has been wrought with friction and hostility since the abolishment of the last Jim Crow laws in the 1960s, and this tension—discussed at length in Chapter 10—is still present in many respects today.

TABLE 2.3

Examples of Jim Crow Laws*

Issue	Law
Interracial marriage	Marriage between a Caucasian person and a Negro, or an individual with any Negro blood, is prohibited.
Buses	All bus stations must have separate waiting rooms and ticket windows for Caucasians and Negros. All buses must have separate sections in which the Caucasians and Negros can sit.
Restrooms	Employers, schools and recreational facilities must provide separate toilet facilities for Caucasians and Negros.
Restaurants	It is prohibited to serve food to Caucasians and Negros in the same room, unless they are separated by a partition.
Education	Caucasian and Negro children will be educated in separate buildings.
Housing	It is a crime for Caucasians to rent rooms in a dwelling to Negros, and vice versa. Caucasians and Negros must not dwell within the same building.
Juvenile detention	White and Negro children in juvenile detention facilities shall be kept completely separated.
Prisons	Caucasian and Negro convicts will eat and sleep separately.
Sports	Particularly with regards to baseball, Caucasian and Negro players must have separate teams, fields, and equipment.
Leisure activities (e.g., theaters)	All individuals operating leisure activity centers (e.g., cinemas, public halls, theaters, etc.) must have separate facilities for Caucasians and Negros.

*Jim Crow laws differed by state. These are general examples of requirements of Jim Crow laws and are not specific to a particular state. For a summary of many laws by state, see www.nps.gov/malu/documents/jim_crow_laws.htm.

The Eras of American Policing

Kelling and Moore (1991) describe American policing as having progressed through three distinct eras—the political era, the reform era, and the community era—each characterized by its own organizational structure, tactics, and focus. The remainder of this chapter examines the political era; Chapter 3 focuses on the reform and community eras. Table 2.4 summarizes the characteristics of each era.

The Political Era (1840–1930)

As in England, industrialization in the United States during the late eighteenth and early nineteenth centuries brought with it rising levels of urban crime and public disorder. As immigration and internal migration led to rapid increases in urban populations—particularly in cities such as New York, Boston, Chicago, and Philadelphia—a new underclass of urban poor emerged. Food riots, labor strikes, and the growing threat of widespread civil disturbance led many local politicians and industrialists to conclude that a new system of law enforcement was needed if the social fabric of the country was to be maintained. However, many were wary of allowing the government to establish a permanent police force, particularly given that Americans had fought the American Revolution to free themselves from just such control by the British. Eventually, however, formal police forces were established, and by the end of the nineteenth century professional policing and law enforcement had become a fact of American life.

Boston was the first city to establish a formal night watch system in 1801, supplemented by a day watch in 1838. The first city to formally employ both day and night watchmen was Philadelphia, though it was New York City that established what is considered the first modern police force in that the day and night watchmen were under the supervision of one police chief. The New York force, loosely modeled on the London Metropolitan police, was organized along military lines, but unlike its counterpart in London, the New York police derived their authority not from an act of Parliament, but rather from the support of local politicians. As a consequence, from the outset, the New York police force was vulnerable to political interference and external pressure.

To exacerbate such problems, early police organizations tended to be highly decentralized. Local stations and officers were rarely supervised or held accountable by anyone except their immediate superiors. During the nineteenth century, most police officers actively worked to further the interests of the local politicians who placed them in power and gave them their resources and authority. These politicians were almost all upper-middle-class white males who worked within a **spoils system**, appointing people to civil service jobs based predominately on patronage, political affiliation, or in return for monetary payments. In addition, they often rewarded their associates by giving them key positions in police departments, and the politicians in turn used the police to help them maintain their political positions. As a result, policing was rife with corruption. Towards the end of the nineteenth century, many public leaders became convinced that something needed to be done to combat increasing levels of corruption and political favoritism within the police that resulted from the spoils system. It was at this point that the police began a period of major reform,

TABLE 2.4

Kelling and Moore's Eras of Policing

Era	Characteristics
The Political Era (1840–1930)	Authority is primarily derived from politicians
	Primary police function is to respond to citizens and politicians, satisfy their needs
	Organization is decentralized
	Intimate relationship with the community
	Much use of foot patrol
	Significant amount of corruption in law enforcement.
The Reform Era (1930–1980)	Authority is primarily derived from the law
	Primary police function is crime control
	Organization is centralized and efficient
	Professional but remote relationship with the community
	Use of motorized patrol, rapid response to emergency calls
	Poor relationship with the community
The Community Era (1980–present)	Authority is derived from both law and the community
	Primary police function is community service and crime control
	Organization is decentralized with special units
	Intimate relationship with the community
	Use of problem-oriented policing, foot patrol and public relations
	Improve citizen's quality of life, but reliance on officer as a social worker

[handwritten annotation: Spoils system, pros. police much closer to politics]

Source: Kelling and Moore (1991).

aimed primarily at making police forces more professional and less susceptible to outside pressures.

The Pendleton Act of 1883   One of the most significant developments at the end of the nineteenth century was the passage of the **Pendleton Act**; its primary purpose was to abolish the spoils system. The Pendleton Act was a federal bill, and its main goal was to reduce the level of corruption endemic within the administration of Ulysses S. Grant (*The Columbia Encyclopedia* 2001). Because it was a federal act, it only applied to federal employees. However, it later set into motion a series of similar proposals at state and local levels calling for the reform of hiring and promotion standards for civil servants in local governments.

[handwritten annotation: Abolished spoils sys.]

The Pendleton Act led to a wave of reforms because it established objective criteria for hiring public officials and it made it unlawful to dismiss civil employees for political reasons. Prior to this, most government positions were politically appointed. Although the Act did not entirely eliminate the influence of politicians, it was an important first step towards regulating the influence of politicians in hiring decisions. For instance, under the Pendleton Act, politicians were prevented from hiring members of the same political party but were instead required to hire equally across all parties. This resulted in less power being vested in individual parties and, thus, less corruption.

However, despite such reform efforts, it should also be stressed that corruption was ever more difficult to combat during this period given that police forces were not particularly **legalistic**, or oriented toward the strict enforcement of the letter of the law. Instead, the police were organizationally decentralized and focused on **order maintenance** and the status quo rather than on creating adequate accountability mechanisms to monitor police use of discretion.

In addition to regulations on hiring and firing of employees, the Pendleton Act also set forth regulations about promotions. The second clause of section two of the Act states that competitive exams must be given to all those applying for a promotion, and only the person with the highest exam score will be promoted. This reform was intended to ensure that promotion would only occur based on an objective evaluation of performance in police departments in hopes that the "best man" would be promoted. This same section goes on to state that "no person in said service has any right to use his official authority or influence to coerce the political action of any person or body," once again establishing a fair system whereby no one from a particular party is favored or punished. As a whole, the Act did not directly address the sources of corruption; however, it did provide honest officers with some degree of protection from political pressure and a degree of job security.

The Wickersham Commission   The turn of the twentieth century brought with it significant social change to the United States. The Industrial Revolution was causing vast urban growth, which coincided with a rise in anonymity within the cities and an increase in crime. It also brought forth different types of crime. Not only were juveniles and women being picked up by the police more than ever before, but there was also an increase in organized crime. This was aggravated in 1920 with the passage of the Eighteenth Amendment, or Prohibition.

In the hope of finding solutions for these and other social ills, Herbert Hoover organized the **Wickersham Commission** in 1929. The purpose of the Commission was to address growing concerns with Prohibition, the increasing crime rate, as well as problems with the juvenile justice and adult criminal justice processes (National Commission on Law Observance and Enforcement 1931). The Wickersham Commission also reported on police misconduct and addressed the increasing awareness of problems between police and minority communities. Though its findings were not remarkable, the Wickersham Commission has come to be regarded as a turning point in the history of policing. The primary reason for this is that it undertook the first large-scale study of the criminal justice system in the United States. Additionally, it was critical of the police in its findings, calling for significant police reforms. In particular, the commission focused on police misconduct, and spurred leaders in the policing community to develop systems whereby citizens could register complaints against the police and to establish internal mechanisms for the investigation of police misconduct. Although the main focus of the Wickersham Commission was on issues other than the police, it nevertheless served as an important precursor to future commissions.

Women and Minorities in Early Policing   It is important to note that although many police forces in the United States were modeled along English lines, America's past meant that these new police officers faced a number of challenges different from those that confronted their counterparts in England. Perhaps most significant was the question of how the police were to deal with issues relating to race and the continuing effects of slavery. The political era of policing was not particularly concerned with the recruitment of women and minorities. When the police did take note of women and minorities, it was based on a narrow view of their potential uses in policing.

African American officers were almost unheard of in the early days of policing, and, as a consequence, accusations of racial bias among the police soon began to emerge. The first known African American police officer served in Washington, D.C., in 1861 (Sullivan 1989), although it was the New Orleans police force that first took steps to actively recruit African Americans during the 1870s. New Orleans had a large African American community at that time, and black police officers were hired to police predominantly black areas. Three African American officers were even appointed to the police board. It was not until the second half of the next century that forces across the country began to deal directly with the question of law enforcement and race. Until that time, most of the forces that hired African American police officers kept them segregated from white officers.

Like ethnic and racial minorities, women were also nearly nonexistent in early police forces. When women were first hired by the police, it was as police matrons in the 1880s. The police matrons, who were for the most part upper-middle-class white women, performed duties such as visiting the sick, making lunches for the male officers, searching female and juvenile suspects, escorting and supervising women in precinct detention facilities, and going to houses of prostitution, theaters, and dance halls, as needed, to reform the wayward women there (Schulz 1995).

The first documented policewoman was Alice Stebbins Wells, who joined the Los Angeles Police Department in 1910. The duties of policewomen, like the matrons, centered on social service activities such as preventive and protection programs for women and children (Schulz 1995). Not surprisingly, the appointment of minority policewomen lagged behind that of whites. The first black female to be hired by a police force was Georgia Robinson, who began working for the Los Angeles Police Department in 1916 as a matron. She was then promoted to policewoman in 1919. Though the hiring of policewomen increased during World War II, women are still significantly underrepresented in police forces. Demonstrating its position as both barometer and enforcer of the external social forces in which it is situated, it was not until Civil Rights and Equal Employment Opportunity legislation during the 1960s that women and minority officers began to take on equal roles within law enforcement, themes that will be developed throughout this book.

The first documented police-woman was Alice Stebbins Wells who joined the Los Angeles Police Department in 1910. However, it was not until the 1960s that women and minority officers began to take on equal roles within law enforcement.

Origins of the Reform Era

Looking back over the history of policing, both in England and the United States, it is possible to see that many of the basic concerns about accountability, independence, and effectiveness that occupied the minds of the first law enforcers continue to be issues today. Deciding on the extent to which a police officer should be a part of the community he or she polices and the role that the public ought to play in the task of law enforcement remain important questions. In an effort to "correct" some of the negative influences in law enforcement, such as entrenched practices of corruption and brutality, reform efforts sought to create a more objective, legalistic profession driven by the rule of law.

Faces of Reform: Early Leaders in Law Enforcement Reform

Although a number of individuals had a significant influence on policing throughout the twentieth century, three in particular were at the forefront of police change during the reform era. August Vollmer, O. W. Wilson, and J. Edgar Hoover all helped to transform law enforcement from a corrupt organization into a respectable profession at the local, state, and federal levels.

August Vollmer: The Father of Police Professionalism

August Vollmer is perhaps best known for linking education with police training. Vollmer established the first police training school in the United States, drawing on the resources of universities in and around Berkeley, California. Having served as the chief of police in Berkeley, California, from 1905 to 1932, August Vollmer is today considered the pioneer of police professionalization and reform. He also helped to develop the School of Criminology at the University of California at Berkeley, which would eventually become the model for law and criminal justice education throughout the United States.

Vollmer is credited with, among other things, introducing the use of intelligence and psychological testing to police selection procedures. He also led the move towards the greater use of the scientific method in police investigations, establishing a forensic laboratory in Berkeley.

Important to understanding the underlying philosophy behind the reformer, Vollmer viewed police officers as "social workers dealing with a range of societal problems which manifested themselves in crime and disorder. In his view, policemen should become college-educated professionals akin to doctors and lawyers" (Reppetto 1978, p. 243). To this end, he was one of the founders of the professional association that later would become the American Society of Criminology.

O. W. Wilson: The Protégé

A protégé of Vollmer, **O. W. Wilson** stands as one of the most influential writers on the subject of policing during the twentieth century. He is the author of the first two books on police management, one of which is described by some authors as being "the Bible of policing for decades" (Dempsey 1999, p. 16).

During his tenure as head of the Wichita, Kansas, police department, Wilson conducted the first systematic study of the effectiveness of one-officer police squad cars. His results showed that they were as efficient and effective as two-person cars, contrary to popular opinion at the time. During his time in

Kansas, Wilson would make major reforms to police training, implementing many of the ideas of his teacher August Vollmer.

Wilson viewed managerial efficiency as central to police administration, believing that police departments should "maximize patrol coverage by replacing foot patrols with one-person auto patrols" (Dempsey 1999, p. 16). Moreover, he saw rapid response to calls as being the best means of measuring the effectiveness of police departments. As such, he developed workload formulas to measure calls for service versus reported crimes on each beat to guide deployment. Both of these views became principles that would guide police management throughout the reform era.

J. Edgar Hoover: The FBI
Even today, the name **J. Edgar Hoover** is synonymous with the Federal Bureau of Investigation in the minds of many Americans. A firm believer in the need for professional law enforcement agencies, Hoover was largely responsible for developing the FBI National Academy in 1935, which is responsible for training police officers from around the country in specialized policing and investigation techniques. Hoover was also responsible for establishing the FBI Crime Laboratory, which, despite controversy surrounding the lab in the 1990s, is generally regarded as one of the best such

J. Edgar Hoover, former director of the FBI, is associated with significant reforms such as the creation of the FBI National Academy in 1935, the Uniform Crime Reports program, and Ten Most Wanted Criminals program.

laboratories in the world.[4] Hoover's other key achievements include the introduction of the FBI Uniform Crime Reports (something we will be turning to shortly), the hiring of accountants and lawyers to serve as special agents, and the development of the FBI's Ten Most Wanted Criminals program.

Although Hoover is well regarded as a reformer and advocate of police professionalism, his reputation since his death has suffered considerably. There are many reasons for this, both professional and personal. On a professional note, Hoover has been accused of harassing alleged Communists using domestic surveillance by the FBI during his time as head of the Bureau, suppressing information from the Warren Commission (the commission that investigated the assassination of John F. Kennedy), protecting individuals involved in organized crime from investigations, and mishandling royalty funds from books and movies (Gentry 1991). On a personal note, there have been many rumors about his sexual proclivities, including his possible homosexuality (despite his vehement opposition to homosexual relationships) and cross dressing (Theoharis 1995), and some biographers speculate that his protection of organized crime families was the result of indecent photos they possessed of him engaging in illicit sexual activities (Summers 1993). It might be beneficial to consider Hoover's harassment of alleged Communists and improper use of surveillance as we consider limits to law enforcement freedoms today in investigating alleged terrorists.

Chapter Summary

- The origins of social control date back to at least 2200 BC. The earliest known formal law is the Code of Hammurabi, which was the first set of laws to establish punishments for specific acts.

- Both England and the United States had informal systems of policing until the nineteenth century. The informal systems were based on the concept of community responsibility. Neighbors would take turns watching each other's houses. In the United States, there were also vigilante committees in the frontier made up of citizens who wanted to actively fight crime.

- The first formal police organization was the London Metropolitan Police, formed by Sir Robert Peel when he signed the Metropolitan Police Act in 1829. This organization was governed by strict standards of conduct and discipline laid out in Peel's Principles of Policing. Many forces worldwide followed the military-like structure.

- Throughout the South (and in some northern cities) policing focused on slave patrols. The primary purpose of slave patrols was to ensure that slaves did not escape from their masters and followed the rules. Once the slave codes were abolished, Jim Crow laws were formed. These required that institutions such as schools and parks have "separate but equal" areas for black and white individuals.

- Kelling and Moore describe three eras of policing: the political era (characterized by corruption, decentralized structure, and intimate relationship with the community); the reform era (characterized by professionalism, centralized structure, rapid response to calls, and poor relations with the community); and the community era (characterized by a focus on service to the community, going back to a decentralized force, an emphasis on foot patrols, and the use of problem-oriented policing).

- Historically, policemen and policewomen held very different roles (though their roles are now equal). Policewomen were originally hired as matrons and worked only with women and juveniles. Their roles were similar to that of a social worker, and their primary concern was the welfare of women and children in the community. The role of minority police officers has also changed from policing "minority communities" only to receiving widespread jobs throughout the department and an increasing number of supervisory roles.

- In an effort to professionalize law enforcement and remove the political influences fueling corruption, the reform movement was born. Key figures in the reform movement were August Vollmer, O. W. Wilson, and J. Edgar Hoover.

KEY TERMS

Bobbies 43
Bow Street Runners 41
Code of Hammurabi 38
Constables 40
J. Edgar Hoover 53
Hue and cry 40
Jim Crow laws 46
Legalistic 50
Lex taliones 38
Metropolitan Police Act 42

Order maintenance 50
Sir Robert Peel 41
Pendleton Act 49
Peterloo Massacre of 1819 41
Posse Comitatus Act 41
Posses 40
Principles of Policing 43
Shire reeves 40
Shires 40
Slave patrols 45

Spoils system 48
Tithings 40
Vigilante 38
Vigilante committees 45
Vigiles 38
August Vollmer 52
Watch systems 45
Wickersham Commission 50
O. W. Wilson 52

Linking the Dots

1. What are the similarities between our current policing system and the watch system? The Code of Hammurabi?
2. In what way can policing be a political issue?
3. Why were there so few women and minority police officers at the turn of the century?

Why are they still so underrepresented?
4. Is there a political/police figure today affecting policing as much as Robert Peel did?
5. Would the U.S. system of policing work in England? Why or why not?

REFERENCES

The Columbia Encyclopedia. 2000. 6th ed. Farmington Hills, MI: Gale Group.

Conser, J. A., and G. D. Russell. 2000. *Law Enforcement in the United States.* Gaithersburg, MD: Aspen Publishers.

Dempsey, J. 1999. *An Introduction to Policing.* Belmont, CA: Wadsworth.

Gentry, C. 1991. *J. Edgar Hoover: The Man and the Secrets.* New York, NY: W.W. Norton & Company.

Howe, R. 1965. *The Story of Scotland Yard.* New York: Horizon.

Kelling, G. L., and M. H. Moore. 1991. "From Political to Reform to Community: The Evolving Strategy of the Police." In *Community Policing: Rhetoric or Reality,* edited by J. R. Greene and S. D. Mastrofsky, 14–15, 22–23. New York: Praeger.

National Commission on Law Observance and Enforcement. 1931. *Report on Lawlessness in Law Enforcement.* Washington, D.C.: National Commission on Law Observance and Enforcement.

Palmer, S. H. 1988. *Police and Protest in England and Ireland 1780–1850.* Cambridge: Cambridge University Press.

Reiner, R. 1994. *The Politics of the Police,* 2d ed. New York: Harvester.

Reppetto, T. A. 1978. *The Blue Parade.* New York: Free Press.

Richardson, J. F. 1970. *The New York Police, Colonial Times to 1901.* New York: Oxford University Press.

Schulz, D. M. 1995. *From Social Worker to Crime Fighter: Women in United States Municipal Policing.* Westport, CT: Praeger.

Silver, A. 1984. "The Demand for Order in Civil Society: A Review of Some Themes in the History of Crime, Police and Riot." In *The Police: Six Sociological Essays,* edited by D. Bordua, 1–24. New York: Wiley.

Stead, P. J. 1985. *The Police of Britain.* London: Macmillan Publishing Company.

Sullivan, P. 1989. "Minority Officers: Current Issues." In *Critical Issues in Policing: Contemporary Readings,* edited by R. Dunham and G. Alpert, 331–345. Prospect Heights, IL: Waveland.

Summers, A. 1993. *Official and Confidential: The Secret Life of J. Edgar Hoover.* New York, NY: Orion Publishing Group.

Tanner, A. R. 2003. "Crime Labs Stained by a Shadow of a Doubt." *LA Times,* July 13, A18.

Theoharis, A. G. 1995. *J. Edgar Hoover, Sex and Crime.* Chicago, IL: Ivan R. Dee, Inc.

Williams, H., and P. V. Murphy. 1990. *The Evolving Strategy of Police: A Minority View.* Washington, D.C.: U.S. Department of Justice.

Wood, B. 1984. *Slavery in Colonial Georgia.* Athens, GA: University of Georgia Press.

NOTES

1. See www.met.police.uk/index.shtml.
2. For a thorough analysis of the history of British policing, see Palmer (1988).
3. *Plessy v. Ferguson*, 163 U.S. 537 (1896).
4. During the 1990s, there were several instances in which contaminated evidence from the FBI Crime Lab was used to convict an individual of serious violent crimes. See Tanner (2003).

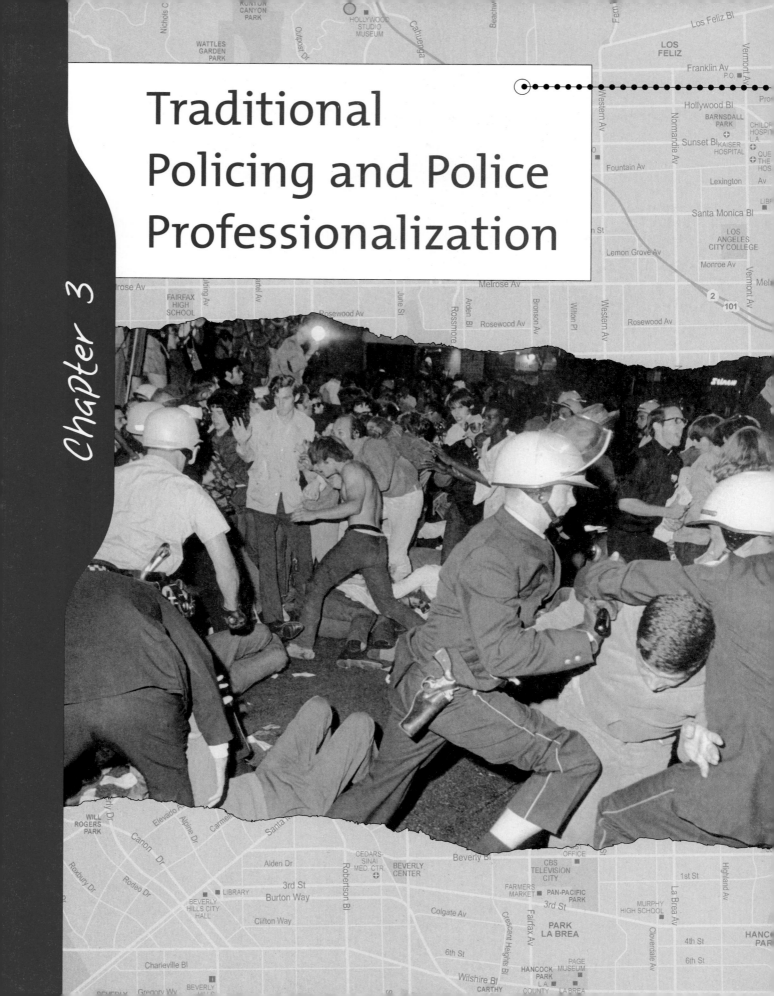

Chapter 3

Traditional Policing and Police Professionalization

Chapter Outline

Chapter Objectives

- Compare and contrast the reform era and the political era.

- Discuss policing as a profession.

- Explain the effect of the reforms of the reform era on crime rate, re-source deployment, and police–community relations.

- Describe the *Uniform Crime Report* (*UCR*), analyze its limitations, and iden-tify other instruments for counting crime.

- Compare the *UCR* and National Incident-Based Reporting System (NIBRS) in terms of similarities, differ-ences, and effectiveness.

- Evaluate the effectiveness of the traditional model of policing that emerged from the reform era.

Introduction

To the middle classes, the police wish to symbolize crime control (of the lower classes), while their actions toward the middle classes are in accord with the middle classes' general moral and social position (that is, they maintain good police/community relations). On the other hand, to the lower classes, the police wish to symbolize, at least on occasion, and as long as it is expedient (as long as there are federal dollars to support the programs), police/community relations, while their conduct is actually crime-repression oriented. (Manning 1977, p. 360)

This quote from the late 1970s emphasizes the new problems that arose from the reform movement in policing. By the end of the political era, significant enthusiasm for reform had grown within policing circles. In an effort to correct the mistakes of the past, a new professionalism was born that would take policing well into the twentieth century. But as with any new movement, even those fueled by a well-intentioned desire for change, there is the danger of "throwing the baby out with the bathwater." In order to create an impartial and independent law enforcement profession that was truly "ruled by the law," and not the corruptive influences of the spoils system, re-formers sought to distance officers from the political machine. An unfortunate by-product of these efforts involved an increasing alienation of the profession from the public, thereby affecting the very core of the Peelian principles upon which modern policing was born.

As the opening quote by Manning suggests, the success of the reform movement in taking officers off the streets and into motor vehicle patrols would only serve to alienate segments of the community in the long run. As the focus of policing truly turned towards that of crime fighting, policing fell victim to the racial divide and political unrest of the tumultuous 1960s and 1970s, leading to violent clashes between the police and citizenry, and, ultimately, a need to re-examine the very foundations upon which the reform era was built.

This chapter examines the advances of the reform era, as well as their long-term effects on the policing profession. The reader is introduced to the birth of social science applications for policing policy and practice. Most important, the chapter provides readers with an analytical basis to learn from the lessons of policing's history and to begin to understand what the twenty-first-century police force should look like, a topic to which Part 4 is devoted.

Policing as a Profession

Although paid professional police forces existed in the United States from 1844 onward, early attempts to professionalize the police benefited greatly from the work of August Vollmer, who was introduced in Chapter 2. According to Abadinsky and Winfree (1992), the key features of a professional police force as imagined by the early reformers such as Vollmer were as follows:

- Replacement of patronage systems with civil service
- Job security for police administrators and leaders
- Centralized policing and recordkeeping

Each of these principles represented positive attempts to move policing out from under the political domination that had consumed its early developmental years. In fact, it is because of the efforts made by pioneers such as Vollmer that policing truly began to be considered a **profession** in the modern sense of the word. Although definitions will vary somewhat, most agree that the following seven criteria must be met in order to qualify as a profession (Swanson et al. 2001, pp. 3–4):

1. An organized body of theoretically grounded knowledge
2. Advanced study
3. A code of ethics
4. Prestige
5. Standards of admission
6. A professional association
7. A service ideal

We will use these criteria to detail the successes of the reform era in modifying police practices.

Advanced Study

As described in Chapter 2, Vollmer began to include law, criminology, and police administration in police training as early as 1908. He also began to actively recruit men with college experience to the police force. Moreover, in a variety of ways, he tried to advance the field through the application of social science methods to policing, a path that O. W. Wilson would continue. To this end, he created the first scientific crime laboratory, mobile patrol, and lie detector. He also began to routinely conduct beat analysis.

In the 1960s, police departments began to require a high school degree or a GED as a minimum entrance requirement. Some even began to require a college degree or credits towards one. The federal government also joined the push for more educated officers in 1964 with the funding of the **Law Enforcement Education Program (LEEP)**. Although LEEP would ultimately be phased out over time, it provided an impetus for police-related training and courses at academic institutions across the country by offering financing for criminal justice professionals seeking post-secondary educational opportunities.

The **National Institute of Justice (NIJ)** was created in 1960 as a research entity specifically targeted at promoting advanced study in the areas of policing and criminal justice reform. A part of the U.S. Department of Justice, its mission is to advance scientific research, development, and evaluation to enhance the administration of public safety both within the United States and internationally (U.S. Department of Justice n.d.). Despite changing political and social contexts in law enforcement and criminal justice, NIJ continues to fund important law enforcement research.

The logic behind this push for higher education standards was the premise that educated officers would be better problem solvers, community relations would be improved by officers' exposure to and appreciation for diversity as a result of the college experience, and therefore corruption would decline. Some studies have demonstrated that officers with higher levels of education have in fact been associated with fewer citizen complaints and overall better performance than their non-college-educated counterparts (Bowker 1980; Sanderson 1977). Higher education has also been linked to fewer physical force allegations (Cascio 1977), greater acceptance of minorities, and decreased use of discretionary arrests (Bowker 1980). Similar results have also been reported with respect to the relationship between ethical decision making and an officer having a college education; the correlation between ethical decisions and a higher education was twelve times greater for police officers than a control group (Tyre and Braunstein 1992).

As evidence of the success of early reform efforts on the field of law enforcement with regards to education, a recent study of the educational levels of police officers in over 700 police departments found that although only 0.4 percent of departments required a four-year college degree, 14 percent of departments required at least some college education. Moreover, 86.1 percent required at least a high school education or its equivalent for appointment (Carter et al. 1989). Although some critics initially argued that higher educational standards would pose unfair barriers for minority recruits, this has not proven to be the case. Programs such as the Cadets continue to encourage the higher education of officers by paying for schooling with the promise of at least two to three years of committed service following degree attainment.

Codes of Ethics

Beginning in the reform era, police departments began to recognize a need for codes of ethics that could assist them in educating officers about the organizational value systems and accountability mechanisms guiding behavior in the organization (Pollack 1993). Codes of ethics include provisions related to the service orientation of an agency, as well as statements formulated much like oaths of office related to corruption, integrity, and the use of force.

Although it is clear that formal codes of ethics assist departments in establishing appropriate accountability and education mechanisms, the formal code of conduct can be very different from the subcultural values of its officers, an issue discussed further in Chapter 9. In addition to individual codes of ethics developed by departments, in 1957 the International Association of Chiefs of Police (IACP) created a Law Enforcement Code of Ethics and a Police Code of Conduct to guide departments in creating their own codes of conduct. This later was revised in 1991 to remove sexist language. As will

Seeking to create officers with a greater appreciation of diversity and ability to solve problems, major efforts throughout the reform era focused on enhanced training and advanced study.

be discussed below, efforts to standardize accountability mechanisms would begin in the 1980s with the creation of the Commission for the Accreditation of Law Enforcement Agencies. Figure 3.1 shows codes of ethics from a number of different police departments.

Prestige

Prestige refers to the degree to which a profession is seen as desirable for employment or worthy of respect. Although prestige will clearly vary significantly from jurisdiction to jurisdiction depending on factors such as the nature of police–community relations, educational requirements of officers, and the local salary of sworn officers, some evidence indicates that the U.S. public views policing as an honest and desirable profession in comparison with others. In a 1995 poll on ethics and various professions, police received an 88 percent positive approval rating (Maguire and Pastore 1995). Business executives, lawyers, U.S. Senators, bankers, journalists, and numerous other professions ranked lower than law enforcement officers, thereby defying the premise that a high level of prestige is associated with a high salary. However, views of the police vary consistently by race. This is a problem for police, especially with regards to minority recruitment. Fraternal organizations within police departments often seek to enhance the prestige of the profession within their communities in order to assist recruitment efforts.

Incidents involving excessive use of force by the police sometimes result in a demoralizing effect on officer morale, in large part due to the resulting negative media coverage. In contrast, some evidence suggests that the tragic events of September 11 led to an increase in the perceived prestige of law enforcement careers, leading to massive surges in applicants for criminal justice programs and agencies (Tyre 2001).

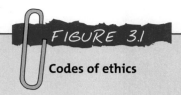

Codes of ethics

Michigan State Police Code of Ethics

As a law enforcement officer, my fundamental duty is to serve the community; to safeguard lives and property; to protect the innocent against deception, the weak against oppression or intimidation and the peaceful against violence, or disorder; and to respect the constitutional rights of all to liberty, equality, and justice.

I will keep my private life unsullied as an example to all and will behave in a manner that does not bring discredit to me or my agency. I will maintain courageous calm in the face of danger, scorn, or ridicule; develop self-restraint; and be constantly mindful of the welfare of others. Honest in thought and deed in both my personal and official life, I will be exemplary in obeying the law and the regulations of my department. Whatever I see or hear of a confidential nature or that is confided to me in my official capacity will be kept ever secret unless revelation is necessary in the performance of my duty.

I will never act officiously or permit personal feelings, prejudices, political beliefs, aspirations, animosities, or friendships to influence my decisions. With no compromise for crime and with relentless prosecution of criminals, I will enforce the law courteously and appropriately without fear or favor, malice, or ill will, never employing unnecessary force or violence and never accepting gratuities.

Law Enforcement Code of Ethics Anaheim, California

As a law enforcement officer, my fundamental duty is to serve mankind; to safeguard lives and property; to protect the innocent against oppression or intimidation, and the peaceful against violence or disorder; and to respect the constitutional rights of all men to liberty, equality, and justice.

I will keep my private life unsullied as an example to all; maintain courageous calm in the face of danger, scorn, or ridicule; develop self-restraint; and be constantly mindful of the welfare of others. Honest in thought and deed in both my personal and official life, I will be exemplary in obeying the laws of the land and the regulations of my department. Whatever I see or hear of a confidential nature or that is confided to me in my official capacity will be kept ever secret unless revelation is necessary in the performance of my duty.

I will never act officiously or permit personal feelings, prejudices, animosities, or friendships to influence my decisions. With no compromise for crime and with relentless prosecution of criminals, I will enforce the law courteously and appropriately without fear or favor, malice or ill will, never employing unnecessary force or violence and never accepting gratuities.

I recognize the badge of my office as a symbol of public faith, and I accept it as a public trust to be held so long as I am true to the ethics of the police service. I will constantly strive to achieve these objectives and ideals, dedicating myself before God to my chosen profession—Law Enforcement.

Adopted 1956

Code of Ethics, Mobile, Alabama

All sworn officers will abide by the following Law Enforcement Code of Ethics:

As a Law Enforcement Officer, I do solemnly swear that my fundamental duty is to serve the community; to safeguard lives and property; to protect the innocent against deception, the weak against oppression or intimidation, and the peaceful against violence or disorder; and to respect the Constitutional rights of all people to liberty, equality and justice.

I will keep my private life unsullied as an example to all and behave in a manner that does not bring discredit to me or to my agency. I will maintain courageous calm in the face of danger, scorn or ridicule; develop self-restraint; and be constantly mindful of the welfare of others. Honest in thought and deed in both my personal and official life, I will be exemplary in obeying the laws of the land and the regulations of my department. Whatever I see or hear of a confidential nature or that is confided to me in my official capacity will be kept ever secret unless revelation is necessary in the performance of my duty.

I will not act officiously or permit personal feelings, prejudices, political beliefs, aspirations, animosities or friendships to influence my decisions. With no compromise for crime and with relentless prosecution of criminals, I will enforce the law

Policing as a Profession

courteously and appropriately, without fear or favor, malice or ill will, never employing unnecessary force or violence and never accepting gratuities.

I recognize the badge of my office as a symbol of public faith, and I accept it as a public trust to be held so long as I am true to the ethics of the police service. I will never engage in acts of corruption or bribery, nor will I condone such acts by other officers. I will cooperate with all legally authorized agencies and their representatives in the pursuit of justice.

I know that I alone am responsible for my standard of professional performance and will take every reasonable opportunity to enhance and improve my level of knowledge and competence.

I will constantly strive to achieve these objectives and ideals, dedicating myself before God to my chosen profession . . . law enforcement.

I do further swear that I will support the constitution of the United States and the constitution of the State of Alabama, that I will faithfully enforce the laws of this state and ordinances of the City of Mobile, and perform the duties of a police officer to the best of my ability. I will obey the rules and regulations of the department and carry out all orders which may be lawfully given me by my superior officers.

I do further swear that I accept this oath as a police officer subject to all the limitations, conditions, and restrictions imposed by the City of Mobile, the ordinances of the City of Mobile, and the regulations of the Police Department.

Source: http://www.lib.jjay.cuny.edu/cje/html/lecet.html

Standards of Admission

In addition to an increase in minimum educational levels during the reform era, departments began to conduct thorough character and background investigations as part of the selection process. Many also began to use psychological testing. The logic for such reforms was that a professional force requires high-caliber applicants. Over time, these requirements were modified to the extent that high-quality candidates were being disproportionately excluded from the force based on standards of admission that had no meaningful relationship to on-the-job performance. Chapter 14 will detail the recruitment and selection process. Figure 3.2 lists common elements of current standards of admission.

Professional Associations

One of the first attempts to professionalize the police came with the creation of the professional society known as the **International Association of Chiefs of Police (IACP)**. The group held its first meeting in 1893 in Chicago, which was attended by fifty-one police chiefs. Initially calling itself the National Chiefs of Police Union, it changed its name to IACP in 1902. From the outset, IACP was devoted to the creation of a professional police force bound by civil service conventions and rules and free from political control and corruption.

Policewomen also founded their own organization around this time. In 1915, Alice Stebbin Wells, appointed in 1910 as the first policewoman in the

Example minimum requirements

Requirements vary from state to state and from jurisdiction to jurisdiction. However, all recruitment standards have provisions for the following characteristics:

Minimum age: Eighteen at time of first application and 21 at time of hire.

Minimum education: High school graduation or G.E.D. equivalency and two or more college courses by date of hire or two years of experience in miliary police.

Citizenship: U.S. citizenship (at hire or in some states within two years of hire).

Background: No felony or misdemeanor convictions (other than traffic violations) that would make it illegal to carry a gun or that involve perjury, false statement, moral turpitude, or domestic violence. No history of criminal or improper conduct. No poor employment, military, or driving record that would affect law enforcement work. Valid driver's license. Responsible financial history. Good moral character.

Health: Good health with no conditions that would restrict ability to perform all aspects of police work. Vision and hearing must be tested and successfully corrected, if necessary; color blindness can be disqualifying. Weight must be proportional to height. There is no height requirement.

Tests: Written civil service examination, medical examination, psychological examination, test of physical fitness or agility, voice stress analysis or polygraph test, drug tests. Background and character investigation. Interview. Employment often is conditional on further testing during the periods of orientation, training, and probation as a police recruit.

Residency: Becoming a resident in the jurisdiction of hire is a requirement. (The range of residency boundaries can vary significantly by jurisdiction.)

United States, founded the **International Association of Policewomen (IAP)**. Wells and other policewomen formed the IAP out of the National Conference of Charities and Correction (NCCC) in order to address issues of police professionalism and the work of policewomen in the social services (Schulz 1995). One of the primary purposes of the IAP was to promote higher educational entry standards and higher work standards in the field. Though some male police chiefs, such as August Vollmer, supported the idea of higher entry standards for policemen and policewomen alike, other police chiefs disagreed, and as a result women had higher educational entry standards than men until 1972. After a surge of economic and social momentum from 1924 to 1928, the IAP eventually disbanded in 1932, and the IACP became the sole national organization for police managers.[1]

Although the IACP was initially established to serve as a voluntary organization for police managers, it soon began to provide specific support services, such as technical assistance and training for local police, and it became a central clearinghouse for criminal identification records (Abadinsky and Winfree 1992). To this day, IACP remains one of the leading police organizations in the United States, but it is now joined by other police research entities such as the Police Executive Research Forum (PERF) and the Police Foundation.

Also essential to the process of professionalizing the police was the establishment of the **Commission for the Accreditation of Law Enforcement**

Agencies (CALEA). CALEA standards stress the importance of running law enforcement agencies according to the traditional criteria for professionalization: centralization, tall hierarchies, and narrowed discretion (Swanson et al. 2001). The core foundation across the CALEA standards is accountability; accreditation can actually shield a department from some civil liability issues. The procedure for becoming accredited involves the police department seeking accreditation to conduct its own self-assessment prior to a site visit review by the CALEA.

Individual officers can also now be accredited in much the same way as their agency through the National Law Enforcement Credentialing Board (NLECB) (Hill 1999).

Today there are many professional organizations for the police. A list of professional organizations is provided in Figure 3.3.

FIGURE 3.3

Professional organizations

The Bellingham, Washington, Police Department belongs to the following professional organizations (www.cob.org/police/source/htm/pro_orgs.htm).

- International Association of Chiefs of Police (ACP)

- Western States Hostage Negotiators Association (WSHNA)

- American Polygraph Association (APA)

- National Tactical Officers Association (NTOA)

- Washington State Tactical Officers Association (WSTOA)

- Washington Law Enforcement Explorer Advisors

- International Association of Bomb Technicians and Investigators (IABTI)

The following list shows examples of national professional organizations and associations that law enforcement officers can choose to participate in independently of their police or sheriff's departments. Similar professional organizations exist for law enforcement officers in specific regions, states, counties, and cities, as well as for other specialties within law enforcement, such as juvenile officers, narcotics offices, and specialists in forensic investigation and analysis.

- American Criminal Justice Association

- American Jail Association

- Fraternal Order of Police *union*

- Association of Certified Fraud Specialists

- International Association of Undercover Officers

- International Union of Police Associations

- Park Ranger

- Police Athletic League

- Patrolmen's Benevolent Association

- National Sheriff's Association

A Service Ideal

Although the professionalization movement focused on crime control rather than on community service, a key characteristic of the community era, policing still had a strong service ideal, albeit with a different focus. As outlined years earlier in the work of O. W. Wilson, an agency would measure the quality of its service according to the speed of its response time and the efficiency with which an incident was handled. (Chapter 6 will discuss the impact of response time on criminal justice outcomes.) By the 1980s, however, clashes between the police and community made it clear that it was necessary to have a true service ideal in which professionalism included the provision of services outside of the traditional crime-control focus of law enforcement. As a result, police–community public relations programs became more prominent throughout the late 1970s and early 1980s, until police leaders began to argue that such programs served only a very basic public relations mechanism that would ultimately do little to reduce crime long-term or even enhance significantly police relations with the community. Despite the successes of so-called crime prevention units and media campaigns in some jurisdictions, creating a special unit with the responsibility for effective community relations had four adverse consequences (Moore 1992):

- Isolating the special unit made it vulnerable to organizational ridicule.

- The presence of the unit created the perception among others in the department that they were free from the responsibility of enhancing community relations.

- Even when such units might gain important information about community concerns, it would be difficult to make this heard in the rest of the department.

- The organization becomes stagnant and refrains from seeking other new and innovative ways to improve police–community relations.

Police leaders and scholars argued for increased partnerships with the community to enhance the quality of life, a mandate that would be met with varying successes as the profession entered the community era discussed in the remaining chapters of the text, primarily in Part 4.

Crime Control as a Focal Concern: Implications for Resource Deployment

With professionalization and the development of new policing models, police departments began to narrowly focus on crime control, believing that department policies should be driven strictly by the enforcement of the law as measured by the reduction of crime rates. The fear of corruption resulting from officers becoming too close to the community residents they served resulted in de-emphasis of foot patrols and a redirection to random motor vehicle patrols, made possible by new automotive and communications technologies. Incident response time became a central concern of what would later be called **traditional policing**, or the reactive policing style epitomized by the reform era. This reliance on incident response time led to the development of **reactive models** of resource deployment. This means that the police would respond to criminal acts by deploying officers to the scene rather than establishing a presence in the community to proactively prevent offenses. Criminal investigations and clearance rates are also important priorities in the traditional professional model of policing. **Clearance rate** refers to the ratio of solved to unsolved cases that are reported to a particular law enforcement agency. Given the tremendous impact that crime measurement had on law enforcement beginning in this era, significant attention will now be paid to the evolution of how crime is measured.

Counting Crime: The *Uniform Crime Reports*

An important measure of a department's effectiveness is its ability to reduce crime within its jurisdiction. Measuring and tracking crime trends became possible during the reform era because of the creation of the *Uniform Crime Reports* (*UCR*).

The seeds for the *UCR* were planted in the 1920s when the IACP created a committee to study crime records in the United States (O'Brien 1985). By the end of the 1920s, the FBI had begun to compile data given to them by local police departments, and in the mid 1930s, Congress passed a bill officially requiring the FBI to compile national crime rate statistics. To address this responsibility, the *UCR* was born, and with its emphasis on crime data measurement and its mechanisms for comparing rates of law enforcement jurisdictions nationally, police departments began to use crime statistics as a key organizational performance measure throughout the reform era, contributing to the redefining of law enforcement agencies away from being strictly about crime control.

Response Rate

The *UCR* is now compiled annually by the FBI, and today it contains data from approximately 17,000 local police departments, covering 97 percent of the total population (Maltz 1999). This is a significant response rate given that law enforcement agencies voluntarily report their data to the FBI. For the "gap" data, or that which is not reported, the FBI uses various estimates and proxies.

Structure of the *UCR*

The *UCR* divides offenses into two major categories: **Part I** and **Part II index crimes**. Part I offenses include **violent personal crimes**—murder, rape, robbery, and aggravated assault—and **property crimes**—burglary, larceny, motor vehicle theft, and arson. These offenses and their definitions are outlined in Table 3.1.

Part II offenses encompass all other crimes: forgery, fraud, embezzlement, vandalism, weapons violations, gambling, sex offenses (other than forcible rape and prostitution), drug abuse, disorderly conduct, and so on. Generally speaking, the more serious offenses as determined by legislatures and public opinion have been classified as Part I crimes. However, some serious offenses, such as kidnapping, are classified as Part II offenses for the purposes of the *UCR*.

TABLE 3.1

UCR Index Offenses

Offense	Description
Crimes Against Persons—Violent Crime	
Murder	Willful killing of a human by another human
Aggravated Assault	Severe bodily harm, often a weapon is involved
Rape	Having sexual intercourse with a female through the use or threat of force
Robbery	Stealing or taking anything of value from the care, custody, or control of a person by force or threat of force
Crimes Against Property	
Burglary	Unlawful entry into a building to commit theft or another felony
Larceny/theft	Unlawful taking and removing another's personal property with the intent of permanently removing it
Motor vehicle theft	Unlawful taking or stealing of a motor vehicle without the authority or permission of the owner
Arson	Intentionally damaging or destroying or attempting to damage or destroy by means of fire, with or without the intent to defraud

When the FBI issues the annual *UCR*, it includes information about each Part I category and an estimate of the percentage of crimes that have been cleared. **Cleared crimes** are those for which an arrest has been made or a person charged. Cleared crimes are also referred to as "solved," although they may not have been adjudicated yet. **Exceptional clearance** refers to a situation whereby the offender's identity has been established and there is enough information to support an arrest, but for whatever reason, the suspect has not been or cannot be arrested (e.g., the suspect suddenly passed away).

Calculating Crime Indices

Given the tremendous diversity in size of jurisdictions across departments, the annual data contained in the *UCR* could not be meaningfully compared across locations without the calculation of **crime indices**. The crime index for a given crime in any jurisdiction is calculated by dividing the total reported crimes by the total population of the reporting area and then multiplying by 100,000 (the index). For instance, if 50 robberies occurred in one year in a city of 10,000 people, the crime rate would be 500 robberies per 100,000 people. This rate could then be compared to robberies in a city of any size. Figure 3.4 shows a map that compares regional crime rates.

Limitations of the *UCR*

When the *UCR* was established, it appeared to be the most effective method by which general crime data could be analyzed. However, by the end of the 1970s, it was clear that the *UCR* needed to be completely revised in order to provide analysis of emerging issues such as domestic violence and hate crimes. The eight summary index offenses used by the *UCR* were not able to show the complexi-

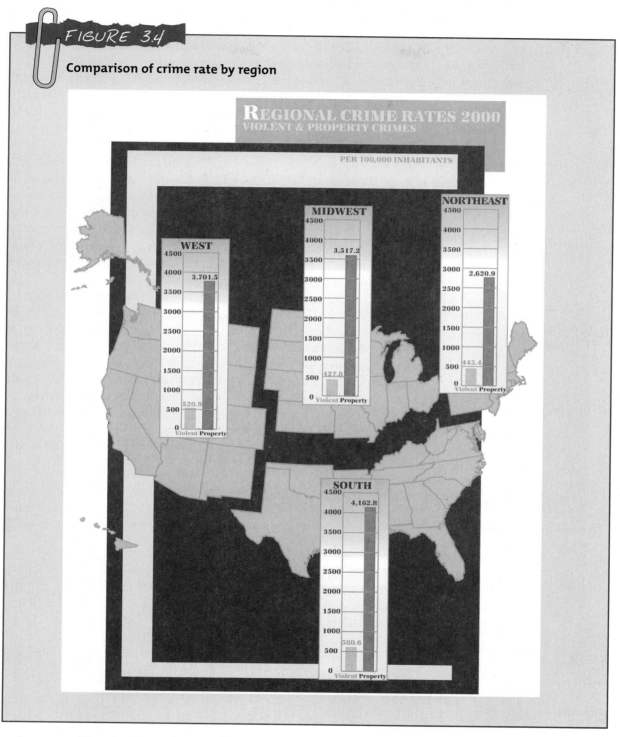

FIGURE 3.4

Comparison of crime rate by region

Source: www.fbi.gov/ucr/cius_00/00crime2.pdf.

ties of crimes, particularly with regards to emerging issues such as domestic terrorism, and the *UCR* no longer seemed capable of capturing the changing trends in crime. In order to address these inadequacies, the FBI and the Bureau of Justice Statistics (BJS) began an evaluation of the *UCR* in 1982. They produced a report in 1986 based on their evaluation, called the *Blueprint for the Future of the UCR Program*, which set out suggestions for a new design and additional reporting requirements.

One major limitation of the *UCR* as a measure of total crime is its reliance on officially **reported crime**, or crimes brought to the attention of the police. Not only must crime be reported to be compiled by the *UCR*, the incident must result in an arrest. As such, it will always underestimate the total volume of crime because not all crimes are reported, and when a crime is reported, it may not end in an arrest. The *UCR* only measures what the police know about crime and the number of arrests made.

The *UCR* is also limited by the application of the **hierarchy rule**. In a multiple-offense situation in which more than one offense is committed at the same time and place, the *UCR* only scores the highest ranking offense and ignores all others, regardless of the number of victims or offenders. So if a man were to break into a house, rape a woman who lives there, and steal her purse, only the rape would be reported (and not the burglary). Arson is the only exception to the hierarchy rule and can be counted along with the other most serious offenses within an incident.

The *UCR* is also limited by the fact that the offense definitions used in the report often do not correspond with other federal and state statutes. For example, many states acknowledge that a man can be the victim of rape, but according to *UCR* definitions, such a case would be classified as a Part II sexual offense (a less serious assault) instead of a Part I forcible rape. Also important is the role that discretionary error can play in limiting the accuracy of *UCR* data. The police report could classify an offense incorrectly or the departmental data clerk may make an error in coding the data. Although many departments have greatly enhanced their data collection/analysis capacities in recent years, for many departments the *UCR* coding process remains a manual effort of coding from the original police report.

The Dark Figure of Crime

The *UCR* has been the primary resource for law enforcement professionals for many years, but given the limitations just outlined, it is clear that the *UCR* alone does not provide a completely accurate picture of total crime in the country. Crime data from law enforcement agencies, such as *UCR* data, require that an incident has first made it to the attention of the police. Crimes are not reported for a variety of reasons, including lack of trust of police in minority communities; shame over offenses such as rape and domestic violence; a perception that the police cannot do anything; and so on. Whatever the reasoning, the level of unreported crime is referred to as the **dark figure of crime**.

To gain a closer understanding of the magnitude of the dark figure of crime, the BJS, in collaboration with the Census Bureau, began in 1972 to conduct an annual survey of a representative sample of approximately 49,000 households for respondents over twelve years old. Referred to as the **National Crime Victimization Survey (NCVS)**, the survey collects self-report data on all crimes against individuals or households, regardless of whether they were reported to the police.

Of great importance is the amount of incident level data, or crime details, that this survey is able to collect, including victim and offender age, race, ethnicity, sex, marital status, the involvement of substance use, victim–offender relationship, use of weapons, time and place, and so on. The NCVS indicates that only about 39 percent of all crime is reported to the police (Bureau of Justice Statistics 2003).

Of course, the NCVS is not without its own limitations, not the least of which is the reliability of self-reported data. Because the survey asks respondents to report all crimes that have occurred in their lives within the last six months, **telescoping** may occur in which serious incidents might be remembered as more recent to the victim than they really are, leading to over reporting in the data. The opposite could be true, too. In addition, self-reporting can lead to misidentification of certain crimes. For example, rape is defined differently in many jurisdictions. In some, the victim can be a male or female, and rape may be vaginal, oral, or anal. If a man is anally penetrated, he may not know whether this offense is rape, assault, or sodomy.

The FBI is also trying to improve the *UCR* to obtain a more accurate picture of the volume and nature of crime in the United States. In so doing, they have created the **National Incident Based Reporting System (NIBRS)**, which is meant to eventually replace the *UCR*; police departments, however, have been very slow to switch over to the more detailed format.

Measuring the Effectiveness of the Traditional Model of Policing

The reform era brought with it many important lasting advances, such as technological developments, greater use of research findings, and an improvement in the status and representation of women and minorities in police departments

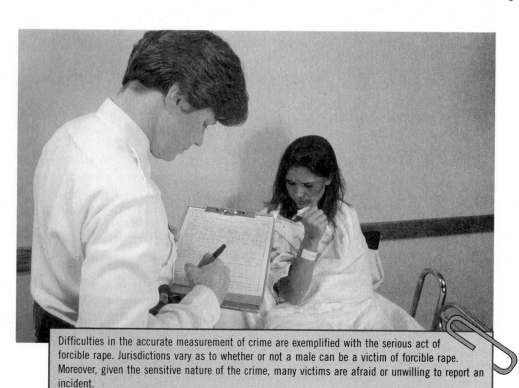

Difficulties in the accurate measurement of crime are exemplified with the serious act of forcible rape. Jurisdictions vary as to whether or not a male can be a victim of forcible rape. Moreover, given the sensitive nature of the crime, many victims are afraid or unwilling to report an incident.

Linkages in Law Enforcement

Incident-Based Reporting and the National Incident-Based Reporting System

The FBI first implemented the National Incident Based Reporting System (NIBRS) in 1989 as a means of improving existing statistical reporting and crime analysis standards nationally (Grant, in press). Unlike the *UCR*, the NIBRS is an incident-based reporting system. NIBRS reporting guidelines define an "incident" as "one or more offenses committed by the same offender or group of offenders *acting in concert*, and *at the same time and place*" (U.S. Department of Justice, FBI, 2000, emphasis added). Such broad definition of an incident allows for the calculation of mul-tiple offenses, multiple victims, multiple offenders, and multiple arrests within a single incident, as well as counting completed and attempted crimes. In defining "same time and place," NIBRS requires that the time and distance between incidents be minimal. "Acting in concert" requires that each of the perpetrators be actively involved in the commission of the crime or assistance in it. If *all* offenders are not involved in the commission of *all* the offenses in the series, then more than one incident is said to be involved. This definition of incident requires that all actions be counted in crime statistics, thereby abolishing the hierarchy rule used in the *UCR*.

In order to calculate crime rates, NIBRS uses detailed data on offenders, victims, locations, properties, and arrests for each single crime incident. NIBRS data is divided into two categories: Group A and Group B crimes. Group A is made up of twenty-two offense categories, with forty-six specific crimes, whereas Group B only uses arrest data for eleven additional offense categories. Because of the level of detail in the data, NIBRS offers law enforcement, legislators, and policy makers increased understanding of national crime trends. Unlike the *UCR*, NIBRS can offer insight into offenses such as gang-related crimes, domestic violence, weapons violations, drug offenses, elder abuse, and bias crimes.

One of the most basic modifications from the old *UCR* system to the new incident-based reporting system was a recognition that a crime data analysis system should be incident based, because incident-based crime analysis is integral to proactive police management. Without an incident-based system, police managers would be hampered in their tactical decision making, strategic planning, and research based on the specific characteristics of the offender, victim, property stolen, and location. In order to address some of the problems with the *UCR*'s summary reporting format, the FBI created NIBRS. Despite the enhanced benefit of having a standardized incident-based reporting system, NIBRS is complicated due to the addition of offense types and incident-based reporting and has taken a long time to implement.

Despite difficulties with its implementation, NIBRS is a significant improvement over the *UCR* with regards to the accuracy of it statistics and its understanding of crime. Unlike the *UCR* summary format, data for NIBRS are collected on individual offender and victim characteristics for all Group A offenses, not just homicide and rape. This allows for the calculation of offending and victimization rates by the type of offense involved. Additionally, annual changes in the number of offenders and victims are now possible rather than simply raw counts of offenses.

The most important result of the implementation of NIBRS is that it allows for a detailed analysis at the incident level, thereby creating a common-denominator language of information that can be shared between agencies. This will create opportunities for regional and local law enforcement agencies to implement proactive strategic for tactical planning and problem identification. Thus, NIBRS offers far greater practical uses (possibly as an additional tool against linkage blindness), as well as more opportunities for research, than the *UCR*.

(detailed in Chapters 10 and 14). However, despite such achievements, several important challenges surfaced during this period that revealed a serious need for the law enforcement profession to reanalyze itself and the changes that had been made, possibly returning to previous policies and strategies while at the same time working to integrate these with important things that had been learned during professionalization.

Rising Crime Rates

Law enforcement agencies had a rejuvenated sense of their role as crime fighters during the reform era, moving away from simply "trying to keep a handle on things," or the order maintenance that was characteristic of the political era. As such, a great deal of attention was paid to overall trends in crime, made possible through the use of tools such as the *UCR*. Although the reform era included many tumultuous events that were not under the immediate control of the police, such as the Civil Rights movement and the Vietnam War, crime rates continued to rise dramatically throughout the period, demonstrating that if law enforcement agencies wanted to hold themselves accountable for crime reductions, they would have to move from a reactive to a more **proactive** stance (i.e., acting before a problem occurs), and develop new strategies and collaborative partnerships. This theme will be explored throughout the remaining sections of this text, laying the groundwork for the shift to the community era.

Traditional Strategies

Much patrol work was carried out behind the wheel of a car during the reform era, the timeline for which is outlined in Table 3.2, based on the belief that random patrols could deter crime by their presence alone. This strategy also seemed perfectly suited to the police need to always be available to respond quickly to incoming calls for service. However, despite the central role random patrols played in policing throughout this period, the now famous Kansas City Preventive Patrol Experiment found that it made no significant difference to crime reduction, fear of crime, or even response time (Kelling et al. 1974). The implications and limitations of this study will be detailed in Chapter 6's overview of the functions of patrol and traffic police.

Just a year after the Kansas City Experiment, the traditional policing model took another serious blow with the Rand Corporation's finding that much of the investigative function of the police was ineffectual, and that patrols might actually be more responsible for clearances than the investigative units (Chaiken et al. 1975). Given the traditional model's reliance on the criminal investigative function, here, too, was another major study that left police administrators and academics looking for new solutions to old problems. The Rand Study will be a focal point of Chapter 8.

Both the Kansas City and the Rand studies challenged the reactive mode of thinking that had dominated the law enforcement field for decades. However, as we will see, getting the bureaucracy of law enforcement to accept a paradigm shift can be a slow process, which we will document throughout the remainder of the text's chapters.

TABLE 3.2

Timeline of the Reform Era

1893	First meeting of the National Association of Chiefs of Police.
1905–1932	Police reformer August Vollmer in Berkeley, CA.
1924–1973	J. Edgar Hoover is Director of the FBI.
1930s	The FBI National Academy, Crime Laboratory, and *Uniform Crime Reports* are founded.
1950; 1957	*Police Administration* and *Police Planning* by Vollmer's protégé O. W. Wilson become classics in law enforcement.
1950s and 1960s	Civil Rights protests; race riots in Detroit, Watts, Harlem, Newark.
1960	National Institute of Justice (NIJ) is founded.
1964	Law Enforcement Education Program (LEEP) is funded.
1960s and 1970s	Anti-Vietnam War protests and War on Drugs.
1974	Results of the Kansas City Preventive Patrol Experiment are presented.
1975	Results of the Rand Study of Detectives is released.
1980s	Crack epidemic hits major urban areas.

Police–Community Relations

It has been argued that during the reform era officers became remote from and "independent" of the community, and as a result the relationship between law enforcement and the community became increasingly hostile. This period saw the civil disobedience associated with the Vietnam War protests and the race riots of Detroit, Watts, Harlem, and Newark. From the standpoint of many Americans, it was readily apparent that the police were not "of the people and for the people," particularly in some neighborhoods. The analogy of there being two Americas was a reality for the law enforcement officer. Moreover, because the civil rights and war protests brought the police into clashes with even middle class youths and families, there was an even stronger call for change and collaboration with the community. Chapter 12 will expand on these issues and the movement towards a return to Peelian principles of community policing. However, it should be noted here that evidence indicated serious flaws in the traditional model of policing.

Back to Basics—The Beginnings of the Community Era of Policing

During the reform era, policing in the United States evolved into the paramilitary structure that we know today. The origins of the centralized, hierarchical departmental structures common throughout the country are rooted in a desire to create professional, accountable models of law enforcement. With varying degrees of success, this was achieved. Moreover, the technological advances of the era, such as crime data collection, sophisticated calls for service mechanisms, automobile patrol, and communication improvements, helped to drive law enforcement's emphasis on quick response to crime incidents and a basing of success on fluctuations in crime rates.

The chapter opened with the argument that with the desire for reform in any profession, there can be a tendency to "throw the baby out with the bathwater." In this case, the police officer of the political era was embedded in the political contexts of his beat, often even residing in the same area he policed. As such, policing had a much greater service orientation with respect to community needs. However, this orientation came with a serious price in the tremendous opportunities it created for corruption and brutality.

In the early 1980s, community policing advocates began to argue for a return to a decentralized policing, returning officers to their community contexts in order to "be of the people" and once again focus on community service needs. With this call for localizing policing came an emphasis once again on foot patrol. Some argued that policing had to "return to its roots." The remainder of this text will discuss ways in which this movement occurred. However, what needs to be stressed here is that the same risks of "throwing the baby out with the bathwater" can be true of community era reforms as well. Turning policing into a proactive force that seeks to address the underlying causes of crime in collaboration with the community is an important and useful emphasis of the community era. Improving police–community relations is an essential ingredient of truly being able to accomplish professional law enforcement goals effectively. However, at the same time, the lessons gained and structures created with respect to accountability and technology needs to be drawn upon and reformed, rather than thrown out altogether. In calls for decentralization and increased officer discretion, the realities of corruption and brutality need to be factored into any implementation plan. In calls for a return to foot patrol, response needs and mobility issues of the motor vehicle patrol must be balanced. The community era offers tremendous potential in its ability to draw upon "the best of both eras." Even with the changing post–911 global context, in which public safety needs are once again rising to the surface, proactive policing models that are in touch with the community offer the greatest chance for a safe environment while maintaining fair and effective law enforcement.

Chapter Summary

- During the reform era, law enforcement increasingly came to be viewed as a profession. Law enforcement now fits the seven-prong test of professionalism: an organized body of theoretically grounded knowledge, advanced study, a code of ethics, prestige, standards of admission, a professional association, and a service ideal.

- Although the police became more professional during the reform era, crime rates actually increased during this time. Additionally, police–community relations became strained due to the lack of communication between the police and the community.

- The primary source of criminal statistics data is the FBI's *UCR*. However, the *UCR* has at least two serious limitations: It only measures reported crime, and crime is seriously under-reported. Also, it conforms to the hierarchy rule, meaning that only the most serious offense is calculated if more than one offense is committed at a given time by one person.

- Two additional sources of criminal justice statistics are the NCVS, a victimization survey that aims to report the dark figure of crime, and the NIBRS, an incident-based reporting system that provides more detail than the *UCR* about the crime, the victim, the location, and the perpetrator.

- During the political era, police officers conducted foot patrols and had an intimate relationship with the community. Though the intimate relationship with the community was beneficial, it also led to corruption. To cut down on corruption and increase efficiency, during the reform era officers were removed from the beat and police–community relations became strained. Leaders began to call for the police to move to more community-oriented policing.

KEY TERMS

Clearance rate   69

Cleared crimes   70

Commission for the Accreditation of Law Enforcement Agencies (CALEA)   66

Crime indices   70

Dark figure of crime   72

Exceptional clearance   70

Hierarchy rule   72

International Association of Chiefs of Police (IACP)   65

International Association of Policewomen (IAP)   66

Law Enforcement Education Program (LEEP)   61

National Crime Victimization Survey (NCVS)   72

National Incident Based Reporting System (NIBRS)   73

National Institute of Justice (NIJ)   62

Part I index crimes   69

Part II index crimes   69

Proactive   75

Profession   61

Property crimes   69

Reactive model   69

Reported crime   72

Telescoping   73

Traditional policing   69

Uniform Crime Reports (UCR)   69

Violent personal crimes   69

Linking the Dots

1. Taking into consideration all of its weaknesses, what are the benefits of using *UCR* data to analyze crime?

2. Compared to professions such as law, medicine, and accounting, do you consider policing to be a profession? Why or why not, and what criteria do you use to make your determination?

3. Studies indicate that patrols do not reduce crime or fear of crime. Why do you suppose that is the case?

4. How can police officers improve their relationship with the public while avoiding the corruption that was rampant during the political era?

REFERENCES

Abadinsky, H., and L. Thomas Winfree, Jr. 1992. *Crime and Justice: An Introduction.* Chicago: Nelson Hall Publishers.

Bowker, L. 1980. "A Theory of Educational Needs of Law Enforcement Officers." *Journal of Contemporary Criminal Justice* 1(4):17–24.

Bureau of Justice Statistics. 2003. *Reporting Crime to the Police, 1992–2000.* Washington, D.C.: U. S. Department of Justice, Office of Justice Protection.

Carter, D., A. Sapp, and D. Stephens. 1989. *The State of Police Education: Policy Direction for the 21st Century.* Washington, D.C.: Police Executive Research Forum.

Cascio, W. 1977. "Formal Education and Police Officer Performance." *Journal of Police Science and Administration* 5(1): 89–96.

Chaiken, J., P. Greenwood, and J. Petersilia. 1975. "The Rand Study of Detectives." *Journal of Policy Analysis and Management* 3(2): 187–217.

Grant, H. (in press). "The National Incident-Based Reporting System." In *Encyclopedia of Law Enforcement,* edited by L. Sullivan, D. M. Schultz, and M. Haberfeld. Belmont, CA: Sage Publications.

Hill, Steven. 1999. "The Significance of Credentialing." *Police* 23(8): 40–42.

Kelling, G., T. Pate, D. Diekman, and C. Brown. 1974. *The Kansas City Preventive Patrol Experiment: A Summary Report.* Washington, D.C.: The Police Foundation.

Maguire, K., and A. Pastore, eds. 1995. *Sourcebook of Criminal Justice Statistics—1995.* Washington, D.C.: National Institute of Justice.

Maltz, M. D. 1999. "Bridging Gaps in Police Crime Data: A Discussion Paper from the BJS Fellows Program." Washington, D.C.: U.S. Department of Justice.

Manning, P. 1977. *Police Work: Essays on the Social Organization of Policing.* Cambridge, MA: MIT Press.

Moore, M. H. 1992. "Problem-solving and Community Policing." In *Modern Policing,* edited by M. Tonry and N. Morris, 293–338. Chicago: University of Chicago Press.

O'Brien, D. M. 1985. *Civil Rights and Civil Liberties,* vol. 2. New York, NY: W. W. Norton & Company.

Pollack, J. 1993. *Ethics in Crime and Justice: Dilemmas and Decisions,* 3d ed. Belmont, CA: Wadsworth.

Sanderson, B. 1977. "Police Officers: The Relationship of a College Education to Job Performance." *Police Chief* 44(11):62.

Schulz, D. M. 1995. *From Social Worker to Crime Fighter: Women in the United States Municipal Policing.* Westport, CT: Praeger.

Swanson, C., L. Territo, and R. Taylor. 2001. *Police Administration: Structures, Processes, and Behavior,* 5th ed. Upper Saddle River, NJ: Prentice Hall.

Tyre, P. 2001. "Turning John Jay into Terrorism U." *Newsweek,* November 12, 52.

Tyre, M., and S. Braunstein. 1992. "Higher Education and Ethical Policing." *FBI Law Enforcement Bulletin* June, 6–10.

U.S. Department of Justice. 2000. *National Incident-Based Reporting System: vol. 1: Data Collection Guidelines.* Washington, D.C.: U.S. Department of Justice.

U.S. Department of Justice. n.d. *National Institute of Justice: About NIJ.* Available at www.ojp.usdoj.gov/nij/about.htm.

NOTES

1. See page 12 of Schulz (1995) for a detailed overview of the history of women in policing.

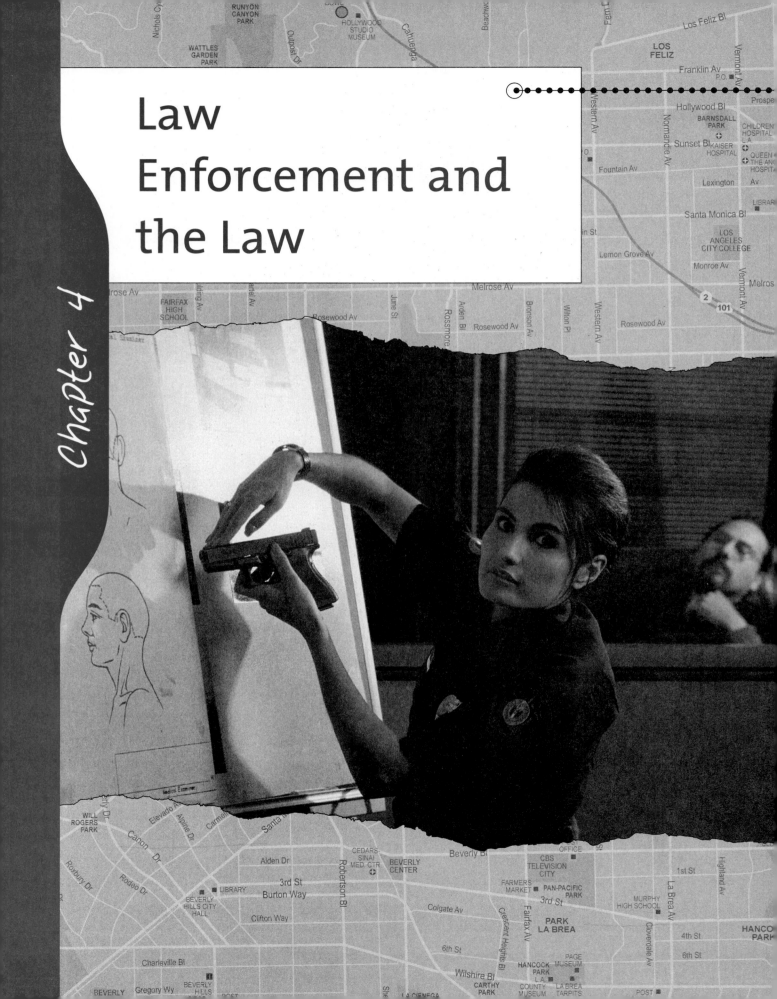

Law Enforcement and the Law

Chapter Outline

Chapter Objectives

- Understand the differences between constitutional, criminal, and civil law and know why these differences are important to law enforcement.

- Understand the significance of the order of authority.

- List the civil rights and liberties guaranteed in each amendment of the Bill of Rights and the Fourteenth Amendment.

- Distinguish between substantive and procedural law.

- Know how criminal law is classified.

- Identify and understand the components of crime.

- Understand the significance of the Civil Rights Act (section 1983) to law enforcement and the types of civil liability law enforcement can face.

Introduction

In *Sorichetti v. City of New York,*[1] Mrs. Sorichetti received an order of protection against her abusive spouse that required that he stay away from the house. However, Mr. Sorichetti was granted visitation rights to see his daughter on the weekends as long as she was picked up and delivered at the precinct house. After threatening his wife and child on the first visit, Mrs. Sorichetti asked the precinct desk officer to arrest her husband for violating the order of protection, but the officer refused. The following day, Mrs. Sorichetti repeated her plea, but even though the desk officer had been told of Mr. Sorichetti's violent history by a fellow officer, he still denied her request for her husband's arrest. That same day, Mr. Sorichetti violently attacked the child, leaving her with permanent physical damage. He was charged with attempted murder. Mrs. Sorichetti filed a civil suit against the New York City Police Department for damages (Sullivan 2000).

The legal question raised in the Sorichetti case is the degree to which an officer or his or her agency can be held liable for failing to protect an individual. In this case, Mrs. Sorichetti received a reward of $2 million. Although there is generally no liability for failure to protect an individual (because the police duty is to protect the public rather than each individual), liability may arise if a **special relationship** is found to exist with the claimant (Sullivan 2000). In this case, the court found that the elements of a special relationship were met as a result of the order of protection, the knowledge of the father's violent history, Mrs. Sorichetti's "reasonable expectation of protection," and the department's failure to respond to her request for help (Sullivan 2000).

This case underscores the importance of law enforcement practitioners and scholars having a suitable understanding of the basics of civil, constitutional, and criminal law. Although some students may at first claim, "Why should I care?" when introduced to the basics of legal principles, this knowledge provides the foundations for both understanding the field of law enforcement and preparing to enter the field as an officer.

As described in Chapter 1, law enforcement officers act as frontline agents of the law, often serving as the first interpreters as to whether a crime has actually been committed (**criminal law**). One of their most important duties is to acquire sufficient evidence during the course of an investigation in order to be able to prove all elements of the offense in a court of law. Similarly, officers must also ensure that their handling and treatment of potential suspects is in accordance with the civil rights and liberties guaranteed to each citizen (**constitutional law**), and that any evidence against a suspect is obtained lawfully. Finally, officers must be careful not to expose either themselves or their department to civil actions for damages or compensation from aggrieved members of the public, victims of crime, or offenders themselves, as in the Sorichetti case described earlier (**civil law**). This chapter will examine various aspects of constitutional, criminal, and civil law, focusing on their application to law enforcement situations.

In order to understand the role of the police in enforcing the law, it is important to first understand their position in the legal system and how this position has developed. The central function and purpose of the police is to enforce laws, and police power is derived from the U.S. Constitution, Supreme Court rulings, statutes, and local ordinances. These sources give the police their powers, including the ability to use force as necessary, but at the same time limit these powers according to the parameters outlined in the U.S. Constitution. As introduced in Chapter 1, the problem of enforcing the law while simultaneously maintaining respect for civil rights and liberties is often referred to as a *delicate balance* (O'Brien 1991). **Civil rights** refer to the rights of citizens to the protection of government (i.e., with regards to freedom of speech, religion, etc.). In contrast, **civil liberties** refer to an individual's freedom from government oppression. Striking a balance between the need to respect and protect rights and liberties with the need for effective law enforcement can be inherently problematic. Some commentators argue, for example, that with too many checks and balances, the police cannot adequately protect the public; others point out that without restrictions on police power, our fundamental rights and freedoms may become threatened or restricted.

Order of Authority

The **Constitution** is the ultimate law of the United States. It was designed to enshrine within the law a respect for certain fundamental principles of justice and to ensure a proper balance between the powers of the individual and the state. It is the document that separates the legislative, executive, and judicial branches of the federal government, as shown in Figure 4.1.

In order to guarantee separation of powers between the branches of government, the framers of the Constitution sought to ensure that no one branch of government could ever become so powerful as to threaten the independence and workings of any of the other branches. Having fought to free themselves from what they saw as the tyranny and injustice of British rule, the founding fathers of the United States were unwilling to entrust any one branch of government or entity with too much power. By creating a system of government in which independent bodies were charged with creating, interpreting, and enforcing the law, the framers of the Constitution also aimed to ensure that the laws themselves could continue to evolve as society itself expanded and changed. This early philosophy of **equity** recognizes that at times the underlying spirit or principles of the law are sometimes more important than the actual "letter of the law."

However, in its original form, the Constitution did not include many of the personal guarantees and rights we now recognize today, and as a result, many of

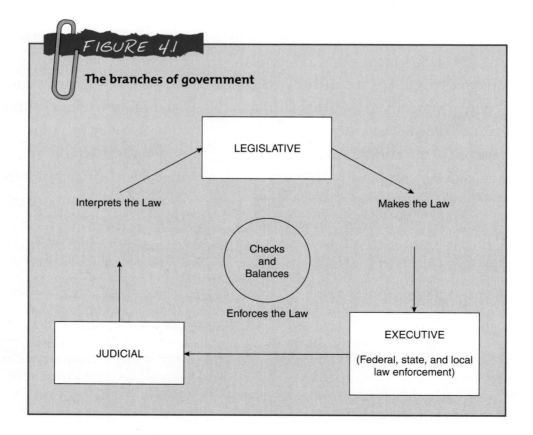

FIGURE 4.1

The branches of government

LEGISLATIVE

Interprets the Law

Makes the Law

Checks
and
Balances

Enforces the Law

JUDICIAL

EXECUTIVE

(Federal, state, and local
law enforcement)

The U.S. Constitution was the product of the Constitutional Convention of 1787, however, it was not ratified until 1789. Not until 1791 were the ten Amendments added that would become collectively known as the Bill of Rights, following resistance on the part of the states to the lack of personal guarantees exhibited in the original draft of the Constitution. This document provides the basis of the powers and duties of law enforcement.

the states initially refused to ratify it. Eventually, a compromise was reached whereby ten amendments—now referred to collectively as the **Bill of Rights**— were added, and the Constitution was accepted. In addition, although states and localities were left to craft their own individual constitutions and pass their own laws, an **order of authority** was established so that conflicts between different federal, state, and local laws could be resolved. In essence, a hierarchy of legal authority was established, with the Constitution at the top as the ultimate and final form of the law (Figure 4.2).

Federal legislation is framed by the U.S. Constitution, state legislation is framed by state constitutions, and local ordinances reflect the immediate public safety and regulatory needs of local jurisdictions. Underlying the application of written law at all levels is the interpretative function of the judiciary, which has led to the development of **case law** that guides decision making. Although no lower level of authority can contradict another, each level has its own unique jurisdiction in certain manners. For example, interstate transport laws are always within the domain of federal government and federal law enforcement, whereas laws related to common theft or robbery within a single jurisdiction are found within state penal codes. Moreover, while all statutory and case law must abide by at least the level of rights guaranteed in the U.S. Constitution, states are free to grant greater rights and liberties to citizens than those the Supreme Court has developed based on the Constitution.

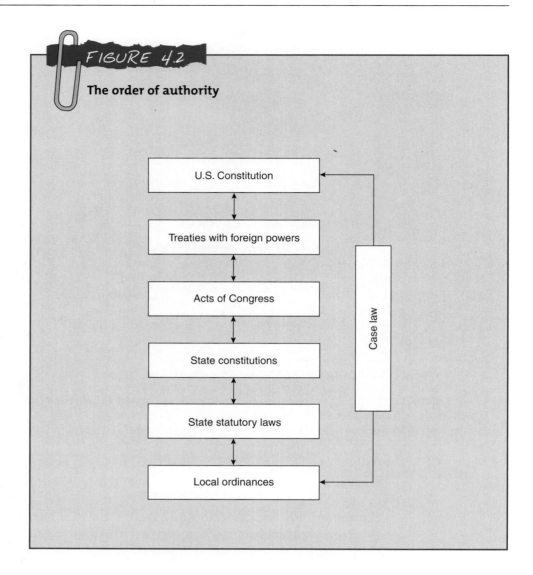

FIGURE 4.2

The order of authority

Law Enforcement and Constitutional Law

Consisting of seven articles and twenty-six amendments, the purpose of the U.S. Constitution is to provide a governmental structure for the federation of states, regulate the relationship between the federation and the member states, and explain the rights of individuals subject to state authority. The strength of constitutional law rests in the power of **judicial review** given to the Supreme Court and the federal judiciary in *Marbury v. Madison* (1803)[2] to "consider and overturn any congressional and state legislation or other official governmental action deemed inconsistent with the Constitution, Bill of Rights, or federal law" (O'Brien 1991, p. 25). The very separation of powers and the principles of federalism outlined earlier as strengths, given the underlying goal of checks and balances, can also lead to ongoing political struggles and debates about enduring Constitutional principles as the Constitution is interpreted over time by the Supreme Court (O'Brien 1991).

One of the central goals of law enforcement is to protect the civil rights and liberties of U.S. citizens. In addition to policing within constitutional parameters, this also requires that individuals do not infringe on the civil rights of others. Table 4.1 presents seven amendments from the Bill of Rights (amendments 3, 7, and 9 are not relevant to law enforcement today) and the Fourteenth Amendment of the U.S. Constitution.

TABLE 4.1

The Bill of Rights and the Fourteenth Amendment

Amendment I	Congress shall make no law respecting an establishment of religion, or prohibiting the free exercise thereof; or abridging the freedom of speech, or of the press; or the right of the people peaceably to assemble, and to petition the government for a redress of grievances.
Amendment II	A well regulated militia, being necessary to the security of a free state, the right of the people to keep and bear arms, shall not be infringed.
Amendment III	No soldier shall, in time of peace be quartered in any house, without the consent of the owner, nor in time of war, but in a manner to be prescribed by law.
Amendment IV	The right of the people to be secure in their persons, houses, papers, and effects, against unreasonable searches and seizures, shall not be violated, and no warrants shall issue, but upon probable cause, supported by oath or affirmation, and particularly describing the place to be searched, and the persons or things to be seized.
Amendment V	No person shall be held to answer for a capital, or otherwise infamous crime, unless on a presentment or indictment of a grand jury, except in cases arising in the land or naval forces, or in the militia, when in actual service in time of war or public danger; nor shall any person be subject for the same offense to be twice put in jeopardy of life or limb; nor shall be compelled in any criminal case to be a witness against himself, nor be deprived of life, liberty, or property, without due process of law; nor shall private property be taken for public use, without just compensation.
Amendment VI	In all criminal prosecutions, the accused shall enjoy the right to a speedy and public trial, by an impartial jury of the state and district wherein the crime shall have been committed, which district shall have been previously ascertained by law, and to be informed of the nature and cause of the accusation; to be confronted with the witnesses against him; to have compulsory process for obtaining witnesses in his favor, and to have the assistance of counsel for his defense.
Amendment VII	In suits at common law, where the value in controversy shall exceed twenty dollars, the right of trial by jury shall be preserved, and no fact tried by a jury, shall be otherwise reexamined in any court of the United States, than according to the rules of the common law.
Amendment VIII	Excessive bail shall not be required, nor excessive fines imposed, nor cruel and unusual punishments inflicted.
Amendment IX	The enumeration in the Constitution, of certain rights, shall not be construed to deny or disparage others retained by the people.
Amendment X	The powers not delegated to the United States by the Constitution, nor prohibited by it to the states, are reserved to the states respectively, or to the people.
Amendment XIV (section 1)	All persons born or naturalized in the United States and subject to the jurisdiction thereof, are citizens of the United States and of the State wherein they reside. No State shall make or enforce any law which shall abridge the privileges or immunities of citizens of the United States; nor shall any State deprive any person of life, liberty, or property, without due process of law; nor deny to any person within its jurisdiction the equal protection of the laws.

First Amendment

There are five elements of the First Amendment: freedom of religion, freedom of peaceable assembly, freedom of petition, freedom of speech, and freedom of the press.

Freedom of Religion   Under the **establishment of religion clause**, a clear separation is made between church and state.[3] Because a large number of early settlers to the United States immigrated to escape government-enforced support of churches, the framers saw a need for a clear division between church and state. No state or federal government can set up a church, and no law or tax can be passed that favors or recognizes one religion over another. This also includes legislation designed to promote a particular dogma or viewpoint within the school system.[4]

Although the First Amendment guarantees the **free exercise of religion**, this does not include exemptions from generally applicable laws,[5] such as the use of illegal drugs or sacrifice of animals. There can never be a private right to ignore general laws.

Freedom of Peaceable Assembly   People are free to assemble in groups for religious, political, or social activities for **expressive purposes** or protests. However, the right to associate for expressive purposes is not absolute. "Infringements on that right may be justified by regulations adopted to serve compelling state interests, unrelated to the suppression of ideas, that cannot be achieved through means significantly less restrictive of associational freedoms."[6]

The right to peaceable assembly can place law enforcement agencies and officers in precarious situations, such as having to protect the rights of groups they may fundamentally disagree with to assemble (i.e., an African American officer at a Ku Klux Klan march that has a legal permit). This can include citizen protests against the police themselves! There are, however, practical limits on the right of assembly. While a crowd of people peacefully protesting in front of police headquarters is within the guidelines of the First Amendment, for example, this right is eliminated as soon as the entrance is blocked. It is constitutional for law enforcement officers to remove people by force if necessary in such a situation because they are violating the rights of others to freely enter and leave the building. It is also constitutional for municipalities to require permits for official assemblies, provided it is for regulatory purposes only and is not disproportionately applied to some groups over others.

Freedom of Petition   As part of the democratic political process, people are free to communicate with the government without obstruction. Such a right obviously only holds, however, until such communications reach the level of threat or stalking. The Secret Service monitors such communications with the President of the United States, using professional threat assessors to determine whether a serious risk is involved.

Freedom of Speech   The right to express one's opinions and perspectives, without the fear of censorship, is a core American value. **Pure speech**, or words that are not accompanied by an action, are clearly protected by the U.S. Constitution. Such protections also extend to the area of **symbolic speech**,

The right to peaceable assembly can place law enforcement in precarious situations, such as having to protect the rights of groups with which they fundamentally disagree.

by which expression takes place through tangible items such as signs, buttons, or flags.

Such protections have even been extended to include antigovernment protests in the form of burning the American flag.[7] In that case (*Texas v. Johnson*), the court held that it is "not simply the verbal or nonverbal nature of the expression, but the governmental interest at stake, that helps determine whether or not a restriction on that expression is valid." Freedom of speech is not absolute, but a "compelling governmental interest" must always be demonstrated before intrusion or restriction is justified.

For example, the landmark case of *Schenck v. United States* (1919)[8] established the **clear and present danger doctrine** that restricts expression in situations where there is a significant likelihood that it will lead to an action or result that the government has the right to prevent (e.g., danger to other citizens, direct obstruction of government military interests in times of war, etc.). Similarly, **fighting words**, or speech that "may have all the effect of force,"[9] are not protected by the Constitution due to the likely resulting violence.

Speech-plus conduct includes activities such as peaceful picketing, boycotts, and demonstrations. Although these activities may receive some First Amendment protection, they do not receive the same protection as those simply engaging in pure speech (O'Brien 1991). When engaging in such conduct, individuals remain subject to generally applicable laws such as trespass, resisting ar-

Linkages in Law Enforcement

Freedom of Speech, Assembly, and Religion and the War on Terror

The War on Terror has brought with it many challenges for even local law enforcement. In addition to the need to be better prepared as potential first responders to terrorist incidents, the resulting conflicts in Israel, Afghanistan, and Iraq have led to large protests throughout the country where public safety concerns are even more heightened because of the potential for terrorist attacks.

Questions

1. Should law enforcement be able to arrest someone who is burning an American flag during a legal protest? Base your answer on the First Amendment cases discussed in this chapter.

2. To what extent should federal law enforcement be able to track Internet usage, book purchases, and religious affiliations of citizens in this country? Again, base your answers on the First Amendment. Should nonresident legal aliens have the same First Amendment rights as U.S. citizens?

rest, inciting riots, and blocking traffic (O'Brien 1991). In such circumstances, it is legally permissible for police to disperse the group without violating the First Amendment.

Freedom of the Press   The ability to access information twenty-four hours a day via news channels, the radio, and, with increasing frequency, the Internet plays a central role in American society. The importance of the freedom of the press within this information age cannot be underestimated. Law enforcement representatives investigating major cases are often pressured to hold press conferences or offer press releases throughout the course of an investigation.

Access to such information, however, can have a price. At some point, the constant release of new investigative leads can hamper an ongoing investigation, just as war reporting can in some cases compromise military action. In *New York Times v. United States* (1971),[10] the Court stated that the courts cannot "make" a law restricting freedom of the press in the name of presidential or national security. Even in a circumstance involving the guarding of military and diplomatic secrets, "to find that the President has the inherent power to halt the publication of the news by resort to the courts would wipe out the Constitution and destroy the fundamental liberties and security of the very people the government hopes to make 'secure.' " Thus, although law enforcement and government officials may choose to not release information about an investigation or military action to the public, once such information is "released" a Department of Justice injunction against the publication of findings would be very difficult to justify.

In addition to affecting the possible integrity of an investigation, the desire for a free press can lead to conflict with the criminal justice system's interests in ensuring that suspects receive a "fair" in addition to "public" trial. Although the case of *Sheppard v. Maxwell* (1966)[11] recognized the fact that a person can be tried in the media in especially sensitive cases and that convictions can be overturned due to the taint of media, the continued use of gag orders by courts following the case was vigorously contested by the press as a First Amendment violation. As a result, in the later ruling of *Nebraska Press Association v. Stuart* (1976),[12] the Supreme Court acknowledged the difficulties inherent in balancing the right to a fair trial according to the Sixth Amendment and the First Amendment freedom of the press. Refusing to ban courtroom orders outright, the Court did "not rule out the possibility of showing the kind of threat to fair trial rights that would justify such restraint." However, such a restriction on the press's access to the court would be very difficult to justify particularly given how difficult it is to predict how media exposure might affect the interests of the accused. The Supreme Court also stressed that even pervasive pretrial publicity may not inevitably prevent the holding of a fair trial.

Second Amendment

The right of the people "to keep and bear arms" continues to be a source of controversy in the United States today. Many are quick to note that over 70,000,000 guns are in private hands, a situation that is not going to go away without highly intrusive measures designed to limit gun ownership (Walker 2001). In addition, it can be argued that efforts at gun control may only result in restricting access to firearms by legitimate owners rather than making a significant dent in the use of guns by criminal entrepreneurs. Others look at the drastically lower violent crime rate in countries with greater gun control restrictions such as Canada, Japan, and the United Kingdom as major examples of the positive effects such legislation can have.

In its original design, as with many elements of the Bill of Rights, the Second Amendment reflected a fear of federal dominance of the states following confederation. As such, the amendment was intended to mean exactly what its words suggest: that the states would have the right to maintain an armed militia to protect their own interests. The Supreme Court itself confirmed this interpretation of the amendment in *United States v. Cruickshank* (1876),[13] ruling that federal gun control legislation was constitutional unless an individual could demonstrate a correlation between possession of an illegal firearm according to federal laws and the ability to maintain a well-armed militia. Cases following this precedent have continued to support the fact that the right to bear firearms is a collective rather than individual right (Kirkland 2003).

While both the federal government and the states have authority to regulate gun ownership, the federal government does not have the jurisdiction to compel state law enforcement agencies to implement federal regulatory procedures related to firearms (such as the 1993 Brady Bill's national five-day waiting period for handgun purchases and mandatory background checks).[14] This is because regulatory procedures are within the jurisdiction of the states themselves. A 1998 modification to the Brady Bill now allows for immediate clearance to purchase a gun. Police agencies that choose to are now able to receive immediate FBI clearance via computer should they have the technological capability.

Many states have since introduced both zero tolerance and other innovative approaches aimed at reducing firearms demand and supply. For example, the **Massachusetts Bartley–Fox laws** mandate a one-year jail term for individuals caught carrying a handgun outside of the home without a permit. These laws are particularly strict as they make no provision for either probation or parole. It is important to note, however, that the right to own a gun in the home is not challenged.

Beginning in Richmond, Virginia, in 1997, **Project Exile** represents a coordinated approach to gun control in which the U.S. Attorney's office works alongside an Assistant Commonwealth Attorney to review cases involving "felons with guns, drug users with guns, guns used in drug trafficking, and gun domestic violence referrals" (OJJDP 1999). Such cases are tried in federal court where possible, resulting in longer sentences for convicted felons in possession of firearms and/or repeat violent offenders. Moreover, when an officer finds a gun during his or her tour, a Bureau of Alcohol Tobacco and Firearms (ATF) agent can be immediately paged, and representatives from the Richmond Police Department, ATF, and U.S. Attorney's office may also become involved. Other comprehensive models for firearms reduction have also proven effective, combining similar zero-tolerance gun control approaches with community mobilization and offender intervention strategies (Sheppard et al. 1999).

Despite the increased focus on gun control, many states over the past decade have adopted **concealed-carry handgun statutes**, or statutes that allow ordinary citizens to apply for a permit to carry a concealed weapon. Such statutes are primarily **shall-issue statutes**, which is when states create a list of objective criteria for obtaining a concealed weapon permit, and if the individual meets those criteria, the state is required to issue him or her a permit. Twelve states have discretionary issue permits, whereby the state can use discretion in determining whether to issue a permit. Only seven states do not allow individuals to apply for a permit to carry a concealed weapon (Andrus 2000). While some researchers suggest that concealed-carry handgun statutes are correlated to a reduction in violent crime (Andrus 2000; Lott 1998), others say that there is no empirical evidence to support such claims (Ludwig 2000). The issues of gun control and concealed weapons laws remain a controversial issue.

Fourth Amendment

Fourth Amendment restrictions on "unreasonable searches and seizures" and its explicit requirement of "probable cause" for the issuance of warrants has perhaps had the greatest impact on the day-to-day activities of law enforcement agencies in the United States. Intended to protect citizens from unwarranted governmental intrusions, the Fourth Amendment has produced a body of case law on the subject of **search and seizure** that is integral to law enforcement practice. As a result, the Fourth Amendment is detailed at length in Chapter 7, with only basic information presented here.

According to the exact wording of the Fourth Amendment, a person cannot be searched in his or her home or person unless a **warrant** based on **probable cause** (facts or proof that a crime has been committed and that the identified individual committed the act) is issued. However, a literal interpretation of the Amendment would make many routine law enforcement activities extremely difficult to carry out. Accordingly, Fourth Amendment case law reflects the need to balance the rights of individuals to be free from unwarranted search with the practicalities of law enforcement.

The controversy over the Second Amendment reflects deeply entrenched values in U.S. history, particularly with regards to fears of the power of a strong, centralized government. In examining the wording of the Amendment, and given the context in which it was framed, do you feel that it refers to an individual right to bear arms, or is it referring to the collective power of the state?

Although ideally a warrant should be obtained before an arrest is made to ensure that probable cause has been judicially determined, if a crime is committed in the immediate presence or **plain view** of an officer, the officer can take the person into custody without a warrant. As soon as the officer has established probable cause sufficient for an arrest, he or she is permitted to search the individual, as well as the immediate area within the suspect's control.[15]

If an officer is simply suspicious of an individual's activities and can offer "specific and articulable reasons to justify a stop," the officer has **reasonable suspicion** and is allowed to conduct a pat-down search limited in scope for weapons.[16] Given the mobile nature of traffic situations, officers are also able to ask all passengers to get out of the car.[17] In such a situation, if the officer has probable cause to believe that contraband is in the car, the officer can search the entire car and its compartments.

Even words can be "seized," as case law surrounding **wiretapping** and **electronic surveillance** indicate.[18] Warrants are required in most situations involving wiretaps and electronic surveillance, with some exceptions. In the wake of the terrorist attacks of September 11, sweeping new antiterror legislation, the USA PATRIOT Act, was passed into law in October 2001. Under the USA PATRIOT Act, investigators are able to apply for court orders approving "roving bugs" to tap any phone a suspected terrorist might use, rather than just a single phone. In addition, agents can also subpoena Internet providers to hand over records of e-mail sent by suspected terrorists (Hentoff 2001).

In order to deter police abuses of Fourth Amendment rights, the **exclusionary rule** states that any evidence obtained in violation of the Fourth

Amendment will be inadmissible in a court of law. Building on federal precedent from 1914,[19] this rule was extended to include the states in 1961.[20]

Fifth Amendment

The Fifth Amendment is a fundamental element of the criminal justice system in general, and law enforcement in particular, as it assures due process and the right against self-incrimination and double jeopardy.

Due Process   Due process of law, which is broadly defined as protection from arbitrary or unfair proceedings against individuals by the criminal justice system, is guaranteed by the Fifth, Sixth, and Fourteenth Amendments. Although it is the Fourteenth Amendment that makes due process binding on the states, it does so by duplicating the wording of the Fifth Amendment, which states that "no person . . . shall be deprived of life, liberty, or property without due process of law." The concept of due process is central to the Bill of Rights, as it mandates equal protection for all individuals within the United States. For instance, during a trial the judge must be impartial, the defendant must be able to present evidence on his or her own behalf, and the defendant must be presumed innocent until proven guilty based upon the evidence presented.

As the meaning of due process is not specifically defined within the U.S. Constitution, the courts have sought to provide guidance on this issue. According to case law, judges are required to interpret the law in accordance with constitutional provisions set forth by the Bill of Rights, and the Supreme Court has described the limits of judicial interpretation as "vague contours of the due process clause." There are two types of due process: **substantive**, which protects against arbitrary or unfair laws, and **procedural**, which protects individuals from arbitrary and unfair *application* of the laws. The majority of due process cases heard by the courts relate to issues of procedural due process, such as police entrapment, questions relating to the composition of lineups, and pretrial motions requesting suppression of evidence by the defense. For instance, the Supreme Court stated that the lineup procedure in *Stovall v. Denno* (1967)[21] violated due process of law because the defendant was the only black man in the lineup presented to the victim. The Court said this procedure was "unnecessarily suggestive and conducive to irreparable mistaken identification" and, thus, denied the defendant due process of law. As described by *Palko v. Connecticut* (1937),[22] the fundamental purpose of the Bill of Rights is to protect basic values "implicit in the concept of ordered liberty."

Double Jeopardy   The Fifth Amendment not only requires due process of law, but also protects individuals against double jeopardy. **Double jeopardy** means that an individual should not be tried twice in either a federal or state court for the same crime once a verdict is given, regardless of whether the person is acquitted or convicted. Double jeopardy does not apply, however, if there is a mistrial, some type of trial error, or if there is a hung jury (no verdict is reached). Additionally, the defendant can be tried in a state and federal court on different charges resulting from the same crime (i.e., if the conduct of the accused violates both state and federal laws) or in criminal and civil courts for the same crime without violating the double jeopardy clause. The O.J. Simpson case exemplifies this point, for although he was acquitted by a criminal court, a civil court held him accountable for the wrongful deaths of his ex-wife and her friend.

Self-Incrimination   The Fifth Amendment also protects against **self-incrimination** such that a person does not have to say anything in a court of law that may implicate his or her guilt. This rule is applicable from the moment an individual is arrested and continues to operate through the entire judicial proceedings. The current interpretation of the Fifth Amendment was established during the 1960s when the Supreme Court considered a number of cases involving civil liberties violations. For example, the case of *Miranda v. Arizona* (1966)[23] established the rule that suspects must be warned of their rights prior to their custodial interrogation. This decision built on the reasoning in previous cases such as *Brown v. Mississippi* (1936)[24] in which the defendants were coerced into confessing to a crime without counsel present. In this case, the convictions rested solely on the defendants' confessions, which were extorted through "brutality and violence," and the Court held that this violated both due process (from the Fourteenth Amendment) and the right against self-incrimination.

Following the *Miranda* decision, the concept of self-incrimination was gradually refined by the courts. In *Brewer v. Williams* (1977),[25] for example, the defendant was indirectly coerced into confiding to produce where he had dumped the body of a ten-year-old girl whom he had abducted on Christmas Eve. Although he was represented by an attorney and had been warned of his *Miranda* rights, a detective transported him by car and began speaking about how the family deserved to give their daughter a Christian burial during the holidays. The detective never directly questioned him, though the Court still considered the defendant's statement to amount to a confession obtained through surreptitious means because the defendant was a religious man. The Court stated that "there can be no doubt that Detective Leaming deliberately and designedly set out to elicit information from Williams just as surely as—and perhaps more effectively than—if he had formally interrogated him." Despite the ruling in *Brewer*, the courts have increasingly allowed the police to use deception, along with broad definitions of custody and interrogation, thereby making exceptions to the *Miranda* rule.

The Court has also examined other types of self-incrimination, and in later cases stated that interrogation refers only to speech and does not include blood samples, handwriting, or voice tests. In *Schmerber v. California* (1966),[26] for example, the defendant was driving while intoxicated, crashed his vehicle, and the responding police officer took a blood sample to determine his blood alcohol content. Although he claimed that this violated his right to due process and privilege from self-incrimination, the Court rejected the argument, finding that driving offered implied consent to such measures.

Sixth Amendment

The Sixth Amendment provides the basis for a number of rights, including the right to a speedy trial, trial by jury, public trial, the right to confront witnesses, and right to counsel. This final right is particularly important for the police because an officer cannot interrogate a person without informing the suspect of his or her rights (as a result of the *Miranda* decision), one of which is the right to counsel.

The right to counsel is a fundamental right, yet the Supreme Court has heard many cases questioning the **critical stage** at which counsel is necessary. The Supreme Court has stated that the critical stage begins when a defendant's rights may be lost or waived, privileges may be lost or waived, or beyond which point the outcome of the case may be otherwise substantially affected. This is a particularly contentious topic in terms of indigent defendants who are unable to afford counsel. Over time, the Court has extended the notion of the critical stage of counsel from application to capital cases (*Powell v. Alabama*[27]) to felony cases (*Gideon v. Wainwright*[28]) to cases that may result in more than six months' imprisonment (*Argesinger v. Hamlin*[29]) to the appeals process (*Douglas v. California*[30]) and back to line-ups (*Escobedo v. Illinois*[31]).

It was only after *Powell v. Alabama* in 1932 that an indigent defendant was allowed to exercise the constitutional right to counsel even in a capital case, though in the 1942 case of *Betts v. Brady*[32] the Court said that indigency alone did not necessitate court-appointed counsel because the appointment of counsel is not a fundamental right. However, the 1963 case of *Gideon* extended the right of counsel to indigent defendants for all felony cases. This was a landmark case and one of the most important changes to the criminal justice system brought about during Warren era. The Court unanimously held that such a rule is necessary in order to establish procedural and substantive safeguards to ensure fair trials, with the judges agreeing that the decision in *Betts* was "an anachronism when handed down."

Eighth Amendment

The Eighth Amendment contains key constitutional provisions for the criminal justice system, though these relate primarily to the field of corrections.

Bail   The Eighth Amendment establishes two further individual safeguards for those accused of a crime: that bail, if given, must not be excessive and that punishment cannot be cruel and unusual. **Bail** is a specified amount of money that a defendant is ordered to pay the court on release from custody to ensure his or her return to court for trial. The purpose of bail, which is paid prior to the trial, is not meant to be punishment, and this has been the subject of a number of court cases. In *Stack v. Boyle* (1951),[33] the Court ruled that a person arrested for a noncapital offense is entitled to bail. Because the purpose of bail is not punishment, if the amount set is higher than reasonably necessary to accomplish this goal, it is considered excessive, and therefore unconstitutional. According to the Supreme Court, bail is not a device for keeping people in jail, but rather one to enable them to stay out of jail.

In *United States v. Salerno* (1984),[34] however, the Court held that no absolute right to bail exists under the Eighth Amendment. The defendants in this case were involved in organized crime activities, including drug trafficking and violence, and it was assumed that if they were given bail they would be a substantial flight risk. The Bail Reform Act (1984) states that if no release conditions "will reasonably assure the safety of any other person and the community, bail pretrial release can be denied." Though the defendants called this punishment before trial, the decision was upheld by the Court.

Cruel and Unusual Punishment   Many issues come up under this clause of the Eighth Amendment, including the type and length of punishment given and prisoners' rights once they are incarcerated. Prisoners' rights are often an issue of contention in the courts. Under the Eighth Amendment, prisoners have the right to decent conditions, including access to medical care and religious services, however, the Court has considered whether further conditions beyond this are necessary. The Court established in *Estelle v. Gamble* (1976)[35] that prisoners not only have the right to medical care, but also that it is unconstitutional for prison officers to show a deliberate indifference to the health care needs of the prisoners.

The death penalty is one particularly controversial punishment that was once deemed unconstitutional and abolished in *Furman v. Georgia*, only to be later reinstated in *Gregg v. Georgia*. The Court analyzed four cases, collectively referred to as *Furman v. Georgia* (1972),[36] relevant to the question of whether capital punishment violates the Eighth Amendment's cruel and unusual statute. The Court looked in particular at the issues of whether capital punishment is unusual because it is seldom imposed and often imposed disproportionately and whether it is cruel because it involves the intentional taking of a human life after a lengthy period of incarceration. Though capital punishment has historically been accepted as constitutional, the Court has recognized that it should be reexamined in terms of an evolving standard of decency.

Although the Court abolished capital punishment in 1972 as a result of *Furman*, it was reinstated just a few years later in *Gregg v. Georgia* (1976).[37] In *Gregg*, the Court set out a number of standards for death penalty application, including the establishment of a bifurcated trial system (one for the trial and another for the sentencing phases of a case); application only to crimes that are proportionate (e.g., murder, but not rape);[38] the existence of aggravating circumstances (e.g., premeditated murder, murder of a peace officer); and the absence of arbitrary application of the punishment (e.g., it should not be applied disproportionately to individuals of a particular race).

Tenth Amendment

Although it often receives less attention than other constitutional guarantees, the Tenth Amendment plays a critical role in the United States through its transference of all remaining powers not covered in the Constitution to the states. Law enforcement thus derives much of its power through the Tenth Amendment's explicit recognitions of state sovereignty.

Fourteenth Amendment

The notion that "all people are created equal" is embodied in the language of the Fourteenth Amendment through the **equal protection clause**, which makes it unconstitutional for states to create arbitrary distinctions between the rights and privileges of different groups of people. As noted earlier, prior to the Fourteenth Amendment, the Bill of Rights remained a document applicable only to the states. In duplicating the language of the Fifth Amendment, the Fourteenth Amendment ensured that all of the rights and protections afforded citizens by federal agencies could not be avoided simply by a government's turning to a state court for refuge.

Law Enforcement and Criminal Law

In order for a crime to be committed, a violation of a written law as passed by a legislature, also referred to as **statutory law**, must occur. Statutory laws are frequently combined to form the **penal codes** or written laws, of the state and federal government, within which there are two components: **substantive law**, which defines the specific elements of the crime committed as well as the parameters available for punishment, and **procedural law**, which specifies how the criminal justice system should deal with violations of the substantive laws in a manner that is both efficient and fundamentally fair (in accordance with the civil rights and liberties described within the Constitution).

The principle that an orderly society needs to be governed by written laws in such a precise and fair manner is known as the *rule of law,* which was discussed in Chapter 1. According to the rule of law, everyone should be held accountable to the same laws, including politicians as high up as the President of the United States. However, differences in interpretation or enforcement of the law can occur as a result of the discretion found at all levels of the criminal justice system.

In order to provide consistency in the interpretation of laws, judges follow precedent from case law (previous trial and appellate decisions). Once a judge makes a decision in a case, it becomes precedent, and all courts of an equal or lower level faced with subsequent cases with similar facts have to follow that decision. This concept is embodied in the principle of ***stare decisis*** (to stand on decided cases). This is the recognition that previous cases should guide to future deliberations, thus allowing for predictability in the enforcement of laws. Precedents can, however, be overturned with new case decisions by higher courts, allowing the justice system to adapt existing laws to changing social and cultural conditions.

Classification of Criminal Laws

Within penal codes, crimes are classified according to their perceived seriousness and the type of punishment prescribed by the legislature. The two primary categories of criminal offenses are felonies and misdemeanors.

Felonies   **Felonies** are serious crimes punishable with at least one year in a state prison or federal penitentiary. Depending on the laws of a particular state, felony crimes can also be punishable by death. Conviction for a felony offense results in the loss of many rights, such as the right to hold public office and the right to own a firearm. The range of felonies is vast, and as a result some states and the federal government now have different degrees, or classes, of felonies. Whereas the federal government assigns felonies scores based on the severity of the offense, states tend to designate the most serious felonies as either Class A or Class 1.

Misdemeanors   **Misdemeanors** are relatively minor crimes subject to less than a year in a jail. Most individuals convicted of misdemeanors, however, are given suspended sentences, fines, or some form of community sentence such as community service.

An important point to note is that the police may make warrantless arrests for both felonies and misdemeanors committed in their presence, which are referred to as **public offenses**. Warrantless arrests can also be made for felony offenses not committed in the presence of the officer, but for which there is probable cause.

Violations   **Violations** are lesser wrongs, such as not obeying a municipal ordinance, that are rarely considered to be part of the criminal law and usually result in fines. An example of a violation is an illegally parked car. Rather than making an arrest, the police are likely to give the violator a traffic ticket with a specified fee to be paid by a particular date.

The Components of Crime

In order for an act to be considered a crime, some specific elements must be present: *actus reus* and *mens rea*. First, there must be some act or omission, known as the ***actus reus***. This is the commission of a wrongful act in violation of written statutory law. The specific statutory elements must clearly define the conditions necessary for the criminal act or omission to have occurred. Acts do not always have to be completed, however, for a crime to occur; attempts are also criminal offenses. For example, if a man attempts to murder a woman by stabbing her to death, the man can be prosecuted for attempted murder even if she does not die. Incomplete crimes are referred to as **inchoate offenses** and may also be prosecuted. Perhaps the most commonly prosecuted inchoate offense is conspiracy, which can be prosecuted in many cases purely on the basis of some intent to commit a crime.

Another component of crime is ***mens rea***, or a guilty mind, and in most cases a crime can only occur if *actus reus* and *mens rea* are formed simultaneously. *Mens rea* refers to whether there was intent to commit an offense. **Intention** is said to exist when the accused intends to commit the act in question or to bring about a certain consequence. Importantly, it does not matter to the formation or determination of intent why the act was committed or what the defendant's **motive** may have been. There are four levels of intent, with decreasing levels of culpability and thus severity of punishment. The four levels of intent as described by the Model Penal Code are (1) purposeful (the act was premeditated, demonstrating a clear and rational decision); (2) knowing (no premeditation, but the act was committed with an awareness of the potential harm that could be caused and there was a near certainty that such a result might occur); (3) recklessly (the individual knows that an act can cause harm, but disregards the risk); and (4) negligently (the individual grossly deviates from the standard of care that a reasonable person would use under the same circumstances). (American Law Institute 2001)

If both *actus reus* and the *mens rea* are present, then there is a body of crime referred to as ***corpus delicti***. For example, the *corpus delicti* of the offense of robbery would include proving that property was taken by force or threat, that the suspect was the same person who took the property by force or threat, and that the suspect had the requisite intention to commit a criminal act.

In addition to the specific requirements of *actus reus* and *mens rea*, a number of principles guide the interactions between the various elements of a crime. There must be **concurrence**, meaning that both the act (*actus reus*) and intent (*mens rea*) must occur at the same point in time for a crime to have been committed (except in the case of strict liability offenses, where no culpable mental state is ever required, such as with routine traffic violations or statutory rape). There also must usually be a legal connection between the act committed and the harm caused (**causation of harm**), though this does not necessarily mean the two have to occur close in time and space. An individual can be held criminally responsible for murder even if the death resulting from the injuries occurs months later. All that needs to be proven is that the death is the direct result of the criminal act committed.

If a crime does occur, a number of defenses can be raised in court. **Defenses** are arguments raised by the accused at trial that either attempt to prove that the prosecution's arguments are flawed and that law enforcement has not collected enough evidence to establish that all elements of a crime were committed or that the wrongful conduct is not necessarily criminal (as in the case of self-defense). Defenses fall into three broad categories: alibi (a denial that the defendant committed the criminal act); excuses (a challenge of the ability of the prosecution to establish the necessary mental state, admitting that the act was committed, but stating that the defendant should not be held responsible because of some personal condition that existed at the time of the crime, for example, provocation or duress); and justifications (admit to committing the criminal act, but challenge the social harm caused because any reasonable person in the same situation would have done the same thing, for example, self defense).

Figure 4.3 illustrates the components required to prove that a crime has occurred and their relationship to different defense strategies. It is the job of law enforcement to collect the necessary evidence to prove all necessary elements of the criminal act or omission.

Law Enforcement and Civil Law

Noncriminal restrictions placed on the freedom of individuals are referred to as **torts** rather than crimes and fall under the jurisdiction of civil law. In contrast with crimes, torts deal with civil wrongs against a person rather than the public, and proceedings are initiated both by and for the privately wronged individual. Torts include situations where one person causes injury to the person or property of another in violation of a legal duty imposed by law.

Rather than seeking punishment, in civil cases the victim seeks restitution or compensation, usually in the form of monetary damages. Typically, civil cases look at the outcome of the situation rather than the intent to do harm. Unlike the standard of proof required in criminal proceedings (beyond a reasonable doubt), civil cases must be proved according to a standard of **preponderance of the evidence**, meaning that the weight of the evidence must be in favor of the complainant. A person charged with a crime can also often be tried in a civil court without violation of the double jeopardy clause outlined in the Fifth Amendment. This is often the case with situations involving medical malpractice, where the patient sues the doctor following any criminal proceedings for criminal negligence or assault.

In some cases, the same set of facts can give rise to both civil and criminal proceedings. The rule against double jeopardy is not violated because the private

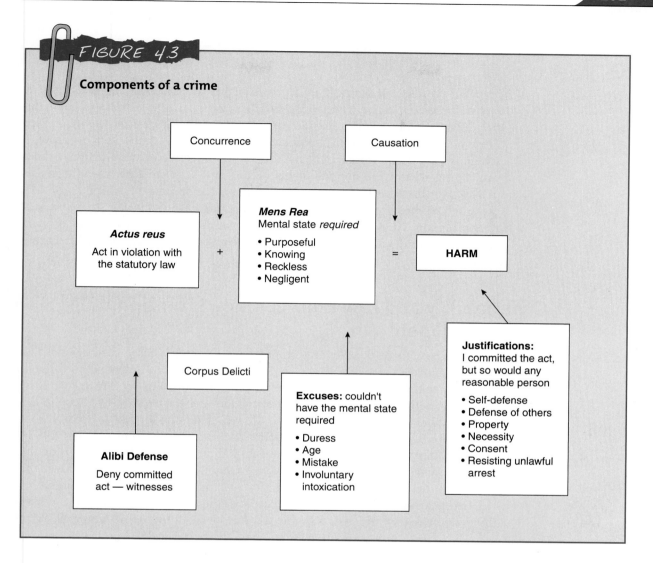

FIGURE 4.3

Components of a crime

individual initiates civil proceedings whereas criminal proceedings are initiated by the state. Additionally, damages received in a civil proceeding are not seen as punishment. As such, civil forfeiture, or seizure of stolen goods or assets following a criminal conviction, is constitutional.[39]

In order to protect themselves from the possibility of civil litigation resulting from an admission or guilty plea in criminal proceedings, many defendants plead ***nolo contendere***, or no contest, at criminal arraignment, a plea that initiates the sentencing proceedings of the criminal justice system but that cannot be used against that same individual in civil proceedings.

Mechanisms for Civil Liability and Law Enforcement

The **Civil Rights Act (section 1983)** states that:

Every person who, under the color of any statute, ordinance, regulation, custom, or usage, of any state or authority, subjects, or causes to be subjected, any citizen of the United States or other persons within the jurisdiction thereof to the deprivation of any rights, privileges, or immunities secured by the Constitution and laws, shall be liable to the party injured in an action at law, suit in equity, or other proper proceeding at redress.

In other words, if a plaintiff is deprived of his or her constitutional right by law enforcement officers or public officials acting in the context of their duties, a lawsuit can be filed for redress. In the landmark case of *Monroe v. Pape* (1961),[40] the Court established that a section 1983 lawsuit can be brought whenever a constitutional right is violated, irrespective of whether the officer was acting within the bounds of his or her authority. In this case, the rights of the Monroe family were violated during the course of a search of Mr. Monroe's home. Previously, Monroe would not have been able to file a suit under section 1983 because the rights violation occurred while the officers were acting under the "color of law," but the Court reinterpreted the statute with this case.

Civil Liability and Law Enforcement: Intentional Versus Negligent Wrongs

Over the past three decades, the number of civil rights cases filed against law enforcement agencies has grown exponentially. In 1966, only one civil liability case resulted in an award exceeding $1 million, but by 1983, over 350 awards exceeding this amount had been made (del Carmen 1991). Despite the large number of cases filed, however, fewer than one-fourth go to trial and less than one in five result in judgment for the plaintiff (del Carmen 1991). Common allegations include both intentional and negligent wrongs, with the greatest damages offered in brutality cases such as the recent case against the New York City Police Department following the attack on Abner Louima.

Intentional wrongs involve crimes against persons or property where the person knew the act was illegal, but decided to do it anyway. With regards to law enforcement agents, these cases typically involve situations where an officer has intentionally inflicted some form of physical or mental harm upon another person. Examples of intentional wrongs that can be committed by law enforcement agents include excessive use of force, false arrest and imprisonment, assault and battery, wrongful death, intentional infliction of emotional or mental distress, misuse of legal procedure, invasion of privacy, illegal electronic surveillance, defamation, and malicious prosecution (del Carmen 1991).

The breach of a common law or statutory duty to act reasonably toward those who may be harmed by an officer's conduct are liable to be tried in a civil court as **negligent wrongs**. Examples of possible negligent wrongs include negligent operation of a motor vehicle, negligent failure to protect an individual or personal property, and negligent failure to respond to calls. Thus, in the case of law enforcement agents, civil litigation can also result from omission or failure to discharge one's duty. For example, if an officer failed to take into custody an individual clearly driving while under the influence of alcohol, the failure to intervene could qualify as a constitutional violation for which the department and/or individual could be held accountable for the resulting harm caused by the drunk driver.

Damages Awarded for Torts and Individual Officer Responsibility

Three types of damages can be awarded to plaintiffs who bring forth a civil action. The first type is **nominal**, whereby the Court acknowledges that the plaintiff proved his or her allegation but suffered no actual injury. As a result, no significant monetary contribution is provided. A second type of damage awarded is **actual**, whereby damages are provided for actual injuries to the victim. This can include medical bills, lost wages, or other such costs. A third type of damage is **punitive**, which is most often sought in cases against law enforcement officials. Here the intent of the award is to punish or make an example of the wrongdoer, and thus, significant monetary awards are often given.

Civil liabilities can result in restitution to the plaintiffs through these three types of damages. However, when **criminal liabilities** are involved, individual officers can be punished. Violations of proper departmental procedure constitute **administrative liabilities** and can result in the dismissal, demotion, transfer, or reprimand of an individual officer. In some cases, officers might be held accountable for liabilities in all three of these areas.

Although damage claims can be pursued against individual law enforcement officers or officials, traditional **good faith immunity** common law protections are usually afforded the individual officer acting in the course of his or her job. This doctrine recognizes that public officials who must exercise discretion daily in the context of their duties should not be penalized for actions pursued in good faith. In the case of *Monell v. Department of Social Services* (1978),[41] the Court ruled that section 1983 was meant to apply to municipalities or governments rather than individuals. Thus, governments themselves will be held liable if their policies and procedures can be found to be responsible for the violation of constitutional rights (Swanson et al. 2001). Policies and procedures that might be held responsible can include negligent recruitment, negligent deployment or retention, negligent supervision, and negligent training. Each of these potential sources of liability will be detailed throughout this book, particularly in Part 4.

Chapter Summary

- The three types of law discussed in this chapter are criminal law (an individual commits a wrong against the state); constitutional law (the civil rights and liberties guaranteed to all individuals); and civil law (also called a tort, a wrong is committed against a person).

- When considering the order of authority between the federal, state, and local governments, the highest form of authority is always the U.S. Constitution. The Constitution en-

sures a proper balance between individual rights and the powers of the state.

- The civil rights and liberties guaranteed in the Bill of Rights are the right to due process; the right to equal protection under the law; the right to be presumed innocent until proven guilty in a court of law; the right to petition and assemble; the right to religious freedom; the right to bear arms; the right against unreasonable searches and seizures;

the right against arrest without probable cause; the right against self-incrimination and double jeopardy; the right to an attorney; the right to a speedy trial and a trial by jury; the right to speak to and cross examine witnesses; the right of a suspect to know the charges against him or her; the right against excessive bail or fines; and the right against cruel or un-usual punishment.

● There are two components of statutory crimi-nal law: substantive law and procedural law. Substantive law defines the specific elements of the crime committed, whereas procedural law specifies how the criminal justice system should deal with the offender.

● There are two main classifications of criminal law: felonies and misdemeanors. A felony is a serious crime subject to at least one year in prison. Some felonies are punishable by death. A misdemeanor is a relatively minor crime subject to a fine or less than one year in a local jail. A person can also receive a vio-lation, such as a parking ticket, which does not fall under either category.

● The Civil Rights Act (section 1983) is signifi-cant to law enforcement because it allows people to sue public officials who deprive them of their constitutional rights. Police offi-cers can therefore be held liable if they act negligently, recklessly, knowingly, or pur-posely and cause harm.

KEY TERMS

Actual damages   103
Actus reus   99
Administrative liability   103
Bail   96
Bill of Rights   85
Case law   85
Causation of harm   100
Civil law   83
Civil liability   103
Civil liberties   83
Civil rights   83
Civil Rights Act (section 1983)   101
Clear and present danger doctrine   89
Concealed-carry handgun statutes   92
Concurrence   99
Constitution 84
Constitutional law   83
Corpus delicti   99
Criminal law   82
Criminal liability   103
Critical stage   96
Defenses   100
Double jeopardy   94

Electronic surveillance   93
Equal protection clause   97
Equity   84
Establishment of religion clause   88
Exclusionary rule   93
Expressive purposes   88
Felony   98
Fighting words   89
Free exercise of religion   88
Good faith immunity   103
Inchoate offense   99
Intention   99
Intentional wrong   102
Judicial review   86
Massachusetts Bartley–Fox laws   91
Mens rea   99
Misdemeanor   98
Motive   99
Negligent wrong   102
Nolo contendere   101
Nominal damages   103
Order of authority   85
Penal code   98
Plain view   93

Preponderance of the evidence   100
Probable cause   92
Procedural due process   94
Procedural law   98
Project Exile   92
Public offense   99
Punitive damages   103
Pure speech   88
Reasonable suspicion   93
Search and seizure   92
Self-incrimination   95
Shall-issue statutes   92
Special relationship   82
Speech-plus conduct   89
Stare decisis   98
Statutory law   98
Substantive due process   94
Substantive law   98
Symbolic speech   88
Torts   100
Violation   99
Warrant   92
Wiretapping   93

Linking the Dots

1. How might policing change if we didn't have the Bill of Rights?
2. Give an example of how a person could be tried in both criminal and civil courts.
3. Can excessive use of force by the police be considered cruel and unusual punishment? Why or why not?
4. Why is it necessary to classify criminal laws?
5. In what type of case might a civil suit be more appropriate than a criminal charge?
6. Should officers individually be held civilly accountable for their actions or for their departments? Why or why not?

REFERENCES

American Law Institute. 2001. *Model Penal Code, Section 2.02.* New York: Aspen Law and Business.

Andrus, R. S. 2000. The Concealed Handgun Debate and the Need for State-to-State Concealed Handgun Permit Reciprocity. *Arizona Law Review* 42(1): 129–156.

del Carmen, R. 1991. *Civil Liabilities in American Policing.* Englewood Cliffs, NJ: Prentice-Hall.

Hentoff, N. 2001. "Has Ashcroft Read the Constitution." *Jewish World Review,* November 19. Available at www.restoringamericas.org/archive/constitution/has_ashcroft_read.html.

Kirkland, M. December 1, 2003. *Court Rejects Second Amendment Case.* United Press International. Available at www.washtimes.com/upi-breaking/2003201-1053337-9133r.htm.

Lott, J. R. 1998. "The Concealed-Handgun Debate." *Journal of Legal Studies* 27(1):221–243.

Ludwig, J. 2000. "Gun Self-Defense and Deterrence." *Crime and Justice: A Review of Research,* edited by M. Tonny. Chicago: University of Chicago Press. 363–417.

Lunney, L. A. 1999. The Erosion of Miranda: Stare Decisis Consequences. *Catholic University Law Review* 48:727–861.

O'Brien, D. 1991. *Constitutional Law and Politics: Civil Rights and Civil Liberties,* Vol. 2. New York: W.W. Norton and Company.

Office of Juvenile Justice and Delinquency Prevention. 1999. *Promising Strategies to Reduce Gun Violence.* Washington, D.C.: Author.

Sheppard, D., H. Grant, and W. Rowe. 1999. *Fighting Juvenile Gun Violence.* Washington, D.C.: Office of Juvenile Justice and Delinquency Prevention.

Sullivan, J. 2000. *Civil Liabilities of N.Y. Law Enforcement Officers,* 4th ed. Flushing, NY: Looseleaf Law Publications.

Swanson C., Walker, S., Territo, L., and Taylor, R. L. 2001. *Police Administration: Structures, Processes, and Behavior,* 5th ed. Upper Saddle River, NJ: Prentice-Hall.

Walker, S. 2001. *Sense and Nonsense about Crime and Drugs: A Policy Guide.* Belmont, CA: Wadsworth.

NOTES

1. *Sorichetti v. City of New York,* 69 N.Y. 2d 255 (1987).
2. *Marbury v. Madison,* 1 Cranch 137 (1803).
3. *Everson v. Board of Education,* 330 U.S. 1 (1947).
4. *Edwards v. Aguillard,* 482 U.S. 578 (1987).
5. *Employment Division, Department of Human Resource of Oregon v. Smith,* 110 S.Ct. 1595 (1990).
6. *Roberts v. United States Jaycees,* 486 U.S. 609 (1984).
7. *Texas v. Johnson,* 109 S.Ct. 2533 (1989).
8. *Schenck v. United States,* 249 U.S. 47 (1919).
9. *Gompers v. Buck's Stove and Range,* 221 U.S. 418 (1911).
10. *New York Times v. United States,* 403 U.S. 713 (1971).
11. *Sheppard v. Maxwell,* 385 U.S. 333 (1966).
12. *Nebraska Press Association v. Stuart,* 427 U.S. 539 (1976).
13. *United States v. Cruickshank,* 92 U.S. 542 (1876).
14. *Printz v. United States,* 521 U.S. 898 (1997).
15. *Chimel v. California,* 395 U.S. 752 (1969).
16. *Terry v. Ohio,* 392 U.S. 1 (1968).
17. *Maryland v. Wilson,* 519 U.S. 408 (1997).
18. *Katz v. United States,* 389 U.S. 347 (1967).
19. *Weeks v. United States,* 232 U.S. 383 (1914).
20. *Mapp v. Ohio,* 367 U.S. 643 (1961).
21. *Stovall v. Denno,* 388 U.S. 293 (1967).
22. *Palko v. Connecticut,* 302 U.S. 319 (1937).
23. *Miranda v. Arizona,* 384 U.S. 436 (1966).
24. *Brown v. Mississippi,* 297 U.S. 278 (1937).
25. *Brewer v. Williams,* 430 U.S. 387 (1977).
26. *Schmerber v. California,* 384 U.S. 757 (1966).
27. *Powell v. Alabama,* 287 U.S. 45 (1932).
28. *Gideon v. Wainwright,* 372 U.S. 335 (1963).
29. *Argesinger v. Hamlin,* 407 U.S. 25 (1972).
30. *Douglas v. California,* 372 U.S. 535 (1963).
31. *Escobedo v. Illinois,* 378 U.S. 478 (1964).
32. *Betts v. Brady,* 316 U.S. 455 (1942).
33. *Stack v. Boyle,* 342 U.S. 1 (1951).
34. *United States v. Salerno,* 481 U.S. 739 (1987).
35. *Estelle v. Gamble,* 429 U.S. 97 (1976).
36. *Furman v. Georgia,* 408 U.S. 238 (1972).
37. *Gregg v. Georgia,* 428 U.S. 153 (1976).
38. This was reinforced in *Coker v. Georgia,* 433 U.S. 584 (1977).
39. *United States v. Ursery,* 518 U.S. 267 (1996).
40. *Monroe v. Pape,* 365 U.S. 167 (1961).
41. *Monell v. Department of Social Services,* 436 U.S. 658 (1978).

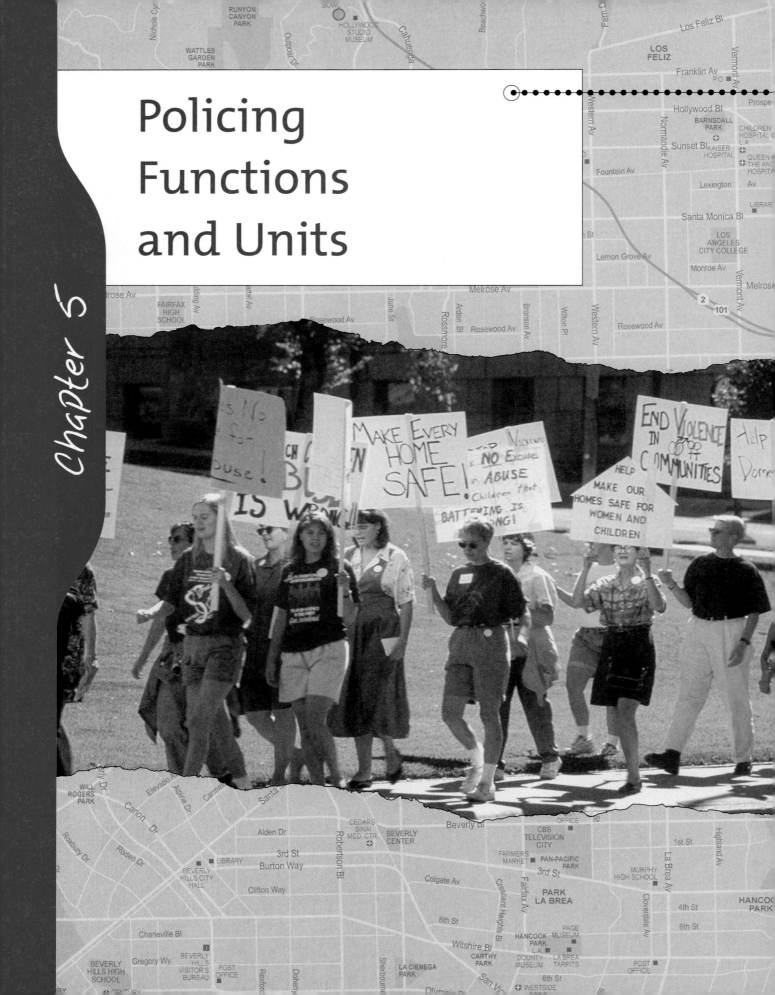

Policing Functions and Units

Chapter Outline

Chapter Objectives

● Understand the relationships between policing goals, policies, and procedures and how these elements influence policing practices within a department.

● Understand the key features of the quasi-military model of policing.

● Become familiar with the structure and operation of police administrative units.

● Identify some of the most important police special units and develop an understanding of how they operate within the overall policing structure.

Introduction

Terrorism has provided a significant impetus for organizational restructuring and increased cross-agency information sharing nationwide. However, in our use of terrorism to highlight key trends in law enforcement in the twenty-first century, it is important not to lose sight of the fact that the issue of linkage blindness has existed since the early days of law enforcement and that it has severe implications for all criminal activity, not simply the most heinous or recent. Looking at the history of criminal justice, it becomes clear that it often takes such events to serve as a catalyst for major reforms or change. A perfect example of this is found in the case of Daniel Funk in Dutchess County.

Despite the fact that the owner of the Little Tikes Day Care Center in the Town of Poughkeepsie reported to the Dutchess County Child Protective Services that his employees strongly suspected that Daniel Funk was being abused, he was allowed to remain in the care of his mother and her live-in boyfriend (Farmer 2002). As a result, the two-year-old boy later died after receiving a severe beating from the couple. One of the central reasons that this was able to occur was the lack of information sharing between the Department of Child Protective Services and law enforcement. Due to confiden-tiality concerns, the agency did not feel it was able to share such information with law enforcement. However, as a result of the incident, a multidisciplinary fatality review team has been developed for reviewing cases of child sexual abuse in the county, modeled on other fatality teams around the nation. The bottom line for the success of this model has been the establishment of information-sharing mechanisms that put the safety of the child first. The National Center of Child Fatality Review (NCFR) investigates cases of "intentional and preventable deaths," and shares their findings with local fatality review teams. The aim is to prevent future deaths through this shared knowledge base (DJJDP 2001).

Before it used to be that "one agency may know about domestic violence in the home, another may be aware of a history of mental illness with a parent, and yet another may know of past injuries suffered by the child" (Farmer 2002, p. 1). Thus, it is only with the sharing of information across agencies that such tragic events can ever hope to be stopped.

This chapter will examine the goals of law enforcement agencies in this country, highlighting the important role that organizational structure can play in attaining these goals. Although

September 11 clearly exposed the problems of poor cross-agency information sharing by modern law enforcement, such problems have existed for a long time, and they are not made any easier by the complex bureaucracies of such agencies, as well as the entrenched cultures of territoriality and interagency rivalry. This chapter will also stress that even within a large agency with many specialized units and functions, linkage blindness can be as significant a barrier as across agencies. Although such communications barriers can be reduced through advances in technology (a subject of Chapters 8 and 13), the organizational structure itself can be modified to ensure that information reaches all relevant parties bearing on a particular problem. In some cases, specialized units or divisions can be created to meet a particular knowledge or communication need. In others, modifications to the department hierarchal structure can facilitate the needed communication.

The creation of the Department of Homeland Security represents the most significant organizational restructuring in years at the federal level. Through such modifications at federal, state, and local levels, it is hoped that fewer tragic cases, such as that of Daniel Funk, will occur.

The Goals of Policing

Every police department, regardless of its size or location, will have an established set of **policing goals** that aim to provide that department with a sense of purpose and direction. Reflecting the underlying values and assumptions of the department, these goals help to inform the development of policing plans and strategies, determine the allocation of departmental resources, and even set the level of discretion exercised by individual police officers. Although the precise objectives will vary from department to department, some commonly stated policing goals (in no particular order) are:

- To prevent crime and protect life
- To uphold and enforce the law
- To combat public fear of crime
- To promote community safety
- To control traffic
- To encourage respect for the law
- To protect the civil rights and liberties of individuals

Order Maintenance Versus Law Enforcement

Policing goals are significant because they help to shape the organizational culture of a police department. Looking back to our discussions of the police function in earlier chapters, we can see that there is an important relationship between ideas about the proper role of the police and the determination of policing goals, policies, and procedures. During the political era of policing, order-maintenance goals dominated; police departments were more concerned about maintaining the status quo with respect to existing political power structures. However, with the advent of professionalization and reform, law enforcement agencies tended to restrict their focus to "upholding and enforcing the law."

As we have seen, however, fear of crime may not be connected to the actual rate of crime in an area, thus reducing the fear of crime is another important goal of policing. Fear of crime will not simply "go away" as a result of the more traditional crime control techniques. Combating the public's fear of crime requires additional service activities that engage the police in interactions with the community, a topic we will examine in Chapter 6. In this manner, the goals of an organization will directly influence particular decisions with respect to resource deployments.

Police departments can also be torn by what might seem to be conflicting goals or demands. On one hand, "promoting community safety" and " enforcing the law" seem like essential goals that should drive an agency's decision making. However, to what extent should these goals be sacrificed to another seemingly important goal, that of "protecting the civil rights and liberties of individuals"? Where these goals clash, which should hold more weight in guiding the decision making of police managers? Similarly, how does a department "encourage respect for the law" at the same time that it engages in aggressive zero-tolerance tactics that seem to alienate the community? Such approaches can ultimately result in long-term reductions in crime, thus meeting the goal of "crime prevention."

Law enforcement operates within the political and social forces in which it is embedded. Viewing the police department as a closed organization solely driven by the need to attack crime will lead to direct conflicts with the community, as witnessed throughout the reform era. However, the extent to which community priorities should drive policy will remain a difficult question as larger public safety needs in response to terrorism rise to the surface. Striking this balance will be the focus of the rest of this book.

Translating Goals into Mission Statements and Policies

Goals will often be stated in writing, either as part of a general mission statement or in the form of specific policies. Typically short and designed to be easily understood and remembered, a **mission statement** is an expression of a department's overall purpose and will usually be accompanied by a list of **values** that summarize the core beliefs and concerns of the department (see Figure 5.1). Ideally, a good mission statement encourages feelings of loyalty and commitment among officers and helps to shape the day-to-day operations of the department. In addition, a mission statement sends a powerful message to the public, fostering confidence in the police and a better understanding of their role in society.

In contrast, a **policy** is a specific statement of principle that aims to guide individual decisions and ensure that those decisions reflect the overall objectives

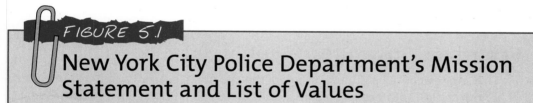

FIGURE 5.1

New York City Police Department's Mission Statement and List of Values

Mission

The mission of the New York City Police Department is to enhance the quality of life in our City by working in partnership with the community and in accordance with constitutional rights to enforce the laws, preserve the peace, reduce fear, and provide for a safe environment.

Values

In partnership with the community, we pledge to:

Protect the lives and property of our fellow citizens and impartially enforce the law.

Fight crime both by preventing it and by aggressively pursuing violators of the law.

Maintain a higher standard of integrity than is generally expected of others because so much is expected of us.

Value human life, respect the dignity of each individual and render our services with courtesy and civility.

Source: NYPD Website (www.nyc.gov/html/nypd/html/mission.html).

of the department. An example of a police policy might be a written directive or **interim order** to all patrol officers prohibiting them from asking witnesses or victims of a crime about their nationality or immigration status or from sharing information with the Immigration and Naturalization Service (INS) without the permission of their supervisor. In such a case, the aim of the policy may be to promote trust between the police and the immigrant community or to clarify the responsibilities of officers when dealing with suspected illegal aliens. It is important to note, however, that such policies do more than simply provide a guide for individual decision making and the use of police discretion. In addition, they also help to maintain consistency of practice within the department and provide the basis for police accountability and external scrutiny of police activities.

Organizational Structure and Accountability

An **organizational chart** reflects the formal structure, in terms of both tasks and authority, that is required to "get a job done." In policing, getting a job done actually refers to the operations of the department, manifested in terms of the patrol, traffic, and investigations divisions, in addition to any other specialized unit required to meet the specialized needs of a given jurisdiction. In small, rural departments (representing the majority of law enforcement agencies in this country), there will be far less diversification or specialization across units. Instead, individual officers are likely to be **generalists**; that is, officers are responsible for carrying out all operations functions. Organizational charts can be organized across many different criteria, including location (i.e., precinct, division, or other jurisdictional boundary), time (i.e., shift structure), and, most typically, hierarchy.

Hierarchical Structures—Centralized Policing

Rising out of the political turmoil of the late nineteenth and early twentieth centuries, law enforcement organizations across all levels of government sought to create **chains of command** to create professional, accountable agencies. To accomplish this, most departments turned to the military model as an example of efficiency and accountability. As a consequence, the vast majority of police departments are organized along rigidly hierarchical **quasi-military** lines. Typically depicted as a pyramid with power and control emanating from the top (see Figure 5.2), the quasi-military model is characterized by strict adherence to formal chains of command and the clear division of personnel into ranks. **Command** and administrative responsibilities are placed in the hands of the chief and his or her deputy chiefs, who exercise direct control over both **middle management**—captains and lieutenants—who in turn are responsible for supervising the day-to-day police work undertaken by **line personnel**, such as that of patrol officers who are themselves immediately supervised by sergeants. Administrative personnel (i.e., human resources, accounting, etc.) within the department are generally considered line personnel and may be supervised by sworn commanding officers according to the rank structure just described or by higher-level civilian staff, depending on the jurisdiction.

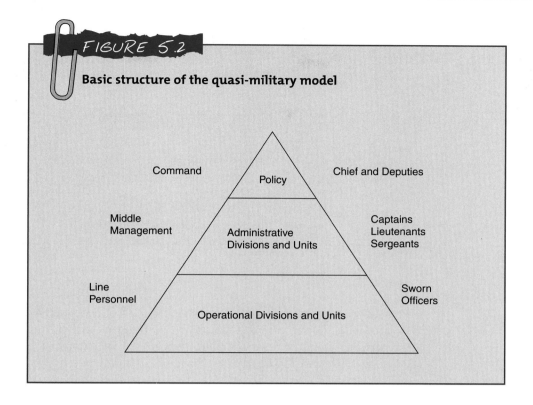

FIGURE 5.2

Basic structure of the quasi-military model

Command   Policy   Chief and Deputies

Middle
Management   Administrative   Captains
                    Divisions and Units   Lieutenants
                                              Sergeants

Line
Personnel   Sworn
                                                   Officers
                    Operational Divisions and Units

Adopted as a replacement for the political patronage model, the quasi-military approach has been favored by the police in part because divisions of responsibility are clearly defined. In principle at least, this division of responsibility helps to ensure that police resources are used effectively and efficiently—by helping to avoid duplication of effort and jurisdictional overlap—and that individuals within the hierarchy can be held accountable for their decisions. Furthermore, the division of officers according to rank tends to foster order and discipline within the department. Line officers are constantly aware that there is someone "above them" in the hierarchy monitoring their performance, just as members of middle management are closely supervised by police command. Power is concentrated at the top of the organization and there are large numbers of intermediary ranks between the top and bottom levels of the pyramid. For this reason, chains of command are extremely important to the police because they ensure that changes in policy and procedure dictated by police command eventually flow down to the line personnel who are expected to implement them.

Although the quasi-military model has many strengths, shown in Table 5.1, some critics of the police have argued that this commitment to military principles leads to serious organizational and cultural problems. According to Goldstein (1977), for example, the use of military style uniforms, military style language, and a strong institutional focus on the value of discipline and solidarity encourages officers to see themselves as a tightly knit group, bound together by a common commitment to fighting crime and apprehending the "enemy." Acutely aware of their organizational uniqueness and convinced that only other police of-

Key Features of the Quasi-Military Model of Policing

- Centralized command structure
- Clearly defined hierarchy of authority and chains of command
- Rigid adherence to rank
- Use of military terminology
- Division of labor according to function and specialization
- Selection and promotion according to merit and competence
- Strictly enforced rules and disciplinary procedures

ficers can ever truly "understand the job," officers soon learn to protect one another and maintain the "Blue Wall of Silence" as a means of deflecting outside scrutiny and criticism of police activities (see Chapter 9). In addition, because such a system favors career advancement based on length of service and rank, the quasi-military style of organization also has a tendency to mismatch jobs with officer skills. As officers advance up the hierarchy, they frequently take on senior positions within divisions they are either unfamiliar with or possibly unsuited to. For this reason, despite its emphasis on promotion according to competency, the quasi-military model can actually prevent skilled officers from advancing and make it difficult for senior management to reform working practices.

Although centralized policing models have the advantage of accountability brought about by the tall bureaucracy noted previously, such systems have an important downside: They create an environment in which information can easily slip through the cracks (linkage blindness). For example, it is often the lower-level line officer who is most in tune with the day-to-day realities of policing within his or her beat. Such an officer is thus more likely to have access to needed information that might have important strategy or policy implications. However, because of the rigid chain of command, important, sometimes time-sensitive, information might become dated or meaningless by the time it is filtered to the appropriate commanding officer that actually has the authority to act on the information. The information blockage that occurs through the chain of command is a product of **vertical differentiation,** or the levels of formal power in an organization. Organizations with many layers in the chain of command are referred to as **tall organizations** and are generally characterized by a small **span of control**, or the number of people reporting to one commanding officer (Figure 5.3).

Flat Organizations—Decentralized Policing

To exchange information more quickly across ranks, some departments have tried to create **flat organizations** (see Figure 5.4), in which unnecessary layers of command are eliminated. **Flattening**, or the elimination of middle ranks, reduces excessive bureaucracy of the chain of command. Although the possibility of creating truly flat organizations in large urban departments is limited, some attempts at creating such organizations have been successful.

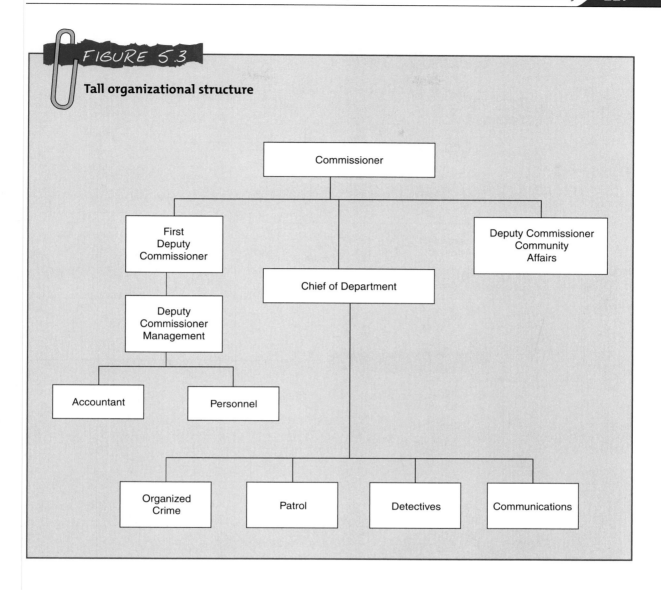

FIGURE 5.3

Tall organizational structure

Former NYPD Police Commissioner William Bratton implemented a form of flat organization within the CompStat model by creating a regular mechanism for direct access and communication between top brass and precinct commanders, detailed in Chapter 13. Additionally, in order to ensure that departments are tied to community needs and information, **decentralizing** commands and providing increased discretion within the precinct unit have also been implemented with varying degrees of success. The implications of both flattening and decentralization on community-policing models will be returned to in the following chapter.

Particularly for large urban police departments, information sharing can be hampered by **horizontal differentiation**. Many departments have become highly specialized as a means of both developing the needed knowledge base in a particular area and maintaining efficiency. However, although such differentiation is in many ways desirable and practical for large departments, it, too, can lead to linkage blindness if not monitored closely. For example, a gang resource officer may have collected important information about youths involved in local drug sales, including developing a rapport with associates of the gang who are always willing to let him know what is going on. At the same time, the narcotics

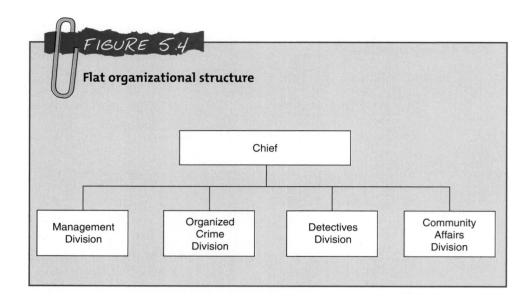

FIGURE 5.4

Flat organizational structure

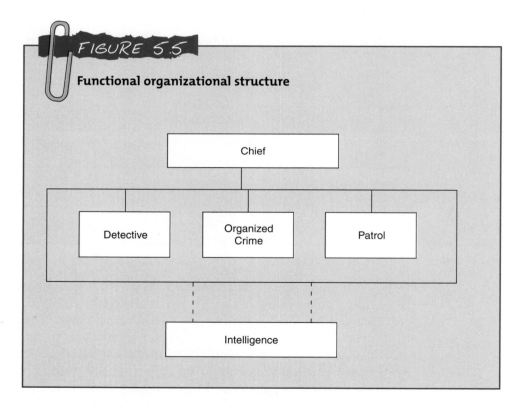

FIGURE 5.5

Functional organizational structure

division might be trying to put together a case to deal with some of the gang's criminal activities, but has proven unable to break through in terms of gaining key witnesses that can support them. Meanwhile, the detective bureau is investigating a murder in the area that they believe to be gang-related based on its modus operandi (the manner in which it was committed), but have no major investigative leads to go on. Although such an extreme lack of communication has been presented for illustrative purposes and is unlikely to occur in reality, it highlights the importance of building proper information-sharing mechanisms even within one agency.

To break down some of these barriers, several organizational structure changes have been advocated and piloted in various forms. **Functional structures** (see Figure 5.5) try to overcome linkage blindness by making specific units that overlap in purpose (such as intelligence) responsible to a variety of commanders. In this manner, the sharing of information is promoted and competing loyalties are diminished. An unfortunate downside of such a structure, however, is the possibility of creating conflict for the unit by having it be responsive to several commanders. As a result, functional structures are seldom used.

Another model that attempts to address linkage blindness is the matrix structure that was used in early attempts at team policing. **Matrix structures** (see Figure 5.6) create a team problem-solving environment in which members of different divisions (i.e., detective bureau, patrol, vice/narcotic) are assigned to specific problem areas, such as counterterrorism, organized crime, and so on.

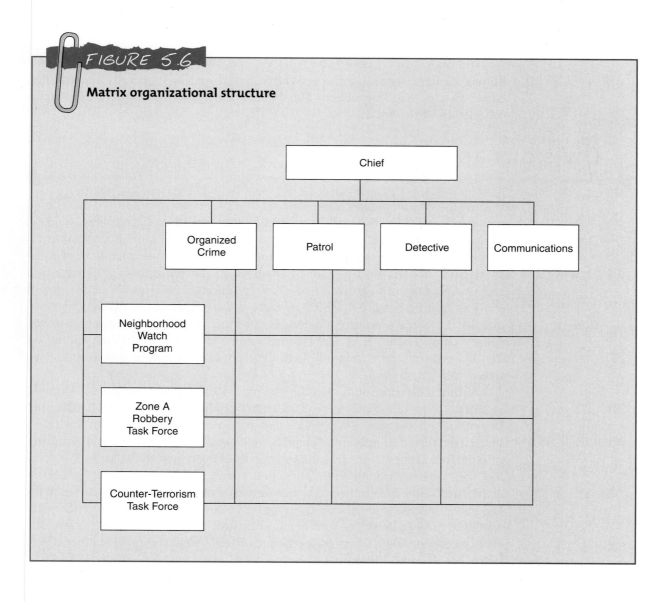

FIGURE 5.6

Matrix organizational structure

Linkages in Law Enforcement

Implications of Cross-Agency Cooperation for Organizational Structure

The challenges of interagency communication, particularly across levels of government, are best served through the task force, or matrix structure, design. Such an approach has been successful with crimes as diverse as organized crime, drug trafficking, serial murder, and terrorism (see Figure 5.7). However, there is a danger for task forces to become ends in themselves, with participants coming to the meeting table to gripe and stall, and nothing meaningful ever being accomplished as a result. Early FBI Counterterrorism Task Forces were one such example. To this extent, sound proactive leadership is required that helps the diverse groups to focus on the data speaking to the issue at hand and to develop and implement sound strategies. Additional examples of the task force model will be the subject of Chapter 12.

Matrix structures are like the task force model and are generally time limited based on a particular problem. Members return to their respective units upon completion of the project.

Divisions and Units

Within the overall quasi-military model, the two most common organizational structures used by the police are the division and the unit (Figure 5.8). Generally speaking, a **division** is a group of police personnel who share responsibility for a particular policing function. For example, members of a department's vice division will all be involved in the prevention of prostitution and other forms of organized sexual exploitation, as well as the enforcement of local gaming laws. Typically, in large departments, each division is commanded by a high-ranking commanding officer who answers directly to the deputy chief. Higher-level command positions can vary in title depending on the department, but commonly include such designations as inspector or assistant superintendent.

Within a division, staff may then be organized into smaller groups—known as **units**—that deal with a specific aspect of the division's overall function. Depending on the size of the police department, a vice division may include a specialized unit that only handles problems associated with illegal gambling and gang-related crime. Units are commanded by officers under the rank of inspector, who report through their divisional commander to the deputy chief. In many small- and medium-sized police departments, the distinction between divisions and units is not always maintained. In such departments, functions will usually be assigned at the unit level, with unit commanders reporting to the deputy chief or some other senior police officer below the rank of chief. Once again, the extent of differentiation in a department will depend on its size and setting (i.e., urban vs. rural).

FIGURE 5.7

Public Safety Fact Sheet
A Publication of the Washington County
Anti-Terrorism Advisory Committee

In response to recent world and national events, Washington County's police and fire agencies, local governments, health officials and emergency managers have increased coordination and communication. The purpose of this effort is two-fold: to ensure an effective countywide response should a major public safety incident occur locally, and to provide residents with timely, consistent information on issues of public concern.

Anti-Terrorism Advisory Committee (ATAC)

In November 2001, representatives from Washington County law enforcement, EMS, 911, fire, emergency management, local government, public health, and hospitals increased their coordination efforts relating to the threat of terrorism. Together they formed the **"Anti-Terrorism Advisory Committee" (ATAC)** to place greater focus on the threat, improve information sharing, and develop guidelines or standards for use throughout the county. At the committee's first meeting, its members defined **ATAC's** purpose with the following mission statement:

> *"To enhance public safety preparedness for response to terrorist-related incidents and threats in Washington County."*

The primary benefit of **ATAC** lies in the professional diversity and experience of its members, which includes individuals from a multitude of organizations likely to be involved in a local terrorist threat or incident. Because of this broad based representation, **ATAC** has been able to significantly improve interagency communication, most notably between public health officials and first responders including fire, EMS, and law enforcement. In addition, **ATAC** has developed recommendations to help improve and standardize local response plans and procedures. This work, in particular, has reduced duplicative efforts among the Washington County agencies who must now anticipate and possibly respond to situations far beyond annual windstorms and flooding.

Issues currently being discussed by ATAC include:

- Recommended minimum prevention and response measures for local governments that are linked to common levels of threat *(e.g., employee measures, facilities security, equipment standards, etc.)*;
- A notification process to ensure timely dissemination of important public safety alert information to police, fire, and other emergency responders;
- Procedures to guide public health officials and law enforcement agencies in decision making related to the use of quarantines to control the spread of epidemics; and
- Safety information for the public

Contacts for More Information:

For more information about the Anti-Terrorism Advisory Committee or terrorism preparedness in Washington County, contact:

The Office of Consolidated Emergency Management at (503) 649-8577 (you may also visit www.ocem.org) or your local enforcement agency.

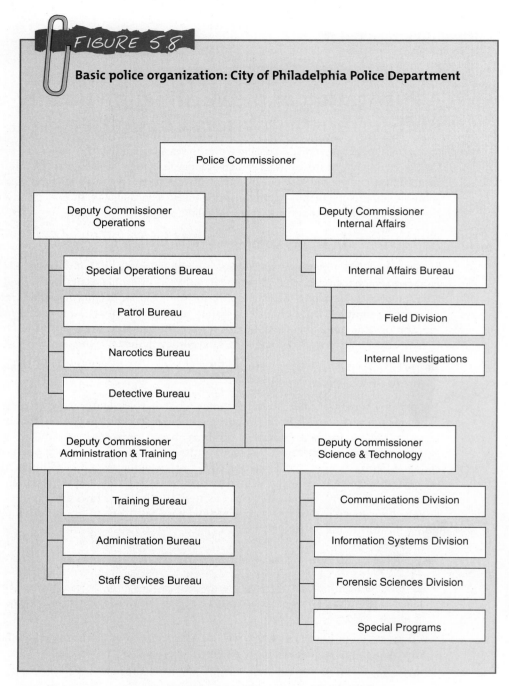

FIGURE 5.8

Basic police organization: City of Philadelphia Police Department

Source: City of Philadelphia Police Department (www.ppdonline.org/ppd2_orgmain.htm).

Administrative Services

Generally speaking, most basic police functions can be classified according to whether they are operational or administrative in nature (see Table 5.2). **Operational units** are engaged in activities performed in direct assistance to

One of the key organizational activities for a police department is the roll call, when line officers are given instruction as to daily priorities and information about changing crime in their areas.

the public, such as police patrol and traffic, and are typically staffed by sworn police officers. In contrast, **administrative units** are responsible for providing support and assistance for the police organization as a whole. Sometimes referred to as support services, administrative units manage such diverse functions as the hiring and training of police personnel, maintaining police records, researching and planning, and overseeing internal affairs. Typically, administrative units are staffed by a mixture of sworn police officers and civilian employees and are housed in the central police headquarters. Patrol, traffic, criminal investigation, and other key police operational units are covered in detail in Chapters 6, 7, and 8. In the following sections, we will look instead at some of the more common administrative units before turning to examine a number of special police units, such as internal affairs and S.W.A.T. teams.

Personnel   The personnel unit or division is responsible for the selection and hiring of staff (officer and civilian), managing the promotion process, and overseeing all aspects of employee performance and welfare. As a result, the personnel unit will typically be in charge of:

- Officer recruitment

- Setting entry level and promotional examinations

- Maintaining personnel records

- Establishing and monitoring standards of employee performance

- Administering employee health, safety, and benefits schemes

- Processing applications for transfers and jobs within the department

TABLE 5.2

Police Organization by Function

Operational Units	Administrative Units
• Patrol	• Clerical
• Traffic	• Finance
• Crime Prevention	• Personnel
• Criminal Investigations	• Training
• Juvenile Service	• Records
• Community Services	• Public Information
• Vice and Narcotics	• Planning and Analysis
• Organized Crime	• Intelligence
• Intelligence and Undercover	• Internal Affairs
• Special Operations	

Source: Sheehan and Cordner (1989).

- Processing applications for extended leaves of absence
- Ensuring that the department adheres to applicable employment and labor laws

In most large police departments, the personnel division will be divided into a number of individual commands, each of which is responsible for managing different aspects of the human resource function. Given that policing is an extremely "human-focused" occupation, personnel units play a crucial role in the day-to-day operation of even the smallest police departments. As we shall see in Chapter 9, police work can place great stress on individual officers, and as a result, making sure that police employees are treated fairly by the department is often essential to the maintenance of staff morale.

Records   Record keeping is an essential aspect of all forms of law enforcement activity. In order to do their job effectively, agencies such as the police must be able to access and cross-reference large quantities of information about past crimes and ongoing investigations quickly and efficiently. The records unit is responsible for storing the vast amounts of information accumulated by the police and for ensuring that these records are kept up-to-date and accessible. Because most interactions between the police and the public are documented as a matter of procedure, the variety and volume of records handled by the records department of even a medium-sized police department can be enormous. As a consequence, in many large departments, records are computerized as much as is practical. The following list gives a sample of the types of records typically maintained by the records unit:

- Arrest reports
- Incident reports
- Accident reports

- Juvenile reports
- Field interrogations
- Witness statements
- Suspect interviews
- Photographic records
- Fingerprint files
- M.O. (modus operandi) files
- Warrant files
- Property damage reports
- Police vehicle damage report
- Public complaints
- Internal investigation reports

Research and Planning   Closely connected to the records division is the research and planning unit. Because the police do not have unlimited resources or perfect information, police managers need to develop and implement law enforcement strategies that address existing patterns of crime and that anticipate future crime trends and problems of disorder. Research and planning units provide the police with information about local social, economic, and political conditions that can be used as the basis for such strategies, as well as with assessments of past law enforcement initiatives and predictions about the likely success of future programs. In addition, the research and planning unit is also responsible for ensuring that the police take advantage of new law enforcement techniques and equipment and for providing the training unit with information that can be used to improve existing policing methods.

Public Information   The public information unit is responsible for communicating with the media and making information about police activities available to the public. Depending on the size of the police department, this task may either be carried out by a separate unit within the administrative services division or managed by staff from some other unit such as the clerical/secretarial unit. Maintaining public confidence is of vital importance to the police, particularly given that they are extremely dependent on the public for information and assistance. Furthermore, in a democracy, it is essential that the activities of the police are open to scrutiny by the media, politicians, and the public at large. The information unit ensures that the public is kept informed about such matters as changing crime rates, new policing strategies, and the progress of high-profile investigations. As the Washington, D.C., sniper case illustrates, however, the task of balancing the public's right to know with the need to keep certain information confidential can at times be an extremely challenging one.

Internal Affairs

In many police departments, the task of handling public complaints against the police is the responsibility of the **internal affairs unit**. In some departments, this unit might be called the Office of Professional Standards. These units typically investigate allegations of (noncriminal) police misconduct—for example, when an officer is accused of breaching departmental rules or standards—and make recommendations to senior police management as to the appropriate punishment or disciplinary action. In some departments, these units also act proactively, working to uncover police corruption and other forms of serious crime committed by serving officers.[1]

Although internal affairs units are typically staffed by sworn police officers, some departments also employ civilian investigators in an effort to reassure members of the public that their complaints are being taken seriously. In addition, a minority of police departments deliberately locate their internal affairs units away from the main police headquarters, in the hope that a less-intimidating setting will encourage citizens to come forward with their complaints. Not surprisingly, internal affairs units are often regarded with suspicion and even hostility by other police officers, and as a result, officers who work for internal affairs can face many of the same problems that confront outsiders who attempt to penetrate the "Blue Wall of Silence" (Thrasher 2001).

Once a complaint has been filed with the internal affairs unit, various steps are taken to determine whether the complaint should be formally investigated and ultimately upheld. Although the procedures used for internal investigations vary from department to department, most follow the key stages set out in Table 5.3, depending on the degree to which civilian oversight is built into the process. The process of investigating civilian complaints will be detailed further in Chapter 11. Possible punishments and disciplinary outcomes are detailed in Table 5.4.

Special Units and Divisions

In addition to operational and administrative divisions, many police departments also maintain a number of specialized units to handle matters beyond the skills and competency of ordinary police officers. Among the most common specialized units are undercover operations, special weapons and tactics, juvenile policing, and police dog (canine) units.

TABLE 5.3

Key Phases in the Investigation of a Complaint Against the Police

1. Initial review and establishment of grounds for complaint
2. Collection of witness and complainant evidence
3. Collection of all other additional relevant evidence, such as police reports and medical records
4. Background check on complainant to establish character and reliability
5. Background check on accused officer, including a review of any prior complaints and past disciplinary actions
6. Interview and take statements from all other departmental personnel involved in the complaint

Source: D'Arcy et al. (1990).

TABLE 5.4

Punishments and Disciplinary Outcomes (in decreasing order of seriousness)

Punishment	Outcome
Termination of employment	Officer is forced to permanently leave the department, losing all salary and benefits.
Loss of rank	Officer is demoted to a lower rank, usually resulting in a fall in salary and some loss of benefits. In most cases, demotion is also likely to affect the officer's chances of future promotion.
Punitive suspension	Officer is forced to take unpaid leave for a set period, typically between one and four weeks, during which time they are also prohibited from undertaking other law-enforcement-related employment.
Punitive probation	Officer remains on duty with full salary and benefits, but risks termination if he or she commits any further acts of misconduct during the probation period.
Reassignment	Officer is removed from his or her current unit or assignment and moved to another division or location within the department.
Mandatory training	Officer is required to receive training designed to help the officer understand why his or her behavior was unacceptable and to teach the officer how best to prevent future instances of misconduct.
Reprimand	Officer receives a formal, written warning from his or her commanding officer, setting out details of the complaint and reprimanding the officer for his or her behavior. This warning is placed in the officer's personnel file and may be referred to when making decisions about the officer's career and any future disciplinary actions.
Supervisory counseling	Officer is required to discuss his or her behavior with either a police counselor or a senior officer within the department, with a view to developing ways of avoiding future instances of misconduct. The least punitive of all of the possible outcomes, counseling is not intended to act as a formal punishment and is rarely noted in an officer's personnel file.

Source: Carter (1994).

Undercover/Intelligence In addition to more traditional forms of investigation, many police departments also routinely engage in **covert**, or **undercover, operations**. During a covert operation, a police officer will assume a false identity—go "undercover"—in order to obtain evidence of criminal activity or gain access to a suspect or known fugitive (Miller 2001; Dumont 2000). In some cases, undercover officers may also work in conjunction with an ongoing police surveillance operation, helping the police to establish the reliability of an informant, prevent a crime from being committed, or make an arrest (Bennett and Hess 2001; Jacobs 1993; Miller 1987). Although undercover work is often portrayed as glamorous and exotic in television dramas and movies—with undercover officers frequently posing as criminals in order to gain access to a gang or some tight-knit criminal organization—in reality, many covert operations are far more mundane. As Hess and Wrobleski (2002) have observed, undercover officers often pass themselves off as utility workers or phone company employees in order to enter a suspect's home or may pretend to be a newspaper reporter or photographer in order to gather evidence without arousing suspicion. This is not to say, however, that undercover work cannot be extremely dangerous. Every year, large numbers of undercover police officers—particularly those involved in the investigation of drug-trafficking and drug-related crime—are either injured or killed while on assignment, often as a result of having their cover "blown" and being exposed as a police officer (DeBlanc and Redman 2000).

There are different forms of covert operations, each with its own unique threats and legal challenges. With **sting operations**, undercover agents pose as buyers of illegal goods or services. For example, in a sting operation by the Stanislaus County Sheriff's Department Special Investigations Unit, an undercover agent entered a convenience store and struck up a conversation with one of its employees, telling him that he had some stolen cigarette cartons and liquor he was looking to sell them at a discounted price. After agreement by the employee, the undercover deputies returned on two other occasions and purchased some of the "stolen" goods now on the public rack for sale. Arrests were subsequently made for the buying and selling of stolen goods (Stanislaus County Sheriff's Department 2002). In sting operations to identify retail operations that sell to minors, a minor (always in the presence of a sworn officer) is instructed to dress age appropriately and attempt to purchase alcoholic beverages. In these operations, the minor is told to be polite and truthful to the sales clerk if asked about his or her age (Texas Alcoholic Beverage Commission 2002). If the minor is sold the goods, an arrest can be made. Undercover agents can also engage in **reverse sting operations** in which officers pose as drug dealers and arrest those who buy drugs from them.

A **decoy operation** involves an officer assuming the identity or physical appearance of a victim or potential victim of a crime with the objective of apprehending a suspect in the commission of a crime. For example, undercover agents might pose as the drivers of livery cabs in an area where livery cab robberies are a major problem. Alternatively, a department might use decoy vehicles that are similar to those targeted for theft. These vehicles might be used to apprehend individuals committing crimes against the vehicle or to locate possible "chop shops" if it is stolen.

Finally, **blending** operations can pose the most significant threat to an undercover agent in that they require the agent to assimilate into the surrounding activities or culture. The penetration of an agent into an organized crime entity or gang would be an example of an undercover blending activity.

The Fine Line Between Entrapment and Encouragement Although undercover operations can be an extremely effective way of gathering evidence and apprehending criminals, the use of covert investigative techniques by the police raises a number of difficult ethical issues. Because an undercover officer is often required to lie to members of the public in order to conceal his or her true identity, the question arises as to how far such lies can be justified and under what circumstances. For example, should officers only be allowed to deceive the public and use undercover methods when investigating major crimes such as racketeering and drug dealing, or are such practices also permissible when it comes to investigating less serious crimes such as shoplifting and petty theft? According to Klockars (1985), the answer to such questions is relatively straightforward, namely if the use of deception means that the police are able to achieve their goals without recourse to the use of force, then lies are morally justifiable, and possibly, even preferable. There are, however, other considerations to take into account in addition to the desirability of avoiding force. As Marx (1995; 1992) has pointed out, the line between legitimate and illegitimate goals is not always a clear one, and there is always a danger that were the use of undercover tactics to become more widespread, that police officers may come to view such methods as a way of circumventing due process controls and engage in illegal, undirected surveillance of the public. Furthermore, it can be argued that greater police reliance on undercover operations might seriously undermine the police's moral authority in the eyes of the public and erode their position of trust within the community.

Traditionally, police undercover operations have not been subject to strict controls, although in recent years many police departments have taken steps to ensure that the use of covert tactics is regulated and that undercover officers are subject to close supervision (Marx 1988). In addition, the Commission on Accreditations for Law Enforcement Agencies (1999) (CALEA—see Chapter 3) currently requires all police departments to have formal written procedures for conducting vice and undercover operations, as well as any activity involving the use of deception. As Walker and Katz (2002) note, these procedures must specifically address issues relating to the use of false identities and credentials by officers and establish a system of effective supervision for all officers working undercover or engaged in covert surveillance.

The legal standard for **entrapment**, or **agent provocateur**, is when an agent incites or counsels a person to commit a crime that he or she would not otherwise have committed; thus, the line between entrapment and encouragement can be very fine indeed.

Unique Stressors and Dangers   In recent years, there have been a number of studies of the effects of undercover work on police officers and other law enforcement agents (Marx 1988, 1995; Pogrebin and Poole 1993). According to the findings of a self-report survey of 271 federal undercover agents administered by Girodo (1991a) in the early 1990s, undercover agents are likely to experience a variety of social and psychological problems as a result of spending long periods in the field.[2] In particular, Girodo found that those working undercover assignments frequently had problems with drugs and alcohol abuse, as well as difficulties with impulse control, discipline, and maintaining interest in the job. These results mirrored the findings of an earlier study by Farkas (1986) of undercover officers in Hawaii that found that more than one-third of those surveyed experienced problems in their relationships with friends and family, often as a result of being unable to discuss their work with those closest to them. In addition to the psychological effects of covert work, undercover police officers also run the risk of being exposed to friendly fire or assaults from other police officers who are unaware of their true identity. One particularly tragic incident of such a shooting occurred in New York during the early 1990s, when a black undercover officer who was holding a suspect at gunpoint was shot and killed by white officers who mistakenly believed that a robbery was in progress (McFaddan 1992; Marx 1995). Incidents such as this have led some police officer groups—particularly those representing officers from racial minorities—to encourage their members to refuse plainclothes assignments and undercover work (Marx 1995). Based on the unique conditions of undercover work, most officers in local departments are not allowed assignments lasting longer than two to three years.

Special Weapons And Tactics (S.W.A.T.) Units   In addition to regular patrol units and other field divisions, many police departments now maintain paramilitary units that specialize in the use of force and aggressive policing techniques. Most commonly referred to as **S.W.A.T. (Special Weapons And Tactics) teams**, these units are responsible for handling high-risk law enforcement situations that are beyond the capabilities of ordinary patrol officers. Such situations typically include:

- Apprehension of barricaded suspects
- Resolution of hostage situations
- Warrant service when there is a chance of a violent confrontation
- Arrest or incapacitation of armed or dangerous suspects
- Provision of security for visiting dignitaries and politicians

Fitted out in body armor and equipped with a variety of specialized weapons—including submachine guns, sniper rifles, and tear gas grenades—members of these teams receive extensive training in a diverse range of skills and are expected to maintain levels of fitness considerably higher than those of regular police officers (Table 5.5). Although in some large police departments, such as the New York Police Department (NYPD) and the Los Angeles Police Department (LAPD), officers are assigned to S.W.A.T. units on a full-time basis, in most departments, special weapons and tactics is a **co-lateral assignment**. In such departments, teams are made up of officers who continue to work regular police assignments and serve as S.W.A.T. members as and when required.

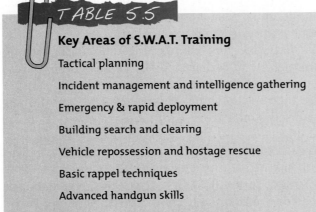

TABLE 5.5

Key Areas of S.W.A.T. Training

Tactical planning

Incident management and intelligence gathering

Emergency & rapid deployment

Building search and clearing

Vehicle repossession and hostage rescue

Basic rappel techniques

Advanced handgun skills

Advanced close-quarter battle skills

Live-fire training

Adapted from the James A. Neal Public Safety Training Center (Georgia) SWAT I-III Curriculum (jamesanealtraining.com).

The Origins of Police S.W.A.T. Teams Although the military use of specialized sharpshooter and tactical units can be traced back as far as the Revolutionary War, the first police S.W.A.T. teams did not begin to appear in the United States until the late 1960s. These units were established in response to a number of high-profile sniper attacks against police and civilians, the most notable of which occurred in Austin, Texas, in 1966. During this particularly shocking episode—sometimes referred to as the "Texas Tower Incident"—a former Marine sharpshooter named Charles Whitman climbed to the top of the University of Texas Tower with a rifle and proceeded to murder fifteen people and wound an additional thirty-one others before eventually being killed by two Austin police officers. Following this incident, many police departments across the country concluded that they were ill-prepared to handle such situations and moved to develop specialized teams trained to deal with similar emergencies. The LAPD is now generally credited with having established the first dedicated S.W.A.T. unit, which consisted of fifteen four-man teams made up of volunteers drawn from regular police assignments, many of whom either had prior military experience or were familiar with special weapons operations. These teams, which were originally referred to as "station defense teams," received regular monthly training in special weapons handling and tactics and were expected to respond whenever an situation emerged that was beyond the capabilities of normal police personnel.

In 1969, the newly formed LAPD station defense team was called to its first major incident. In the course of attempting to carry out a search for illegal weapons at the Los Angeles headquarters of the Black Panther Movement, a gun battle broke out between the police defense team and members of the Panthers.

During the ensuing siege of the Panthers' headquarters—which lasted over four hours—three Black Panthers and three police officers were wounded and thousands of rounds of ammunition were fired before the Panthers eventually surrendered. Remarkably, no one was killed in the shootout, and as a consequence, the LAPD was widely praised for its handling of what was an extremely charged and dangerous situation. By 1971, the volunteer system was abandoned by the LAPD, and officers were placed on full-time assignment to the teams, which were renamed Special Weapons And Tactics (S.W.A.T.).

Over the past three decades, hundreds of police departments have established their own S.W.A.T. units, many of them based on the original LAPD model. According to recent studies, approximately 90 percent of all medium- and large-sized police departments (i.e., those responsible for policing areas with a population in excess of 25,000) now maintain S.W.A.T. teams or similar special units (Kraska & Kappeler 1997). Although the acronym S.W.A.T. is commonly used, alternative names for such units include Special Response Team (S.R.T.) and Emergency Response Team (E.R.T.).

In addition to receiving advanced weapon and tactics training, SWAT officers are also required to maintain high levels of fitness and preparedness.

New Trends and Controversies Although the use of S.W.A.T. teams has come to be seen as an essential part of modern policing, some commentators have raised concerns about the growing use of such specialized units. According to Kraska and Cubellis (1997), for example, in 1995 alone there were a total of 29,929 paramilitary deployments by the police and other law enforcement agencies, more than nine times the number of similar deployments recorded in 1980.[3] Although it has been suggested that this increase in activity can be attributed to similar increases in the rate of violent crime over the same period, this argument is rejected by Kraska and Cubellis (1997). Instead, they claim that S.W.A.T. teams and other special police units have become increasingly proactive in recent years, gradually moving away from their original emergency role and becoming more akin to specialized search and patrol units. Moreover, they argue that the increasing reliance on specialized, essentially paramilitary units is indicative of a return to the military models that dominated policing for much of the first half of the twentieth century and a shift away from a commitment to the ideals of community policing (Kraska and Cubellis 1997):

> [W]e find strong support for the thesis that the military model is still a powerful force guiding the ideology and activities of the American police. This should not be surprising considering the war/military paradigm remains an authoritative framework for crime-control thinking and action by politicians, bureaucrats, the media, and much of the public. (p. 622)

If it is true that S.W.A.T. teams are being used more proactively, then the question arises as to whether these units should continue to be regarded as special units or instead be treated as a form of specialized patrol. Finally, in the wake of the September 11 attacks, some commentators have argued that there is a need for local police S.W.A.T. units to be more involved in national antiterrorism operations. In large cities such as New York and Los Angeles—cities particularly at risk from terrorist attack—police administrators have already begun to take steps to expand existing special operations training programs to include a greater emphasis on antiterrorist tactics and strategies.

In summary, it should also be stressed that although the military style of S.W.A.T. teams has been emphasized throughout this chapter, most units are also heavily trained in **hostage-negotiation techniques** to minimize the likelihood of having to resort to lethal force. For example, during a hostage situation during a bank robbery, trained hostage negotiators will try to persuade the suspect to release the hostages and/or surrender without bursting in on the scene and risking more lives.

Juvenile Units

In recent years, the police have become increasingly aware of the need to provide young children and juveniles with special care and protection (Krisberg and Austin 1993). In most states, juvenile offenders do not have the same rights as adult offenders and are processed by specialized institutions (such as youth courts) within the criminal justice system. As a consequence, many police departments around the country now maintain dedicated juvenile crime units that only handle juvenile offenders and victims and are responsible for ensuring that children who come into contact with the law receive specialized attention (Bittner 1976; National Institute for Juvenile Justice and Delinquency Prevention 1997; Kobetz and Borsage 1973). In addition to dealing with cases of juvenile crime and investigating crimes against children, one of the key functions of these units is to work with schools, social services, child welfare services, and voluntary organizations to develop strategies for protecting children and keeping young people out of the criminal justice system.

In many instances, these units will include officers who specialize in particular aspects of juvenile crime and victimization, such as homelessness, gang violence, child prostitution, and juvenile drug use. Some juvenile units also employ **school liaison officers** (also referred to as school resource officers in some jurisdictions), who are permanently assigned to local high schools to investigate juvenile crime and serve as a resource to school staff and students. School liaison officers provide students and teachers with direct access to police services as well as information, counseling, and referrals and frequently assist with such activities as:

- Juvenile offender counseling

- Counseling of family members of juvenile offenders

- Placement of juvenile offenders into drug/alcohol treatment programs

- Voluntary fingerprinting of juveniles, toddlers, and infants at the request of parents

- Lectures to schools and youth groups on drug/alcohol awareness and detection

Although most juvenile units exist primarily to investigate crimes, an increasing amount of police time and resources is being spent on youth education and crime prevention programs. In recent years, for example, many juvenile crime units have become actively involved in the **D.A.R.E. (Drug Abuse Resistance Education)** program, which consists of a series of police-officer-led classroom lessons designed to teach children and young people how to avoid becoming involved in drugs, gangs, and violence. Founded in 1983 by the LAPD and the Los Angeles Unified School District, the program can be found in almost

Policing juveniles requires officers to employ a range of skills and to be ready to work with vulnerable young people at risk of committing crimes.

75 percent of schools and is taught from kindergarten through the twelfth grade (D.A.R.E. America 1996). Although a number of recent studies have questioned its effectiveness, the program is widely regarded as one the most successful collaborations between the police and the community ever devised in the United States (Rosebaum and Hanson 1998; LaFree et al. 1995; Sigler and Talley 1995). The D.A.R.E. program can now be found in many other countries, including Mexico.

As mentioned, a number of scholars have criticized the actual preventive success of D.A.R.E. programming. In contrast, recent studies have demonstrated the promise of a similar model targeting youth involvement in gangs (Grant n.d.). Called Gang Resistance Education and Training (GREAT), this model also puts officers into the classroom to discuss the negative implications of gang involvement. It has been shown to have a significant effect on youth behavior several years after participation in the program. Future study and replication is, of course, necessary.

Canine (K9) Units   The use of police dogs is now widespread throughout the United States, with **canine (K9) units** being deployed in a vast array of situations and emergencies ranging from public order incidents to drug investigations and the tracking of suspects.[4] Although dogs were regularly used by the police in Europe from the end of the nineteenth century (most notably in Belgium and Holland), it wasn't until the early 1900s that a small number of U.S. police departments began to look into the feasibility of establishing dedicated K9 units. The NYPD is now generally credited with setting up the first dedicated police dog unit in 1907, although almost from the outset the unit was regarded as a mixed success and was eventually disbanded in 1951. Between the

In large departments, officers that specialize in juvenile crime and victimization have become an important resource, with activities ranging from investigation and counseling, to include crime prevention classes in the schools, such as the well-known D.A.R.E. program begun by the LAPD in 1983.

Over time, police handlers develop extremely close relationships with their dogs.

first and second World Wars, numerous other police departments also experimented with the use of dogs, but as in the case of New York, these units were frequently plagued by problems of inadequate funding, a shortage of competent trainers, and difficulties finding suitable animals. In addition, K9 units were initially regarded with considerable suspicion by members of the public, many of whom feared that the police might begin to use dogs for such things as crowd control and disabling suspects who resisted arrest.

During the 1950s, however, police and public attitudes towards K9 units began to change. Rising crime rates led a number of departments to reevaluate the use of police dogs. In 1957, the Baltimore Police Department established a highly effective K9 unit. Its success in combating certain types of crime prompted numerous cities to follow its example. By 1970, over eighty police departments were employing dogs as part of their patrol force, with most departments favoring the use German Shepherds, Dobermans, and Labradors. As drugs began to become an increasing problem in many major cities, K9 units began to further expand their operations beyond the use of dogs for public order and police protection and developed sophisticated training programs designed to teach dogs how to identify certain types of narcotics and other prohibited substances.[5] Today, it is rare to find a police department that doesn't either keep trained dogs or have ready access to them if needed (ACLU, NAACP Legal Defense Fund 1992; Stitt 1991; Bird 1996).

Police dogs can be used for the following activities:

- Tracking of suspects and victims
- Area, building, and vehicle searches
- Drug identification
- Officer backup

Given the amount of injury a dog can inflict on a suspect (including even lethal levels of force), K9 officers are taught to command their charges according to the same principles governing the use of all other types of force detailed in Chapter 10. Failure to exercise proper command over a police dog can itself be a civil liability concern for a department.

Chapter Summary

- Every police department has a set of organizational goals and values that provide officers with a sense of direction and purpose. These goals are often framed in the form of a mission statement and form the basis of police polices and rules.

- Traditionally, police departments in the United States have been organized along quasi-military lines and have favored a hierarchical bureaucracy based on clear chains of command and the division of police personnel into ranks.

- Police units and divisions can be classified according to whether they are operational or administrative. Typical operational units include police patrol, traffic, and criminal investigation; administrative units include personnel, records, research and planning, and public information. In addition, many police departments now have specialized units that deal either with specific crimes or certain types of offenders.

- According to some commentators and researchers, the increasing importance placed on special units such as S.W.A.T. by police departments in the United States may be indicative of a shift to a more militaristic style of policing and away from the community-policing strategies that have been popular for the past three decades.

KEY TERMS

Administrative unit 123
Agent provocateur 129
Blending 128
Canine (K9) units 134
Chains of command 114
Co-lateral assignment 130
Command 114
Covert (undercover) operations 127
D.A.R.E. (Drug Abuse Resistance Education) 133
Decentralizing 117
Decoy operation 128
Division 118
Entrapment 129

Flat organizations 116
Flattening 116
Functional structures 118
Generalists 114
Horizontal differentiation 117
Hostage-negotiation techniques 132
Internal affairs unit 125
Interim order 114
Line personnel 114
Matrix structures 118
Middle management 114
Mission statement 113
Operational unit 122

Organizational chart 114
Policies 113
Policing goals 112
Quasi-military 114
Reverse sting operations 128
S.W.A.T. (Special Weapons And Tactics) teams 130
School liaison officers 133
Span of control 116
Sting operations 128
Tall organizations 116
Unit 120
Values 113
Vertical differentiation 116

Linking the Dots

1. Explain the difference between a goal, a policy, and a procedure. How are the decisions of individual police officers guided by policies and procedures?

2. What is the purpose of a mission statement? How do mission statements help to shape the working culture of a police department?

3. What is the difference between a police division and a police unit? What are the functions of each?

4. What is the difference between an operational unit and an administrative unit? Name and describe the basic functions of two operational units and two administrative units.

5. What are the eight basic outcomes of a police complaint?

6. What is the basic function of a S.W.A.T. unit? Do you think that such units should only be reactive?

REFERENCES

ACLU of Southern California. 1992. *Analysis and Recommendations: Los Angeles Police Department K9 Program.* Los Angeles, CA: NAACP Legal Defense Fund, Police Watch.

Bennett, W. W., and K. M. Hess. 2001. *Criminal Investigation,* 6th ed. Belmont, CA: Wadsworth.

Bird, R. C. 1996. "An Examination of the Training and Reliability of the Narcotics Detection Dog." *Kentucky Law Journal* 85(2):405–433.

Bittner, E. 1976. "Policing Juveniles: The Social Context of Common Practice." In *Pursuing Justice for the Child,* edited by M. K. Rosenheim, 351–372. Chicago: University of Chicago Press.

Carter, D. 1994. "Police Disciplinary Procedures: A Review of Selected Police Departments." In *Police Deviance,* 3d ed., edited by T. Barker and D. Carter, 351–372. Cincinnati: Anderson Publishing.

Chapman, S. G. 1990. *Police Dogs in North America.* Springfield, IL: Charles C. Thomas.

Commission on Accreditations for Law Enforcement Agencies. 1999. *Standards for Law Enforcement Agencies,* 4th ed. Fairfax, VA: CALEA.

D'Arcy, S. 1990. *Internal Affairs Units Guidelines.* San Jose, CA: San Jose Police Department.

D.A.R.E. America. 1996. *The Official D.A.R.E. Web site: D.A.R.E. America.* Available at www.dare.com/D_offi/DD_DARE/DU_DARE.htm

DeBlanc, D., and W. Redman. 2000. "Officer Safety for Undercover Violence." *The Law Enforcement Trainer* 15(4):34–35.

Dumont, L. F. 2000. "Minimizing Undercover Violence." *Law and Order* 48(10):103–109.

Farkas, G. 1986. "Stress in Undercover Policing." In *Psychological Services for Law Enforcement*, edited by J. T. Reese and H. A. Goldstein, 433–440. Washington, D.C.: U.S. Government Printing Office.

Farmer, A. 2002. "Law Fosters Interagency Cooperation: Evidence of Abuse Not Always Shared." *Poughkeepsie Journal,* April 7. Available at www.poughkeepsiejournal.com/projects/cps/1_04070_4.shtml

Girodo, M. 1991a. "Drug Corruption in Undercover Agents: Measuring the Risk." *Behavioral Sciences and the Law* 9 (3):361–370.

Girodo, M. 1991b. "Personality, Job Stress, and Mental Health in Undercover Agents: A Structural Equation Analysis." *Journal of Social Behavior and Personality* 6 (3):375–390.

Goldstein, H. 1977. "Directing Police Agencies Through the Political Process." In *Policing a Free Society,* edited by H. Goldstein, 131–156. Cambridge, MA: Ballinger.

G.R.E.A.T. n.d. *2005 Plan: No Violence is Great.* Available at www.aff.gov/grat/2000/htm.

Grennan, S. 2001. "Historical Perspective of Police Corruption in New York City." In *Police Misconduct: A Reader for the 21st Century,* edited by M. Palmiotto, 117–131. Upper Saddle River, NJ: Prentice-Hall.

Hart, L. A., and R. L. Zasloff. 2000. "The Role of Police Dogs as Companions and Working Partners." *Psychological Reports* 86 (1):190–202.

Hess, K. M., and H. M. Wrobleski. 2002. *Police Operations: Theory and Practice,* 3d ed. Belmont, CA: Wadsworth.

Jacobs, B. 1993. "Undercover Deception Clues." *Criminology* 31 (2):281–299.

Klockars, C. 1985. *The Idea of Police.* Beverly Hills, CA: Sage Publications.

Kobetz, R., and B. Borsage. 1973. *Juvenile Justice Administration.* Gaithersburg, MD: International Association of Police Chiefs (ICAP).

Kraska, P. B., and L. J. Cubellis. 1997a. "Militarizing Mayberry and Beyond: Making Sense of American Paramilitary Policing." *Justice Quarterly* 14 (4): 607–629.

Kraska, P. B., and V. E. Kappeler. 1997b. "Militarizing American Police: The Rise and Normalization of Paramilitary Units." *Social Problems* 44 (1):1–18.

Krisberg, B., and J. Austin. 1993. *Reinventing Juvenile Justice.* Newbury Park, CA: Sage.

LaFree, G., C. Birkbeck, and N. Wilson. 1995. "Policemen in the Classroom: Albuquerque Adolescents' Opinions About the Drug Awareness and Resistance Education Program." Albuquerque, NM: New Mexico Criminal Justice Statistical Analysis Center.

Marx, G. T. 1988. *Undercover: Police Surveillance in America.* Berkeley: University of California Press.

Marx, G. T. 1992. "Under-the-Covers Undercover Investigations: Some Reflections on the State's Use of Sex and Deception in Law Enforcement." *Criminal Justice Ethics* 11(1):13–24.

Marx, G. T. 1995. "Recent Developments in Undercover Policing." In *Punishment and Social Control: Essays in Honor of Sheldon Messinger,* edited by T. Blomberg and S. Cohen, 88–101. New York, NY: Aldyne de Gruyler.

McFaddan, R. D. November 20, 1992. "Darkness and Disorder in Subway: Questions Swirl in Police Shooting." *New York Times,* A1.

Miller, C. 2001. "The Art of the Ruse: Does Winning a Battle Mean Losing a War?" *Law Enforcement Technology* 18(1):26–32.

Miller, G. 1987. "Observations on Police Undercover Work." *Criminology* 25 (1):27–46.

National Institute for Juvenile Justice and Delinquency Prevention. 1997. *Police–Juvenile Operations: A Comparative Analysis of Standards and Practices,* Vol. 2. Washington, D.C.: Government Printing Office.

Office of Juvenile Justice and Delinquency Prevention. 2001. *The National Center on Child Fatality Review.* Washington, D.C.: Department of Justice, Office of Juvenile Justice and Delinquency Prevention.

Pogrebin, M., and E. Poole. 1993. "Vice Isn't Nice: A Look at the Ethics of Working Undercover." *Journal of Criminal Justice* 21(4):383–394.

Rosenbaum, D. P., and G. S. Hanson. 1998. "Assessing the Effects of School-based Drug Education: A Six-year Multilevel Analysis of Project D.A.R.E." *Journal of Research in Crime and Delinquency* 35 (4): 381–412.

Sheehan, R., and G. W. Cordner. 1989. *Introduction to Police Administration,* 2d ed. Cincinnati: Anderson Publishing.

Sigler, R. T., and G. B. Talley. 1995. "Drug Abuse Resistance Education Program Effectiveness." *American Journal of Police* 14 (3/4): 111–121.

Stanislaus County Sheriff's Department. 2002. "Sheriff's Undercover Unit Has Many Faces." Available at www.stanislaussheriff.com/pub_info/2002/n021102. Accessed February 11, 2002.

Stitt, B. G. 1991. "Practical, Ethical, and Political Aspects of Engaging 'Man's Best Friend' in the War on Crime." *Criminal Justice Policy Review* 5 (1): 53–65.

Texas Alcoholic Beverage Commission. 2002. "Minor Sting Operations." Available at www.tabc.state.tx.us/enforce/minor.htm.

Thrasher, R. 2001. "Internal Affairs: The Police Agencies' Approach to the Investigation of Police Misconduct." In *Police Misconduct: A Reader for the 21st Century,* edited by M. Palmiotto, 396–408. Upper Saddle River, NJ: Prentice-Hall.

Walker, S., and C. Katz. 2002. *Police in America: An Introduction,* 4th ed. Boston: McGraw-Hill.

NOTES

1. A good example of an internal affairs unit that has been successful in helping to combat police corruption is the NYPD Internal Affairs Bureau (IAB). See Grennan (2001).

2. See also Girodo (1991b).

3. See also Kraska and Kappeler (1997b).

4. For a good overview of the role played by police dogs, see Chapman (1990) and Hart and Zasloff (2000).

5. For a more detailed discussion of the history of police dogs units, see the City of Toronto Police Department Website at www.torontopolice.on.ca/pds/histdog1.html.

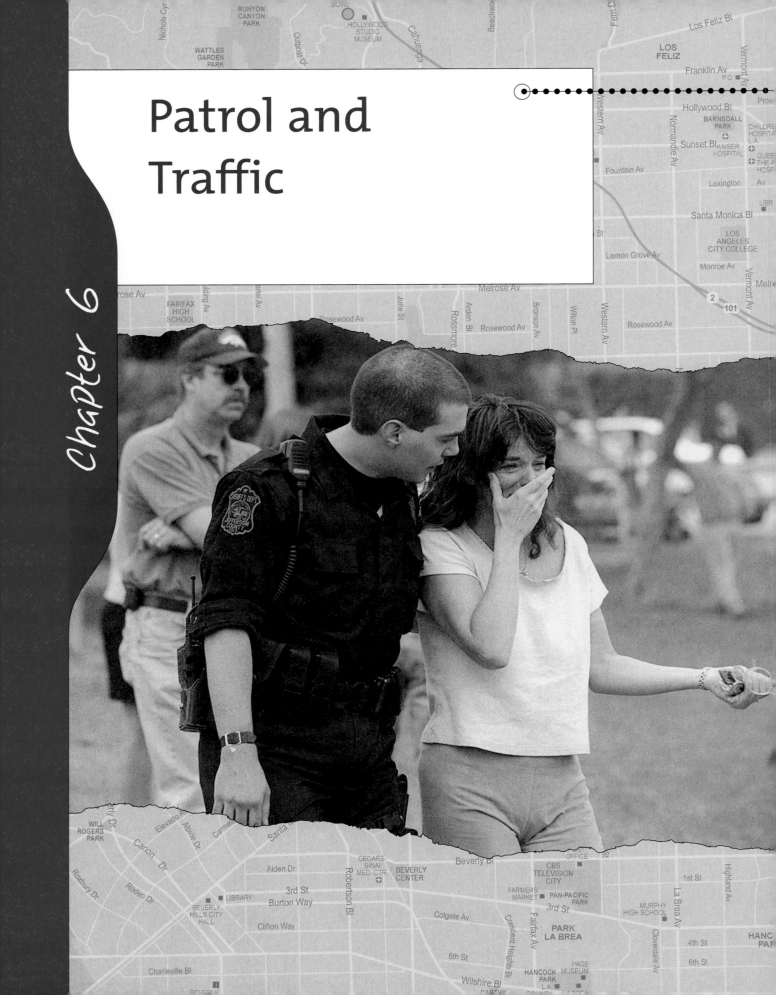

Patrol and Traffic

Chapter 6

Chapter Outline

Chapter Objectives

● Appreciate the nature of patrol work and be familiar with empirical data related to the use of time by patrol officers and officer productivity.

● Become familiar with the various types of patrol, including random, directed, and aggressive patrol.

● Understand the implications of the Kansas City Preventive Patrol Experiment to the traditional model of policing and recognize the experiment's weaknesses.

● Articulate the various types of patrol deployments, as well as studies related to their effectiveness.

● Know the nature and importance of the traffic function and its unique dangers.

Introduction

In Akron, Ohio, two women were attacked within two months of each other. Only one of these women survived. The first attack took place in May 2002, and the victim had an order of protection against her ex-husband. Despite the order forbidding him to contact her or come within 100 yards of her, Karen Hunter's ex-husband decided to pay her an unfortunate visit.

A neighbor saw Mrs. Hunter's ex-husband dragging her into the home and called 911 immediately upon hearing her scream. Unfortunately, the police did not arrive at the home until forty minutes after the 911 call, finding the victim stabbed to death on the kitchen floor.

The Akron Police Department did not react to this incident lightly. They made all domestic violence calls involving a court order a higher priority. In July, the police had to respond to an incident similar to that of Karen Hunter and her ex-husband. Within minutes after receiving an emergency call, the police arrived at the house of Tracy Stoyer. Upon arriving at the scene, the responding officers heard screams, leading them to kick down the door and enter the home. When they reached Mrs. Stoyer, they found her bruised and bloody with impressions of fingers on her neck. But she was alive. In this case, the victim claimed that police response time saved her life (Associated Press 2002).

Police response time to emergencies has traditionally been viewed as a central measure of departmental effectiveness. Although the patrol officer can make the life-saving difference in cases such as the above example, the realities of patrol are such that more often than not, quick response time will not make a significant difference in the outcome of the incident. This chapter will examine the essential role of patrol within policing. Patrol is often referred to as the "backbone of policing" because of its predominance over the designation of departmental resources (Walker 2002). For example, in 1997, 63 percent of all sworn officers were assigned to patrol duty (Bureau of Justice Statistics 1997).

Patrol officers are also the most visible ambassadors for the police department. The nature of police–community relations can be shaped by citizen interactions with the patrol division more than any other part of the department. Even with the best-intentioned police chief, if departmental controls do not significantly affect patrol officer behavior, individual policies will fail. Moreover, citizen interactions with the patrol are often used to frame analysis of departmental priorities and policies.

This chapter will examine the critical role of patrol in contemporary policing. Although patrol plays a significant role in the department, very few large-scale evaluations of its effectiveness have been carried out. Despite this, we know a great deal more about what works for patrol than in the past, thanks to an explosion in police research throughout the 1970s and 1980s.

The Realities of Patrol

Patrol officers are the most visible symbol of the law; they must conduct themselves in a manner that inspires confidence and respect in the law. When the average person envisions a career in law enforcement, he or she usually thinks of the patrol function as depicted on television: high-speed pursuits, chasing offenders through back alleys and crowded nighttime streets, or arriving at the scene of a robbery in progress to arrest and bring in the "bad guy." It is also common for aspiring law enforcement professionals to have a glamorized version of the FBI, CIA, or CSI roles based on media imagery. Although entertaining, such activities do not represent the day-to-day realities of the patrol function.

Use of Time by Patrol Officers

Despite our perceptions about the nature of policing, empirical evaluations of the patrol function have consistently demonstrated that responding to crime is not the primary activity engaged in by officers on patrol. Some studies have suggested that only about 20 percent of all assigned calls involve active Part I and Part II offenses, as defined by the *UCR* (see Chapter 3) (Boydstun et al. 1977). Of those calls involving more serious offenses, 15 percent involve officers taking reports of crimes that had already occurred, and 8 percent involve checking on suspicious circumstances or individuals (Boydstun et al. 1977).

The **Police Services Study (PSS)** examined how officers from twenty-four departments spent their time and their interactions with citizens in sixty residential neighborhoods. The PSS found that, on average, two-thirds of an officer's shift was "unassigned" (Whitaker 1982). Most of this time was spent patrolling the beat and engaging in officer-initiated contacts with citizens; more often than not, these citizen encounters involved traffic-stop situations. In support of Boydstun et al.'s (1977) findings, the PSS found that only 38 percent of all observed encounters involved crime as the primary problem (Whitaker 1982).

Overall, the activity that officers spent the most time on was information gathering, either from the standpoint of an officer helping a citizen or controlling an offender. Despite the central role of force discussed in Chapter 1, the PSS found that actual force was only used in 5 percent of all encounters, and that this involved taking a suspect by the arm or handcuffing them (Whitaker 1982). The threat of force, however, was more common, occurring in 14 percent of all encounters (Whitaker 1982). Interestingly, arrests occurred in only one out of every twenty PSS encounters. Other studies have found that officers can sometimes go months without ever reporting an arrest. One such study of Washington, D.C., officers found that 46 percent made no arrests in a year (Forst et al. 1978)!

Productivity Measures

In light of these findings, one obvious question that emerges is how officer productivity should be measured. Are arrest quotas a sufficient gage of an officer's average job performance given that so little of officers' time is spent dealing with crime problems? In the absence of other indicators, how should command staff

Although required to be both reactive and proactive, officers typically spend considerable amounts of time dealing with routine administration arising from patrol.

evaluate their line officers? Despite the reported successes of the NYPD's Compstat model, there have also been a significant number of reports about the demoralizing effects of the "pressure to produce" arrests on the average officer (see Chapter 13).

Response time to calls for service has also been used as a measure of officer effectiveness, but here, too, one can run into some difficulties in practice. Although the public is generally thought to desire a quick response to their calls, the reality is that most of the time the speed of the officer's arrival will make little difference to the outcome of the incident. Obviously a speedy response is a necessity in situations where the crime is in progress, such as with the examples at the beginning of this chapter. However, according to a Police Executive Research Forum (PERF) study, only 25 percent of cases are cases in which there is an ongoing confrontation between victim and offender (Skogan and Attunes 1979). Thus, in most situations, particularly property offenses, the chance of case clearance is almost nonexistent without adequate information being provided to the officer. If a patrol officer's time might be better spent engaged in meaningful interactions with the community, should response time be such a significant determinant of effectiveness on the job?

Some departments, such as the Indiana State Police, no longer use arrest or ticket quotas as measures of officer performance. Instead, district commanders work with their troopers to craft performance goals that include community activities that most departments traditionally do not use as performance measures, such as interactions with the community and evidence of problem solving (Niederpruem 2000).

In sum, productivity and performance measures are ways of evaluating the effectiveness of police agencies, and therefore they need to be based on an understanding not only of *what* the police actually do, but also on what the police *should* do (Fridell 2000). According to Moore (1999), agencies should identify "what matters" for the purposes of performance evaluation by considering overall accountability needs from the perspective of internal command structures as well as from the vantage point of citizen needs and those of other **external authorizing environmental stakeholders**. The external authorizing environment refers to all individuals or agencies outside of the police department that can influence its strategy or policy decisions. Future research needs to determine:

- How to link performance evaluation to accountability mechanisms within the department

- How best to incorporate the needs and expectations of community residents and external agencies into the performance evaluation system

- The impact of performance evaluation systems on departmental achievement of goals and objectives

Community policing activities require significant resource expenditures on tasks not captured by traditional performance measures. For example, collaborative problem-solving efforts can require attendance at community meetings, outreach to other city agencies and businesses, and the addressing of "noncrime" community problems. Community police officers often complain about the conflicting demands upon them to meet arrest quotas at the same time as they are to engage in these types of activities (Moore 1999). Even in departments where community police officers are excluded from regular response to calls for service, they may be the focus of resentment or ridicule from regular patrol line officers, with the result that morale among such officers is compromised.

The Patrol Function

Whatever the incident, from the minor squabble between a cab driver and a patron to a serious domestic assault, an officer is generally the first to arrive at the scene, highlighting how the job can turn from mundane to life-threatening in the blink of an eye. Given this wide range of possible daily interactions, the patrol officer serves many functions, including crime fighter, mediator, social worker, and service provider. Adams (2001) identifies several objectives of police field operations and patrol:

- Protection and defense of lives and property
- Repression of criminal and delinquent behavior
- Identification, apprehension, and conviction of offenders
- Traffic flow and collision reduction
- Maintenance of order and public safety

In a newly developed training curriculum for both recruits and in-service officers, Kenney et al. (2003) categorize central patrol functions into three non-mutually exclusive types of interactions:

1. Information gathering

2. Conflict resolution

3. Maintenance/restoration of control

As noted by Bittner (1990), at some level, policing is always going to be about force or control, even when an officer is engaging in simple information-gathering activities. Conflict resolution is also a regular component of an officer's interactions, and as such, good communication and problem-solving skills are also crucial to success. In many situations, such skills will also allow the officer to maintain control without often having to resort to the use of force. However, once physical force becomes necessary, it can safely be said that the officer has lost control of the situation (not necessarily as a fault of his or her own actions), and the range of possible options for problem resolution narrows significantly (Kenney et al. 2002).

Types of Patrols

Although the image of a police vehicle cruising slowly through a neighborhood is what we most often think of as patrol activity, there are several different types of patrol commonly used by contemporary police departments, each with varying degrees of effectiveness.

Random Patrol

With **random**, or **routine**, **patrol**, officers are assigned to a specific area and are asked to move around in an "unsystematic" way (usually by motor vehicle)

One of the most significant technological developments of the 20th century, the invention of the automobile revolutionized policing and gave officers the ability to respond to incidents both quickly and efficiently.

(Cordner and Trojanwicz 1992). The central goals of this type of patrol include the detection of crimes in progress, as well as the hope of deterring crimes through presence. It is because of the presumed deterrence effect of this type of patrol that it is also often referred to as *preventive patrol*. Random patrol is said to be **incident driven**, or reactive, in that officers respond to crimes only after they occur, either through rapid response to calls for service or to a violation or call in progress. Because officers are constantly moving while awaiting calls, the logic of random patrol dictates that officers will be ready to respond to 911 calls, thereby reducing the time between call and response. The specific activities an officer engages in while on random patrol will vary significantly across officers, times, locations, and departments in that much of the time spent on patrol is officer initiated.

Directed Patrol

Directed patrol involves the focusing of patrol resources on targeted hot spots, crime problems, and/or offenders. Crime statistics are used to assess patterns of crime for strategic purposes. In addition to using such data to isolate high-crime areas and peak times, directed patrol addresses the problem-identification component of the problem-solving process, which is detailed further in Chapter 12. Sometimes a form of directed patrol can occur on an informal level with an experienced officer self-initiating "directed" patrol by regularly driving past hot spots during random wanderings. Similarly, parking the squad car in a specific location when writing reports and using the restroom at the back of a 7-Eleven that has been a source of problems represents such informal directed activity.

To the extent that it attempts to target problems rather than simply respond to them, directed patrol can be viewed as a form of **proactive patrol**. Cordner (1981) notes that although directed patrol can have an immediate effect on certain crimes (i.e., gun crimes, street robberies), over time there may be a point of diminishing returns in terms of factors such as police–community relations. Additionally, it remains unclear as to whether such activities only serve to displace crime activities to other locations. Table 6.1 details the differences between random and directed patrol.

A major downside to directed patrol is the significant costs attached to operating such activities on a continued basis. Directing greater police resources to one specific location and/or time often means that resources are taken away from somewhere else or that the department must rely on overtime to meet patrol needs. As such, to run directed patrol operations extensively, departments often have to engage in differential response strategies. **Differential response** involves the more efficient screening of calls for service at dispatch. Rather than treating all calls as deserving of the same priority, dispatchers screen incidents based on need for immediate response time. Some possible options involved in differential response include:

- Have dispatch provide the caller with an estimate of how long it will take the patrol officer to respond
- Have a civilian personnel or dispatcher rather than sworn officer take a report over the phone or have the complainant submit it via fax or the Internet

TABLE 6.1

Differences Between Random and Directed Patrol

Random Patrol	Directed Patrol
• **Random**—Patrol officers begin their shifts by driving unsystematically throughout their sector in the hopes of detecting crimes in progress and deterring crime through their presence	• **Proactive**—Focus on hot spots, targeted locations, problems and people (e.g., gun crimes)
• **Incident driven**—Reactive	• Puts more **officers in peak areas** at **times** when crime committed
• **Rapid response to calls for service**	

- Have a civilian rather than a sworn officer respond to the crime scene for less serious or cold cases

Although we are often quick to judge the police based on how quickly they respond to our needs, the empirical research is somewhat mixed regarding the degree to which this affects overall dissatisfaction with police services. Although it is true that response time plays a part in overall satisfaction, researchers have found that such an evaluation is more related to the civilians' expectations of how quickly the police should arrive rather than just the actual response time (Percy 1980). Thus, departments that cannot afford the significant resources it would take to improve response time may be better served by a community relations campaign that stresses realistic arrival expectations for certain types of offenses. This can also be a component of differential response strategies.

Aggressive Patrol

Often considered a form of directed patrol, **aggressive patrol** refers to the use of high-profile patrol activities such as frequent traffic stops and regular field interrogations. Aggressive patrol also often involves crackdowns aimed towards drawing media attention in the hope that this will enhance any deterrent effect (Cordner and Trojanwicz 1992). For example, the targeting of known "crack rows" for the apprehension of offenders and later clean-up usually brings significant media attention. Strategies such as closing down street access to high drug trafficking locations have proven successful, such as the NYPD's Model Block Program or similar efforts by Weed and Seed programs by departments nationwide (Grant and Jacobs 1998; Grant 2000).

Sheppard et al. (2000) point to the need for community collaboration when engaging in aggressive patrol activities because of the seemingly disproportionate affect such strategies can have on certain segments of the population. In this case, a zero-tolerance program for gun violence in a predominantly low income African American community in Baton Rouge, Louisiana, was implemented successfully after receiving community approval from clergy leaders and organizations such as 100 Black Men (Sheppard et al. 2000). In addition, the degree to which such aggressive tactics successfully target offenders rather than the average citizen can go a long way towards reducing community dissatisfaction (Boydstun 1975).

The results of the **Kansas City Gun Experiment**, in which intensive patrols targeted an eighty-block high-crime area with traffic stops and field interrogations, revealed that aggressive patrol can significantly reduce gun crimes such as drive-by shootings and homicides. Most important, no displacement effects were measured (at least in the short term of the study) (Sherman et al. 1995).

Saturation Patrol

Placing extremely high levels of patrol within a narrowly defined geographic area is referred to as **saturation patrol**. Although empirical findings are mixed, some immediate suppressive effects of saturation patrol on crime have been evidenced (Wilson 1975), but it can be limited to certain times of day (Carr et al. 1980) and can be dependent on reaching a certain "tipping point" in terms of number of officers. In the latter case, increases from one to two officers in a beat made no difference, but as more were added, there were increasingly greater effects on crime (Bright 1969).

The Effectiveness of Patrol

As our previous discussion indicates, different types of patrol will be more effective depending on the specific crime and location being targeted. An **integrated patrol**, combining random patrol with any of the other more intensive tactics, might be successful in suppressing open-air activities, but the degree to which this lasts over time or leads to crime displacement is difficult to gauge. What we do know, however, based on the patrol studies of the 1970s and 1980s, is that random patrol on its own does not significantly affect criminal activity. The study most responsible for bringing this point home to the police community and that forced a reconsideration of the role of random patrol as a policing strategy was the **Kansas City Preventive Patrol Experiment**.

At the request of the Kansas City Police Department, and funded by the Police Foundation, the Kansas City Patrol Experiment was conceived of in 1972 as a means of evaluating the true ability of random patrol to reduce crime and fear of crime. At that point in time, random patrol's ability to meet those two goals had been accepted on faith.

To conduct the quasi-experiment, researchers divided fifteen patrol beats in the south side of the city into three types of intervention activities (Kelling et al. 1974) (Figure 6.1). In the **reactive beats**, all random patrol activity was suspended. Patrol officers only responded to calls for service in the area and then would quickly retreat. Normal levels of patrol were maintained in the **control beats**, allowing patrol to function as it had prior to the intervention. Finally, **proactive beats** were established that had three times the level of random patrol activity.

Over the course of the study between 1972 and 1973, the researchers closely monitored whether displacement effects were occurring or if the pattern of crime was significantly changing in the reactive beats. Should this be the case,

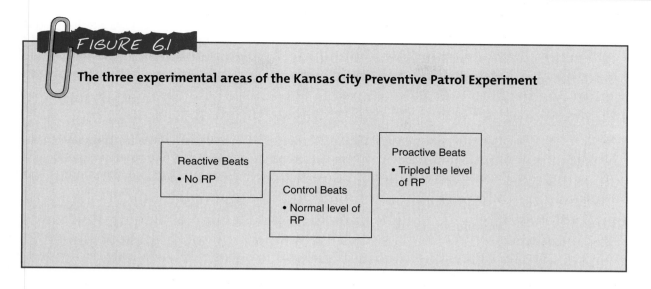

FIGURE 6.1

The three experimental areas of the Kansas City Preventive Patrol Experiment

Reactive Beats
• No RP

Control Beats
• Normal level of RP

Proactive Beats
• Tripled the level of RP

as many Kansas City officers and personnel predicted, the experiment would have been called off immediately for ethical reasons.

This never occurred. In fact, no significant differences were found between the three areas in terms of either crime, fear of crime, or even attitudes towards the police. The assumption by policing experts that random patrol necessarily had a deterrent effect faced its first real challenge. Based on the results of the experiment, varying the levels of random patrol appeared to have no effect on crime.

The authors of the study were quick to point out that the findings in no way suggested that patrol was unnecessary or could operate effectively with significantly fewer resources (Wilson 1975). In the years since the study was completed, some critics have since questioned the experiment's central findings. For example, it has been argued that a visible presence was inadvertently maintained in the reactive area by specialized units not participating in the experiment, as well as by a higher incidence of such activities as siren use and more than one unit responding to a call for service (Larson 1975). Some authors claim that a heightened perception of presence also resulted in residual deterrence, which is when people believe patrol is working in their area because they had seen the police recently, either responding to a call the previous day or in another beat of the city (Sherman 1990).

Walker (2001) argues that the Kansas City Preventive Patrol Experiment could only meaningfully serve as an evaluation of the level of patrol. Whether or not certain types of patrol are more effective than others was not examined by the study. For example, officers who engage in activities outside of the "traditional box" of patrol might see greater reductions in both fear of crime and/or actual crime. In fact, some of the studies discussed in this chapter with respect to aggressive, saturation, and directed patrol would indicate that there is some validity to this statement.

Others have argued that the analysts in the study only looked at overall numbers in the experimental areas rather than factoring in different styles of policing (Cordner 1992). The fact that "aggressive" order maintenance and hotspot policing have been associated with less criminal activity offers some support for these assertions. Despite such challenges to the study's validity and implications, the results of the Kansas City Preventive Patrol Experiment largely have been accepted by the policing community in the years following their explosive release. Very few efforts have since attempted to verify or refute the study's findings.

It is important to use caution in generalizing from any one study to all areas without being aware of all the factors involved in the study and their related reliability and validity concerns. However, the challenges these findings present to the traditional model of policing propagated during the reform era cannot be underestimated. In many ways, later developments related to community and problem-oriented policing reflect a sentiment that innovations are necessary if policing is ever able to contribute meaningfully to crime or fear reduction in the community. As Goldstein (1990) notes:

> Upon discovering that their traditional methods were not as effective as previously assumed, the police realized the need to enlist the community in preventing crime. But it was clear that this would not be accomplished simply by renewing the old campaigns. The police were going to have to cultivate an entirely different type of relationship with the people that they served. (p. 23)

These findings thus went a long way towards laying the foundations of the community-policing movement that will be detailed in Chapter 12.

Patrol Methods

There are many methods of patrol in use today, depending greatly on the terrain being covered and the specific needs of the jurisdiction. However, unquestionably the two most common patrol methods are automobile and foot patrol.

Automobile Patrols

Automobile patrol is by far the most common patrol method used, covering 84 percent of all patrol activities as of 1997 (Bureau of Justice Statistics 1997). Probably the greatest reason for the predominance of this method of patrol is the significant mobility and flexibility it offers to the patrol officer. Not only does the method allow for wider coverage, especially with improvements in communication and information technology, automobile patrol also offers quick response to calls for service. Moreover, it is far easier to transport suspects back to the precinct when an officer is in an automobile. In areas without accessible or manageable roads, such as beaches, some jurisdictions rely heavily on alternatives to the automobile, such as all-terrain vehicles (ATVs) and dirt bikes.

Automobile patrol is not without its limitations, however. For example, officer vision is significantly restricted during automobile patrol, and unless an officer gets out of the car, he or she is unable to view many of the activities taking place on the street. Moreover, as the Kansas City Preventive Patrol Experiment demonstrates, random patrol by automobile alone has a limited deterrent effect. Part of this may be due to the fact that a great number of Part I crimes occur indoors, outside of the scope of motor vehicle patrol efforts (Walker 2001). Some policing experts have also argued that where there might be an initial deterrent effect resulting from random automobile patrol, crime will either be displaced from regularly patrolled areas or simply return as soon as the vehicles have passed.

As noted in Chapter 3, a major problem with an over-reliance on automobile patrol is the distancing of law enforcement from the community it serves. Although this may have the benefit of "professionalizing" the police, removing many of the corruptive influences associated with the intimate connection to the community prevalent during the political era, it has also contributed to a great divide between law enforcement and their beats. With automobile patrols, officers no longer know the specific contexts and issues of the community, as well as its politics and personality dynamics, as they did when they interacted on foot with the community each shift.

Safety concerns have also arisen due to the fact that the majority of automobile patrol activities consist of **one-officer cars**. A central reason for departmental preference for one-officer as opposed to **two-officer cars** is the overall cost-efficiency of this approach. With one-officer cars, a department can cover twice as much area and respond to twice as many calls as a two-officer deployment system (Walker 2001). Although many patrol officer unions have protested against departmental shifts from two-officer to one-officer systems based on safety grounds, a Police Foundation study found that one-officer cars were actually involved in fewer assaults and fewer arrest incidents than two-person cars (Boydstun et al. 1977).

Of course, such a finding can be explained by other factors than that one-officer cars are simply equally safe. For example, one-officer cars might be less likely to observe crimes in progress or may be reticent to get involved before first calling for a backup. In response to such claims, Boydtsun et al. (1977) note that in only 2.8 percent of all incidents did one-officer cars have to call for back-up following arrival to the scene.

Foot Patrols

Although there has been a significant push for a return to foot patrol following the Kansas City Preventive Patrol Experiment, and with the corresponding impetus for **community policing** and problem-solving models, as of 1997, foot patrol only represented roughly 4 percent of all patrol activities (Bureau of Justice Statistics 1997). Foot patrol obviously seriously limits the area an officer can cover on his or her shift. Similarly, although communications technology (e.g., radios and cellular phones) has significantly improved interactions between the foot patrol officer and the precinct, response time is generally slower with foot patrol officers for obvious reasons.

However, despite the challenges of limited mobility, patrol officers deployed on foot are better poised to monitor and identify crimes in progress within buildings or in areas that would be out of the visual path of a passing cruiser.

Patrol studies following the Kansas City Preventive Patrol Experiment have also identified an additional significant ad-

Foot patrol has less mobility than automobile patrol, but has important benefits in terms of monitoring and identifying crimes in buildings or places that would not be readily visible from behind the wheel of a cruiser.

At the core of the community-policing philosophy, police–citizen interactions provide the police with vital information and can greatly improve their responsiveness to local problems.

vantage to foot patrol: the ability to influence fear of crime in the community. Using a design similar to that used in Kansas City with random patrol, the **Newark Foot Patrol Experiment** found that, as with earlier patrol studies, increased foot patrol did not appear to have a significant effect on overall crime levels in the community (The Police Foundation 1981). However, citizens in the intensive foot patrol beats reported significantly more positive attitudes toward the police as well as reductions in fear of crime (The Police Foundation 1981). Such findings led to a resurgence in the use of foot patrol officers in many pilot community-policing programs throughout the 1980s and early 1990s.

Motorcycle and Bicycle Patrols

Foot patrol is generally limited to small, clearly defined areas that automobile patrol cannot reach given the general issues with mobility noted earlier. However, where patrol officers need to cover greater distances than would be pos-sible on foot, many departments offer the use of motorcycles and bicycles. **Motorcycles** are particularly useful in traffic-enforcement activities given their ability to negotiate heavy traffic situations (Adams 2001). Motorcycles are also indispensable in cases of high-profile police escorts and parades.

In tighter areas, such as pedestrian-only streets, malls, or parks, **bicycles** may also be used by patrol officers (Adams 2001). The use of bicycles maintains the foot patrol's benefits of high visibility and approachability while increasing the overall mobility of the officer.

Horse Patrols

Similarly, but used far less frequently, **horse patrol** offers mobility to officers in places that are inaccessible to automobiles or even motorcycles, such as parks and wild terrain. In urban crowd settings, such as during a parade or protest, the horse patrol can offer officers greater visibility of masses of people in crowd-control situations due to the height of the horse.

Water and Helicopter Patrols

Harbor or **water patrol** is a necessity for jurisdictions bordering shorelines, beaches, and lakes given the tremendous amount of illegal activity that can begin on the water. Because "the smuggling of people and contraband from coastal waters into inland harbor areas is a constant problem . . . investigation and apprehension can be accomplished only with the aid of boats and helicopters" (Adams 2001, p. 129).

Patrol Deployment

As evidenced throughout the chapters so far, patrol deployment practices have developed considerably since the earliest days of law enforcement in the United States. The reliance on up-to-date statistics to inform decision making related to patrol deployment and resource distribution enables departmental planners to have a greater chance to understand and resolve crime-related problems across diverse contexts. In addition to methods of patrol, **patrol deployment** has provided the military with insight into the effective use of military troops in occupation circumstances.

Rotating Versus Assigned Shifts

Rotating shifts were developed during the reform era as a means of combating police corruption. **Rotating shifts** refers to the rotation of officers across either different working hours or different divisions within the department. In contrast, **assigned shifts** involve officer assignment to the same shifts and/or areas for extended periods of time.

Time of Day and Shift Hours

Most jurisdictions have a three-shift structure, sometimes referred to as *tricks* or *watches*. For example, the NYPD organizes its shifts across three eight-hour periods:

1. 7 AM to 3 PM (watch)
2. 3 PM to 11:30 PM (swing watch)
3. Midnights (11 PM to 7 AM) (dog watch)

If a department uses a rotating shift structure for working hours, an officer will gradually progress through each of the shift periods. For example, an officer might work the swing watch, progress to dog watch, and finally day watch, staying on each shift generally for a period of a few weeks.

The most popular shift plan is an **eight-hour shift structure**. With an eight-hour plan, officers generally work five days a week for eight hours and then get two days off. Following an additional five days, the officer will receive four days off. Some jurisdictions use a **twelve-hour plan** where officers work for twelve hours a day for three days before having the next four days off.

Fatigue is a problem with shift work. PERF has conducted a series of studies to measure the effects of officer fatigue on job performance. In addition to the obvious health costs, they have found that fatigue can lead to severe impairment of cognitive and motor coordination, thereby lowering productivity and/or leading to accidents (Vila 2000). The important role of discretion in policing was emphasized in Chapter 1. Given the discretionary powers of officers, and the fact that they may at any time be called upon to use force, the potential dangers of patrol officer fatigue cannot be underestimated.

Not surprisingly, the problems of fatigue need to be considered when deciding on appropriate shift structures for patrol, both in terms of rotating versus assigned and the length of the shift. Unfortunately, only a limited amount of research in this area with regards to patrol has been conducted (Vila 2000), with the majority of empirical studies related to fatigue coming in the fields of nursing and public health. Constantly rotating officers through each of the three shifts can ultimately take a toll on an officer's health, ability to manage stress, interpersonal relationships, and daily functioning (Vila 2000). Anyone who has ever flown an international flight across time zones knows how difficult it can be to adjust to significant changes in one's sleep patterns. Research on our internal biological clocks, or **circadian rhythms**, supports the claim that at least six months is required to adjust to changes in sleep patterns (Broughton 2000). Rotating shifts alter circadian rhythms, with long-term negative consequences. The toll that rotating structures can have on one's family life is also worth mentioning. The many other stressors related to shift work and the nature of policing are detailed in Chapter 9.

Interestingly, some research has indicated that officers on an eight-hour shift structure can be more sleep deprived than those working twelve-hour shifts (Vila, 2000). The likely reason for this finding is that following a three-day work week, officers in the twelve-hour structure have the next four days off to rejuvenate. However, before one should take these findings as indicative of a need to change departmental shifts over to twelve hours (which would be a significant move given that most departments follow an eight-hour system), an important word of caution is necessary: Officers towards the end of a twelve-hour shift also exhibit signs of sleep deprivation, thereby diminishing their effectiveness and productivity (Vila 2000).

Allocating Personnel

Proactive police departments make decisions about the level and target of patrol deployments based on a review of all available data sources (Thibault et al. 2001). Peak times and areas thus receive proportionately larger numbers of patrol officers per shift. In some cases, it may be that increased deployment decisions are made on the basis of a specific crime problem or issue rather than overall crime rates.

However, the collaborative effort and proactive problem solving required by community-policing models requires more than simply directing resources to an area or specific time. An intimate knowledge of the community is essential for true problem solving to occur, an issue that will be detailed at length in Chapter

12. Part of this intimate knowledge includes an acquaintance with key leaders in the community who might be important collaborators in addressing the issues at hand. As such, many departments are opting for assigned shifts in which officers patrol the same beat and time period for extended periods of time. Having the same officers working the same shifts is important in that a community can change significantly depending on the time of day, as can the influence of key players in the community. Thus, officers on assigned shifts can become more acquainted with the concerns of their beat, with regards to both location and time.

Some departments have taken lessons from the corporate model, seeking to provide officers with a wide range of experiences across divisions that can help them as they move towards advancement in the agency. Following rotation across divisions, officers are returned to patrol in a senior status, such as **field training officers** for new recruits (Thibault et al. 2001).

Foot Patrol Versus Automobile Patrol Assignments

In most departments, police officers are assigned a sector each shift at roll call, which is called a **tour**. Interestingly, in many departments, rookie officers are assigned to foot patrols. Although in many small- and medium-sized departments foot patrol is a desired assignment, some large departments need to work to remove the stigma that foot patrol is undesirable and to be avoided. Importantly, some research has demonstrated that officers on foot patrol or who have the opportunity to interact frequently with the community actually have higher levels of job satisfaction (Grant and Jacobs 1998). These officers report a sense of accomplishment from their interactions, learning that even in the most high-crime areas, the majority of citizens are respectable and law abiding.

As noted, automobile patrol has important benefits that will continue to make it essential to patrol activities, even if by itself it cannot reduce crime or fear of crime. The need to cover large distances in a short amount of time is critical in emergency situations. Additionally, one needs to remember that the vast majority of municipal police departments in the country are small agencies covering large, rural areas with as few as ten officers on staff. Under such circumstances, foot patrol is not a practical option.

The finding that foot patrol can play an important role in reducing fear of crime as well as enhancing police–community interactions has made it an important element of community-policing models. The **1994 Violent Crime Control and Law Enforcement Act** provided funding for an additional 100,000 officers nationally to increase the availability of officers for foot patrol and other community-policing functions.

Traffic Goals and Enforcement

Traffic enforcement is arguably the most undervalued division within law enforcement in terms of status, primarily because it does not fit into the traditional "crime enforcer" image many members of the public hold. Moreover, most members of the public feel resentment when interacting with officers engaged in the traffic function because such interactions often result in a ticket and corresponding fine. However, the importance of the professional handling of a traffic stop even in the face of an irritable public cannot be underestimated in that this is the most common interaction the average citizen has with law enforcement. The nature of the interaction can thus carry weight in terms of police–community relations.

Public safety on streets and highways is the overarching goal of traffic enforcement. The majority of state and municipal law enforcement agencies have responsibility for the enforcement of traffic regulations, or **moving violations**, to ensure this safety (Dempsey 1999).

Thibault et al. (2001) outlined a number of the more important functions performed by the traffic division:

- The elimination of accident causes and congestion
- The identification of potential traffic problems and hazards
- The regulation of parking on street and municipal facilities
- The investigation of property damage and personal injury automobile accidents
- Directing public awareness toward the proper use of automobiles, bic-ycles, and motorcycles
- The arrest of offenders

Another important function of traffic patrol is to route traffic around special events such as parades and protests. It is important to emphasize that although the largest police departments in the country have specialized traffic patrol functions, these duties are covered by regular patrol in the majority of small- to medium-sized departments.

Traffic enforcement became a very important part of American law enforcement in the early urban environment of cities such as New York and Chicago. Johnson (1981) notes how the movement of people and goods throughout cities was constantly jeopardized by massive disorder:

> Horsecar drivers frequently raced one another through the streets, paying no attention to the discomfort of their passengers or the danger to pedestrians. Wagon drivers and coachmen often disputed rights-of-way, sometimes to the point of assaulting one another. Pedestrians wandered haphazardly across the streets. At busy intersections, it was every man for himself as dozens of drivers sought to force their way through a maze of competing vehicles. (p. 36)

In order to eliminate such disorder, cities created numerous ordinances to regulate proper traffic behavior through fines and penalties. However, as Johnson stresses, compliance was not an instantaneous development with "thousands of people unaccustomed to these kinds of laws providing enough work to keep as much as one-third or more of the city's police busy writing citations" (p. 39).

Traffic enforcement became even more complicated with the advent of automobiles, particularly as they moved from being "toys for the wealthy" to being cheap and commonly owned following the introduction of Ford's Model T. With such developments, law enforcement also had to evolve. For example, as travel outside of the city became more popular for the average citizen and criminal alike, state police had to evolve to meet a changing, increasingly mobile, enforcement context.

The Dangers of Traffic Stops

The dangers inherent to traffic stops are often not fully appreciated by members of the public. However, many officers are killed each year, and thousands more injured in the course of traffic stops gone wrong. In 1999, over half of all officers killed in the line of duty were killed in a traffic-related incident (Onder 2002). When traffic stops require the use of officers' weapons, the percentage of officer fatalities increases significantly Onder 2002).

What might start out as a **routine traffic stop** for a minor violation can very quickly escalate when an officer learns that he or she is dealing with a wanted offender, an impaired driver, or a car containing contraband. Under such circumstances, an officer might find him or herself faced with a desperate (and potentially armed) offender. The fact that many major offenders in U.S. law enforcement history (e.g., Timothy McVeigh, Ted Bundy, Randall Kraft) were captured as a result of a routine traffic stop should drive this point home to the reader.

High-risk traffic stops are those where the officer is aware that the driver has committed a felony. Such stops are often the finale of a high-speed pursuit. In these cases, the vehicle may have been identified as stolen or people in the car may be suspected of being involved in a serious offense such as murder, rape, or robbery. The fact that such stops are extremely dangerous needs little explanation. Unlike the routine traffic-stop situation, the danger of stopping such a vehicle is known in advance.

The Supreme Court has recognized the inherent dangers involved in traffic stops, granting officers the right to order all passengers out of the car for officer safety concerns in the case of *Maryland v. Wilson.*[1] This case will be addressed in more detail in Chapter 7, along with a much more detailed analysis of the legal complexities involved in traffic-stop situations.

Traffic enforcement became an important means of reducing the severe disorder in the early urban environment of cities such as New York and Chicago.

Automated Traffic Enforcement

One of the most interesting developments in the area of traffic control and traffic policing has been the growing use of automated tracking technology. Typically based on a system of cameras (positioned at or near cross-streets) fitted with sophisticated motion detectors, these systems are able to monitor traffic flow and provide traffic authorities with accurate information on road usage. Where these cameras are also linked to some form of video-monitoring system, they can also be used by law enforcement agencies to conduct searches for particular types of vehicles or even individual suspects. Even small municipalities may be able to afford this equipment; manufacturers are using a fee system in which free equipment and installation are offered with a percentage of the revenue generated through tickets to be paid to the company.

A good example of such a system is currently in operation in New York City. Originally established to help improve traffic flows on Manhattan Island, the system is now used by the police for such things as monitoring street sellers,

Linkages in Law Enforcement

Role of Patrol in Detecting Terrorist Activities

The role of federal law enforcement agencies in combating terrorism would never have been a surprise to anyone, even prior to September 11. The need for global intelligence activities seemed well-suited for the international FBI field offices, but of little use to the local police department.

One of the most disturbing facts that resonated in the U.S. law enforcement community with the collapse of the two towers was the fact that the reach of terrorism actually extended much further than we had thought. And we now realize that local law enforcement has a significant role in responding to and combating terrorism. The first responders to a terrorist act will invariably be local law enforcement, fire fighters, and emergency services. On September 11, a total of 343 New York firefighters and 23 NYPD officers died at the World Trade Center.

The law enforcement community has moved quickly to revise its training, deployment, and communication strategies in order to be better prepared for future terrorist attacks. For example, in response to an extensive citywide review of the events of September 11 in New York City, changes in deployment strategies were made that involve controlling the number of personnel who respond at any one time to an event (ABC News 2002). On September 11, dozens of firefighters and police officers went directly to the scene and died in the aftermath of the attack.

September 11 also highlighted the need for specialized knowledge within police operations, leading to the creation of special counterterrorism units in many departments. Although the FBI had created localized task forces to coordinate law enforcement resources related to terrorism, clearly information was slipping through the cracks, as noted in Chapter 1.

The importance of law enforcement being in touch with the community, which was important even before September 11, is even more important now as President Bush calls for the "vigilance" of residents to serve as the eyes and ears of law enforcement. Patrol officers are faced with renewed cultural challenges as they try to connect with segments of the Muslim community in the face of a rising tide of misunderstandings and accusations of racial profiling, particularly as the federal government has turned to the registration of people of Middle Eastern origin. However, it is only with the trust of the community that law enforcement can hope to get needed information related to suspicious activities. The reality that there are active terrorist cells in the United States cannot mean that all members of a group become suspects. This very difficult issue will be addressed further in Chapter 10.

An important issue for the patrol officer is how the "war" on terrorism affects his or her typical response. The delicate balance remains that officers still must operate within legal norms, even as military style tactics and/or assistance may be needed (White 2001). Although public safety will always be a pertinent goal with respect to dealing with terrorism, law enforcement cannot be encouraged to act with impunity. In some Latin American countries, semimilitary police have justified the practice of "disappearances" of suspected citizens on the basis of terrorist groups being too strong.

Questions

1. What are the most significant changes to the role of patrol officers post–September 11?

2. What specific strategies can police operations develop to be able to collaborate more effectively with the Muslim community?

3. What tactics might you use to gain information on suspected terrorist cells in the community? What tactics would be going too far?

The multiagency investigation of the Washington, D.C., area sniper case highlights the important use of automated traffic surveillance technology in attempts to identify offenders' vehicles.

searching for stolen vehicles, and policing public demonstrations. Indeed, the use of such systems by the police has led some civil libertarians to complain that such monitoring threatens individual privacy, particularly in light of the fact that this form of police surveillance activity is almost completely unregulated.

The potential uses of such technology recently became apparent in the five-jurisdiction search for the sniper in Washington, D.C., who killed ten individuals and injured two more. Hundreds of hours of traffic surveillance tapes were reviewed at locations and times near each of the crime scenes (where such cameras are located) to try and identify the sniper's vehicle and license identification. Although the surveillance tapes were not ultimately involved in the October 2002 capture of the snipers, John Allen Muhammad and John Lee Malvo, their use demonstrates the need to better integrate such technologies into the routine and daily work of large police departments.

Chapter Summary

- Despite common perceptions of the patrol function, responding to crime is not the primary activity engaged in by patrol officers. The majority of an officer's time is spent "unassigned," or patrolling. Only rarely is force ever used or an arrest even made. Patrol observation studies, such as the Police Services Study (PSS) have played an important role in aiding our understanding of patrol operations.

- Response time to calls for service will only make a significant difference to the outcome of involvement crimes, which a PERF study indicates are only about 25 percent of all incidents.

- There are several types of patrol, each varying in effectiveness. Random patrol involves officers driving "unsystematically" around their assigned beats looking for crimes in progress, waiting for calls for service, or deterring crimes through their presence. Random patrol is an incident-driven, or reactive, form of patrol. Directed patrol involves targeting patrol resources on hot spots, crime problems, and/or offenders, usually based on an analysis of crime trends. Aggressive patrol refers to the use of high-profile activities such as intensive traffic stops and field interrogations. Finally, saturation patrol is when a department places extremely high numbers of patrol in a very narrowly defined area.

- The Kansas City Gun Experiment and other studies indicate that directed, aggressive, and saturation patrols can have immediate effects on crime. However, such strategies can reach a point of diminishing returns in effectiveness.

- Given the finding that not all calls require equal response time priority and the need to free up patrol resources for more proactive or directed patrol activities, many departments use differential response strategies. In such cases, dispatchers will either take the report over the phone, send a civilian to take the report, or explain to the caller that a sworn officer will be there in a specified (but longer) period of time.

- The Kansas City Preventive Patrol Experiment found that random patrol alone has no significant effect on crime, fear of crime, or even attitudes towards the police. This finding was significant given the reliance on this type of patrol at the time, forcing the law enforcement community to reexamine its methods. The movement towards proactive community-policing models began following this and a series of other key findings.

- Although foot patrol represents only a small proportion of total patrol resources, studies such as the Newark Foot Patrol Experiment have found that it can have a significant effect on reducing fear of crime, even if it too does not significantly reduce crime itself.

- Decisions related to shift structure (i.e., rotating vs. assigned, number of hours) need to be made cautiously because studies have demonstrated the serious effects fatigue can play on officers' cognitive and motor skills, possibly leading to serious mistakes on the job. The type and structure of patrol can also impact the success of community-policing models in an area.

- The traffic division is an often underestimated function and can be one of the most potentially dangerous to officers regardless of whether they are dealing with a routine or high-risk (felony) stop situation. Recent Supreme Court decisions have recognized the importance of officer safety in traffic-stop situations.

KEY TERMS

Aggressive patrol   149
Assigned shifts   155
Bicycle patrol   154
Circadian rhythms   156
Community policing   153
Control beats   150
Differential response time   148
Directed patrol   148
Eight-hour shift structure   155

External authorizing environmental stakeholders   146
Fatigue   156
Field training officers   157
Harbor patrol   155
High-risk traffic stop   159
Horse patrol   154
Incident-driven policing   148
Integrated patrol   150

Kansas City Gun Experiment   150
Kansas City Preventive Patrol Experiment   150
Motorcycle patrol   154
Moving violations   158
Newark Foot Patrol Experiment   153
One-officer cars   153

Linking the Dots

1. Explain the significance of the Kansas City Preventive Patrol Experiment to policing. How did it help move policing methods from reactive to proactive strategies?
2. What productivity measures should be used to track the effectiveness of patrol officers?
3. How can a patrol officer's job be affected by issues of linkage blindness within the department?
4. Explain the role of foot patrol in community policing. What other patrol deployment and shift-structure decisions should a department consider when deciding to implement community policing?

REFERENCES

ABC News. 2002. "Report Recommends FDNY Response Changes." August 19, 1992. Available at abcnews.go.com/sections/us/DailyNews/homefront 020819.htm.

Adams, T. 2001. *Police Field Operations,* 5th ed. Upper Saddle River, NJ: Prentice-Hall.

Associated Press. 2002. "Response Time Proves Crucial When Protection Order Violated." August 25. Available at www.wkyc.com/news/morelocal/akron/ 020825dispatch.asr.

Bittner, E. 1990. *Aspects of Police Work.* Boston, MA: Northeastern University Press.

Boydstun, J., M. Sherry, and N. Moelter. 1977. *Patrol Staffing in San Diego.* Washington, D.C.: The Police Foundation.

Boydstun, J. E. 1975. *San Diego Field Interrogation: Final Report.* Washington, D.C.: The Police Foundation.

Bright, J. A. 1969. *Beat Patrol Experiment.* London: Home Office.

Broughton, M. 2000. *Circadian Rhythms and Shift Work.* Available at http://www.ifpo.org.

Bureau of Justice Statistics. 1997. *Law Enforcement Management and Administrative Statistics, 1997.* Washington, D.C.: Bureau of Justice Statistics.

Carr, A. F., J. F. Schnelle, and J. F. Kirchner. 1980. "Police Crackdowns and Slowdowns: A Naturalistic Evaluation of Changes in Police Traffic Enforcement." *Behavioral-Assessment* 2:33–41.

Cordner, G. 1981. "The Effects of Directed Patrol: A Natural Quasi-Experiment in Pontiac." In *Contemporary Issues in Law Enforcement,* edited by J. J. Fyfe, 37–58. Beverly Hills, CA: Sage.

Cordner, G. W., R. C. Trojanwicz. 1992. "Patrol." In *What works in policing? Operations and Administration Examined,* edited by G. W. Cordner and D. C. Hale, 3–18. Cincinnati, OH: Anderson Publishing.

Dempsey, J. 1999. *An Introduction to Policing.* Belmont, CA: Wadsworth Publishing.

Forst, B., J. Lucianovic, and S. Cox. 1978. *What Happens After Arrest?* Washington, D.C.: U.S. Government Printing Office.

Fridell, L. 2000. *Measuring What Matters: Designing, Implementing and Evaluating a Comprehensive Model of Police Performance.* Unpublished manuscript. Police Executive Research Forum.

Goldstein, H. 1990. *Problem-oriented Policing.* Boston, MA: McGraw-Hill.

Grant, H. 2000. "The Buffalo Weed and Seed Program." In *Comprehensive Strategies to Reduce Juvenile Gun Violence.* Washington, D.C.: Office of Juvenile Justice and Delinquency Prevention.

Grant, H., and N. Jacobs. 1998. *The Brooklyn North Neighborhood Safety Project.* Washington, D.C.: Office of Community-Oriented Policing Services.

Johnson, D. 1981. *American Law Enforcement: A History.* St. Louis, MO: Forum Press.

Kelling, G., T. Pate, D. Dieckman, and C. E. Brown. 1974. *The Kansas City Preventive Patrol Experiment: A Summary Report.* Washington, D.C.: The Police Foundation.

Kenney, D., H. Grant, and N. Allen. 2002. *Policing a Diverse Society: Curriculum II.* Washington, D.C.: PolicyLab.

Larson, R. C. 1975. "What Happened to Patrol Operations in Kansas City? A Review of the Kansas City Preventive Patrol Experiment." *Journal of Criminal Justice* 3 (4): 267–297.

Moore, M. 1999. *Recognizing and Realizing Public Value in Policing: The Challenge of Measuring Police Performance.* Unpublished manuscript, Kennedy School of Government.

Niederpruem, K. 2000. "Downplaying Patrols and Embracing Communities, the State Police Sets Its Sights on Being a Force of Change." *Indianapolis Star,* January 9.

Onder, J. 2002. "Traffic Safety." Available at www.sussexcountysheriff.com/traffic_safety.htm.

Percy, S. L. 1980. "Response Time and Citizen Evaluation of Police." *Journal of Police Science and Administration* 8 (1): 75–86.

The Police Foundation. 1981. *The Newark Foot Patrol Experiment* Washington, D.C.: The Police Foundation.

Sheppard, D., H. Grant, W. Rowe, and N. Jacobs. 2000. *Fighting Gun Crime.* Washington, D.C.: U.S. Department of Justice.

Sherman, L. 1990. "Police Crackdowns: Initial and Residual Deterrence." In *Crime and Justice: A Review of Research,* edited by M. Tonry and N. Morris, 1–49. Beverly Hills: Sage.

Sherman, L., J. Shaw, and D. Rogan. 1995. *The Kansas City Gun Experiment.* Washington, D.C.: Government Printing Office.

Skogan, W., and G. Attunes. 1979. "Information, Apprehension, and Deterrence: Exploring the Limits of Police Productivity." *Journal of Criminal Justice* 7 (3): 217–241.

Thibault, E., L. Lynch, and R. McBride. 2001. *Proactive Police Management,* 5th ed. Upper Saddle River, NJ: Prentice-Hall.

Vila, B. 2000. *Tired Cops: the Importance of Managing Police Fatigue.* Washington, D.C.: Police Executive Research Forum.

Walker, S. 2001. *Police in America: An Introduction.* Boston, MA: McGraw-Hill.

Whitaker, G. 1982. "What Is Patrol Work?" *Police Studies* 4 (2): 13–22.

White, J. 2001. *Terrorism,* 3d ed. Belmont, CA: Wadsworth Publishing.

Wilson, J. Q. 1975. *Thinking About Crime.* New York, NY: Basic Books.

NOTE

1. 519 U.S. 408 (1997).

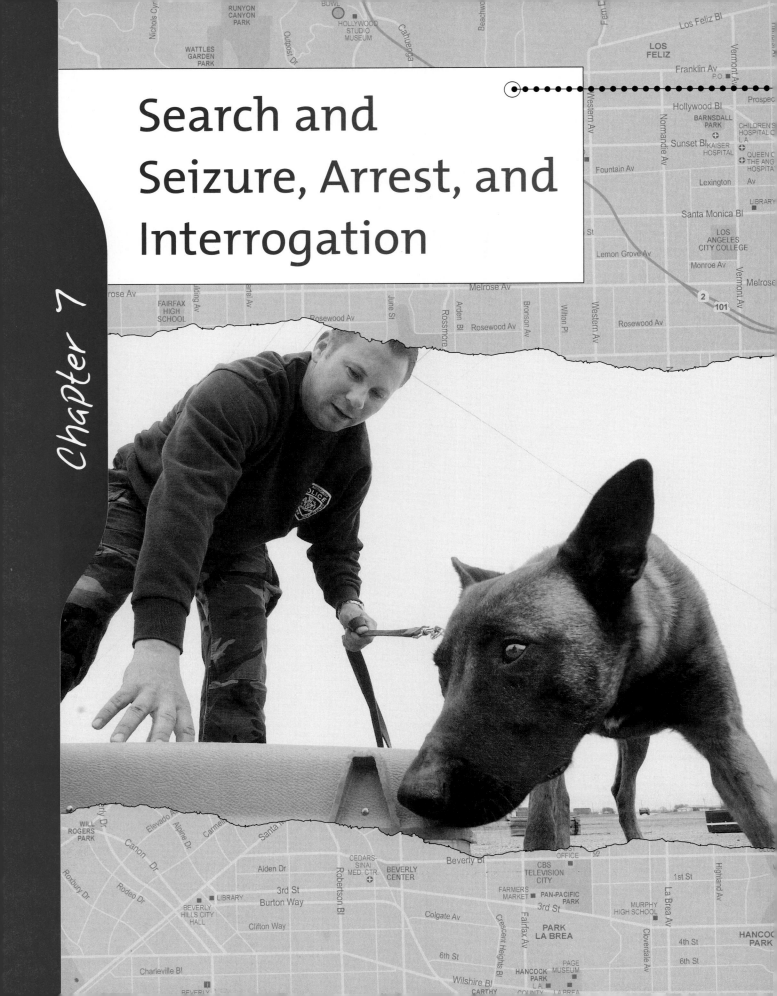

Chapter 7

Search and Seizure, Arrest, and Interrogation

Chapter Outline

Chapter Objectives

● Understand how the Fourth and Fifth Amendments affect search and seizure.

● Learn about different types of searches and requirements for those searches.

● Understand *Miranda*, the implications of this ruling to arrest and interrogation, and its limitations.

● Recognize the difference in standards of proof and know what is necessary for various types of searches.

● Become familiar with case law relating to search and seizure, arrest, and interrogation and understand how case law shapes the role of the police in these processes.

Introduction

On February 4, 1999, a bus driver en route from Florida to Michigan allowed three plain clothes police officers to board the bus and conduct a search for weapons and drugs. The search was voluntary, and they asked each individual passenger to consent to the search. On the bus, the officers stood so that they were not blocking the door or the aisle to assure passengers that they could leave at any time. One officer approached two passengers, Clifton Brown, Jr. and Christopher Drayton, identified himself as a police officer, and asked if he could search them and their luggage. The passengers consented to the search, and the officer found packets of drugs. Both passengers were led from the bus and arrested, charged with conspiring to distribute cocaine and possessing cocaine with intent to distribute it. Though convicted, the passengers argued that they did not realize they had the ability to refuse the search. The Court, looking at the totality of the circumstances, upheld the conviction and said that while they may not have realized they could refuse to cooperate, the passengers' consent to this suspicionless search was nevertheless voluntary. The Court found that a reasonable person in such circumstances would have understood that he or she was free to refuse the search, and the search was therefore not coercive. Thus, the search was constitutional under the Fourth Amendment.[1]

The U.S. Supreme Court found that the searches of Brown and Drayton were constitutional. But what is a constitutional search and, subsequently, seizure, under the Fourth Amendment? This is one of the most complicated issues in law enforcement, as will be shown in this chapter. There are numerous types of searches, and case law is constantly evolving in this area. Post–September 11, the Court may allow the police more leniency as to who is searched, despite the constitutional requirement that people have a right to "be secure in their persons, houses, papers and effects, against unreasonable searches and seizures." The question is, what is reasonable, and how has this definition changed?

Search and Seizure

The Fourth Amendment is critical to policing because it structures how police investigate crimes and suspects. It was only during the Warren Court era of the 1960s that the Court put systematic restrictions on the police and promoted the ideal of human rights. The Court refused to accept confessions that were coerced or evidence that was obtained improperly. It also recognized that the police routinely violated the rights of individual suspects, and that in order for a court to function democratically, it must curb the power of the state.

In order to conduct a search, police officers must have probable cause. **Probable cause** is an ambiguous concept that is difficult to define in specific terms. A literal definition from *Black's Law Dictionary* is that it is "a set of probabilities grounded in the factual and practical considerations which govern the decisions of reasonable and prudent persons and is more than mere suspicion but less than the quantum of evidence required for conviction." (p. 1201). The Court has decided several cases that relate to a definition of probable cause, dating back to *Locke v. United States*[2] in 1813. However, the often-accepted definition of probable cause comes from *Carroll v. United States*,[3] which was later solidified in *Brinegar v. United States*.[4] Procedurally, the Court defined probable cause as existing where "the facts and circumstances within their [the officers'] knowledge and of which they had reasonably trustworthy information [are] sufficient in themselves to warrant a man of reasonable caution in the belief that an offense has been or is being committed."[5] In *Draper v. United States*,[6] the Court devised a definition of probable cause that is still relevant today. It referred to probable cause as being more than suspicion, saying that it requires the existence of facts that would lead a person of reasonable caution to believe that a crime has been committed, yet it does not require proof of guilt.

Though the courts still refer to the definition of probable cause set out in *Draper*, they have since further clarified the definition. The Court set out a two-pronged test in *Spinelli v. United States*,[7] whereby both the information and source of the information had to be verified in order for probable cause to exist. In *Illinois v. Gates*,[8] the Court expanded upon the *Spinelli* decision by stating that the two-pronged test may be abandoned in some cases if the totality of the circumstances indicates that there is probable cause to search. Specifically, information obtained from an anonymous informant would not be sufficient to warrant probable cause under *Spinelli*. Yet, by looking at the specific case in *Gates*, the Court said that the information obtained from the informant was sufficient despite its anonymous nature.

There are three primary ways in which officers can discern whether or not probable cause exists. The first is observational probable cause, where the officer sees, hears, or smells something that indicates that a crime is being committed. For instance, an officer may observe a person robbing a store, smell marijuana, or hear a gun being fired. The second way in which an officer can establish probable cause is through his or her expertise. With expertise, the officer's previous policing experience leads him or her to believe that people who are acting suspiciously but who are not at the time doing an illegal act have committed or are about to commit an offense. Chapter 10 will discuss the fine, and at times difficult, line between relying on experience and using stereotypes. The third type of probable cause is informational, meaning that the officer receives information about a crime from victims, witnesses, informants, or police bulletins or broadcasts. However it is attained, probable cause must exist before a full-scale search can take place.

Stop and Frisk

Police officers do not need probable cause for a stop if a full-scale search of a person, dwelling, or automobile will not be conducted. There are two situations in which the police may stop an individual when they do not have probable cause to determine that that individual committed a crime: field interrogations and frisks. In these situations, the officer needs only to have **reasonable suspicion**. Reasonable suspicion requires articulable facts that warrant minor intrusion and investigation into a situation where criminal activity may be afoot. If officers have reasonable suspicion, they can stop an individual, or conduct a **field interrogation**. In a field interrogation, the police will stop and question an individual about his or her actions in regard to the suspicious activity. During this brief period of questioning, an officer must rely on the cooperation of the person he or she has stopped. The officer cannot detain the person, and the person must not feel as though he or she is "in custody."

The police can also stop a person based on reasonable suspicion to conduct a **stop and frisk**. A frisk is a pat-down search of the suspect on the outside of the clothing in order to determine whether the individual is carrying a weapon. An officer can frisk a person only if the officer believes that he or she is in imminent danger of life or limb. A frisk is not a full-scale search, which is why the officer only needs reasonable suspicion to conduct it. The pat down for weapons

Stop and frisk is one of the most common and controversial investigative techniques available to the patrol officer.

must occur on the outside the clothes. The officer can ask the individual to take off outer clothes, such as a jacket, but the officer cannot reach into the clothing for any contraband other than a weapon, unless he or she, without added manipulation, simultaneously recognizes the item is not a weapon and is contraband (Plain Feel Doctrine).

Like the definition of probable cause, reasonable suspicion is an ambiguous term and the courts have wavered in their definition of it. The landmark case in which the Court articulated a standard for reasonable suspicion is *Terry v. Ohio.*[9] Cleveland police detective Martin McFadden, a thirty-nine-year veteran of the police force, observed two men whom he perceived to be "casing" a store. After they walked back and forth past the store twenty-four times, they briefly met with a third man. Officer McFadden approached the men, identified himself as a police officer, and asked them for identification. Based on his experience as a police officer, he assumed that they would have weapons if they were, in fact, casing the store, so he frisked them. The Court upheld this stop, despite the fact that no crime had taken place and the officer only had his expertise to rely upon. The judge not only said that McFadden conducted the search properly—making sure that the search was minimally intrusive and served only to determine if the men were armed—but that it would have been irresponsible *not* to stop them based on his expertise.

Other cases since *Terry* have supported a standard of reasonable suspicion in order to conduct a minimally intrusive stop or frisk. In *United States v. Arvizu,*[10] the Court allowed an investigatory stop of a vehicle by Border Patrol officers based on reasonable suspicion. However, the Court emphasized that race alone does not constitute reasonable suspicion.[11] The Court has also addressed the issue of drug-courier profiles and whether these are sufficient in order to establish reasonable suspicion for a field interrogation. In *United States v. Sokolow,*[12] the Court explained that based on the totality of the circumstances, it was acceptable to use such a profile. The Court has also confirmed that fleeing at the sight of police officer does not, in itself, constitute reasonable suspicion, even if the person is fleeing in a high-crime area.[13]

The Exclusionary Rule

The Fourth Amendment places considerable restrictions on police power; if evidence is obtained improperly during any type of search, it is excluded in a court of law. Searches can be conducted prior to, incident to, or after an arrest. Whenever the search occurs, officers must follow specific procedures, and they are usually required to obtain a search warrant stipulating what they are to search and what they are searching for. The **exclusionary rule**, which prohibits the admission of illegally obtained evidence in court, was established at the federal level in 1914.[14] This rule includes any physical or verbal evidence that was obtained while violating an individual's Fourth, Fifth, or Sixth Amendment rights.

There was no statewide exclusionary rule until 1961. However, in 1952, the Court did put some restrictions on improper **seizure** of evidence in the case of *Rochin v. California.*[15] After a tip that an individual was selling narcotics, police officers went to question him and illegally entered his home. At this time, the suspect put two capsules of morphine in his mouth. The officers attempted to forcefully extract the capsules, but he swallowed them. They handcuffed the suspect, took him to a hospital, and had a doctor pump his stomach against his

Officers usually are required to first obtain a warrant prior to searching individuals or homes according to the Fourth Amendment. However, the practical realities of law enforcement make many exceptions necessary.

will. He was convicted based upon this "seizure" of evidence. The U.S. Supreme Court later overturned the finding and said:

> We are compelled to conclude that the proceedings by which this conviction was obtained do more than offend some fastidious squeamishness or private sentimentalism about combating crime too energetically. This is conduct that shocks the conscience. . . . This course of proceeding by agents of government to obtain evidence is bound to offend even hardened sensibilities.[16]

The "shocks the conscience" standard remained the only check on statewide police search and seizure powers until 1961, when the exclusionary rule became applicable on a state level with the case of *Mapp v. Ohio.*[17] In this case, the police illegally entered the house of Mapp because they thought she was harboring a fugitive. While in the house, they found and seized a trunk full of obscene material. The Court claimed that this material was inadmissible because the search was not conducted following proper police procedures. The judge said, "nothing can destroy a government more quickly than its failure to observe its own laws."[18]

All illegally obtained evidence is excluded from a court of law, as is anything that an officer seizes as a result of the tainted evidence or search. For instance, if a police officer conducts an illegal interrogation and violates an individual's Fifth Amendment right against self-incrimination, that confession would be thrown out. If, based on that confession, the suspect tells the police where the weapon is that he used to kill his victim, the weapon would also be excluded during the trial because the police learned about the weapon through illegal means. The weapon would be considered **fruit of the poisoned tree**. The fruit of the poisoned tree doctrine was established in *Wong Sun v. United States,*[19] in which the Court explained that police misconduct does not require the entire case to be dismissed, but only the tainted evidence, or "fruit," resulting from that misconduct.

The most common poisoned fruits are derived from an interrogation that has been conducted improperly, during which the suspect discloses information about evidence from his or her offense. The Court explained in *Michigan v. Tucker,*[20] however, that when a suspect's *Miranda* rights are violated, this does not automatically result in the exclusion of the fruits from that confession. The case of *New York v. Quarles*[21] supported this decision, creating a public safety exception to the exclusionary rule. In *Quarles*, a woman approached two officers and told them that an individual with a gun had just raped her. She also pointed out the supermarket into which her assailant went. Upon entering the store and finding the alleged perpetrator, they frisked him and found only an empty holster. Out of concern for public safety, the officer asked where the gun was. The suspect told him, and that statement was later used against the suspect in court. Because the officers had not yet read him his *Miranda* rights, the trial court excluded the statement under the exclusionary rule and the gun as a "fruit of the poisoned tree." However, the Supreme Court allowed both to be entered as evidence, explaining that public safety takes precedence over individual rights when there is an imminent danger to life or limb.

Although the exclusionary rule remains an important check on police powers, there are exceptions to it. First, there is a **good faith exception**, which was established in *United States v. Leon.*[22] The good faith exception establishes that if officers believe in good faith that their actions are authorized by warrants that turn out to be defective, the evidence should still be admissible. The Court in *Leon* claimed that the exclusionary rule should not be applied as a blanket solution to improper searches and should not serve to deter reasonable law enforcement activity.

Another exception to the exclusionary rule is that of **inevitable discovery**. This holds that evidence obtained illegally can be admitted if the police could have legally found it anyway. This occurred in the case of *Nix v. Williams,*[23] in which the defendant was accused of murdering a ten-year-old girl. The police drove the suspect from Davenport to the police station in Des Moines. He explained that, on advice of counsel, he wanted to invoke his Fifth Amendment right to remain silent. During the three-hour drive, the officers spoke to each other about the case and how badly the family felt that they wouldn't be able to give their daughter a proper Christian burial. Although they never asked him directly about the offense, he confessed to the killing and explained where he buried the body. The Court said that the officer's "Christian burial" speech was tantamount to interrogation, and the evidence (the child's body) was considered the fruit of an illegal search. However, the Court also later found in *Nix v. Williams* that the police would have found the child's body through legal means even without Williams' confession, and the evidence was therefore admissible. Such after-the-fact justifications illustrate the sometimes difficult balance between crime control and due process concerns discussed in Chapter 1. The Supreme Court was justifiably concerned about asking law enforcement agencies to "turn the other way" with respect to the body of a little girl, despite apparent improper actions on the part of a detective.

Searches of Persons and Premises

Full-scale searches of premises generally require a **search warrant**, or a written order to search for and seize any property that is evidence of a crime. Searches can be done either before or after arrest, depending on the circumstances. In order to get a search warrant, the officer must prepare an affidavit for a judge that contains information on the area to be searched, what the police are searching for, and what facts establish probable cause. The judge can then issue a warrant for the police to search for specific property in a particular area, seize it, and return it to the court.

When searching a house with a warrant, officers are generally required to "knock and announce," or knock on the door and announce their presence. The Fourth Amendment protects against unannounced police entry. This concept dates back to 1756 (*Curtis' Case*), at which time the Crown Court in England stated that "peace-officers, having a legal warrant to arrest for a breach of the peace, may break open doors, after having demanded admittance and given due notice of their warrant."[24] Most warrants will be secured for a daytime search; however, searches may be legal at night if the officers believe that there will be either an imminent consumption or movement of the evidence or that the officer's safety is in jeopardy during the day. If the officer perceives the situation to be dangerous or that the suspect may not cooperate with the search procedure, the officer may not need to follow the normal knock-and-announce procedure. This is often the case when police raid the residence of a suspected drug dealer, though the Court has stated that there is no blanket dismissal of knock-and-announce procedures for such cases.[25]

The police do not always need warrants to search premises. When there are **exigent circumstances**, or emergency circumstances, the officers can search premises without a warrant. There are several types of exigent circumstances, the most common being that evidence is going to be destroyed. When in question, the Court will almost always uphold the individual's right to be free from unwarranted searches over the power of the police if there is a question about the legitimacy of the exigency. A search without a warrant will be considered illegal if there was no probable cause or if the officers had time to secure a warrant.

For instance, in *Kirk v. Louisiana*,[26] the Supreme Court claimed that the police erred in searching the petitioner prior to securing a warrant because there were no obvious exigent circumstances. The police had received an anonymous complaint that drug sales were occurring in an apartment, and so they placed the apartment under surveillance. The police watched what they thought were several drug transactions and stopped an individual leaving the premises. After finding illegal drugs on this buyer, they immediately knocked on the door, found Kennedy Kirk in possession of drugs and money, and found contraband in plain view in the apartment. They arrested Kirk and then called for a search warrant before searching the rest of the house. The Court found, however, that their original entrance into the house was not legal, and that they should not have searched Kirk without a warrant because there were no seemingly exigent circumstances. A similar error occurred in the case of *Payton v. New York*,[27] in which the officers suspected Payton of a homicide and conducted a warrantless search of his home. The Court declared this search illegal and the evidence seized as poisoned fruit even though the evidence was in plain view.

If evidence is in plain view, it can be seized without a warrant. The **plain view doctrine** states that evidence of criminal activity can be seized if it is "immediately apparent" and the officer has a legal right to be in the place where the contraband can be viewed. It is also necessary for the contraband to be immediately recognizable. In a similar vein, the Court allows evidence to be seized if it is in "plain smell" or an officer experiences "plain feel." In the case of *Minnesota v. Dickerson*,[28] the Court upheld the concept of plain feel but said that the officer did not immediately recognize the contraband. Rather, when an officer did a *Terry* frisk on Dickerson and realized that there was no weapon, he felt a lump in the suspect's pocket and determined that it was a narcotic substance. The Court rejected this evidence because the officer had to manipulate the substance with his fingers in order to determine what the substance was, and the substance was not therefore immediately recognizable.

Another type of search is one of voluntary consent. Officers can ask a person for consent to search his or her house, and if the person agrees, this type of search is legal without a warrant. The consent must be knowing, free, and voluntary, and not a result of deceit or trickery. The only individuals who can give consent to search a residence are the adults who live there, including roommates, a husband, a wife, or an individual who is temporarily staying at the residence.[29] Guests, juveniles, and landlords cannot legally give consent to search a dwelling.

Another type of search of premises involves sense-enhancing technology, namely thermal imaging. With **thermal imaging**, a device is used to determine the amount of heat emanating from premises. Although thermal imaging can be used to detect body heat, it is more likely to be used to detect lights that give off a particularly high level of heat and are used to grow marijuana plants. In the case of *Kyllo v. United States*,[30] the petitioner questioned the use of a thermal imaging device on his home, which he claimed was intrusive and violated his Fourth Amendment rights. The Court stated that the use of thermal imaging would be constitutional within the confines of a legal search. However, as used in *Kyllo*—at 3 AM, aimed at a private home from a public street, and without a warrant—thermal imaging is unconstitutional. The Court said that this search turned up information that the police could not have otherwise found without a physical intrusion into the home.

In addition to searching premises, the police can search a person **incident to arrest**, or at the time of arrest, as well as the area that is in the immediate wingspan (reach) of the victim. The case that set a precedent for this was *Chimel v. California*,[31] in which case officers arrested Chimel for the burglary of a coin shop. The officers searched his entire three-bedroom house at the time of his arrest, and they seized evidence, including coins, that were admitted as evidence and used to help convict him. Though the appellate court upheld his conviction because the search was incident to a lawful arrest, the Supreme Court overturned the decision because the search of the defendant's home went far beyond the immediate area of the suspect in which he might have been able to obtain a weapon or destroy evidence. The Court said that without a search warrant there was no constitutional jurisdiction to search

As the technology of surveillance continues to develop, the meaning of a "police search" has evolved over time in an effort to balance the rights of citizens with the need for law enforcement.

beyond the immediate area, and the search was therefore unconstitutional. If, however, the officer believes that the suspect poses a danger, the officer can do a protective sweep of the immediate surroundings. A protective sweep is limited and can only last as long as is necessary to secure the immediate area and dispel the suspicion of danger.[32]

Another case involving search of a person is *Schmerber v. California*.[33] Schmerber was pulled over while driving under the influence of alcohol. Upon stopping Schmerber, the police officer drew blood, which Schmerber later claimed was an improper "seizure" of his person. The court disagreed, claiming that so long as experienced medical personnel draw the blood this is an acceptable seizure of evidence.

Searches of Motor Vehicles

As with searching premises and persons, police officers must have probable cause in order to search an automobile. However, unlike other full-scale searches, officers generally do not need a warrant to search automobiles, and they can search all areas of the car—including the trunk and glove compartment. The reason that officers do not need a warrant to search cars follows the idea of mobility: In the time that it would take to obtain a warrant, the individual can move the car and possibly destroy evidence. The concept of mobility was introduced in 1924 in *Carroll v. United States*,[34] and further supported in many subsequent cases. In *Chambers v. Maroney*,[35] the Court extended the concept of mobility to include those cars that have been impounded. They decided that the

Motor vehicle stops are among the most common, yet potentially hazardous, police–citizen interactions.

warrantless search of a car after it had been taken to the police station did not violate the petitioner's Fourth Amendment rights because a car can maintain its mobility even when impounded. If there is probable cause, an automobile, because of its mobility, may be searched without a warrant in circumstances that would not justify a warrantless search of a house or office. However, there is not blanket ability for police officers to search impounded cars. The Court in *Coolidge v. New Hampshire*[36] claimed that mobility only applies if there is a danger the car will be moved.

The protection of an automobile is not as stringent as that of a home. Whereas "a man's home is his castle" and will be protected to the utmost, the Court is more lenient on officers with regards to searching cars and the passengers within them. In addition to warrantless searches of a vehicle based on mobility, the Court has also decided that warrantless searches are constitutional when the car is used in the commission of a felony.[37] At this time, everything in the automobile may be searched, including closed containers.[38] It is constitutional to seize an auto from a public place without a warrant as well, as happened in *Florida v. White*[39] when the officers seized White's car in order to search it for narcotics. Because the warrantless seizure of the car was deemed constitutional, the narcotics found in the car were not fruits of a poisoned tree. If an officer is conducting a stop of a vehicle, the officer can ask both the driver and the passenger to step out of the car in order to ensure that evidence is not destroyed.[40] Though the majority of searches on cars are considered legal once the auto has been stopped, there has been considerable debate about what constitutes a legal stop.

Pretextual Stops

Many searches of autos arise from pretextual stops. A **pretextual stop** occurs when an officer ostensibly stops a vehicle for some traffic violation (e.g., a broken taillight or speeding) and proceeds to use that stop to conduct a full-scale search of the vehicle.[41] The Court has upheld pretextual stops, calling them a constitutionally acceptable policing tactic. The first formal acknowledgment of pretextual stops occurred in 1996 in the case of *Whren v. United States*.[42] A police officer pulled Whren over for a vehicular violation, though the true intention of the stop was to investigate drug-dealing activity. The officer saw drug-related contraband in plain view when he approached the car. The Court said that this stop was constitutional, even though the traffic violation was only a pretext to the real reason for the stop. The Court said the stop was reasonable because the officers had probable cause to believe that the petitioner had violated the traffic code. Therefore, the seizure of the evidence was constitutional and admissible in court. The Court went on to say that the law could not be selectively enforced; to do so would violate the Equal Protection clause of the Constitution. However, it would not violate the Fourth Amendment search and seizure laws, and the pretextual stop was therefore constitutional on those grounds.

Because many people could conceivably be pulled over for a traffic violation, it is likely that officers may use race, or racial profiling, as a factor to decide whom they will pull over. At the center of the racial profiling controversy is the allegation that police officers exercise their discretionary power to stop based on race, and this is primarily used against African Americans and Latinos (ACLU 1999). Lawsuits have been filed against police agencies in New Jersey, Illinois, and Maryland because of alleged racial disparities in stops (Gibbons 2003). Following the terrorist attacks on September 11, renewed justifications for targeting based on race or ethnicity have surfaced with respect to Arab Americans, particularly with regards to air travel. We will return to this very difficult issue in Chapter 10.

Systematic Stops and Searches

The police are allowed to stop and search individuals without probable cause if there is a systematic method to the searches. One method through which **systematic stops** occur is through roadblocks for border patrol areas or sobriety checkpoints. The Court has ruled that temporary roadblocks are constitutional and a reasonable tool in law enforcement based on the fact that 1.5 percent of the drivers stopped at sobriety checkpoints are legally drunk.[43] Additionally, these checkpoints are not aimed at a particular group of people, but rather follow a systematic method as to who is stopped (i.e., every fifth car). The key to systematic searches is that there is no reasonable suspicion or probable cause that a particular individual has committed an offense. Rather, the purpose of these stops is to prevent crime. Such justifications again illustrate the need to balance individual liberties with public safety concerns. In the case of *Michigan Department of State Police v. Sitz*,[44] the Court found the intrusion to be minor while at the same time providing a significant benefit to society.

Another type of systematic search is like that of the opening case in this chapter, in which the police boarded a bus and asked the passengers to voluntarily consent to a search. Police officers can board any form of public transportation to conduct such searches of luggage and persons aboard for either weapons or some other form of illegal contraband. Similarly, individuals at an airport can be stopped prior to boarding a plane or upon landing, and their luggage can be checked. As with roadblocks, this is constitutional so long as airport personnel follow a systematic method in choosing individuals to be stopped and searched. The stops must be random, and race cannot be a factor that determines whether a person is stopped and searched.[45]

Though random sobriety checkpoints are legal, random drug checkpoints are not. The Court declared these unconstitutional in *City of Indianapolis v. Edmond*,[46] calling them an unconstitutional means to a justified end. The Court recognized that drug use, particularly while driving, may be dangerous, but to allow such roadblocks would set a precedent for interrogating people about any illegal activity. The Court claimed that this would be intrusive and unconstitutional under the Fourth Amendment.

Searches of Public Places

The key concept of the Fourth Amendment is privacy, though it only protects **reasonable expectations of privacy**. Common land, or that which is open to the public, can be searched without a warrant because there is no reasonable expectation of privacy. Generally, there is a reasonable expectation of privacy within the **curtilage**, or the immediate area surrounding a residence. However, some areas are not easily defined as either private or public, for instance, public telephone booths, garbage cans, driveways, and vacated hotel rooms. The courts have decided many cases that have helped to define what is considered private.

The case that determined the recognized standard of reasonable expectation of privacy was *Katz v. United States*.[47] Katz used a public telephone booth to wager money on a gambling deal. Police officers had wiretapped the booth and introduced the evidence from his conversation into the court. Katz claimed that he should have a reasonable expectation of privacy in a phone booth and that the evidence should therefore be inadmissible. The Supreme Court agreed, and set forth a two-prong test in order to determine privacy in future cases. First, the individual must show that he or she expected privacy, and second, that that expectation should be reasonable.

Whereas driveways fall within the general definition of curtilage, garbage that is placed out on the street does not. In *California v. Greenwood*,[48] the Court stated that Greenwood did not have a reasonable expectation of privacy with his garbage when he put the garbage in front of his house. Investigators who looked through the garbage to determine whether Greenwood was involved in drug trafficking did not violate Greenwood's right to privacy. Similarly, individuals do not have a reasonable expectation of privacy with regard to abandoned property—such as vacated hotel rooms—and the police can search such property without violating an individual's Fourth Amendment rights.

Arrest

If a police officer has probable cause to believe that an individual has committed a criminal act, the officer can arrest the individual. An **arrest** occurs when an officer takes a person suspected of criminal activity into custody. Officers are allowed to use coercive force when arresting an individual. Although the force cannot be excessive, police officers are allowed to use the minimum amount of force necessary to ensure the arrest and control the situation.

Arrests Versus Stops

An arrest is more intrusive on civil liberties than a stop, during which individuals are not in custody and can leave. An arrest is generally defined as the point at which a suspect is taken into custody and detained or the point at which a reasonable person believes that he or she is not able to leave. Several cases have supported the opinion that an individual is in custody when he or she does not perceive the ability to leave as opposed to being in the physical custody of the police. This was the argument of Clifton Brown, Jr. and Christopher Drayton from the case at the beginning of the chapter. They argued that the police officers conducted a stop that was custodial in nature, thereby exceeding the legality of a stop and voluntary search. Though the court disagreed in this particular case, several other cases have deliberated over the perception of a custodial condition. They can be summed up by the decision in *Florida v. Bostick*,[49] in which the Court explained that a stop does not become custodial as long as a reasonable person would be free to leave the situation. This supports the concept of custody discussed in *Miranda v. Arizona*,[50] in which the Court described custody as psychologically rather than physically oriented.

Linkages in Law Enforcement

Searches and Terrorism—the USA PATRIOT Act of 2001

On October 26, 2001, the USA PATRIOT Act of 2001 was signed into law, expanding all four traditional surveillance tools—wiretaps, search warrants, pen/trap orders, and subpoenas. Powers under the Foreign Intelligence Surveillance Act (FISA), which applies to spying within the United States by foreign intelligence agencies, were also expanded (Electronic Frontier Foundation 2001). The 342-page bill includes many provisions that are meant to facilitate law enforcement's ability to investigate terrorist activities in the interest of public safety. Some of the key provisions of the USA PATRIOT Act are discussed below:

- The FBI and CIA can now conduct nationwide roving wiretaps. Law enforcement is no longer limited to specific phones or specific computers. Instead, the government can issue one wiretap order that will allow investigators to extend the search to different phones and computers without having to prove in court that the information being accessed is specifically relevant to the investigation.

- The government can now receive all "noncontent" information voluntarily given to them by an Internet Service Provider (ISP) without the need for a court order or subpoena. Additionally, court order review is not required to access records of session times and durations and means and sources of payments.

- Simply by telling any single judge in the United States that the information collected would be relevant to an ongoing criminal investigation, the government can now spy on an individual's use of the Internet, including the key terms that person enters into search engines. This is re-

gardless of whether or not the person being monitored is the target of the investigation.

- FISA has been expanded and given greater powers, including less-stringent standards for searches that are based on counterterrorism measures.

- Where the standard of probable cause is not met for domestic surveillance, the U.S. Attorney General can obtain a FISA wiretap for the monitoring of an American citizen. All information from the search can subsequently be shared with the FBI.

- The Act addresses money laundering and includes RICO-style provisions for the seizure of property and assets.

Questions

1. No one can argue with the public safety concerns raised by September 11. Do you feel that these concerns warrant increased law enforcement powers to combat terrorism?

2. Which of the new USA PATRIOT Act provisions do you feel "water down" civil liberties beyond the public safety justifications? What are the risks involved in "watering down" respect for civil liberties?

3. Should FISA be used against U.S. citizens? What are the implications of this?

4. Research past allegations of spying against the FBI and foreign intelligence agencies. What precipitated the allegations and/or investigations? Are the concerns being raised about the USA PATRIOT Act similar or different to previous cases?

The Arrest Warrant

An arrest can occur with or without a warrant. Generally, an officer is supposed to obtain a warrant if the suspect is not yet in police custody. The process for obtaining an arrest warrant is similar to that of a search warrant; both require a set of facts that indicate probable cause to believe the person committed the act. The Court in *Wong Sun* stated that an arrest must stand upon firmer ground than mere suspicion, though it is not necessary to prove guilt at this stage.[51] It is actually more common for officers to arrest suspects without a warrant than with one. In order to make a warrantless arrest of a suspect who has committed a misdemeanor, the officer must be present during the commission of the crime (with the exception of shoplifting or domestic violence incidents). Otherwise, the arrest would not be valid. An arrest for a felony can be made without a warrant if the officer witnesses a crime, has probable cause to believe that an individual committed a crime that the officer knows was committed, or if there are exigent circumstances. Exigent circumstances for arrest are similar to those discussed with regard to searches. Exigent circumstances may involve a suspect who is armed, violent, or threatening or who is destroying evidence. If any of these circumstances exist, the officer does not need to announce his or her presence before entering premises to arrest the suspect. The Court has deliberated upon several cases in order to determine the validity of a suspect's warrantless arrest. In *People v. Ramey*,[52] officers made an arrest without a warrant when there were no exigent circumstances present. The Court invalidated the arrest and the subsequent search (as a fruit of an invalid arrest). The Court further supported this decision in *Payton v. New York*,[53] claiming that officers can only make a warrantless arrest in a dwelling if there are exigent circumstances. Once a legal arrest has been made, the officer must inform the suspect of his or her rights before an interrogation.

Interrogation

Upon arrest, it is necessary for the police to question the suspect about the crime they believe the suspect has committed. This goes beyond the field interrogation, discussed earlier, where it is only necessary for the police to have reasonable suspicion that a crime is afoot. Field interrogations require cooperation between the police and the suspect, whereas an interrogation is not voluntary. The suspect in an interrogation does not have the right to leave. Before the police can conduct an **interrogation**, or a questioning of the suspect after an arrest, they must read the suspect his or her *Miranda* rights. Most people in the United States know the *Miranda* rights well, because they have been documented in police dramas on television and in movies since the late 1960s. The ***Miranda rights*** and waiver state:

> You have the right to remain silent. If you give up that right, anything you say can and will be used against you in a court of law. You have the right to speak with an attorney and to have the attorney present during questioning. If you so desire and cannot afford one, an attorney will be appointed for you without charge and before questioning. Do you understand each of these rights I have read to you? Having these rights in mind, do you wish to give up your rights as I have explained them to you and talk to me now?

The common perception, based on television docudramas, is that the police read individuals their rights as they are handcuffing them and taking them into custody. Such a dramatic occurrence is unlikely, and the rights must only be read prior to interrogation. So how did these rights come to being and what is their significance?

Miranda v. Arizona

Ernesto Miranda was arrested in Phoenix, Arizona, in 1963 on charges of kidnapping and rape. He was identified by the victim in a lineup, arrested, and subsequently interrogated for two hours without being advised of his right to remain silent or his right to counsel. He confessed to the crimes, and this statement was later admitted into evidence. He was convicted of the offenses, though the conviction was overturned because the U.S. Supreme Court recognized that Miranda's constitutional rights had been violated.

The basis of *Miranda* is that coerced confessions are unconstitutional and may not be true. To avoid coerced confessions, the Court listed specific steps for the police officers to follow prior to interrogation. It is necessary for the police to explain to each suspect that he or she has the right not to incriminate him or herself under the Fifth Amendment, as well as the right to counsel under the Sixth Amendment. Though many suspects waive their rights and speak to the police, the waiver must be knowing and voluntary. In order for a suspect to waive his or her *Miranda* rights, the suspect must agree orally or in writing that they wish to speak without counsel present. If the suspect indicates that he or she wants a lawyer present, the police must stop the questioning immediately. However, they can later ask the suspect again whether he or she wants to waive the *Miranda* rights. It is important to note, however, that the request to waive rights cannot be made every day and cannot be made if the suspect has asked to speak to a lawyer, unless at the initiation of the suspect.

Problems can arise, however, if the suspect does not understand his or her *Miranda* rights or does not waive them voluntarily. For instance, the suspect may not understand English, may be intoxicated, under the control of mind-altering substances, or even mentally ill. An alternative version of the *Miranda* warnings (Figure 7.1) is used in some jurisdictions to determine whether or not an officer is dealing with a mentally ill offender incapable of comprehending his or her rights. The police must be careful in such a situation, because any confession must be voluntary and knowing in order to be admissible in court. If it is not, then the confession (and any of the fruits resulting from it) is excluded.

Police are allowed to use cunning tactics to work around *Miranda* rights in order to get a suspect to confess. For example, upon the recommendation of an offender profiler (see Chapter 8), an interrogator left pictures of the victim and crime scene in the room an offender was being held in, in order to make the suspect feel guilty and be more likely to confess (Douglas 1994). However, the police must respect the suspect's right to counsel if so asked. In the case of *Brewer v. Williams*[54] (see the rehearing of *Nix v. Williams,* presented earlier, for the inevitable discovery doctrine), the police officers tricked Williams into confessing about where he buried the body of the girl he had killed. Because the police were driving Williams to a police station three hours away, he was essentially "in custody" while in the car. This, combined with the fact that he asked for counsel immediately, invalidated the confession that he made about the body. The confession was thrown out in the trial, though the girl's body was admitted as evidence due to inevitable discovery.

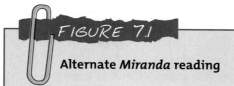

FIGURE 7.1

Alternate *Miranda* reading

1. You have the right to remain silent.
   "You do not have to talk to anyone.
   Tell me in your own words what I just said."

2. Anything you say can and will be used against you in a court of law.
   "If you talk, I can tell others what you said. Tell me in your own words what I just said."

   "What you say can get you in trouble. Tell me in your own words what I just said."

3. You have the right to talk to a lawyer and have him present at any time during questioning.
   "You can talk to a lawyer. Tell me in your own words what I just said."

   "Your lawyer can be with you if you talk to anyone. Tell me in your own words what I just said."

4. If you cannot afford a lawyer, one will be appointed for you without cost.
   "If you cannot pay for a lawyer, the judge will get you one for free. Tell me in your own words what I just said."

When *Miranda* Rights Must Be Read

The police are required to read a suspect his or her *Miranda* rights prior to interrogation. This usually occurs when the police take the suspect into custody, but the definition of custody is not always clear. Though it was indirect, the discussion between the police and Williams, above, was considered an interrogation. In his opinion in *Miranda*, Chief Justice Warren stated that a custodial interrogation can be psychological as well as physical, and that coercion can be mental as well as physical. This was also clear in *Williams*, because the tactic used by the police was to impose guilt upon Williams. They convinced him that the morally correct thing to do was to lead them to the body so that her parent's could organize a Christian burial. This psychological tactic, while "in custody" in the police car, is equivalent to a custodial interrogation, and the confession was thereby invalidated because Williams had asked for counsel.

Unless there is an arrest and an interrogation, it is not necessary for the police to read the suspect his or her Miranda rights. It is not necessary to read Miranda warnings during a traffic stop, a stop and frisk, or when the suspect volunteers information to the police prior to an arrest. The police can also use voluntary information that a suspect tells an acquaintance, though the police cannot encourage the acquaintance in order to extract such information for their purposes. If the suspect does not directly ask for questioning to cease and ask for a lawyer, the police do not have to grant the suspect a lawyer.

The Court has debated the necessity of *Miranda* on several occasions, but upheld its necessity in *Dickerson v. United States*[55] in 2000. *Dickerson* deemed that statutes that conflict with *Miranda* (specifically, 18 USCS 3501) are invalid. Prior to *Dickerson*, a number of cases allowed for exceptions to *Miranda*. For example, *New York v. Quarles*, discussed earlier, established that a confession given prior to the reading of *Miranda* rights is valid and admissible if there is a necessary public safety exception. In another case, *Arizona v. Fulminante*,[56] the Court held that a coerced confession can be considered a fruit of the poisoned tree, but that it will not automatically require a conviction to be overturned. Though these cases may diminish *Miranda*'s worth through the establishment of their many exceptions, the warnings are still "embedded in routine police practice to the point where the warnings have become part of our national culture. . . . If anything, subsequent cases have reduced *Miranda*'s impact on legitimate law enforcement while reaffirming the decision's core ruling."[57]

Privacy and the Internet

Along with the many benefits of the Internet has come a new type of crime: cyber crime. A **cyber crime** is any offense that occurs via the Internet as opposed to in the real world. This is not the same as computer crime, which is any wrongful act occurring on or directed against a computer, though this can include cyber crime. The emergence of cyber crime has challenged traditional law enforcement in many ways, ranging from creating problems of jurisdiction to difficulties in investigation. It has also produced new rules and regulations on what information can be searched and seized and how such information can be gathered without a violation of privacy.

How private is the Internet? What information can law enforcement officers retrieve from your computer or your computer server (i.e., America Online), and how can they legally monitor your time on the Internet? Who has jurisdiction over cyber space? These are questions that are just now being answered in the courts.

Cyber Offenses

A number of different offenses can be committed in cyber space. Many of these offenses are not new, but are now being committed via the Internet rather than in the real world. Cyber crimes include (but are not necessarily limited to): cyber stalking, cyber fraud, cyber theft (including identity theft), cyber terrorism, hacking, cyber money laundering, pirating intellectual property, online gambling, and child pornography (Gaines and Miller 2003). These offenses are difficult to investigate, and laws against cyber crimes are difficult to enforce. There are over 600 million Internet users worldwide, and it is thus difficult to regulate all aspects of cyber crime. **Cyber sleuths**, or individuals who regulate Internet use and enforce cyber laws, therefore focus their attentions on certain

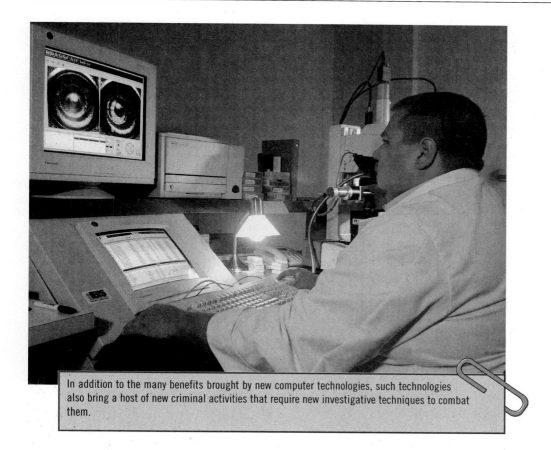

In addition to the many benefits brought by new computer technologies, such technologies also bring a host of new criminal activities that require new investigative techniques to combat them.

serious crimes. One of the most important crimes to track over the Internet is the possession and distribution of child pornography.

Child Pornography Investigations

Child pornography is the depiction of sexually explicit behavior involving a minor, including actual or simulated intercourse; oral or anal intercourse; bestiality (sexual behavior involving animals); masturbation; sexual sadism and masochism; penetration of the vagina or rectum digitally or with foreign objects; exhibition of the genitals or pubic or rectal areas for the purpose of sexually stimulating the viewer; excretory functions performed in a lewd manner; and lascivious exhibition of the genitals. Images are also considered pornographic if the child is the focal point of a sexually suggestive setting, is in an unnatural pose or inappropriate attire, or is depicted to suggest coyness or willingness to engage in sexual activity or where the depiction is intended to elicit a sexual response in the viewer (Terry, in press). Despite the benefits of the Internet, it is unfortunately responsible for the increased circulation of child pornography (and adult pornography, but that is, for the most part, legal).

Another issue of contention is that of "virtual child pornography." This is where images appear to depict minors engaging in sexual activity, but the images are produced by some means other than the use of real children (such as computer-generated images of children or images of adults who look like children). Virtual or fictitious children are not protected by the Child Pornography Prevention Act of 1996, and several court cases have upheld this Act in order to protect free speech. In the case of *Ashcroft v. Free Speech Coalition*,[58] the Supreme Court said that acts banning virtual child pornography go overboard and violate the First Amendment. While the Court recognized that there are dangers in allowing such material to be produced, it also acknowledged that the virtual images are not fundamentally related to the sexual abuse of children.

Legal Implications of Cyber Crime

Because of the anonymity of the Internet, cyber crimes are difficult to investigate. It is often not clear who has the jurisdiction to investigate particular offenses. Jurisdiction generally relates to physical geography; yet, there is no geographical boundary for the World Wide Web. Although local agencies have some duties to investigate cyber crimes, jurisdiction will usually fall upon federal agencies. This is because much of the crime in cyberspace crosses state and even international boundaries, and therefore many of the crimes are cross-jurisdictional. Here, problems of linkage blindness can intensify even further.

With cyber crimes, there is little hard physical evidence, as would be found at a traditional crime scene, and cyber sleuths must target offenders through their "conversations" and electronic "fingerprints." Any computer, computer system, computer network, or any software or data owned by the suspect that is used during the commission of any public offense involving pornography (or any other cyber crimes) or that which is used as a repository for the storage of illegal software is subject to forfeiture. A suspect does not have to be convicted in order for the computer to be seized; rather, there must be probable cause to show that the material is obscene. When officers do seize a computer, they must show that the removal is reasonable, and they must return anything that is not evidence. That said, there are few established boundaries as to how cyber searches can legally take place and what types of searches would be considered constitutional under the Fourth Amendment.

One way to conduct searches is through wiretaps. Appendix A is a summary of legislation proposed or enacted relating to the legality of wiretaps. Additionally, the provider can disclose information that it inadvertently comes across if the information pertains to a crime. In terms of the Fourth Amendment, computers are equivalent to "containers"; the user does not have a special expectation of privacy, even though data can be erased.[59] As with a container, the officer must have probable cause to search the computer, which usually requires a warrant specifying exactly what is to be searched and what the officer is searching for. Once the officers look for material beyond the scope of their specified search, they violate the individual's Fourth Amendment rights. For instance, in the case of *United States v. Carey*,[60] the officers had a warrant to search the suspect's computer for drug-related information. Upon finding images of child pornography, the officers continued to search for further such images in the .jpeg files. The Court invalidated the search, claiming that the officers should have stopped the search and obtained a warrant once they found the pornographic images.

Chapter Summary

- There are many different types of searches, including stop and frisk, searches of persons, searches of premises, searches of vehicles, searches of public places, and plain view searches. In order to conduct a search, the officer must have probable cause to believe that a particular person committed a crime.

- Officers usually need a warrant to conduct a search. However, under exigent circumstances a warrant is not necessary. Additionally, officers usually do not need a warrant to search a car because of the issue of mobility. An officer does not need a warrant when the suspect consents to a search, when searching public places, when there is a systematic search, or when searching incident to arrest.

- A frisk is a type of search, though it is less invasive than a full search. It is only a pat down for weapons. To conduct a frisk, an officer only needs reasonable suspicion, rather than probable cause, that crime is afoot.

- After arrest and prior to custodial interrogation, officers must warn suspects that they have the right to remain silent and that they have the right to counsel. This precedent, established in *Miranda v. Arizona,* helps to reduce the likelihood of coerced confessions from suspects.

- A new and challenging type of search is one conducted via the Internet. These are more difficult than searches in the "real world" because of jurisdictional issues, the changing nature of cyber crimes, and the anonymity of the Internet.

Linking the Dots

1. What are the most important cases that limit police powers with regard to searches and seizures?

2. Should police officers be able to make pretextual stops of vehicles? What are the costs and benefits of this practice?

3. Do officers have to tell individuals during systematic searches that they are free to leave? Should they be required to explain to the individuals that this type of search is consensual?

4. What are the most significant challenges of investigating the possession and distribution of child pornography on the Internet? How do investigations in the real world differ from those in the virtual world? What are the similarities?

5. How are searches different since the passing of the USA PATRIOT Act? For what type of searches are search standards more lenient now?

KEY TERMS

Arrest 179

Child pornography 185

Curtilage 178

Cyber crime 184

Cyber sleuths 184

Exclusionary rule 171

REFERENCES

American Civil Liberties Union. 1999. *An American Civil Liberties Union Special Report: Driving While Black: Racial Profiling on Our Nation's Highways.* New York, NY: American Civil Liberties Union.

Black's Law Dictionary. 1990. St. Paul, MN: West Publishing.

Douglas, J. 1994. *Mind Hunter.* New York, NY: Scribner.

Electronic Frontier Foundation. 2001. "EEF Analysis of the Provisions of the USA Patriot Act." Available at: www.eff.org/Privacy/Surveillance.../20011031_eff_usa_patriot_analysis.html.

Gaines, L. K., and R. L. Miller. 2003. *Criminal Justice in Action,* 2d ed. Belmont, CA: Wadsworth.

Gibbons, M. 2003. "Profiling—More than a Euphemism for Discrimination: Legitimate Use of a Maligned Investigative Tool." In *Policing and Minority Communities: Bridging the Gap,* edited by D. J. Jones-Brown and K. J. Terry, 36–51. Upper Saddle River, NJ: Prentice-Hall.

Terry, K. J. (in press). *Sexual Offenses and Offenders: Theory, Practice and Policy.* Belmont, CA: Wadsworth.

NOTES

1. *United States v. Drayton,* 122 S. Ct. 2105 (2002).
2. *Locke v. United States,* 11 U.S. 339 (1813). Probable cause in this case is defined vaguely as prima facie evidence, which is less than that which would justify condemnation.
3. *Carroll v. United States,* 267 U.S. 132 (1925).
4. *Brinegar v. United States,* 338 U.S. 160 (1949).
5. *Carroll v. United States,* 267 U.S. 132 (1925) at 162. n15; *Brinegar v. United States,* 338 U.S. 160 (1949) at 175–176.
6. *Draper v. United States,* 358 U.S. 307 (1959).
7. *Spinelli v. United States,* 393 U.S. 410 (1969).
8. *Illinois v. Gates,* 462 U.S. 213 (1983).
9. *Terry v. Ohio,* 392 U.S. 1 (1968).
10. *United States v. Arvizu,* 534 U.S. 266 (2002).
11. *United States v. Brignoni-Ponce,* 422 U.S. 873 (1975).
12. *United States v. Sokolow,* 490 U.S. 1 (1989).
13. *Illinois v. Wardlow,* 528 U.S. 119 (2002).
14. *Weeks v. United States,* 232 U.S. 383 (1914).
15. *Rochin v. California,* 342 U.S. 165 (1952).
16. Ibid., at 210.
17. *Mapp v. Ohio,* 368 U.S. 871 (1961).
18. Ibid. at 659. If there is any question as to the legality of a police officer's actions in terms of a search, the judge will exclude the evidence seized. For example, when a New York City police officer saw a suspect toss a bag of marijuana onto the floor of his car—which was illegally parked in front of a fire hydrant in a well-known drug neighborhood—he approached the suspect to ask some questions. When the suspect mumbled, the officer pinched the suspect's cheeks until the drugs he had put in his mouth fell out. The judge excluded the four bags of marijuana from the trial, stating that forcing the suspect to open his mouth was unnecessarily intrusive. See *New York v. Cooper,* 2002 NY Slip Op 50399U. Cited *Schmerber v. California,* 384 U.S. 757 (1966); the judge said that there was no "clear indication" that the officer would find evidence through such actions.
19. *Wong Sun v. United States,* 371 U.S. 471 (1963).
20. *Michigan v. Tucker,* 417 U.S. 433 (1974).
21. *New York v. Quarles,* 467 U.S. 649 (1984).
22. *United States v. Leon,* 468 U.S. 897 (1984).
23. *Nix v. Williams,* 430 U.S. 387 (1977).
24. Originally from *Curtis' Case,* Fost. 135, 168 Eng. Rep. 67 (1756), the Court cited this decision in *Ker v. California,* 374 U.S. 23 (1963). This was further supported in *Wilson v. Arkansas,* 514 U.S. 927

(1995), in which the Court cited the necessity of an officer to knock and announce unless there are exigent circumstances.

25. *Richards v. Wisconsin,* 520 U.S. 385 (1997).

26. *Kirk v. Louisiana,* 122 S. Ct. 2458 (2002).

27. *Payton v. New York,* 445 U.S. 573 (1980).

28. *Minnesota v. Dickerson,* 508 U.S. 366 (1993).

29. *United States v. Matlock* (1974) states that a roommate can give consent to search the common areas of the residence; *People v. Cosme* (1979) states that either the husband or the wife can give consent; *Illinois v. Rodriguez* (1990) states that an individual who by all appearances is staying at the residence, even if they are not living there permanently, can give consent. This does not, however, include overnight guests (*Minnesota v. Olsen,* 1989).

30. *Kyllo v. United States,* 533 U.S. 27 (2001).

31. *Chimel v. California,* 395 U.S. 752 (1969).

32. *Maryland v. Buie,* 494 U.S. 325 (1989).

33. *Schmerber v. California,* 384 U.S. 757 (1966).

34. *Carroll v. United States,* 267 U.S. 132 (1924).

35. *Chambers v. Maroney,* 399 U.S. 42 (1970).

36. *Coolidge v. New Hampshire,* 403 U.S. 443 (1971).

37. *United States v. Ross,* 456 U.S. 798 (1982).

38. Supra note 32; *California v. Acevedo,* 500 U.S. 565 (1991).

39. *Florida v. White,* 526 U.S. 559 (1999).

40. *Maryland v. Wilson,* 519 U. S. 408 (1997).

41. The Court in *Knowles v. Iowa,* 525 U.S. 113 (1998), 525 U.S. 113, confirmed that the police can legally conduct a full-scale search of the car even if they pull over the individual for a traffic citation.

42. *Whren v. United States,* 517 U.S. 806 (1996).

43. *Michigan Department of State Police v. Sitz,* 496 U.S. 444 (1990).

44. *Department of State Police v. Sitz,* 496 U.S. 444 (1990).

45. Randomized searches of passengers prior to boarding a plane is different from the stop and search of those who fit a drug-courier profile, which was discussed in the previous section. With drug courier profiles, race can be one factor, though not the sole factor, for a stop.

46. *City of Indianapolis v. Edmond,* 531 U.S. 32 (2000).

47. *Katz v. United States,* 389 U.S. 347 (1967).

48. *California v. Greenwood,* 486 U.S. 35 (1988).

49. *Florida v. Bostick,* 501 U.S. 429 (1991).

50. *Miranda v. Arizona,* 384 U.S. 436 (1966).

51. *Wong Sun v. United States,* supra n. 19.

52. *People v. Ramey,* 16 Cal. 3d 263 (1976).

53. *Payton v. New York,* 445 U.S. 573 (1980).

54. *Brewer v. Williams,* 430 U.S. 387 (1977).

55. *Dickerson v. United States,* 530 U.S. 428 (2000).

56. *Arizona v. Fulminante,* 499 U.S. 279 (1991).

57. *Dickerson v. United States,* supra note 36 at 419–420.

58. *Ashcroft v. Free Speech Coalition,* 122 S. Ct. 1389 (2002).

59. *Commonwealth of Pennsylvania v. Copenhefer,* 587 Atl. 2d 1353 (Pa. 1991).

60. *United States v. Carey,* 172 F.3d 1268 (1999).

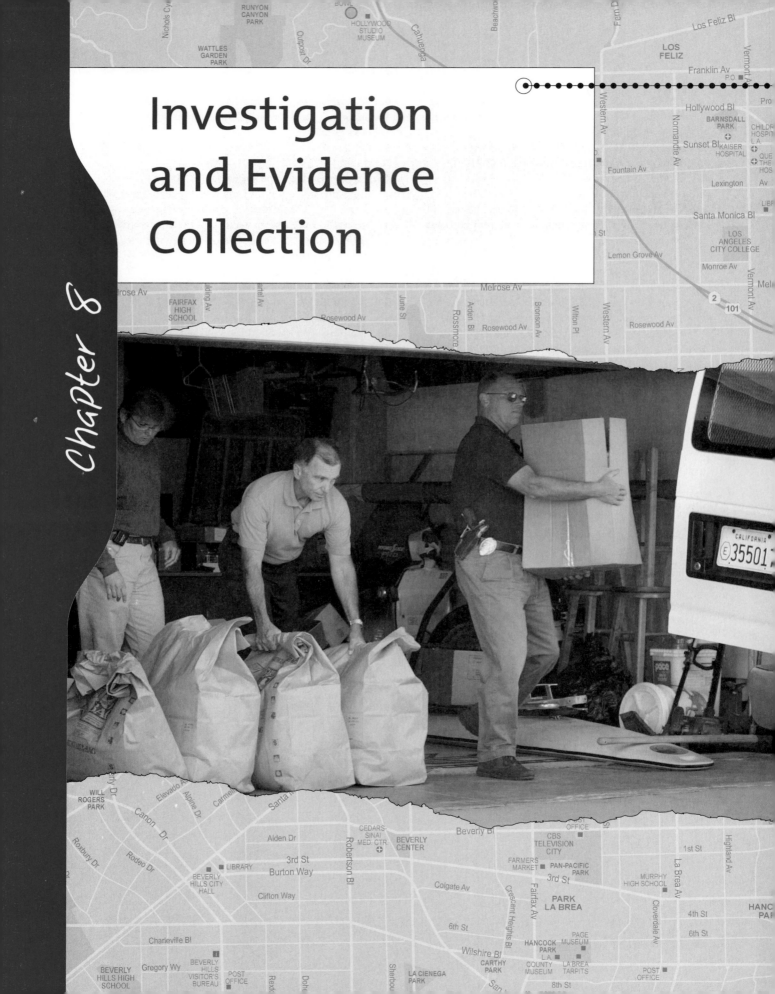

Chapter 8

Investigation and Evidence Collection

Chapter Outline

Chapter Objectives

● Learn about the development of the investigative function and how it has evolved.

● Understand the Locard exchange principle and its importance to investigations.

● Know the different types of evidence and how they affect an investigation.

● Understand the concept of behavioral profiling and how police officers can use it to identify a perpetrator.

● Know how new technologies are being used to solve investigations.

● Learn about different models of counterterrorism on local, state, and federal levels.

● Appreciate the challenges and issues involved in police–prosecutor collaboration.

Introduction

Early on the morning of February 2, 2002, seven-year-old Danielle van Dam disappeared from her bedroom in San Diego, California. David Westerfield, who lived two houses away from the van Dams, quickly emerged as a suspect following the abduction. The prosecutors obtained warrants to search for child pornography and any DNA evidence linking Danielle to Westerfield's house or vehicles. Westerfield was arrested nearly three weeks later and charged with murder, kidnapping, and possession of child pornography. At the time of his arrest, Danielle's body had not yet been found.

The prosecution referred to evidence found in Westerfield's home during these initial searches as the "smoking gun" linking him to Danielle's abduction and suspected murder. Such evidence included fiber, hair, and fingerprint samples found in his motor home and a small amount of her blood on his jacket. Even though the body was not found until four days after Westerfield's arrest, the trace evidence found in the searches was used to form the probable cause necessary for his arrest. In addition to this physical evidence, investigators also brought to trial circumstantial evidence linking Westerfield to the death, such as his collection of child pornography, his 600-mile meandering trip immediately following her abduction, and his unusual actions such as cleaning all of his bed linen and profuse sweating while the police searched his house.

Even in cases where investigators have strong reason to believe in the potential guilt of a suspect, incidental evidence such as the strange behavior of David Westerfield after the abduction of Danielle van Dam is not enough. The criminal justice system requires an establishment of credible evidence to meet the standards of probable cause necessary for full searches and an arrest. The case of David Westerfield is an example of this. The investigators were able to demonstrate Danielle's connection to the Westerfield motor home through fingerprints, blood, hair, and fibers, which was enough to obtain an arrest warrant, even in the absence of finding the body. In addition to strong physical evidence, however, behavioral evidence can help to solidify a case and sway jurors towards a guilty verdict. This chapter will introduce readers to the investigative process, highlighting key issues and topics in this very central function of law enforcement.

The Development of the Investigative Function

As discussed in Chapter 2, Henry Fielding's Bow Street Runners were a significant first step towards the creation of the London Metropolitan Police, or law enforcement as we know it today. In the London of 1750 (the year the Runners were formed), thieves were the central criminal figures, with individuals and families turning to theft as a profession when access to industrial jobs proved to be more elusive than initially promised. In the face of this perceived crime wave, the constable system proved inadequate, leaving local businesses and residents responsible for crime prevention or even the recovery of stolen property. Those individuals who could afford the service would often hire a **thief catcher** to find lost property. Similar to a law enforcement officer who moonlights as a security guard in modern times, the thief catcher was often a constable in his primary job. However, even where successful in finding stolen property, thief catchers were unable to reduce general crime levels in a seemingly besieged city (Emsley 1996).

Taking on the position of London Magistrate in a city bereft with crime and disorder, Fielding sought to revitalize the government's crime-fighting arsenal by appointing a group of parish constables to his court. This group quickly began to demonstrate effective thief-catching functions as a result of implementing criminal investigative activities, such as using informants with close ties to the criminal underworld. Despite these successes, which led to them being hailed as the leading law enforcement agency in the metropolitan London area (Johnson and Wolfe 1996), the Bow Street Runners also faced issues of corruption and abuse (Osterburg and Ward 1997). In 1790, ten years after the Metropolitan Police Act, the Runners became an officially recognized force of trained and paid detectives. The Runners continued to fight criminal behavior for nearly fifty years.

It was not long after the disbandment of the Runners that Sir Robert Peel recognized the need to create an investigative division within the Metropolitan Police. Recruited directly from the patrol ranks, Peel sought to encourage foot patrol (beat) officers to develop the observational skills and intelligence networks important for promotion to the detective role. Housed in Scotland Yard, these officers were soon dubbed the "detective force" (Osterburg and Ward 1997). Johnson and Wolfe (1996) note that this method of selecting officers is very similar to contemporary police practices.

In the United States, the detective function was also recognized as a necessity early on. Thomas Byrnes was appointed as the first detective bureau chief for the NYPD in 1880. However, as was the case with Fielding's Bow Street Runners, Byrnes' close ties to the underworld often led him to walk a fine ethical line. Theodore Roosevelt forced Byrnes out of his role immediately upon becoming president of the Board of Police Commissioners in 1895.

The detective function, as with law enforcement in general, has become professionalized with the application of science and technology over time. Part of this professionalization has involved a shift of the detective role from being intimately tied to the underworld to one that is principally undertaken by a police officer, even though the use of criminal informants has remained an important tool.

The Realities of Investigation

When one thinks of an *investigation,* a number of things might come to mind. One might think of Sherlock Holmes and his skills of deduction—meticulously taking notes of seemingly meaningless elements of a crime scene and then brilliantly using those notes to get from the "what" to the "why" and ultimately to the "who." Or, perhaps one might think of the television show *CSI,* in which detectives evaluate forensic evidence from crime scenes and are nearly always able to identify violent perpetrators based on this evidence. And no one can forget in *Silence of the Lambs* the chilling "quid pro quo" exchange between Hannibal Lector and the newly recruited FBI agent Clarice Starling, which ultimately led to her finding a killer who had eluded teams of law enforcement agents. In fact, such portrayals of detectives in movies, books, and television have caused the public to equate investigation with policing itself, despite that fact that 60 percent of departmental resources are dedicated to patrol and only 15 percent are devoted to investigation (Bayley 1994). Popular crime dramas such as *NYPD Blue* focus on the detectives chasing down suspects through a combination of intellect and physical prowess; they do not focus on the officer on patrol offering directions or writing reports. Detectives also have a certain special status within many police departments, receiving higher salaries than ordinary officers and having the freedom to choose their own hours and not wear a uniform (Bayley 1994).

As glamorous and exciting as media portrayals of investigation may be, the reality of investigation for may detectives and agents is often far more mundane and routine.

In 1977, the **Kansas City Response Time study**, which analyzed the time it takes police officers to respond to calls, found that citizens take longer to report crimes to police than it takes police to respond (Kansas City Police Department 1977). Additionally, the likelihood of arrest is more significantly related to the citizen's time to report than to police response time. Given that 75 percent of crimes are **discovery crimes** (Wrobleski and Hess 2002), in which the police respond after the crime was committed, how significant a role can investigation play in solving the majority of offenses? **Involvement crimes,** in which the police arrive during the commission of the offense, only account for 25 percent of all cases.

Researchers first examined the realities of investigation in a study by the Rand Corporation in 1975 (Greenwood and Petersilia 1975). Researchers examined how serious crimes such as rape, robbery, murder assault, theft, and burglary were solved, using a variety of data sources from 153 jurisdictions nationwide serving populations over 100,000. Seeking to understand the contribution that investigation ultimately makes to the resolution of crimes, the researchers examined clearance rates by organizational structure, technology, and departmental role.

Clearance rate is the ratio of successful identification and apprehension of offenders to unsolved crimes. The results of the Rand study had a similar impact on thinking about investigation as the Kansas City Preventive Patrol Experiment had on patrol (see Chapter 6). Figure 8.1 presents the percentage of Part I crimes that were solved by traditional detective work.

Results indicate that *no more than 2.7 percent* of all Part I crime clearances can be attributed to special investigative techniques. Thus, 97 percent of all cleared crimes were cleared crimes no matter what the investigators did or did not do. Of course, that 2.7 percent often includes the most interesting and publicly visible crimes, such as homicides (Greenwood and Petersilia 1975).

How can this be? In reality, patrol officers are responsible for most clearances. Thirty percent of all clearances are the result of pickup arrests by patrol officers responding to the scene of the crime (Greenwood and Petersilia 1975). These are the "smoking gun" situations in which the offender has not left the immediate crime area before the first responding officer arrives at the scene. Such cases are obvious examples of involvement crimes, in which fast law enforcement response to the scene is crucial.

In 50 percent of the cleared cases, the offender was already known when the crime report was taken at the scene. Greenwood and Petersilia (1975) offer three examples of such cases:

1. The offender was arrested at the scene.

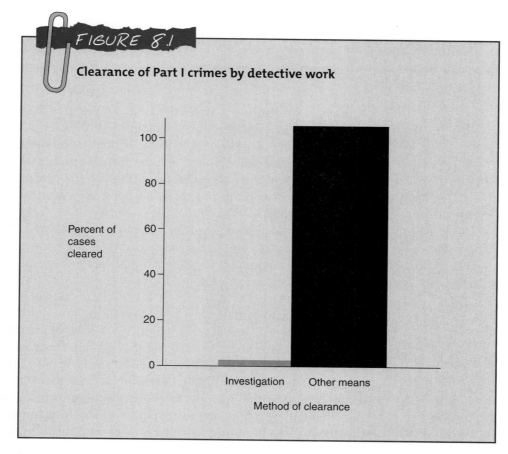

FIGURE 8.1

Clearance of Part I crimes by detective work

Percent of cases cleared (y-axis: 0, 20, 40, 60, 80, 100)

Investigation   Other means

Method of clearance

Source: Data from Greenwood and Petersilis. 1975. The Criminal Investigation Process, Vol. 1.

2. The victim and/or other witnesses identified the offender by name and address.

3. There was unique evidence to identify a perpetrator, such as a license plate.

In cases such as these, no amazing sleuth work is necessary to solve the crime. Instead, the principal efforts of the investigation will be pulling together enough facts for the successful prosecution of the case and locating the offender to take him or her into custody.

Although this leaves 20 percent of cleared crimes that could still potentially be solved by good "detective work," the reality remains that a good number of these are actually solved by patrol officers or members of the public who later reveal critical information. In other cases, simple clerical work plays the central role in identifying the perpetrator. Another surprising finding revealed by the Rand study was that although crimes such as homicide, rape, and suicide certainly received some investigative attention, over half of all serious offenses received only superficial investigative work. Additionally, organizational changes related to staffing, workload, or even training appeared to have no effect on clearance rates.

Does this mean that investigative units are unnecessary? No. The quality of investigative work can still affect the clearance rates of homicide, robbery, and commercial theft. However, what is evident is that the role of the patrol officer who conducts the preliminary investigation needs to be given important consideration; the patrol officer's role in initially documenting the crime scene evidence needed for the legal resolution of a case is indispensable.

The Preliminary Investigation

The first uniformed officer (usually a patrol officer) to arrive at the crime scene conducts a **preliminary investigation**. Duties involved upon arrival at the crime scene include determining whether the offender is at the scene or in the area, responding to the victim's needs, and ensuring the general safety of anyone in the immediate vicinity. The percentages presented earlier demonstrate the importance of the first responder's training and professional response given that what initially occurs at a scene can determine whether the crime will eventually be cleared.

As such, the processing of the initial crime scene and the recording of relevant evidence and information are critical. In addition to securing the scene from possible contaminants, detailed and methodical note taking and record keeping are essential in order to document everything at the scene exactly as it was found. Some departments even have sophisticated computer software available on laptops to assist in this process, making it easy for even the most artistically challenged investigator to produce a true-scale drawing.

Contaminants include anything that can alter a crime scene. This can involve someone taking something from the scene, leaving something behind, or moving things from their original position. Because all elements of a crime scene can be critical in the process of **reconstruction**, or determining exactly what happened and by whom, the introduction of any foreign items to the scene can send the investigation in many wrong (and time-consuming) directions. This is why careful documentation and monitoring is required at the point of first entry. For example, if an officer enters a murder scene, picks up three kitchen chairs that had been knocked over, and casually smokes a cigarette, he or she might lead the investigators to make some false initial conclusions. Rather than seeing the obvious signs of a struggle, the investigator might see a scene that was calm and methodical, to the point where the offender even took the time to smoke a cigarette immediately following the event, not to mention the fact that the cigarette will be sent to the crime lab for costly testing.

The patrol officer who first arrives at the scene will pass on a report to the detective unit regarding all evidence found at the scene. Based on **solvability factors**, a decision is made whether or not to assign a follow-up investigation to investigative services. Solvability factors are anything that can potentially affect the probability of successfully concluding the case (e.g., presence of witnesses and/or physical evidence) (Skogan and Attunes 1979).

The Follow-up Investigation

The Rand study showed that more than half of serious reported crimes do not receive full investigative attention, and when full attention is given, this may only include reading over the incident report once (Greenwood and Petersilia 1975). Although crimes such as homicide, rape, and suicide are almost guaranteed to get some subsequent investigative activity, less than half of reported felonies will not, with many receiving less than a day of investigative work (Greenwood and Petersilia 1975).

Types of Crime Scenes

Before proceeding, it may be useful to clarify what we mean by *crime scene*. A **crime scene** is the area from which the majority of the physical evidence associated with the crime is obtained (Lee et al. 2002). This is often, although not al-

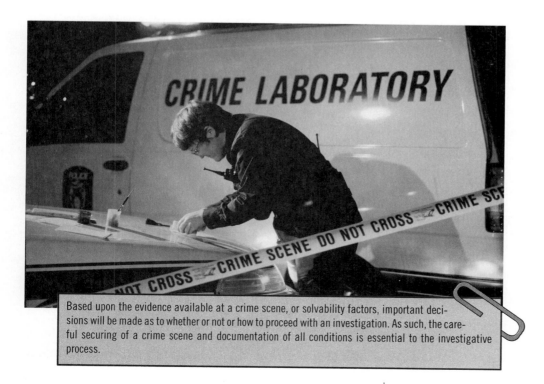

Based upon the evidence available at a crime scene, or solvability factors, important decisions will be made as to whether or not or how to proceed with an investigation. As such, the careful securing of a crime scene and documentation of all conditions is essential to the investigative process.

ways, the starting point for an investigation. Lee (2002) identifies two types of possible crime scenes: primary and secondary. The **primary scene** is where the original crime took place. Any subsequent scene is referred to as the **secondary scene**. See Figure 8.2 for an illustration of the two types of crime scenes.

The Danielle van Dam case introduced at the beginning of this chapter demonstrates the differences between primary and secondary crime scenes. Although the little girl's body was found wrapped in a blanket in the desert, this would be classified as a secondary scene. Any trace evidence located in the car used to transport her from the site of her death (Westerfield's motor home) to the dump site would also be classified as a secondary scene. The motor home itself would be classified as the primary scene because that is where Westerfield allegedly raped and killed her, leaving behind the majority of evidence. Hair, fingerprints, and blood were found on the bed and walls in the bedroom. Blood was found on Westerfield's jacket. Even though Danielle was originally abducted from her own home, this would also likely not be classified as a primary scene given the lack of evidence and the fact that most of the serious action took place once Westerfield transported her to his own quarters. To the extent possible, investigators need to make an effort to find the primary scene because that is where the bulk of the evidence will be. As will become clearer in the following text, the lack of trace evidence is what makes dumping scenes so difficult to investigate.

The Locard Exchange Principle

The most effective way to prosecute a case is to collect reliable and sufficient evidence linking an offender to a crime scene. As a consequence, crime laboratories must be able to examine evidence in a scientific manner. Edmond Locard

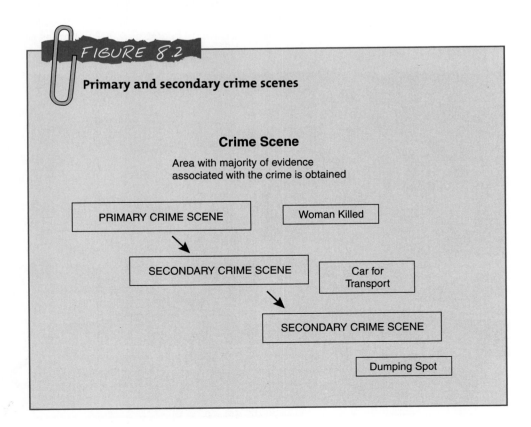

FIGURE 8.2

Primary and secondary crime scenes

Crime Scene

Area with majority of evidence
associated with the crime is obtained

| PRIMARY CRIME SCENE | Woman Killed |

| SECONDARY CRIME SCENE | Car for Transport |

| SECONDARY CRIME SCENE |

| Dumping Spot |

established the first "crime laboratory" in Lyon, France, in 1910, followed by others in the 1920s and 1930s. Since the 1930s, the number of crime laboratories operating in the United States has exploded, so much so that it is difficult to find a major city without such a facility.

Named after the founder of the first crime lab, the **Locard exchange principle** recognizes that it is simply impossible for anyone to enter a location without changing it in some way, either by bringing something to it or removing something from it (see Figure 8.3). This principle is essential to linking an offender and weapon to a crime scene (e.g., through blood, carpet fibers, soil, etc.), but it also explains why it is crucial to shield the crime scene from possible contaminants. It is also why the importance of detailed, meticulous note taking throughout all phases of the investigation cannot be overemphasized. The crime scene is usually photographed, measured, and sketched in great detail. The photographs need to show the scene as it was found, taken in a series to reconstruct the crime. Scale and dimension is critical, which is why computer programs, photographs, and even videotaping are all used.

The importance of strict procedures guiding the investigation process was never more apparent than during the O. J. Simpson case. The bulk of testimony in Simpson's trial focused on the admissibility and relevance of DNA evidence. The accusation against Detective Mark Fuhrman in that case highlighted the need to maintain a chain of evidence as soon as the first officer enters the scene; evidence must be maintained from its initial collection to its analysis and presentation in court. **Chain of evidence** refers to the meticulous documentation and tracking of all physical evidence taken from a crime scene. In the O. J. Simpson case, the fact that the exact whereabouts of key evidence such as the bloody glove and blood traces found in the suspect's car went a long way toward helping the defense plant a seed of reasonable doubt in the minds of the jurors.

Establishing a Physical Link

Obtaining **physical evidence** is a central function of the investigation. From Locard's exchange principle, we know that physical evidence links an offender and weapon to the crime scene. In property crimes, the investigator

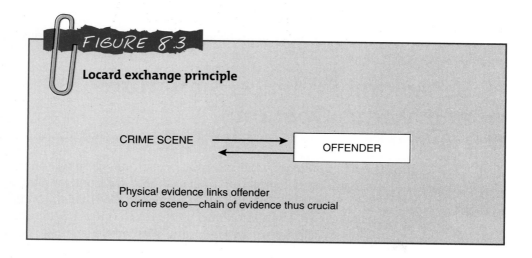

FIGURE 8.3

Locard exchange principle

CRIME SCENE ⟶ OFFENDER
⟵

Physical evidence links offender
to crime scene—chain of evidence thus crucial

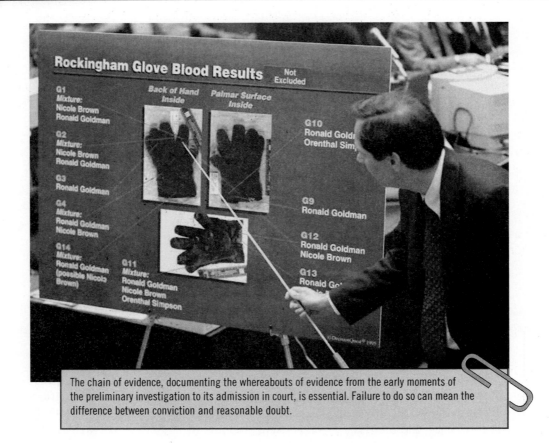

The chain of evidence, documenting the whereabouts of evidence from the early moments of the preliminary investigation to its admission in court, is essential. Failure to do so can mean the difference between conviction and reasonable doubt.

will generally look for signs of forcible entry, such as marks on a door from the implement used to pry the door open. Physical evidence in a violent crime may include blood, hair, fibers, fingerprints, and weapons. Depending on the type of offense, investigators may also expect to find evidence such as semen or bite marks on the victim. Table 8.1 offers examples of several types of physical evidence.

Associative evidence is a nonlegal term for the laboratory work used to establish linkages between the crime scene, victim, and offender (Osterburg and Ward 1997). In contrast, **criminalistics** encompasses the application of scientific technology to the minute details of a crime scene to reconstruct what happened, as well as to establish the connections between people, places, and things that is the core of associative evidence (Saferstein 1995).

Behavioral Evidence: Signature and Modus Operandi

In addition to physical evidence, investigators also rely on interrogating suspects whom they believe to be connected with the crime, relying on **nonverbal cues** (e.g., tone, pitch, inflection) and **kinesics** (body language) to support or confirm a suspect's statements. Remember the **behavioral evidence**, or nonphysical evidence, used in the van Dam case: Westerfield's strange behavior following the

TABLE 8.1

Types of Physical Evidence

Physical Evidence	Investigative Significance
Fingerprints	• When a person grasps an item with reasonable pressure, grease oozing out of the pores under the ridges leaves latent fingerprints.
	• No two persons have the same fingerprints. Fingerprints are a combination of eight possible patterns.
	• In the past, investigators matched paper fingerprint cards with the fingerprints of persons previously arrested. Investigators now use automated fingerprint identification systems (AFISs).
Blood Saliva Semen Skin	• DNA profiling uses genetic material to identify individuals. No two people have the same DNA structure, except for identical twins.
	• The National DNA Identification System (NDIS) is an FBI database of approximately 600,000 offenders. The database allows states to exchange profiles and make comparisons.
	• Federal law allows police to take blood samples from convicted felons.
Weapon	• When a weapon is fired, the bullet picks up tiny imperfections of the bore as it passes through. Scratches are caused by the imperfections in the lands and grooves placed in the barrel at the time of manufacture and caused through use. These marks allow experts to determine that rounds are fired by the same gun. Ballistics studies the motion of bullets.
	• The make of the weapon, determined by riflings (spiral grooves) in the barrel, varies from manufacturer to manufacturer.

disappearance, his meandering journey, his sweating, and his obsessive need to clean all bed linen.

Although very important, reliance on nonverbal cues can also be misleading when the investigator or police officer comes from a different culture than the suspect. Nonverbal cues can actually vary across cultures, leading some authors to refer to them as cultural cues (Kenney et al. 2002). **Cultural cues** are the alternative meanings of nonverbal cues that can vary by culture. For example, the inability to make eye contact is often viewed by investigators as a clear sign of suspiciousness or guilt. However, in some Asian cultures, a lack of eye contact (a form of kinesics) can actually mean deference to authority (NCPC 1999). Automatically jumping to conclusions based on one's cultural framework may potentially lead an investigation in the wrong direction. Law enforcement officers should receive diversity training to help them to recognize potentially misleading cues, a subject we return to in Chapter 10.

Criminal profiling involves the use of behavioral evidence found at the scene to predict what type of person committed the crime. Profiling is based on past experience with patterns identified in similar crimes. Despite the mythological presentation of profiling in the media, it can never replace true investigative work. Profiling should only be viewed as an additional tool in the arsenal of the investigator to narrow the field of investigation, particularly in cases in which there is no connection between the victim and offender. In the end, even with the most accurate criminal profile, it will take investigative skills to identify a perpetrator.

To determine a behavioral profile, it is helpful to ascertain whether the perpetrator of the crime follows a particular modus operandi or has an identifiable signature. Though sometimes discussed interchangeably, these are different but equally important concepts in establishing a behavioral profile.

Modus operandi (MO) refers to "how" a crime is committed. Although MO analysis is useful in linking crimes by the same suspect, this must be done with caution (Gerberth 1996). For example, sexual homicide can involve the escalation of acts as the offender becomes more comfortable with his behavior. What starts out as being an act of voyeurism may progress into burglary, rape, and ultimately homicide. Where an offender is in this cycle can influence the commonalities in MOs across crime scenes. Moreover, it may not be the type of weapon that is important to the offender, but some other fantasy element that is difficult for an untrained investigator to detect. Sex offender registries are a useful medium for monitoring and controlling such suspects. Police agencies now have computerized databases containing descriptions, addresses, and MOs of local offenders to, among other things, help in the investigation of new offenses and pinpoint emerging patterns in a geographical area.

Signature refers to the "what" instead of the "how" at a crime scene. Specifically, the offender's signature is what the offender needs or takes from a crime scene (Gerberth and Douglas 1995). FBI agent John Douglas has referred to this as the "behavioral fingerprint" of the offender because it is directly tied to his or her fantasy element regarding the crime. Though the fantasy may evolve over time, this element is likely to remain consistent from scene to scene and is therefore more reliable than the MO (Douglas and Munn 1992). For example, one rapist's signature may be to have his victims say "I love you" during the act, whereas another rapist may enjoy the torture and humiliation of his victims (Hazelwood 1987). These signatures indicate two very different types of individuals and may give investigators a clue as to the type of perpetrator for whom they are searching.

Following a now classic, but hotly contested, study of sexual homicide offenders, FBI agents John Douglas and Robert Ressler developed a typology to guide and classify the examination of physical evidence at a sexual homicide (also referred to as lust murders) crime scene (Douglas et al. 1985). Correlating crime scene elements with key personality characteristics is a key function of the **organized–disorganized typology**, described in Table 8.2.

The organized offender takes great care in the planning of his or her offense, ensuring that there is little or no evidence remaining at the crime scene (Holmes and Holmes 1999). As a result, the weapon of choice will usually be brought to the scene by the offender and taken away following the completion of the act. The victim is likely to be a stranger, eliminating the connection between victim and offender that increases the likelihood of getting caught. Victims tend to be selected opportunistically, and as such may include prostitutes, hitchhikers, homosexuals, and others with "deviant" lifestyles. This creates a minimal risk of the killer being caught (Gerberth 1996).

In contrast, disorganized offenders often engage in a chaotic, unplanned style of attack in which substantial amounts of evidence are left behind at the crime scene. Although the victims of such attacks are also likely to be strangers,

TABLE 8.2

The Organized–Disorganized Crime Scene Typology

	Crime Scene Indicators	Personal Characteristics	Postoffense Behavior	Interview Techniques
Organized offender	Planned offense Targeted stranger Personalizes victim Controlled conversation Controlled crime scene Submissive victim Restraints used Aggressive acts Body moved Weapon taken Little evidence	High intelligence Socially adequate Sexually competent Lives with partner High birth order Harsh discipline in childhood Controlled mood Masculine image Charming Situational cause Geographically mobile Occupationally mobile Follows media	Returns to crime scene Volunteers information Police groupie Anticipates questioning May move body May dispose of body to advertise crime	Use direct strategy Be certain of deaths Be aware that offender will admit to only what he or she must
Disorganized offender	Spontaneous event Victim unknown Depersonalizes victim Minimal conversation Chaotic crime scene Sudden violence No restraints Sex after death Body not moved Weapon left Physical evidence	Below average intelligence Socially inadequate Unskilled worker Low birth order status Father's work unstable Lives alone Lives/works near scene Nocturnal Poor personal hygiene High school dropout	Returns to crime scene May attend victim's funeral May change job May have personality change May turn to religion May keep diary or news clippings	Show empathy Introduce information indirectly Use counselor approach Interview at night

Source: Modified from Holmes, R., and S. Holmes. 1996. *Profiling Violent Crimes: A Practical Tool for Homicide Investigation,* Reprinted with permission.

they are less likely to be selected based on a likelihood of being caught. In fact, with disorganized offenders, the victims tend to be distant acquaintances, such as residents in the same building. Unlike the organized offender who is more likely to have traveled great distances to the scene, the spontaneous nature of a disorganized killer's act makes him or her more likely to either live or work within his or her original zone of comfort (Rossmo 2000).

Holmes and Holmes (1999) argue for the maintenance of the FBI's original distinction between the organized **nonsocial offender** and disorganized **asocial offender** due to their closer match to the specific profile characteristics suggested by the typology. The organized nonsocial offender is likely to meet the classification of a **psychopath**, one who is able to charm his or her victims but who has a complete void of empathy that is often manifested in sadistic sexual pleasure. Control of the victim and the scene is the central signature element for many organized offenders. The disorganized asocial offender is closer in profile to a **schizoid personality**, or someone who is withdrawn from society. Their inability to relate to others can explain the reliance on sudden attack for such offenders, as well as the disordered nature of their crime scenes.

The ability to use crime scene information to suggest personality type is controversial. Even those who subscribe to the possibilities of profiling are quick to refute the organized–disorganized typology (Turvey 2001), largely because offenders rarely fit into such mutually exclusive categories. Few meaningful evaluations of the effectiveness of either the organized–disorganized typology or profiling in general have been completed to date.

Information, Clearance Rates, and Investigation

As described earlier, clearance rates vary significantly from crime to crime. Only crimes involving some level of interpersonal vigilance have at least some chance of positive resolution. Some of this has to do with factors related to the circle of investigation. The **circle of investigation** is the pool of possible suspects in a crime (Skogan and Attunes 1979). Crimes involving personal contact and/or an acquaintanceship with the victim have a much narrower circle of investigation, and consequently, a greater chance of being solved.

Although people expect the police to dust their homes for fingerprints following a burglary, the unfortunate reality is that such crimes are very rarely solved. When they are, it is often due to the confessions of an offender caught during the commission of another crime. The solution of any particular property crime has been referred to as "a chance event, insensitive to the amount of investigation conducted" (Greenwood 1970, p. 37).

Skogan and Antunes (1979) note that these investigative realities (i.e., Rand Study findings) clearly demonstrate the importance of information to policing. Without adequate information being obtained by the first patrol officer responding to the scene, the likelihood of successful clearance is dramatically reduced. Following the Rand Study, in the 1970s many departments began to alter their perceptions of patrol officers. Training procedures for patrol began to emphasize the importance of gathering all pertinent information at the crime scene. However, Greenwood and Petersilia (1975) point out that the departmental practice of creating long check lists of crime scene data for officers to wade through and record can actually be a hindrance. Too much information can be as bad as too little; the key to collecting information is to only collect that which is likely to be useful in the resolution of the immediate offense. The selection of information is related to "case construction," a factor that can be related to police attitudes. For example, police often emphasize or downplay pieces of information depending on whether it fits with their preconceived ideas about the crime and offender, which can significantly throw off the course of an investigation.

Ultimately, the Rand study showed that, contrary to public perception, the responsibility for resolving crime lies in the hands of the community as much or more than it does with the police. This citizen responsibility is reflected in both the initial reporting of a crime and in providing adequate information about the crime and perpetrator to the responding officers. This is one reason why barriers to police–community communications may have a detrimental effect on the police, even as it relates to such measures as arrest productivity and clearance rates. This is an issue we will return to in Chapters 10 and 12.

Investigating Terror: Models of Counterterrorism

Task forces, which bring together multiple agencies from different jurisdictions to study the same problem, are a very important tool in counterterrorism efforts. Each major jurisdiction in the United States had a counterterrorism task force in place even prior to September 11. For instance, several incidents of violence by the Puerto Rican Armed Forces for National Liberation (FALN) in the late 1970s and early 1980s led to the creation of the New York Terrorism Task Force. This task force combined the efforts of federal, state, and local police departments. The task force successfully investigated and charged key members of FALN involved in the murder of an armored truck driver and two law enforcement officers. The central task post–September 11 is to revitalize such efforts and increase their effectiveness. (See Chapter 5 for more on the logic of task force structures.)

The investigation of terrorism involves all of the same techniques that are used to investigate other crimes; there are no techniques that are specific to terrorism itself (Dyson 2001). Dyson (2001) notes that the key factors of successful terrorism investigation include:

- The task force concept
- The recognition of terrorism as a specialty
- A focus on people committing crimes rather than those exercising their constitutional rights
- The exercise of great care with respect to gathering evidence

Because local law enforcement officers are often the first responders to the scene of a terrorist act, it is essential that they are adequately trained to recognize the incident as being the result of terrorism, are able to understand and deal with the use of possible weapons of mass destruction, and are able to adequately document the crime scene. Problems in identifying the true significance of the 1993 World Trade Center bombing may have contributed to a time delay in successfully resolving the case. Moreover, it was not until much later that connections would be made between this event and the worldwide efforts of the Al Qaeda network (White 2001).

Because of its global nature, terrorism blurs jurisdictional boundaries, even international ones. The NYPD recently deployed officers to Israel to learn first hand how to respond to terrorist activity. NYPD officers now scan newspapers from around the world to learn about global trends and issues, a task previously thought to only be within the domain of the FBI or CIA (Grant 2000). Departments across the country are reexamining their practices, creating specialized counterterrorism units and revising training procedures.

Linkages in Law Enforcement

The Role of Technology in Reducing Linkage Blindness

Many factors in an investigation can contribute to linkage blindness, or the inability to analyze and link critical information across or within an agency. Specific concerns include the many overlapping jurisdictions between and even within organizations that can lead to inadequate communication and coordination. In most cases, linkage blindness occurs when two or more jurisdictions are investigating the same crime from different perspectives but are not sharing information. This inability to "connect the dots" can stop certain crimes from being solved or prevent the linking of incidents to recognize larger problems. For example, the Bridgeport, Connecticut Police Department might have an open murder case that they have been investigating for years. If they ran ballistics tests on spent shell casings found at the scene and then shared this information with the NYPD, they may find that the same weapon had been involved in an assault case in that jurisdiction. The NYPD knows the identity of the weapon's owner. If the Bridgeport department knew this information, they would be able to solve the case. National efforts to reduce linkage blindness through technological advancements have been developed and are constantly evolving.

National Crime Information Center

The **National Crime Information Center (NCIC)** is a national computerized system run by the FBI. It contains items such as a fingerprint database, a list of individuals on supervised release (parole), and a sex offender database. Officers out in the field can call into operators in their department to run checks on stopped individuals for wanted persons, stolen guns, stolen vehicles, and so on (Federal Bureau of Investigation 1999). This would, for example, allow an officer in California to know that a person he or she has pulled over on a highway is wanted for a felony offense in Connecticut, thereby allowing the individual to be arrested and cleared.

Violent Criminal Apprehension Program

In response to fears of serial murders and child kidnappings in the 1980s, the **Violent Criminal Apprehension Program (VICAP)** was created by the FBI to help identify national homicide patterns. VICAP is a comprehensive database of solved and unsolved violent crimes that includes significant details related to the crime scene, victim characteristics, and offender characteristics (when known). In practice, VICAP is meant to draw connections between similar incidents even if they took place in opposite parts of the country. For example, a series of prostitute murders occurring in Seattle, Washington, might be linked to a similar series that had occurred two years previously in New York City. By drawing this connection, the two police departments can now share information they previously would not have, perhaps through the establishment of a joint investigative task force. It may be that each department is holding different pieces of the puzzle, which when put together, can lead to the successful apprehension of the offender. The usefulness of VICAP has been limited, however, by the unwillingness of departments to regularly submit their cases to the FBI.

Drugfire System

Similar in principle to both NCIC and VICAP, Drugfire was a pilot project that established a digital database of shell casings to match guns used in crimes across different jurisdictions. Departments wishing to participate in Drugfire had to first demonstrate a forensic examiner capacity for dealing with firearms (Grant 1996). Recent proposals by some senators, such as Chuck Schumer of New York, seek to have data from all new, legally purchased firearms entered into such a system. In this way, matches would not have to rely on whether or not the gun was used in two separate incidents. A database would have each new gun's "ballistic fingerprint" that could be matched with spent shell casings.

Automated Fingerprint Identification Systems

A significant advance from the days when latent fingerprint matches had to be done by comparing paper cards, **automated fingerprint identification systems (AFISs)** involve the matching of digitized fingerprints found at different crime scenes. The larger the number of jurisdictions that participate in sharing AFIS data, the greater the probability of identifying offenders that operate outside of the boundaries of just one jurisdiction (see Chapter 13 for a more detailed explanation of this technology).

National DNA Identification System

Operated by the FBI, the **National DNA Identification System (NDIS)** is a database that includes the DNA of over 600,000 felons. As with the other systems, NDIS is able to make a computerized match between the DNA profiles of hair, blood, semen, and saliva found at one scene and that found at a different crime scene. If there is a successful "hit" in the database, then a successful identification has been made.

The success of such management information systems greatly depends on the quality and volume of data put into them. Successful mechanisms for sharing and utilizing such systems are key to their success.

Questions

1. What are the strengths of these technologies in eliminating linkage blindness? What are their weaknesses?

2. Which technology could best be adapted to communicate to a patrol officer in a routine traffic stop that the individual in the car is on an FBI terrorist watch list?

3. Should all U.S. citizens be required to submit DNA and fingerprint samples to be stored in AFIS and NDIS systems? Why or why not? What about firearms databases? Should firearms owners be required to submit ballistics samples for a national Drugfire system? What opposition will law enforcement face in implementing such policies?

Challenges of Police–Prosecutor Collaboration

As noted throughout this chapter, the importance of successfully documenting a crime scene and maintaining a sound chain of evidence cannot be underestimated. Failure to do so can lead to the outright dismissal of a case by the time it gets to the prosecutor. The inability of a responding officer to write sound, descriptive reports can play a major role in a detective's decision not to proceed to a follow-up investigation or to waste valuable time reinterviewing witnesses, an effort that more often than not will prove to be futile (Skogan and Attunes 1979).

A lack of communication or collaboration between the prosecutor and police department might also lead to a significant number of dismissals and voided arrests. In such cases, police organizational practice can be affected. For example, if the chief perceives that the district attorney consistently does not prosecute a certain type of crime, he or she may divert enforcement efforts and resources elsewhere (Swanson et al. 2001).

Although the prosecutor is technically the chief law enforcement officer under the statutes of some states, he or she does not have overall responsibility for police supervision. However, close collaboration between the agencies over chain of evidence in an investigation is required. One needs only to look at the problems evidenced in such cases as the O. J. Simpson trial for this point to be driven home. In some jurisdictions, postarrest investigations are handled by the prosecutor's office to avoid tension and conflict. Tensions between the prosecutor and the police can be particularly salient when there are indictments against police for criminal acts such as corruption or brutality. Similar tensions can also arise as a result of judicial practices. For example, sometimes a motion to suppress will be granted by a judge who feels that a particular case should not be prosecuted because it is too minor. These practices may confuse officers, leading them to stop enforcing laws in similar cases in the future (Swanson et al. 2001).

Chapter Summary

- The investigative function evolved from the success of Henry Fielding's Bow Street Runners, who often walked a fine line between developing an underground informant network and actually participating in criminal activities. The Bow Street Runners lasted until Sir Robert Peel created Scotland Yard following the creation of the London Metropolitan Police Force.

- As with patrol, the realities of the investigation function are not as they are portrayed in the media. In fact, according to the Rand study, most clearances result from patrol and victim activities at the scene of the crime.

- Although the patrol officer conducts the preliminary investigation, it is usually up to the detective whether or not to proceed to a follow-up investigation. Detectives will make a decision as to whether or not to investigate further as a result of solvability factors.

- Meticulous detail and a sound chain of evidence are essential to ensure that no contaminants have entered a crime scene, potentially throwing off the credibility of the entire case. The Locard exchange principle recognizes that just as an offender can never leave a crime scene without taking some part of it with him or herself or leaving a part of him or herself behind, a sloppy investigator can destroy or alter physical evidence.

- Criminalistics are used to establish the physical link between victim and offender. In contrast, profiling often relies on behavioral evidence to identify the "type" of offender likely to have committed such an offense.

- Technological advances have played a significant role in reducing linkage blindness, such as AFIS, VICAP, NCIC, and Drugfire.

- Although involving many of the same techniques common to other crimes, terrorism investigations present special challenges, particularly related to the need for information sharing on a global level. The task force model has proven particularly useful for both national and international collaborations related to terrorism.

- Given the importance of chain of evidence concerns in the establishment of guilt in court, police–prosecution collaboration is a necessary (though often difficult) reality. Judicial practice related to the suppression of evidence and the investigation of police corruption both can aggravate existing tensions.

KEY TERMS

Asocial offender   203
Associative evidence   200
Automated fingerprint identification system (AFIS)   207
Behavioral evidence   200
Chain of evidence   199
Circle of investigation   204
Clearance rate   195
Contaminants   196
Crime scenes   197
Criminal profiling   201
Criminalistics   200
Cultural cues   201

Discovery crimes   194
Involvement crimes   194
Kansas City Response Time study   194
Kinesics   200
Locard exchange principle   199
Modus operandi   202
National Crime Information Center (NCIC)   206
National DNA Identification System (NDIS)   207
Nonsocial offender   203
Nonverbal cues   200

Organized–disorganized typology   202
Physical evidence   199
Preliminary investigation   196
Primary scene   198
Psychopath   203
Reconstruction   196
Schizoid personality   204
Secondary scene   198
Signature   202
Solvability factors   197
Thief catcher   193
Violent Criminal Apprehension Program (VICAP)   206

Linking the Dots

1. Explain the importance of the Locard exchange principle as a justification for creating sound investigation policies.

2. What were the key findings of the Rand study? How were these similar to or different from the findings of the Kansas City Preventive Patrol Experiment?

3. What factors might influence an investigator's decision to pursue a follow-up investigation? How might this vary by crime scene? How might this vary based on the investigator's own personal characteristics?

REFERENCES

Bayley, D. 1994. *Police for the Future.* New York, NY: Oxford University Press.

Cassidy, J. 2000. Personal interview by Grant on June 6, 2000.

Douglas, J., and C. Munn. 1992. "Violent Crime Scene Analysis: Modus Operandi, Signature and Staging." *FBI Law Enforcement Bulletin* 61(2):1–10.

Douglas, J., R. Ressler, A. Burgess, and C. Harman. 1985. "Criminal Profiling from Crime Scene Analysis." *Behavioral Sciences and The Law.* 4(3):401–421.

Dyson, W. 2001. *Terrorism: An Investigator's Handbook.* Cincinnati, OH: Lexis Nexis.

Emsley, C. 1996. *The English Police: A Political and Social History.* Harrow: Addison Wesley Longman.

Federal Bureau of Investigation. 1999. *NCIC Operating Manual.* Washington, D.C.: Federal Bureau of Investigation.

Gerberth, V. 1996. *Practical Homicide Investigation: Tactics, Procedures and Forensic Techniques,* 3d ed. Boca Raton, Fl: CRC Press.

Grant, H. 1996. *Evaluation of the Bridgeport Youth Firearms Violence Initiative*. Washington, D.C.: Office of Community Oriented Policing Services.

Greenwood, P. 1970. *An Analysis of the Apprehension Activities of the New York City Police Department*. New York: Rand Institute.

Greenwood, P. W., and J. Petersilia. 1975. *The Criminal Investigative Process*, Vol. 1, *Summary and Policy Implications*. Santa Monica, CA: RAND Corp.

Hazelwood, R. 1987. *Practical Aspects of Rape Investigation: A Multidisciplinary Approach*, 3d ed. Boca Raton, FL: CRC Press.

Holmes, R., and S. Holmes. 1999. *Profiling Violent Crimes*. Thousand Oaks, CA: Sage.

Johnson, H., and N. T. Wolfe. 1996. *History of Criminal Justice,* 2d ed. Cincinnati, OH: Anderson Publishing Company.

Kansas City Police Department. 1983 *Response Time Analysis*. Washington, D.C.: The Police Foundation.

Kenney, D. H., H. Grant, and T. Allan. 2002. *Policing in a Diverse Society*: Washington, D.C.: Bureau of Justice Assistance.

Lee, H., T. Palmback, and M. Miller. 2001. *Henry Lee's Crime Scene Handbook*. San Diego, CA: Academic Press.

NCIC. 2001. *When Law and Culture Collide*. Washington, D.C.: NCPC.

Osterburg, J. W., and R. H. Ward. 1997. *Criminal Investigation: A Method for Reconstructing the Past,* 2d ed. Cincinnati, OH: Anderson Publishing Company.

Rossmo, K. 2000. *Geographic Profiling*. Boca Raton, FL: CRC Press.

Saferstein, C. 1995. *Criminalistics*. Englewood Cliffs, N.J.: Simon and Schuster.

Skogan, W., and G. Attunes. 1979. "Information, Apprehension, and Deterrence: Exploring the Limits of Police Productivity." *Journal of Criminal Justice* 7(3): 217–241.

Swanson, C., L. Territo, and R. Taylor. 2001. *Police Administration: Structures, Processes, and Behavior*. 5th ed. Upper Saddle River, NJ: Prentice-Hall.

Turvey, B. 2001. *Criminal Profiling: An Introduction to Behavioral Evidence Analysis*. San Diego: Academic Press.

White, J. 2001. *Terrorism,* 3d ed. Belmont, CA: Wadsworth.

Wrobleski, H. M., and K. Hess. 2002. *Introduction to Law Enforcement and Criminal Justice*. St. Paul, MN: West Publishing.

Chapter 9

Police Discretion and Behavior

Chapter Outline

Chapter Objectives

- Understand what the term police discretion means.

- Identify and examine the factors that influence police decision making and the exercise of discretion.

- Examine different theories of police behavior and address the question of whether there is such a thing as a "police personality."

- Become familiar with Wilson's three styles of policing and explore the relationship between police organization and the behavior of individual officers.

- Examine the causes of police stress and police suicide.

Maria Teresa Macias lived in fear. After separating from her husband, she continued to be terrorized and abused by him as a result of repeated stalking and harassment, despite her having successfully obtained a restraining order against him. On April 15, 1996, the abuse finally ended when her husband showed up at her home for the last time, ultimately shooting and killing her. Above and beyond the disturbing facts related to the steady progression of violence found in this and many other domestic violence cases, what raises even more questions is the fact that in the year and a half leading up to her death, Maria Macias had contacted the Sonoma County Sheriff's Department on more than twenty-two occasions for help in dealing with her husband, including making them aware of his repeated threats to kill her. According to expert testimony "the Sheriff's Department brushed Teresa off at every turn" (Women's Justice Center n.d.).[1]

Despite the husband's known violent history, and the escalating seriousness and fear on the part of Maria Macias, the sheriff did not come to her aid. Expert testimony in the $15 million federal civil rights wrongful death lawsuit filed by the Macias family claimed that the failure of the sheriff's office to respond, and in many incidents properly investigate the seriousness of the occurrences, contributed to the escalation of violence because the suspect was sent the message that he could continue his actions and that Macias' life was expendable. Sergeant Anne O'Dell testified that "long gone are the days when the criminal justice system has to speculate on how and why people are murdered" (Women's Justice Center n.d.). Domestic violence homicide is preventable. O'Dell went on to cite that in jurisdictions where responding officers do not have complete discretion to treat domestic incidents as "family affairs," formerly common practice in law enforcement, domestic violence homicides have decreased by more than 50 to 60 percent (Women's Justice Center n.d.).

In the case of domestic violence, then, practices to reduce the amount of officer discretion involved might appear to make sense. However, in reality, discretion can never completely be eliminated from policing given the complex realities of policing, just as it will always play a central role within the courts and correctional agencies across this country as well. Even with domestic violence, the answer is not always as simple as implementing **mandatory arrest policies** to eliminate officer discretion. Studies such as the **Minneapolis Domestic Violence Experiment** have pointed to a more cautious interpretation of mandatory arrest policies; such arrests might decrease the escalating violence of those males who have a lot to lose by criminal justice attention, such as the employed or political figures in a community. For others, however, such a practice can lead to further anger, and ultimately, aggression (Worthington 1991).

The good news in the case of Maria Macias is ultimately its legacy. After an initial dismissal of the case by the Ninth District Court judge on grounds that there was not a "direct causal link" be-tween the murder and the response of the sheriff's department, the U.S. Ninth Circuit Court of Appeals ruled to reverse the dismissal, finding that women have a constitutional right to nondiscriminatory protection. Although not eliminating the complexities of officer discretion in domestic violence altogether, even with mandatory arrest policies, the Macias case evidences that "proper care" in such cases on the part of law enforcement will be a standard for jurisdictions to follow in the future.

The Role of Discretion in Policing

Along with the right to use force, one of the defining characteristics of policing as a profession is the amount of discretion given to individual officers, which was introduced in Chapter 1. Although the organizational structure of most police departments follows a traditional bureaucratic model—with power concentrated at the top of a hierarchical pyramid and clear lines of accountability running up from the base—police organizations differ from many other public institutions in that low-ranking individuals are given considerable decision-making power, much of which is unsupervised. Although senior police management makes decisions about police strategy, departmental policy, and the allocation of police resources, the great majority of day-to-day policing decisions are in fact made by ordinary officers. These police officers decide who to stop, who to question, and who to arrest, as well as how best to deal with public concerns and complaints.

In this sense, the formal organization of traditionally oriented police departments offer support for the Iron Law of Oligarchy proposed by Michels (1966). The **Iron Law of Oligarchy** suggests that the formal organization of bureaucracies inevitably leads to oligarchy, in which even organizations that were originally proposed to be based upon democratically oriented philosophies eventually come to be dominated by a small, self-serving group of people who have achieved positions of power. Over time, this group will become more distant from the needs and realities of the rank and file. The depersonalizing effect of police bureaucracies has often been cited as a major contributing factor to the development and maintenance of a distinct police subculture.

Because so much power is concentrated in the hands of individual officers, no matter how rigid the formal bureaucracy of a department, how and why police officers exercise their discretion continues to be of great interest to policy makers, researchers, and the media. Studying police discretion is, however, problematic. Many important police decisions are made on the job and on the street and, as a consequence, are not open to easy scrutiny. For example, although police departments record all of the arrests made by their officers, they rarely, if ever, keep track of police–public interactions that do not lead to an arrest or some other type of formal response. Although this is changing significantly with concerns over racial profiling, police officers do not inform their superiors every time they decide to let a speeding motorist off with a warning or choose to overlook some minor incident of public disorder or illegality. For this reason, criminologists and sociologists interested in police discretion have tended to concentrate their efforts on identifying those factors most likely to influence the exercise of police discretion, especially as it relates to the power of arrest and the use of force.

Defining Police Discretion

Although a number of writers have attempted to define police discretion, one of the most widely accepted definitions is that used by Kenneth Culp Davis in his book *Discretionary Justice* (1969).[2] According to Davis:

> A police officer or police agency may be said to exercise discretion whenever effective limits on his, or her, or its power leave the officer or agency free to make choices among possible courses of action or inaction. (p. 4)

Put another way, a police officer is said to have discretion when he or she has a choice over how to respond to a specific problem or situation.[3] In the majority of cases, officer discretion is expressly provided for by the law or by police procedure. For example, although New York City police officers are given the power to arrest citizens for jaywalking by the city's traffic rules and regulations, they are not required by the statute to make an arrest in every case.[4] As a consequence, the officer can exercise his or her discretion when dealing with a pedestrian who has broken the law and choose whether to arrest that individual or issue a warning or some other verbal reprimand. In other cases, police discretion exists because the law does not expressly cover the situation facing the officer. As Bittner (1990) notes in his famous article on the function of the police, officers frequently find themselves in the role of society's problem solvers of last resort, called in to deal with situations that "ought not to be happening and about which someone had better do something now!" (p. 249).[4]

Discretion is regarded as an essential aspect of policing because individual police officers are required to deal with a vast range of different problems and situations, many of which are not precisely regulated by the law. Indeed, so important is the exercise of discretion to police work that it is hard to imagine what policing would be like without it. In a world in which individual police officers had no discretion, every type of possible police–public interaction would have to be governed by clear policies, guidelines, and rules, which the officer would then be required to follow precisely and without deviation. Police officers would walk the streets with a book of laws and rules that they would enforce without exception, irrespective of their own personal judgments or feelings. This is hardly a model of policing that many would regard as either realistic or desirable.

Although such extreme examples help to highlight the importance and necessity of discretion, there are situations in which "nondiscretionary" policing tactics are employed in the real world. **Zero tolerance policing**, for example, is often used by the police as a means of combating certain forms of minor crime, such as urinating in public, aggressive begging, and fare dodging. When zero-tolerance policies are in effect, police officers are required to stop anyone they see committing such offenses and have little or no discretion as to whether to make an arrest. According to advocates of zero-tolerance policing, limiting or removing police discretion in this way is justified because strict enforcement of the law sends a powerful deterrent message to potential offenders and increases public confidence in the police (Kelling and Coles 1996; Greene 1999; Bratton 1996). Critics, however, argue that such policies rarely have a lasting effect on crime rates and can cause considerable harm to fragile police–public relations (Harcourt 1998).[5] Ironically perhaps, critics argue that it is the existence of police discretion that protects the public from abuse and helps to ensure that the police respect the rights of citizens.

Factors Affecting the Exercise of Officer Discretion

Over the past fifty years, a large number of studies have examined police decision making and have attempted to identify factors that influence the exercise of officer discretion (see, for example, Reiss 1968; Black 1971; Davis 1975; Klinger 1995; Worden 1995). Broadly speaking, these factors can be grouped as follows (see Figure 9.1).

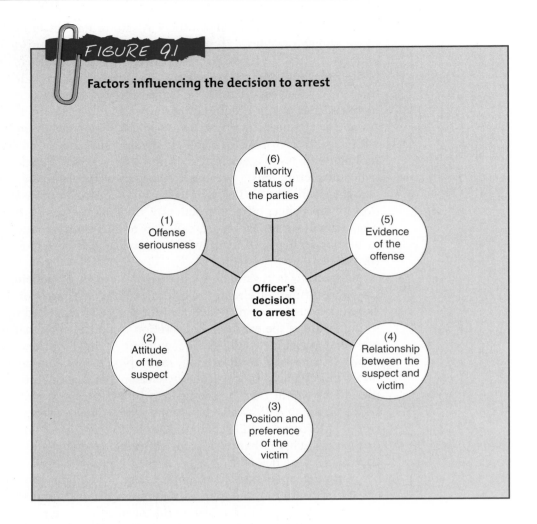

FIGURE 9.1

Factors influencing the decision to arrest

Seriousness of the Offense According to research undertaken by Black (1971) in the late 1960s and early 1970s, one of the most important factors that police officers take into consideration when deciding whether or not to arrest a suspect is the seriousness of the alleged offense.[6] As might be expected, the police are far more likely to arrest an individual they believe to have committed a major crime, such as assault or robbery, than one who has committed a relatively minor offense, such as ignoring parking regulations or littering. In Black's study, for example, the police chose to arrest a suspect in 58 percent of all felony cases, as opposed to only 44 percent of all misdemeanors (Black 1971).[7] More recent statistics on arrest rates also appear to bear out this basic relationship. As Roberg et al. (2000) observe, approximately half of all violent crimes result in an arrest, as compared with only less than a quarter of all property offenses. Other factors related to offense seriousness that may influence an officer's decision making include the use or presence of weapons and the type of property concerned (when the offense is property related).

There are, of course, obvious reasons for why the seriousness of an offense influences an officer's decision making. Given that one of the primary aims of the police is to maintain order and promote public safety, in cases of serious crime arrest is one way that the police can incapacitate a suspect and ensure that he or she does not have an opportunity to reoffend. In addition, from the perspective of both the police and the public, arresting those suspected of committing serious crimes is far more important than apprehending those responsible for minor offenses and misdemeanors. Yet there are, however, other reasons why serious offenses are more likely to lead to an arrest. Many instances of violent crime, for example, involve an identifiable victim who can serve as both a complainant and a witness to the offense, increasing the likelihood that arrest will lead to prosecution and eventually conviction of the suspect. Furthermore, as Black and others have observed, the decision to arrest is frequently based on questions of probable cause, which is generally easier for an officer to establish in the case of a serious crime (Black 1980).

Attitude of the Suspect

How a suspect reacts to being stopped and questioned by the police can also have a significant effect on an officer's decision to arrest, particularly if the suspect appears aggressive or disrespectful. As Black (1971) notes, "disrespect in a police encounter is much the same as 'contempt' in a courtroom hearing" (p. 1092) in that it represents a challenge to the position and authority of the police officer. Just like a judge in the courtroom, the police need to maintain the public's respect in order to do their job, and as a result, they can be expected to vigorously defend that authority when threatened. Some authors have referred to a disrespectful attitude as **contempt of cop (COC)**.

Studies of police discretion have also found that the demeanor of the suspect is an important factor in an officer's decision to use force. Research by Reiss (1968) in the late 1960s found, for example, that police officers were far more likely to use physical force against suspects who they felt had not shown the proper amount of respect to them either as individuals or to the police in general. Similarly, a later study by Worden (1995) suggested that disrespect was a key factor in the decision to use force, as was the perception that the suspect was being uncooperative or was attempting to resist arrest. The conclusions drawn by both Reiss and Worden, have, however, been the subject of some debate. According to Klinger (1994), for example, in many cases disrespect and friction between the police and the suspect emerges after the arrest has taken place, and as a result, such behavior cannot be said to have influenced the initial decision to arrest. However, later studies have found the opposite: that disrespect is not a key predictor of behavior with respect to force (Terril and Mastrofski 2002).

Characteristics, Position, and Preference of the Victim

Although offense seriousness and suspect demeanor appear to play an important part in the decision to arrest, research has also shown that the characteristics of the victim may also be significant. In a study of police attitudes towards rape victims, for example, LaFree (1989) found evidence to suggest that officers may be less likely to arrest a suspected offender when they disapprove of the victim or her lifestyle in some way. Furthermore, when the victim of a crime does not want the suspect to be arrested, the police are likely to take this into account, particularly if the victim is the sole witness to the crime. Of course, many studies have demonstrated that the presence of a witness (or willingness to report of a witness) is a key factor influencing discretionary decisions to pursue an allegation or incident (Black 1971; Greenwood and Petersilia 1975). Officers are far more likely to arrest or cite the offender if there are witnesses present.

Given the many complexities inherent to police work, officer decision making on the street can be influenced by numerous factors that are often difficult to control through departmental hierarchy, policy, or training strategies. Ultimately, discretion will remain a core force in police work.

Relationship Between the Suspect and the Victim

Another factor that can have an effect on a police officer's decision to arrest is the relationship between the suspect and the victim. In situations in which the parties are close—for example, where the suspect and victim are husband and wife—the officer may feel that there is little chance that the victim will be willing to testify against the suspect in court, and as such, an arrest is unlikely to lead to a conviction (Enstermaker, Berk and Loeske 1980–1981).[8] In such cases, the officer may choose to regard the incident as a "private matter" and simply decide to issue the suspect a warning (Black 1971). Mandatory arrest policies target just such discretionary factors. There are also a number of other reasons why an officer may choose not to arrest when the relationship between the suspect and complainant is close, namely:

- When the officer believes that the complainant does not actually want the suspect arrested, but merely wants to "teach them a lesson" by calling in the police

- In suspected cases of domestic violence, where there is a strong possibility that the suspect may reoffend as a way of punishing the victim for making the complaint

- When an arrest would deprive a family of it's major income earner ("breadwinner")

Evidence of the Offense

According to work by Black and others, police officers are more likely to arrest a suspect when there is clear evidence of wrongdoing. In cases in which there is little or no physical evidence or when the only evidence available to the police is the testimony of the complainant or victim, the officer must decide whether there is enough evidence for there to be a reasonable chance of conviction if the case ends up going to court (Black 1971).

The Race and Gender of the Parties to the Offense

Of all the factors that can influence an officer's decision to arrest, questions of race and gender are by far the most controversial. Based on studies of racial profiling and the impact of race on police decision making, many criminologists and police researchers now believe that a suspect's race is an important factor in the decision to arrest. Although Black did not find any clear evidence of racial discrimination in his study of police discretion, subsequent work by Maurer (1993), Kappeler et al. (1994), and Chambliss (1997) indicate that African American suspects are not only more likely to be stopped and arrested than whites, but that they are also more likely to be subjected to police use of force. In efforts to explain these findings, some criminologists (Worden 1995) have suggested that this difference in treatment may not simply be a product of police racism, but rather a consequence of poor police–minority relations or miscommunication between white officers and African American suspects. It is also worth noting that although there may be a broad consensus regarding the existence of racial profiling and gender bias, there is, however, considerable disagreement over the relative importance that police officers attach to race when making the decision to arrest. Is, for example, a suspect's race more important than the suspect's attitude or the seriousness of the alleged offense? Are officers more likely to take a victim's complaint if the victim is a member of an ethnic or racial majority? To what extent does race outweigh or "trump" other considerations?

In contrast to the issue of race, few studies have been conducted on the impact of a suspect's or victim's gender on the decision to arrest. One widely held belief is that male police officers are generally more lenient when it comes to dealing with women and have a tendency to act out of a sense of "chivalry" when dealing with female victims or complainants. Research by Visher (1983) suggests that the level of chivalry extended depends largely on whether the woman's appearance, demeanor, and behavior conforms to the male officer's traditional gender stereotypes and conception of how a woman "ought to behave." In those cases in which the woman does not conform to that ideal image, they may in fact be treated more severely than a man on the basis that they are "doubly deviant"; that is, they offend both the law and the officer's idea of what constitutes normal female behavior. Although many police departments in the United States continue to be dominated by men, what evidence there is appears to suggest that women are no more (or less) likely to be stopped or arrested by the police than men (Martin 1980).[9] Perhaps the one exception to this general finding is with regards to traffic violations. According to a study undertaken by Kappeler et al. (1994), attractive young women are more likely to be stopped for traffic offenses by male police officers than men, in many cases simply because the male officer is looking to initiate personal contact with the female driver in question.[10]

According to early studies by LaFave (1965) and Davis (1969), there are a number of additional reasons why police officers choose not to arrest. In many cases, a police officer will not arrest a suspected offender either because the officer believes that the legislature did not intend the law in question to be enforced in all cases or because the officer feels that the general community would not be in favor of the arrest. As both LaFave and Davis observed, laws that officers feel are out of date, ambiguous, or overly harsh are often not enforced, particularly if those laws deal with questions of community standards or "victimless crimes." Similarly, because the police are aware of the need to maintain good relations with the public, where strict enforcement of an unpopular law may lead to serious conflict with the community, the police may choose to use less-formal means of discouraging the unlawful behavior. In addition, police officers may choose not to enforce a certain law because it would mean drawing time and resources away from other more important tasks. The police cannot arrest every person who breaks a law, and as a result, they have to make choices about which laws they enforce and under what circumstances. Time spent arresting jaywalkers could, for example, be spent preventing or investigating more serious crimes such as assaults and burglaries.

Finally, research has suggested that many individual factors also affect the exercise of police discretion. According to a number of studies, female officers tend to be less aggressive when dealing with suspects than their male counterparts, particularly when it comes to the use of force (Martin 1990; Grennan 1988). Some of this difference has been attributed to the higher tendency of female officers to use more-developed mediation skills in tense situations, as compared with their male counterparts. In contrast, evidence indicates that African American officers are stricter when dealing with the African American community than they are with other racial and ethnic groups and are more likely to arrest African American suspects than whites or Hispanics (Brooks 1989).

The devalued status of minority groups has also historically been said to influence police decision making, as will be discussed further in Chapter 10. Depending on the degree of tolerance of the responding officer, he or she may have difficulties dealing with members of the gay, lesbian, bisexual, or transgendered community (GLBT). One particularly disturbing example of such differential treatment is how two officers responded to a bleeding, disoriented Laotian boy on the streets of Milwaukee after receiving a call from a disturbed neighborhood resident. After learning that the fifteen-year-old boy was gay, the officers dismissed the incident as a "lover's quarrel" and returned him to the apartment of Jeffery Dahmer, now widely known as a depraved serial killer. The taped communications of the two responding officers revealed horrible references to needing to "delouse" following contact with the "gay couple."

The Importance of Police Behavior

Since the early 1960s, researchers in the United States have become increasingly interested in police behavior and the possibility that there may be a distinct "police personality." According to a number of prominent sociologists and criminologists—such as Neiderhoffer (1969), Skolnick (1966), and Goldstein (1968)—it is possible to identify certain core beliefs, values, and behavioral traits that are common to many police officers and that help to explain how individual officers exercise their discretion, how they deal with members of the public, and how police organizations function. Many studies argue the existence of a police subculture with its own characteristics, such as cynicism, authoritarianism, and suspiciousness of the general public, and suggest that these traits often affect the way in which the police deal with particular groups, such as women and racial minorities (Leftkowitz 1973; 1975).

In their efforts to explain how the police personality and subculture develops and why certain beliefs are more prevalent than others, researchers have tended to favor one of four main explanations. Broadly speaking, these theories can be summarized as follows:

- *Psychological theories* argue that core attitudes are formed *before* the individual enters the police force and are a function of such things as family background, social status, and prior education.

- *Educational theories* argue that core attitudes are acquired during police training and early years on the street and are usually passed on to recruits by older, more experienced police officers.

- *Sociological theories* argue that police attitudes are shaped by the daily demands of police work and reflect the "working culture" of policing.

- *Organizational theories* argue that police attitudes and values are shaped by the organizational and working culture of policing and the demands placed on officers by their police colleagues.

Before moving into a discussion of these theories, however, it is important to note that the idea of the "police personality" or subculture remains an extremely controversial one. Many of the key studies in this area were conducted during the 1960s and 1970s, and as a result, their relevance to policing today must be questioned. Although most criminologists and sociologists appear to accept that the police are indeed more conservative than the average citizen, many remain unconvinced that the police are necessarily more authoritarian or more prone to racism and sexism (Worden 1995).

Psychological Explanations: Predisposition and Police Behavior—Police Personality or Culture?

As noted by Bonifactio (1991), most predispositional theories focus on exploring the reasons why people join the police and whether there is a particular **police personality** pattern common to police applicants that distinguish them from members of the general public. In an effort to identify these patterns, a number of researchers have looked at the reasons why people join the police and have asked whether there is some link between the motivation to join and certain key personality traits. For example, various studies have suggested that most people who apply to become police officers do so either because they want to help society or because they want a job that will offer challenges and excitement (Lester 1983). According to work by Reiser (1973), Arcuri (1976), Lester (1983), and Stratton et al. (1984), such individuals tend to see themselves as "brave" and "powerful" and are both more conservative and **authoritarian** in their thinking than the average person. In addition, it has also been argued that because many police recruits are drawn from traditional working-class backgrounds, they are naturally more inclined towards conservative attitudes. However, Bayley and Mendelson (1969) found that working-class recruits were no more or less authoritarian than recruits drawn from other social backgrounds.

The emerging consensus in the literature is that career socialization is a stronger influence on police behavior than preexisting differences in temperament (Wiederhoffer 1969; Worden 1995). However, famed police personality researcher Lefkowitz (1975) found that although police do not differ from other groups in terms of psychological disorders or intelligence, a constellation of traits/attitudes does emerge with officers, such as authoritarianism, suspiciousness, conservatism, loyalty, secretiveness, physical courage, and self-assertiveness. These traits are more likely influenced by a strong **police subculture** than by a predisposed personality type. For example, one of the key elements stressed in police subculture literature is the sense of mission felt by police that corresponds with each of the cluster traits noted by Lefkowitz. This sense of mission is characterized by the perception that the police are a **thin blue line** between anarchy and order in a society (Reiner 1992). The peer solidarity and loyalty so often noted in the literature are also seen as outcomes of this sense of mission and the type of work that police do (Waddington 1999).

Chan (1997) argues that the majority of the academic literature related to police culture is too simplistic. Instead, she argues that police culture is the result of history and learned dispositions (socialization) that mold the police officer's sense of what constitutes suspicious activities, and thus police work itself. These sociological processes have been categorized within educational, sociological, and organizational domains depending on the background of the researcher.

Educational Explanations: Police Recruits and the Effects of Police Training

According to traditional educational theories of police personality, the character traits typically observed in serving police officers are the direct result of the process of police training and early experiences on the job. Perhaps the most well-known and influential advocate of this explanation of police attitudes is Arthur Niederhoffer. In a study that attempted to measure levels of job satisfaction and cynicism among recruits and serving police officers, Niederhoffer (1963) found that after less than three months, levels of cynicism among serving recruits rose dramatically. For example, in Niederhoffer's study, nearly half of all first-day recruits polled believed that the average police superior was "very interested in the welfare of his subordinates." Two months later, the number of recruits who still believed this to be true had fallen to just 13 percent. Similarly, nearly 80 percent of first-day recruits believed that their department was an "efficient, smoothly operating organization." Two months later, less than a third of experienced recruits held that same opinion. Lastly, nearly three-quarters of all new recruits questioned believed that police training does "a very fine job of preparing the recruit for life in the precinct." Two months later, less than a quarter of the experienced recruits believed that was the case.[11] It is important to note that such cynicism may be the result of psychological shielding against the realities faced by officers on a regular basis.

Based on these results, Niederhoffer concluded that the quasi-military style of police training caused police recruits to become cynical about themselves, others, and the department they were joining. A parallel study undertaken later by Van Maanen (1997) returned similar results. For his study, Van Maanen sought to determine how much a recruit's feelings about a department changed during the course of the police training process. To test this, Van Maanen developed a questionnaire to measure the motivational level and organizational commitment of recruits. Note that Van Maanen also did participant observation, thus lending greater weight to his final results. According to Van Maanen, as recruits' careers progressed, there were significant changes in attitudes and beliefs. Recruit motivation declined significantly, as did organizational commitment.

In summary, these studies suggest that the person who completes police training is clearly different from the person who begins it. At the outset of the training experience, the recruit identity is eagerly embraced. A few months later, however, the typical recruit is disenchanted with the recruit role and the department. In light of the changes that have taken place in police training practices since the 1960s and 1970s, however, these findings need to be treated with caution.

Sociological Explanations: Skolnick's "Working Personality"

In contrast to the approach taken by Neiderhoffer and others, some sociologists, most notably Jerome Skolnick and William Westley, have sought to explain various aspects of police behavior in terms of the relationship between individual officers and the police organization. One of the most influential writers on the subject of police personality, Skolnick published his first book, *Justice Without Trial* (1966), at the height of the Civil Rights movement, a time when the public was becoming increasingly concerned about racial bias in law enforcement and the problem of police brutality. Having examined the subculture of policing and police deception in his book, Skolnick came to the conclusion that the ways in which police officers view the world fit into a distinct occupational category and that it was possible to identify a number of elements that combine to form a police officer's "working personality," most notably danger and authority.

According to Skolnick (1966), because police officers are constantly faced with dangerous, sometimes life-threatening, situations, many officers tend to become suspicious when dealing with members of the public. Taught to regard civilians as potential offenders or even as threats to their personal safety, officers have difficulty trusting anyone other than their police colleagues or forming friendships with people outside of their department. In addition, because they exercise considerable power and authority over the civilian population, the police also tend to be regarded by the public as outsiders, with the result that officers also feel isolated from the general community. These two factors—danger and authority—lead many police officers to conclude that the only way for the police to protect themselves from the outside world is to be loyal to one's fellow officers, even if this means lying or covering up acts of police misconduct.

Drawing on this account of the police **working personality**, Skolnick argues that police behavior and many undesirable police practices can be explained by the emphasis on solidarity within police culture. From the officer's perspective, lying to protect another officer is seen as acceptable, even if this means deliberately deceiving one's superiors or police investigators (Skolnick 2000). As Skolnick (2000) notes in a recent article, new police officers quickly learn to back up their fellow officers when dealing with the authorities and expect to be backed up in return. Equally, officers who do not support their fellow officers are regarded as "rats" who are not to be trusted and deserve to be excluded from the group.

Although Skolnick's work has had an enormous influence on thinking about the police and police working culture over the past thirty years, he does have his critics. In 1967, for example, the criminologist David Bordua (1967) argued in a review of *Justice Without Trial* that Skolnick's account of police behavior was somewhat misleading and overly negative. While agreeing with many of Skolnick's conclusions, according to Bordua, Skolnick's concern with the police work ethic leads Skolnick to understate the positive effect that professionalism has had on police efficiency and formal legality. On a similar note, the John Birch Society has continued to argue since the 1960s that it is important to recognize that the same subculture that Skolnick sees as the source of police deception and brutality also provides individual officers with the support they need to do their job effectively and with confidence (Grant 1995).

Organizational Explanations: Wilson's Three Styles of Policing

In addition to these various sociological and psychological theories of individual officer behavior, attempts have also been made to explain police attitudes in terms of the history of the policing function and changes in the organization of policing in the United States. By the beginning of the 1960s, most theories of police management focused primarily on the importance of bureaucracy, hierarchy, and authoritarianism.[12] According to this view, the police were almost exclusively concerned with the tasks of law enforcement and crime control, a fact reflected in the militaristic organization of police departments and the strict emphasis placed on formal chains of command. In the 1970s, however, this view of policing began to give way to new theories of police organization. These theories—sometimes referred to as behavioral management theories—emphasized the importance of looking at what police officers actually do and acknowledging just how complex the modern police department had become. Research during the 1960s had revealed, for example, that less than 20 percent of police time was devoted to law enforcement; police officers were more likely to spend their days engaged in community service activities than arresting criminals or preventing crimes (Cumming et al. 1965; Goldstein 1968; Bercall 1970). Furthermore, researchers observed that while many police departments were organized along similar lines, they often adopted very different approaches to basic policing problems and their relationship with the public (Wilson 1978). These findings prompted a number of police researchers—most notably the American criminologist J. Q. Wilson (1978)—to reexamine existing ideas about the police function, to develop new theories about how police organizations worked, and to look for new explanations of individual officer behavior.

According to Wilson (1978), all police departments were faced with two fundamental but different types of problems: problems of law enforcement and problems of order maintenance. Law enforcement problems typically involved illegal conduct that could lead to an arrest (such as a felony), whereas order maintenance problems involved less serious behavior that in many cases could be dealt with informally by the police. Based on a study of eight police departments, Wilson concluded that police organizations could be divided into one of three basic categories depending on how they approached these problems: the watchman style; the legalistic style; and the service style (see Table 9.1). The key features of each of these policing styles follow.

TABLE 9.1

Key Features of Wilson's Typology of Policing

Watchman Style	Legalistic Style	Service Style
Policing as order maintenance	Policing as law enforcement	Policing as public service
Few policies and procedures	Emphasis on legal rules	Emphasis on community relations
Individual approach to problems	Formal resolution of problems	Informal resolution of problems
Emphasis on "curbside" justice	Commitment to professionalism	Commitment to public service

Source: Wilson, J. Q. 1978. *Varieties of Police Behavior*. Cambridge, MA: Harvard University Press, p. 33.

The Watchman Style   Based primarily on the use of the uniformed police patrol, the **watchman style** places great emphasis on order maintenance and individual officer discretion. Because most policing activity takes place on the street, officers are less concerned with law enforcement than keeping the peace in their patrol areas, with the result that minor infractions of the law are generally overlooked. According to Lundman (1980), for example, one of the defining characteristics of the watchman style of policing is the tendency of officers to "avoid trouble" and to rely on informal, nonlegalistic means of resolving conflicts. Police departments adopting this style rarely engage in research or systematic planning and tend to suffer from problems of discriminatory arrests and corruption because there are few effective restraints on the activities of individual officers.

The Legalistic Style   The **legalistic style** of policing emphasizes the importance of law enforcement and the maintenance of clear and impartial legal standards for both the police and public alike. Police departments organized along legalistic lines tend to be bureaucratic, use performance indicators as a means of promoting professional standards, and place considerable importance on research and planning. In addition, individual officers are less inclined to exercise curbside discretion, preferring instead to refer to the law and make arrests. Corruption—at least at the operational level—is far less pervasive and discrimination less institutionalized than under the watchman model. Looked at historically, the legalistic style of policing replaced the watchman approach as the police became more professional, more technologically advanced, and more proactive.

The Service Style   According to Wilson's typology, the **service style** of policing sees the police primarily as servants of the community. Although law enforcement and order maintenance remain priorities, particular emphasis is placed on maintaining good police–public relations and on the use of informal policing methods aimed at keeping offenders out of the criminal justice system. As a consequence, service-style departments tend to favor strategies that are proactive and heavily oriented towards crime prevention, with individual officers preferring to avoid reference to the law when dealing with the public. As Lundman (1980) has observed, service-style police departments are most likely to be found in affluent, middle-class communities.[13]

By dividing police organizations according to this typology, Wilson was able to explain the differences he observed in terms of both police functions and in-

The style of policing exhibited by a department can be seen as a reflection of the history of the police function in society, moving from watchman to legalistic to service style models. What will be the dominant model post-911?

dividual officer behavior. In addition, one of the great strengths of Wilson's approach was that he did not abandon previous theories of police organization, but instead argued that the "legalistic model" favored by many departments in the 1960s and early 1970s was better understood as a stage in the overall development of policing. Although elements of all three styles can be found in most police departments, according to Wilson, as society becomes more complex and begins to demand more of its police, police organizations tend to go through stages of evolution, moving more towards the service-style model.

Reconciling the Theories

Attempting to account for and explain why police officers appear to share certain values and personality traits, criminologists, sociologists, and psychologists have approached the subject of police personality from a variety of angles. Clearly, the reality is that all of the factors and influences identified in this section play a part in shaping how police officers think, behave, and exercise their discretion. One thing that is apparent from this discussion is that there is a pressing need for more work to be done in this area and for many of the seminal studies, such as those by Niederhoffer and Skolnick, to be updated to account for the very real changes that have taken place in policing over the past thirty years.

Police Stress

In addition to being interested in how police officers behave, police researchers have also devoted considerable time to looking at how individual officers are affected by the demands of police work and how police officers deal with stress. It is generally accepted by the public that policing is one of the most stressful occupations in contemporary society. Many police officers deal with potentially dangerous situations on a daily basis and are required to handle a wide range of different and challenging tasks as a matter of routine. Furthermore, because they occupy a unique position in relation to the public they exist to serve and protect, the police are required to maintain high standards and are frequently subjected to intense scrutiny and criticism from the media and the public at large.

Although police work is clearly extremely stressful, recent research in the United States and overseas has suggested that policing may not be the most stressful profession. According to a study conducted by Pendleton (1983) in the 1980s, although police work can be extremely stressful, members of many other occupations—including emergency medical personnel and correctional service officers—face stress levels at least equal to and in many cases in excess of those confronting police officers (Patterson 1992). Regardless of whether policing is any more or less stressful than other forms of work, however, officer stress and its consequences for the health and well-being of individual officers is a serious problem for many police departments across the country.

Sources of Police Stress

Police officers experience stress for a variety of reasons.[14] There are two categories of occupational stress: **eustress** (stress that is normal and good, even providing on-the-job motivation) and **dis-stress** (stress that is outside of the normal range and very harmful over time). Often referred to as stressors, the causes of police stress can be broadly categorized according to the source of the stress, that is, whether the cause is produced by the police organization itself or by the on-the-job pressures of actual police work.

Internal and External Organizational Stressors   These are stress factors that stem either from the relationship between the individual police officer and his or her department (**internal stressors**) or from outside pressures placed on the police as a group by the criminal justice system or the community at large (**external stressors**). The following are common internal and external stressors:

External Stressors

- Lack of interagency cooperation or community support
- Ineffective criminal justice system
- Overly lenient courts
- Political interference in police policy and decision making
- Overly critical media coverage of police actions
- Poor police–minority relations

Internal Stressors

- Overly tough supervision
- Absence of promotional opportunities
- Troublesome or offensive internal policies and procedures
- Excessive paperwork
- Poor or substandard equipment

Linkages in Law Enforcement

Post-Traumatic Stress Disorder Following Response to Stress—Law Enforcement and Other Emergency Workers

Although police work often involves its share of mundane activities, such as report writing or having to respond to minor disputes, there can be no question that the job always holds the threat of difficult and dangerous situations. In addition to the often insular nature of the profession (Blau 1994), many officers often feel alone when they have to work in a "thankless" environment for a community that does not support their efforts. Moreover, police often have to see the very worst in people or communities, more often responding to the violent or disturbed elements of a community than having a chance to meaningfully interact with those that are truly supportive.

In the course of their duties, patrol officers may have to confront highly disturbing or stressful situations, such as responding to a particularly gruesome accident, taking testimony from a sexually abused child, or having had their own personal encounter with serious injury. In situations where officers have had to use lethal force, the months afterwards can be filled with sorrow and the second-guessing of one's own actions. The response of police officers, firefighters, and other emergency workers to the horrific events of domestic and international terrorism evidenced in the Oklahoma City Bombing and the September 11 attacks demonstrates both the courage of those in these professions as well as the gravity of the situations they can be called upon to face in the course of their duties.

Post-Traumatic Stress Disorder

In some cases, traumatic incidents can lead to the development of **post-traumatic stress disorder (PTSD)** in law enforcement or other emergency personnel. The diagnostic criteria for PTSD are the following (American Psychological Association 1994):

- The person experiences a traumatic event that involved the actual or threatened death or injury to self or others.

- The traumatic event is persistently re-experienced through recurrent and intrusive recollections or dreams, acting or feeling as though the event were reoccurring.

- Intense psychological distress and physiological reactivity upon exposure to internal or external cues resembling an aspect of the traumatic event.

In some cases, officers may break down under the cumulative weight of numerous stressors rather than a single traumatic event. Officers develop numerous coping mechanisms for dealing with these stressors, including the isolation of feelings, use of seemingly callous humor, and the shutting off of the outside world. These coping mechanisms are characteristic of the insular police subculture (Blau 1994). In many cases, however, these coping and defense mechanisms are not enough, and the affected officer may require more formal intervention services. Some of these interventions might consist of a day-long workshop; some officers may require more intensive interventions.

Strategies for Dealing with PTSD

To avoid the possible stereotyping of police officers who access mental health services, interventions are usually referred to as **critical incident stress debriefings (CISDs)** (Belles and Norvell 1990). A CISD is a "structured intervention designed to promote the emotional processing of traumatic events" through the discussion and normalization of reactions, as well as preparing officers to be able to cope with other possible traumatic events in the future (Miller 1999). A CISD consists of seven phases (Miller 1999):

1. Introduction: A debriefing in a group setting about the CISD approach.

2. Fact phase: A group discussion as to the facts surrounding exactly what happened during the traumatic event.

3. Thought phase: Group members begin to discuss what was going through their minds during the event.

4. Reaction phase: Group members begin to comprehend the emotional consequences of the event, highlighting what the worst part of the event was for them.

5. Symptom phase: Group members work past the incident to begin to deal with their experiences since the event occurred.

6. Education phase: Information is provided to the group as to the stress response and the related psychological and physiological symptoms.

7. Reentry phase: Coping strategies are provided to prepare members for the eventuality of future traumatic events.

In order to prevent the possibility of group participants being subpoenaed as witnesses, it is recommended that the CISD process not begin until after the initial investigation and collection of formal statements in the case of officer-involved shooting investigations (Solomon 1995).

1. In your opinion, what are the most stressful aspects of police work? Have these stressful conditions changed since September 11? Why or why not?

2. What interventions might you introduce as a police manager to help officers deal with stress?

3. What characteristics/background might you look for in new recruits that might be predictive of a better ability to cope with stress? Remember your answer when you read Chapter 14.

Work-Related Stressors   Work-related stressors include stress factors that result from the day-to-day work done by police officers, and although these stressors often affect officers who are not engaged in routine patrol or investigative work, they are most likely to have a negative impact on officers on the street or otherwise engaged in more "traditional" policing tasks such as public order maintenance and crime prevention. These stressors include, but are not limited to:

- Work fatigue
- Rotating shift patterns
- Having to maintain conflicting roles in the community (i.e., both law enforcer and public servant)
- Persistent fear and danger associated with police work
- Dealing with victims and the families of victims
- Lack of control over the progress of cases within the department
- Internal review boards and ongoing performance assessments

In terms of the relative importance of individual stress factors, research by Violanti and Aron (1995) found that the single most stressful event a police officer is ever likely to face in the course of his or her career is killing someone in the line of duty. Closely behind this was the death of a fellow police officer, followed by being subjected to injury or physical attack. Although the majority of officers are rarely, if ever, forced to deal with such events, the fact that they are all incidents that occur on the job reinforces the point that policing is an inherently dangerous and stressful profession.

How police officers respond to these different forms of stress will vary according the personality of the individual concerned; the level of support they receive from friends, family, and their department; and other factors, such as their level of experience on the job, years of service, ability to develop effective coping strategies, and the nature of the stressful event itself. According to an early study by Niederhoffer (1969), most police officers respond to stress by withdrawing into themselves and becoming more cynical.

Police Suicide

In recent years, police suicide has become a major concern for many departments throughout the United States. Although it is difficult to get an accurate picture of the problem, most studies suggest that suicide rates among serving police officers are considerably higher than those of the general population. In one of the first studies of the problem, Guralnick (1963) compared suicide rates for police officers with those for 130 other occupations and found that police officers were almost twice (1.8 times) as likely to take their own lives as members of the general public. These results were later confirmed by a similar study conducted by Richard and Fell in 1975, which concluded that policing had the third-highest suicide rate of any profession. While more recent studies by Heiman (1979), Terry (1981), Ivanoff (1994), Violanti (1996), and Hoenig and White (2000) have returned marginally different results, in each case police officers were found to be more likely to commit suicide than almost any other group in society. Perhaps even more disturbingly, Violanti (1996) found that more police officers—over 8.3 times more—die at their own hands than at the hands of criminals or in the line of duty.

As disturbing as such figures are, however, there is reason to believe that the problem of police suicide is far more pervasive than these studies suggest. According to Violanti (1996), many officer suicides are intentionally misclassified by police departments as "accidental," either to protect the reputation of the individual officer or the department as a whole. For example, police investigators may deliberately misclassify an apparent gun-related suicide as a case of careless weapon handling or instead conclude that the gun had misfired while the officer was cleaning his or her weapon. Such misclassification allows the deceased officer to be treated as having died in the line of duty, entitling him or her to burial with police honors and the officer's surviving family to full insurance and benefits (Bonifacio 1991). Alternatively, a suspected suicide may be misclassified in an effort to protect the officer's department from criticism, particularly with regards to the provision of mental health services and officer support. Although the courts have ruled that police departments are responsible for ensuring that all police personnel are psychologically fit, many departments do not have the resources to effectively monitor the mental health of their officers (Meredith 1984). As a result, there is a strong incentive for departments to "cover up" the problem of police suicide, both to protect themselves from possible legal actions and from external investigations that may harm the department's reputation. In either case, there is reason to believe that many police suicides go unreported. According to an FBI study of the Chicago Police Department (see Cronin 1982), it was possible that as many as 67 percent of all police suicides in Chicago had been misclassified, a finding that suggests reported police suicide rates may seriously underestimate the extent of the problem.

Over the past forty years, researchers have advanced a number of theories for police suicide, each of which attempts to explain why police officers kill themselves in such numbers. One of the earliest explanations can be found in the work of Friedman (1967), who looked at incidences of police suicide in the NYPD between 1934 and 1940. Having examined ninety-three individual cases, Friedman concluded that while approximately two-thirds of the officers who committed suicide could be said to have had "passive" personalities, the remaining one-third could be classified as "overtly aggressive, impulsive, and reckless" in nature. This led Friedman (1967) to conclude that police suicide is primarily the result of emotional displacement, with officers turning their aggressive impulses onto themselves in an effort to deal with feelings of frustration or inadequacy:

> The policeman is permitted to kill and receives praise from his superiors, peers, and even the public for carrying out these acts. The aggressive and controlling drives, which are no doubt the primary motivations for his choice of occupation, are often in collision with the command to refrain and repress, therefore causing tremendous conflict within him. (p. 430)

This explanation—sometimes referred to as the displaced aggression theory—was later challenged by Farber (1968), Heiman (1977), and Danto (1978), all of whom argued that it was too simplistic and failed to adequately explain why officers in the "passive" category also took their own lives. More recently, theories of police suicide have sought to explain the problem in terms of stress, substance abuse, and the personal lives of officers. Based on their examination of police suicides in Buffalo between 1950 and 1990, for example, Violanti and Vena (1995) concluded that many officers commit suicide because of work-related stress and problems with their social and martial relationships. Violanti and Vena also found—like Cronin (1982) and Wagner and Brzeczek (1983) before them—that the majority of officers who committed suicide had a history of alcohol abuse. In contrast, while Ivanoff's 1994 study of police suicide in New York also found that many of the deceased officers had abused alcohol, there was little evidence to suggest that job-related stress was a major cause of police suicide. Instead, Ivanoff concluded that personal problems—such as depression and martial difficulties—were far more likely to result in feelings of depression among officers than the challenges they faced on the job.

Chapter Summary

- One of the key features that distinguishes the police and other criminal justice agencies from other public institutions and organizations is the extent to which serving police officers possess and exercise discretion. Although efforts can be made to reduce officer discretion, such as zero tolerance or mandatory arrest policies, the complexities of police work will ensure that discretion will always remain a central component of policing.

- Police decision making can be influenced by many factors related to the officer's own disposition or the nature of the unlawful act itself. Factors commonly cited in the literature as influencing police discretion include the seriousness of the offense, the attitude of the suspect, the characteristics of the victim, the relationship between the suspect and the victim, evidence of the offense, and the minority status of the parties to the offense.

- Whether officers exhibit similar personality traits and the extent to which these are caused by predisposing factors or by socialization into the police culture is the subject of many diverse explanations: psychological, ed-

ucational, sociological, and organizational. The influence of historical factors on officer perceptions of suspiciousness must also be considered in discussing the origins of police culture. Police are in many ways a reflection of the larger societal forces in which they are embedded.

- The nature of police work can bring with it many serious stressors requiring complex coping mechanisms that themselves can contribute to the maintenance of police culture. However, following particularly serious traumatic incidents, officers can develop post-traumatic stress disorders. Such disorders require serious intervention strategies. To avoid negative perceptions of such interventions, in policing these often are referred to as critical incident stress debriefing.

- Policing has been consistently found to have an exceptionally high suicide rate as compared to other professions. However, the reliability of measures used to document the incidence of police suicide often is difficult to assess. Causes of police suicide have ranged from the police personality, displaced aggression, and a reaction to job-related stressors.

KEY TERMS

Authoritarian 223
Contempt of cop (COC) 219
Critical incident stress debrief-
    ings (CISD) 230
Dis-stress 229
Eustress 229
External stressors 229
Internal stressors 229

Iron Law of Oligarchy 216
Legalistic style 227
Mandatory arrest policies 214
Minneapolis Domestic Violence
    Experiment 214
Police personality 223
Police subculture 224

Post-traumatic stress disorder
    (PTSD) 230
Service style 227
Thin blue line 224
Watchman style 227
Working personality 225
Zero-tolerance policing 217

Linking the Dots

1. Why do police officers need to use discretion? Where is the majority of discretionary
power concentrated in the typical police
department?

2. What is zero-tolerance policing? Why do
some commentators believe that limiting
police discretion can damage police–public
relations?

3. Name four factors that may influence an officer's decision to make an arrest. Which factor do you think should be given the most
weight by the officer? Which should be given
the least weight? (Explain your reasons in
each case.)

4. Explain the difference between the psychological and sociological theories of police behavior. Which of these theories do you find to
be the most convincing?

5. What are the major causes of police stress?
Do you think that limiting the amount of
discretion given to individual police officers would help to reduce levels of police
stress?

6. What causes of police suicide discussed in
the chapter do you feel provide the best explanation of this problem? What might be
done to best reduce this behavior?

REFERENCES

Acuri, A. F. 1976. "Police Pride and Self-Esteem: Indica-
tions of Future Occupational Changes." *Journal of
Police Science and Administration* 4 (4): 295–305.

American Psychological Association. 1994. *Diagnostic
and Statistical Manual, Version IV.* Washington, D.C.:
American Psychological Association.

Bayley, D. H., and H. Mendelson. 1969. *Minorities and
the Police: Confrontation in America.* New York, NY:
The Free Press.

Belles, D., and N. Norvell. 1990. *Stress Management for
Law Enforcement Officers.* Sarasota, FL: Professional
Resource Exchange.

Bercall, T. E. 1970. "Calls for Police Assistance." *American Behavioral Scientist* 13(4): 681–691.

Bittner, E. 1990. *Aspects of Police Work*. Boston, MA: Northeastern University Press. (Note that this quote originally appeared in a 1974 article by Bittner entitled "Florence Nightingale in Pursuit of Willie Sutton" in *The Potential for Reform of Criminal Justice* Vol. 3, 3d ed., edited by H. Jacob, 17–44. Beverly Hills, CA: Sage.)

Black, D. 1971. "The Social Organization of Arrest." *Stanford Law Review* 23:1087–1111.

Black, D. 1980. *The Manners and Customs of the Police*. New York, NY: Academic Press.

Blau, T. H. 1994. *Psychological Services for Law Enforcement*. New York, NY: Wiley.

Bonifacio, P. 1991. *The Psychological Effects of Police Work: A Psychodynamic Approach*. New York, NY: Plenum Press.

Bordua, D. 1967. "Review of *Justice Without Trial: Law Enforcement in Democratic Society*." *American Sociological Review* 32(3): 492–493.

Bratton, W. J. 1996. "New Strategies for Combating Crime in New York City." *Fordham Urban Law Journal* 23: 781–795.

Brooks, L. W. 1989. "Police Discretionary Behavior: A Study of Style." In *Critical Issues in Policing: Contemporary Readings*, edited by R. G. Dunham and G. P. Alpert, 121–145. Prospect Heights, IL: Waveland Press.

Chambliss, W. 1997. "Policing the Ghetto Underclass: The Politics of Law and Law Enforcement." In *Public Policy: Crime and Criminal Justice*, edited by B. Handcock and P. Sharp, 146–166. Upper Saddle River, NJ: Prentice-Hall.

Chan, J. 1997. *Changing Police Culture*. Sydney: Cambridge University Press.

Crank, J. 2004. *Understanding Police Culture*, 2d ed. City: Anderson.

Crank, J., J. Hewitt, B. Regoli, and R. Culbertson. 1993. "An Assessment of Work Stress Among Police Executives." *Journal of Criminal Justice* 21(4): 313–324.

Cronin, T. J. 1982. *Police Suicides: A Comprehensive Study of the Chicago Police Department*. Masters thesis, Lewis University, Chicago, I Department of Criminal Justice.

Cumming, E., I. Cumming, and L. Edell. 1965. "Policeman as Philosopher, Guide, and Friend." *Social Problems* 12:276–286.

Danto, B. L. 1978. "Police Suicide." *Police Stress* 1 (1): 32–36, 38–40.

Davis, K. C. 1969. *Discretionary Justice*. Chicago, IL: University of Illinois Press.

Davis, K. C. 1975. *Police Discretion*. St. Paul, MN: West Publishing.

Enstermaker Berk, S., and D. R. Loeske. 1980–1981. "'Handling Family Violence: Situational Determinants of Police Arrest in Domestic Disturbances." *Law and Society Review* 15 (2): 317–346.

Farber, M. 1968. *Theory of Suicide*. New York,, NY: Funk and Wagnalls.

Friedman, P. 1967. "Suicide Among Police: A study of Ninety-three Suicides Among New York City Policemen, 1934–1940." In *Essays in Self-Destruction*, edited by E. Shneidman, 414–449. New York, NY: Science House.

Friedrich, R. J. 1980. "Police Use of Force: Individuals, Situations, and Organizations." *The Annals* 452 (November): 82–92.

Goldstein, H. 1968. "Police Response to Urban Crisis." *Public Administration Review* 28(July/August): 417–418.

Goldstein, J. 1998. "Police Discretion Not to Invoke the Criminal Justice Process: Low Visibility Decisions in the Administration of Justice." In *The Criminal Justice System: Politics and Policies*, 7th ed., edited by G. F. Cole and M. G. Gertz, 85–103. Belmont, CA: Wadsworth Publishing.

Greene, J. A. 1999. "Zero Tolerance: A Case Study of Police Policies and Practices in New York City." *Crime and Delinquency* 45(2): 171–187.

Grennan, S. A. 1988. "Findings on the Role of Officer Gender in Violent Encounters with Citizens." *Journal of Police Science and Administration* 15(1): 78–85.

Guralnick, L. 1963. "Mortality by Occupation and Cause of Death Among Men 20–64 Years of Age." *Vital Statistics Special Reports* 53. Bethesda, MD: Department of Health, Education, and Welfare.

Harcourt, B. 1998. "Reflecting on the Subject: A Critique of the Social Influence Conception of Deterrence, the Broken Windows Theory, and Order Maintenance Policing New York Style." *Michigan Law Review* 97(2): 291–389.

Harcourt, B. 2001. *Illusion of Order: The False Promise of Broken Windows Policing*. Cambridge, MA: Harvard University Press.

Heiman, M. F. 1975. "Police Suicide." *Journal of Police Science and Administration,* 3(3): 267–273.

Hoenig, A., and E. White. 2000. "By Their Own Hand." *The Police Chief* 2000. 67(10): 156–161.

Ivanoff, A. 1994. *The New York City Police Suicide Training Project*. New York, NY: Police Foundation.

Kappeler, V. E., R. D. Sluder, and G. Alpert. 1994. *Forces of Deviance: Understanding the Dark Side of Policing*. Prospect Heights, IL: Waveland Press.

Kelling, G. L., and C. Coles. 1996. *Fixing Broken Windows*. New York, NY: The Free Press.

Klinger, D. A. 1994. "Demeanor or Crime? Why 'Hostile' Citizens Are More Likely To Be Arrested." *Criminology* 32(3): 475–493.

Kroes, W. 1976. *Society's Victim, The Policeman: An Analysis of Job Stress in Policing.* Springfield, IL: Charles C. Thomas.

LaFave, W. 1965. *Arrest: The Decision to Take a Suspect into Custody.* Boston, MA: Little, Brown and Company.

LaFree, G. 1989. *Rape and Criminal Justice.* Belmont, C.A.: Wadsworth.

Leftkowitz, J. 1973. "Attitudes of Police Towards Their Job." In *The Urban Policeman in Transition*, edited by R. J. Snibbe and H. M. Snibbe, 203–232. Springfield, IL: Charles C. Thomas.

Leftkowitz, J. 1975. "Psychological Attributes of Policemen: A Review of Research and Opinion." *Journal of Social Issues* 31(1): 3–26.

Lester, D. 1983. "Why Do People Become Police Officers: A Study of the Reasons and Their Predictions of Success." *Journal of Police Science and Administration* 11(2): 170–174.

Lord, V. 1996. "An Impact of Community Policing: Reported Stressors, Social Support, and Strain Among Police Officers in a Changing Police Department." *Journal of Criminal Justice* 24(6): 503–522.

Lundman, R. J. 1980. *Policing the Police.* New York, NY: Holt, Reinhart, and Winston.

Manning, R. 1977. *Police Work: The Social Organization of Policing.* Prospect Heights, IL: Waveland Press.

Martin, S. E. 1980. *Breaking and Entering: Policewomen on Patrol.* Berkeley. CA: University of California Press.

Martin, S. E. 1990. *On the Move: The Status of Women in Policing.* Washington, D.C.: Police Foundation.

Maurer, M. 1993. *Young Black Men and the Criminal Justice System: A Growing National Problem.* Washington. D.C.: U.S. Government Printing Office.

Meredith, N. 1984. "Attacking the Roots of Police Violence." *Psychology Today* 18(1): 20–26.

Michels, R. 1966. *Political Parties.* New York, NY: The Free Press.

Miller, L. 1999. *Law Enforcement Traumatic Stress: Clinical Syndromes and Intervention Strategies.* Available at www.aaets.org/arts/art87.htm.

Niederhoffer, A. 1963. *A Study of Police Cynicism.* Garden City, NY: Doubleday.

Neiderhoffer, A. 1969. *Behind the Shield.* Garden City, NY: Doubleday.

Niederhoffer, A. 1977. *The Police Family: From Station House to Ranch House.* Lexington, MA: Lexington Books.

Niederhoffer, A. 1985. *The Ambivalent Force: Perspectives on the Police.* New York, NY: Holt, Rinehart, and Winston.

Patterson, B. 1992. "Job Experience and Perceived Job Stress Among Police, Correctional, and Probation/Parole Officers." *Journal of Criminal Justice and Behavior* 19(3): 260–285.

Pendeleton, M. 1983. *Police Stress: Value Disparity, Self-esteem and Occupational Strain.* Unpublished dissertation, University of Washington.

Reiner, R. 1992. *The Politics of the Police,* 2d ed. Oxford: Oxford University Press.

Reiser, M. 1973. *Practical Psychology for Police Officers.* Springfield, IL: Charles C. Thomas.

Reiss, A. 1968. "Police Brutality—Answers to Key Questions." *Transactions* 5(8): 10–19.

Richard, W., and R. Fell. 1975. "Health Factors in Police Job Stress." In *Job Stress and the Police Officer*, edited by W. W. Kroes and J. J. Hurrell, 172–185. Washington, D.C.: U.S. Government Printing Office.

Roburg, R., J. Crank, J. Kuykendall. 1999. *Police and Society.* Los Angeles, CA: Roxbury.

Roburg, R., J. Crank, and J. Kuykendall. 2000. *Police and Society,* 2d ed. Los Angeles, CA: Roxbury.

Skolnick, J. H. 1966. *Justice Without Trial.* New York, NY: John Wiley & Sons.

Skolnick, J. H. 2000. "Code Blue." *The American Prospect* 11(10): 49.

Smith, B. 1960. *Police Systems in the United States,* 2d ed. New York, NY: Harper and Row.

Solomon, R. 1995. "Critical Incident Stress Management in Law Enforcement." In *Innovations in Disaster and Trauma Psychology: Applications in Emergency Services and Disaster response,* edited by G. S. Everly, 123–157. Elliott City, IA: Chevron.

Stratton, J. G., D. A. Parker, and J. R. Snibbe. 1984. "Posttraumatic Stress: Study of Police Officers Involved in Shootings." *Psychological Reports* 55(7): 127–131.

Terrill, W. and S. Mastrofski. 2002. "Reassessing Situational and Office-Based Determinants of Police Coercion." *Justice Quarterly* 19(2): 215–248.

Terry, W. C. 1981. "Police Stress: The Empirical Evidence." *Police Science and Administration* 9(1): 61–75.

Van Maanen, D. 1997. "Making Rank: Becoming an American Police Sergeant." In *Critical Issues in Policing: Contemporary Readings,* 3d ed., edited by R. G. Dunham and G. P. Alpert, 167–183. Prospect Heights, IL: Waveland Press.

Violanti, J. 1996. *Police Suicide: Epidemic in Blue.* Springfield, IL: Charles Thomas.

Violanti, J., and F. Aron. 1995. "Police Stressors: Variations in Perceptions Among Police Personnel." *Journal of Criminal Justice* 23(2): 280–291.

Violanti, J. M., and J. E. Vena. 1995. "Epidemiology of Police Suicide." *Research in Progress.* NIMH Grant MH47091-02.

Visher, C. A. 1983. "Gender, Police Arrest Decisions, and Notions of Chivalry." *Criminology* 21(1): 5–28.

Waddington, P. 1999. *Policing Citizens: Authority and Rights.* London: UCL Press.

Wagner, M., and R. J. Brzeczek. 1983. "Alcoholism and Suicide: A Fatal Connection." *FBI Law Enforcement Bulletin* 52(3): 8–15.

Wilson, J. Q. 1978. *Varieties of Police Behavior.* Cambridge, MA: Harvard University Press.

Wilson, O. W. 1950. *Police Administration.* New York, NY: McGraw-Hill.

Women's Justice Center. N. D. Available at www .justicewomen.com/witness.html.

Worden, R. E., and A. A. Pollitz. 1984. "Police Arrest in Domestic Disturbances: A Further Look. *Law and Society Review.* 18(1): 105–119.

Worden, R. E. 1995. "The 'Causes' of Police Brutality: Theory and Evidence on Police Use of Force." In *And Justice for All*, edited by W. A. Geller and H. Toch, 31–60. Washington, D.C.: Police Executive Research Forum.

Worthington, R. 1991. "Value of Mandatory Arrest for Women Beaters Questioned." *Chicago Tribune*, November 19, 5.

NOTES

1. The story of Maria Macias is summarized from the expert testimony of retired San Diego Police Sergeant Anne O'Dell. O'Dell's testimony can be found at the Women's Justice Center Web site at www.justicewomen.com/witness.html.

2. For a more condensed account of Davis' thinking about the issue of police discretion, see also Davis (1975).

3. Another excellent definition is provided by Goldstein (1998), who argues that discretion is the decision not to impose a sanction in a situation where a sanction is available to the police.

4. New York City Traffic Rules and Regulations 2002, Section 4-04(c).

5. For a more detailed critique of zero-tolerance policing, see also Harcourt (2001).

6. See also Black (1980).

7. See also Friedrich (1980).

8. See also Worden and Pollitz (1984).

9. See also Martin (1989; 1990).

10. See also Roburg et al. (1999).

11. See also Niederhoffer (1977; 1985).

12. Two of the most important books on police management at this time were both firmly rooted in the "classic" tradition. See Wilson (1950) and Smith (1960).

13. See also Manning (1977).

14. Some of the more notable studies of police stress in recent years include Kroes (1976), Crank et al. (1993), and Lord (1996).

Chapter 10

Policing Multicultural Communities

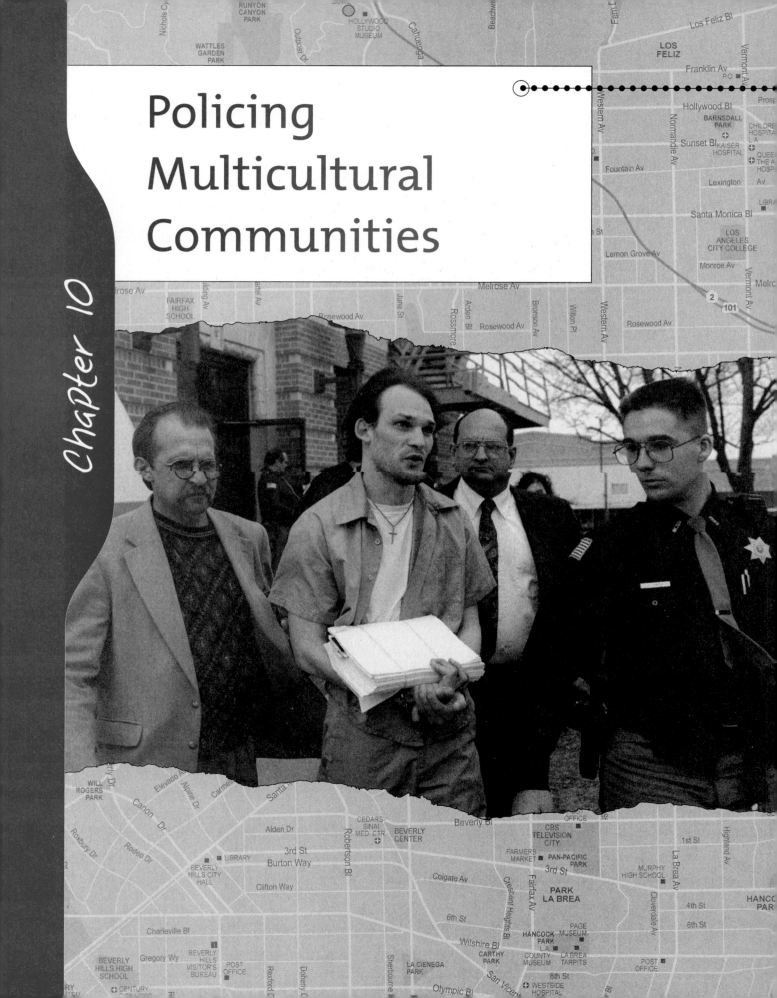

Chapter Outline

Chapter Objectives

● Become familiar with the state of relations between the police and racial and ethnic minorities in the United States.

● Identify some of the key challenges facing police in their efforts to provide law enforcement services to diverse communities.

● Examine the problem of police racism and understand the current debate over the use of racial profiling by the police and other law enforcement agencies.

● Consider some of the ways in which police departments in the United States have attempted to improve their relationships with immigrant and other minority communities and understand what is meant by the phrase "cultural diversity in policing."

Brandon Teena lived the life of many troubled youths, compulsively forging checks in order to win the affections of his girlfriends, leading to a series of convictions for forgery and theft by 1993 (Reardon 2000).[1] However, there was one important difference between Brandon and other teenage boys: Brandon Teena was originally born as Teena Brandon. Feeling that his gender by birth did not correspond with his perception of himself as a male, he changed his name to Brandon Teena as a teenager and began a full-time life as a man. Brandon's frustration at being remembered as a female, particularly within his growing number of petty theft records, led to his decision to move away from his home town for a new future as an unknown in Falls City, Nebraska. Although quickly finding love prospects in Lana Tisdel, as well as the acceptance and friendship of her ex-convict male companions, Brandon's luck was soon to run out. Brandon was arrested again when he resorted back to stealing to support himself, leading to the revelation of his true female identity to the small town he now called home. This revelation would enrage his new companions, John Lotter and Tom Nissen, leading both to violently rape and beat Brandon for his deception. Police investigating the attack on Brandon were more preoccupied with his true identity than with apprehending his attackers, thus failing to protect him from future harm. One week after the initial assault, Brandon was shot and killed by Lotter and Nissen on New Year's Eve.

In another case, plaintiffs of the Mohawk Indian reservation alleged that the New York State Police had failed to provide protection on the reservation from the violent actions of a private security force for illegal casinos. The situation was complicated by the fact that, according to the New York State Police, the tribe exercises a considerable amount of self-governance and the police felt that the violence on the reservation put their officers at risk, and therefore they did not intervene. The Court of Appeals denied the claim, finding that a claim under the Equal Protection Clause for discriminatory denial of police protection does not depend on whether or not it can be demonstrated that other "similarly situated individuals" received better protection, or even that it involved an express racial classification. Rather, what must be demonstrated is a "discriminatory motivation for the denial" (*Pyke v. Cuomo*[2]).

Providing effective policing for minority communities is one of the greatest challenges facing law enforcement agencies in the United States today. Language barriers, racial stereotyping, and cultural differences are all factors that can prevent minorities from gaining access to justice or taking advantage of important criminal justice services. In addition, the failure of certain groups—such as recent immigrants—to report crimes to the police means that many minority communities in the United States currently receive inadequate levels of funding for local crime control and law enforcement initiatives.

Today, a key question for the police and public is how to improve relations between the police and the various racial, ethnic, and other cultural communities that make up the United States. Unfortunately, highly publicized incidents of police misconduct and brutality have done little to improve matters, and in some cases—as in the mishandling of the Brandon Teena case—have made them considerably worse. Nor are these high-profile cases always an accurate reflection of the true sensitivity or concern for cultural issues of police nationally or even within one jurisdiction. This chapter explores some of the issues surrounding the policing of diverse communities and examines some of the ways in which the police are trying to improve relations with minority communities in the United States. Although the picture that emerges is not always a positive one, it is clear that significant—if perhaps slow—progress is being made towards ensuring that all citizens—regardless of race or ethnic background—receive equal protection from the police and other law enforcement agencies.

Key Problems and Sources of Tension

Ever since the first organized police forces were established during the second half of the nineteenth century, the police have been faced with the challenge of providing law enforcement services and protection to a vast range of racial and ethnic communities. Frequently called upon to uphold laws seen by many as racist and discriminatory, such as the Jim Crow laws discussed in Chapter 2, and often accused by critics of engaging in racist tactics and behavior themselves, the police have repeatedly found themselves drawn into some of the most divisive racial struggles in American history. According to many historians, police involvement in the suppression of **race riots** during the 1930s and 1940s and open clashes with Civil Rights activists in the 1960s severely damaged police–minority relations in the United States, leaving many convinced that the police exist to protect the interests of only white communities. Furthermore, although police racism and poor minority relations have long been a problem, there is now an even greater need to address these issues than ever before.

According to the most recent national census, between 1990 and 2000 the total population of the United States increased by 13.2 percent, and while the majority white population, representing 75.1 percent of the total, increased by 5.9 percent during this period, the African American and Hispanic communities increased by more than 15 and 50 percent, respectively (U.S. Census Bureau 2001a).[3] If U.S. Census Bureau predictions prove to be accurate, within the space of a few generations no single racial or ethnic group will hold a clear majority in the United States. Instead, the country will be made up of a collection of significant "minorities," namely black, white, and Hispanic. In certain communities across the United States (particularly on the West coast), Asian and Pacific Islander communities also continue to see significant growth. (See Table 10.1.)

Despite the fact that police departments across the country have worked hard to improve relations with **minority communities** in recent years, research suggests that many racial and ethnic minorities continue to encounter considerable difficulties in their dealings with the police and the criminal justice system in general. In the following sections, we look briefly at some of the major sources of tension that currently exist between the police and minorities in the United States, including problems stemming from the use of racial profiling and

TABLE 10.1

Projected Ethnic Composition of the United States by Year

Year	White	Black	Hispanic	Asian	Minority Total
1980	80.0%	11.5%	6.4%	1.5%	19.4%
1995	73.9	12.0	10.2	3.3	25.5
2030	60.5	13.1	18.9	6.6	38.6
2050	52.8	13.6	24.5	8.2	46.3

Source: U.S. Census Bureau (2001a).

difficulties arising from linguistic and cultural barriers between the police and many minority communities.

Police Racism and Racial Profiling

One of the most common explanations offered for the poor state of **police–minority relations** in the United States is **racism** on the part of individual officers. Generations of racial minorities throughout the United States have repeatedly complained of being treated more harshly than whites, and while it is notoriously difficult to measure the impact of race on police behavior, figures recently released by the Department of Justice suggest that racial profiling and police discrimination continue to be significant problems (Rennison 2001). As Tables 10.2 and 10.3 show, blacks and Hispanics are more likely to be searched, handcuffed, and arrested during traffic stops than whites and minorities in general are more likely to be subjected to the threat or actual use of force in contacts with the police. Blacks and other minorities also experience higher rates of victimization than whites—particularly for violent crime and theft—leading some to conclude that the police are less concerned with protecting minorities and are unwilling to devote the necessary resources to the policing of minority communities (Rennison 2001).

In light of these figures, it is perhaps unsurprising that surveys within minority communities reveal a widespread belief that differential treatment by the police is simply a fact of life (Morin and Cottman 2001). According to public opinion polls recently commissioned by the Bureau of Justice Statistics, only 58 percent of blacks said that they held a favorable opinion of the police (as compared with 81 percent of whites), while only 38 percent reported having "a great deal or quite a lot of confidence in the police" (Langan et al. 2001). Perhaps even more disturbing, however, is the extent to which conflict with the police is regarded as unavoidable by many minorities. For young black men in particular, a dangerous and sometimes fatal encounter with the police has almost come to be seen as a rite of passage, while within the larger black community, jokes about

TABLE 10.2

Police Actions During Traffic Stops by Race and Ethnicity of Stopped Drivers (1999)*

Race/ Ethnicity of Stopped Driver	Ticketed the Driver	Driver or Vehicle Searched	Driver Searched	Vehicle Searched	Handcuffed the Driver	Arrested the Driver	Used Force Against the Driver	Used Excessive Force Against the Driver
White	51.8%	5.4%	3.5%	4.3%	2.5%	2.6%	0.6%	0.4%
Black	60.4	11.0	8.0	8.5	6.4	5.2	1.5	1.0
Hispanic	65.6	11.3	7.0	9.7	5.0	4.2	1.4	1.4
Other	61.9	6.5	3.2	5.4	1.7	2.1	0.0	0.0

*Percentages may not sum to 100 due to rounding.
Source: Lagan et al. (2001).

TABLE 10.3

Experience of Force by Race and Ethnicity (1999)*

Race/ethnicity	Percentage of all Police Contacts	Percentage of Persons Experiencing Force in Contact with the Police	Experience of Force as a Percentage of *All* Contacts with the Police
White	78.25%	58.9%	0.72%
Black	10.56	22.6	2.06
Hispanic	8.10	15.5	1.85
Other	3.08	3.0	0.90

*Percentages may not sum to 100 due to rounding.
Source: Lagan et al. (2001).

being stopped for the offense of "driving while black" frequently hide considerable resentment and hostility towards the police (Wycliff 1987).

According to some critics of the police, police officers routinely discriminate against members of racial minorities because they regard them as second-class citizens, unworthy of the same legal protections and rights enjoyed by members of the majority white community. In support of this view, critics of the police point out that the vast majority of police officers are white and typically drawn from some of the more conservative sections of the community. According to such an argument, armed with racist attitudes before they enter the force, individuals are free to harass and discriminate against minorities without fear of reprisals or censure from their presumably like-minded colleagues once they join the force. In contrast, other critics contend that it is the police **socialization process** that plays a critical role in promoting racist attitudes and cultural insensitivity amongst serving officers (Shusta et al. 2002). As a number of researchers have observed, one of the key characteristics of police working culture is the use of **stereotypes** when dealing with members of the public (Goldstein 1990; Walker 1992). New officers quickly learn from their colleagues how to "recognize" actual or potential offenders and to discriminate between those citizens who are regarded as generally law-abiding and those who are not. Where these stereotypes are informed by ideas about race and criminality—for example, a belief that black people are more prone to violence than whites—racist attitudes can be passed from one generation of officers to the next in the guise of received wisdom or operational knowledge, although in reality these stereotypes hold no truth.

Both of these views of police behavior are, however, overly simplistic, and there is now a vast body of research to suggest that police racism is an extremely complex phenomenon. As Blakemore et al. (1995) have observed, police prejudices are often based on "a lifetime of personal and professional experience, along with a multiplicity of ideological influences" (p. 79). Both **predisposition** and **socialization** play major roles in the formation and promotion of racist attitudes within the police, but understanding how they affect actual police behavior and decision making is extremely difficult, in part because officers may be motivated by reasoning that is subconscious and essentially unknown even to themselves (Lumb 1995). Police officers are given considerable discretion when making decisions about whether to stop, search, or arrest individual citizens. Although in principle they are expected to exercise this discretion without regard to extra-legal factors such as class, race, gender, or age, in practice, all of these factors have a bearing on how individual officers deal with members of the public.

Police discrimination can also be the result of **fundamental attribution errors** on the part of serving officers and police managers. According to Winkel (1991), there is a tendency for police officers to explain criminal behavior in terms of "internal factors," such as race or membership of a particular ethnic group, rather than by reference to external or situational factors, such as poverty or marginal social position. Often based on a genuine misunderstanding of the causes of crime, this type of reasoning frequently lies behind the practice of racial profiling and is used by officers who do not otherwise consider themselves or their conduct to be racist. Fundamental attribution errors can also be compounded by ignorance of minority cultures. In Das's (1993) study of the Canadian police and their views on the policing of minorities, for example, officers complained about what they perceived to be the "poor upbringing" of minority children and of the disregard shown by immigrants from "Third World" countries for traffic regulations and other minor laws.

Complaints such as these often mask mistaken assumptions—such as the belief that individuals from certain cultures are inherently less law-abiding—that arise from a lack of cultural understanding on the part of the police. Such assumptions can soon become part of the **operating stereotype** used by officers when dealing with members of particular minority communities. Again, while officers holding such views may not consider themselves to be racist, such stereotypes can provide the basis for unwitting but serious discrimination on the grounds of race or ethnicity. Finally, it is important to remember that few, including even the most critical, researchers suggest that the majority of police officers hold racist or discriminatory views. Indeed, most of the studies cited in this section point to the fact that while police racism is a serious problem, the vast majority of police officers are extremely sensitive to issues of race and the need to treat all citizens equally. Unfortunately, however, as the Rodney King and Abner Louima cases demonstrate, incidents of police misconduct are not only more likely to receive attention than proper behavior, but also have a significant effect on minority attitudes towards and images of the police.

Aggressive Patrol Tactics and Minority Communities

Related to the issue of racial profiling is the use of aggressive patrol techniques in minority communities. As discussed in Chapter 6, **aggressive patrolling** is designed to reduce crime in a given neighborhood or area by raising the immediate police presence and sending a signal to offenders in the community that a failure to obey the law will no longer be tolerated. Although welcome in many neighborhoods that have experienced persistently high crime rates, the use of this technique of policing in minority communities has attracted some criticism. On the one hand, while aggressive patrolling can reduce crime, it necessarily increases the likelihood of cultural misunderstandings and possible conflicts be-

Linkages in Law Enforcement

Terrorism, Racial Profiling, and the Arab Community

Although polls provide conflicting results, some have indicated that as many as 70 percent of Americans believe that some form of racial profiling of the Arab American community is necessary, and acceptable, to ensure public safety (Davis 2001). Eighty percent of Americans were opposed to the practice prior to September 11 (Davis 2001). Other polls have indicated that respondents are more suspicious of people of Arab descent. As a result they are even willing to tolerate such intrusive practices as special identification cards unique to this population.

Questions

1. Do you feel that the post–September 11 climate justifies the racial profiling of Arab Americans? Justify your argument with respect to the concepts and cases related to the Fourth and Fourteenth Amendments covered throughout Chapter 7.

2. In what specific ways do you feel that the practice of racial profiling actually helps law enforcement keep society safe? How is this argument different from what you would argue about the use of racial profiling to apprehend drug offenders?

3. What are the potentially negative consequences of racially profiling persons of Arab descent?

tween the police and certain minority groups such as recent immigrants. More significantly, however, when the aggressive patrolling is directed at an area that contains a mixture of communities, there is a danger of the police being perceived to favor one group over another. Such favoritism can lead to accusations of racism and harassment on the part of the police.

As a consequence, although in certain situations aggressive patrol techniques are extremely effective at bringing down the overall level of crime in an area, the police need to be aware of the concerns of all of the residents affected by such tactics and ensure that law enforcement is being carried out in an even-handed and unbiased manner. Failure to do so can lead to an increase in police–community tensions and lead to discrimination against minority groups.

Policing Diversity: Cultural and Linguistic Barriers to Communication

Although much of the research on police minority relations has tended to focus on the problem of police racism and the use of discriminatory policing tactics, **cultural** and **linguistic barriers** can also have a profound effect on dealings between the police and racial and ethnic minorities. Gardenswartz and Rowe (1998) argue that **diversity** includes all ways that human beings are both similar and different; these factors create the commonalities we feel with others, as well as areas in which we can conflict.

Many minority communities in the United States have—for a variety of historical and social reasons—developed and continue to maintain cultures that are

Linkages in Law Enforcement

Myths About Immigrant Communities and the Criminal Justice System

One of the most abiding myths about immigrants in the United States is that they are more likely to commit crimes than native-born American citizens. In the past, this assumption drove the police and other law enforcement agencies to adopt particularly aggressive tactics when dealing with these communities, often at the expense of building good relations despite the fact that many immigrant communities were in desperate need of more effective policing. When compared to the population at large, however, there is little evidence to suggest that immigrants are any more criminal than native-born citizens. Indeed, recent studies appear to show that immigrants—far from being "inherently criminal"—are in fact more law-abiding than members of the general population (Aronson 1997).

According to research undertaken by researchers at Harvard's Kennedy School of Government, for example, immigrant men are far less likely to be in correctional institutions than native-born residents, while rates of imprisonment for recent immigrants are considerably lower than those for earlier arrivals (Butcher and Piehl 1998).[4] Data compiled by the INS also suggests that recidivism rates for immigrant offenders are considerably lower than those for the population at large. According to INS figures (Goold 2002), of the 35,318 immigrant offenders released from custody during the period October 1994 to May 1999, 11,605 went on to reoffend. This puts the rate of recidivism for immigrants at approximately 37 percent, some 30 percent lower than the 66 percent rate for the U.S. criminal population as a whole. Far from being major contributors to the U.S. "crime problem," it appears that immigrants are less likely to offend or reoffend than many other groups, a fact that is being increasingly focused upon by the police in their efforts to improve relations with these communities.

Questions

1. Why have many Americans throughout history traditionally associated immigrant populations with crime? Is this justified?

2. What are the positive and negative impacts of aggressive policing tactics in immigrant communities?

3. To what extent should local law enforcement be in partnership with Federal Immigration and Naturalization Service (INS) agents?

unique to them and often significantly different from those of the general community. A typical example of this can be found in **immigrant communities**. Because many immigrants continue to observe the cultural beliefs and practices of their native country after they settle in the United States, officers working in immigrant communities are often confronted with the task of maintaining order and providing protection for groups of people whose behavior and basic values may be unfamiliar to them. In extreme cases, these cultural differences between the police and the communities they serve can lead to serious misunderstandings and accusations of bias or lack of concern. Immigrants who have come to the United States to escape political persecution may, for example, view the police with suspicion based on experiences in their native country (Vrij et al. 1991). As one police officer interviewed by Das (1993) observed, minorities were often "afraid of the police as they carried at the back of their minds their conception about the police from their countries of origin" (p. 142). Similarly, for recent arrivals from countries where police corruption and malpractice are rife—such as parts of Eastern Europe and the former Soviet Union—trusting the police to help them rather than make their problems worse may be extremely difficult. In either case, interactions between these individuals and local police officers are likely to be colored by these beliefs, and possibly fraught with peril as a result.

In addition to the need to be aware of potential cultural differences, the police are also regularly confronted with the perennial problem of language. In an effort to solve this problem, almost every major police department in the United States has, at one time or another, experimented with short language courses for patrol officers (Taft 1982). Research has consistently shown, however, that requiring police officers to undergo intensive language training, typically in the form of so-called "crash courses," frequently does little more than provide them with a few key words and phrases. Although useful, knowing how to tell a suspect to "Put your hands up" is unlikely to help an officer whose primary concern is not with asserting authority, but rather with establishing trust. Being able to speak to ethnic minorities and recently arrived immigrants in their own language not only improves the ability of the police to gather information and carry out investigations, but more importantly, it demonstrates a commitment to the community in question and a willingness to at least try to understand their culture. Furthermore, in many cases linguistic barriers do more than simply make it difficult for officers and minorities to communicate with each other. Perhaps more importantly, they also undermine the ability of the police officer to assert his or her authority through the use of spoken commands and gestures.

Making things even more complex, according to Kenney et al. (2002), police have to be able to perform their duties professionally when interacting with groups that are cross cultural in nature. **Cross-cultural populations** include many layers of diversity that can be viewed as both enriching the lives of those

Attendance by law enforcement representatives at important cultural events can be an important first step towards enhancing police–community relations.

in the community but at the same time pose their own unique challenges. Examples of such groups in the community include the deaf and hearing impaired community, the mentally ill, and the Gay, Lesbian, Bisexual, and Transgendered (GLBT) communities.

Policing the Deaf and Hard of Hearing Community

"You lose a lot of the impact of surprise, a lot of your knowledge, a lot of your gut feelings. You lose all of your years of experience working through an interpreter" [Lt. William Lamb, Miami Beach Police Department, quoted in Taft (1982, p. 14)].

Contrary to popular belief, the deaf and hard of hearing community represents a diverse community in terms of their ability to hear and communicate vocally. Whereas the **profoundly deaf** are incapable of any hearing, those who are **hard of hearing** have some ability to hear and often try to hide their inability to hear through reliance upon lip reading or closed captioning (Stolba and Stilman 2002). Encounters with the deaf population can be potentially dangerous for an officer who does not recognize signs that indicate that he or she is interacting with a member of the population, and thus misperceive the situation at hand. For example, Stolba and Sliman (2002) note the following difficult encounters:

- A deaf person who has not seen an officer approach or seen his or her lips move when issuing a command might appear to the officer to be disregarding a direct order.

- It is a misperception that written warnings from law enforcement will be a suitable substitute because the average deaf person in the United States writes at near a fourth-grade level.

- A police officer may misperceive communication among deaf individuals as other activity, as was the case with a Chicago police officer who arrested a group of teenagers at a bus stop on the grounds that they were making gang signals when, in fact, they were using **American Sign Language (ASL)**.

Deaf individuals themselves can benefit from an understanding of the precautions officers need to take in their interactions so that misunderstandings might be avoided.

Although officer understanding of ASL is of course desirable, it is entirely impractical to believe that the average officer will ever have enough training to be competent in this complex language. As a result, new efforts in cultural diversity training seek to educate officers about the signs to recognize when dealing with a deaf or hard of hearing individual and offer available interpretation services and alternative strategies as necessary.

Policing the Mentally Ill

People have many misconceptions of the mentally ill, particularly the belief that they usually are violent and uncontrollable (Durham 1989). This being said, officers must be familiar with a variety of techniques for dealing with the mentally ill, recognizing the tremendous scope of the population. Police officers need to recognize that responding to a call for an emotionally disturbed or mentally ill individual will often require a significant amount of time and patience and in some cases require the transfer of the individual to a hospital (Glenn and Hadfield 2002). Moreover, in many circumstances, the assistance of a specially trained mental health professional may be necessary.

Because of these issues, many police departments, such as those in Los Angeles, Memphis, and Houston, have created special crisis intervention teams with specially trained officers to respond to calls involving the mentally ill. However, these agencies also offer condensed recruit and in-service training so that all officers are better able to respond to the unique needs of this population, and thereby prevent situations from escalating needlessly.

Policing the Gay, Lesbian, Bisexual, and Transgendered (GLBT) Community

The history of police relations with the GLBT population is not a very positive one. Police interactions with the community often focused on the invocation of laws against disorderly conduct, public lewdness, and solicitation to arrest GLBT individuals, including gay men hitting on individuals in public bars and, on occasion, private parties in homes (D'Emilio 1983). It is in large part because of this history that few GLBT individuals feel comfortable reporting their victimizations to the police, even though many reports indicate that gays and lesbians continue to be one of the most stigmatized and victimized minorities in the United States (Leinen 1993).

Homophobia can greatly increase the effects of domestic violence from a partner due to the reluctance of members of the community to come forward for fear of a homophobic reaction from police. Even where called, however, responding to domestic violence incidents can pose great complexities in ascertaining who the primary aggressor is in cases involving a GLBT couple.

Few police departments have attempted to develop strategies aimed specifically at combating hate crimes directed at homosexuals or improving police handling of victims of such crimes. Furthermore, it is rare for police departments to classify the gay community as an identifiable minority, and as a result, diversity programs designed to improve police–minority relations often focus on issues of race and ethnicity rather than sexual identity and orientation.

The Underreporting of Crime

Similar to the challenges noted in the GLBT community, one of the major challenges facing the police is how to increase the reporting of crime in minority and immigrant communities. There is good reason to believe, for example, that immigrant victims are far less likely to report crimes than other victims, despite the fact that immigrants are victimized at rates comparable with those for the population at large. Although it is notoriously difficult to measure the extent of underreporting, based on a national survey of police chiefs, prosecutors, and court administrators, researchers have concluded that the underreporting of serious crimes—such as sexual assault and gang violence—is particularly endemic in communities of recent immigrants (Davis and Erez 1998).

Aside from the fact that underreporting means that many crimes go unpunished and offenders are left free to reoffend (often against the same victim), underreporting also has serious implications for the allocation and use of resources within the criminal justice system as a whole. As noted by approximately one-third of the officials surveyed by Davis and Erez (1998), underreporting leads to the undercounting of crimes in immigrant communities, with the result that

Watching over the
ty and County of San Francisco

The San Francisco Sheriff's Department
rs you a rewarding career as a Deputy Sheriff

Become a
San Francisco
Deputy Sheriff!

A rare
career opportunity

Oportunidad para una
magnifica carrera

一個很難得的
事業機會

Pagkakataon sa
nalibang propesyon

www.sfsheriff.com

Police outreach materials in languages representative of the community are an essential means of getting out information and breaking down barriers.

these communities often receive inadequate levels of policing and other law enforcement resources. This is not a problem that can be solved simply by putting more officers on the streets or improving levels of cultural awareness or linguistic competence. As many commentators have noted, underreporting stems from two main sources: internal cultural pressures within immigrant communities that discourage individuals from seeking police help and a general lack of trust in the police and other law enforcement agencies by immigrants.

For example, what most Americans might call a crime, members of a particular immigrant community may consider a tradition, or if it is a crime, it is a "family matter" not requiring outside interference. In this view, police are not supposed to supplant patriarchal authority in resolving disputes, however evident that the "conflict" in question is a case of prey needing protection from predator (Horowitz 2001).

While underreporting has made it difficult for both the police and independent researchers to develop an accurate and detailed picture of crime in minority communities, in recent years it has become increasingly clear that violent crime is an especially serious problem for immigrants. Researchers from the UCLA School of Public Health found that although immigrants make up approximately 17 percent of the overall population in California, between 1970 and 1992 they accounted for roughly 23 percent of all recorded homicides (Roback 1996). As Susan B. Sorenson, one of the chief authors of the report notes, these findings "demonstrate the urgent need to establish violence-prevention programs geared specifically towards immigrant groups. . . . We need to find ways to intervene early to keep immigrants from becoming victims of violence" (Chu and Sorenson 1996, p. 120).

Underrepresentation of Racial Minorities in the Police

Finally, it is important to note that the state of police–minority relations has not been helped by the fact that police departments have, until recently, been slow to acknowledge and eliminate racial discrimination in their own hiring practices. Although the numbers of African American and Hispanic officers have been rising steadily since the 1960s, according to recent figures from the Bureau of Justice Statistics (BJS) (Reeves 1996), both groups together still comprise less than 20 percent of the total number of officers in service (see Table 10.4).

Evidence also suggests that minority officers still do not receive the same promotional opportunities as white officers. While it is true that considerable variations exist across different police departments—in Chicago and Detroit, for example, black officers are far more likely to hold supervisory positions than in New York or Philadelphia—only some of this disparity can be explained by differences in local demographics. What is clear is that some degree of racial bias continues to play a part in determining what opportunities

Race and Ethnicity of Full-time Officers in Local Police Departments by Size of Population Served (1993)

Population Served	White	Black	Hispanic	Other*	Total of All Minorities
All sizes	80.9%	11.3%	6.2%	1.5%	19.0%
1,000,000 or more	69.2	17.7	12.0	1.2	30.9
500,000–999,999	66.2	21.0	7.0	5.8	33.8
250,000–499,999	71.9	17.7	9.0	1.4	28.1
100,000–249,999	80.6	12.4	5.4	1.6	19.4
50,000–99,999	86.3	7.2	5.1	1.4	13.7
25,000–49,000	89.8	5.4	4.3	0.6	10.3
10,000–24,999	91.6	5.1	2.6	0.6	8.3
2,500–9,999	92.8	4.1	2.6	0.5	7.2
Under 2,500	91.7	5.3	1.9	1.2	8.4

* Includes Asians, Pacific Islanders, American Indians, and Alaska Natives.
Source: Reeves (1996).

are available to minorities within the police. As has already been noted earlier in this chapter, fostering trust is an essential precursor to the development of good police–community relations. According to some minority leaders, this trust will only result once the police and other law enforcement agencies demonstrate that they are open to minority recruitment and that they are aware of the importance of being representative of the communities they are charged with serving and protecting.

Finding Solutions: Cultural Diversity and Policing

Despite the fact that the state of police–minority relations in the United States remain a source of concern, over the past three decades many police departments across the country have worked extremely hard to address the issues raised in the first part of this chapter. As a result of a growing emphasis on the need for greater cultural diversity in police training and recruitment policies, considerable progress has been made in a number of major cities—such as New York and Los Angeles, which have historically suffered from poor police–minority relations—and in many other cities and towns with significant minority and immigrant populations. In addition, positive changes to police complaint procedures have also helped to build trust and instill greater levels of confidence in the police.

Cultural Diversity Training and Education

Over the past fifty years, of the various efforts that have been made to improve police–minority relations in the United States, perhaps the greatest amount of reform has come in the area of police training and education. As Blakemore et al. (1995) have observed, "the preparation of police officers for work in a multicultural society has become a major concern for police departments, local governments, and the general community" (p. 71), with the result that most city and state police departments now provide some form of ongoing cultural diversity training for their officers. The emergence of community policing as the dominant philosophy in contemporary law enforcement has also led to an increased emphasis on diversity training based on the assumption that "to achieve better relationships, knowledge of people, their motivations, beliefs and behaviors are necessary compliments to officer training and increased understanding" (Lumb 1995, p. 42).

For the most part, the police approach to cultural diversity training and education has not changed dramatically since the 1960s (Blakemore et al. 1995). Generally speaking, police thinking about cultural diversity training has been based on two key assumptions: (1) that police officers can be more effective social control agents if they are able to secure community support through better communication skills and (2) that police officers will be more responsive to all members of the community and less likely to be abusive if they have an understanding of marginalized groups. Furthermore, this thinking has been underpinned by a particularly pragmatic approach to the problem of transforming attitudes and beliefs. Although many programs attempt to explain to officers how cultural stereotypes develop, and go to great lengths to present principled arguments against prejudice, most accept that one of the best ways to promote

Cultural diversity training for law enforcement makes officers aware of the practical implications of cultural boundaries; immediate attitude change is generally not a practical expected outcome on its own—emphasis on awareness, human dignity, and sensitivity is.

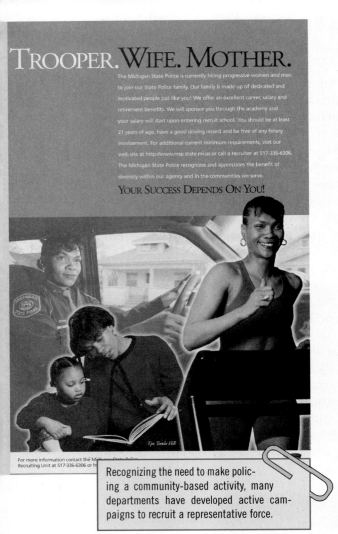

TROOPER. WIFE. MOTHER.

The Michigan State Police is currently hiring progressive women and men to join our State Police family. Our family is made up of dedicated and motivated people just like you! We offer an excellent career, salary and retirement benefits. We will sponsor you through the academy and your salary will start upon entering recruit school. You should be at least 21 years of age, have a good driving record and be free of any felony involvement. For additional current minimum requirements, visit our web site at http://www.msp.state.mi.us or call a recruiter at 517-336-6306. The Michigan State Police recognizes and appreciates the benefit of diversity within our agency and in the communities we serve.

YOUR SUCCESS DEPENDS ON YOU!

For more information contact the Michigan State Police Recruiting Unit at 517-336-6306 or h...

Recognizing the need to make policing a community-based activity, many departments have developed active campaigns to recruit a representative force.

change is to convince officers that they also stand to benefit from improved police–minority relations (Barlow and Barlow 1993).[5]

Today, police cultural diversity training programs typically include substantial sections on such issues as race, cultural, and interethnic relations; migration, minority integration, and cultural evolution; the dynamics of prejudice; group traditions, values, and attitudes; police intervention strategies; human rights; and police ethics and behavior (Lumb 1995; Normandeau and Leighton 1990). Although diversity training aims to challenge police prejudices and assumptions about minorities, sophisticated programs also strive to bring about organizational and institutional changes and to fundamentally reorient police–minority relations (Lumb 1995).

Improving the Representation of Minorities in the Police

In addition to attempting to change police culture and combat discriminatory attitudes through education and officer training, many police departments have also begun to take steps towards ensuring that minorities are better represented among their own ranks. It is now generally accepted by most policy makers and police administrators that part of community policing involves "making the police as representative of the community as possible" (Cox 1990, p. 169). According to some commentators, if we are committed to the idea that policing should be a community-based activity, then it follows that the police should strive to represent the society they are sworn to serve and protect (Lumb 1995). Perhaps even more fundamentally, however, it can be argued that the very legitimacy of the police depends on the extent to which they are representative of society at large.

In keeping with the recommendations of the National Advisory Commission's *Report on Police* (1973), most U.S. police departments have sought to increase the number of minority police officers through the use of **affirmative action** policies. According to some estimates, almost two-thirds of all police departments in the United States now have affirmative action employment policies in place. As a number of commentators have argued, however, there is a danger that the practice of hiring or promoting minorities without proper regard to individual qualifications is ultimately detrimental to the officers themselves, their colleagues, and the community at large (Alpert and Dunham 1992). According to Cox (1990):

> Only when all new police recruits meet the same, basic qualifications will there be any chance that race and gender will cease to be the controversial issues that they have traditionally been in American law enforcement (which simply reflects the larger society). If, and only if, this happens, will the difficulties in recruiting qualified women and minorities be eased and the goal of a community police partnership which includes all segments of the community be achievable. (p. 176)

Regardless of whether one accepts such objections to affirmative action in police recruitment, it is clear much remains to be done before the police manage to achieve a ratio of minority group employees that approximates its proportion in the larger population (National Advisory Commission 1973). As has already been noted, despite the fact that significant progress has been made in terms of the **recruitment and promotion of minorities**, it remains that African Americans, Hispanics, and other ethnic minorities remain underrepresented in police departments at both the local and state level. In order to ensure that the police continue to become more representative over time, it is necessary for departments to continue to reassess their hiring and promotion policies and ensure that all officers are treated equally irrespective of their race or ethnic background. In addition, such attempts at reform need to be accompanied by a range of other proactive measures aimed at improving levels of diversity and encouraging understanding within departments. Simply hiring more minority officers is not enough; personnel practices, officer evaluation methods, and disciplinary procedures must all be examined and restructured to ensure that institutional biases and discriminatory polices are eliminated. These issues will be elaborated upon in Chapter 14.

Chapter Summary

- Providing effective policing for minority communities is one of the greatest challenges facing law enforcement agencies in the United States today. Despite the fact that police departments across the country have worked hard to improve their relations with minority communities in recent years, research suggests that many minorities continue to encounter considerable difficulties in their dealings with the police and the criminal justice system in general.

- One of the most common explanations offered for the poor state of police–minority relations in the United States is racism on the part of individual officers and the use of racial profiling in police decision making. In support of this view, critics of the police point out that the vast majority of police officers are white and typically drawn from some of the more conservative sections of the community.

- Cultural and linguistic barriers to communication can also pose a problem for police working in minority communities and can hinder the development of good police–minority relations. In recent years, the police

have devoted considerable resources to overcoming these problems, and many departments across the country have well-established language and cultural diversity programs that attempt to address these issues.

- Although the numbers of minorities entering careers in law enforcement has been rising steadily, many racial and ethnic groups are still significantly underrepresented within policing. While the numbers of African American and Hispanic officers have been rising steadily since the 1960s, both groups together still comprise less than 20 percent of the total number of officers in service. Evidence also suggests that minority officers still do not receive the same promotional opportunities as white officers, a fact that has led some to argue that racial bias plays a significant part in determining what opportunities are available to minorities within the police.

- Despite police efforts, the underreporting of crime continues to be a problem in many minority communities. According to a number of recent studies, recent immigrants are particularly reticent about reporting crime to the police, in part because many fear contact with the authorities and because of the "closed" nature of their communities.

- Many strategies have been attempted since the 1960s to address the problems associated with policing diverse communities, particularly in the areas of training and recruitment. Diversity training has not changed signifi-

cantly over the years; typically it attempts to explain to officers the nature and impact of stereotypes and prejudice on the profession. Although most police managers recognize the importance of a representative police force, there are many challenges to achieving this in reality.

KEY TERMS

Affirmative action 256
Aggressive patrolling 247
American Sign Language (ASL) 251
Cross-cultural populations 250
Cultural barriers 248
Diversity 248

Fundamental attribution errors 247
Hard of hearing 251
Immigrant communities 249
Linguistic barriers 248
Minority communities 244
Minority recruitment 257
Operating stereotype 247

Police-minority tensions 245
Predisposition 246
Profoundly deaf 251
Race riots 244
Racism 245
Socialization 246
Stereotype 246

Linking the Dots

1. How have critics of the police sought to explain the phenomena of police racism? What steps can police departments take to eliminate racism within their ranks?

2. What is racial profiling? Do you think that racial profiling is a legitimate police tactic? Are there any circumstances under which racial profiling can never be justified?

3. Why do many minority leaders object to the use of aggressive patrol tactics? What sorts of communities are most likely to be affected by the use of such police tactics?

4. Can you think of an example of a common cultural barrier that might provide difficulties for police officers working in a minority or immigrant community?

5. Aside from taking language courses, what

can individual police officers do to overcome the problem of linguistic barriers?

6. Why is the underreporting of crime a problem? Why are certain minority communities particularly prone to underreporting? What can the police do to combat this problem?

7. Do you believe that the police in your city or town are representative of the entire community? Do you think that affirmative action recruitment policies are appropriate in policing and law enforcement?

8. What is cultural diversity training? What areas do such programs typically cover?

9. What do you think is the greatest challenge currently facing the police in their efforts to improve relations with minority communities?

REFERENCES

Alpert, G. P., and R. G. Dunham. 1992. *Policing Urban America*, 2d ed. Prospect Heights, IL: Waveland Press.

Aronson, D. 1997. "Immigration and the Criminal Justice System." *Research Perspectives on Migration* 1(5): 1–14.

Barlow, D. E., and M. H. Barlow. 1993. "Cultural Diversity Training in Criminal Justice: A Progressive or Conservative Reform?" *Social Justice* 20(1): 69–85.

Barlow, D. E., and M. H. Barlow. 1994. "Cultural Sensitivity Rediscovered: Developing Training Strategies for Police Officers." *Justice Professional* 8(1): 97–116.

Blakemore, J. L., D. Barlow, and D. L. Padgett. 1995. "From the Classroom to the Community: Introducing Process in Police Diversity Training." *Police Studies* 18(1): 71–83.

Butcher, K. F., and A. M. Piehl. 1998. "Cross-City Evidence on the Relationship Between Immigration and Crime." *Journal of Policy Analysis and Management* 17(3): 457–493.

Chul, L. D., and S. Sorenson. 1996. "Trends in California Homicide, 1970 to 1993." *Western Journal of Medicine* 165:119–125.

Cox, S. M. 1990. "Policing into the Twenty-first Century." *Police Studies* 13(2): 168–177.

D'Emilio, J. 1983. *Sexual Politics, Sexual Communities: The Making of a Homosexual Minority in the United States.* Chicago: University of Chicago.

Das, D. K. 1993. "Canadian Police Perception of Minority Problems." *Police Studies* 16(2): 138–146.

Davis, N. 2001. "The Slippery Slope of Racial Profiling." *ColorLines,* December 13, 2001. Available at www.arc.org.

Davis, R. C., and E. Erez. 1998. "Immigrant Populations as Victims: Toward a Multicultural Criminal Justice System." *Research in Brief,* May 1998. National Institute of Justice.

Durham, M. 1989. "The Impact of Deinstitutionalization on the Current Treatment of the Mentally Ill." *International Journal of Law and Psychiatry* 12(1)): 117–131.

Gardenswartz, L., and M. Barlow. 1993. *Managing Diversity: A Complete Desk Reference and Planning Guide.* New York: McGraw-Hill.

Glenn, J., and K. Hadfield. 2002. *Policing Persons with Mental Illness.* Washington, D.C.: Bureau of Justice Assistance.

Goldstein, H. *1990. Problem-Oriented Policing.* New York, NY: McGraw-Hill.

Goold, B. 2002. *Policing Immigrant Communities.* Washington, D.C.: Bureau of Justice Assistance.

Hagan, J., and A. Palloni. 1998. "Immigration and Crime in the United States." In *The Immigration Debate: Studies on the Economic, Demographic, and Fiscal Effects of Immigration,* edited by J. P. Smith and B. Edmonston, 367–387. Washington D.C.: National Academy Press.

Horowitz, C. 2001. *An Examination of U.S. Immigration Policy and Serious Crime.* Washington, D.C.: Center for Immigration Studies.

Kenney, D., H. Grant, and T. Allen. 2002. *Policing a Diverse Society.* Washington, D.C.: Bureau of Justice Assistance.

Langan, P. A., L. A. Greenfeld, S. K. Smith, M. R. Durose, and D. J. Levin. 2001. *Contacts Between Police and the Public: Findings from the 1999 National Survey.* Washington, D.C.: Bureau of Justice Statistics.

Leinen, S. 1993. *Gay Cops.* New Brunswick, NJ: Rutgers University Press.

Lumb, R. C. 1995. "Policing Culturally Diverse Groups: Continuing Professional Development Programs for Police." *Police Studies* 18(1): 23–43.

Morin, R., and M. H. Cottman. 2001. "Discrimination's Lingering Sting: Minorities Tell of Profiling, Other Bias." *The Washington Post,* June 22, 6.

National Advisory Commission on Criminal Justice. 1973. *Report on Police. Standards and Goals.* Washington, D.C.: U. S. Government Printing Office.

Normandeau, A., and B. Leighton. 1990. *A Vision of the Future of Policing in Canada: Police Challenge 2000.* Ottawa: Minister of Supply and Services Canada.

Reardon, L. 2000. "Brandon's Murder Thrusts Trans Issues into the Spotlight." *Gay.com.* Available at: wysiwyg://5/http://content.gay.com/channels/home/history_brandon.htm.

Reeves, B. A. 1996. *Local Police Departments, 1993.* Washington, D.C.: Bureau of Justice Statistics.

Rennison, C. M. 2001. *Criminal Victimization 2000: Changes 1999–2000 with Trends 1993–2000.* Washington, D.C.: Bureau of Justice Statistics.

Roback, W. 1996. "Immigrants More Likely to be Victims of Homicide." *UCLA School of Public Health Web Bulletin.* January 26, 1996. Available at: www.ph.ucla.edu/sph/pr/wr038.html.

Shusta, R., D. Levine, P. Harris, and H. Wong. 2002. *Multicultural Law Enforcement.* Upper Saddle River, NJ: Prentice-Hall.

Stolba, C., and M. Stilman. 2002. *Policing the Deaf and Hard of Hearing Community*. Washington, D.C.: Bureau of Justice Statistics.

Taft, P. B. 1989. "Policing the New Immigrant Ghettos." In *Crime and the New Immigrants*. H. Launer and J. Palenski, eds. Springfield, IL: Charles C. Thomas.

U.S. Census Bureau. 2001a. *Census 2000 Projections of the Resident Population by Race, Hispanic Origin, and Nativity*. Washington, D.C.: U.S. Census Bureau.

U.S. Census Bureau. 2001b. *Census 2000 Redistricting Data*. Washington, D.C.: U.S. Census Bureau.

U.S. Census Bureau. 2001c. *Census 2000: Overview of Race and Hispanic Origin*. Washington, D.C.: U.S. Census Bureau.

Vrij, A., F. W. Winkle, and F. Willen. 1991. "Encounters Between the Dutch Police and Minorities: Testing the Non-cooperation Hypothesis of Differential Treatment." *Police Studies* 14(1): 17–21.

Walker, S. 1992. *The Police in America*. New York, NY: McGraw-Hill.

Winkel, F. W. 1991. "Interaction Between the Police and Minority Group Members: Victimization Through the Incorrect Interpretation of Nonverbal Behavior." *International Review of Victimology* 2 (1): 15–27.

Wycliff, D. 1987. "Blacks and Blue Power." *New York Times*, February 8.

NOTES

1. The following account of the Brandon Teena story is summarized from details presented in Reardon (2000).
2. *Pyke v. Cuomo*, F.3d (2110 WL 822327, 2nd Cir., 2001).
3. See also U.S. Census Bureau (2001b; 2001c).
4. See also Hagan and Palloni (1998).
5. See also Barlow and Barlow (1994).

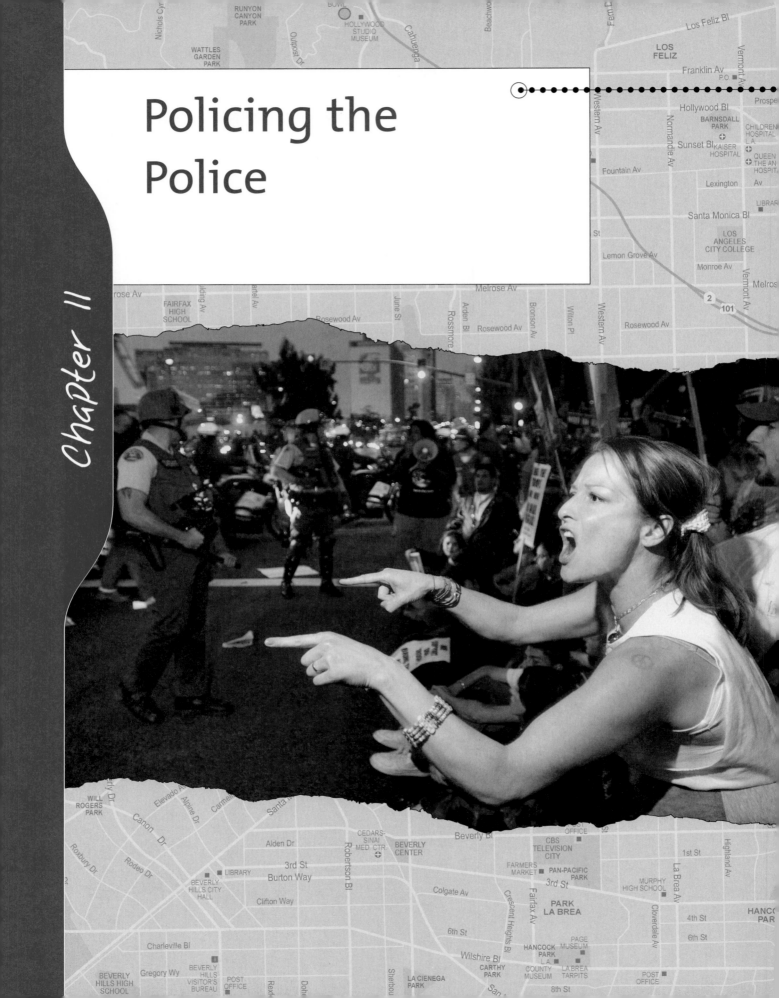

Policing the Police

Chapter Outline

Chapter Objectives

- Understand the continuum of force and recognize when legitimate force becomes excessive force.

- Explain when deadly force is legitimate and the guidelines under which officers can use lethal force.

- Understand how force, brutality, and corruption differ.

- List the types of oversight for police officers and explain which type is best for a particular situation.

- Recognize the common problems that lead to police corruption, as well as recommendations to combat such corruption.

Introduction

During an April 2000 protest by anarchists and other groups against the policies of the World Bank and the International Monetary Fund (IMF), what had largely started as a peaceful protest turned sour (Vest 2000). The protesters were parading without a permit. As the police and protestors approached each other from opposite sides of the street, the police continued to show restraint in the face of inflammatory comments from some angry protesters. Some members of the crowd began to throw and kick newspaper boxes into the street. One individual hurled an object at an officer. Shortly after, at least half a dozen police motorcycles entered the melee, and officers carrying drawn billy clubs emerged behind them. Several officers began to swing at members of the crowd. In the midst of all of this, the police fired tear gas into the crowd, and many of the protestors quickly put on gas masks. Protest medics were immediately on the scene to attend to those affected by the gas. Other individuals began to shower the officers with a steady flow of tulips. Angered by the changing tide, the anarchists began to leave. In total, nearly six hundred arrests were made throughout the day for parading without a permit.

As is often the case, both the protestors and the police have their own version of whether the police exercised legitimate use of force. However, as we will see, the answer is not always clear cut. And when it comes to the use of force, interpretation of the facts is essential.

Use of Force

As discussed in Chapter 1, the use of force is central to the role of the police (Klockers 1985). The police are authorized to use coercive force to control a variety of situations, and this authority defines the police role (Bittner 1970). Although the police are allowed to use coercive force, there are limits as to how much force an officer can legitimately use. Use of force is **legitimate** if it is the minimum amount of force necessary to control a situation. However, the word *necessary* is ambiguous and is certainly subject to the discretion of any officer who responds to a situation.

The Force Continuum

Officers are not always justified in using force, and for the use of force to be legitimate, they must abide by a number of criteria. Officers are only allowed to use force to protect themselves and others around them. They must follow the **force continuum**, or begin with the least amount of force needed and progress to more physical force as necessary (Figure 11.1). The first type of force is simply **command presence**, meaning that the presence of an officer is considered a manner of force in and of itself. This is **nonphysical force** (i.e., use of body language, eye contact, presence, and even the mere significance of the uniform). The next level of force is the **command voice**, or **verbal force**. As is indicated by the name, verbal force requires the officer to speak to the person(s) at whom the officer is applying force. At the very least, the officer should indicate to the person that he or she is a police officer. Verbal force is also appropriate when the officer must tell suspects to put down any weapons or to come out of their home or vehicle.

The use of force is a central, though often complex, function of the police role in society.

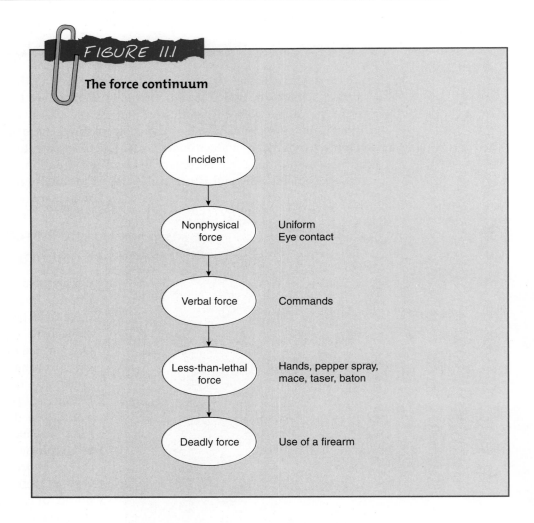

FIGURE 11.1

The force continuum

Incident

↓

Nonphysical force — Uniform / Eye contact

↓

Verbal force — Commands

↓

Less-than-lethal force — Hands, pepper spray, mace, taser, baton

↓

Deadly force — Use of a firearm

If verbal force does not accomplish the task of controlling the situation, the officer can use **less-than-lethal force**. This includes minimal physical force such as with hands, pepper spray, mace, a taser, a baton, or rubber bullets. This level of force is not intended to be deadly, but rather to subdue the suspect so as to avoid harm to the officer or anyone in the surrounding area. Officers are generally allowed to use less-than-lethal force in order to prevent the escape of a fleeing felon, to control a suspect who is resisting arrest, or to protect the officer or anyone in the immediate area from harm. If this level of force is ineffective at controlling a suspect, the officer can use **lethal force**, or force with a firearm. An officer can only use lethal force if he or she is in imminent danger of life or limb or to protect a citizen. This is an officer's last resort, and officers generally only use it when confronted by a suspect with a firearm. However, every situation differs, as does an officer's use of the force continuum. It is important to note that an officer can move in both directions along the force continuum in terms of both escalating and declining tensions.

As an example of the complexities of the force continuum, take the example of Gideon Busch (Marzulli and Hoyle 2003). Police officers responded to a complaint that a mentally disordered man from Brooklyn was acting "strangely." The police arrived to find the 6'4" Gideon Busch wielding a hammer, screaming incoherently, and threatening neighbors and the police with the hammer. Four officers surrounded him and shouted at him to put down the hammer. He did not respond to the verbal force, so they used pepper spray in an attempt to subdue him. Rather than its intended effect, the pepper spray appeared to agitate him, and he reportedly began hitting a police sergeant with the claw hammer. After exhausting the verbal and less-than-lethal means of force, the four officers shot him a total of twelve times. The family filed a wrongful death suit, but the courts came back with a finding that the officers did not use unreasonable force. So how much force *is* unreasonable? This chapter introduces the standards governing law enforcement use of force in the United States.

Objective Reasonableness: *Graham v. Connor*

Reasonable is an ambiguous term. How much force is reasonable in any given situation? Without precise definitions, it is difficult to explain when an officer has used coercive force legitimately or when the force has been excessive. The Court attempted to define legitimate use of force in the case of *Graham v. Connor*.[1]

Dethorne Graham, a diabetic man, had an insulin reaction. He asked a friend to drive him to a convenience store to buy a carton of orange juice to counteract the effect of the insulin. He quickly walked into the store, saw a long line, and then quickly walked back out to the car and asked his friend to drive him elsewhere. After witnessing this strange behavior, Officer Connor pulled over the vehicle and asked Graham and his friend to step out of the car. Confusion ensued, and the officers (Connor had called backup officers to the scene) handcuffed Graham, told him to shut up, and withheld orange juice from him while waiting to find out what Graham had done at the store. Upon receiving information that he had not done anything wrong, the officers drove him home. Graham sustained several injuries, such as bruises, cuts, and a broken foot, and he subsequently claimed excessive use of force.

The Court sought to determine whether Officer Connor's behavior, based upon what he witnessed, was reasonable under the Fourth Amendment. Though he acknowledged using force, the officer claimed that Graham's erratic behavior justified the need to detain him in a forceful manner. The Court agreed, explaining that reasonableness could not be specifically defined and that the Court would be required to look at the issue of reasonableness on a case-by-case basis. The Court found that Connor used force appropriate under the circumstances, and that force was used for the purpose of securing a potentially volatile scene rather than for the purpose of causing harm. **Objective reasonableness**, then, is based on the circumstances of the case. The Court is required to judge whether the force used is legitimate based on the perspective of a "reasonable officer" on the scene who is required to make quick decisions on the amount of force that may be necessary to control a situation.

Excessive Force: The Road to Brutality

Officers sometimes use more than the minimum amount of force necessary to control a situation, and that is when legitimate force becomes **excessive force**. There is no distinct line between behavior that is acceptable and that which is too aggressive. In many cases, force that appears to be excessive may, in fact, be required in a particular situation. That is why the Court applies the objective reasonableness standard on a case-by-case basis.

Although police officers partake in some behavior that is questionably reasonable, other behavior is clearly a violation of an individual's human rights. For instance, compare the cases of Rodney King and Abner Louima. In 1991, the country watched an amateur videotape of four Los Angeles police officers beating Rodney King after he allegedly violated traffic laws and led the police on a pursuit.[2] The police claim that King, a twenty-five-year-old black male, was driving 115 miles per hour in his Hyundai. After stopping King, the police claimed that he appeared to be on PCP and of "superhuman" power. They beat him with nightsticks, fists, and eventually hit him with tasers. He sustained skull fractures and broken bones in his face, and the officers knocked out some of his teeth. The officers in the case claimed that King threatened them, and that, combined with the reaction to the alleged drugs, is why they used such a high degree of force.

The case of Abner Louima was by all intents and purposes more severe than even the King beating. Louima, a Haitian immigrant, was arrested on charges that he assaulted a police officer outside a nightclub. After the police took him into custody, Louima claims that two officers took him into the precinct bathroom and one sodomized him with the broken handle of a toilet plunger while the other held him down.[3] Just prior to this, Louima had been doing nothing to provoke such an attack; he was not even verbally abusing the officers. Yet Justin Volpe, angered by his earlier outburst outside the nightclub, brutally committed an act of torture on him, rupturing Louima's rectum, injuring his bladder, and requiring him to be hospitalized for several weeks. Additionally, Volpe lied about the attack and said that Louima likely sustained such injuries as a result of homosexual activity that night, claiming he was afraid to tell his wife so he made up the story of abuse. Later, with the weight of evidence against him, Volpe pleaded guilty to the offense.

The case of Rodney King quite clearly shows an excessive use of force by police officers. Anyone who witnessed the videotaped beating would likely agree. Although coercive force was arguably justified, King's eleven skull fractures and broken facial bones lead one to believe that the beating was excessive. The case of Abner Louima, however, clearly goes beyond excessive force and would be considered police brutality. People often equate excessive use of force with police brutality, but the most common type of excessive force is actually pushing or grabbing by the officer (Bureau of Justice Statistics 2001). **Brutality**, on the other hand, is when officers express malicious intent to harm. Generally, we think of brutality as intent to physically harm, as in the case of Abner Louima. However, officers can also use verbal brutality, or the intent to use words to harm. This harassment may be psychological, if not physically, damaging.

It is not clear what causes an officer to go from law-abiding rookie officer to ruthless oppressor. Perhaps it is the development of a police personality, discussed in Chapter 9, that leads the officer into a life of stress, cynicism, and authoritarianism. As these police officers develop an "**us versus them**" attitude towards members of the community, the members of the community that the officers abuse develop the same attitude towards them. Unfortunately, such behavior does not usually come to the attention of the police manager until it is too late. After the Rodney King beating, the Christopher Commission was formed to investigate excessive force within the LAPD. Even though Chief Darryl Gates said it was an isolated incident, they found that the excessive use of force was widespread.

Deadly Force

The police rarely use **deadly force**, and most officers do not even draw their guns while on duty. However, many highly trained officers such as SWAT team members (see Chapter 5) are far more likely to use their guns. The police are allowed to use deadly force, though only if it is the minimum amount of force necessary to control a situation. Because this is the ultimate ban on a person's civil liberties, the courts have regulated use of deadly force and consider it to be reasonable only as an absolute last resort.

Deadly force is most often used in high-crime, urban areas. In fact, because of the prevalence of deadly force incidents in New York City in the mid-1980s, then-mayor Mario Cuomo appointed a task force to review all cases where police used their firearms. The duty of this task force was to investigate the causes of deadly force and the effect of the use of such force on the community. The task force determined that minorities were more likely to be victims of deadly force than whites, and this had a negative impact on police–community relations (Condon 1986).

The Fleeing Felon Rule: *Tennessee v. Garner*

Elsewhere, police use of deadly force was also rarely regulated until the mid-1980s. Until 1985, the police could legitimately shoot a **fleeing felon,** or an individual suspected of committing a felony who was fleeing the scene of the crime, in twenty-three states. In 1985, however, the U.S. Supreme Court invalidated the fleeing felon rule and imposed a set of uniform rules governing the use of deadly force, which reflected their ruling in *Tennessee v. Garner*.[4]

Even when an individual suspected of committing a felony has fled the scene (on foot or in vehicle), the use of deadly force must be balanced against the safety concerns to the officer or others following the *Tennessee v. Garner* decision.

One evening, the police were called to investigate a prowler in a Memphis, Tennessee, neighborhood. They came upon an individual, who turned out to be a fifteen-year-old boy, Edward Garner, who ran away from them after they told him to halt. Obeying the fleeing felon laws, the police officer shot and killed Garner. In Court, the officer testified that he did not think the boy was armed but he shot him so that he would not get away. He testified that he could not have caught the suspect any other way because he was old and overweight. Moreover, the officer claimed that he believed that Garner was an adult. The Supreme Court called the shooting of felons to prevent their escape constitutionally unreasonable under the Fourth Amendment. The Court explained that deadly force is unjustified when the suspect poses no immediate danger to the officer or public.

As a result of *Garner*, the federal government and most states established guidelines on the acceptability of deadly force. Generally, the police can only use deadly force when

- An individual commits a felony and uses deadly force or a threat of deadly force during the commission of a felony (i.e., the suspect has committed an armed robbery and is threatening to use deadly force)

- When the officer reasonably believes there is a substantial imminent risk that the person to be arrested will cause death or serious bodily harm to the officer or to another person in the vicinity

- When such force must be used to prevent the escape of a prisoner from prison[5]

- To suppress a riot after sufficient warning has been given.

High-Speed Pursuits as Deadly Force

High-speed vehicle pursuits are dangerous to the police, the public, and the suspect who is fleeing from the police. A pursuit can be defined as a situation in which an officer attempts to initiate a stop, but the suspect flees and the officer pursues the suspect (Welch 2002). A suspect may flee an officer who is initiating a stop for a number of reasons. For instance, the suspect may have stolen the car, have an arrest warrant outstanding, or is leaving the crime scene (Dunham et al. 1998). Whatever the reason, pursuits constitute a high risk, and approximately one in five individuals who initiates a pursuit is injured (Dunham et al. 1998).

High-speed pursuits most often end in one of four ways. First, the suspect can voluntarily stop the pursuit and surrender to the police. Second, the police can damage the fleeing suspect's car or tires (e.g., by planting spikes on the road or by shooting the tires) so that the suspect is forced to stop. This is more common than the first option, though this may be dangerous and the suspect may try to

High-speed vehicle pursuits are dangerous to the police, public, and the fleeing suspect.

flee once the car has been stopped. The most common method by which vehicle pursuits end, however, is when the fleeing suspect crashes the vehicle into an inanimate object (e.g., a tree or light pole) or into another motorist. When the pursuit ends this way, it can result in serious injury or death to both the suspect and the individual into whom he or she crashes. For this reason, many police departments have policy guidelines governing high-speed pursuits (Rayburn 2001). A fourth way in which high-speed pursuits end is when the police officer terminates the pursuit because it is endangering the lives of others. More police departments are beginning to adopt the policy that when the public safety risk outweighs the risk of the fleeing offender getting away, the pursuit must stop.

Though dangerous, high-speed pursuits are not unconstitutional. In the case of *County of Sacramento v. Lewis*[6] in 1998, the Court decided that high-speed pursuits, though dangerous, do not constitute a deliberate indifference or a reckless disregard for human life. The Court reviewed whether such pursuits, when they end in death, violate the Fourteenth Amendment Due Process clause of the Constitution. The Court in *Lewis* claimed that liabilities for injuries resulting from high-speed pursuits arise only if the officer involved in the pursuit intended to harm the suspect physically. The Court claimed that the majority of high-speed pursuits do not go as far as to "shock the conscience," and that they are therefore constitutional. Despite this fact, cases have continued to come before the Court to test this concept.[7] As of yet, no cases have overridden the important precedent set in *Lewis*.

Corruption

Police corruption, or the misuse of authority by a police officer, has been a concern in policing since the time of the watch system. Corruption involves an entire range of actions involving an officer's misuse of his or her authority for personal gain. These actions can include both passive and active behaviors on the part of the officer. There are many types and levels of corruption, but the Knapp Commission (which will be discussed later in detail) described corruption by placing corrupt officers into one of two categories: grass eaters and meat eaters. **Grass eaters** are officers who accept gifts or favors from individuals, but who do not actively seek out or demand such activities. In contrast, **meat eaters** aggressively demand bribes in exchange for protection (or lack of) of the person from whom they are seeking the favor. Studies have shown that in environments where meat eater activity is allowed to persist with impunity, a greater number of grass eaters in the department will be the inevitable result (Swanson et al. 2000).

Investigative Commissions: From Wickersham to Christopher

One way to investigate corruption or brutality in a department is to form a commission. A **commission** is a group of individuals, generally appointed by a governor, mayor, or the president, who come together to investigate police misconduct. Since the 1930s, many investigative commissions have been appointed to investigate allegations of police abuse of power. The purpose of such commissions is to find the source of misconduct and hold the police, either individually or collectively, accountable for their actions. Commissions offer recommendations for improving the accountability of the police. However, a review of various commission recommendations indicates that commissions are cyclical in nature.

There are three main recurring themes to commission reports: (1) improve recruitment and training, (2) improve police–community relations, and (3) improve the existing police complaints system (Terry and Grant 2003). Commissions are often formed as a reaction to specific incidents of misconduct, yet their recommendations tend to lack any recognition of the underlying issues that caused the triggering incident. As a result, the changes suggested by the commission are rarely effective in the long-term.

The first commission to fully analyze police conduct (and misconduct) was the Wickersham Commission in the 1930s. Since that time, the most influential commissions have included the Kerner Commission, the Knapp Commission, the Mollen Commission, and the Christopher Commission. Commissions are not only an American phenomenon, however. In England, the McPherson Report was written in response to an inquiry into the police investigation of the death of Stephen Lawrence, a black teenager, at the hands of four white teenagers. Specifically, the inquiry aimed to determine whether the British police showed a systemic racial bias in their investigative duties. The McPherson Report indicated that Lawrence's death was not only racially motivated, but that the police response was grossly inadequate and that the police needed to implement long-term, systemic changes in order to combat such problems in the future (McPherson 1999). The British inquiry investigated several of the same issues as those examined by American commissions, and its findings were surprisingly analogous.

The Wickersham Commission (1931)

By the end of the 1920s, the United States faced a number of social and criminal problems such as crime stemming from Prohibition, a rise in organized and juvenile crime, and discord between the police and the community. President Herbert Hoover organized the Wickersham Commission in 1929 to investigate these problems. The commission produced a total of fourteen volumes of reports that analyzed social problems and the criminal justice response to those problems.

In terms of police abuse of power, the commission examined the investigative technique of the "third degree" (National Commission on Law Observance and Enforcement 1931).[8] The third degree was a technique whereby officers would inflict pain upon the suspect in order to elicit a confession (Walker et al. 1996). At this point in time, state police could still legally get coerced confessions.[9] However, the report contained a scathing analysis of such techniques, which soon fell into disuse.

The Wickersham Commission provided the first national analysis of police misconduct, and for the first time, police reform leaders formed a system whereby civilians could register complaints against the police. These were internal systems, consisting of specialized officers whose sole duty was to investigate misconduct by fellow officers. Though there were problems with the system, it was the first true system of police accountability.

The Kerner Commission (1965)

The 1960s was an era of civil unrest in the United States. Riots occurred in many cities, stemming largely from the deteriorating relationship between the police and the people in the communities they patrolled, particularly in minority communities. Police misconduct was rampant, and there was still no adequate way to hold police accountable for their actions. The police routinely violated the constitutional rights of individuals, and the Court finally took notice. Under the leadership of Chief Justice Earl Warren, the Supreme Court decided a number of landmark cases at this time that limited the powers of the police and held them accountable for their actions.[10] Individuals were registering complaints with the police in record numbers, but the only means by which these complaints were investigated was by the police themselves. To the community, this was not acceptable.

As a result of community discord, riots, and increasing reports of police misconduct, the government sponsored the formation of a number of commissions. Lyndon Johnson formed the Kerner Commission in 1965 to investigate these problems, and the Commission reported widespread racial injustices by the police and general dissatisfaction with the internal review procedures of police practices (Morris and Hawking 1970).

The report published by the Kerner Commission suggested many reforms (National Advisory Commission on Civil Disorder 1968). Similar to those before and after it, the report suggested the need to eliminate aggressive policing tactics (which largely targeted minorities), to implement effective mechanisms of police accountability, to increase minority recruitment for and promotion within the police, and to improve police relations with the community through the establishment of community policing programs. Despite the implementation of many of the suggestions, as well as the Court's curb on police power, there was no long-term reduction of police brutality or corruption (Bureau of Justice Statistics 2001).

The Knapp Commission (1972)

In the 1970s, the police were embroiled in a number of corruption scandals. The alleged "blue wall of silence" kept officers from testifying against the corrupt practices, though in 1972 that silence was broken. Frank Serpico, a plainclothes officer from the Bronx, exposed the widespread corruption within the NYPD and testified against his fellow officers in the resulting Knapp Commission (Knapp Commission Report 1972). The Knapp Commission found significant forms of police misconduct at all levels of the NYPD, including corruption, bribery, and participation in illegal activities such as gambling and prostitution.

The Knapp Commission recognized that the existing system of police accountability was inadequate. Though the NYPD had an Internal Affairs Division (IAD), it was ineffective and needed to be reorganized. Additionally, the commission stated that police officers should be criminally prosecuted for

Serpico remains an important symbol in the fight against police corruption.

any type of misconduct. As with the Kerner Commission, these recommendations were implemented but were largely ineffective, with the post of special prosecutor dissipating by 1990.

The Mollen Commission (1994)

After the scandal of the Knapp Commission findings, the NYPD vowed to reform its organizational structure, crack down on misconduct, and eliminate corruption. Yet just over twenty years later they were embroiled in yet another scandal. Six NYPD officers were arrested on drug charges in 1992, prompting another inquiry into police misconduct in New York City. The Mollen Commission, formed to investigate the new revelations of abuse, found that corruption was still widespread and that the types of misconduct were more serious than those found by the Knapp Commission. The many crimes included protecting narcotics traffickers, conducting illegal searches and seizures, falsifying records, and committing crimes such as robbery and drug trafficking (Mollen Commission Report 1994). The Mollen Commission found a link between corruption and brutality, and this was particularly prevalent in minority communities. The misconduct had continued for an extended period of time, and it was able to continue because of the code of silence among officers. It was apparent at all levels of the NYPD, from the top managers to the rank and file officers, and there was no system to adequately address complaints.

Like the Knapp Commission before it, the Mollen Commission suggested sweeping changes to both the structure of and practice within the NYPD.

Though both commission reports recommended increased accountability, the Mollen Commission specifically suggested the implementation of a system of external oversight. It recognized that the IAD was not sufficient to combat the problems within the department and that the managerial officers in charge of the department were themselves corrupt. Though the NYPD has not yet convened any new commissions since the Mollen Commission, it has still been witness to acts of misconduct and brutality. The case of Abner Louima is an example of how police misconduct can escalate to severe cases of brutality—and, as some officers have said, it is the most severe case of brutality the department has ever witnessed.

The Christopher Commission (1992)

The LAPD, like the NYPD, has also been subject to independent review by a commission. In 1991, the world witnessed four white officers beating Rodney King, a black motorist, who was allegedly on PCP and displaying "superhuman" powers. This case was highly publicized because a civilian videotaped the beating and sent the tape to a television station.[11] The Christopher Commission was formed as a result of the King beating, and subsequently found evidence indicating that racism and bias were rampant within the LAPD. The commission also noted the lack of accountability, both within the department and to the community, and suggested extensive reforms such as changes in structure, recruitment, and accountability mechanisms (Christopher Commission 1992). The Commission also found that police management was poor and rarely reprimanded officers for complaints of excessive force.

Recommendations from the Commissions

Commissions all offer similar recommendations: minority recruitment, education and residency requirements, and police accountability (specifically, civilian oversight of the police). Despite their cyclical nature, reforms are rarely implemented and, when they are, they rarely result in the sweeping changes suggested. See Table 11.1 for a summary of the cyclical nature of commission reports.

The most significant recruitment push resulting from investigative commissions has been towards greater representation of both ethnic minorities and women in law enforcement agencies. Despite this push over the past decade, as discussed in Chapter 10, minorities are still underrepresented. Racial and ethnic minorities represented about one-fifth of the local police department populations in 1997 (Bureau of Justice Statistics 2001). This constitutes a significant increase from the previous decade, but it is still not representative in urban areas such as Los Angeles and New York City.

Educational and residency requirements are other topics frequently touched upon by the commissions. Many police departments have educational standards whereby officers are required to have either a college degree or a certain number of college credits towards a degree in order to join a police force. Although the majority of departments still do not require college credit, over one-quarter of all departments require some college education for entry-level positions, a number double what it was a decade ago (Terrill 1991).

In addition to education requirements, some departments have residency requirements mandating that officers live within the jurisdiction in which they are

TABLE 11.1

Major Commission Findings and Recommendations

Commission/Task Force	Precipitating Incident	Underlying Problem	Recommendations
Wickersham	Prohibition, increasing crime rate, need to reevaluate juvenile justice, need to evaluate the adult criminal justice process	Increasing crime rate, particularly organized crime, need for evaluation of governmental agencies and adequacy of the criminal justice process	• Social awareness of problems between police and minority communities • Establish a complaints system
Kerner	Riots of the 1960s, complaints by minorities about police abuse of power	Police misconduct, lack of accountability to all citizens, no oversight of police procedures	• Better recruitment and training standards • Accountability to the community • Establish mechanisms for registering complaints
Knapp	Widespread corruption and bribery, particularly among undercover units in New York City	Lack of oversight of police procedures, decreasing hierarchical accountability, identification of "blue wall of silence"	• Reorganize IAD • Civilian oversight of the police • Create post of state special prosecutor
Christopher	Excessive use of force by the police against a black motorist, subsequent riots and inability of the LAPD to adequately control the situation.	Lack of accountability, lack of repercussions for misconduct, concealment of brutality	• Implement structural changes in recruitment, selection, training, and evaluation • Establish a new system for handling complaints and improve civilian oversight • Implement a community-based policing model
Mollen	Corruption scandal in specific undercover units, linking of corruption and brutality	Lack of accountability in undercover units, concealment of corruption and brutality by officers and management	• Improve screening, recruitment and training (for new and in-service officers) • Increase and improve police supervision • Reform internal/external oversight • Enhance sanctions for brutality and corruption

Source: Terry and Grant (2003).

policing. This recommendation has surfaced from many of the commissions in the hopes that by living in the communities they police, officers will be better equipped to understand, and thereby interact with, its citizenry. Despite all of these suggestions, the commissions discussed here were most adamant about their recommendations for accountability. Specifically, they called for a system of civilian oversight so that the police could be held accountable for their actions.

Models of Civilian Oversight

Prior to the 1960s, only one body reviewed complaints against the police—the police. This internal investigation process began after publication of the Wickersham Report, which acknowledged the fact that someone needed to police the police. It was at this time that police departments began to form **internal affairs bureaus (IABs)**, or specialized police units with whom citizens could register complaints. The IAB, which was comprised entirely of police officers, would then investigate the complaints. Most complainants were encouraged to withdraw their complaints, and those that were investigated were found to be unsubstantiated or the officer was **exonerated** (found not liable for the conduct with which they were charged) (Terrill 1991). By the 1960s, with outbreaks of urban rioting in response to police misconduct, various citizen groups began vocalizing their dissatisfaction with the police complaint process. They claimed that the police cannot effectively police themselves, and that the existing means for seeking redress were ineffective (Goldstein 1977). Therefore, citizens groups, as well as various commissions, suggested that external review boards should be set up so that civilians could hold the police accountable for their actions.

An external review board will not completely eliminate police misconduct, brutality, or prejudicial discretion, but it can provide one level of **democratic accountability**, or accountability to the community, over a group of individuals with the power to use coercive force. This system of accountability should alert police management to potential problems with officers in the force, thus allowing for actions to be taken to deter future misconduct. IABs also provide a type of accountability—**hierarchical accountability**—or accountability to those structurally higher within the department (e.g., accountability to the police chief). Both types of accountability are important and can help to reduce misconduct among officers.

A satisfactory police complaints system can help to instill public confidence in the police, because those who register complaints are likely to consider the effectiveness of the police complaints system based on the way they are treated as well as on the outcome of their cases. Studies have found that individuals who file complaints against the police are more likely to be satisfied with the outcome if they view the process through which the outcome was derived to be fair and impartial. This concept is called **procedural justice**, and explains situations in which the outcome is less important than the procedure by which the outcome is produced (Kerstetter 1995).[12] Maguire and Corbett (1991) and Brown (1987) showed that most individuals do not consider internal investigations about police complaints to be fair and impartial, because they seemingly exist within a closed institution and the police will protect each other from the public. In order to allow a greater public confidence in the police and satisfaction from complainants, some form of external review over police actions is necessary.

Civilian oversight of the police has four goals: (1) to deter future misconduct, (2) to remove deviant officers, (3) to satisfy individual complainants, and (4) to maintain public confidence in the police (Walker 2001). Since external review boards were first implemented in the 1960s, they have varied in their accomplishment of these goals. The fact that a civilian oversight committee exists is not enough to eradicate tensions between the police and the community. The board must be created so that it is suitable for the community it is serving, and it must have adequate powers to make the process satisfactory to the citizens making the complaints.

History of Civilian Oversight

The first civilian review boards emerged in Philadelphia (The Philadelphia Advisory Board, 1958–1967) and in New York City (New York Civilian Complaint Review Board, 1953–present) (Walker et al. 1996). In order to combat the increasing tension between the police and the community, the Philadelphia branch of the ACLU called for the creation of the civilian review board in 1957. Although the police were strongly opposed to civilian oversight, Mayor Richard Dilworth created an entirely civilian body called the Philadelphia Police Advisory Board. The members of the Board had the responsibility to assess complaints of police brutality, false arrest, discrimination charges, or any other wrongful conduct against citizens. The board faced many problems, such as lack of legal standing, political backing, and cooperation from the police (Goldstein 1977).

The police were dismayed by the fact that their actions would be judged by individuals who were not police officers and who had no experience with what they went through on a daily basis (Brown 1983) and considered the boards to be a type of political interference in their police duties (Morris and Hawking 1970). The police also believed that they would not be able to use the amount of initiative, aggressiveness, and discretion necessary in their police work for as long as the lay board scrutinized them. Their worst fear was that a civilian board would view those making the complaints to be more credible than the officers (Van Maanen 1978). Most important, they did not believe that lay individuals would be able to understand the necessity of discretion in a police officer's job (Reiner 1993).

Despite police opposition to civilian review boards, more cities began to implement some form of civilian oversight over the next few decades. Most of the early boards eventually disbanded, and individuals began turning to the courts in the 1970s for restitution (Cheh 1995). In turn, the government focused on eliminating the misconduct that led to complaints and accusations of police malpractice.

The concept of an ombudsman was also introduced in the 1970s. An **ombudsman** is a neutral figure who reviews complaints against all public servants, not just the police, in an effort to combat organizational or systemic misconduct. Today, the role of mediation is similar to the practice used by an ombudsman in the 1970s.

It was in the 1970s that a number of prominent review boards were formed. The most influential of these boards were in Detroit (Board of Police

Commissioners), Chicago (Office of Professional Standards), Berkeley (Police Review Commission), and Kansas City (Office of Citizen Complaints). The 1980s brought forth a conservative period of law enforcement practice, with a primary focus on crime control instead of due process. Nonetheless, fifteen cities established civilian review boards at this time (Petterson 1991). In these cities, the implantation of such boards tended to be sparked by an emotionally charged case of police brutality, as in the case of Arthur Duffie, a black insurance salesman. Four white police officers in Dade County, Florida, all with previous complaints of misconduct, followed Duffie in a high-speed car chase and beat him to death when they caught him (Porter and Dunn 1974). It was after this incident that Dade County established its Independent Review Panel (IRP).

By 1995, 66 police departments had some form of civilian complaint review process, and by 2000, the number had increased to 100 (Walker 2001). Civilian review boards could be found in large- and medium-sized cities, as well as rural areas. Some civilian review boards that had already been in place were modified to incorporate changes suggested by the various commission reports. For example, the Civilian Complaint Review Board (CCRB) in New York City was transformed into an all-civilian review board in July 1993. Prior to 1987, it had been composed solely of nonsworn police personal (e.g., police dispatchers), and from 1987–1993 the board members consisted of both civilians and nonsworn police personnel. This change resulted from suggestions by the Mollen Commission.

Walker's Typologies of Civilian Oversight

What do civilian oversight committees look like today? Each city is unique, but according to Walker (2001) they follow four primary systems: Class I, Class II, Class III, and Class IV. With Class I systems, an independent body has jurisdiction for receiving and investigating complaints. Though the police chief can make recommendations based upon the findings of the independent body, his or her role is that primarily of approval and oversight. New York City, Washington, D.C., San Francisco, and Minneapolis have this type of external complaint system. With Class II systems, internal affairs units are in charge of the investigation, but an oversight agency reviews the results of the investigation. Kansas City is one city with this type of police complaints system. With Class III systems, internal affairs departments investigate the complaints. The complaint goes on to a civilian oversight agency only if the complainant is dissatisfied with the results of the investigation, at which point the complainant can appeal the decision. Omaha is one city with this type of review system. With Class IV systems, the responsibility of reviewing police complaints remains entirely within the department. The only role of the oversight agency is to assure quality control throughout the complaint process. Portland, San Jose, and the Los Angeles Sheriff's department have this type of system. Table 11.2 outlines each class of system.

Problems with the Complaint Process: Is There a "Best Practice"?

Each type of police complaint system has costs and benefits. Walker (2001) explains seven ways in which civilian oversight is both beneficial and problematic, shown in Table 11.3.

TABLE 11.2

Walker's Class System of Civilian Oversight

Class	Description
Class I	• An independent agency has original jurisdiction for receiving and investigating complaints.
	• Staff investigators are not members of the police department.
	• Results of the investigation are forwarded by the oversight agency to the police chief for appropriate disciplinary action, if sustained.
Class II	• Complaints are investigated by an internal affairs or professional standards unit.
	• Results of the investigation are reviewed by an oversight agency.
	• Decision of the oversight agency is forwarded to the police chief.
Class III	• Complaints are investigated by an internal affairs or professional standard unit.
	• Complainant can appeal decision if not satisfied with the result.
	• Oversight agency handles appeals.
Class IV	• Responsibility for investigating complaints lies within the department.
	• Oversight agency audits or monitors the complaint process (quality control).

Source: Walker (2001).

The primary ground of dissatisfaction with any police complaints system is the low number of **substantiated complaints**, or those in which the officer is found guilty of the action alleged. The more serious the complaint is, the less likely it is to be substantiated. This difficulty in substantiating complaints is due to several important factors. First, the charges must be proven "beyond a reasonable doubt," the same standard of proof required in criminal courts, and if the evidence does not meet this standard, the charge is dismissed. In order to prove a charge beyond a reasonable doubt, there must be corroborating evidence. The majority of complainants cannot substantiate their statements, because there are rarely witnesses to the officers' actions except perhaps other officers or friends of the complainant. Thus, the only statements that exist are those of the complainant and the officer, which often directly contradict each other. Individuals registering complaints are usually unaware of the high standard of proof required and are subsequently disappointed in the results of the process.

With serious complaints, the corroborating evidence is particularly important because of the potentially serious consequences if the results are substantiated. Such allegations are important to substantiate if the charges are true, and they are also the most damaging to the officer's career if they are not. The use of coercive force is a tactic that the police use to maintain social order. There is a delicate balance between the amount of force that is legitimate and that which is excessive, and what may be excessive in one circumstance might be necessary in another. Complaints of assault and excessive force are most likely to come about in situations where danger is present and force was a necessary action to protect the officer, the public, or the suspected offender (Cheh 1995; Goldstein 1977).

TABLE 11.3

Walker's Arguments For and Against Civilian Complaint Review Boards

Arguments for Civilian Review	Arguments Against Civilian Review
Police misconduct widespread	Police misconduct not a serious problem
More thorough and fair investigations	Less thorough and less fair investigations
Higher sustain rate	Lower sustain rate
More disciplinary actions	Fewer disciplinary actions
Deter police misconduct	Deter effective police work
Improve public attitudes	Less public satisfaction
Promote police professionalism	Undermine police professionalism

Source: Walker (2001).

In most cases, the police conduct complaint investigations, even when civilian review boards exist. The public is likely to be skeptical of investigative outcomes when the police investigate themselves, even when civilian review boards oversee the investigation. Unfortunately, the police *and* the public are not likely to be satisfied with any one complaint system; the public views police investigations as unfair, feeling that the police will protect each other (Niederhoffer 1967; Reiner 1994), and the police feel that civilian investigations are unfair because the word of the complainant might be accepted over that of the officer (Van Maanen 1978; Walker 2001). However, the police are often able to investi-

Mediation offers important benefits to both police and citizens, including an increased understanding of the others' perspective.

gate accusations more thoroughly than civilian boards, and their investigations are thus more likely to be substantiated (Walker 2001). This is because the police have access to the information necessary to conduct a thorough investigation. Boards employing civilian investigators have almost universally collapsed, and those that still exist regularly utilize police investigators to conduct their investigations (Walker 2001).

Another beneficial system of review is the Early Warning System (EWS), which allows the department to keep track of all complaints against officers, the outcome of the complaints, and repetitive behavior patterns that are potentially problematic (Alpert and Dunham 1992). If problematic behavior is noted or the officer receives multiple complaints, his or her entire record is reviewed and action is taken to address the problem (Gaines et al. 1994). This is an internal procedure, providing a means of assistance rather than punishment for potential behavioral problems. It is based on the assumption that officers will be more likely to respond positively to constructive criticism from their peers than to an external review committee.

Another positive development in some larger police agencies is the use of **mediation**, or alternative dispute resolution. Several departments are implementing mediation systems so that minor complaints (e.g., verbal abuse) can be resolved quickly and with preferred outcomes. Following on the concept of procedural justice, many citizens are more satisfied with informal resolution than with fully investigated complaints because the process is more satisfactory (Corbett 1991). Maguire and Corbett (1991) showed that for cases that were in-

Linkages in Law Enforcement

Civilian Oversight of the War on Terror

In addition to the USA PATRIOT Act of 2001, Congress also passed the Terrorism Tribunal Act of 2001 in order to "support the President and the United States Armed Forces in their actions to deter and prevent acts of international terrorism by providing appropriate mechanisms for the United States to prosecute individuals suspected of committing or supporting terrorism." As a tool against terrorism, the Act seeks to "put accused terrorists on trial faster and in greater secrecy than in an ordinary criminal court" (Fournier 2001). Although the Department of Justice insists that with either a military trial, the right to a lawyer and jury will remain, the composition of the jury will not be civilians. In other words, these acts are intending to ensure that there will not be any civilian oversight over terrorist investigations or trials.

Questions

1. What reasons do you feel the government has for creating a more secret investigation or adjudicatory process for terrorists? Do you agree or disagree with these reasons?

2. What role should citizen oversight play in the war on terrorism? At what point do you feel citizen oversight should be sacrificed for public safety interests?

3. How much should law enforcement warn the public about possible terrorist threats? What criteria would you develop?

formally resolved, over half of the complainants were at least fairly satisfied and 30 percent were very satisfied. This can be compared with only 10 percent of complainants for investigated cases being even fairly satisfied and 68 percent being very dissatisfied.

Who should police the police? This is an age old question that is difficult to answer because no answer will satisfy all the parties involved. Many of the commissions discussed in this chapter evaluated the issue of police accountability and claimed that there must be some system of internal and external review so that officers are held democratically and hierarchically accountable. The police have in the past opposed the initiation of civilian review over their actions, and yet few forces have increased the amount of hierarchical accountability so that civilian review would not be necessary. As the Christopher Commission stated in its report after the Rodney King beating, "The failure to control these officers is a management issue that is at the heart of the problem" (Skolnick and Fyfe 1993, p. 3).

Chapter Summary

- Officers have the legal power to use coercive force, but when doing so they must follow a force continuum from verbal force to less-than-lethal force to lethal force.

- There is no clear definition of excessive force. In order to determine whether a police officer's use of force is excessive, the Court uses the Fourth Amendment standard of "objective reasonableness."

- Specific rules apply as to when officers are allowed to use deadly force. Generally, the officer or the public must be in imminent danger of life or limb. The Court set out standards for use of deadly force in *Tennessee v. Garner*, a case that also abolished the fleeing felon rule.

- When a police force experiences a serious case of misconduct (or when the misconduct exists throughout the department), a commission is often appointed to investigate the abuse of power. Several commissions throughout the twentieth century have published recommendations for reducing corruption and brutality, the most common being better recruitment and training standards, increased accountability, and a better complaint system.

- By the year 2001, more than 100 departments had implemented a civilian review board. This external oversight system should help make police accountable to the communities they police. However, many citizens are still not satisfied with the complaint structure.

KEY TERMS

Brutality 268
Command presence 265
Command voice 265
Commission 271
Deadly force 269
Democratic accountability 277
Excessive force 267
Exonerated 277
Fleeing felon rule 269

Force continuum 265
Grass eaters 271
Hierarchical accountability 277
Internal affairs bureau (IAB) 277
Legitimate force 265
Less-than-lethal force 266
Lethal force 266
Meat eaters 271

Mediation 282
Nonphysical force 265
Objective reasonableness 267
Ombudsman 278
Police corruption 271
Procedural justice 277
Substantiated complaints 280
Us versus them 268
Verbal force 265

Linking the Dots

1. What are the different levels of legitimate force that an officer can use? How can the Court tell if an officer uses legitimate or excessive force? Can reasonable force be defined?

2. What is more important, democratic or hierarchical accountability? Why?

3. What would be a proactive way to combat police corruption, force, and brutality? What is currently being done to combat these problems?

REFERENCES

Alpert, G. P., and R. C. Dunham. 1992. *Policing Urban America*, 2d ed. Prospect Heights, IL: Waveland Press.

Bittner, E. 1970. *The Functions of Police in Modern Society*. Washington, D.C.: National Institute of Mental Health.

Brown, D. C. 1983. *Civilian Review of Complaints Against the Police: A Survey of the United States Literature*. Home Office Research and Planning Unit. London: H.M.S.O.

Brown, D. C. 1987. *The Police Complaints Procedure: A Survey of Complainants' Views*. Home Office Research Study No. 93. London: H.M.S.O.

Bureau of Justice Statistics. 2001. *Contacts Between the Police and the Public*. Washington, D.C.: Bureau of Justice Statistics.

Cheh, M. M. 1995. "Are Lawsuits an Answer to Police Brutality?" In *And Justice For All: Understanding and Controlling Police Abuse of Force*, edited by W.A. Geller and H. Toch, 233–259. Washington, D.C.: Police Executive Research Forum.

Christopher Commission. 1991. *Christopher Commission Report*. Los Angeles, CA:Independent Commission on the Los Angeles Police Department.

Condon, 1986. *New York City Report on Deadly Force*. Albany, NY: Department of Criminal Justice Services.

Corbett, C. 1991. "Complaints Against the Police: The New Procedure of Informal Resolution." *Policing and Society* 2(1): 47–60.

Dunham, R., G. Alpert, G. Kenny, and P. Cromwell. 1998. "High-Speed Pursuit: The Offenders' Perspective." *Criminal Justice and Behavior* 25(1): 30–45.

Fournier, R. 2001. "USA: Bush Orders Terrorist Trials by Military Tribunal." Available at www.yale.edu./lawweb/avalon/sept_11/hr3564_ih.htm.

Gaines, L. K., V. E. Kappeler, and J. B. Vaughn. 1994. *Policing in America*. Cincinnati, OH: Anderson Publishing Company.

Goldstein, H. 1977. *Policing a Free Society*. Cambridge, MA: Ballinger.

Kerstetter, W. A. 1995. "A 'Procedural Justice' Perspective on Police and Citizen Satisfaction with Investigations of Police Use of Force: Finding a Common Ground of Fairness." In *And Justice For All: Understanding and Controlling Police Abuse of Force*, edited by W. A. Geller and H. Toch. Washington, D.C.: Police Executive Research Forum.

Klockars, C. 1985. *The Idea of the Police*. Beverly Hills, CA: Sage.

Knapp Commission. 1972. *Knapp Commission Report*. New York, NY: Independent Commission on the New York City Police Department.

Lind, E. A., and T. R. Tyler. 1988. *The Social Psychology of Procedural Justice*. New York, NY: Anchor Press.

MacPherson, W. 1999. *The Stephen Lawrence Inquiry: Report of an Inquiry*. London: The Stationery Office.

Maguire, M., and C. Corbett. 1991. *A Study of the Police Complaints System*. London: H.M.S.O.

Marzulli, J., and R. Hoyle. 2003. "A Killing in Dispute." *Daily News*, October 12, 2003, 10.

Mollen Commission. 1994. *Commission Report: Commission to Investigate Allegations of Police Corruption and the Anti-Corruption Procedures of the Police Department.* New York, NY: Mollen.

Morris, N., and G. Hawking. 1970. *The Honest Politicians Guide to Crime Control.* Chicago: University of Chicago Press.

National Advisory Commission on Civil Disorder. 1968. Report of the National Advisory Commission on Civil Disorder. Washington, D.C.: Government Printing Office.

National Commission on Law Observance and Enforcement. 1931. *The Wickersham Commission Report.* Washington, D.C.: Government Printing Office.

Niederhoffer, A. 1967. *Behind the Shield: The Police in Urban Society.* Garden City, NY: Doubleday.

Petterson, W. E. 1991. "Police Accountability and Civilian Oversight of Policing: An American Perspective." In *Complaints Against the Police: The Trend to External Review*, edited by A. J. Goldsmith, 259–290. Oxford: Clarendon Press.

Porter, B., and M. Dunn. 1984. *The Miami Riot of 1980: Crossing the Bounds.* Lexington, MA: Lexington Books.

Rayburn, M. 2001. *Advanced Patrol Tactics.* Flushing, NY: Looseleaf Law.

Reiner, R. 1993. *The Politics of the Police*, 2d ed. Sussex: Wheatsheat Books.

Reiner, R. 1994. "Policing and the Police." In *The Oxford Handbook of Criminology,* edited by M. Maguire, R. Morgan, and R. Reiner, 705–772. Oxford: Oxford University Press.

Skolnick, J. H., and J. J. Fyfe. 1993. *Above the Law: Police and the Excessive Use of Force.* Toronto: Free Press.

Swanson, C., L. Territo, and R. Taylor. 2000. *Police Administration: Structures, Processes and Behavior.* Upper Saddle River, NJ: Prentice-Hall.

Terrill, R. J. 1991. "Civilian Oversight of the Police Complaints Process in the United States: Concerns, Developments, and More Concern." In *Complaints Against the Police: The Trend to External Review,* edited by A.J. Goldsmith, 291–322. Oxford: Clarendon Press.

Terry, K. J., and H. B. Grant. 2004. "The Roads Not Taken: Improving the Use of Civilian Complaint Review Boards and Implementation of the Recommendations from Investigative Commissions." In *Policing and Minority Communities: Bridging the Gap,* edited by D. J. Jones-Brown and K. J. Terry, 160–182. Upper Saddle River, NJ: Prentice-Hall.

Van Maanen, J. 1978. "The Asshole." In *Policing: A View From the Street*, edited by P. Manning and J. Van Maanen, 21–38. New York, NY: Random House.

Vest, J. 2000. "Police Use Limited Force as Protesters Perturb IMF Meetings." Alternet.org. Available at www.atlernet.org.

Walker, S. 2001. *Police Accountability: The Role of Civilian Oversight.* Belmont, CA: Wadsworth Publishing.

Walker, S. C. Spohn, and T. DeLone. 1996. *The Color of Justice: Race, Ethnicity and Crime in America.* Belmont, CA: Wadsworth.

Welch, M. 2002. "Police Pursuits: Just One Form of Violence." In *Policing and Violence,* edited by R. G. Burns and C. E. Crawford, 147–166. Upper Saddle River, NJ: Prentice-Hall.

NOTES

1. *Graham v. Connor,* 490 U.S. 386 (1989).
2. Only four officers actually beat King, but twenty-three officers in total responded to the incident (see Skolnick and Fyfe 1993).
3. The identity of the officer who held him down is still an issue of contention. Charles Swartz was accused and tried three times, then after another hung jury, he pled out to a lesser offense. It is likely that the identity of the second officer will never be known.
4. *Tennessee v. Garner,* 471 U.S. 1 (1985).
5. However, this is only constitutional if deadly force is not excessive punishment for the prisoner's actions. In other words, it would be excessive force for an officer to shoot an offender convicted of misdemeanor larceny who escapes from jail because deadly force is not proportionate to the offender's prior act.
6. *County of Sacramento v. Lewis,* 523 U.S. 833 (1998).
7. For instance, see *Epps v. Lauderdale County,* 2002 U.S. App. LEXIS 16575.
8. According to Skolnick and Fyfe (1993), the first degree is arrest, the second degree is the transport to a place of confinement, and the third degree is the interrogation. The Wickersham Commission describes the third degree process as a situation that encourages police brutality, equating the process with torture.

9. This ended in 1936 with the case of *Brown v. Mississippi*, 297 U.S. 278 (1936).

10. For example, see *Mapp v. Ohio*, 368 U.S. 871 (1961); *Wong Sun v. United States*, 371 U.S. 471 (1963); *Miranda v. Arizona*, 384 U.S. 436 (1966); *Katz v. United States*, 389 U.S. 347 (1967); *Terry v. Ohio*, 392 U.S. 1 (1968); and *Chimel v. California*, 395 U.S. 752 (1969).

11. King's brother and the civilian who taped the beating attempted to register complaints with the police. Both were dissuaded from doing so, and a formal complaint was only registered after the civilian sent the tape to the media, who played it on national television. See Skolnick and Fyfe, (1993).

12. See also Lind and Tyler (1988).

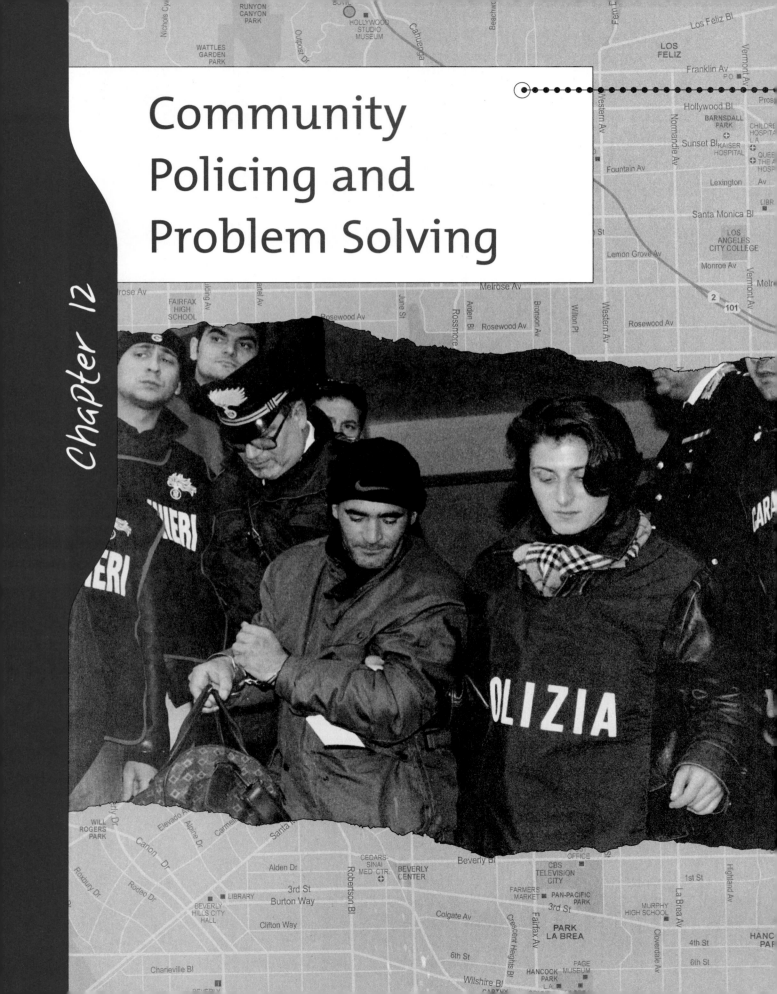

Chapter 12

Community Policing and Problem Solving

Chapter Outline

Chapter Objectives

- Know how community is defined.

- Understand the theoretical underpinnings of community policing.

- Recognize the key components
  and theoretical underpinnings
  of community policing and their
  implications to the organization's
  management.

- Identify key operational barriers to
  implementing community policing in
  practice and articulate ways that they
  can be overcome.

- Understand the problem-solving
  process and its relevance even in the
  current law enforcement context.

- To understand the practical applications of criminological theory on
  modern law enforcement practice.

Introduction

Our struggle showed that the law court is only one front in the campaign against violence and lawlessness. The other is culture. An image that occurred to me early in my own fight against the Mafia was of a cart with two wheels, one law enforcement and the other culture. If one wheel turned without the other, the cart would go in circles. If both turned together, the cart would go forward. So, at the same time as brave lawmen were dying in order to establish a rule of law, we were trying to rebuild our civic life. (Orlando 2001, p. 7)

Leoluca Orlando,
former mayor of Palermo, Sicily

When thinking about how law enforcement can respond to a threat as large and subversive as organized crime, many of us think of images direct from Hollywood. Indeed, there is a long history of films about the fight against organized crime, with characters such as the idealistic Eliot Ness of the *Untouchables* being among the most popular. The media is filled with such glamorized portrayals of law enforcement efforts to combat the Mafia; such portrayals have all of the makings of the action-packed, romantic entertainment that American audiences crave. There is a kernel of truth to some of these stories (the *Untouchables* was, after all, based upon the autobiographical accounts of the real-life Eliot Ness), and organized crime divisions across the country use sound investigative techniques in their efforts against organized crime.

Few would claim that the community, too, can have an important role in anticrime and anticorruption efforts against an enemy as large as the Mafia. However, the success of community policing strategies in Palermo, Sicily, once the "heartland of the Mafia," clearly shows the tremendous role that community participation can play in fighting crime and corruption. Beginning with the example of Palermo, Sicily, this chapter discusses the importance of police partnerships with the community in achieving long-term crime reductions. The important proactive role of the proper application of theory and best practice to law enforcement strategy is also highlighted.

Throughout the 1980s and early 1990s, there were more victims of organized crime violence in Palermo than there were victims of terror in such war-torn places as Palestine and Belfast, numbering into the thousands (Orlando 2001). Palermo's fallen included a general in charge of security forces, the chief of detectives, the chief of police, and two of the most famous magistrates in

Hollywood films are rife with dramatic portrayals of law enforcement's efforts to combat organized crime, such as *The Untouchables*.

Europe. Beginning as a struggle for control between Gaetano Badalamenti and Stefano Bontate—the heads of rival organized crime networks of major Sicilian cities—and including new rivals such as the Corleionisi faction, infighting soon escalated to such a level that it became known as the "Mafia War" (Orlando 2001). Indeed, so fierce was the fighting that even many Mafiosi considered the fighting extreme.

Existing as an institution in Sicily since the nineteenth century, the Mafia had come to permeate all aspects of civil society, including social, political, and cultural life (Orlando 2001). Over time, the established networks eventually began to take on the functions of government, collecting taxes, creating a complex organizational hierarchy, and developing its own groups of "enforcers" to ensure compliance with its demands. It was considered the right of the Mafia families to extort a tax (known as a *pizzo*) on all business activities within its territory in addition to ensuring that employers hire selected Mafia dependents if asked. The Mafia also served the role as mediator, even returning stolen goods (for a fee) on occasion.

Former mayor of Palermo Leoluca Orlando notes that the Mafia was able to dominate Sicilian life in such a complete way in part because of its ability to shroud itself in mystique. Its members were portrayed as men of honor who were integral to the smooth functioning of society (Orlando 2001). This mythology allowed them to regard their jobs as a "call to duty" in much the same way as one might think of becoming a police officer or firefighter. As a subculture, Mafia values were transmitted through a rule of secrecy embodied in the word *omerta,* or "silence before the law." So complete was this secrecy, that the Mafia was virtually unheard of or openly discussed for many years. In fact, it was not until 1982, after over a hundred years of Mafia domination, that the Catholic hierarchy began to speak out against the "evil institution" on the island (NSIC 2000).

Because political and economic life had adjusted to the presence of the Mafia, law enforcement agencies were faced with a dual challenge in their efforts to control organized crime. In addition to traditional investigative and prosecutorial approaches, agencies such as the police first had to convince the public that members of the Mafia were "criminal" (Orlando 2001). Following a particularly violent period in Mafia history, citizens finally began to raise their voices in protest. Eventually, a "Committee of the Sheets" sprang up in some of the worst Mafia controlled areas, in which housewives hung sheets out of windows denouncing the presence and activities of the Mafia. Teachers began to teach schoolchildren about the negative impact of organized crime on society,

and, in an effort to take back the communities that had been allowed to decline under Mafia domination and corruption, began an "Adopt a Monument" program in which children researched decayed monuments throughout the city and took part in their restoration.

As a result of corruption and Mafia domination, Palermo had become a wasteland of sorts, with deteriorating public services, crumbling monuments, overcrowded schools, and high crime. However, the end product of the collaborative efforts of civic organizations (i.e., schools, businesses, and churches) and a revival in fair and effective law enforcement practices was a city transformed. Walking the streets of Palermo just ten years later paints an entirely different picture of the city:

> *The sidewalks are packed—every day and every night. Underscoring the upbeat tempo, music blares from loudspeakers atop utility poles. Shoppers patronize storefronts that line the streets of a city that has never experienced such prosperity—even though the unemployment rate is 29 percent. (Wood 2001, p. 1)*

Further testament to such a sea change in such a short time, which has now been characterized as the "Sicilian Renaissance" (Godson 2000), is the fact that the municipal debt rating service, Moody's, upgraded Palermo's bond rating to Triple A, noting the tremendous political, legal, and economic reforms that have helped to restore investor faith in its integrity and potential for economic development.

The story of Palermo clearly demonstrates the importance of community participation in even the most difficult crime reduction efforts. Although many think of community policing as being "soft on crime," public support is vitally important, and community involvement, when implemented properly, can actually have further-reaching, longer-term impacts than more traditional attempts to control crime such as sting operations, undercover operations, and large-scale arrests. Orlando's analogy of the "two wheels

Known for a time as the "Walking Corpse" for his courageous stand against the Mafia in Sicily, former Mayor of Palermo, Leoluca Orlando, recognized that long-term, sustainable reductions in crime and corruption required the joint efforts of both the police and the community's cultural centers.

of the cart" needing to move forward at the same time captures the idea that both law enforcement and community responsibility are necessary to tackle crime and disorder.

What Is Community?

As any resident of a large city knows without having to turn to crime data, crime varies by neighborhood. The correlation between communities and crime has long been recognized by criminologists, beginning with early work of Shaw and McKay (1931) on the relationship between social disorganization and crime, discussed in the next section.

Before we examine the relationship between communities and crime or the principles of community policing, it is important to have a clear understanding of what is meant by the term **community**. Although this word brings to mind many different ideas and images, defining community has proven to be an enormous challenge to both law enforcement agencies trying to implement community policing policies and to researchers trying to evaluate the effectiveness of such policies.

Many police scholars have taken a broad view of the issue, preferring to define a community as a population or area affected by some particular problem or a specific police strategy (Goldstein 1990). Although defining community based on geographical boundaries or police deployment makes immediate sense to the individual police manager, administrator, or researcher, it clearly represents a significant oversimplification that could lead to major difficulties in strategy implementation or in understanding why a particular approach to policing is or is not working. Community is clearly much more than a geographic boundary; a very small area can encompass a diversity of values, cultures, and available resources or problems (Community Policing Consortium 1994).

For this reason, other authors have emphasized the need to view a community as a shared sense of ownership and pride in a given place or environment (Miller and Hess 1998). In order for people living within a distinct geographical area to develop common beliefs and values, as represented in such a conception of community, members of the community generally must share a common history and a shared process of socialization (Klockars 1991).

Although such distinct communities may exist in suburban areas, where there is a significant likelihood that individuals will know and look out for each other, in most large urban centers it is common for residents of the same housing complex to not know each others' names. It is also true that those areas that are the least well integrated are also most likely to have higher rates of crime, disorder, and poor relations with the police (Skogan 1996). Such communities stand to benefit the most from community policing (Skogan 1996). However, it is often very difficult to implement community policing in such neighborhoods.

Sampson and Groves (1989) have identified a number of key variables in their efforts to define and understand the structure of local communities in the United Kingdom:

- **Socioeconomic composition**: Percent college educated, percent in professional and managerial positions, percent with high incomes

- **Residential stability**: Percentage of residents brought up in the area within a fifteen-minute walk from home

- **Racial/ethnic heterogeneity**: Index based on percent of each racial/ethnic category

- **Local friendship relational networks**: Average number of friends living within a fifteen-minute walk of the respondents' homes

- **Organizational participation**: Percentage of residents who participated in meetings in the week before the interview

- **Supervisory capacity**: Percentage of residents who reported that disorderly teenagers were a very common neighborhood problem (see also Bursik and Grasmik 1993)

On one level, supervisory capacity is a difficult, though essential, gauge of the degree of integration in an area, and thus a sense of community. This can range from direct intervention whereby residents know each other and actively question strangers and other residents about suspicious activities to casual but active observation of neighborhood activities to the complete avoidance of areas viewed as unsafe (Greenberg et al. 1982). Of course, community policing benefits from the active participation and monitoring behaviors of area residents—a large factor behind the creation of Neighborhood Watch programs throughout the country. However, over-vigilance of community members can have its downside, as evident in some cases of racial profiling.

Harris's (2002) important work on the problem of racial profiling, *Profiles in Injustice,* is full of case examples of negative citizen encounters with law enforcement on the basis of race. As in the following example, in some cases citizen participation in the supervision of a community can itself involve elements of racial profiling. Police response is often a reaction to citizen concerns or complaints.

The active engagement of community residents in citizen patrols can play an important role in sending the message that crime and disorder will not be tolerated in a neighborhood.

> Suron Jacobs, a construction worker in his twenties who is African American, had a construction job as part of a crew in a nearly all-white suburban area outside of Toledo, Ohio. One day, Jacobs made arrangements to meet his brother on a corner near the construction site during his lunch break to exchange an apartment key. Unbeknownst to Jacobs, a resident who saw him waiting on the corner for his brother called 911 and reported him as a suspicious person. Responding to the call, a police officer drove by, stopped, and began to question Jacobs. What was he doing? Where was his brother, and how long had he been waiting? After a number of these questions, Jacobs became irritated. He refused to answer any more questions and began walking back to the construction site. Jacobs immediately learned the price of defying the police in a place where "he didn't belong"; the officer grabbed him, while another who arrived on the scene handcuffed him. . . . Though charges were eventually dropped, the police responses to the resident's 911 call told Jacobs everything he needed to know about his presence in a white area. (p. 104)

Thus, there can be a negative side to the overvigilance or participation of citizens. While community policing practices are actually thought to minimize such situations due to a greater familiarity between the police and community, whether residents or businesses, there remains a need to balance collaborations with concerns of professionalism and human dignity at all times. Trojanowicz et al. (2002) provide a useful summary of the eight attributes of a community:

1. It has a particular geographic area or location.
2. It is a recognized legal entity.
3. Social interactions within it include a division of labor and a sense of interdependence.
4. It is composed of citizens with a shared culture, interest, outlook, or perspective.
5. It possesses a moral dimension whereby values are transmitted.
6. Social interactions within it collectively shape its character.
7. It is defined by the processes of inclusion and exclusion.
8. Its citizens possess a shared sentiment, a sense of belonging, and interdependence.

Police departments will likely have a head start in implementing community policing as a philosophy in an area that meets each of these criteria. However, many communities in need of the potential benefits of the model are themselves characterized by crime, disorder, and mistrust of the police, making it difficult to implement community policing.

Theoretical Underpinnings of Community Policing

Communities can be distinguished by their degree of organization. Geographical areas that are said to be more integrated tend to have the sense of **community ownership** evidenced by self-policing and informal surveillance activities; upkeep of homes, streets, and businesses; and participation in local activities.

In what has now become a classic article in police scholarship, Wilson and Kelling (1982) used the analogy of a broken window to describe the relationship between disorder and crime. One broken window left unrepaired shows others that no one cares about the property. Consequently, others are less likely to respect the property. Over time, more and more of the windows are broken, forcing those in the area that do care about their property to leave. In the words of Wilson and Kelling (1982):

> A stable neighborhood of families who care for their homes, mind each other's children, and confidently frown on unwanted intruders can change, in a few years or even a few months, to an inhospitable and frightening jungle. A piece of property is abandoned, weeds grow up, and a window is smashed. Adults stop scolding rowdy children; the children, emboldened become more rowdy. Families move out, unattached adults move in. Teenagers gather in front of the corner store. The merchant asks them to move; they refuse. Fights occur. Litter accumulates. People start drinking in front of the grocers; in time, an inebriate slumps to the sidewalk and is allowed to sleep it off. (p. 32)

Even though the above activities can be characterized as low-level, nonserious offenses, more serious criminals may be attracted to the area by its minimal self-policing and lack of interest in combating illegal activities. According to Wilson and Kelling, there is a direct correlation between residents withdrawing from the streets, getting to know less and less of each other, and an increase in crime in an area. The **broken windows theory** suggests that in order for policing to have a lasting effect on serious crime in a neighborhood, the lower-level quality-of-life offenses need to be addressed in order to restore a sense of community in an area.

Writing in a similar vein, Skogan (1996) describes what he refers to as a **contagion proposition,** whereby certain disorders generate more disorder unless they are quickly stamped out. Current levels of disorder thus produce future levels of disorder. Putting this theory to the test, Skogan found that perceived crime problems, fear of crime, and actual victimization were all linked to the extent of social and physical disorder in an area. He also found that disorder was linked to residential satisfaction and commitment, two factors that are indicative of the overall stability of the housing market. As disorder increased, residents were more likely to seek opportunities to leave.

The case example of Palermo, Sicily, appears to provide considerable support for the broken windows theory. As organized crime gradually took control of the city through corruption and violence increased, the city (and certain neighborhoods in particular) began to decline. However, once the residents finally decided that they had had enough and embarked on a campaign of protest and community reclamation, a transformation began to take place that would eventually free Palermo from Mafia domination. In this case, citizen participation, community cooperation, and fair and effective law enforcement eventually brought about the demise of the Mafia in the city.

Even small levels of disorder in a community can lead to a spiral of decay over time that might eventually result in high levels of crime.

Although the idea that communities need to participate in the fight against crime and disorder is at the heart of most theories of community policing, this new approach to policy sprang from the failure of the professional model of policing to halt rising crime rates during the 1960s and 1970s. Efforts to encourage impartiality and to make law enforcement agencies more professional during the reform era caused a serious rift between the police and the community (particularly minority citizens) that would reach a peak during the riots of the 1960s and 1970s. Although placing patrol predominately behind the wheel of a patrol car may have increased the mobility of police, it failed to reduce crime or even fear of crime (as was evidenced in the Kansas City Preventive Patrol Experiment) (Kelling et al. 1974). Other challenges to the traditional model came from the Rand study of investigations, which revealed how dependent detectives and other officers were on information from citizens during the preliminary investigation (Greenwood 1977). However, perhaps the most significant push for change came from the police and public realization that, despite a renewed focus on crime control, crime continued to rise even though technology and professionalization had transformed the typical police department.

Around the same time, studies of foot patrols in Newark, New Jersey (Police Foundation 1981), and Flint, Michigan (Trojanowicz 1982), began to reveal that the police themselves were more likely to develop a positive attitude toward the community if they spent time on foot patrol and the residents were more likely to be satisfied with police services. In accordance with the broken windows theory, the police began to encourage community residents to take a more active role in restoring and revitalizing their communities (Community Policing Consortium 1994).

As a result of these changes in practice, a **public health model** of policing began to emerge that differed from the strict emphasis on crime control of the past:

The doctor (police officer) talks to the patient (community) to identify a problem. Sometimes the solution lies solely with the patient (community) for example, a change of diet (the owner agrees to remove an eyesore or abandoned automobile). Sometimes it calls for the doctor (police officer) and patient (community) to work together, i.e., a change of diet plus medication (organizing the community to shut down a blight establishment). Sometimes only the doctor (police) alone can solve the problem, i.e., surgery (heavy suppression). Sometimes we have to accept the fact that the problem simply cannot be solved, e.g., terminal illness (poverty). (Braiden 1992, p. 21)

The public health perspective encourages law enforcement agencies to look at crime from a preventive standpoint. Just as people are responsible for their own health (through diet and exercise), communities can take ownership of their neighborhoods and reject disorder and criminality. For example, citizens can become involved in organizing citizen patrols, reporting crime to the police, developing community clean-up activities, as well as numerous other possibilities. A need to focus on the underlying causes of a problem, rather than simply responding to the symptoms, is another central pillar of the public health model.

Community Partnerships and Problem Solving

At the core of community policing strategy is the establishment of mutually beneficial ties between the community and the police in which both become partners in crime prevention and reduction. According to the Community Policing Consortium (1994), "the growing trend within communities to participate in the fight against crime and disorder has paralleled a growing recognition by police that traditional crime-fighting tactics alone have a limited impact on controlling crime. Community policing is the synthesis of these two movements" (p. 34).

Although the term *community policing* has been widely used within law enforcement circles over the last twenty years, a great deal of confusion exists as to what it actually means. As a result of this lack of consensus among both practitioners and those in academic circles, the term has come to mean many different things (Rosenbaum 1989). Some departments have simply molded the term to encompass more traditional law enforcement strategies, whereas others have taken it to include community-relations activities (Bayley 1988). For example, in their in-service training program for law enforcement, entitled the *Fundamentals of Community Policing*, the New York State Regional Community Policing Institute (NYSRCPI1990) proposes its own definition and rejects many of the "myths" of community policing, which are summarized in Table 12.1.

TABLE 12.1

Myth Versus the Reality of Community Policing

Myth	Reality
It is a specialized technique or program.	It involves a customer focus and requires officers to embrace a philosophy to provide high-quality services.
It is a limited or specialized style of policing.	It is full-service policing that gives attention to the old line of business (traditional, call-driven responses) in addition to proactive type prevention. This combination of aggressive policing with community-based orientation is known as *integrated patrol*.
It only involves foot or bicycle patrols.	It involves an officer becoming knowledgeable about the area and familiar with its businesses/residents. It incorporates problem-solving approaches ranging from working with organized neighborhood associations to making referrals to other community resource services.
It is soft on crime.	Traditional law enforcement duties continue. Other responsibilities are "in addition to" and not a substitute for existing ones.
It involves a specialized unit.	Each member of the agency needs to be involved, trained, and committed to the program. Too often it is relegated to a specific group of officers.

Community policing is based on two core beliefs that emerge from a broader perspective than that found in traditional law enforcement efforts: community partnership and problem solving (Community Policing Consortium 1994). Once one recognizes that the police cannot combat crime alone, particularly many quality-of-life concerns, it becomes clear that partnerships with outside organizations must become an important part of policing (community partnership). Partnership does not simply refer to the community residents and organizations becoming the "eyes and ears" of the police, although increasing citizen trust in coming forward to the police is certainly an important first step.

According to the NYSRCPI (1999), **partnership** involves several important elements:

- Working together on a common problem
- Identifying common goals
- Steady and consistent communication and information sharing
- Having a shared perception of problems and benchmarks for when problems are solved
- All parties contributing work towards accomplishing shared goals and objectives or solving the problem

Where partnership is really present, the police, residents, and other service agencies are involved in all phases of planning problem resolution (Peak and Glensor 1999). Moreover, a sense of **empowerment** must also be facilitated in which all parties feel that they have equal input into decisions and the commitment of needed resources (Eck and Spelman 1987). Given the host of underlying causes of community problems, the police would not be able to deal with them effectively in the absence of such committed partnerships. Depending on the problem being addressed, police can partner with many different community organizations, including the following:

- Merchant associations
- Neighborhood and civic groups
- Youth-serving agencies
- Tenant associations
- Block associations
- Community development corporations

At its most basic, **problem solving** involves the collaborative identification of problems and their underlying causes, rather than simply responding to incidents. In this sense, community policing moves departments beyond the **reactive** stance of waiting for calls for service or citizen complaints into a more **proactive** mode of addressing problems before they occur and attacking the underlying causes of crime.

Eck and Spelman (1987) offer a useful visual representation of the important differences between the reactive, incident-driven focus of traditional policing and the proactive model encompassed within community policing. Incident-driven policing is depicted in Figure 12.1. Just as a flu might be man-

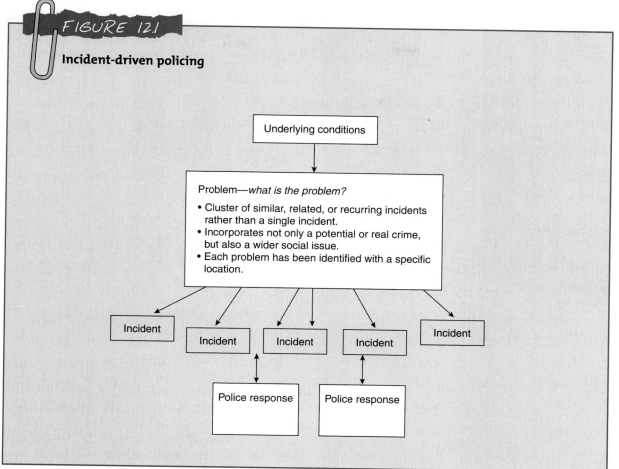

FIGURE 12.1

Incident-driven policing

Underlying conditions

Problem—*what is the problem?*

- Cluster of similar, related, or recurring incidents rather than a single incident.
- Incorporates not only a potential or real crime, but also a wider social issue.
- Each problem has been identified with a specific location.

Incident   Incident   Incident   Incident   Incident

Police response   Police response

Source: Modified from Eck and Spelman (1987).

ifested by various disturbing or uncomfortable symptoms, such as a runny nose, fever, headaches, and so on, community problems also have distinctive conditions manifested as incidents that might reflect the nature of the underlying problem.

For example, a late-night gathering of youths in front of a bowling alley could result in repeated calls to the police to deal with unruly behavior and disperse the group. However, if the police were to examine the issue more closely in an effort to identify underlying conditions and consult with local residents and businesses, they might discover that the bowling alley offers late-night specials that attract the youths, who are subsequently left to walk home due to the lack of public transport. Instead of just continually reacting to incidents, as a result of collaboration, the police and business leader may be able to choose an alternative approach, such as arranging for adequate public transportation on those nights when late-night specials are offered, reducing the likelihood of future disturbances or incidents. Without adequately addressing the underlying causes of a problem, incidents will continue to occur. Although reactive police response is required to alleviate *immediate* issues, it can only be a temporary response to larger, more intractable problems.

The CAPS community policing model in Chicago has institutionalized the problem-solving process by requiring regular beat officer attendance at community problem-solving meetings.

Figure 12.2 is based on Eck and Spelman's summary of the benefits offered by police problem solving. By recognizing that there is a problem, rather than simply a series of unrelated incidents, police can begin to analyze a situation and hopefully identify underlying conditions and causes that might be contributing to the problem. In standard policing terminology, **problems** refer to two or more incidents capable of causing harm in which there is an expectation that the police and community can do something about it (National Strategy Information Center 2000). Generally, it is not necessary to go through a detailed problem-solving process in the case of a single incident that is unlikely to be repeated. In such circumstances, a quick police response may be all that is required. However, when there is a series of harmful and related incidents, the only way to ultimately prevent future occurrences is to identify and address the underlying conditions. The recognition that crime problems can be affected by altering certain precipitating factors is referred to as **crime prevention through environmental design (CPTED)** and is a direct outgrowth of the problem-oriented policing model (Crowe 2000).

By partnering with other public and private resources, the police greatly increase their likelihood of success and the chance of finding a permanent solution to a given problem. It is important to recognize that in addition to collaboration, the police and the community must have sufficient resources to attack the identified causes of a problem. No matter how committed and creative a police department and its partners may be to resolving poverty, for example, rarely do they have the means to remedy it. However, while they might not be able to eliminate poverty as a cause of crime, by providing offenders on probation with skills training and job placement schemes, the police and the community may be able to weaken the economic incentive to reoffend.

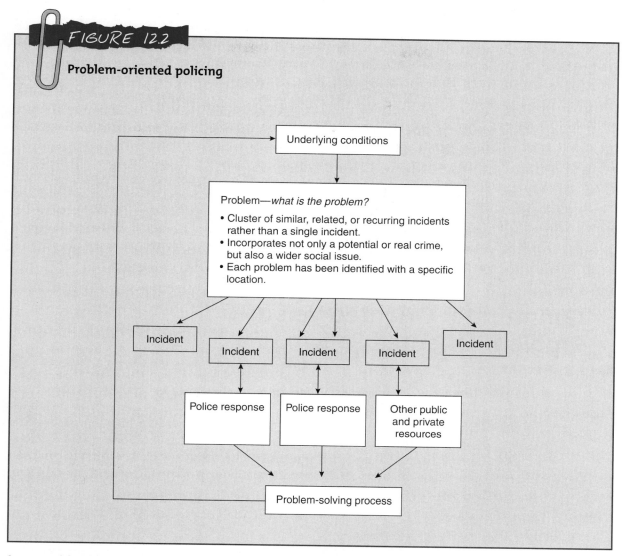

FIGURE 12.2

Problem-oriented policing

Source: Modified from Eck and Spelman (1987).

Networking: Coordination and Collaboration

Collaborative problem solving through partnerships requires a great deal more commitment from both the police and its partners than simply hosting joint meetings or sharing information. Community-relations activities introduced by police departments throughout the 1970s and 1980s were an important first step towards building the foundations for community policing, but in many cases amounted to little more than public-relations activities for the department (Hunter et al. 2000). Examples of community relations activities include citizen academies, neighborhood newsletters, spouse academies, or police athletic leagues (Gaines et al. 2003).

The police must develop positive relationships with the community in order to successfully marshal public support for community policing. In some communities, particularly those where aggressive policing strategies have not been well-received by residents, the level of trust required as a precondition for such relationships will often be absent. Moreover, the path to building relationships is often gradual, requiring a tremendous amount of patience and commitment from both the police and their intended partners. A Department of Justice monograph (U.S. Department of Justice 1994) depicts the partnership building process as cyclical in nature: trust facilitates increased community contact, which in turn leads to better communication, a key ingredient for increased trust, and so on (see Figure 12.3).

As a mutual trust is developed, community policing can also help foster increased accountability, with all partners understanding and recognizing their specific roles and tasks that emerge from the problem-solving process (Peak and Glensor 1999). By identifying the multiple causes of specific problems, it becomes clear to all parties not only that the police cannot alone be held responsible for remedying all problems, but also that their own agencies can play an essential role in problem resolution.

Community-Oriented Versus Problem-Oriented Policing

The term *problem-oriented policing* is generally attributed to the work of Herman Goldstein, who outlined the basic principles of this approach in his book *Policing a Free Society* (1977) and carried it through into his more recent title *Problem-Oriented Policing* (1990), which is one of the most often cited explanations of the problem-solving process to date. Many people are initially confused with the distinctions made between community-oriented policing and problem-

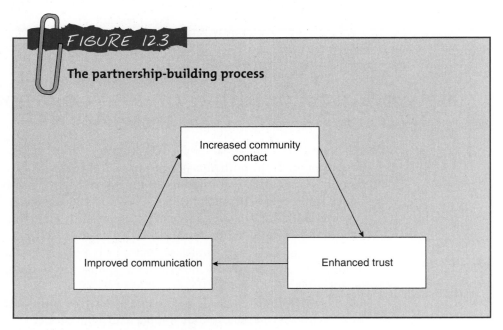

FIGURE 12.3

The partnership-building process

Increased community contact

Improved communication

Enhanced trust

Source: U.S. Department of Justice (1994).

Linkages in Law Enforcement

Collaboration with the Courts—Community Prosecution

Prosecutors across the country are also seeing their role extend beyond the effective and efficient handling of cases. In redefining their methods and their mission with respect to crime, a new approach known as **community prosecution** has emerged. According to this approach, prosecutors work with citizens and police to identify high-priority cases and offenders, recognizing that the goal of prosecution should be to eliminate or manage problems rather than simply prosecute cases (Coles and Kelling 1999). In this sense, community prosecution efforts seek to partner with other agencies and resources in the community, including law enforcement, making it a useful complement to community policing strategies.

By focusing on problem reduction or elimination, prosecution partnerships with the police can extend to the use of civil remedies such as nuisance abatement for gang offenders, restraining orders to keep persistent offenders out of certain neighborhoods, trespass statute prosecutions, and health and safety code enforcement (Coles and Kelling 1999).

As an example of a successful community prosecution program, the Buffalo, New York, Weed and Seed initiative created a fifteen agency "Save Our Streets" task force that included the Narcotics Division of the Buffalo Police Department, the District Attorney's Office, probation services, the Department of Social Services, parole services, the U.S. Marshals, and the U.S. Attorney's Office to target houses suspected of drug use and harboring criminal activity (Grant 1999). Through a creative application of federal asset forfeiture laws, each agency on the task force is responsible for the en-

forcement of specific ordinance violations within their jurisdictions, holding tenants and owners accountable. In the case of continued problems, the task force uses prosecution to reclaim the property and place it back into more productive community use, such as through the creation of community gardens or parks.

Another such partnership exists in Washington, D.C., where the Metropolitan Police of the District of Columbia (MPDC) partners with the U.S. Attorney's Office and other private and public agencies to enhance the prosecutorial function (Metropolitan Police District of Columbia n.d.). As part of their role within this partnership, the Community Prosecution Section of the U.S. Attorney's Office geographically assigns attorneys to assist the police in criminal investigations, in the review of arrest warrants, and with the presentation of arrested cases in court. A major outcome of this partnership thus includes the increased flow of information among the community, police department, and U.S. Attorney's Office.

Questions

1. For what type of crime problems would community prosecution models be most relevant? Research whether or not such a model has already been implemented.

2. What are some potential negative sides to community prosecution?

3. Examine the success of the Drug Court model around the country. What role do the police play (if any) in such efforts?

oriented policing. We have said that the two core components of community policing are partnership and problem solving, so how is it that we are now making a distinction between community-oriented policing (COP) and problem-oriented policing (POP)?

Whereas **community-oriented policing** is meant to be the overriding philosophy guiding departmental change, problem-oriented policing is often viewed as one of the principle means to put this philosophy into practice (Peak and

Linkages in Law Enforcement

Collaboration with Corrections— Community Corrections

Over the last several years, the police and correctional agencies have also begun to form mutually beneficial partnerships based primarily on the goal of enhancing community safety. The movement towards establishing such partnerships is a direct response to the community policing movement's recognition of the need to make better use of community resources in order to achieve long-term reductions in crime and disorder.

The National Institute of Justice (NIJ) recently funded a comprehensive study of police–corrections partnerships in the interest of helping administrators and policymakers replicate such models in their jurisdictions. Following an intensive case study review of fourteen police–corrections partnerships across the country, the authors categorized the partnerships into the following five implementation categories (Parent and Snyder 1999).

Enhanced-Supervision Partnerships

The most common form of partnership, enhanced–supervision partnerships seek to increase the odds of detecting offender violations of probation or parole by conducting joint supervision activities. Random home visits involving police, probation, and parole is a common means of increasing supervision, made famous by the Boston's Operation Night Light successes. Following Night Light and other related projects, homicides decreased from a high of 152 in 1990 to 23 in the first eight months of 1998 (Office of Juvenile Justice and Delinquency Prevention 2000). Increased citywide collaborations in response to gang violence were also outcomes of the Boston strategy (Office of Juvenile Justice and Delinquency Prevention 2000). An additional benefit of increased supervision is an increased awareness of offender needs/risks on the part of correctional agencies, allowing them to better match offenders with needed social services.

Fugitive-Apprehension Units

With this model, police and corrections jointly seek to locate and apprehend offenders who have absconded from probation or parole supervision.

Information-Sharing Partnerships

With this model, procedures are implemented that enhance the exchange of information. Formal processes such as shared databases and regular meetings to discuss correctional populations under community supervision within geographic boundaries are examples of partnerships in this category. Sex offender registries and gang intelligence databases are commonly utilized resources in this type of partnership.

Specialized-Enforcement Partnerships

Working together with relevant community agencies, specialized enforcement partnerships involve collaborative problem-solving efforts related to the individual concerns of particular communities.

Interagency Problem-solving Partnerships

Both police and corrections identify mutual problems in their jurisdiction. Together they prioritize strategy selection and implementation in a mutually beneficial manner.

Police–corrections partnerships produce numerous benefits for the communities in which they are implemented and provide both agencies with more creative means to solve problems than would be the available if each agency acted on its own. For example, while a police officer may have no power to stop a gang member from associating with other gang members, a probation officer could arrest the individual and begin revocation hearings for the violation of the conditions of probation (Parent and Snyder 1999). Similarly, in Baton Rouge, Louisiana, a specialized detail of police officers were familiar-

Police/probation partnerships have helped the criminal justice system more effectively monitor offenders without sacrificing the public safety interests of probation officers. These partnerships have also increased information sharing between police and probation in the jurisdictions in which they are implemented.

ized with the members of a hard-core group of probationers and provided with a list of names and photos to take with them when they are out on their tour. If they saw a probationer out on the streets in violation of his or her curfew, the police officer could pass the information of the violation onto the respective probation officer, thus dramatically increasing the level of available supervision (Sheppard et al. 2000). Other benefits of such partnerships include an increased ability of police departments to investigate crimes by probationers/parolees, as well as increased information for correctional authorities about the associations of the offenders in their charge provided by the specialized knowledge and contacts offered by the police (Parent and Snyder 1999).

However, police–corrections partnerships are not without risk. For example, there can be a temptation to circumvent many of the constraints of the Fourth Amendment by creatively utilizing the distinct role of the parole or probation officer.

Although the police may have reason to suspect that an offender's home might contain evidence of a crime, they may not have sufficient probable cause to obtain the necessary search warrant; however, by having the probation officer search the residence (which is within their authority) and report this information to the police, Fourth Amendment restrictions can be avoided (Parent and Snyder 1999).

Questions

1. For what types of crime problems do you feel that police–corrections partnerships are most relevant? Research whether or not such a model has already been implemented.

2. What are some potential negative sides to police–corrections partnerships?

3. How can these models be merged with the community prosecution approach to law enforcement?

Glensor 1999). **Problem-oriented policing** involves proactive policing strategies and focuses on the identification of underlying causes of problems and the selection of solutions or remedies to prevent a problem from occurring again in the future (Goldstein 1999). Problem-oriented policing involves getting police officers and departments to think outside of the box, recognizing connections across like incidents that they may not have been able to see when responding to a seemingly random incident from an incident-based, reactive perspective.

The SARA Model

In focusing on the resolution of the underlying causes of problems, problem-oriented policing relies on the process of problem solving. Once again, *problem solving* involves the process of moving toward a goal when the path to that goal is uncertain. Spelman and Eck (1987) have developed an acronym for the problem-solving process to facilitate teaching these skills to both law enforcement practitioners and community residents. They coined the term **SARA**, referring to four separate components of the problem-solving process: scanning, analysis, response, and assessment.

Although SARA is usually presented in a linear fashion, Figure 12.4 shows it as a cyclical pattern to provide a more meaningful description of the continuous nature of the problem-solving process.

Scanning involves the clustering of incidents into meaningful problem units. This stage is the recognition that a series of incidents are in fact connected and could be alleviated through common responses. In order to understand the underlying causes leading to the problem, a meaningful **analysis** is then conducted. This stage is often considered the heart of the problem-solving

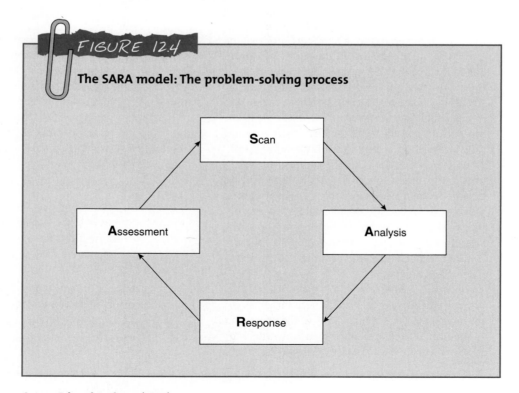

FIGURE 12.4

The SARA model: The problem-solving process

Source: Eck and Spelman (1987).

model because any mistakes made here can lead to inappropriate responses or strategies. At this stage, many practitioners use a conceptual framework referred to as the **crime triangle** (provided in Figure 12.5). The triangle begins with three known facts derived from studies such as the **Serious Habitual Offender Criminal Apprehension Program (SHOCAP)**, which was developed by the Office of Juvenile Justice and Delinquency Prevention (OJJDP 1995):

1. Ten percent of offenders account for 55 percent of all crimes.

2. Ten percent of victims account for 42 percent of all victimization.

3. Ten percent of all locations account for 60 percent of the call load to the police.

Thus, by targeting the specific problem areas, offenders, and victims through the analysis stage, police departments and communities can work to identify the true underlying causes of a given problem and be better poised to achieve a successful resolution.

Once a comprehensive analysis has been completed, a strategy (**response**) can be selected based on what is actually causing the problem. However, not until **assessment** does the community policing practitioner actually evaluate whether the implemented response actually works. For example, after implementation, the community policing practitioner may better understand the problem and recognize the need to reconsider the initial analysis. If so, the practitioner may then redesign the current strategy or select a new approach alto-

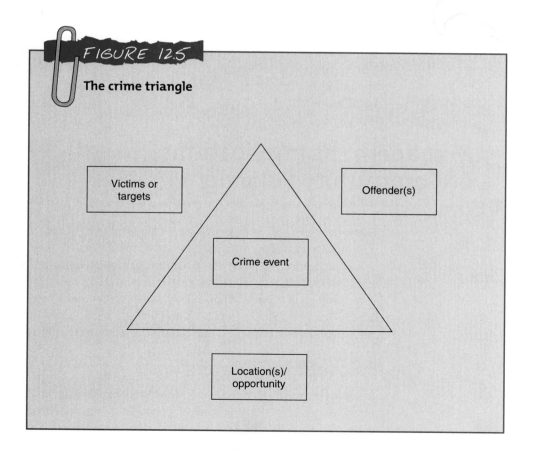

FIGURE 12.5

The crime triangle

gether. In some cases, as agencies go through the process, the practitioner may even come to the conclusion that the nature of the problem was completely misidentified and recommence the process accordingly.

Focusing on Problem Locations

As Pease (1998) has observed, much of the focus on the role of location origi-nated with a number of pioneering studies in the United Kingdom on the phe-nomenon of **repeat victimization** in crimes ranging from burglary to domestic violence to racial violence. The most significant finding to come from these stud-ies was that repeat victimization may be preventable, especially if the problem-solving process involves focusing analysis and strategy on repeat locations, victims, and offenders. Moreover, because some locations are responsible for sig-nificant amounts of crime, addressing them can also lead to significant decreases in overall crime rates (Davis and Taylor 1997).

These studies also confirmed the importance of **crime analysis**, which in-volves the statistical review of incident data, calls for service, and so on to iso-late trends and patterns in order to focus strategy. Chapter 13 will detail advances in technology that have significantly aided proactive policing strategy. When attempting to address a problem such as gun violence within a city (**prevalence** refers to the overall incidence of a problem in a geographical area), the first stage is to identify the particular neighborhood within the city (**target area**) in which the problem is occurring most frequently so that the police and community can get a better idea of the underlying conditions that could inform strategy. Focusing analysis even further to specific blocks and locations (**hot spots**) can also be important in gaining an appreciation of the kinds of problem dynamics that can inform strategy. Figure 12.6 graphically displays the process of location analysis. Once a target area or hot spot is identified, problem solvers can identify possible contextual conditions or the target population most re-sponsible for the problem, allowing strategy to be developed, selected, and tai-lored accordingly.

Management Implications of Community Policing

Even for the most innovative and energetic police departments, implementing community policing policies has proven difficult. A major reason for this has been the confusion over what community policing actually is and the fact that implementation can cause strain or resentment among both line officers and command staff (Gaines et al. 2003). In an effort to address these problems, how-ever, Cordner (1999) offers a framework of three important dimensions that are each necessary in order to adequately implement community policing.

The Philosophical Dimension

In many departments, it is commonly believed that community policing nec-essarily requires the creation of specialized units whose function is to work with the community, attend meetings, and identify community concerns.

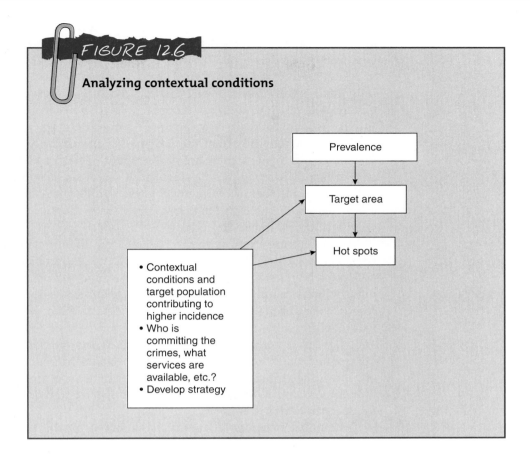

FIGURE 12.6

Analyzing contextual conditions

Prevalence

Target area

Hot spots

- Contextual conditions and target population contributing to higher incidence
- Who is committing the crimes, what services are available, etc.?
- Develop strategy

However, community policing requires a more fundamental philosophical transformation in policy practices from a reactive crime-fighting mentality to a broader approach based on proactive problem-solving and resource deployment (Goldstein 1997). When only a small portion of departmental resources are devoted to this mission, resentment towards the specialized group of officers can develop among other officers. Moreover, if the majority of officers function within a traditional model of policing, there will be far less exposure to the benefits of the community model within the community. Most of the officers with whom the community continues to interact will not seek citizen input beyond the most basic of reporting functions. As a result, efforts at implementing community policing policies must begin with a reorientation of officer attitudes and police culture.

The Strategic Dimension

Shifting the focus of policing from responding to incidents to proactive crime prevention has important strategic implications, many of which involve **structural changes**. A key ingredient of successful community policing requires that officers become familiar with the residents and businesses in the area to which they have been assigned and with their particular concerns and problems. As such, an assigned shift structure (based on geographical areas as well as time of day) becomes most desirable. However, even more than this, police operational units must make combined use of foot patrols, directed patrols, and citizen surveys in order to ensure that they are able to target the crime and disorder issues judged to be of greatest concern by both the police and community (Gaines et al. 2003).

Additionally, it can be argued that proactive decision making requires that individual patrol officers have increased discretion to respond to problems creatively and quickly, without having to rely on receiving detailed directions through a complex chain of command. As a result, many practitioners argue for **decentralization**, in which the designation of authority and responsibility is widened so as to allow for more independent, localized decision making on the part of line officers. Similarly, **flattening** the organizational structure involves reducing the number of hierarchical levels in order to reduce unneeded bureaucracy that could stand in the way of proactive policing. Both of these concepts were introduced in Chapter 5.

Pooling officers into **teams** and decreasing the number of specialized units (**despecialization**) can also be compatible with the objectives of community policing. Having officers from patrol, traffic, and the detective divisions working together as a unit can ensure that linkage blindness is minimized and needed resources are brought to bear on a problem. Officers operating under a departmental philosophy of community policing are required to think outside the box and stay on top of area problems, constantly interacting with residents, businesses, and other agencies. Too much specialization can hamper this process and encourage officers to think that certain issues are "not their concern," even though problems in an area may be interconnected and symptomatic of some of the same underlying issues.

The failed attempts of team policing models in the 1970s suggest the need for police managers to plan ahead thoroughly before implementing a community policing program (Walker 1992). Although many of the elements currently touted as essential to community policing have their origins in the **team policing model** (assigned shift structures, increased officer discretion, team management, despecialization), this model proved to be unsustainable because most of the jurisdictions in which it was piloted failed to first gain the support of middle management within the notoriously hierarchical and militaristic police structure. Consequently, when middle managers began to feel threatened by the increased responsibilities granted to line officers and feared a reduction in their own roles within the department, efforts were made to sabotage the viability of the model. Moreover, team policing models generally occurred as specialized units rather than department-wide practice.

Under community policing, management is ideally based on a **participatory management model** in which line officers are encouraged to be creative and resolve problems rather than simply following directives. More freedom is given to officers to interact with the community and work as partners with relevant stakeholders to resolve crime and quality-of-life concerns. However, increased discretion can bring with it certain risks and dangers. Accountability always remains a concern, particularly in light of the corruption that characterized the political era of policing. Thus, despite the concern of middle managers over moves towards team policing, such a shift does not necessarily lead to a reduction in their importance within the policing organization. Strong middle managers are needed to transmit skills and to provide experience with proactive strategy development. Furthermore, although officers may not be judged solely on arrest quotas and response time, new performance measures will need to be developed that better correlate with the changing expectations of the new model—measures that middle management will be called upon to devise and monitor.

The Programmatic Dimension

The programmatic dimension of community policing involves "nuts and bolts" activities such as problem-solving and community-mobilization activities. Tied directly with the strategic dimension, programmatic activities need to be clearly planned out with a long-term plan for departmental change in mind. Innovative police managers need to think long-term with respect to piloting new approaches that will gradually introduce and change everyday policing practices and outlooks in a department. In response to federal youth firearms prevention funding, a former chief of the Bridgeport Police Department sought to instill his officers with proactive problem-solving experience. Although the central objectives of the initiative did not directly target community policing practices, the chief saw the federal money as an opportunity to infuse the department with the concepts of community policing and problem solving by instituting a rotating overtime structure that allowed a significant number of officers to participate in firearms suppression details that would offer the needed exposure and resources to reduce firearms violence in the hot spots of the city (Grant and Jacobs 1997). Rather than simply having a small group of officers acquire this specialized knowledge, he drew on officers from regular patrol, ensuring that they would return to their regular tours and transmit these new skills to other officers. This strategy was just one of numerous complementary pilot initiatives implemented by the chief over a period of years.

Barriers to Implementing Community Policing

Internal departmental resistance to community policing can be overcome through the careful long-term planning efforts of police managers. Techniques thought to help move departments toward a department-wide philosophy and practice of commmunity policing include involving line officer and middle management input into the early planning process, and beginning implementation with multiple pilot projects (Sadd and Grine 1996). However, resource demands often lead departments to give community policing a special unit status that is capable of producing interdepartmental rivalry, defeating any momentum toward true community policing implementation. External barriers are also a signification cause for concern. In areas where there is a history of mistrust between the community and the police, the requisite **community mobilization** required for partnership can be daunting. Departments must be aware of residents' fears of retaliation from area drug dealers as a barrier to participation. Rather than becoming overwhelmed by the need to reach the entire community, research suggests that police departments wishing to move towards community policing should first target the critical mass in a community most likely to engage in civic activities promoting public safety (Correia 2000). This, in combination with collaboration with other city agencies, can slowly build a sense of trust in the department's commitment to change.

The Relationship Between the Causes of Crime and Strategy

The community policing movement began with the realization that the police alone could not be expected to bring about long-term reductions in the crime rate. Given the many causes of crime empirically identified throughout the criminology literature, it is important for proactive policing strategy to begin with a **needs assessment** to identify the most likely sources of any local problem. No two communities are the same or have the same crime-producing conditions.

Implications of Criminology Theory for Law Enforcement Practice

A needs assessment is a comprehensive review of the factors underlying a given problem based on multiple data sources. Once community needs have been identified, additional partnering agencies can be selected based on the varying levels of expertise each has in dealing with the factors at hand, as well as the potential resources available to remedy the problem.

Predictor variables found to be associated with delinquent or criminal activity are termed **risk factors** (Hawkins et al. 1995). Hawkins et al. (2000), in their review of the major long-term studies on violence predictors, converted the strength of correlations between risk factors and later violence into odds ratios, highlighting the practical applications of the resiliency-theory literature. Odds ratios "express the degree of increased risk for violence associated with the presence of a risk factor in a population" (Hawkins et al. 2000, p. 2). For example, an odds ratio of 3.0 refers to a tripling of risk due to the presence of a particular risk factor.

Risk factors can be categorized across five domains: individual, family, school, peer related, and community/neighborhood factors, as summarized in the following list (Hawkins et al. 2000):

Individual factors

- Pregnancy and obesity complications
- Low resting heart rate
- Internalizing disorders
- Hyperactivity, concentration problems, restlessness, and risk taking
- Aggressiveness
- Early initiation of violent behavior
- Involvement in other forms of antisocial behavior
- Beliefs and attitudes favorable to deviant or antisocial behavior

Family factors

- Parental criminality
- Child maltreatment
- Poor family management practices

- Low levels of parental involvement
- Parental attitudes favorable to substance use and violence
- Parent–child separation

School factors

- Academic failure
- Low bonding to school
- Truancy and dropping out of school
- Frequent school transitions

Peer-related factors

- Delinquent siblings
- Delinquent peers
- Gang membership

Community and neighborhood factors

- Poverty
- Community disorganization
- Availability of drugs and firearms
- Neighborhood adults involved in crime
- Exposure to violence and racial prejudice

A plethora of studies (McKnight and Loper 2002; Rutter 1987; Tiet and Huizinga 2000) provide empirical support for the relationship between these risk factors and violence or other criminal activity. Representing the connections across problem behaviors, these risk factors can play a role in predicting behaviors such as substance abuse and teen pregnancy (Hawkins et al. 1992).

The logic of **resiliency theory** is that the larger the number of risk factors influencing an individual at any given moment, the greater is the likelihood of criminal activity or other problem behavior. Thus, programs seeking to reduce or prevent such activities will be most successful if they target multiple risk factors at the same time. A needs assessment clearly documenting the presence of all possible risk factors is an essential ingredient in selecting or tailoring programs that will have the greatest likelihood of success (Wasserman and Seracini 2001).

The Suppression–Intervention–Prevention Continuum

Once the combination of underlying factors is known, a comprehensive plan of action for long-term problem solving can be developed based on matching strategies and activities to particular risk factors. Because most problems have more than one factor contributing to their occurrence, **comprehensive plans** should address as many underlying conditions as both resources and political contexts will allow.

A useful framework for the development of comprehensive strategies with police–community partnerships is that proposed by Sheppard et al. (2000). According to their model, once a needs assessment has been developed, strategy selection occurs within three domains: suppression, intervention, and prevention.

Suppression Strategies

Suppression strategies target specific offenders and locations. Recognizing that problem areas and chronic offenders can be readily identified with criminal justice data and that such areas are generally responsible for the majority of crime, strategies identifying key offender and location hot spots are an important component of any comprehensive plan. Suppression strategies generally involve the more traditional law enforcement activities such as directed patrol, intensive supervision, street sweeps, and so on.

Intervention Strategies

Once a chronic group of offenders has been identified, partners will be better equipped to understand the factors influencing offender behavior and location vulnerability. **Intervention strategies** involve matching offenders to needed services in their community that can help to reduce their likelihood of recidivism.

Prevention Strategies

Prevention strategies try to stop a problem before future incidents can occur. Community development techniques addressing the quality of life in an area are important prevention activities. Matching the siblings of gang offenders to needed services prior to their becoming involved in criminal activity is another example.

The OJJDP's Partnership to Reduce Juvenile Gun Violence (2000) program illustrates this continuum and the need to link causes with strategy. Following a review of where the hot spots for gun violence were in the city of Baton Rouge, Louisiana, city planners identified two high-crime areas by zip code to serve as a pilot target area for a demonstration project to reduce gun violence. Examination of records of the gun violence incidents occurring within these areas indicated that the vast majority of gun offenses were being committed by a small group of repeat juvenile offenders, many of whom were actually being supervised in the community on probation. As a result, a suppression strategy was developed involving intensive and random police–probation supervision of the target group for probation violations, a strategy described in one of the Linkage Boxes in this chapter. This hard-core group of juvenile offenders was referred to as "Eigers," named after a mountain in Switzerland that is difficult, though not impossible, to climb.

Although this was a great starting point for a strategy, city planners recognized that it was not enough, particularly as they came to know the needs of the target population itself. A case planner was hired to work with each Eiger and the probation officer to develop an integration plan that would reduce each individual's chance of reoffending, including such needed **intervention services** as job skills training and placement, counseling, conflict resolution skills, and so on. In addition, based on a common service need of the whole target group, a Life Skills Academy was created for skills training for both the Eigers and their families. Moreover, as the city became increasingly knowledgeable about the service needs of this population, new programs and services were identified and/or created to fill in these gaps. Finally, in recognition that younger children often look up to their older siblings, a special menu of mostly school-based preventive services was created over time, trying to get to these kids before they, too, make bad decisions in their lives. For more on this and other similar programs, refer to Sheppard et al. (2000).

Situational Crime Prevention **Routine activities theory** states that in order for a crime to occur three elements must intersect at the same time and place (Cohen and Felson 1979):

1. A motivated offender
2. Absence of capable guardianship
3. Suitable target

These three components also provide a useful framework from which to engage in strategy selection. It follows from routine activities theory that if any one of these three components can be removed, crime will not occur. For example, if a problem analysis indicates that a pattern of rapes are occurring along a dimly lit section of the city, police strategists might opt to increase surveillance in the area and thereby create a guardianship that did not exist previously. Such a strategy might include increasing lighting in the area and directing more foot and random patrols to the location during the problem time periods.

Chapter Summary

- The term *community* can mean many things, from its simplest reference to geographical boundaries to more complex relationships such as supervisory capacity, interdependence, and shared values. Such distinctions are not arbitrary; crime and disorder will be less common and police—community partnerships more easily facilitated in those areas demonstrating a greater amount of cohesion.

- The broken windows theory and the contagion proposition document the connections between disorder and crime. Police departments need to engage the community in the resolution of even low-level quality-of-life offenses in order to make meaningful, long-term impacts on more serious crime.

- Community policing is not soft on crime. Rather, through partnership and problem solving, community policing can have a serious impact on crime in an area. A shift to community policing involves moving departments from a reactive view of crime-fighting responsibilities to a more proactive commitment to remedying the underlying causes of crime.

- To be effective, community policing requires partnerships with all available stakeholders that have both knowledge and resources related to a particular problem. Partnerships with both the courts and corrections can be particularly important. Community policing should be implemented across three dimensions: philosophical, strategic, and programmatic.

● Problem solving requires the targeting of particular offenders and locations and gaining a complete understanding of all of the conditions, or risk factors, perpetuating a given problem. Resulting strategies must be comprehensive, covering the complete spectrum of suppression, intervention, and prevention.

● Barriers to community policing exist on both internal and external levels. Improper planning and a failure to involve the participation of all ranks can lead to poor outcomes with respect to community policing. Externally, poor police–community relations, high crime and disorder, and inadequate community networks can all impede a department's efforts at community mobilization, and thus community policing.

● Part of the strategic planning or problem-solving process often begins with a needs assessment in order to get an adequate understanding of the causes of problems in a specific area. Situational crime prevention involves altering the connection between victim, offender, and location that are creating crime problems in a given community.

KEY TERMS

Analysis 308
Assessment 309
Broken windows theory 297
Community 294
Community mobilization 313
Community ownership 296
Community-oriented
  policing 305
Community policing 300
Community prosecution 305
Comprehensive plans 315
Contagion proposition 297
Crime analysis 310
Crime prevention through experimental design (CPTED) 302
Crime triangle 309
Decentralization 312
Despecialization 312
Empowerment 300
Enhanced-supervision
  partnerships 306

Flattening 312
Fugitive-apprehension
  units 306
Hot spots 310
Information-sharing
  partnerships 306
Interagency problem-solving
  partnerships 306
Intervention services 316
Needs assessment 314
Participatory management
  model 312
Partnership 300
Philosophical dimension 310
Prevalence 310
Proactive 300
Problem solving 300
Problem-oriented policing 308
Problems 301
Programmatic dimension 313
Public health model 298

Reactive 300
Repeat victimization 310
Resiliency theory 315
Response 309
Risk factors 314
Routine activities theory 317
SARA 308
Scanning 308
Serious habituation offender
  criminal apprehension program (SHOCAP) 309
Specialized-enforcement
  partnerships 306
Strategic dimension 311
Structural changes 311
Suppression–intervention–
  prevention 316
Target area 310
Team policing model 312
Teams 312

Linking the Dots

1. A commitment to broad social service functions and community interaction were also characteristics of the political era of policing. How does community policing differ from policing methods of the political era? What are the potential negative implications of community policing approaches?

2. Is community policing still relevant post–September 11 and for serious issues such as terrorism? Should law enforcement now focus more on public safety than on building police–community partnerships?

3. When a department shifts to community policing, how are average line officers affected? Are any new expectations realistic?

4. How would you address a gang problem in a high-crime neighborhood? What information would you need to combat the problem? What groups would you partner with? What strategies might be relevant?

REFERENCES

Bayley, D. 1988. "Community Policing: A Report from the Devil's Advocate." In *Community Policing: Rhetoric or Reality,* edited by J. Greene and S. Mastrofski, 225–238. New York, NY: Praeger.

Braiden, C. 1992. "Community Policing: Nothing New Under the Sun." In *Community Oriented Policing and Problem Solving.* Sacramento, CA: California Department of Justice.

Bursik, R., and H. Grasmik. 1993. *Neighborhoods and Crime: the Dimensions of Effective Community Control.* New York, NY: Lexington Books.

Cohen, L., and M. Felson. 1979. "Social Change and Crime Rate Trends: A Routine Activity Approach." *American Sociological Review* 44(4): 588–608.

Coles, C., and G. Kelling. 1999. "Prevention Through Community Prosecution," *The Public Interest.* 136(2): 124–137.

Community Policing Consortium. 1994. *Understanding Community Policing.* Washington, D.C.: Bureau of Justice Assistance.

Cordner, G. W. 1999. "Elements of Community Policing." In *Policing Perspectives: An Anthology,* edited by L. Gaines and G. Cordner, 137–149. Los Angeles, CA: Roxbury.

Correia, M. 2000. *Social Capital and a Sense of Community Building: Building Social Cohesion.* Los Angeles, CA: Roxbury.

Crowe, T. 2000. *Crime Prevention Through Environmental Design,* 2d ed. Boston, MA: Butterworth-Heinemann.

Davis, R., and B. Taylor. 1997. "A Proactive Response to Family Violence. The Results of a Randomized Experiment." *Criminology.* 35(3): 307–333.

Eck, J., and W. Spelman. 1987. *Problem Solving: Problem-Oriented Policing in Newport News.* Washington, D.C.: National Institute of Justice.

Gaines, L., J. Worrall, M. Southerland, and J. Angel. 2003. *Police Administration,* 2d ed. New York, NY: McGraw-Hill.

Godson, R. 2000. "Guide to Developing a Culture of

Lawfulness." Unpublished paper presented at the Symposium on the Role of Civil Society in Countering Organized Crime: Global Implications of the Palermo, Sicily Renaissance, December 14, Palermo, Italy.

Goldstein, H. 1990. *Problem-Oriented Policing.* New York, NY: McGraw-Hill.

Goldstein, H. 1979. *Policing in a Free Society.* Cambridge, MA: Ballinger.

Grant, H., and N. Jacobs. 1997. *The Bridgeport Youth Firearms Violence Initiative.* Washington, D.C.: Office of Community-Oriented Policing Services.

Grant, H. 1999. "Buffalo Weed and Seed Initiative." In *Promising Practices to Reduce Juvenile Gun Violence,* edited by D. Sheppard, 34–40. Washington, D.C.: Office of Juvenile Justice and Delinquency Prevention.

Greenberg, S., J. Williams, and W. Rohe. 1982. "Safety in Urban Neighborhoods: A Comparison of Physical Characteristics and Informal Territorial Control in High and Low Crime Neighborhoods." *Population and Environment* 5(3): 147–148.

Greenwood, P., J. Chalken, and J. Petersilia. 1977. The Criminal Investigation Process. Lexington, MA: D. C. Heath and Company.

Harris, D. 2002. *Profiles in Injustice: Why Racial Profiling Cannot Work.* New York, NY: The New Press.

Hawkins, J., R. Catalano, and J. Miller. 1992. "Risk and Protective Factors for Alcohol and Other Drug Problems in Adolescence and Early Adulthood." *Psychological Bulletin.* 112(2): 343–427.

Hawkins, J., M. Arthur, and R. Catalano. 1995. "Preventing Substance Abuse." In *Building a Safer Society: Strategic Approaches to Crime Prevention.* Vol. 19, *Crime and Justice: A Review of Research,* M. Tonry and D. Farrington, eds., 343–427. Chicago, IL: University of Chicago Press.

Kelling G., T. Pate, D. Dieckman, and C. Brown. 1974. the Kansas City Preventive Patrol Experiment: A Summary Report. Washington, D.C.: The Police Foundation.

Klockars, C. 1991. "The Rhetoric of Community Policing." In *Community Policing: Rhetoric and Reality.* J. Green and S. Mastrofski, eds. New York, NY: Praeger.

McKnight, L., and A. Loper. 2002. "The Effects of Risk and Resilience Factors on the Prediction of Delinquency in Adolescent Girls." *School Psychology International.* 23: 186–198.

Metropolitan Police District of Columbia, n.d. *Community Prosecution.* Available at wysiwig://20/ http://mpoc.oc.gov/info/comm./commpros.shtn.

Miller, L., and K. Hess. 1998. *The Police in the Community: Strategies for the 21st Century,* 2d ed. Belmont, CA: Wadsworth.

National Strategy Information Center. 2000. *School-Based Curriculum to Counter Crime and Corruption, 3rd Draft.* Washington, D.C.: National Strategy Information Center.

New York State Regional Community Policing Institute. 1999. *Fundamentals of Community Policing,* Module II, Handout 3.2. New York, NY: New York State Regional Community Policing Institute.

Office of Juvenile Justice and Delinquency Prevention. 1995. *The Serious Habitual Offender Comprehensive Action Program.* Washington, D.C.: Office of Juvenile Justice and Delinquency Prevention.

Office of Juvenile Justice and Delinquency Prevention. 2000. "Boston Strategy to Prevent Youth Violence." In *Promising Strategies to Reduce Gun Violence.* Washington, D.C.: Office of Juvenile Justice and Delinquency Prevention.

Orlando, L. 2001. *Fighting the Mafia.* New York, NY: Encounter Books.

Parent, D., and B. Snyder. 1999. *Police–Corrections Partnerships: Issues and Practices.* Washington, D.C.: National Institute of Justice.

Peak, K., and R. Glensor. 1999. *Community Policing and Problem Solving: Strategies and Practices.* Upper Saddle River, NJ: Prentice Hall.

Pease, K. 1998. *Repeat Victimization: Taking Stock. Crime Detection and Prevention Series, Paper 90.* London: Home Office Police Research Group.

Police Foundation. 1981. *The Newark Foot Patrol Experiment.* Washington, D.C.: The Police Foundation.

Rosenbaum, D. 1994. "Community Crime Prevention: A Review of What is Known." In *Police and Policing: Contemporary Issues.* D. Kenny, ed., 203–218. New York, NY: Praeger.

Rutter, M. 1987. "Psychosocial Resilience and Protective Mechanisms." *American Journal of Orthopsychiatry.* 57: 316–331.

Sadd, S., and R. Grinc. 1996. "Implementation Challenges in Community Policing: Innovative Neighborhood-Oriented Policing in Eight Cities." *National Institute of Justice, Research in Brief,* February.

Shaw, C., and H. McKay. 1931. "Social Factors in Juvenile Delinquency." *National Commission on Law Observation and Enforcement,* No. 13, *Report on Causes of Crime,* Volume II. Washington, D.C.: U.S. Government Printing Office.

Sheppard, D., H. Grant, W. Rowe, and N. Jacobs. 2000. *Fighting Gun Violence. OJJDP Bulletin in Brief.* Washington, D.C.: Office of Juvenile Justice and Delinquency Prevention.

Skogan, W. 1996. *Disorder and Decline.* Berkeley, CA: University of California Press.

Tiet, Q., and D. Huizinga. 2002. "Dimensions of the Construct of Resilience and Adaptation Among

Inner City Youth." *Journal of Adolescent Research*. 17: 260–276.

Trojanowicz, R. 1982. *An Evaluation of the Neighborhood Foot Patrol Program in Flint, Michigan*. East Lansing, MI: State University Press.

Walker, S. 1992. *The Police in America: An Introduction*, 2d ed. New York, NY: McGraw-Hill.

Wasserman, G., and A. Seracini. 1995. "Family Risk Factors and Interventions." In *Child Delinquents: Development, Intervention, and Service Needs*.

R. Loeber and D. Farrington, eds., 165–189. Thousand Oaks, CA: Sage Publications.

Wilson, J., and G. Kelling. 1982. "The Police and Neighborhood Safety." *Atlantic Monthly* (March): 29–38.

Wood, L. 2001. "Palermo Creates a Culture of Legality; Economic Growth Follows." *The Business Journal Online*, January. Available at wysiwig://16/ http://www.business-journal.com/sicilytour/ Palermo.htm.

Chapter 13

Advances in Policing—New Technologies for Crime Analysis

Chapter Outline

Chapter Objectives

● Identify the stages of technological advancement in policing and the implications of technology utilization in the field.

● Understand the different types of crime analysis and the technologies available for them, such as GIS.

● Know the variety of applications of GIS technology.

● Appreciate the many types of technology available to modern law enforcement.

Introduction

Throughout its history, the U.S. Border Patrol has faced the seemingly insurmountable task of detecting and apprehending an ever-present stream of drug traffickers and illegal immigrants. The 60-mile area around the U.S.–Mexico border in the San Diego area alone requires the management of more than 2,000 agents and 900 seismic sensors (DeAngelis 2000).[1] To aid them in their efforts, the U.S. Border Patrol San Diego Sector has many high-tech tools at their disposal, such as geographic information systems (GIS), seismic sensors, and infrared night vision equipment.

Agents use GIS technology to map the locations of alien apprehensions to determine why certain areas are higher in illegal migration and drug trafficking than others. Using real-time sensor feeds from the Intelligent Computer Aided Detection System (ICAD), agents monitor "hits" corresponding to potential illegal migrant entry into the country. Armed with the knowledge of a possible entry point, agents are able to map out the travel route that has the highest probability of leading to the apprehension of the illegal border crossers.

Illegal traffic has also found underground avenues of escaping detection. To combat this, the Border Patrol has used global positioning system (GPS) receivers and GIS to plot storm drain and sewer systems that are facilitating traffic from Mexico into the United States.

The application of such technologies to the practice of law enforcement has revolutionized the capacity of police to both *respond* to crime that is taking place in real time and to proactively identify problems, analyze their causes, and develop strategic plans that truly enhance an agency's *crime prevention* capabilities. For example, the U.S. Border Patrol also targets high-risk areas with warning signs in Spanish informing immigrants of the dangers of crossing the border illegally.

In this technological era, law enforcement has had to evolve to fulfill its mandate of contributing to overall public security. Technology has proven invaluable in responding to the problem of linkage blindness across jurisdictions as well as with other criminal justice agencies and sectors of the community. In an age faced with the continuing threats of transnational crime and terrorism, the importance of continued technological advances cannot be ignored.

However, the increasing reliance upon and availability of technology to law enforcement can be intimidating.

The struggle to manage our borders is made increasingly easier through the use of high-tech equipment such as GPS, GIS, and night vision.

This technology brings with it new legal challenges, particularly with regard to the balance between crime control and the private interests of citizens, which was discussed at the beginning of this book. This chapter will begin with a brief overview of the development of technological advances in law enforcement, followed by descriptive coverage of key technological applications in policing. Particular attention will be paid to the use of GIS in facilitating proactive police management in the twenty-first century.

The Stages of Technological Advancement in Policing

Soulliere (1999) provides a useful conceptual framework for describing the advancement of technology in policing since its early professional origins. Although there is significant overlap with Kelling and Moore's (1987) three eras of policing (see Chapter 2), Soulliere (1999) offers four useful stages that help to conceptualize technological development in policing. Table 13.1 summarizes **Souillere's stages of technological advancement**.

The First Stage (1881–1945)

As described in Chapters 2 and 3, many of the initial technological advances in policing can be attributed to the work of August Vollmer, who headed the early twentieth-century police department (1909–1932) in Berkeley, California. Under his guidance, law enforcement increased its mobility through motor vehicle patrol and enhanced officer–precinct communications through telephone and radio. With his establishment of the first forensic laboratory, criminal investigators had access to an increasing array of technological expertise that would continue to increase exponentially throughout the development of law enforcement. For example, Vollmer's crime laboratory pioneered the use of the polygraph as well as fingerprint and handwriting classification systems (Seaskate 1998). Souillere (1999) cites several ways in which these early technological advances had an impact on police organization, including:

- The development of increasingly complex police organizations through the creation of specialized sections within large police organizations to handle the new technology, such as radio communications and forensic labs.
- Increased mobility for patrol activities offered by the use of automobiles.

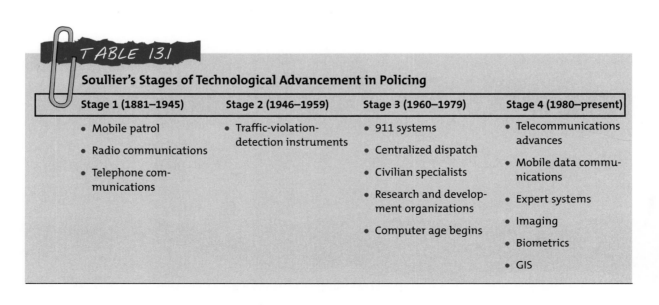

TABLE 13.1

Soullier's Stages of Technological Advancement in Policing

Stage 1 (1881–1945)	Stage 2 (1946–1959)	Stage 3 (1960–1979)	Stage 4 (1980–present)
• Mobile patrol • Radio communications • Telephone communications	• Traffic-violation-detection instruments	• 911 systems • Centralized dispatch • Civilian specialists • Research and development organizations • Computer age begins	• Telecommunications advances • Mobile data communications • Expert systems • Imaging • Biometrics • GIS

- Increased officer safety made possible with enhanced communications and the use of automobiles.

The Second Stage (1946–1959)

Roughly corresponding with the beginnings of Kelling and Moore's (1987) reform era of policing, Soulliere (1999) notes that the second stage of advancement saw the bureaucratization of policing organizations that, to some degree, was a result of technological advancements. During this stage, traffic police received a significant boost with the advent of the first instruments to measure both speeding violations and the condition of the driver. Although early instruments were rather crude indicators, they would grow over time to include the significant automobile surveillance mechanisms and blood-alcohol measures discussed briefly in Chapter 6.

The Third Stage (1960–1979)

As society in general entered the computer age, Soulliere (1999) claims that police technology began to truly emerge. It is during this stage that call distribution centers, computerized databanks, and **computer-aided dispatch (CAD)** became commonplace in police agencies. Some of the significant technological advancements in this stage can be attributed to President Lyndon B. Johnson. In 1967, Johnson created the President's Commission on Law Enforcement and the Administration of Justice to analyze U.S. crime patterns and provided resources to combat crime. Importantly, the report generated by the Commission on Law Enforcement highlighted the slow infusion of societal technological advances into the criminal justice system, with particular attention paid to policing. To this end, the report stated (President's Commission on Law Enforcement and the Administration of Justice 1967):

> The police, with crime laboratories and radio networks, made early use of technology, but most police departments could have been equipped 30 or 40 years ago as well as they are today. . . . Of all criminal justice agencies, the police have had the closest ties to science and technology, but they have called on scientific resources primarily to help in the solution of specific serious crimes, rather than for assistance in solving general problems of policing. (p. 125)

A notable gap existed between the technologies that were currently available that had potential law enforcement applications and what police agencies were actually using. In response to this gap, the Johnson administration began "the flow, a trickle at first, of what eventually became billions of dollars in direct and indirect assistance to local and state law enforcement" (Seaskate 1998, p. 2).

Importantly, the commission argued for the establishment of a single telephone number that citizens across the country could use to contact the police in the case of an emergency. In only a matter of years following AT&T's announcement of the first **911 system** in 1968, its use became a driving force for police departments across the country (Seaskate 1998). As highlighted throughout earlier chapters, this increasing emphasis on calls for service would have both benefits (the seeming ease of access to the police in times of emergency), as well as detriments (this became the principal means of determining police resource deployment and performance evaluation). Skolnick and Bayley (1986) point out that patrol personnel can easily be exhausted by rushing between calls for service, rather than taking the time needed to truly digest and understand the human situations into which they are thrown constantly.

During this third stage of development, large municipalities began to centralize the dispatch of all fire, police, and medical services (Seaskate 1998). The over-reliance of the average citizen on the use of 911, regardless of the nature or seriousness of the problem, has led to the establishment of **311 systems** in many metropolitan areas to try and decrease the significant burden 911 has had on city emergency resources. The 311 system is available for all calls to police and fire personnel that are not emergencies. Other recent strategies for handling the call volume brought about by 911 include the differential response approaches described in Chapter 6.

Increased research on law enforcement applications and technological development was also a key characteristic of the third stage. The National Institute of Justice (NIJ) was created in 1968 and it continues to play a leading role in enhancing the field of law enforcement both nationally and internationally (Soulliere 1999). An increasing reliance on civilian specialists within large police organizations also continued throughout this stage because of developments in the areas of forensics and communication technologies.

The Fourth Stage (1980–present)

Information access and use characterize Soulliere's (1999) fourth stage of technological development. In addition to simply amassing a volume of information—a task that law enforcement agencies have been successful at since their creation—technological advancement now focuses on the speed and ease of information use. Moreover, technology developed throughout the fourth stage now provides law enforcement with access to data that would be unavailable to them without these tools. Collaboration between traditional law enforcement and the military has resulted in many of the technologies introduced in this stage. Examples of such new tools include those in telecommunications, mobile computing, expert systems, imaging, and biometric technologies (Soulliere 1999). Each of these areas will be described further in this chapter.

The importance of law enforcement access to such technological advancements is in many ways a balancing act between concerns for personal liberties and public security, as illustrated by Cowper (2003) (Figure 13.1).

Kurzweil (2001) discusses the significant rate of technological development in modern society. He notes that although technology has always increased exponentially, earlier generations were at such early stages of development that the trends appear flat due to the low baseline. Kurzweil argues that although everyone in society generally expects technological progress to continue, the rate of change is accelerating. Rather than incremental increases every year, technological advancement is characterized by exponential growth, doubling every year. He organizes these observations into the **law of accelerating returns**:

- The enhanced methods resulting from one stage of progress are used to create the next stage.

- Consequently, the rate of progress of an evolutionary process increases exponentially over time.

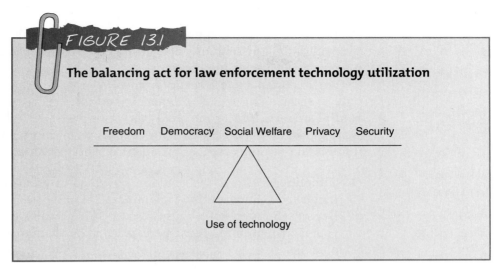

FIGURE 13.1

The balancing act for law enforcement technology utilization

Freedom   Democracy   Social Welfare   Privacy   Security

Use of technology

Modified from Cowper (2003).

- In addition, the speed and cost-effectiveness of a technological advancement will also increase exponentially over time.

- Finally, current methods of solving a problem in technology (such as shrinking transistors on an integrated circuit as an approach to making more powerful computers) will provide exponential growth until the method exhausts its potential. At this time, a fundamental change will result that will allow the exponential growth to continue.

Cowper (2003) summarizes the law of accelerating returns by saying that we will have 100 years of progress in the next 25 years and 20,000 years of progress in the next 100 years. Thus, the technology of science fiction that we often think of as being so far in the future is perhaps not as distant as it might seem. The applications available to policing now or in the near future might seem more the work of science fiction than reality. Certainly the applications of technology to policing have greatly enhanced the ability of law enforcement organizations to meaningfully engage in the problem-solving process. Although many police departments continue to be behind the curve in terms of integrating new technologies into day-to-day operations, the success of many applications to sound policing will make ignoring progress increasingly difficult over time.

Crime Analysis

Integral to the process of problem solving discussed in Chapter 12 is crime analysis. **Crime analysis** has been defined as involving "the collection and analysis of data pertaining to a criminal incident, offender, and target" (Canter 2000, p. 4). Ideally, crime analysis will guide police managers in making deployment and resource allocation decisions that are linked to a true understanding of the nature of the problem. The more important data collected and analyzed related to all components of the crime triangle (victim, offender, location) (see Chapter 12), the better equipped police organizations will be to develop innovative, out-of-the-box solutions that include the full spectrum of suppression, intervention, and prevention options.

An important note of caution must be stressed here. Crime analysis will only be as good as the data or information that is collected. There are three **essential criteria for crime analysis** that departments should use when designing data collection processes as well as when interpreting the meaning of information resulting from crime analysis. These criteria are:

1. **Timeliness**: Does the pattern or trend presented reflect a current problem or issue or is it more representative of a previous situation? Deployment decisions with respect to both prevention and offender-apprehension efforts must be based on information that is as current as possible.

2. **Relevancy**: Do the measures used in the analysis accurately reflect what is intended? For example, whether a pattern is based upon **calls-for-service data** or **incident data** can be a very important determination depending on what the police manager is trying to understand.

3. **Reliability**: Would the same data, interpreted by different people at different times, lead to the same conclusions?

Canter (2000) categorizes crime analysis into both strategic and tactical functions.

Strategic Crime Analysis

The collection and analysis of data spanning a long period of time is **strategic crime analysis**. This type of analysis is said to be *research focused* because it includes the use of statistics to make conclusions (Canter 2000). This form of analysis can be useful to departments in terms of **crime-trend forecasting**, or using data to estimate future crime based on past trends (Canter 2000). With crime-trend forecasting, important decisions can be made as to the deployment of patrol as a reflection of the changing volume of criminal activity.

Another important benefit of strategic crime analysis is the analysis of changing community dynamics and risk factors that might be contributing to the particular crime trends of a specific area (Canter 2000). Once again, this type of analysis over time can result in more informed decision making that can lead to police partnerships with other city and community agencies that can help create more long-term, sustainable reductions in criminal activity.

Tactical Crime Analysis

Whereas strategic crime analysis involves the review of data spanning generally a year or more, **tactical crime analysis** uses real-time data spanning several days. One of the principal uses of this type of analysis involves problem identification, or the **pattern detection** of multiple offenses over a short period of time that have common characteristics, such as the type of crime, modus operandi, and type of weapon used (Canter 2000). One example of tactical crime analysis that will be discussed later in this chapter is geographic profiling, which can be used to suggest the likelihood of where an offender lives based on the pattern of where victims and offenses occur. Tactical crime analysis can occur on as large an area as a department's entire jurisdiction or as small as the few block radius of a hot spot.

Linkage analysis involves connecting a suspect to a series of incidents based on commonalities in modus operandi and suspect description as well as known offenders that live in close proximity to a given area (Canter 2000). Following a nationwide effort by state legislatures to implement sex offender registration laws (Terry and Furlong 2004), many police departments regularly search their databases of registered sex offenders when a known series of sexual offenses is identified.

Finally, **target profiling** involves the use of data to determine the potential risks certain areas may have for criminal victimization based on known offense patterns in the area. Following the previous example, some departments have experimented with community-risk profiles (i.e., day care centers, presence of parks, etc.) as a means of notifying the community of the presence of registered sex offenders.

Geomapping Crime Patterns: Moving Beyond Push Pins

Based on the previous discussion of the applications of crime analysis to policing, the integral role that **geographic information systems (GIS)** play in the process is readily apparent. A GIS is an automated system for the capture, storage, retrieval, analysis, and display of spatial data (Clarke 1990). Others have noted that "GIS technology is to geographical analysis what the microscope, the telescope, and computers have been to other sciences" (Cowen 2001, p. 3). By visually representing diverse data sources that can be geographically located, such as crime events, land usage, property values, racial ethnic composition, and so on, GIS enables planners to "manipulate and display geographical knowledge in new and exciting ways" (Cowen 2001, p. 3). Despite its diverse applications across various fields, the common focus of GIS is the enhancement of decision making.

In law enforcement, GIS has revolutionized the practice of electronic **crime mapping**, or visually displaying crime incidents on a mapped surface of a particular jurisdiction. However, the use of crime maps has a long history within policing. For example, the NYPD used pin maps to represent crime patterns at least as far back as 1900 (Harries 1999). Moreover, criminologists and sociologists have examined the spatial trends of crime and delinquency since as far back as mid-nineteenth-century France's Quetelet (Phillips 1972) and the **social ecology of crime** efforts pioneered by Shaw and McKay (1942). The difference is, of course, that until the use of GIS became more commonplace in policing practice throughout the 1990s, crime patterns were literally represented by inserting push pins into the map of a jurisdiction that was usually mounted on the wall.

Although these early crime maps proved to be useful in visually showing where crimes occurred, patterns would be lost over time as more and more pins

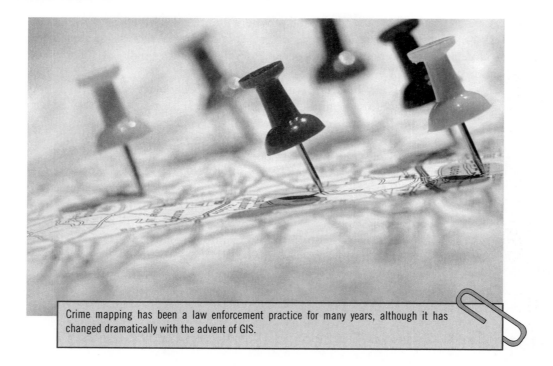

Crime mapping has been a law enforcement practice for many years, although it has changed dramatically with the advent of GIS.

were added to the map. Additionally, these maps were very difficult to archive for later retrieval and analysis unless they were photographed (Shaw and McKay 1942).

What Crime Maps Do: GIS as a Technical Aid to Problem-oriented Policing

GIS has revolutionized the way in which problem-oriented policing is conducted internationally. This is largely due to the police's ability to now overlay seemingly diverse types of data that all contribute to a true understanding of a particular problem. For example, a series of burglaries taking place between the hours of 1:00 AM and 3:00 AM might be the first thing visually displayed on a crime map. This would correspond with the scanning (problem-identification) part of the problem-solving model detailed in Chapter 12. However, getting at the underlying causes of the burglary problem requires deeper probing and innovative thinking. In this case, the crime analyst might overlay the burglary incident data with available data about land usage in the area. The crime analyst might then learn that the burglaries are occurring within walking distance of an area high school.

Although this might seem to be an obvious linkage to many, individuals often overlook such connections. By visually displaying overlays of various potential data combinations, GIS can play a critical role in jump-starting the analysis process. With the current example, the police manager might begin to develop a series of hypotheses related to the fact that the burglaries might be caused by troublemaking youths playing hooky from their afternoon classes. In addition to providing a large pool of individuals from which investigators might seek to learn information about the incidents, police planners may also begin to

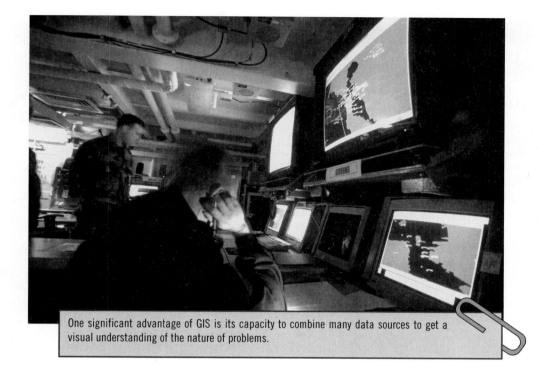

One significant advantage of GIS is its capacity to combine many data sources to get a visual understanding of the nature of problems.

collaborate with the school to develop responses that increase **truancy enforcement** in area schools.

Types of Data with Mapping Applications

Many types of data can be used for mapping purposes. Any data that can be **geocoded**, or for which there is geographic reference information, can be used for GIS analysis (Harries 1999). Although early forms of geocoding only permitted street addresses as the geographic unit upon which to map data, blocks and census tracts can now be used. Crime incidents are readily applicable for geocoding purposes given that they are almost always available as street addresses or are otherwise locationally based (Harries 1999).

To summarize, direct crime mapping pattern applications of GIS can include (Harries 1999):

- Mapping incident types and modus operandi
- Mapping attributes of victims and suspects

Based on the initial pattern analysis, overlays of other forms of data can help to present a broader understanding of the problem. For example, a pattern analysis might indicate a problem of disorderly conduct and assaults in an area. An overlay with available liquor stores and bars in an area may present the planner with a series of hypotheses as to what factors might be driving the problem. An additional benefit of GIS is that they are directly compatible with statistical analyses to further refine causal projections. Thus, a city planner might be able to statistically link the rate of disorderly conduct and assaults in city jurisdictions with the overall density of alcohol availability or other possibilities.

Linkages in Law Enforcement

GIS Applications to Sex-offender Management

GIS applications can also help to increase law enforcement's capacity to engage in the collaborative problem-solving process with other criminal justice and community agencies. The visual representation of information can be a powerful tool in coming to a common understanding of the nature of problems even across planning groups with diverse perspectives.

The authors of this text participated on a citywide task force in New York City composed of representatives from law enforcement, probation and parole, family and criminal courts, mental health, treatment providers, and victim advocates to examine the issue of sex-offender management in the community (Grant and Terry 2000). Although New York City had a large registered sex offender population at the time (over 3,000 offenders), there was no comprehensive plan for the management of these offenders in the community involving collaboration between each of the key stakeholders. Building on the recognition across team members of the clear need for such a collaborative approach to sex-offender management, as well as a need to better understand the dynamics of the problem through data collection, the New York City Sex Offender Management Team had tremendous momentum from the start, with agencies opening their doors to facilitate the data collection process.

Beginning at the first team meeting, partners sought to identify a mechanism for gaining a complete understanding of the sex offender population currently residing in the community. Although it was initially suggested that each of the five District Attorneys represented conduct searches on sex offenders within their own databases to form an initial population for study, it became immediately apparent that the most efficient access to such data would be to use a database of all registered sex offenders in the city.

Based on this initial database, the team sought to get complete information on probation conditions, employment, treatment, living situation, probation officer contacts, mental status, substance abuse history, and so on. In addition, complete criminal histories on the offenders were requested in order to gain a true understanding of the nature of the population being managed so that accurate comprehensive strategies could be devised. At all points, ethical considerations were paramount in the use of this information, which was always presented in aggregate form and never published beyond the law enforcement planning team purposes.

In a city the size of New York, and with such a large number of offenders, GIS mapping of offender residences is essential for two reasons: First, depending on the plan developed by the team, it might have been necessary to pilot the demonstration project within one borough given the tremendous task and the resources required for a citywide approach. Having a visual display of where offenders are most concentrated can help aid planners in making decisions as to where to target initial resources. Second, offender mapping had the tremendous ability to demonstrate to the team the scope of the problem, particularly given the obvious clustering of offenders in several city locations. Mapping allowed researchers to present the planning team with **buffer zones** around each offender, combining offender density in a given area with overlays of key risk factors for reoffending drawn from the relapse-prevention literature and connected to each offender residence location. Examination of this data by school and daycare locations, parks, available treatment resources, and so on were all part of the process for meaningful informed problem solving, to which GIS proved to be the essential core tool.

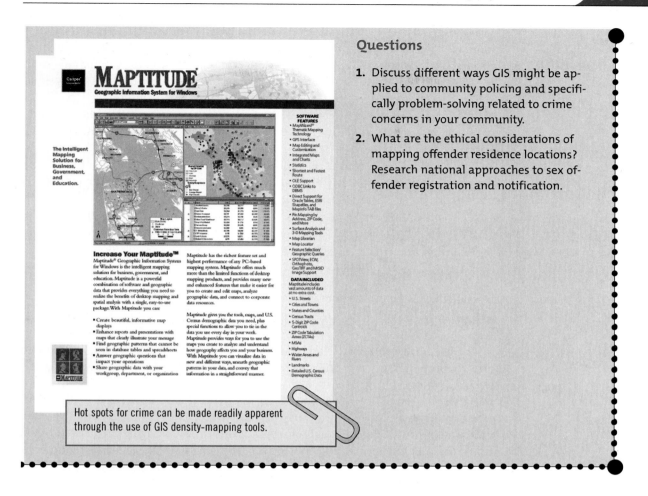

Questions

1. Discuss different ways GIS might be applied to community policing and specifically problem-solving related to crime concerns in your community.

2. What are the ethical considerations of mapping offender residence locations? Research national approaches to sex offender registration and notification.

Hot spots for crime can be made readily apparent through the use of GIS density-mapping tools.

Although such analyses can only show planners of possible relations between two variables, or **correlations**, rather than saying conclusively that X causes Y (**causation**), there can be no doubt that such findings greatly enhance the level of informed decision making by law enforcement and other key stakeholders in a city.

Mapping and Accountability: GIS in Action

Crime mapping can greatly increase the accountability of a department by visually demonstrating incident patterns for which departmental administrators can hold commanding officers accountable for over time. A proactive police manager should use GIS and other problem-solving tools to create sound strategic and tactical decisions related to such things as officer deployment, resource allocation, and partnerships with other agencies for sustained crime reductions. The CompStat model of the NYPD institutionalized the use of GIS for departmental planning purposes. The program was such a success that similar versions of CompStat have been implemented in departments across the country.

The NYPD Crime Control Model, or CompStat, cannot be oversimplified to simply refer to quality-of-life policing, aggressive policing, or even data-driven policing, as is commonly found in the literature about the model. Rather, as police scholar Phyllis McDonald (2002) emphatically states, "this proliferation of singularly focused descriptors does a disservice to the management principles of CompStat and its potential for use in other jurisdictions. CompStat (from "computer-driven crime statistics") is a comprehensive, continuous analysis of results for improvement and achievement of prescribed outcomes" (p. 7). In other words, **CompStat** involves managing police operations by institutionalizing accountability and analysis processes that are the embodiment of the problem-oriented policing model.

McDonald (2002) offers a concise overview of the key elements of the CompStat model and issues involved in its replication in other departments. To summarize, these elements include:

- Specific objectives
- Accurate and timely intelligence
- Effective tactics
- Rapid deployment of personnel and resources
- Relentless follow-up and assessment

As we have seen in earlier chapters, police organizations, like any other form of bureaucracy, are often extremely resistant to change. How then, did such a seemingly proactive, forward-looking model become implemented in the country's largest police department? In his prior position as head of the New York City Transit Police in the early 1990s, former NYPD police commissioner William Bratton had seen tremendous successes in focusing departmental operations on specific measurable objectives and an ongoing review of outcome achievement. Following a series of complementary strategies in the notoriously dangerous New York City subways, such as increased undercover and uniformed police presence and the removal of graffiti and other signs of disorder, dramatic declines in robberies, fare evasion, and general disorder resulted. New Yorkers once again began to feel safe about riding the subways.

When Bratton came to the helm of the NYPD in 1994, he began a dramatic reengineering effort that included interviews and focus groups involving representatives of every rank and bureau in order to assess the state of command in the department (Silverman 1999a). Seven specific objectives were created to guide the future direction of the department (McDonald 2002):

1. Get guns off the street.
2. Curb youth violence in the schools and on the streets.
3. Drive drug dealers out of NYC.
4. Break the cycle of domestic violence.
5. Reclaim the public spaces of NYC.
6. Reduce auto-related crime in NYC.
7. Root out corruption and build organizational integrity in the NYPD.

In order to achieve these outcomes, as well as to measure departmental progress towards them, ready access to timely data was essential. However, a significant problem became immediately apparent: The NYPD was not equipped to provide up-to-date crime reports. In fact, there was generally a reporting lag of three to six months for crime statistics, and even then, any meaningful analysis at the incident-based level was near impossible (Silverman 1996). Headquarters was not systematically tracking crime activity in the precincts, let alone using such information to evaluate the performance of its commanding officers (Silverman 1999a). As a result, precinct commanders did not view crime reduction as a primary job responsibility. Common to departments across the country, efficiency concerns in responding to crime were seen as more important. Detective bureaus and other specialized functions thus only rarely collaborated with patrol, and often directly clashed over territory and other concerns.

CompStat was devised as a means of reforming these organizational issues by pushing all precincts to generate weekly crime activity reports so that they could be held accountable for the achievement of the seven specific objectives outlined in the reengineering process (McDonald 2002). In the beginning, the Patrol Bureau staff computerized this data and compiled it into the "CompStat Book," offering year-to-date crime complaints and arrests for every major felony category in addition to gun arrests (Silverman 1999a). These data would then be compared at citywide, patrol-borough, and precinct levels. In addition, precinct commanders quickly became accountable for not only crime activity, but also for any inaccuracies in the data. Over time, these data became even more readily available and could be downloaded directly from the department's On-Line Booking Service (OLBS). Headquarters would come to rank order the precincts in terms of overall crime changes within their jurisdiction.

By providing timely and accurate data it quickly became clear to precinct commanders that their role had changed; they were now being held accountable for the crime under their charges. As such, they began to realize that they had to stop simply responding to crime and had to begin to proactively think about ways to deal with it from all angles: suppression, intervention, and prevention.

In order to solidify this message, NYPD headquarters began to hold regularly scheduled CompStat meetings in which precinct commanders and their staff met directly with top departmental brass to discuss crime trends and issues in their precincts. In a very intimidating environment, precinct commanders must stand before a lectern in front of three large video screens that flash GIS-generated maps of recent crime patterns (Figure 13.2). During this meeting, commanders are asked about what **tactics** they have tried to address the patterns, what resources they have tried or need, and with whom they have collaborated. The session thus becomes a brainstorming problem-solving session about how better to proactively respond to crime. Suggestions for strategy directives are made and at subsequent meetings are relentlessly followed up by top brass to further ensure accountability. Having the top brass available as part of this process ensures that departmental resources will be directed to precinct needs, even across precinct and unit lines. Thus, in addition to implementing accountable problem solving, CompStat seeks to reduce the problem of linkage blindness, which has been an important theme of this book.

In order to better prepare for CompStat meetings, each borough implemented **Pattern Identification Modules (PIMS)** composed of housing, transit, patrol, detective, organized crime, and robbery squads to review daily index

FIGURE 13.2

Layout of CompStat room

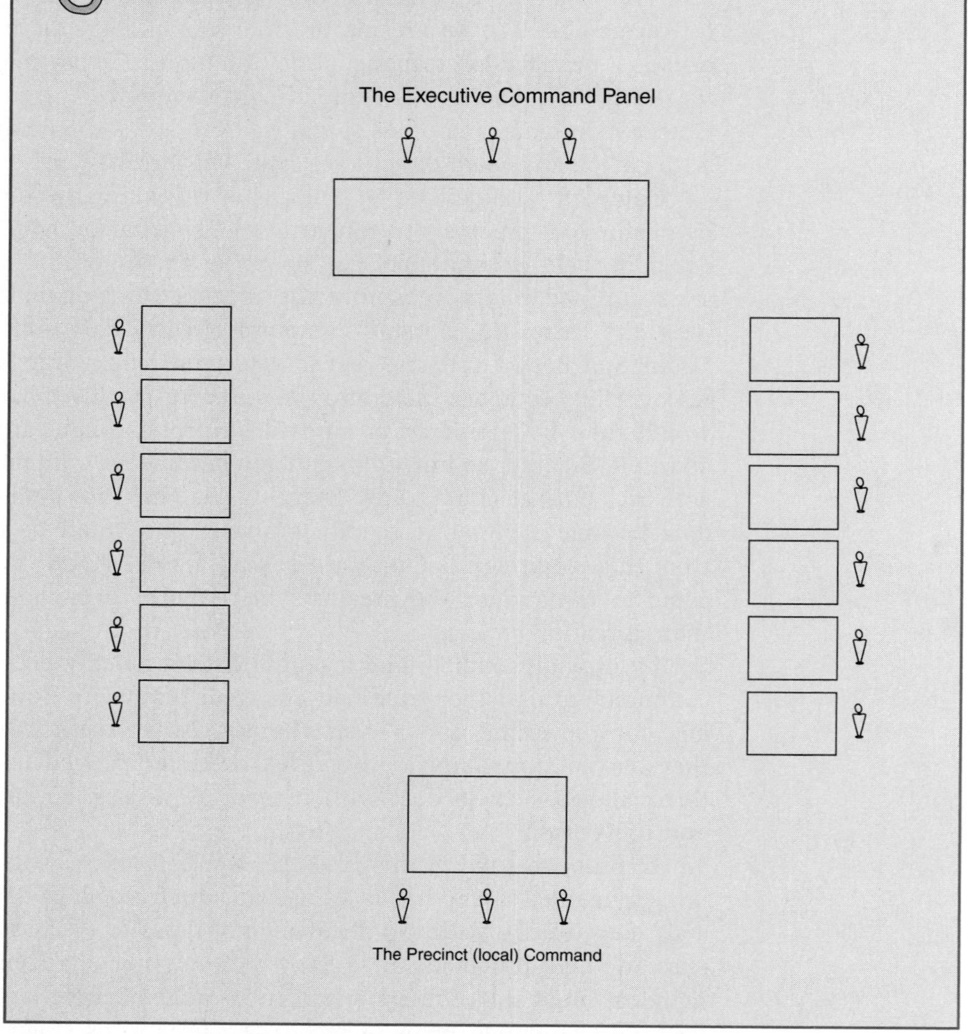

The Executive Command Panel

The Precinct (local) Command

Source: NYSRCPI.

crime reports and thus identify crime clusters or patterns that need to be addressed. Figure 13.3 provides a conceptual framework of this planning process.

Over time, CompStat has evolved to include other data: Census demographics, arrest and summons activity, available resources, average response time, domestic violence incidents, unfounded radio runs, and personnel absences (Silverman 1999a). Former Commissioner Howard Safir also added citizen complaints and charges of officer misconduct to the process. Time-of-day photos might also be presented in CompStat meetings to monitor changes in precinct dynamics by shift period.

Many scholars and practitioners have argued that CompStat has played a critical role in the significant crime reductions witnessed by New York City fol-

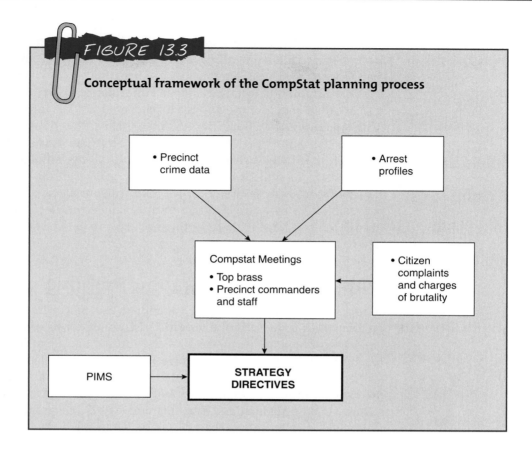

FIGURE 13.3

Conceptual framework of the CompStat planning process

lowing its implementation (Silverman 1999a). Others are more skeptical of these claims, arguing that the crime reductions in New York City can be attributed to larger patterns in society (Karmen 1996). The answer is likely somewhere in the middle; however, the tremendous impact CompStat has had on police management practices cannot be denied. Although some reports have pointed to the demoralizing effects of the process on precinct commanders and officers who feel a pressure to produce numbers, many others cite the significant increases in job satisfaction found by those who feel empowered by the problem-solving aspects brought to the job.

An important concern that has been raised is whether the pressure to keep crime statistics low has led to a zero-tolerance policing style that loses sight of community concerns, damaging police–community relations. The answer to this issue is unclear, as it is probably too soon to come to concrete conclusions. These questions will have to be tracked by practitioners and academicians alike as the model is implemented across diverse contextual conditions within the United States and abroad.

GIS and the Patrol Officer

As GIS crime mapping became recognized as an important tool in both tracking and responding to crime at the neighborhood level, departments across the country sought to expand its use beyond administrative planning to patrol officers and community residents. For example, the Camden New Jersey Police Department began providing officers with access to crime-mapping information on desktop computers and even on wireless laptops in patrol cars (American City and Country 2002). The department allowed officers to access information on crime based on location, type, and time in order to better focus their patrol efforts. The maps have also been designed to allow officers to pinpoint business contact information when an alarm is sounded, rather than having to call a dispatcher for the information (American City and Country 2002). Moreover, in 1998 the NIJ awarded the leading GIS software provider, **Environmental Systems Research Institute, Inc. (ESRI)**, a $500,000 grant to work with local law enforcement agencies and universities to effectively use GIS as a crime-fighting tool (Carney 1998). Collaborating with several local law enforcement agencies, ESRI developed an accessible GIS software program with a simple interface that would be easily transferable to large-scale departmental use outside of a specialized civilian analyst capacity.

Other Applications: Geographic Profiling

Geographic profiling, or the combined use of geography, psychology, and mathematics to identify the location of an offender, is most commonly associated with tracking down serial killers, rapists, and arsonists. However, it is a useful investigative tool in any case in which an individual offender has committed criminal activity across a series of locations (including crimes as diverse as robbery, burglary, theft, and fraud). Building from the significant empirical efforts of Brantingham and Brantingham (1981), geographic profiling suggests investigative alternatives based on the "hunting behavior" of the offender. Leading geographic profiler Kim Rossmo argues that criminals are no different in their pattern of carrying out their offenses as ordinary citizens are in going about their day-to-day activities (Onion 2002).

Following this logic, geographic profiling uses the nearness principle as a key rule. The **nearness principle** argues that offenders will remain within a limited range that is comfortable to them when committing their offenses (Rossmo 1998), just as animals will tend to forage within a limited range from their base (Onion 2002). Geographic profiling incorporates all possible methods of transportation available to an offender when calculating the area in which the offender is most likely to reside.

This research has led to the creation of a computerized geographic profiling workstation called **Rigel** that includes statistical analyses, GIS features, and database management functions to aid in the process of offering calculated investigative suggestions. Crime scenes are broken down by type (remember the primary and secondary distinctions discussed in Chapter 8) and then entered by location. Based on the theoretical principles of geographic profiling, addresses of suspects can be evaluated based on their probability of being the actual offender (Harries 1999). This can help investigators sort through their existing databases, such as those of registered sex offenders, and other investigative information available to them. When a specific suspect pool is not known, geographic profiling can help to pinpoint the highest probability areas in which to focus the search. As with the offender-profiling process discussed in Chapter 8, geographic profiling should only be considered as an additional tool for investigators; solving a series of offenses ultimately requires a sound investigative strategy.

Linkages in Law Enforcement

GIS Applications to Community Policing

Beginning in 1995, the Chicago Police Department (CPD) implemented one of the most easy to use and accessible GIS systems in the country as a complement to its department-wide **Chicago Alternative Policing Strategy (CAPS)** community policing approach. Called **Information Collection for Automated Mapping (ICAM)**, the program enables departmental personnel to generate maps of reported offenses by type in particular areas, including charts of the ten most frequently reported offenses through a series of easy clicks with a mouse (Rich 1996).

CAPS was implemented in 1993 in pilot districts and has since expanded to all twenty-five of the city's policing districts. This formula for community policing emphasizes officer problem solving by assigning officers to their beats for at least a year, altering dispatch schedules so that the time spent responding to crime outside of their beats is limited, and requiring regular beat officer attendance at meetings with community residents (Rich 1996). Early evaluation of CAPS demonstrated that it had affected significant declines in reported crime, victimization, and fear of crime (Skogan 1996).

ICAM was seen as a complement to CAPS by helping officers to better understand the problems in their assigned areas and, therefore, be better facilitators of collaborative problem-solving efforts with community residents to develop strategies to address these problems (Rich 1996). As part of the ICAM development process, focus groups were held with officers and detectives to seek their understanding and cooperation and to ensure that the completed program suited their information needs. Once the department got the officers' buy-in, they regularly shared generated maps at beat meetings. In the years following its introduction, a Citizen ICAM program was developed. This program enables citizens to generate much of the same information (without specific identifiers) that an officer can, thereby facilitating joint police–community planning efforts even more. Initially, confidentiality issues slowed citizen access to ICAM due to the specific details of street locations. However, it is now running for anyone to see at www.cicam.cpd.org.

Other departments across the country have produced their own mapping programs, including Web-based citizen crime reports, as will be discussed later.

Questions

1. How does your department's Web site compare to ICAM?
2. Which GIS elements would you include on a department Web site?
3. What applications of available GIS crime data are there for the community?

Twenty-first Century Technologies in Policing

In addition to the introduction of GIS into everyday crime-fighting activities, over the past decade numerous other technologies have become available, from **record management systems (RMS)** that help departments to store and readily retrieve the immense amounts of data they receive on a day-to-day basis to sophisticated weaponry and intelligence technologies that have reached law enforcement by way of the military. Covering all of these advances in significant detail is beyond the scope of this text; however, the remainder of this chapter will provide an overview of some significant technological developments that are becoming part of everyday law enforcement activities.

Surveillance Technologies

Surveillance technologies represent the wide array of systems currently available to law enforcement, the military, and even private entities, to track the movements of individuals and/or provide capable guardianship to a specific location. Examples of advancements in this area include, CCTV, GPS, Biometrics, and APIS systems.

Closed-Circuit Television The use of **closed-circuit television (CCTV)** and other forms of public-surveillance technology in the United States has grown significantly in recent years as not only police departments, but also airport security and other public entities, have increasingly turned to video surveillance in their efforts to reduce crime and increase public safety. The use of this technology may not be nearly as prevalent in the United States as it is in countries such as Britain, where there is a camera on every street corner and in every public building. However, it is becoming increasingly popular, particularly following the events of September 11. Law enforcement is now turning to surveillance systems such as CCTV as a means of trying to sort through the tremendous traffic at our borders, airports, and dense city streets.

After spending almost two years in CCTV control rooms across England, Goold (2001) concluded that in many cases actual surveillance outcomes have less to do with technological factors than they do with the working culture and the attitudes of individual camera operators. In particular, Goold found that, once established, many public-area surveillance systems quickly become prone to institutional inertia, with both camera operators and scheme managers being either unwilling or unable to update their systems or change their working practices in response to technological advances. Technology does not exist in a vacuum; it is both socially shaped and it shapes the attitudes and practices of those who use it (Bijkker et al. 1987). In addition, technical workers, such as CCTV operators, often shape the implementation of new technology by fitting it into their existing routines. Technological change may as often be subsumed into existing organizational structures as it affects organizational change (Barley 1986).

No one can erase the images caught on airport CCTV cameras of the September 11 hijackers boarding their plane in Boston. Certainly such retrospective images can be used as evidence of what transpired in a given incident, but law enforcement has become increasingly more interested in finding better ways to harness CCTV technology to readily identify known offenders passing through a checkpoint, such as a wanted felon or individual on a terrorist watch list. As such, new advances have sought to merge CCTV systems with promising approaches in the field of biometrics, as will be discussed later.

Some agencies have also developed innovative ways of using private security systems to aid responding units at the scene of an incident. For example, the Seal Beach Police Department, which is located in a high-robbery-incident suburb of Los Angeles, installed a network that transmits the output of bank security cameras directly to dispatch and to responding units in real time (Garcia 2001). This

New technology research seeks to merge facial recognition software with CCTV surveillance cameras.

network transmits video over the air in the same manner that images are sent over the Internet through encrypted wireless communication paths.

Global Positioning Systems   Global positioning systems have been used to enhance the tracking of offenders and officer deployments. **Global positioning systems (GPS)** use satellite-based technologies for the purpose of tracking the movement of patrol cars or specially equipped stolen vehicles. In some cases, an officer's cell phone can be equipped with GPS technology, providing an important alternative to conventional address-matching for an officer responding to a call. GPS technology has also proven to significantly enhance aerial photography of crime incident locations, allowing for greater visualization of the complete context of a situation (Harries 2001). The state of Iowa has capitalized on the surveillance capacity of GPS to monitor the real-time location of high-risk offenders released from prison. With offender-monitoring systems, law enforcement and correctional agencies can "prevent offenders from venturing near schools, daycare centers, and other restricted areas" (Greene 2001).

The Escambia County Sheriff's Department's SWAT team in Florida used a broadband-via-satellite system when responding to an emergency call involving a shooting victim and a barricaded suspect. Communicating through the Mobile Command Center's satellite system, the SWAT officers were able to determine that the suspect had fled the scene and the victim was likely dead (Hughes Network Systems 2002). Pictures of the suspect were immediately obtained via satellite and distributed to patrol, rather than taking hours or days, which was the norm before such technology was available to law enforcement agencies.

Even sophisticated tracking technology, such as GPS, can now fit into the palm of an officer's hand!

Biometrics

Biometric technologies involve the automatic, real-time identification of individuals based on their physiology or behavior (Cowper 2003). Biometrics thus covers a diversity of technologies, including voice/speech recognition, fingerprint scanning, lip movement recognition, retinal scanning, facial recognition software, DNA profiling, and thermal imagery, to name just a few.

Facial Recognition Software
The field of biometrics, particularly **facial recognition software**, is seen as offering the chance to overcome the limitations of CCTV systems, both by reducing the need for expensive human operators and by making the process of suspect identification faster and more reliable. Several promising studies support the potential applications of facial recognition software; however, little is known about how they will function in practical situations (Norris and Armstrong 1999).

Like any technology, the potential impact of facial recognition technology on preventing crime versus infringing on civil liberties rests upon the quality of the database from which possible "hits" are derived. For example, an underinclusive database might exclude potential terrorists but "catch" a child-support violator; whereas, a mistargeted database may send out too large a net that might unnecessarily infringe civil liberties and reduce the effective application of the technology. Cole's (2001) groundbreaking analysis of the history of identification technologies highlights the need for further study of the information elements being used to comprise biometric databases.

Fingerprint Identification Systems
Automated fingerprint identification systems (AFISs) were introduced in Chapter 8 and require little additional explanation here. An advanced system to aid in the processing, storage, and match-

ing of fingerprints has been introduced by the FBI. Called the **Integrated Automated Fingerprint Identification System (IAFIS)**, this enhanced technology offers a two-hour turnaround on electronically submitted criminal print searches from federal, state, and local law enforcement agencies (Smith 1998).

Interjurisdictional Communication Technology

At the core of linkage blindness is the lack of or minimal amount of critical communication that occurs between different law enforcement jurisdictions as well as other sectors of the criminal justice system and community at large. Given the diversity of criminal justice core functions, including community policing, crime prevention and investigation, prosecution, adjudication, punishment, restitution, release, and rehabilitation, the gathering and sharing of criminal justice information is particularly complex (Tomek 2001). The need to build information-sharing capacities, both technological and organizational, is evidenced by the NIJ's recent decision to make information sharing the number one priority for information technology solutions among state and local agencies, as well as internationally (Tomek 2001).

The need for information continuity and access is key to informed decision making by all criminal justice stakeholders. One of the biggest challenges to larger information-sharing collaborations, however, is the large differences across agencies in terms of agency protocols, standards, and even measures for the collection and utilization of data (Tomek 2001).

Offender Databases   Efforts have been made in recent years to develop sufficient technologies capable of overcoming many of the barriers involved in cross- and interjurisdictional information sharing.

The San Diego County **Automated Regional Information System (ARJIS)** warrants further description as to the possibilities in interjurisdictional information sharing. ARJIS compiles information from thirty-eight state, local, and federal law enforcement agencies into one Web site that registered police, court, and correctional officials can access (Walsh 2003). ARJIS includes crime-incident data that are updated every twenty-four hours, most-wanted lists, and interactive maps. Similarly, the Pennsylvania Integrated Justice Network (JNET) connects all of the state's criminal justice agencies together for the sharing of critical information, including offender photos and images of distinguishing marks. In one case, an offender was able to be apprehended because a victim was able to describe the perpetrator's tattoo to the police (Walsh 2003).

Cross-Jurisdictional Radio Communications   Federal efforts to improve cross-jurisdictional radio communications include the NIJ's development of the **Advanced Generation of Interoperability for Law Enforcement (AGILE)** program in 2001. AGILE provides direct connections across the radio systems of neighboring law enforcement agencies with overlapping or adjacent jurisdictions (Kaluta 2001). The possibilities of such technologies for enhancing national security needs has been demonstrated by early evaluation successes of the system as an enhancement to communication in San Diego County (ARJIS) (Scanlon 2000). AGILE has also been used to establish an emergency-only radio channel for presidential inaugurations, linking the Secret Service, the FBI, the Capitol Police, the U.S. Park Police, and the Metropolitan Police Department (Kaluta 2001).

Electronic Warrant Processes   A number of jurisdictions have responded to the numerous problems involved in the arrest-warrant process. This cumbersome process has traditionally involved the issuance of paper warrants by courts that are subsequently used by law enforcement agencies to create a wanted person record in their own system, which can then be checked by law enforcement officials throughout the country through the use of the FBI's National Crime Information Center (see Chapter 8). What is most problematic about this process is that there is often a delay between the time the court either issues or cancels a warrant, which can create serious officer safety concerns if an officer comes in contact with a dangerous individual that has not yet been entered into the NCIC system (Perbix 2001). Additional concerns arise from the lack of synchronization across the systems, in which warrants entered into one system are not entered into the other.

Electronic warrant processes, such as the Colorado Integrated Criminal Justice Information System (CICJIS), link the state's main criminal justice systems (including law enforcement, prosecutors, courts, adult and juvenile corrections) so that data entered by one agency's system is automatically transferred and loaded into another agency's system, thereby reducing concerns of linkage blindness and inconsistent data (Perbix 2001).

Information Security Through Encryption   Given the confidential information being shared by criminal justice agencies through these enhanced technologies, serious privacy concerns inevitably arise. Secure law enforcement communication over the Internet or an intranet can be achieved through **virtual private networking (VPN)** technologies. VPNs involve the use of encryption software to scramble the contents of communications so that even if the system becomes available to hackers, they are unable to read the information (Taylor 2000). In addition to an advanced encryption algorithm that is virtually impossible to break, VPNs pass encrypted communications through a "tunnel" between communicating agencies, ensuring that users meet a high level of identification to be able to access the information (Taylor 2000). With the establishment of proper identification and access protocols, VPNs offer law enforcement agencies the ability to exchange and track important information over a secure channel.

The World Wide Web and Community Policing

With its focus on collaborative problem solving and communication with the public, community policing is even more information intensive than traditional policing methods (Monahan 1998). New communication technologies such as the Internet have proven to be important mechanisms for furthering departmental–community policing objectives. Important features that are used by many departmental Web sites in reaching their constituent audiences include (Hart 1996):

- Officer photo galleries, including photos and biographical sketches
- Libraries devoted to crime prevention and safety tips, including information about known scam cases operating within the jurisdiction

- Virtual tours of the department

- Recruitment tool with links to personnel information about the hiring process

- Recent citywide and neighborhood crime statistics, including crime mapping capabilities on the more advanced pages

- Departmental wanted lists and upcoming court cases

- Capacity for anonymous and/or confidential reporting of crime information or complaints about officer conduct

It should be noted that department home pages on the Internet have moved beyond the realm of being public relations tools and towards the true support of community policing activities to the extent that the department shares important details about activities and arrests rather than the filtered information generally provided to citizens by the media (Price 2001). Departmental posting of such information, however, should be balanced against the privacy needs of victims and nonconvicted offenders.

Improving Accountability—Mobile Communications with Patrol

Radio communications with patrol cars revolutionized the ability of departments to monitor the activities of line officers. Although such technology did not take away the high level of discretion available to officers, enhancements to dispatch communications capabilities had a profound effect on the nature of their job. More recently, cellular phone technology has provided an alternate communication forum for some jurisdictions.

Mobile Digital Communications **Mobile digital communications (MDC)** offer nonverbal means of communicating information between communication centers and patrol (Thibault et al. 2001). Such communication is achieved through the use of a mobile digital terminal in the patrol car. In some jurisdictions, MDC options allow for electronic submission of reports, thereby reducing the volume of paperwork. More recently, some departments have installed new laptop computers into patrol cars, allowing officers instant access to information, such as notes from the communications officer and even the Internet. Soon officers will not have to leave their cars to write even the most detailed reports (Johnson 2003). Available Internet capabilities will also facilitate interjurisdictional information exchange opportunities, providing an important tool in the reduction of linkage blindness.

Automatic Vehicle Monitoring   Through the use of **automatic vehicle monitoring (AVM)** technologies, departments are able to know the location and status of patrol vehicles, including whether the door of the vehicle has been left open (Thibault et al. 2001). AVM systems are thus vitally important in aiding officers in high-speed pursuit situations and determining whether an officer is in need of back-up.

Chapter Summary

- There has been significant advancement in technology in the past twenty years, and the application of this technology to policing has benefited law enforcement officers in both proactive and reactive methods of policing.

- The most important factors in crime analysis are timeliness, relevancy, and reliability, all of which are necessary in order to effectively examine data.

- GIS crime mapping is a virtual map that allows police officers to analyze the areas in which crime occurs. It has many benefits, particularly in proactive policing. It can help the police to understand spatially where crimes occur and how to make strategies to combat crime, particularly in hot spots.

- Advanced technology enables the collection of more timely and accurate data, and it helps patrol officers respond more quickly and effectively to crimes in neighborhoods.

- One of the leading technologies of twenty-first-century policing is CompStat, which envelopes the problem-oriented policing model and assists in more effective management of areas where crime occurs.

- Surveillance technologies such as CCTV are extremely beneficial in tracking all types of criminals, from shoplifters to terrorists. Through the taped monitoring of movements, combined with emerging biometrics of face recognition technology, there are many potential applications of CCTV. GPS also has proven important in facilitating law enforcement operations in both investigatory and deployment capacities. Fingerprint identification systems have aided in the identification of individuals who have offended across boundaries. Other interjurisdictional communication technologies include offender databases and electronic warrants system.

KEY TERMS

311 system   328
911 system   327
Advanced Generation of Interoperability for Law Enforcement (AGILE)   345
Automated Regional Information System (ARJIS)   345
Automatic vehicle monitoring (AVM)   347
Biometrics   344
Buffer zones   334
Calls-for-service data   330
Causation   335
Chicago Alternative Policing Strategy (CAPS)   341
Closed-circuit television (CCTV)   342
CompStat   336
Computer-aided dispatch (CAD)   327
Correlations   335
Crime analysis   329
Crime mapping   331
Crime-trend forecasting   330

Electronic warrant processes   346
Environmental Systems Research Institute, Inc. (ESRI)   340
Essential criteria for crime analysis   330
Facial recognition software   344
Geocoded   333
Geographic information systems (GIS)   331
Geographic profiling   340
Global positioning systems (GPS)   343
Incident data   330
Information Collection for Automated Mapping (ICAM)   341
Integrated Automated Fingerprint Identification System (IAFIS)   345
Law of accelerating returns   328
Linkage analysis   331

Mobile digital communications (MDC)   347
Nearness principle   340
Pattern detection   330
Pattern Identification Modules (PIMS)   337
Record management systems (RMS)   341
Relevancy   330
Reliability   330
Rigel   340
Social ecology of crime   331
Souillere's stages of technological advancement   326
Strategic crime analysis   330
Surveillance technologies   342
Tactical crime analysis   330
Tactics   337
Target profiling   331
Timeliness   330
Truancy enforcement   333
Virtual private networks (VPN)   346

Linking the Dots

1. What have been some of the most significant technological advancements in policing since 1980?

2. What are some of the dangers associated with advancements in police technology? How are these dangers balanced with the benefits of such technology?

3. Do you think CompStat is partially responsible for the significant drop in crime in New York City over the past decade?

4. How does police technology benefit the community?

5. How can technology be used to help combat terrorism?

REFERENCES

American City and Country. 2002. "Crime Maps Improve Patrols in Camden." *American City and County*. October 1, 2002. Available at http://www.americancityandcountry.com/ar/government_crime_maps_improve.

Barley, S. 1986. "Technology as an Occasion for Structuring Evidence from Observations of CT Scanners and the Social Order of Radiology Departments." *Administrative Science Quarterly*. 31(1): 78–108.

Bijkker, M., T. Hughes, and T. Pinch. 1987. *The Social Construction of Technological Systems. New Directions in the Sociology and History of Technology*. Cambridge, MA: MIT Press.

Brantingham, C., and B. Brantingham. 1981. *Environmental Criminology*. Thousand Oaks, CA: Sage Publications.

Canter, P. 2000. "Using a Geographic Information System for Tactical Crime Analysis." In *Analyzing Crime Patterns: Frontiers of Practice,* edited by V. Goldsmith, P. McGuire, J. Mollenkopf, and T. Ross, 3–10. Thousand Oaks, CA: Sage.

Carney, D. 1998. "Arming Beat Cops with GIS Weapons." Civic.com, April 13, 1998. Available at www.civic.com.

Clarke, K. C. 1990. *Analytical and Computer Cartography*. Upper Saddle River, NJ: Prentice-Hall.

Cole, S. 2001. *Suspect Identities: A History of Fingerprinting and Criminal Identification*. Cambridge, MA: Harvard University Press.

Cowen, D. 2001. "Why Is GIS Important?" Available at www.env.duke.edu/lel/enn351/images/uoi.txt/.

Cowper, T. 2003. "Emerging Technology and the Future of Policing." Paper presented at the International Police Studies Conference, June 12–15, Eastern Kentucky University, Richmond, Kentucky.

DeAngelis, T. 2000. "GIS: Answering the Why of Where?" *Police Chief*. February 2000. Available at www.iactechnology.org/library/techtal/techtalk0200.htm.

Goold, B. 2001. *CCTV in the United Kingdom*. Unpublished dissertation. Oxford University, Oxford, United Kingdom.

Garcia, M. 2001. "Force Protection Using Wireless Internet Technology." *Technology Talk*. Available at http://www.loronit.com/solutions/casestudies/iactechtalk1201.pdf.

Grant, H., and K. Terry. 2000. *The New York City Sex Offender Management Team: Summary Progress Report*. New York, NY: John Jay College of Criminal Justice.

Greene, K. 2003. "Global Positioning Systems Used for Some Offenders." *Noble News Online,* April 4. Available at www.nonlenatl.org/news/publish/article_501.shtml.

Harries, K. 2001. *Demonstration of Orthophotographic Representation and Analysis*. Washington, D.C.: National Institute of Justice.

Harries, K. 1999. *Mapping Crime: Principle and Practice*. Washington, D.C.: National Institute of Justice.

Hart, F. 1996. "How and Why to Implement the Worldwide Web for Community Policing." *Police Chief*. 3(1): 55.

Hughes Network Systems. 2002. *Case Study*. Germantown, MD: Hughes Network Systems.

Johnson, M. 2003. "City Vehicles Receive Laptops." *Daytona Beach News Journal,* April 15, 1.

Kaluta, R. 2001. "New Developments in Interjurisdictional Communication Technology." *Police Chief.* Available at http://www.iacptechnology.org/library/techtalk/techtalk0401.htm.

Karmen, A. 1996. *New York City Murder Mystery.* New York, NY: NYU Press.

Kelling, G., and M. Moore. 1987. "The Evolving Strategy of Policing." *Perspectives on Policing.* 4(1): 1–15.

Kurzweil, R. 2001. "The Law of Accelerating Returns." Available at www.kurzweilai.net.

McDonald, P. 2002. *Managing Police Operations: Implementing the New York Crime Control Model—CompStat.* Belmont, CA: Wadsworth.

Monahan, M. 1998. "Technology Management for Community Policing." *Police Chief.* September 1998. Available at http://www.iacptechnology.org/library/techtalk/techtalk0998.htm.

Norris, C., and G. Armstrong. 1999. *The Maximum Surveillance Society: The Rise of CCTV.* New York, NY: NYU Press.

Onion, A. 2002. "Coordinates of a Killer: A Mathematical Method Can Help Investigators Locate Killers." ABCnews.com, October 8. Available at www.abcnews.com.

Perbix, M. 2001. "Automating Arrest Warrants Between Courts and Law Enforcement." *Police Chief.* October 2001. Available at http://www.iacptechnology.org/library/AutomatingArrestWarrantsBTCountsandLE.pdf

Phillips, P. 1972. "A Prologue to the Geography of Crime." *Proceedings, Association of American Geographers* 4(1): 86–91.

Presidents Commission on Law Enforcement and the Administration of Justice. 1967. *Final Report of the President's Commission on Law Enforcement and the Administration of Justice.* Washington, D.C.: Presidents Commission on Law Enforcement and the Administration of Justice.

Price, C. 2001. "The Police Web Site as a Community Policing Tool." *Police Chief.* December 2001. Available at http://www.iacptechnology.org/library/PoliceWebsiteasaCommunity PolicingTool.pdf.

Rich, T. 1996. *The Chicago Police Department's Information Collection for Automated Mapping (ICAM) Program.* Washington, D.C.: National Institute of Justice Program Focus.

Rossmo, K. 1998. *Geographic Profiling.* Boca Raton, FL: CRC Press.

Scanlon, P. 2000. "A Successful Partnership: When Police and the Feds Team for Technology." *Police Chief.* October, 2000. Available at http://www.iacptechnology.org/library/techtalk/techtalk/co.

Seaskate, Inc. 1998. *The Evolution and Development of Police Technology.* Washington, D.C.: National Institute of Justice.

Shaw, C., and H. McKay. 1942. *Juvenile Delinquency and Urban Areas.* Chicago, IL: University of Chicago Press.

Silverman, E. 1996. "Mapping Change: How the New York City Police Department Reengineered Itself to Drive Down Crime." *Law Enforcement News* 23. December 15, 1996. Available at http://www.lib.jjay.cuny.edu/len96/15Dec/?/htm.

Silverman, E. 1999. *NYPD Battles Crime.* Boston, MA: Northeastern University Press.

Skogan, W., and S. Hartnett. 1996. *Community Policing Chicago Style.* New York, NY: Oxford University Press.

Skolnick, J., and D. Bayley. 1986. *The New Blue Line: Police Innovation in Six American Cities.* New York, NY: The Free Press.

Smith, K. 1998. "Integrated Automated Fingerprint Identification System: Twenty-first-century Technology for Law Enforcement." *Police Chief.* 62(6): 23.

Soulliere, N. 1999. *Police and Technology: Historical Review and Current Status.* Ottawa: Canadian Police College.

Taylor, B. 2000. "Virtual Private Networking: Secure Law Enforcement Communication on the Internet." *Police Chief.* 67(1): 13.

Terry, K., and J. Furlong. 2004. *Sex Offender Registration and Community Notification,* 2d ed. Kingston, NJ: Civic Research Institute.

Thibault, E., L. Lynch, and R. McBride. 2001. *Proactive Police Management,* 5th ed. Upper Saddle River, NJ: Prentice-Hall.

Tomek, W. 2001. "Information Sharing: A Strategic Necessity." *Police Chief.* February, 2001. Available at http://www.iacptechnology.org/library/techtalk/techtalk0201.pdf.

Walsh, T. 2003. "Data Sharing Tightens Net for the Law—Agencies Put Criminal Justice Data On-line for Sharing." *Government Computer News,* July 10. Available at www.gcn.com.

NOTE

1. This introduction draws upon information found in DeAngelis (2000).

Chapter 14

New Standards for Police Recruitment

...ARD AND UPWARD

years! And the benefits... ...positively impact the community where you serve. You'll also receive a month of paid vacation a year, excellent dental and health care coverage, and a great retirement package. Why settle for a boring job when you can enjoy an exciting, challenging and rewarding career in the Michigan State Police?

YOUR SUCCESS DEPENDS ON YOU!

...Moore. 15 years   Capt. Marie Waalkes. 22 years   F/Lt. Cheryl Strayhorn. 20 years   Insp. Diane DeWitt. 22 years

Chapter Outline

Chapter Objectives

● Explain the basic recruitment and selection standards for police officers and how they have developed over the past fifty years.

● Develop an understanding of the difficulties of specific selection requirements for minority populations.

● Explain the effect of legislation on recruitment and selection standards.

● Understand the benefits and problems with affirmative action policies in policing.

● Compare the benefits of academic education and police training from an academy.

● Describe five assessment areas upon which officers are promoted. Explain the effect of affirmative action on promotion.

Introduction

Every police department seeks to recruit, select, train, and maintain the best officers possible. However, what characteristics of an officer are "the best"? The ideal qualities of a police officer have evolved over time and have been adapted to represent a changing society. During the political era, the only important characteristic of new recruits was that they belong to a particular political party. Until fifty years ago, the "ideal" police officer was a strong, white male who would follow commands from superior officers. Both minorities and women were significantly underrepresented until the 1970s when legislation was passed requiring equal opportunities for them in the field of policing. Still, approximately 78 percent of police officers in local departments are white and nearly 90 percent are male (Bureau of Justice Statistics 2000).

This chapter discusses current standards for the recruitment, selection, training, and promotion of police officers and how these standards have evolved. There is no specific formula for recruiting and maintaining the ideal officer. However, now that you have completed this book, it is hoped that you have a better understanding of the types of officers you feel are most suited to the law enforcement profession. This chapter will summarize some of the key themes introduced throughout the text to focus on recruitment and selection needs.

Linkages in Law Enforcement

Who Is the "Ideal" Law Enforcement Officer?

Throughout this textbook, we have discussed the duties of police officers, the tasks they must perform while on the job, and how this role has changed throughout history. Now it is time to consider who you think would make an ideal police officer. Here are some questions to consider:

- What would be your ideal composition of police officers in one department, considering issues of background, age, race, education, agility, and gender? Explain your reasoning.

- From where would you recruit officers?

- What type of selection process would you have?

- Should police officers be held to higher ethical standards than individuals in other professions?

- How would you retain officers in your police department?

- What would be your standards for promotion?

It is difficult to define the characteristics of an "ideal" police officer. It might be better to ask how departments should recruit, select, and train officers in order to produce an ideal police department, creating opportunities for promotion and encouraging retention. This chapter will help you to analyze these issues while utilizing knowledge gained from previous chapters.

Recruitment of Candidates

The job of a police officer involves stressful situations and entails interactions with many individuals in the community. It also requires quick decision making and good judgment. Police duties vary from writing reports to maintaining order to responding to criminal situations, all of which require critical thinking skills. Because of the range of an officer's duties, an officer should possess certain traits: he or she should be physically agile, be able to cope with difficult situations, write articulately, have good communication skills, use good judgment, be compassionate towards victims, be observant, and be able to exert and respect authority. Unfortunately, it is difficult to find an ideal candidate with every one of these qualities (Sharp 1994).

Recruitment standards vary depending on the area being policed, and each department will aim to recruit the best person for that community. Each department recruits officers in different ways, though there are some standard recruitment techniques. These include passing out flyers in the community, going to job fairs at universities, advertising in newspapers or on radio or television, and in larger cities, putting up posters in subways and on billboards (Strandberg 1996). Many of the larger police departments have cadet programs or internships that offer college credit, both of which serve as recruitment tools (Leach 1998). The key to recruiting a qualified group of individuals is advertising to a large audience. Within that broad group, each department is likely to find what it is seeking in terms of educational background, diversity, and residency.

Bona Fide Job Requirements

There are few articulated standards for officer selection because every department sets its own standards. Most departments require that officers, at a minimum:

- Be at least twenty-one years of age
- Have a driver's license in the state (or be eligible for one)
- Have no prior felony convictions
- Pass a written exam, a medical exam, an interview, a physical agility test, and psychological screening

Individuals who become police officers must have or be eligible to receive a driver's license because their primary duty is motor vehicle patrol and they must be able to drive to respond to incidents. Police officers must also be able to possess a firearm. In order to qualify to own a firearm, a person must be at least twenty-one years of age. For that reason, a police officer will not have full police powers until at least that time, and most police departments do not even allow recruits to begin the police academy until they are at least twenty-one. Convicted felons are also prohibited from possessing a firearm, which would thereby bar them from becoming police officers. Individuals with any convictions for domestic violence are no longer able to possess a firearm, thereby prohibiting them from becoming police officers as well (Clark 1997).

Education

Many police departments in the United States now have educational standards for recruits. Nearly all departments now require officers to have at least a high

The police department today represents a culturally diverse group of people. This is much different from the early twentieth century, when police officers were almost all white males.

school diploma, and many also require at least some college credit. Such high standards in education were not always the norm, however.

At the beginning of the twentieth century, the majority of male officers lacked a high school diploma. The male officer was expected to understand English well enough to speak intelligently, and read and write reports (Schulz 1999). The standards for women were different from those for men. The International Association of Policewomen (IAP)—the female equivalent of the International Association of Chiefs of Police, which was begun by Alice Stebbins Wells in 1916—suggested that policewomen have minimum educational qualifications equivalent to high school graduates (Schulz 1995). The IAP also suggested that this minimum requirement should be combined with two years of experience in social service or educational work or with training as a nurse. This educational double standard existed until 1972 when congress amended Title VII of the 1964 Civil Rights Act (discrimination policies). At that time, the educational standards for men did not rise. Rather, the educational standards for women were lowered.

Although most police departments in the early twentieth century did not require college-level education for police officers, entities such as the Wickersham Commission began pushing for higher educational standards as early as 1931. In 1967, the Kerner Commission recommended that police officers should have four-year college degrees. The **Law Enforcement Assistance Administration (LEAA)** began to emphasize the need for police officers to attend college at this time as well, going so far as to implement a grant system for individuals who were or planned to be police officers upon graduation. The Law Enforcement Education Program (LEEP) lasted for more than a decade and was responsible for a mass increase in individuals with degrees in criminal justice throughout the United States.

Despite the efforts of the LEAA, which ended its LEEP program in the early 1980s, the rise of educational standards has only become apparent in the past decade. Table 14.1 shows that educational standards across police departments in the United States in 1997 were nearly double the standards in 1990 (LEMAS 1992, 1999). Still, less than one-quarter (23.8 percent) of all police agencies require their recruits to have some level of college education.

Experts continue to debate whether higher education makes an officer better at his or her job or whether vocational experience (e.g., police academy, on-the-job training) is all that is necessary. Cao and Huang (2000) conducted one

TABLE 14.1

Educational Requirements for New Officer Recruits in City, County, and State Agencies

Educational Requirement	1990 (*N* = 584)	1997 (*N* = 651)
Four-year degree	3 (0.51%)	13 (2.0%)
Two-year degree	29 (4.9%)	50 (7.7%)
Some college	41 (7.0%)	92 (14.1%)
Total	73 (12.5%)	155 (23.8%)

Source: Terry and Grant (2003).

empirical study and found that educational standards did not make a difference in the number of complaints filed against officers. Additionally, some believe that education alone does not make a good police officer; an individual is only a good police officer if he or she possesses all the other characteristics that make a good police officer (e.g., keen powers of observation, physical agility, ability to handle stressful situations), though education can help one who does possess these qualities (Molden 1999). (See also Chapter 3.)

Other researchers, however, believe that education is beneficial in a number of ways. They believe that advanced learning increases the officers' decision-making skills and may help them handle difficult situations through negotiation as opposed to force. They propose that fewer complaints are filed against officers who have a higher degree of education, and those with some college education have fewer disciplinary problems than those with a high school education (Carter and Sapp 1988). Additionally, educated officers, as a whole, seem to have better knowledge of the law, human behavior, and social situations and have better communication and writing skills (Ferriera 1997). Police officers with college degrees believe that they are more prepared for the job than officers without degrees (Krimmel 1996). These officers believe that they have better interpersonal skills and problem-solving abilities and that the quality of their work is better than less-educated officers (Krimmel 1996). Nonetheless, no documented studies have shown that a college education alone makes for more effective police officers or better crime fighters.

Technology

The increasing use of technology in policing is another reason why education is now an important job requirement. Not only has computer technology been adapted into the daily routine of many police officers, but officers must also be able to understand technological advances such as crime mapping and CompStat. By looking at computerized maps of the city, the police can pinpoint geographic areas where the majority of crime occurs, or the hot spots (Bratton and Knobler 1988). This technology is used to hold police officers accountable for crime increases or reductions in their neighborhoods. Though over one-third of all large police departments are currently using some sort of crime-mapping technology, it is likely that this number will increase significantly in the near future because of the dramatic drop in crime in some of the cities that have applied such technology. (See Chapter 13.)

Technology also is used to assist in criminal identification. Computer software is now used to generate composites for identifying suspects. Such programs have a library of facial features and accessories to help a witness construct an accurate picture of a perpetrator (Senna and Siegal 2002). Computer technology not only assists in accuracy, but also in efficiency. For instance, as highlighted in Chapter 8, an automatic fingerprint identification system helps to identify unique marks and ridges with accuracy and speed. For these reasons, it is important that police officers be knowledgeable about such systems or have the capacity to be trained to use them.

Legal Knowledge

Though education may not assist the officer in all aspects of his or her job, it may increase an officer's knowledge of legal issues. Legal knowledge is integral to the job of a police officer. It was argued in Chapter 7 that the officer should have an understanding of constitutional law, criminal law, criminal procedure, rules of evidence, and even civil law in case he or she is the subject of litigation. Training in the police academy covers the legal issues central to the duties of a police officer, such as the Fourth Amendment and an individual's right to be free from illegal searches and seizures. Many university-based criminal justice programs, however, cover legal issues more extensively than the police academy and give police officers a broader understanding of the issues they may encounter on a daily basis.

Residency

In addition to education requirements, some departments have residency requirements mandating that officers live within the jurisdiction in which they are policing. This is a recommendation that surfaced from many of the commissions in the hopes that by living in the communities they police, officers will be better equipped to understand, and thereby interact with, its citizenry. There are many benefits for officers to live in the community where they police, such as knowing the problems in that community that need to be addressed and being able to identify with residents of that community.

However, there are a few drawbacks to a police officer living in the community that he or she polices. First, the police officer may not be able to live in the area in which he or she is policing if it is one of the higher income communities, since police officers usually do not receive an income that is in the highest socioeconomic tax bracket. A second drawback to residency requirements is the possibility of corruption. If an officer is patrolling or responds to a situation that involves an acquaintance, he or she is less likely to uphold the law with that individual. Despite the drawbacks of not knowing the community well that he or she is policing, there is a general consensus that it is best for an officer to live in or near the area he or she is policing.

Diversity

Perhaps the greatest recruitment push resulting from the various commissions has been towards greater minority representation within law enforcement agencies. (See Chapters 10 and 11.) Although there has been some improvement in this area within the last ten years, ethnic representation in most police forces is still disproportionate. Racial and ethnic minorities represented 21.5 percent of local police departments in 1997, compared to just 14.8 percent in 1987 (Bureau of Justice Statistics 2000). Broken down, 11.7 percent of police officers in 1997 were African American, while they represented over 12 percent of the U.S. population (Census Bureau 2000). Officers of Hispanic or Latino origin accounted for 7.8 percent of the police force, though they comprised over 12 percent of the population. Women, who account for 46.5 percent of the U.S. population, accounted for only 6.3 percent of full-time sworn personnel.

When recruiting a diverse police force, one must question why an individual wants to become a police officer. Historically, policing was a job for white males. Women who were hired as police officers worked more as social workers, and it took many decades for them to become crime fighters. (See Chapter 2.) Several studies in the late 1970s and early 1980s analyzed why women were interested in entering a male-dominated career such as law enforcement. In 1978, Ermer found that job security was the primary factor that women were choosing careers in law enforcement, as well as the fact that the starting salaries at this time were higher than for most other equivalent jobs. Meagher and Yentes (1986) also found job security to be an important factor in choosing policing as a career, and they found this to be true for both men and women. They studied whether men and women joined the police force for the same reasons, and they found that, contrary to preconceptions, the two groups shared similar reasons for choosing policing as a career. Whereas men are perceived to join the police for reasons of excitement, authority, and the ability to fight crime, they actually join primarily to help people—the same reason that women cited for joining the force (Meagher and Yentes 1996). Lester (1983) supported these results, finding that women tend to join the police force because of the nature of police work, the variety of assignments, and the salary benefits.

Agencies can use a variety of methods to recruit ethnic and racial minorities as well as women. Many larger departments have recruiting officers. Those officers should represent the minorities that the department is trying to attract (Milgram 2002). Recruiting officers should attend community meetings and try to interact with the individuals they are trying to recruit. Such positive interactions are necessary, because many individuals from minority groups lack trust in the police due to negative personal interactions or negative media attention. Recruiting officers can also seek out college students and even high school students for internships, cadet programs, youth programs, or other community programs in order to develop their interest in eventually becoming a police officer. It is necessary to take these additional steps beyond the traditional methods of recruitment in efforts to diversify the police force. In the interest of reaching minorities, many departmental fraternal organizations often have activities and mentoring programs within their respective communities.

Selection of Candidates

Once a candidate is recruited, he or she must go through an extensive selection process in order to be hired as a police officer. This is a lengthy, competitive process involving multiple phases. In most police departments, the candidate must pass a written exam, an interview, a physical exam, a psychological exam, a background check, and a polygraph.

The selection process has been modified considerably over the past twenty-five years, due in large part to equal opportunity criteria. The Court has heard several cases related to hiring standards for police, and it has mandated that the process not be arbitrary or discriminatory in any way but rather focus on job-related criteria. Several selection procedures have been modified as a result of these cases. For example, the physical agility tests used in the selection process were originally designed in a way that was prohibitory toward women, therefore very few women were able to pass the physical agility phase of the selection process. Similarly, it was difficult for candidates from other states or whose native language was not English to pass the written exam; these issues are now addressed in exam preparation courses.

The Written Exam

The written exam is generally the first phase of the selection process once a formal application has been submitted. The exam differs depending on the jurisdiction. The exam may be produced by an individual police department or by a private company. In addition, it may also be a civil service exam. The purpose of this exam is not to test specific legal or criminal justice knowledge, but rather the candidate's basic reading, writing, and comprehension skills. The exam is likely to contain a number of different sections, whereby the candidate must be able to understand and write in English, write a sample essay, understand basic mathematics, memorize facts, show sound reasoning and logic, and analyze potential scenarios. Candidate's scores are ranked, and only those who receive above a particular benchmark score will be able to move to the next phase of selection.

Because of the exam's focus on the reading, writing, and comprehension of English, applicants that are non-native English speakers may be eliminated from the prospective pool of candidates. Though some departments have attempted to avoid this predicament by offering exam preparation courses, there is still a strong possibility that many non-native recruits who are otherwise capable of becoming police officers are eliminated at this stage of the selection process (Rafilson 1997). Though it is difficult to overcome this obstacle, one suggestion is to offer non-native English speakers extra time on exams (National Crime Prevention Council 1995).

Background Checks

Once a candidate submits a formal application to become a police officer, the police department conducts a background check on the candidate. The primary purpose of the background check is to determine if the candidate has been convicted of any felonies or serious misdemeanors and to make sure that he or she is of "good moral character" (Fagin 2003). Police departments consider a number of factors in relation to a police candidate's moral character. The candidate should not only be free of prior criminal convictions, but also should not partake in drug use, violent activity, excessive alcoholism, or display prejudicial attitudes of any kind. Though these factors would not necessarily disqualify individuals from attaining other jobs, police officers are often held to higher moral standards than the general population. The reason for this is that police officers must abide by a code of ethics and exhibit moral behavior in their job. When officers lack ethics, they may digress into corruption or mistreat the individuals they are policing. Most police departments explain in their recruitment brochures what type of moral behavior is expected from potential candidates. For instance, the Los Angeles recruitment flyer reads:

> You must have no felony convictions or any misdemeanor conviction that would prevent your carrying a gun. You must not have a history of criminal or improper conduct, or a poor employment, military, or driving record that would affect your suitability for law enforcement work. You must also have a responsible financial history and a pattern of respect and honesty in your dealings with individuals and organizations. A valid California driver's license is required prior to appointment.

The person who is in charge of conducting the background investigation should be professional and unbiased and should exhibit the characteristics the agency is seeking. Although the background investigation will consist of a specified set of questions, such as whether the candidate has ever been convicted of a crime, the background investigator should also be aware of moral and ethical issues that may potentially screen out candidates for a policing job. For instance, the candidate should not express prejudicial views about any particular race, gender, ethnicity, or sexual identity.

The Interview Process

The interview process is designed to evaluate a candidate's suitability for becoming a police officer. With a panel consisting of three to five skilled interviewers in a variety of fields (e.g., policing, psychology), the interview can be structured, unstructured, or a combination of both. In a structured interview, the candidate is asked a series of questions regarding the job and his or her abilities. Structured questions usually require specific answers to direct questions (e.g., Do you drink alcohol?). The other alternative is to conduct a semi-structured interview, with open-ended questions on particular topics (e.g., How much alcohol do you consume weekly?). Whereas structured interviews allow for a better comparison between candidates on specific topics, open-ended questions are likely to elicit more information.

Although the interview board may need to eliminate candidates at this stage because of particular answers they may give (e.g., a candidate admits to drinking excessive quantities of alcohol on a daily basis), the purpose of the interview is to assess other issues, such as the candidate's professionalism, social and communication skills, level of reasoning, appearance, composure, and poise. Whereas the written exam is designed to measure basic comprehension skills, the goal of the interview is to find out more about the candidate's desire to become a police officer and how he or she can handle scenarios that a police officer may encounter. The candidate is scored based on his or her answers and compared with other candidates on a range of criteria. Though the candidate must pass all phases of the selection process in order to be hired as a police officer, the interview process is critical in the assessment of the candidate's attitudes, appearance, and demeanor.

Psychological and Polygraph Tests

The purpose of the psychological screening process is to assess the candidate's intelligence and personality characteristics and to detect mental disorders that may lead to problematic behavior in the future. Studies show that between 80 to 90 percent of police departments use some sort of psychological screening tool to determine whether a candidate is fit to become a police officer (Langworthy et al. 1995; Reaves and Goldberg 1999).[1] It is important to screen out individuals who may exhibit mental or personality deficits because police officers interact with individuals on a daily basis and often in high-stress situations.

The most common psychological assessment tool used is the **Minnesota Multiphasic Personality Inventory (MMPI)**. The primary purpose of the MMPI is to assess an individual's psychopathology and to determine whether he or she should be diagnosed with a mental disorder as well as to identify problems with social adjustment, neuroses, psychoses, phobias, and delusions. This test is used by many occupations to determine whether candidates are suitable for high-risk positions, such as policing. The MMPI was recently revised and is now in its second edition. It consists of 567 true/false questions about attitudes, beliefs, and ideas.[2] The test is presumed to be reliable and valid, with built-in mechanisms that determine if a test taker is lying.

Some police departments use multiple psychological tests or tests other than the MMPI. One other common inventory is the California Psychological Inventory (CPI), which contains 434 questions relating to personality that aim to measure individual differences. The Rorschach test is also common.

Originally published in 1921, it consists of ten inkblots that are meant to identify particular personality traits. This is a controversial test that some psychologists consider subjective, as a result, it is usually only used to supplement other screening tools.

Approximately half of U.S. police departments use a **polygraph**, or lie detector, examination in the selection process.[3] Information obtained by a polygraph is not legally admissible in court because it has an accuracy of only 85 to 90 percent (Board on Behavioral, Cognitive, and Sensory Sciences and Education 2003). However, it is used in the assessment process to determine whether the candidate is in any way trying to answer questions deceptively. A polygraph records involuntary physiological changes in the body that occur when an examinee is partaking in conscious deceit. It simultaneously measures respiration, changes in blood pressure and pulse rate, and electrical resistance of the skin.

Physical Agility

Measuring a police candidate's level of physical agility is a crucial part of the selection process. The physical agility test has been controversial and has undergone significant changes since its inception. Until the 1970s, the physical agility test required substantial upper-body strength, which kept a lot of women from passing the test and thereby eliminated them as police candidates. These tests, which consisted largely of push-ups, pull-ups, and sit-ups, measured rapid reflexes, speed and coordination, dexterity, endurance, and strength. The Court invalidated such tests, however, saying that these standards of agility were not job related.

In 1972, Title VII of the 1964 Civil Rights Act declared that all applicants for a position requiring physical strength and agility must be given an oppor-

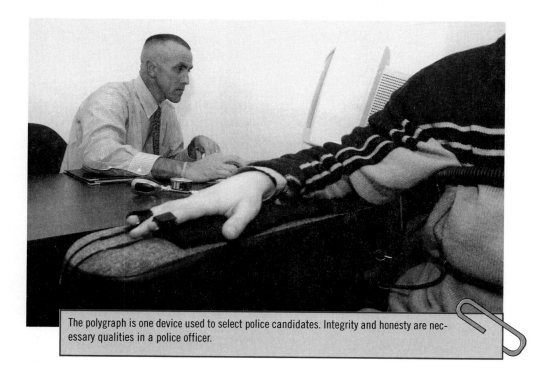

The polygraph is one device used to select police candidates. Integrity and honesty are necessary qualities in a police officer.

Physical agility tests have changed significantly since the 1970s. At that time, it was difficult for women to pass the agility tests, which required a lot of upper-body strength.

tunity to demonstrate their ability to perform the work in question. The Equal Employment Opportunity Commission (EEOC) guidelines on sex discrimination barred the refusal to hire a female applicant because of characteristics attributed to women as a class. Both of these regulations suggest that women must be given a chance to show that they can do the required duties of the police job and that physical tests must not be applied in a manner that is discriminatory to women. Police agencies must demonstrate the job relatedness of the criteria, and for that reason physical agility tests have changed considerably over the past few decades.

San Francisco is one example of a city that used a physical agility test with a substantial disparate impact on the hiring of women. The test, which only about 1 percent of the women taking it passed, consisted only of physical skills that were not applicable to daily situations that a police officer would likely face. The tests were considered by the courts to be invalid at measuring the skills of patrol officers. Similarly, the police department in Houston, Texas, had a physical agility test requiring recruits do a pull-up on a 7'6" wall, and yet there are no walls 7 feet or higher in Houston. Alternatively, Miami assesses the agility potential of a candidate and gives the candidate training if he or she cannot pass the test the first time. The majority of women who fail the test the first time later complete it successfully (95%). Thus, women are able to pass the test at the same rate as male candidates (Lonsway et al. 2003).

Most agility tests now consist of an obstacle course that simulates a potential police experience. Candidates must complete activities such as climbing a 4- to 6-foot wall, crawling under a bar that is about 24 inches high, dragging a 150- to 170- pound dummy, sprinting, and climbing stairs, ropes or ladders, all within a specified amount of time. Whether this time is the same for all candidates or whether it varies depending on the candidate's characteristics (e.g., male or female, different heights, etc.) depends on the jurisdiction.

The key to passing the physical agility test appears to be in the training. With modifications in training, women are as likely to pass the new agility tests as men. Modification does not mean that standards of physical fitness must be lowered. However, with modified tests, females can emphasize their lower-body weight, because women generally have less upper-body strength than men. Women also tend to be weaker with firearms, largely because their hands are smaller, thereby making it difficult to grip the firearm with the same strength as a man. With extra training to strengthen their grips, however, they can improve their accuracy and agility with firearms.

Research on the Job Performance of Female Officers When police departments began to modify their physical agility tests, police officers and researchers alike questioned whether women could perform the duties of a police officer as well as men. In the 1970s, many studies were conducted to study women's performance on the job. These studies showed that in nearly every area of law enforcement, women performed as well as their male counterparts (Bloch and Anderson 1974). By the mid-1980s, studies had looked at a number of different issues, including the attitudes of male officers towards female officers and the way that female officers perceived their roles in the department.

Many studies throughout the 1970s focused on how policewomen compared with men in a variety of areas (e.g., urban versus rural) and with a variety of tasks (particularly patrol). Researchers published articles that showed the following results (Charles 1982; Fry and Greenfield 1980; Johns and Barclay 1979; C. Martin 1979).

- Policemen and policewomen perform similarly on patrol, and there is no discernible difference in how they handle incidents.

- Women often are assigned to different duties than men. Generally, they are assigned to lighter duties than their male counterparts, or they are assigned to lower crime areas.

- Policewomen are similar to policemen in how they respond to and handle arrests and summons.

- Policewomen and policemen are different in three key areas. Policewomen do not draw their weapons as frequently, they use less physical force, and they are better at handling domestic violence and house calls.

Affirmative Action

Physical agility tests were not the only barrier to women becoming police officers, and the police department was strikingly lacking in women and minorities in the 1960s. Because policing was almost universally a white male profession, states and the federal government began enacting laws that created political pressure for law enforcement to hire racial minorities and women. **Affirmative action** policies required that police departments do more than simply create equal opportunities for everyone. They mandated that the police department take extra steps to hire minorities. Many affirmative action policies established

quotas for minorities, or a specified number of jobs that had to be filled with minorities and women.

The purpose of creating affirmative action policies was to ensure that individuals who previously had been excluded from particular types of employment would have access to these jobs. Law enforcement agencies that did not comply with affirmative action policies could face civil suits from the parties being excluded, and they could also face a loss of funding from major grant bodies if their hiring and promotional policies were deemed unlawful. Affirmative action policies are very controversial, because despite the positive motivation behind them—equal opportunity in the workplace—they also bring charges of **reverse discrimination** (hiring minorities at the expense of those in the majority). In addition, some believe that those of minority background who are hired are "tokens" and that such policies conflict with social integration within the police department.

Legal Issues

Affirmative action policies began appearing in the 1960s and were largely the result of court-mandated legislation. Several federal laws were passed in order to assist women and minorities with attaining jobs dominated by white males, one of which was policing. Table 14.2 presents several of these acts and the purpose of each.

Though these acts set policies mandating that women and minorities have equal access to employment opportunities, it was the case of *Griggs v. Duke*

TABLE 14.2

Acts Requiring Equal Opportunities for Women and Minorities in the Workplace

Act	Purpose
Equal Pay Act, 1963	Passed by Congress, this act prohibited unequal pay for men and women who did the same work. Prior to its enactment, policewomen were paid far less than their male colleagues.
Executive Order, 1969	Passed by President Richard Nixon, this order stated the federal government could not use sex as a qualification for hiring. This had an impact on federal agencies such as the FBI, and the municipal police departments were soon to follow.
Title VII of the 1964 Civil Rights Act, 1972	This prohibited employment discrimination on the basis of race, color, religion or sex for recruitment, hiring, working conditions, promotion, or benefits in any governmental agency. Prior to this, it was nearly impossible for women and minorities to attain a job in policing.
Crime Control Act, 1973	Ensured that police departments did not discriminate against women in employment practices. It did so by withholding funds from the LEAA, the major funding body of the municipal governments.
Americans with Disabilities Act, 1990	Ensures that agencies do not discriminate against any person otherwise qualified for a job because of a disability.

Power [4] in 1971 that firmly established equal opportunity guidelines. The Court stated that employment criteria that excluded minorities or women disproportionately were illegal unless the standards for exclusion were job related. For the first time, the Court declared that the burden of proof was on the employers, not the applicants, to show that exclusion from the job was due to job-related reasons. This burden-of-proof test has since been swapped, however, and the burden of proof now lies upon the person excluded from the job to show that the exclusion is not job related (*Wards Cove Packing Company, Inc. v. Antonio*).[5]

Barriers for Women and Minorities

In the 1970s and 1980s, the percentage of minorities in policing increased significantly. While, in 1970, the percentage of black police officers was 6.35 percent (double the percentage of 1960) (Kuykendall and Burns 1980), by the early 1990s black police officers represented nearly 11 percent of the police force (Bureau of Justice Statistics 1996). This was due to a number of factors, including the demand for black police officers after the race riots in the 1960s, the civil rights movement, and affirmative action policies (Kuykendall and Burns 1980). This increase in black police officers was critical in improving police–community relations in minority communities.

The role of affirmative action policies on the increasing number of minorities was significant (Walker 1985). Police agencies specifically sought out individuals from classes of people who were historically underrepresented or were discriminated against as a result of these affirmative action policies. The rate of racial minorities, particularly African Americans, increased. Although many of these policies became effective in the 1970s, it was the cumulative effect of the policies that made an impact by the 1980s (Lewis 1989).

Affirmative action policies also had a significant impact on the number of women in police agencies at this time. According to Susan Martin (1989), by the late 1980s women comprised 10.1 percent of police departments with affirmative action policies. In comparison, they comprised 8.3 percent of forces with affirmative action policies but no court orders to support them, and 6.1 percent of forces with no affirmative action policies.

Though women and minorities were accepted into the department at much higher rates due to affirmative action policies, there were some negative consequences to this. Both racial and gender minorities accepted under affirmative action policies were considered **tokens**, or officers that the departments were legally required to hire due to affirmative action policies. Had a department not accepted women applicants, it would have faced legal repercussions. Unfortunately, those on the force often treated the "tokens" differently from officers of the dominant race and gender. This often led to discrimination in assignments and evaluations, as well as exclusion from the police culture. In addition, many affirmative action hires also faced harassment.

Policewomen at this time found it particularly difficult to fit in, and they had to change their characteristics in order to socially interact with the male officers. Susan Martin wrote a classic article on the role dilemmas of female police officers in 1979, which also analyzed the effects of affirmative action policies on these officers. She noted two distinct roles of female officers: that of the *police-*woman, the defeminized officer who emphasizes her physical skills, and the po-lice*woman*, the deprofessionalized officer who emphasizes her femininity.

Martin (1979) explained that the defeminized woman seeks acceptance by acting in an exceptional manner. She does not identify with the other women, but rather with her male counterparts. She tries to fulfill the same work norms as them and not stand out in any way that would allow them to put her down personally or professionally. She shows professional competence above that of many colleagues and closely adheres to the norms of behavior governing male police officers. The defeminized woman adopts coping strategies to maximize her effectiveness as an officer. She acts with self-confidence and tries not only to meet the production norms of the department, but to surpass them. She accepts the fact that women have to try harder than men, and she goes out of her way to show courage and willingness to take action even if it is dangerous. She is comfortable on the street and enjoys patrol, is generally ambitious, and tries to make political friends to get ahead. She denies or minimizes the existence of discrimination against women by the department and is likely to blame other female officers for the problems they encounter. Finally, she does not feel that her work threatens her gender identity outside of the department.

The deprofessionalized woman, in contrast, plays up her femininity. She functions as a junior assistant to the policemen, even though she has an equal title to them. She consistently acts in a feminine manner and is satisfied to do less work than her counterparts. She does not like patrol and is not comfortable on the street. Instead, she prefers the social-work aspect of policing. She does not necessarily believe that women are physically equipped to be on patrol. She also believes that it is better to do work that is not dangerous, because the pay is the same either way. When she is on patrol, she relies on the male partner to do most of the patrol work. Unlike the defeminized officer, the deprofessionalized officer emphasizes her femininity, thereby making police work difficult. She is not interested in a career and promotions within the department, has no desire to supervise men or add additional responsibilities, and she does not want more shift work. She has few chances for promotion; however, she knows this and is not disappointed when she does not receive the promotion. Finally, she is critical of the defeminized policewoman because she feels such women have objectionable morals, like the policemen.

Based on this information, policewomen seem to find themselves in a paradoxical situation. If they don't defeminize themselves, they will fit only a feminine stereotype and not allow themselves room for promotion. If they do defeminize themselves, they will be competing with men for their promotional opportunities and they become a career threat. Several studies have analyzed this socialization problem. Sherman (1975) showed that if women do not sacrifice at least some of their femininity, they will not be accepted by the male officers. Gross (1984) observed that female academy recruits displayed masculine characteristics and few feminine characteristics. This may be due to the fact that they are subjected to standardized behavior in training, which is essentially masculine.

In their study on women's perceptions of policing, Daum and Johns (1994) found that most policewomen felt accepted by civilians and other female officers. However, 42 percent did not feel accepted by other male officers. Also, 55 percent of the policewomen felt as though their male supervisors did not accept them. On other factors, 76 percent thought they perform their job as well as the policemen; 68 percent felt they had to do more work than their male colleagues to be given the same credit; 58 percent of the women thought they faced tougher standards of conduct than the men (including grooming standards); 57 percent saw no difference in morale between female or male officers; and 35 percent thought that morale was lower for women. Some of the women wanted the department to recognize that women have special needs even though they do the job as well as the men. Others did not want any pampering or special attention at all.

Both African American and white male officers tended to have negative views about policewomen at the outset of affirmative action, marginalizing women on the force. Women tended to be placed on early shifts where the duties were light or they were made to go on dead-end calls, issue tickets, work as dispatchers or desk attendants, or take missing persons reports.

Two major barriers for women in policing are sexual harassment and poor maternity leave policies. Daum and Johns (1994) found that 62 percent of the women they spoke to said that they had experienced some form of sexual harassment in the form of jokes, inappropriate touching, requests for sex, sexually degrading comments, or sexual gestures. Policewomen are generally not happy about their police force's maternity policy, claiming that despite legislation, pregnant policewomen are discriminated against. The Pregnancy Discrimination Act was passed in 1978, with an amendment to Title VII of the Civil Rights Act 1964. It prohibits discrimination "because of or on the basis of pregnancy, childbirth, or related medical conditions," and its purpose is to allow women to participate equally in the workforce while still being able to have a child because the right to a family life is a fundamental right. The police department cannot discriminate against a woman based upon pregnancy, though the department can legally change the policewoman's duties in order to prevent harm to her or her child (Higginbotham 1993).

There has been much litigation concerning the assignment of duties to pregnant women or the leave that these women are forced to take when they are pregnant, and the courts have not been consistent in their rulings. The courts often refer to the case of *O'Loughlin v. Pinchback*.[6] In this case, a pregnant corrections officer was told that she was discharged because her work assignment endangered her health and that of her unborn child and because she could not perform her duties adequately. The courts said that this was a violation of the Pregnancy Discrimination Act for two reasons: First, there was no evidence that she could not do her duties or respond to security threats just as other employees would; second, there was no medical evidence that this assignment was dangerous to the health of her unborn child. Though legislation in this area has come a long way, women still lack equality in a male-dominated field.

Training

Once a police candidate has passed through the selection process, he or she is hired on **probation**, or a trial period of one or two years during which the officer is evaluated. This probationary period begins with training at the **police academy**, or a school where officers learn on-the-job techniques prior to receiving full police powers. Officers must train at the academy for up to 1,100 hours, and they receive full pay and benefits from the time they enter the academy (Reaves and Goldberg 1999). While at the academy, the officer receives educational as well as practical physical training. The officer must learn

Constitutional law, and well as the criminal laws specific to the state in which he or she is policing.

Police academies vary by jurisdiction, though there are certain standard instructional categories. All police academies have lectures from which the officers learn about the law and the criminal justice system. They have physical training, training in the use of firearms, and training in the systems of patrol and traffic. They must also learn about the police department, its policies, and its relationships with other agencies (e.g., state/county/federal agencies). This training serves a number of purposes; namely, it standardizes the training of all officers in the jurisdiction while encouraging the safety of the officers and the community they will be policing. The extended time in training should aid the officer's confidence in his or her ability to use police powers, to make quick decisions, and to apply the appropriate level of discretion when approaching a situation.

Once out of the academy, the police officer is assigned a **field training officer (FTO)**. The FTO assists the new officer in applying the knowledge and skills learned at the academy to the job of the police officer.

The FTO also assists the new officer to acclimate into the police culture, or experience the socialization process. **Socialization** includes learning the values, social processes, and behaviors associated with the police institution. It involves the patterns of interaction that are dependent on the relations of the individuals in a particular setting. Because police culture is so unique, the new officer is likely to adapt his or her personality to those of other police officers who have experience on the job. It is during the rookie period that a new officer can begin to develop an "us versus them" attitude. However, the FTO can have a significant influence over the new officer and assist him or her in dealing with the inevitable stress and cynicism of the job. It is even more difficult for women to adapt to the socialization process, and both women and minorities are often excluded from the police subculture and may face harassment. Affirmative action

Education is part of the training process for police officers. They must learn about sociological, psychological, and legal issues, as well as critical thinking and writing skills.

and equal opportunity policies can mandate equal hiring, but they do not assist in the socialization process.

Retention

Many individuals are drawn to a policing career because of the job opportunities and benefits. However, the job also leads to stress and **burnout** for many of the officers. The key to job retention is to accentuate the positive aspects of the job (e.g., positive community relations, helping people) and to provide services that can help to reduce the level of stress experienced by police officers. In studies assessing job strain, Johnson (1991) showed that women experienced more "internal" burnout whereas men experienced more "external" burnout. Johnson described internal burnout as being emotionally exhausted by the job, and he described external burnout as lacking compassion due to emotional hardening. In practical terms, policemen would be more likely to take out the stress of the job on others, such as the individuals they are policing. The tangible result of internal burnout was that policewomen described having difficulty or no desire to wake up each day and face the duties of their job. Despite the problems they face, Daum and Johns (1994) point out that 80 percent of women plan to stay in the department until retirement and 71 percent said that if they had to do it all over they would again choose to be police officers.

The Bureau of Justice Assistance (2001) has examined the issue of recruitment and retention of female police officers and has issued guidelines for police departments on how to so increase their retention. The guidelines state that the retention of female officers is more difficult than male officers, because they face additional challenges such as sexual harassment, gender discrimination, and isolation. The guidelines go on to explain, however, the advantages to departments who retain women on the force. These advantages include (Bureau of Justice Assistance 2001):

- Women are competent. Female officers are as competent as their male counterparts.

- Women are not likely to use physical force. Subsequently, they are less likely than men to be accused of excessive use of force.

- Women help focus on community-oriented policing tactics. This helps build positive police–community relations.

- Women help in domestic violence incidents. The highest volume of calls to the police are related to domestic violence, and female officers assist in the response to these calls.

- Less discrimination and harassment. The more female officers there are in a department, the less likely the female officers will be harassed because they will have a higher representation in the department.

- Changes in policy. The increasing number of women in departments creates the need for a previously male-only profession to modify outdated policies in relation to selection criteria, performance standards, and supervision.

Standards for Promotion

The promotion process for police officers is very competitive (Garner 1998). There are several methods by which officers may be promoted. Although these differ by jurisdiction, officers must typically take a written exam, be interviewed, and then be assessed on qualities relating to the job. The written exam, though not common across all departments, is particularly common in the larger urban departments such as in New York, Los Angeles, and Chicago. The written exam is in a multiple-choice format, and though it is meant to be objective, there has been a lot of litigation against it for its alleged bias against minorities. For instance, in the case of *Acosta v. Lange,*[7] the court stated that if the answers of the candidates are as good or better than the established answers, they must be accepted.

Candidates for promotion must also have an oral interview, during which a board of several (generally three to six) members asks the candidates a variety of questions. These questions range from information about their background and personal characteristics to judgments about policing situations. After the interview, the candidates are assessed, during which time they are observed, tested, rated, and evaluated. Areas of assessment generally include:

- An "in-basket" exercise, where the person is tested on desk tasks and paperwork issues

- An oral presentation, where the candidate presents an overview of his or her work history and personal strengths

- A creative writing project, where the candidate prepares and delivers a paper on a specialized topic

- A peer-group-rating exercise, where the candidate rates his or her peers based on specific criteria

- Group dialogue, where the candidate acts as the leader of a group discussion

The purpose of these assessment tools is to determine how well the candidate would perform at a supervisory level. The promotion is not based on the candidate's performance on these assessments alone, but these factors are considered in combination with a performance evaluation. Performance evaluations examine, among other things, quantity and quality of work, work habits, human relations, and adaptability to new situations.

As could be expected, up until the mid-1980s nearly all of those promoted were white males. However, from the mid-1980s on there has been an increase in the number of women in the ranks above patrol officer. Despite this increase, few women are in supervisory positions. Affirmative action policies helped the promotion of female supervisors considerably. In the 1980s in departments where there were court ordered affirmative action policies, females comprised 3.5 percent of supervisory positions; where there were affirmative action policies with no court orders, they comprised 2.4 percent; where there were no specific affirmative action policies, they comprised 2.2 percent of the supervisors

(Martin 1989). Gavin and Price (1979) noted that promotional opportunities for women prior to this time were limited and that the police management hierarchy is rigid and restricted at the top. They claimed that the most important indicator for promotion was crime fighting and a good arrest record, qualities associated with male officers.

Many police departments in the 1980s adopted **dual promotion lists**, or separate promotional instruments for white male officers and all other officers. Though these lists helped in the promotion of women and minorities, it negatively affected their integration with other police officers. Such policies created tension among all groups of officers. The white male and female officers felt resentment towards officers of racial minorities, feeling that they received advancement only because of a court-mandated policy rather than merit. Alternatively, African American officers felt that the promotional exams were culturally biased and that that is why the African American officers received lower exam scores. The purported cultural bias of these exams continues to be a contentious topic.

Between 1980 and the mid-1990s, promotional opportunities for women increased. Women continued to be significantly more likely to be eligible for promotion to sergeant in departments with affirmative action. Today, several factors relate to whether women apply for and receive a promotion. According to Whetstone (2001) the biggest impact on the number of women applicants in the departments was the number of women already serving there. Women who were considered effective officers were often given desirable positions above men who were similarly qualified. Additionally, many women choose not to apply for a promotional position but rather remain patrol officers. Reasons for this include poor work conditions, poor assignment and work-hour flexibility, and lack of child care and family concerns (Whetstone 2001).

Though still underrepresented, women are increasingly being promoted into management positions within the police department.

Chapter Summary

- During the late 1970s and early 1980s, police departments began to actively recruit women and minorities and implemented affirmative action policies to help give them equal opportunities to be hired as police officers.

- Though more representative of the community today than ever before, police departments still employ a selection process with controversial requirements.

- Debates continue about the benefits of higher education, residency requirements, necessary levels of physical agility, and the lengths and types of training.

- Recruitment of police candidates has evolved significantly over the past two decades, utilizing technology and educational institutions to seek out a diverse population.

- Selection of police candidates is based on many criteria. Prior to the 1980s, selection was based primarily on physical agility, whereas selection now is based on a combination of psychological assessments, written examinations, and interviews.

KEY TERMS

Affirmative action   365

Burnout   371

Dual promotion lists   373

Field training officer
   (FTO)   370

Law Enforcement Assistance
   Administration (LEAA)   357

Minnesota Multiphasic
   Personality Inventory
   (MMPI)   362

Police academy   369

Polygraph   363

Probation   369

Quotas   366

Reverse discrimination   366

Socialization   370

Tokens   367

Linking the Dots

1. How have recruitment and selection standards changed since the early twentieth century?

2. Why is it important to have so many selection procedures? Are any of these processes more important than others?

3. Compare male and female officers. What are their different strengths and weaknesses?

4. How have legal issues affected police departments over the last forty years? How has the law assisted gender and racial minorities? Have these legal requirements hindered minorities in any way?

5. What can police managers do to increase officer retention?

REFERENCES

Bloch, P. B., and D. Anderson. 1974. *Policewomen on Patrol: Final Report*. Washington, D.C.: The Police Foundation.

Board on Behavioral, Cognitive and Sensory Sciences and Education. 2003. *The Polygraph and Lie Detection*. Washington, D.C.: National Academies Press.

Bratton, W. W., and P. Knobler. 1988. *Turnaround: How America's Top Cop Reversed the Crime Epidemic*. New York: Random House.

Bureau of Justice Assistance. 2001. "Recruiting and Retaining Women: A Self-Assessment Guide for Law Enforcement." *Bureau of Justice Assistance Bulletin*, Washington, D.C.: NCJ 188157.

Bureau of Justice Statistics. 1996. *Local Police Departments, 1993*. Washington, D.C.: U.S. Department of Justice.

Bureau of Justice Statistics. 1999. *Law Enforcement Management and Administrative Statistics, 1997*. Washington, D.C.: U.S. Department of Justice.

Bureau of Justice Statistics. 2000. *Local Police Departments, 1997*. Washington, D.C.: U.S. Department of Justice.

Cao, X. and X. Huang, 2000. "Determinants of Citizen Complaints Against Police Abuse of Power." *Journal of Criminal Justice*. 28(2): 203–213.

California Psychological Inventory (CPI). Palo Alto, CA: Consulting Psychology, Inc.

Carter, D., and A. Sapp. 1988. *The State of Police Education: Critical Findings*. Washington, D.C.: Police Executive Research Forum.

Clark, J. R. 1997. "Police Careers May Take a Beating from Federal Domestic Violence Law." *Law Enforcement News* 23(1): 23–47.

Daum, J. M., and C. M. Johns. 1994. "Police Work from a Woman's Perspective." *The Police Chief*. 9: 46–49.

Ermer, V. B. 1978. "Recruitment of Female Police Officers in New York." *Journal of Criminal Justice*. 6(4): 327–338.

Fagin, J. A. 2003. *Criminal Justice*. Boston, MA: Allyn and Bacon.

Ferriera, B. R. 1997. "The Importance of Law Enforcement Education." *Law and Order* 26(1): 26, 30–32.

Fry, L., and S. Greenfield. 1980. "An Examination of Attitudinal Differences Between Policemen and Policewomen." *Journal of Applied Psychology*. 65(2):123–126.

Garner, G. 1998. "Are You Ready for Promotion?" *Police* 28(1): 22–24.

Gross, S. 1984. "Women Becoming Cops: Developmental Issues and Solutions." *Police Chief*. 51: 32–35.

Higginbotham, J. 1993. "Pregnancy and Maternity Leave Policies: The Legal Aspects." *FBI Law Enforcement Bulletin*, March, 27–32.

Johns, C. J., and A. M. Barclay. 1979. "Female Partners for Male Police: The Effect on Shooting Responses." *Criminal Justice and Behavior*. 6(4): 327–337.

Johnson, L. B. 1991. "Job Strain Among Police Officers: Gender Comparisons." *Police Studies* 14 (1): 12–16.

Krimmel, J. T. 1996. "The Performance of College-Educated Police: A Study of Self-rated Police Performance Measures." *American Journal of Police* 15(1): 85–96.

Kuykendall, J. L., and D. E. Burns. 1980. "The Black Police Officer: An Historical Perspective." *Journal of Contemporary Criminal Justice*. 1(4): 4–12.

Langworthy, R. H., B. Anders, and T. Hughes. 1995. *Law Enforcement Recruitment and Selection: A Survey of Major Police Departments in the U.S.* Highland Heights, KY: Academy of Criminal Justice Sciences.

Leach, T. 1998. "College Internship: An Aid to Recruitment." *Law and Order* 46(1): 57–59.

Lester, D. 1983. "Why Do People Become Police Officers: A Study of Reasons and Their Predictions of Success. *Journal of Police Science and Administration* 11(2): 170–174.

Lewis, W. G. 1989. "Toward Representative Bureaucracy: Blacks in City Police Organization, 1975–1985." *Public Administration Review*. 49(3): 257–267.

Longway, K., K. Spillar, and S. Tejani. 2003. *Tearing Down the Wall: Problems with Consistency, Validity, and Adverse Impact of Physical Agility Testing in Police Selection*. Washington, D.C.: National Center for Women and Policing.

Martin, C. A. 1979. "Women Police: A Survey of Education, Attitudes and Problems." *Journal of Studies in Technical Careers*. 1(3): 220–227.

Martin, S. E. 1979. Policewomen and Equality: Occupational Role Dilemmas and Choices of Female Officers. *Journal of Police Science and Administration* 7(4): 314–322.

Martin, S. 1989. *Women on the Move? A Report on the Status of Women in Policing*. Washington, D.C.: Police Foundation Reports.

Meagher, M. S., and N. A. Yentes. 1986. "Choosing a Career in Policing: A Comparison of Male and Female Perceptions." *Journal of Police Science and Administration* 14(4): 320–327.

Milgram, D. 2002. "Recruiting Women to Policing: Practical Strategies That Work." *The Police Chief*. 69(1): 31–34.

Molden, J. B. 1999. "College Degrees for Police Applicants." *Law and Order* 7(1): 21–22.

National Crime Prevention Council. 1995. *Lengthening the Stride: Employing Peace Officers From Newly Arrived Ethnic Groups.* Washington, D.C.: National Crime Prevention Council.

Price, B. R., and S. Gavin. 1979. "A Century of Women in Policing." In *Modern Police Administration,* edited by D. O. Schultz, 109–122. Houston: Gulf Publishing Company.

Rafilson, F. M. 1997. "Everything You Always Wanted to Know About Written Exams . . . but Were Afraid (Really) to Ask!" *Law and Order* 45(2): 100–102.

Schulz, D. M. 1995. *From Social Worker to Crime Fighter: Women in United States Municipal Policing.* Westport, CT: Praeger.

Senna, J. J., and L. J. Siegal. 2002. *Introduction to Criminal Justice,* 9th ed. Belmont, CA: Wadsworth.

Sharp, A.G. 1994. "Recruiting Quality Applicants: The Ideal Police Officer Candidate Does Not Exist." *Law and Order* 42(2): 100–108.

Sherman, L. 1975. "An Evaluation of Policewomen on Patrol in A Suburban Police Department." *Journal of Police Science Administrator.* 3(4): 434–438.

Strandberg, K.W. 1996. "Police Recruiting: Hiring Strategies." *Law Enforcement Technology* 23(1): 38–42.

Terry, K. J., and H. B. Grant. 2003. "The Roads Not Taken: Improving the Use of Civilian Complaint Review Boards and Implementation of the Recommendations from Investigative Commissions." In *Policing and Minority Communities: Bridging the Gap,* edited by D. Jones-Brown and K. J. Terry, 160–182. Upper Saddle River, NJ: Prentice-Hall.

U.S. Census Bureau. 2000. U.S. Census 2000. Available at www.census.gov.main/www.cen2000/html.

Walker, S. 1985. "Racial Minority and Female Employment in Policing: The Implications of 'Glacial' Change." *Crime and Delinquency.* 31: 535–572.

Whetstone, T. S. 2001. "Copping Out: Why Police Officers Decline to Participate in the Sergeant's Promotional Process." *American Journal of Criminal Justice* 25 (2): 147–159.

NOTES

1. Langworthy et al. (1995) state that over 91 percent of police departments use psychological screening tools such as the MMPI or conduct psychological interviews with trained psychologists or psychiatrists. Reaves and Goldberg (1999) state that approximately 80 percent of police departments use psychological screening tools.

2. The first edition consisted of 680 questions. In addition, the MPPI is only meant for adults, however, there is an MMPI-A designed for adolescents.

3. Although many departments use the polygraph as an assessment tool, they are prohibited from requiring candidates to submit to a polygraph exam on the basis that the candidate will not be hired without taking this test. The Employee Polygraph Protection Act of 1988, 29 U.S.C.A. §2001, was enacted because of concerns that employers were using polygraph exams and relying on information that may be inaccurate, inconclusive, or unfounded to make employment decisions

4. *Griggs v. Duke Power Company,* 401 U.S. 424 (1971).

5. *Wards Cove Packing Company Inc. v. Antonio,* 490 U.S. 642 (1989).

6. *O'Loughlin v. Pinchback,* 579 So. 2d 788 (1991).

7. *Acosta v. Lang,* 16 N.Y. 2d 668.

Wiretaps (CALEA)/Cybersecurity Legislation, 106th U.S. Congress

Appendix A

Bill No.	Name (Sponsor)	Summary	Status
H.R. 3048	Presidential Threat Protection Act of 2000 (McCollum)	"Authorizes the use of administrative subpoenas (subpoenas without the oversight of a judge) by the FBI, DEA, INS or any other agency within the Department of Justice to seize information relating to the apprehension of fugitives, and by the Secret Service to seize information relating to threats against the President and other officials. This would permit the government to obtain private records without notifying the individuals who own the records."	**10/7/99:** Introduced and referred to House Judiciary Committee. **10/15/99:** Referred to Subcommittee on Crime. **3/16/00:** Amended and reported back to Judiciary Committee. **5/24/00:** Amended and reported back to the floor. **6/26/00:** Passed the House under suspension of the rules. **6/27/00:** Received by the Senate. **10/13/00:** Passed the Senate with an amendment by Unanimous Consent.

Source: Copyright © 2001 by Center for Democracy and Technology. Available at http://www.cdt.org/legislation/106th/wiretaps/.

Bill No.	Name (Sponsor)	Summary	Status
S. 2516	Fugitive Apprehension Act of 2000 (Thurmond)	"Authorizes the use of administrative subpoenas (subpoenas without the oversight of a judge) by the FBI, DEA, INS, and other agencies within the Department of Justice to seize information relating to the apprehension of fugitives. This would permit the government to obtain private records without notifying the individuals who own the records."	**5/8/00:** Introduced and referred to Senate Judiciary Committee. **7/20/00:** Amended and reported back to the floor. **7/26/00:** Passed the Senate with an amendment by Unanimous Consent. **7/27/00:** Received by the House; referred to House Judiciary Committee. **8/3/00:** Referred to Subcommittee on Crime.
HR 5018	Electronic Communications Privacy Act of 2000 (Canady/Hutchinson)	Establishes provisions for the public reports on law enforcement's interception of stored communications; Places new restrictions on the use of pen registers and trap and trace devices.	**7/27/00:** Introduced and referred to Judiciary Committee. **8/23/00:** Referred to the Subcommittee on the Constitution. **9/6/00:** Subcommittee hearing held. CDT *testified*. **9/14/00** - Passed out of subcommittee, referred to full committee. **9/26/00** - Amended and reported by full committee. **10/4/00** - Reported by the Committee on Judiciary. H. Rept. 106-932.
HR 4987	Digital Privacy Act of 2000 (Barr/Emerson)	Strengthens restrictions on the issuance of pen register and trap and trace device orders; requires a showing of probable cause for the disclosure of location information by mobile service providers.	**7/27/00:** Introduced and referred to Judiciary Committee. **9/6/00:** Subcommittee hearing held. CDT *testified*.
HR. 4908	Notice of Electronic Monitoring Act (Canady/Barr) (see also S. 2898)	Requires that employers monitoring their employees' wire, oral, or electronic communications give annual notice to that effect.	**7/20/00:** Introduced and referred to Judiciary Committee. **7/25/00:** Referred to Subcommittee on the Constitution. **9/6/00:** Subcommittee hearing held. CDT *testified*.

Bill No.	Name (Sponsor)	Summary	Status
S. 2898	Notice of Electronic Monitoring Act (Schumer)	Requires that employers monitoring their employees' wire, oral, or electronic communciations give annual notice to that effect.	**7/20/00:** Introduced and referred to Judiciary Committee.
S. 2448	Internet Integrity and Critical Infrastructure Protection Act of 2000 (Hatch/Schumer)	Increases penalties for computer crimes and eliminates threshold for federal prosecution. Makes it illegal to send spam with false identification information. Sets privacy standards for satellite TV subscriber info. Requires websites to give notice and opt-out. Makes fraudulent access to personal information a crime.	**4/12/00** Introduced and referred to Judiciary Committee. **5/25/00** *Hearing held. CDT testimony.* **10/5/00** Senate Judiciary Committee reported *substitute version of S.2448*
S. 2092	(Schumer)	Amends title 18, United States Code, to extend the use of pen registers and trap and trace devices to the Internet, to give such orders nation wide reach, and modify computer crime law. *CDT analysis.*	**2/24/00** Referred to the Committee on the Judiciary.
HR 4246	*Cyber Security Information Act of 2000* (Davis-Moran)	Creates FOIA exemption for cybersecurity information. *CDT analysis.*	**4/12/00:** Introduced and referred to the Judiciary Committee and Committee on Government Reform. **5/8/00:** Referred by Committee on Government Reform to the Subcommittee on Government Management, Information and Technology. **6/22/00:** Subcommittee hearings held.
S 2430	Internet Security Act of 2000 (Leahy)	Amends computer crime law, strengthens privacy standards for pen registers.	**4/13/00** Referred to the Committee on the Judiciary.

Bill No.	Name (Sponsor)	Summary	Status
S 1769 **Enacted!**	Continued Reporting of Intercepted Wire, Oral, and Electronic Communications Act (Leahy)	Preserves the important reporting requirements for wiretapping which were set to expire.	**10/22/99** Introduced and referred to the Committee on Judiciary. **10/28/99** Reported favorably with amendment. **11/5/99** Passed Senate by unanimous consent. **11/8/99** Referred to House Judiciary Committee. **11/18/99** Passed by House with amendment. **5/2/2000** Enacted as Public Law No: 106-197
S 9	Safe Schools, Safe Streets and Secure Borders Act of 1999 (Daschle)	Omnibus crime bill of Senate Democrats, includes sec. 8312, enhancing privacy protections for stored electronic data.	**1/19/99** Referred to Judiciary Committee.
HR 514	Wireless Privacy Enhancement Act of 1999 (Wilson)	To amend the Communications Act of 1934 to strengthen and clarify prohibitions on electronic eavesdropping	Introduced **2/3/99**. Referred to the Commerce Committee Subcommittee on Telecommunications. **2/3/99** Subcommittee hearing. *CDT Testimony.* **2/11/99** Approved by House Commerce Committee. **2/25/99** Amended and passed by the House. **3/3/99** Received in the Senate, referred to Commerce Committee.
HR 438 **Enacted!**	Wireless Communications and Public Safety Act of 1999 (Shimkus)	Establishes 911 as nationwide emergency number, limits commercial disclosure or reuse of location information from mobile telephones. Senate Companion: S. 800.	**2/2/99** Introduced and referred to Commerce Committee. **2/3/99** Telecommunications Subcommittee hearing. *CDT testimony.* **2/11/99** Approved by full Committee. **2/24/99** Amended and passed by the House. Enacted as S. 800 (See below).
S 411	Clone Pager Authorization Act of 1999 (DeWine)	Requires court order for use of clone pagers by law enforcement.	**2/11/99** Introduced and referred to the Committee on Judiciary.

Bill No.	Name (Sponsor)	Summary	Status
HR 1159	Protection of Children From On-Line Predators and Exploitation Act of 1999 (Johnson)	Creates Child Cyber-smuggling Center, expands use of wiretaps.	**3/17/99** Introduced and referred to Committee on Ways and Means and Committee on the Judiciary. **3/25/99** Referred to Subcommitee on Crime.
S. 781	Telephone Privacy Act of 1999 (Feinstein)	Requires 2 party consent for recording telephone calls.	**4/13/99** Introduced and referred to Judiciary Committee.
S. 854	E-RIGHTS (Leahy)	Establish standards for law enforcement access to location information, decryption assistance for encrypted communications, and stored electronic information. Affirms right to use and sell encryption products.	**4/21/99** Introduced and referred to Judiciary Committee.
S. 782	Patients' Telephone Privacy Act of 1999 (Feinstein)	Limits health care providers recording of patients' phone calls.	**4/13/99** Introduced and referred to Judiciary Committee.
S. 800 **Enacted!**	Wireless Communications and Public Safety Act of 1999 (Burns)	Establishes 911 as nationwide emergency number, limits commercial disclosure or reuse of location information from mobile telephones. (House companion: HR 438.)	**4/14/99** Introduced and referred to the Commerce Committee Communications Subcommittee. **5/12/99** Hearing held. **8/4/99** Reported to Senate with amendments on. **8/5/99** Passed Senate with amendments by unanimous consent. **10/12/99** Passed House 424-2. **10/26/99** Signed by President, Public Law 106-81.

Sec. 1385.
Use of Army and
Air Force as
Posse Comitatus

Whoever, except in cases and under circumstances expressly authorized by the Constitution or Act of Congress, willfully uses any part of the Army or the Air Force as a posse comitatus or otherwise to execute the laws shall be fined under this title or imprisoned not more than two years, or both

USA PATRIOT Act of 2001

To deter and punish terrorist acts in the United States and around the world, to enhance law enforcement investigatory tools, and for other purposes. *Be it enacted by the Senate and House of Representatives of the United States of America in Congress assembled,*

SECTION 1. SHORT TITLE AND TABLE OF CONTENTS.

(a) SHORT TITLE–This Act may be cited as the 'Uniting and Strengthening America by Providing Appropriate Tools Required to Intercept and Obstruct Terrorism (USA PATRIOT ACT) Act of 2001'. (b) TABLE OF CONTENTS–The table of contents for this Act is as follows:

Source: Complete text of USA PATRIOT Act of 2001 available at http://www.epic.org/privacy/terrorism/usapatriot/.

TITLE IV—PROTECTING THE BORDER

Subtitle A—Protecting the Northern Border

TITLE V—REMOVING OBSTACLES TO INVESTIGATING TERRORISM

Sec. 903. Sense of Congress on the establishment and maintenance of intelligence relationships to acquire information on terrorists and terrorist organizations.

Sec. 904. Temporary authority to defer submittal to Congress of reports on intelligence and intelligence-related matters.

Sec. 905. Disclosure to Director of Central Intelligence of foreign intelligence-related information with respect to criminal investigations.

Sec. 906. Foreign terrorist asset tracking center.

TITLE II—ENHANCED SURVEILLANCE PROCEDURES

SEC. 201. AUTHORITY TO INTERCEPT WIRE, ORAL, AND ELECTRONIC COMMUNICATIONS RELATING TO TERRORISM.

Section 2516(1) of title 18, United States Code, is amended—

(1) by redesignating paragraph (p), as so redesignated by section 434(2) of the Antiterrorism and Effective Death Penalty Act of 1996 (Public Law 104-132; 110 Stat. 1274), as paragraph (r); and

(2) by inserting after paragraph (p), as so redesignated by section 201(3) of the Illegal Immigration Reform and Immigrant Responsibility Act of 1996 (division C of Public Law 104-208; 110 Stat. 3009-565), the following new paragraph:

'(q) any criminal violation of section 229 (relating to chemical weapons); or sections 2332, 2332a, 2332b, 2332d, 2339A, or 2339B of this title (relating to terrorism); or'.

SEC. 202. AUTHORITY TO INTERCEPT WIRE, ORAL, AND ELECTRONIC COMMUNICATIONS RELATING TO COMPUTER FRAUD AND ABUSE OFFENSES.

Section 2516(1)(c) of title 18, United States Code, is amended by striking 'and section 1341 (relating to mail fraud),' and inserting 'section 1341 (relating to mail fraud), a felony violation of section 1030 (relating to computer fraud and abuse), ' .

SEC. 203. AUTHORITY TO SHARE CRIMINAL INVESTIGATIVE INFORMATION.

(a) AUTHORITY TO SHARE GRAND JURY INFORMATION-

(1) IN GENERAL–Rule 6(e)(3)(C) of the Federal Rules of Criminal Procedure is amended to read as follows:

'(C)(i) Disclosure otherwise prohibited by this rule of matters occurring before the grand jury may also be made—

'(I) when so directed by a court preliminarily to or in connection with a judicial proceeding;

'(II) when permitted by a court at the request of the defendant, upon a showing that grounds may exist for a motion to dismiss the indictment because of matters occurring before the grand jury;

'(III) when the disclosure is made by an attorney for the government to another Federal grand jury;

'(IV) when permitted by a court at the request of an attorney for the government, upon a showing that such matters may disclose a violation of state criminal law, to an appropriate official of a state or subdivision of a state for the purpose of enforcing such law; or

'(V) when the matters involve foreign intelligence or counterintelligence (as defined in section 3 of the National Security Act of 1947 (50 U.S.C. 401a)), or foreign intelligence information (as defined in clause (iv) of this subparagraph), to any Federal law enforcement, intelligence, protective, immigration, national defense, or national security official in order to assist the official receiving that information in the performance of his official duties.

'(ii) If the court orders disclosure of matters occurring before the grand jury, the disclosure shall be made in such manner, at such time, and under such conditions as the court may direct.

'(iii) Any Federal official to whom information is disclosed pursuant to clause (i)(V) of this subparagraph may use that information only as necessary in the conduct of that person's official duties subject to any limitations on the unauthorized disclosure of such information. Within a reasonable time after such disclosure, an attorney for the government shall file under seal a notice with the court stating the fact that such information was disclosed and the departments, agencies, or entities to which the disclosure was made.

'(iv) In clause (i)(V) of this subparagraph, the term 'foreign intelligence information' means—

'(I) information, whether or not concerning a United States person, that relates to the ability of the United States to protect against—

'(aa) actual or potential attack or other grave hostile acts of a foreign power or an agent of a foreign power;

'(bb) sabotage or international terrorism by a foreign power or an agent of a foreign power; or

'(cc) clandestine intelligence activities by an intelligence service or network of a foreign power or by an agent of foreign power; or

'(II) information, whether or not concerning a United States person, with respect to a foreign power or foreign territory that relates to—

'(aa) the national defense or the security of the United States; or

'(bb) the conduct of the foreign affairs of the United States. ' .

(2) CONFORMING AMENDMENT–Rule 6(e)(3)(D) of the Federal Rules of Criminal Procedure is amended by striking '(e)(3)(C)(i)' and inserting '(e)(3)(C)(i)(I)'.

(b) AUTHORITY TO SHARE ELECTRONIC, WIRE, AND ORAL INTERCEPTION INFORMATION-

(1) LAW ENFORCEMENT–Section 2517 of title 18, United States Code, is amended by inserting at the end the following:

'(6) Any investigative or law enforcement officer, or attorney for the Government, who by any means authorized by this chapter, has obtained knowledge of the contents of any wire, oral, or electronic communication, or evidence derived therefrom, may disclose such contents to any other Federal law enforcement, intelligence, protective, immigration, national defense, or national security official to the extent that such contents include foreign intelligence or counterintelligence (as defined in section 3 of the National Security Act of 1947 (50 U.S.C. 401a)), or foreign intelligence information (as defined in subsection (19) of section 2510 of this title), to assist the official who is to receive that information in the performance of his official duties. Any Federal official who receives information pursuant to this provision may use that information only as necessary in the conduct of that person's official duties subject to any limitations on the unauthorized disclosure of such information. ' .

(2) DEFINITION–Section 2510 of title 18, United States Code, is amended by—

(A) in paragraph (17), by striking 'and' after the semicolon;

(B) in paragraph (18), by striking the period and inserting '; and'; and

(C) by inserting at the end the following:

'(19) 'foreign intelligence information' means—

'(A) information, whether or not concerning a United States person, that relates to the ability of the United States to protect against—

'(i) actual or potential attack or other grave hostile acts of a foreign power or an agent of a foreign power;

'(ii) sabotage or international terrorism by a foreign power or an agent of a foreign power; or

'(iii) clandestine intelligence activities by an intelligence service or network of a foreign power or by an agent of a foreign power; or

'(B) information, whether or not concerning a United States person, with respect to a foreign power or foreign territory that relates to—

'(i) the national defense or the security of the United States; or

'(ii) the conduct of the foreign affairs of the United States. ' .

(c) PROCEDURES–The Attorney General shall establish procedures for the disclosure of information pursuant to section 2517(6) and Rule 6(e)(3)(C)(i)(V) of the Federal Rules of Criminal Procedure that identifies a United States person, as defined in section 101 of the Foreign Intelligence Surveillance Act of 1978 (50 U.S.C. 1801)).

(d) FOREIGN INTELLIGENCE INFORMATION-

(1) IN GENERAL–Notwithstanding any other provision of law, it shall be lawful for foreign intelligence or counterintelligence (as defined in section 3 of the National Security Act of 1947 (50 U.S.C. 401a)) or foreign intelligence information obtained as part of a criminal investigation to be disclosed to any Federal law enforcement, intelligence, protective, immigration, national defense, or national security official in order to assist the official receiving that information in the performance of his official duties. Any Federal official

who receives information pursuant to this provision may use that information only as necessary in the conduct of that person's official duties subject to any limitations on the unauthorized disclosure of such information.

(2) DEFINITION–In this subsection, the term 'foreign intelligence information' means—

(A) information, whether or not concerning a United States person, that relates to the ability of the United States to protect against—

(i) actual or potential attack or other grave hostile acts of a foreign power or an agent of a foreign power;

(ii) sabotage or international terrorism by a foreign power or an agent of a foreign power; or

(iii) clandestine intelligence activities by an intelligence service or network of a foreign power or by an agent of a foreign power; or

(B) information, whether or not concerning a United States person, with respect to a foreign power or foreign territory that relates to—

(i) the national defense or the security of the United States; or

(ii) the conduct of the foreign affairs of the United States.

SEC. 204. CLARIFICATION OF INTELLIGENCE EXCEPTIONS FROM LIMITATIONS ON INTERCEPTION AND DISCLOSURE OF WIRE, ORAL, AND ELECTRONIC COMMUNICATIONS.

Section 2511(2)(f) of title 18, United States Code, is amended—

(1) by striking 'this chapter or chapter 121' and inserting 'this chapter or chapter 121 or 206 of this title'; and

(2) by striking 'wire and oral' and inserting 'wire, oral, and electronic'.

SEC. 206. ROVING SURVEILLANCE AUTHORITY UNDER THE FOREIGN INTELLIGENCE SURVEILLANCE ACT OF 1978.

Section 105(c)(2)(B) of the Foreign Intelligence Surveillance Act of 1978 (50 U.S.C. 1805(c)(2)(B)) is amended by inserting ', or in circumstances where the Court finds that the actions of the target of the application may have the effect of thwarting the identification of a specified person, such other persons,' after 'specified person'.

SEC. 208. DESIGNATION OF JUDGES.

Section 103(a) of the Foreign Intelligence Surveillance Act of 1978 (50 U.S.C. 1803(a)) is amended by—

(1) striking 'seven district court judges' and inserting '11 district court judges'; and

(2) inserting 'of whom no fewer than 3 shall reside within 20 miles of the District of Columbia' after 'circuits'.

SEC. 209. SEIZURE OF VOICE-MAIL MESSAGES PURSUANT TO WARRANTS.

Title 18, United States Code, is amended—

(1) in section 2510—

(A) in paragraph (1), by striking beginning with 'and such' and all that follows through 'communication'; and

(B) in paragraph (14), by inserting 'wire or' after 'transmission of'; and

(2) in subsections (a) and (b) of section 2703—

(A) by striking 'CONTENTS OF ELECTRONIC' and inserting 'CONTENTS OF WIRE OR ELECTRONIC' each place it appears;

(B) by striking 'contents of an electronic' and inserting 'contents of a wire or electronic' each place it appears; and

(C) by striking 'any electronic' and inserting 'any wire or electronic' each place it appears.

SEC. 210. SCOPE OF SUBPOENAS FOR RECORDS OF ELECTRONIC COMMUNICATIONS.

Section 2703(c)(2) of title 18, United States Code, as redesignated by section 212, is amended—

(1) by striking 'entity the name, address, local and long distance telephone toll billing records, telephone number or other subscriber number or identity, and length of service of a subscriber' and inserting the following: 'entity the—

'(A) name;

'(B) address;

'(C) local and long distance telephone connection records, or records of session times and durations;

'(D) length of service (including start date) and types of service utilized;

'(E) telephone or instrument number or other subscriber number or identity, including any temporarily assigned network address; and

'(F) means and source of payment for such service (including any credit card or bank account number),

of a subscriber'; and

(2) by striking 'and the types of services the subscriber or customer utilized, '.

SEC. 213. AUTHORITY FOR DELAYING NOTICE OF THE EXECUTION OF A WARRANT.

Section 3103a of title 18, United States Code, is amended—

(1) by inserting '(a) IN GENERAL–' before 'In addition'; and

(2) by adding at the end the following:

'(b) DELAY–With respect to the issuance of any warrant or court order under this section, or any other rule of law, to search for and seize any property or material that constitutes evidence of a criminal offense in violation of the laws of the United States, any notice required, or that may be required, to be given may be delayed if—

'(1) the court finds reasonable cause to believe that providing immediate notification of the execution of the warrant may have an adverse result (as defined in section 2705);

'(2) the warrant prohibits the seizure of any tangible property, any wire or electronic communication (as defined in section 2510), or, except as expressly provided in chapter 121, any stored wire or electronic information, except where the court finds reasonable necessity for the seizure; and

'(3) the warrant provides for the giving of such notice within a reasonable period of its execution, which period may thereafter be extended by the court for good cause shown. ' .

SEC. 214. PEN REGISTER AND TRAP AND TRACE AUTHORITY UNDER FISA.

(a) APPLICATIONS AND ORDERS–Section 402 of the Foreign Intelligence Surveillance Act of 1978 (50 U.S.C. 1842) is amended—

(1) in subsection (a)(1), by striking 'for any investigation to gather foreign intelligence information or information concerning international terrorism' and inserting 'for any investigation to obtain foreign intelligence information not concerning a United States person or to protect against international terrorism or clandestine intelligence activities, provided that such investigation of a United States person is not conducted solely upon the basis of activities protected by the first amendment to the Constitution';

(2) by amending subsection (c)(2) to read as follows:

'(2) a certification by the applicant that the information likely to be obtained is foreign intelligence information not concerning a United States person or is relevant to an ongoing investigation to protect against international terrorism or clandestine intelligence activities, provided that such investigation of a United States person is not conducted solely upon the basis of activities protected by the first amendment to the Constitution.';

(3) by striking subsection (c)(3); and

(4) by amending subsection (d)(2)(A) to read as follows:

'(A) shall specify—

'(i) the identity, if known, of the person who is the subject of the investigation;

'(ii) the identity, if known, of the person to whom is leased or in whose name is listed the telephone line or other facility to which the pen register or trap and trace device is to be attached or applied;

'(iii) the attributes of the communications to which the order applies, such as the number or other identifier, and, if known, the location of the telephone line or other facility to which the pen register or trap and trace device is to be attached or applied and, in the case of a trap and trace device, the geographic limits of the trap and trace order. ' .

(b) AUTHORIZATION DURING EMERGENCIES–Section 403 of the Foreign Intelligence Surveillance Act of 1978 (50 U.S.C. 1843) is amended—

(1) in subsection (a), by striking 'foreign intelligence information or information concerning international terrorism' and inserting 'foreign intelligence information not concerning a United States person or information to protect against international terrorism or clandestine intelligence activities, provided that such investigation of a United States person is not conducted solely upon

the basis of activities protected by the first amendment to the Constitution'; and

(2) in subsection (b)(1), by striking 'foreign intelligence information or information concerning international terrorism' and inserting 'foreign intelligence information not concerning a United States person or information to protect against international terrorism or clandestine intelligence activities, provided that such investigation of a United States person is not conducted solely upon the basis of activities protected by the first amendment to the Constitution'.

(A) in subparagraph (A)—

(i) by inserting 'or other facility' after 'telephone line'; and

(ii) by inserting before the semicolon at the end 'or applied'; and

(B) by striking subparagraph (C) and inserting the following:

'(C) the attributes of the communications to which the order applies, including the number or other identifier and, if known, the location of the telephone line or other facility to which the pen register or trap and trace device is to be attached or applied, and, in the case of an order authorizing installation and use of a trap and trace device under subsection (a)(2), the geographic limits of the order; and'.

(3) NONDISCLOSURE REQUIREMENTS–Section 3123(d)(2) of title 18, United States Code, is amended—

(A) by inserting 'or other facility' after 'the line'; and

(B) by striking ', or who has been ordered by the court' and inserting 'or applied, or who is obligated by the order'.

(c) DEFINITIONS-

(1) COURT OF COMPETENT JURISDICTION–Section 3127(2) of title 18, United States Code, is amended by striking subparagraph (A) and inserting the following:

'(A) any district court of the United States (including a magistrate judge of such a court) or any United States court of appeals having jurisdiction over the offense being investigated; or'.

(2) PEN REGISTER–Section 3127(3) of title 18, United States Code, is amended—

(A) by striking 'electronic or other impulses' and all that follows through 'is attached' and inserting 'dialing, routing, addressing, or signaling information transmitted by an instrument or facility from which a wire or electronic communication is transmitted, provided, however, that such information shall not include the contents of any communication'; and

(B) by inserting 'or process' after 'device' each place it appears.

(3) TRAP AND TRACE DEVICE–Section 3127(4) of title 18, United States Code, is amended—

SEC. 316. ANTI-TERRORIST FORFEITURE PROTECTION.

(a) RIGHT TO CONTEST–An owner of property that is confiscated under any provision of law relating to the confiscation of assets of suspected international terrorists, may contest that confiscation by filing a claim in the manner set forth in the Federal Rules of Civil Procedure (Supplemental Rules for Certain Admiralty and Maritime Claims), and asserting as an affirmative defense that—

(1) the property is not subject to confiscation under such provision of law; or

(2) the innocent owner provisions of section 983(d) of title 18, United States Code, apply to the case.

(b) EVIDENCE–In considering a claim filed under this section, a court may admit evidence that is otherwise inadmissible under the Federal Rules of Evidence, if the court determines that the evidence is reliable, and that compliance with the Federal Rules of Evidence may jeopardize the national security interests of the United States.

(c) CLARIFICATIONS-

(1) PROTECTION OF RIGHTS–The exclusion of certain provisions of Federal law from the definition of the term 'civil forfeiture statute' in section 983(i) of title 18, United States Code, shall not be construed to deny an owner of property the right to contest the confiscation of assets of suspected international terrorists under—

(A) subsection (a) of this section;

(B) the Constitution; or

(C) subchapter II of chapter 5 of title 5, United States Code (commonly known as the 'Administrative Procedure Act').

(2) SAVINGS CLAUSE–Nothing in this section shall limit or otherwise affect any other remedies that may be available to an owner of property under section 983 of title 18, United States Code, or any other provision of law.

(d) TECHNICAL CORRECTION–Section 983(i)(2)(D) of title 18, United States Code, is amended by inserting 'or the International Emergency Economic Powers Act (IEEPA) (50 U.S.C. 1701 et seq.)' before the semicolon.

SEC. 317. LONG-ARM JURISDICTION OVER FOREIGN MONEY LAUNDERERS.

Section 1956(b) of title 18, United States Code, is amended—

(1) by redesignating paragraphs (1) and (2) as subparagraphs (A) and (B), respectively, and moving the margins 2 ems to the right;

(2) by inserting after '(b)' the following: 'PENALTIES-

'(1) IN GENERAL–';

(3) by inserting ', or section 1957' after 'or (a)(3)'; and

(4) by adding at the end the following:

'(2) JURISDICTION OVER FOREIGN PERSONS–For purposes of adjudicating an action filed or enforcing a penalty ordered under this section, the district courts shall have jurisdiction over any foreign person, including any financial institution authorized under the laws of a foreign country, against whom the action is brought, if service of process upon the foreign person is made under the Federal Rules of Civil Procedure or the laws of the country in which the foreign person is found, and—

'(A) the foreign person commits an offense under subsection (a) involving a financial transaction that occurs in whole or in part in the United States;

'(B) the foreign person converts, to his or her own use, property in which the United States has an ownership interest by virtue of the entry of an order of forfeiture by a court of the United States; or

'(C) the foreign person is a financial institution that maintains a bank account at a financial institution in the United States.

'(3) COURT AUTHORITY OVER ASSETS–A court described in paragraph (2) may issue a pretrial restraining order or take any other action necessary to ensure that any bank account or other property held by the defendant in the United States is available to satisfy a judgment under this section.

'(4) FEDERAL RECEIVER–

'(A) IN GENERAL–A court described in paragraph (2) may appoint a Federal Receiver, in accordance with subparagraph (B) of this paragraph, to collect, marshal, and take custody, control, and possession of all assets of the defendant, wherever located, to satisfy a civil judgment under this subsection, a forfeiture judgment under section 981 or 982, or a criminal sentence under section 1957 or subsection (a) of this section, including an order of restitution to any victim of a specified unlawful activity.

'(B) APPOINTMENT AND AUTHORITY–A Federal Receiver described in subparagraph (A)—

'(i) may be appointed upon application of a Federal prosecutor or a Federal or State regulator, by the court having jurisdiction over the defendant in the case;

'(ii) shall be an officer of the court, and the powers of the Federal Receiver shall include the powers set out in section 754 of title 28, United States Code; and

'(iii) shall have standing equivalent to that of a Federal prosecutor for the purpose of submitting requests to obtain information regarding the assets of the defendant—

'(I) from the Financial Crimes Enforcement Network of the Department of the Treasury; or

'(II) from a foreign country pursuant to a mutual legal assistance treaty, multilateral agreement, or other arrangement for international law enforcement assistance, provided that such requests are in accordance with the policies and procedures of the Attorney General. ' .

SEC. 318. LAUNDERING MONEY THROUGH A FOREIGN BANK.

Section 1956(c) of title 18, United States Code, is amended by striking paragraph (6) and inserting the following:

'(6) the term 'financial institution' includes—

'(A) any financial institution, as defined in section 5312(a)(2) of title 31, United States Code, or the regulations promulgated thereunder; and

'(B) any foreign bank, as defined in section 1 of the International Banking Act of 1978 (12 U.S.C. 3101). ' .

SEC. 320. PROCEEDS OF FOREIGN CRIMES.

Section 981(a)(1)(B) of title 18, United States Code, is amended to read as follows:

'(B) Any property, real or personal, within the jurisdiction of the United States, constituting, derived from, or traceable to, any proceeds obtained directly or indirectly from an offense against a foreign nation, or any property used to facilitate such an offense, if the offense—

'(i) involves the manufacture, importation, sale, or distribution of a controlled substance (as that term is defined for purposes of the Controlled Substances Act), or any other conduct described in section 1956(c)(7)(B);

'(ii) would be punishable within the jurisdiction of the foreign nation by death or imprisonment for a term exceeding 1 year; and

'(iii) would be punishable under the laws of the United States by imprisonment for a term exceeding 1 year, if the act or activity constituting the offense had occurred within the jurisdiction of the United States. ' .

SEC. 405. REPORT ON THE INTEGRATED AUTOMATED FINGER-PRINT IDENTIFICATION SYSTEM FOR PORTS OF ENTRY AND OVERSEAS CONSULAR POSTS.

(a) IN GENERAL–The Attorney General, in consultation with the appropriate heads of other Federal agencies, including the Secretary of State, Secretary of the Treasury, and the Secretary of Transportation, shall report to Congress on the feasibility of enhancing the Integrated Automated Fingerprint Identification System (IAFIS) of the Federal Bureau of Investigation and other identification systems in order to better identify a person who holds a foreign passport or a visa and may be wanted in connection with a criminal investigation in the United States or abroad, before the issuance of a visa to that person or the entry or exit from the United States by that person.

(b) AUTHORIZATION OF APPROPRIATIONS–There is authorized to be appropriated not less than $2,000,000 to carry out this section.

Subtitle B—Enhanced Immigration Provisions

SEC. 411. DEFINITIONS RELATING TO TERRORISM.

(a) GROUNDS OF INADMISSIBILITY–Section 212(a)(3) of the Immigration and Nationality Act (8 U.S.C. 1182(a)(3)) is amended—

(1) in subparagraph (B)—

(A) in clause (i)—

(i) by amending subclause (IV) to read as follows:

'(IV) is a representative (as defined in clause (v)) of—

'(aa) a foreign terrorist organization, as designated by the Secretary of State under section 219, or

'(bb) a political, social or other similar group whose public endorsement of acts of terrorist activity the Secretary of State has determined undermines United States efforts to reduce or eliminate terrorist activities;';

(ii) in subclause (V), by inserting 'or' after 'section 219, ' ; and

(iii) by adding at the end the following new subclauses:

'(VI) has used the alien's position of prominence within any country to endorse or espouse terrorist activity, or to persuade others to support terrorist activity or a terrorist organization, in a way that the Secretary of State has determined undermines United States efforts to reduce or eliminate terrorist activities, or

'(VII) is the spouse or child of an alien who is inadmissible under this section, if the activity causing the alien to be found inadmissible occurred within the last 5 years,';

(B) by redesignating clauses (ii), (iii), and (iv) as clauses (iii), (iv), and (v), respectively;

(C) in clause (i)(II), by striking 'clause (iii)' and inserting 'clause (iv)';

(D) by inserting after clause (i) the following:

'(ii) EXCEPTION–Subclause (VII) of clause (i) does not apply to a spouse or child—

'(I) who did not know or should not reasonably have known of the activity causing the alien to be found inadmissible under this section; or

'(II) whom the consular officer or Attorney General has reasonable grounds to believe has renounced the activity causing the alien to be found inadmissible under this section.';

(E) in clause (iii) (as redesignated by subparagraph (B))—

(i) by inserting 'it had been' before 'committed in the United States'; and

(ii) in subclause (V)(b), by striking 'or firearm' and inserting ', firearm, or other weapon or dangerous device';

(F) by amending clause (iv) (as redesignated by subparagraph (B)) to read as follows:

'(iv) ENGAGE IN TERRORIST ACTIVITY DEFINED–As used in this chapter, the term 'engage in terrorist activity' means, in an individual capacity or as a member of an organization—

'(I) to commit or to incite to commit, under circumstances indicating an intention to cause death or serious bodily injury, a terrorist activity;

'(II) to prepare or plan a terrorist activity;

'(III) to gather information on potential targets for terrorist activity;

'(IV) to solicit funds or other things of value for—

'(aa) a terrorist activity;

'(bb) a terrorist organization described in clause (vi)(I) or (vi)(II); or

'(cc) a terrorist organization described in clause (vi)(III), unless the solicitor can demonstrate that he did not know, and should not reasonably have known, that the solicitation would further the organization's terrorist activity;

'(V) to solicit any individual—

'(aa) to engage in conduct otherwise described in this clause;

'(bb) for membership in a terrorist organization described in clause (vi)(I) or (vi)(II); or

'(cc) for membership in a terrorist organization described in clause (vi)(III), unless the solicitor can demonstrate that he did not know, and should not reasonably have known, that the solicitation would further the organization's terrorist activity; or

'(VI) to commit an act that the actor knows, or reasonably should know, affords material support, including a safe house, transportation, communications, funds, transfer of funds or other material financial benefit, false documentation or identification, weapons (including chemical, biological, or radiological weapons), explosives, or training—

'(aa) for the commission of a terrorist activity;

'(bb) to any individual who the actor knows, or reasonably should know, has committed or plans to commit a terrorist activity;

'(cc) to a terrorist organization described in clause (vi)(I) or (vi)(II); or

'(dd) to a terrorist organization described in clause (vi)(III), unless the actor can demonstrate that he did not know, and should not reasonably have known, that the act would further the organization's terrorist activity.

This clause shall not apply to any material support the alien afforded to an organization or individual that has committed terrorist activity, if the Secretary of State, after consultation with the Attorney General, or the Attorney General, after consultation with the Secretary of State, concludes in his sole unreviewable discretion, that this clause should not apply.'; and

(G) by adding at the end the following new clause:

'(vi) TERRORIST ORGANIZATION DEFINED–As used in clause (i)(VI) and clause (iv), the term 'terrorist organization' means an organization—

'(I) designated under section 219;

'(II) otherwise designated, upon publication in the Federal Register, by the Secretary of State in consultation with or upon the request of the Attorney General, as a terrorist organization, after finding that the organization engages in the activities described in subclause (I), (II), or (III) of clause (iv), or that the organization provides material support to further terrorist activity; or

'(III) that is a group of two or more individuals, whether organized or not, which engages in the activities described in subclause (I), (II), or (III) of clause (iv).'; and

(2) by adding at the end the following new subparagraph:

'(F) ASSOCIATION WITH TERRORIST ORGANIZATIONS–Any alien who the Secretary of State, after consultation with the Attorney General, or the Attorney General, after consultation with the Secretary of State, determines has been associated with a terrorist organization and intends while in the United States to engage solely, principally, or incidentally in activities that could endanger the welfare, safety, or security of the United States is inadmissible. ' .

(b) CONFORMING AMENDMENTS-

(1) Section 237(a)(4)(B) of the Immigration and Nationality Act (8 U.S.C. 1227(a)(4)(B)) is amended by striking 'section 212(a)(3)(B)(iii)' and inserting 'section 212(a)(3)(B)(iv)'.

(2) Section 208(b)(2)(A)(v) of the Immigration and Nationality Act (8 U.S.C. 1158(b)(2)(A)(v)) is amended by striking 'or (IV)' and inserting '(IV), or (VI)'.

(c) RETROACTIVE APPLICATION OF AMENDMENTS-

(1) IN GENERAL-Except as otherwise provided in this subsection, the amendments made by this section shall take effect on the date of the enactment of this Act and shall apply to—

(A) actions taken by an alien before, on, or after such date; and

(B) all aliens, without regard to the date of entry or attempted entry into the United States—

(i) in removal proceedings on or after such date (except for proceedings in which there has been a final administrative decision before such date); or

(ii) seeking admission to the United States on or after such date.

(2) SPECIAL RULE FOR ALIENS IN EXCLUSION OR DEPORTATION PROCEEDINGS-Notwithstanding any other provision of law, sections 212(a)(3)(B) and 237(a)(4)(B) of the Immigration and Nationality Act, as amended by this Act, shall apply to all aliens in exclusion or deportation proceedings on or after the date of the enactment of this Act (except for proceedings in which there has been a final administrative decision before such date) as if such proceedings were removal proceedings.

(3) SPECIAL RULE FOR SECTION 219 ORGANIZATIONS AND ORGANIZATIONS DESIGNATED UNDER SECTION 212(a)(3)(B)(vi)(II)–

(A) IN GENERAL-Notwithstanding paragraphs (1) and (2), no alien shall be considered inadmissible under section 212(a)(3) of the Immigration and Nationality Act (8 U.S.C. 1182(a)(3)), or deportable under section 237(a)(4)(B) of such Act (8 U.S.C. 1227(a)(4)(B)), by reason of the amendments made by subsection (a), on the ground that the alien engaged in a terrorist activity described in subclause (IV)(bb), (V)(bb), or (VI)(cc) of section 212(a)(3)(B)(iv) of such Act (as so amended) with respect to a group at any time when the group was not a terrorist organization designated by the Secretary of State under section 219 of such Act (8 U.S.C. 1189) or otherwise designated under section 212(a)(3)(B)(vi)(II) of such Act (as so amended).

(B) STATUTORY CONSTRUCTION-Subparagraph (A) shall not be construed to prevent an alien from being considered inadmissible or deportable for having engaged in a terrorist activity—

(i) described in subclause (IV)(bb), (V)(bb), or (VI)(cc) of section 212(a)(3)(B)(iv) of such Act (as so amended) with respect to a terrorist organization at any time when such organization was designated by the Secretary of State under section 219 of such Act or otherwise designated under section 212(a)(3)(B)(vi)(II) of such Act (as so amended); or

(ii) described in subclause (IV)(cc), (V)(cc), or (VI)(dd) of section 212(a)(3)(B)(iv) of such Act (as so amended) with respect to a terrorist organization described in section 212(a)(3)(B)(vi)(III) of such Act (as so amended).

(4) EXCEPTION–The Secretary of State, in consultation with the Attorney General, may determine that the amendments made by this section shall not apply with respect to actions by an alien taken outside the United States before the date of the enactment of this Act upon the recommendation of a consular officer who has concluded that there is not reasonable ground to believe that the alien knew or reasonably should have known that the actions would further a terrorist activity.

(c) DESIGNATION OF FOREIGN TERRORIST ORGANIZATIONS–Section 219(a) of the Immigration and Nationality Act (8 U.S.C. 1189(a)) is amended—

(1) in paragraph (1)(B), by inserting 'or terrorism (as defined in section 140(d)(2) of the Foreign Relations Authorization Act, Fiscal Years 1988 and 1989 (22 U.S.C. 2656f(d)(2)), or retains the capability and intent to engage in terrorist activity or terrorism' after '212(a)(3)(B)';

(2) in paragraph (1)(C), by inserting 'or terrorism' after 'terrorist activity';

(3) by amending paragraph (2)(A) to read as follows:

'(A) NOTICE–

'(i) TO CONGRESSIONAL LEADERS–Seven days before making a designation under this subsection, the Secretary shall, by classified communication, notify the Speaker and Minority Leader of the House of Representatives, the President pro tempore, Majority Leader, and Minority Leader of the Senate, and the members of the relevant committees of the House of Representatives and the Senate, in writing, of the intent to designate an organization under this subsection, together with the findings made under paragraph (1) with respect to that organization, and the factual basis therefor.

'(ii) PUBLICATION IN FEDERAL REGISTER–The Secretary shall publish the designation in the Federal Register seven days after providing the notification under clause (i).';

(4) in paragraph (2)(B)(i), by striking 'subparagraph (A)' and inserting 'subparagraph (A)(ii)';

(5) in paragraph (2)(C), by striking 'paragraph (2)' and inserting 'paragraph (2)(A)(i)';

(6) in paragraph (3)(B), by striking 'subsection (c)' and inserting 'subsection (b)';

(7) in paragraph (4)(B), by inserting after the first sentence the following: 'The Secretary also may redesignate such organization at the end of any 2-year redesignation period (but not sooner than 60 days prior to the termination of such period) for an additional 2-year period upon a finding that the relevant circumstances described in paragraph (1) still exist. Any redesignation shall be effective immediately following the end of the prior 2-year designation or redesignation period unless a different effective date is provided in such redesignation.';

(8) in paragraph (6)(A)—

(A) by inserting 'or a redesignation made under paragraph (4)(B)' after 'paragraph (1)';

(B) in clause (i)—

(i) by inserting 'or redesignation' after 'designation' the first place it appears; and

(ii) by striking 'of the designation'; and

(C) in clause (ii), by striking 'of the designation';

(9) in paragraph (6)(B)—

(A) by striking 'through (4)' and inserting 'and (3)'; and

(B) by inserting at the end the following new sentence: 'Any revocation shall take effect on the date specified in the revocation or upon publication in the Federal Register if no effective date is specified.';

(10) in paragraph (7), by inserting ', or the revocation of a redesignation under paragraph (6),' after 'paragraph (5) or (6)'; and

(11) in paragraph (8)—

(A) by striking 'paragraph (1)(B)' and inserting 'paragraph (2)(B), or if a redesignation under this subsection has become effective under paragraph (4)(B)';

(B) by inserting 'or an alien in a removal proceeding' after 'criminal action'; and

(C) by inserting 'or redesignation' before 'as a defense'.

SEC. 412. MANDATORY DETENTION OF SUSPECTED TERRORISTS; HABEAS CORPUS; JUDICIAL REVIEW.

(a) IN GENERAL–The Immigration and Nationality Act (8 U.S.C. 1101 et seq.) is amended by inserting after section 236 the following:

'MANDATORY DETENTION OF SUSPECTED TERRORISTS; HABEAS CORPUS; JUDICIAL REVIEW

'SEC. 236A. (a) DETENTION OF TERRORIST ALIENS-

'(1) CUSTODY–The Attorney General shall take into custody any alien who is certified under paragraph (3).

'(2) RELEASE–Except as provided in paragraphs (5) and (6), the Attorney General shall maintain custody of such an alien until the alien is removed from the United States. Except as provided in paragraph (6), such custody shall be maintained irrespective of any relief from removal for which the alien may be eligible, or any relief from removal granted the alien, until the Attorney General determines that the alien is no longer an alien who may be certified under paragraph (3). If the alien is finally determined not to be removable, detention pursuant to this subsection shall terminate.

'(3) CERTIFICATION–The Attorney General may certify an alien under this paragraph if the Attorney General has reasonable grounds to believe that the alien—

'(A) is described in section 212(a)(3)(A)(i), 212(a)(3)(A)(iii), 212(a)(3)(B), 237(a)(4)(A)(i), 237(a)(4)(A)(iii), or 237(a)(4)(B); or

'(B) is engaged in any other activity that endangers the national security of the United States.

'(4) NONDELEGATION–The Attorney General may delegate the authority provided under paragraph (3) only to the Deputy Attorney General. The Deputy Attorney General may not delegate such authority.

'(5) COMMENCEMENT OF PROCEEDINGS–The Attorney General shall place an alien detained under paragraph (1) in removal proceedings, or shall charge the alien with a criminal offense, not later than 7 days after the commencement of such detention. If the requirement of the preceding sentence is not satisfied, the Attorney General shall release the alien.

'(6) LIMITATION ON INDEFINITE DETENTION–An alien detained solely under paragraph (1) who has not been removed under section 241(a)(1)(A), and whose removal is unlikely in the reasonably foreseeable future, may be detained for additional periods of up to six months only if the release of the alien will threaten the national security of the United States or the safety of the community or any person.

'(7) REVIEW OF CERTIFICATION–The Attorney General shall review the certification made under paragraph (3) every 6 months. If the Attorney General determines, in the Attorney General's discretion, that the certification should be revoked, the alien may be released on such conditions as the Attorney General deems appropriate, unless such release is otherwise prohibited by law. The alien may request each 6 months in writing that the Attorney General reconsider the certification and may submit documents or other evidence in support of that request.

'(b) HABEAS CORPUS AND JUDICIAL REVIEW-

'(1) IN GENERAL–Judicial review of any action or decision relating to this section (including judicial review of the merits of a determination made under subsection (a)(3) or (a)(6)) is available exclusively in habeas corpus proceedings consistent with this subsection. Except as provided in the preceding sentence, no court shall have jurisdiction to review, by habeas corpus petition or otherwise, any such action or decision.

'(2) APPLICATION-

'(A) IN GENERAL–Notwithstanding any other provision of law, including section 2241(a) of title 28, United States Code, habeas corpus proceedings described in paragraph (1) may be initiated only by an application filed with—

'(i) the Supreme Court;

'(ii) any justice of the Supreme Court;

'(iii) any circuit judge of the United States Court of Appeals for the District of Columbia Circuit; or

'(iv) any district court otherwise having jurisdiction to entertain it.

'(B) APPLICATION TRANSFER–Section 2241(b) of title 28, United States Code, shall apply to an application for a writ of habeas corpus described in subparagraph (A).

'(3) APPEALS–Notwithstanding any other provision of law, including section 2253 of title 28, in habeas corpus proceedings described in paragraph (1) before a circuit or district judge, the final order shall be subject to review, on appeal, by the United States Court of Appeals for the District of Columbia Circuit. There shall be no right of appeal in such proceedings to any other circuit court of appeals.

'(4) RULE OF DECISION–The law applied by the Supreme Court and the United States Court of Appeals for the District of Columbia Circuit shall be regarded as the rule of decision in habeas corpus proceedings described in paragraph (1).

'(c) STATUTORY CONSTRUCTION–The provisions of this section shall not be applicable to any other provision of this Act. ' .

(b) CLERICAL AMENDMENT–The table of contents of the Immigration and Nationality Act is amended by inserting after the item relating to section 236 the following:

'Sec. 236A. Mandatory detention of suspected terrorist; habeas corpus; judicial review. ' .

(c) REPORTS–Not later than 6 months after the date of the enactment of this Act, and every 6 months thereafter, the Attorney General shall submit a report to the Committee on the Judiciary of the House of Representatives and the Committee on the Judiciary of the Senate, with respect to the reporting period, on—

(1) the number of aliens certified under section 236A(a)(3) of the Immigration and Nationality Act, as added by subsection (a);

(2) the grounds for such certifications;

(3) the nationalities of the aliens so certified;

(4) the length of the detention for each alien so certified; and

(5) the number of aliens so certified who—

(A) were granted any form of relief from removal;

(B) were removed;

(C) the Attorney General has determined are no longer aliens who may be so certified; or

(D) were released from detention.

SEC. 413. MULTILATERAL COOPERATION AGAINST TERRORISTS.

Section 222(f) of the Immigration and Nationality Act (8 U.S.C. 1202(f)) is amended—

(1) by striking 'except that in the discretion of' and inserting the following: 'except that—

'(1) in the discretion of'; and

(2) by adding at the end the following:

'(2) the Secretary of State, in the Secretary's discretion and on the basis of reciprocity, may provide to a foreign government information in the Department of State's computerized visa lookout database and, when necessary and appropriate, other records covered by this section related to information in the database—

'(A) with regard to individual aliens, at any time on a case-by-case basis for the purpose of preventing, investigating, or punishing acts that would constitute a crime in the United States, including, but not limited to, terrorism or trafficking in controlled substances, persons, or illicit weapons; or

'(B) with regard to any or all aliens in the database, pursuant to such conditions as the Secretary of State shall establish in an agreement with the foreign government in which that government agrees to use such information and records for the purposes described in subparagraph (A) or to deny visas to persons who would be inadmissible to the United States. ' .

SEC. 414. VISA INTEGRITY AND SECURITY.

(a) SENSE OF CONGRESS REGARDING THE NEED TO EXPEDITE IMPLEMENTATION OF INTEGRATED ENTRY AND EXIT DATA SYSTEM-

(1) SENSE OF CONGRESS–In light of the terrorist attacks perpetrated against the United States on September 11, 2001, it is the sense of the Congress that—

(A) the Attorney General, in consultation with the Secretary of State, should fully implement the integrated entry and exit data system for airports, seaports, and land border ports of entry, as specified in section 110 of the Illegal Immigration Reform and Immigrant Responsibility Act of 1996 (8 U.S.C. 1365a), with all deliberate speed and as expeditiously as practicable; and

(B) the Attorney General, in consultation with the Secretary of State, the Secretary of Commerce, the Secretary of the Treasury, and the Office of Homeland Security, should immediately begin establishing the Integrated Entry and Exit Data System Task Force, as described in section 3 of the Immigration and Naturalization Service Data Management Improvement Act of 2000 (Public Law 106-215).

(2) AUTHORIZATION OF APPROPRIATIONS–There is authorized to be appropriated such sums as may be necessary to fully implement the system described in paragraph (1)(A).

(b) DEVELOPMENT OF THE SYSTEM–In the development of the integrated entry and exit data system under section 110 of the Illegal Immigration Reform and Immigrant Responsibility Act of 1996 (8 U.S.C. 1365a), the Attorney

General and the Secretary of State shall particularly focus on—

(1) the utilization of biometric technology; and

(2) the development of tamper-resistant documents readable at ports of entry.

(c) INTERFACE WITH LAW ENFORCEMENT DATABASES–The entry and exit data system described in this section shall be able to interface with law enforcement databases for use by Federal law enforcement to identify and detain individuals who pose a threat to the national security of the United States.

(d) REPORT ON SCREENING INFORMATION–Not later than 12 months after the date of enactment of this Act, the Office of Homeland Security shall submit a report to Congress on the information that is needed from any United States agency to effectively screen visa applicants and applicants for admission to the United States to identify those affiliated with terrorist organizations or those that pose any threat to the safety or security of the United States, including the type of information currently received by United States agencies and the regularity with which such information is transmitted to the Secretary of State and the Attorney General.

SEC. 415. PARTICIPATION OF OFFICE OF HOMELAND SECURITY ON ENTRY-EXIT TASK FORCE.

Section 3 of the Immigration and Naturalization Service Data Management Improvement Act of 2000 (Public Law 106-215) is amended by striking 'and the Secretary of the Treasury,' and inserting 'the Secretary of the Treasury, and the Office of Homeland Security'.

SEC. 416. FOREIGN STUDENT MONITORING PROGRAM.

(a) FULL IMPLEMENTATION AND EXPANSION OF FOREIGN STUDENT VISA MONITORING PROGRAM REQUIRED–The Attorney General, in consultation with the Secretary of State, shall fully implement and expand the program established by section 641(a) of the Illegal Immigration Reform and Immigrant Responsibility Act of 1996 (8 U.S.C. 1372(a)).

(b) INTEGRATION WITH PORT OF ENTRY INFORMATION–For each alien with respect to whom information is collected under section 641 of the Illegal Immigration Reform and Immigrant Responsibility Act of 1996 (8 U.S.C. 1372), the Attorney General, in consultation with the Secretary of State, shall include information on the date of entry and port of entry.

(c) EXPANSION OF SYSTEM TO INCLUDE OTHER APPROVED EDUCATIONAL INSTITUTIONS–Section 641 of the Illegal Immigration Reform and Immigrant Responsibility Act of 1996 (8 U.S.C.1372) is amended—

(1) in subsection (a)(1), subsection (c)(4)(A), and subsection (d)(1) (in the text above subparagraph (A)), by inserting ', other approved educational institutions,' after 'higher education' each place it appears;

(2) in subsections (c)(1)(C), (c)(1)(D), and (d)(1)(A), by inserting ', or other approved educational institution,' after 'higher education' each place it appears;

(3) in subsections (d)(2), (e)(1), and (e)(2), by inserting ', other approved educational institution,' after 'higher education' each place it appears; and

(4) in subsection (h), by adding at the end the following new paragraph:

'(3) OTHER APPROVED EDUCATIONAL INSTITUTION–The term 'other approved educational institution' includes any air flight school, language training school, or vocational school, approved by the Attorney General, in consultation with the Secretary of Education and the Secretary of State, under subparagraph (F), (J), or (M) of section 101(a)(15) of the Immigration and Nationality Act. ' .

'd) AUTHORIZATION OF APPROPRIATIONS–There is authorized to be appropriated to the Department of Justice $36,800,000 for the period beginning on the date of enactment of this Act and ending on January 1, 2003, to fully implement and expand prior to January 1, 2003, the program established by section 641(a) of the Illegal Immigration Reform and Immigrant Responsibility Act of 1996 (8 U.S.C. 1372(a)).

SEC. 503. DNA IDENTIFICATION OF TERRORISTS AND OTHER VIOLENT OFFENDERS.

Section 3(d)(2) of the DNA Analysis Backlog Elimination Act of 2000 (42 U.S.C. 14135a(d)(2)) is amended to read as follows:

'(2) In addition to the offenses described in paragraph (1), the following offenses shall be treated for purposes of this section as qualifying Federal offenses, as determined by the Attorney General:

'(A) Any offense listed in section 2332b(g)(5)(B) of title 18, United States Code.

'(B) Any crime of violence (as defined in section 16 of title 18, United States Code).

'(C) Any attempt or conspiracy to commit any of the above offenses. ' .

SEC. 504. COORDINATION WITH LAW ENFORCEMENT.

(a) INFORMATION ACQUIRED FROM AN ELECTRONIC SURVEILLANCE–Section 106 of the Foreign Intelligence Surveillance Act of 1978 (50 U.S.C. 1806), is amended by adding at the end the following:

'(k)(1) Federal officers who conduct electronic surveillance to acquire foreign intelligence information under this title may consult with Federal law enforcement officers to coordinate efforts to investigate or protect against—

'(A) actual or potential attack or other grave hostile acts of a foreign power or an agent of a foreign power;

'(B) sabotage or international terrorism by a foreign power or an agent of a foreign power; or

'(C) clandestine intelligence activities by an intelligence service or network of a foreign power or by an agent of a foreign power.

'(2) Coordination authorized under paragraph (1) shall not preclude the certification required by section 104(a)(7)(B) or the entry of an order under section 105. ' .

(b) INFORMATION ACQUIRED FROM A PHYSICAL SEARCH–Section 305 of the Foreign Intelligence Surveillance Act of 1978 (50 U.S.C. 1825) is amended by adding at the end the following:

'(k)(1) Federal officers who conduct physical searches to acquire foreign intelligence information under this title may consult with Federal law enforcement officers to coordinate efforts to investigate or protect against—

'(A) actual or potential attack or other grave hostile acts of a foreign power or an agent of a foreign power;

'(B) sabotage or international terrorism by a foreign power or an agent of a foreign power; or

'(C) clandestine intelligence activities by an intelligence service or network of a foreign power or by an agent of a foreign power.

'(2) Coordination authorized under paragraph (1) shall not preclude the certification required by section 303(a)(7) or the entry of an order under section 304. '.

SEC. 506. EXTENSION OF SECRET SERVICE JURISDICTION.

(a) Concurrent Jurisdiction Under 18 U.S.C. 1030–Section 1030(d) of title 18, United States Code, is amended to read as follows:

'(d)(1) The United States Secret Service shall, in addition to any other agency having such authority, have the authority to investigate offenses under this section.

'(2) The Federal Bureau of Investigation shall have primary authority to investigate offenses under subsection (a)(1) for any cases involving espionage, foreign counterintelligence, information protected against unauthorized disclosure for reasons of national defense or foreign relations, or Restricted Data (as that term is defined in section 11y of the Atomic Energy Act of 1954 (42 U.S.C. 2014(y)), except for offenses affecting the duties of the United States Secret Service pursuant to section 3056(a) of this title.

'(3) Such authority shall be exercised in accordance with an agreement which shall be entered into by the Secretary of the Treasury and the Attorney General. '.

(b) Reauthorization of Jurisdiction under 18 U.S.C. 1344–Section 3056(b)(3) of title 18, United States Code, is amended by striking 'credit and debit card frauds, and false identification documents or devices' and inserting 'access device frauds, false identification documents or devices, and any fraud or other criminal or unlawful activity in or against any federally insured financial institution'.

SEC. 507. DISCLOSURE OF EDUCATIONAL RECORDS.

Section 444 of the General Education Provisions Act (20 U.S.C. 1232g), is amended by adding after subsection (i) a new subsection (j) to read as follows:

'(j) INVESTIGATION AND PROSECUTION OF TERRORISM-

'(1) IN GENERAL–Notwithstanding subsections (a) through (i) or any provision of State law, the Attorney General (or any Federal officer or employee, in a position not lower than an Assistant Attorney General, designated by the Attorney General) may submit a written application to a court of competent jurisdiction for an ex parte order requiring an educational agency or institution to permit the Attorney General (or his designee) to—

'(A) collect education records in the possession of the educational agency or institution that are relevant to an authorized investigation or prosecution of an offense listed in section 2332b(g)(5)(B) of title 18 United States

Code, or an act of domestic or international terrorism as defined in section 2331 of that title; and

'(B) for official purposes related to the investigation or prosecution of an offense described in paragraph (1)(A), retain, disseminate, and use (including as evidence at trial or in other administrative or judicial proceedings) such records, consistent with such guidelines as the Attorney General, after consultation with the Secretary, shall issue to protect confidentiality.

TITLE VII—INCREASED INFORMATION SHARING FOR CRITICAL INFRASTRUCTURE PROTECTION

SEC. 701. EXPANSION OF REGIONAL INFORMATION SHARING SYSTEM TO FACILITATE FEDERAL-STATE-LOCAL LAW ENFORCEMENT RESPONSE RELATED TO TERRORIST ATTACKS.

Section 1301 of title I of the Omnibus Crime Control and Safe Streets Act of 1968 (42 U.S.C. 3796h) is amended—

(1) in subsection (a), by inserting 'and terrorist conspiracies and activities' after 'activities';

(2) in subsection (b)—

(A) in paragraph (3), by striking 'and' after the semicolon;

(B) by redesignating paragraph (4) as paragraph (5);

(C) by inserting after paragraph (3) the following:

'(4) establishing and operating secure information sharing systems to enhance the investigation and prosecution abilities of participating enforcement agencies in addressing multi-jurisdictional terrorist conspiracies and activities; and (5)'; and

(3) by inserting at the end the following:

'(d) AUTHORIZATION OF APPROPRIATION TO THE BUREAU OF JUSTICE ASSISTANCE–There are authorized to be appropriated to the Bureau of Justice Assistance to carry out this section $50,000,000 for fiscal year 2002 and $100,000,000 for fiscal year 2003. '.

TITLE VIII—STRENGTHENING THE CRIMINAL LAWS AGAINST TERRORISM

SEC. 801. TERRORIST ATTACKS AND OTHER ACTS OF VIOLENCE AGAINST MASS TRANSPORTATION SYSTEMS.

Chapter 97 of title 18, United States Code, is amended by adding at the end the following:

'Sec. 1993. Terrorist attacks and other acts of violence against mass transportation systems

'(a) GENERAL PROHIBITIONS–Whoever willfully—

'(1) wrecks, derails, sets fire to, or disables a mass transportation vehicle or ferry;

'(2) places or causes to be placed any biological agent or toxin for use as a weapon, destructive substance, or destructive device in, upon, or near a mass transportation vehicle or ferry, without previously obtaining the permission of the mass transportation provider, and with intent to endanger the safety of any passenger or employee of the mass transportation provider, or with a reckless disregard for the safety of human life;

'(3) sets fire to, or places any biological agent or toxin for use as a weapon, destructive substance, or destructive device in, upon, or near any garage, terminal, structure, supply, or facility used in the operation of, or in support of the operation of, a mass transportation vehicle or ferry, without previously obtaining the permission of the mass transportation provider, and knowing or having reason to know such activity would likely derail, disable, or wreck a mass transportation vehicle or ferry used, operated, or employed by the mass transportation provider;

'(4) removes appurtenances from, damages, or otherwise impairs the operation of a mass transportation signal system, including a train control system, centralized dispatching system, or rail grade crossing warning signal without authorization from the mass transportation provider;

'(5) interferes with, disables, or incapacitates any dispatcher, driver, captain, or person while they are employed in dispatching, operating, or maintaining a mass transportation vehicle or ferry, with intent to endanger the safety of any passenger or employee of the mass transportation provider, or with a reckless disregard for the safety of human life;

'(6) commits an act, including the use of a dangerous weapon, with the intent to cause death or serious bodily injury to an employee or passenger of a mass transportation provider or any other person while any of the foregoing are on the property of a mass transportation provider;

'(7) conveys or causes to be conveyed false information, knowing the information to be false, concerning an attempt or alleged attempt being made or to be made, to do any act which would be a crime prohibited by this subsection; or

'(8) attempts, threatens, or conspires to do any of the aforesaid acts,

shall be fined under this title or imprisoned not more than twenty years, or both, if such act is committed, or in the case of a threat or conspiracy such act would be committed, on, against, or affecting a mass transportation provider engaged in or affecting interstate or foreign commerce, or if in the course of committing such act, that person travels or communicates across a State line in order to commit such act, or transports materials across a State line in aid of the commission of such act.

'(b) AGGRAVATED OFFENSE–Whoever commits an offense under subsection (a) in a circumstance in which—

'(1) the mass transportation vehicle or ferry was carrying a passenger at the time of the offense; or

'(2) the offense has resulted in the death of any person,

shall be guilty of an aggravated form of the offense and shall be fined under this title or imprisoned for a term of years or for life, or both.

'(c) DEFINITIONS–In this section—

'(1) the term 'biological agent' has the meaning given to that term in section 178(1) of this title;

'(2) the term 'dangerous weapon' has the meaning given to that term in section 930 of this title;

'(3) the term 'destructive device' has the meaning given to that term in section 921(a)(4) of this title;

'(4) the term 'destructive substance' has the meaning given to that term in section 31 of this title;

'(5) the term 'mass transportation' has the meaning given to that term in section 5302(a)(7) of title 49, United States Code, except that the term shall include schoolbus, charter, and sightseeing transportation;

'(6) the term 'serious bodily injury' has the meaning given to that term in section 1365 of this title;

'(7) the term 'State' has the meaning given to that term in section 2266 of this title; and

'(8) the term 'toxin' has the meaning given to that term in section 178(2) of this title. ' .

(f) CONFORMING AMENDMENT–The analysis of chapter 97 of title 18, United States Code, is amended by adding at the end:

'1993. Terrorist attacks and other acts of violence against mass transportation systems. ' .

SEC. 802. DEFINITION OF DOMESTIC TERRORISM.

(a) DOMESTIC TERRORISM DEFINED–Section 2331 of title 18, United States Code, is amended—

(1) in paragraph (1)(B)(iii), by striking 'by assassination or kidnapping' and inserting 'by mass destruction, assassination, or kidnapping';

(2) in paragraph (3), by striking 'and';

(3) in paragraph (4), by striking the period at the end and inserting '; and'; and

(4) by adding at the end the following:

'(5) the term 'domestic terrorism' means activities that—

'(A) involve acts dangerous to human life that are a violation of the criminal laws of the United States or of any State;

'(B) appear to be intended—

'(i) to intimidate or coerce a civilian population;

'(ii) to influence the policy of a government by intimidation or coercion; or

'(iii) to affect the conduct of a government by mass destruction, assassination, or kidnapping; and

'(C) occur primarily within the territorial jurisdiction of the United States. ' .

(b) CONFORMING AMENDMENT–Section 3077(1) of title 18, United States Code, is amended to read as follows:

'(1) 'act of terrorism' means an act of domestic or international terrorism as defined in section 2331;'.

SEC. 803. PROHIBITION AGAINST HARBORING TERRORISTS.

(a) IN GENERAL–Chapter 113B of title 18, United States Code, is amended by adding after section 2338 the following new section:

'Sec. 2339. Harboring or concealing terrorists

'(a) Whoever harbors or conceals any person who he knows, or has reasonable grounds to believe, has committed, or is about to commit, an offense under section 32 (relating to destruction of aircraft or aircraft facilities), section 175 (relating to biological weapons), section 229 (relating to chemical weapons), section 831 (relating to nuclear materials), paragraph (2) or (3) of section 844(f) (relating to arson and bombing of government property risking or causing injury or death), section 1366(a) (relating to the destruction of an energy facility), section 2280 (relating to violence against maritime navigation), section 2332a (relating to weapons of mass destruction), or section 2332b (relating to acts of terrorism transcending national boundaries) of this title, section 236(a) (relating to sabotage of nuclear facilities or fuel) of the Atomic Energy Act of 1954 (42 U.S.C. 2284(a)), or section 46502 (relating to aircraft piracy) of title 49, shall be fined under this title or imprisoned not more than ten years, or both. ' .

'(b) A violation of this section may be prosecuted in any Federal judicial district in which the underlying offense was committed, or in any other Federal judicial district as provided by law. ' .

(b) TECHNICAL AMENDMENT–The chapter analysis for chapter 113B of title 18, United States Code, is amended by inserting after the item for section 2338 the following:

'2339. Harboring or concealing terrorists. ' .

SEC. 806. ASSETS OF TERRORIST ORGANIZATIONS.

Section 981(a)(1) of title 18, United States Code, is amended by inserting at the end the following:

'(G) All assets, foreign or domestic—

'(i) of any individual, entity, or organization engaged in planning or perpetrating any act of domestic or international terrorism (as defined in section 2331) against the United States, citizens or residents of the United States, or their property, and all assets, foreign or domestic, affording any person a source of influence over any such entity or organization;

'(ii) acquired or maintained by any person with the intent and for the purpose of supporting, planning, conducting, or concealing an act of domestic or international terrorism (as defined in section 2331) against the United States, citizens or residents of the United States, or their property; or

'(iii) derived from, involved in, or used or intended to be used to commit any act of domestic or international terrorism (as defined in section 2331) against the United States, citizens or residents of the United States, or their property. ' .

SEC. 807. TECHNICAL CLARIFICATION RELATING TO PROVISION OF MATERIAL SUPPORT TO TERRORISM.

No provision of the Trade Sanctions Reform and Export Enhancement Act of 2000 (title IX of Public Law 106-387) shall be construed to limit or otherwise affect section 2339A or 2339B of title 18, United States Code.

SEC. 808. DEFINITION OF FEDERAL CRIME OF TERRORISM.

Section 2332b of title 18, United States Code, is amended—

(1) in subsection (f), by inserting 'and any violation of section 351(e), 844(e), 844(f)(1), 956(b), 1361, 1366(b), 1366(c), 1751(e), 2152, or 2156 of this title,' before 'and the Secretary'; and

(2) in subsection (g)(5)(B), by striking clauses (i) through (iii) and inserting the following:

'(i) section 32 (relating to destruction of aircraft or aircraft facilities), 37 (relating to violence at international airports), 81 (relating to arson within special maritime and territorial jurisdiction), 175 or 175b (relating to biological weapons), 229 (relating to chemical weapons), subsection (a), (b), (c), or (d) of section 351 (relating to congressional, cabinet, and Supreme Court assassination and kidnaping), 831 (relating to nuclear materials), 842(m) or (n) (relating to plastic explosives), 844(f)(2) or (3) (relating to arson and bombing of Government property risking or causing death), 844(i) (relating to arson and bombing of property used in interstate commerce), 930(c) (relating to killing or attempted killing during an attack on a Federal facility with a dangerous weapon), 956(a)(1) (relating to conspiracy to murder, kidnap, or maim persons abroad), 1030(a)(1) (relating to protection of computers), 1030(a)(5)(A)(i) resulting in damage as defined in 1030(a)(5)(B)(ii) through (v) (relating to protection of computers), 1114 (relating to killing or attempted killing of officers and employees of the United States), 1116 (relating to murder or manslaughter of foreign officials, official guests, or internationally protected persons), 1203 (relating to hostage taking), 1362 (relating to destruction of communication lines, stations, or systems), 1363 (relating to injury to buildings or property within special maritime and territorial jurisdiction of the United States), 1366(a) (relating to destruction of an energy facility), 1751(a), (b), (c), or (d) (relating to Presidential and Presidential staff assassination and kidnaping), 1992 (relating to wrecking trains), 1993 (relating to terrorist attacks and other acts of violence against mass transportation systems), 2155 (relating to destruction of national defense materials, premises, or utilities), 2280 (relating to violence against maritime navigation), 2281 (relating to violence against maritime fixed platforms), 2332 (relating to certain homicides and other violence against United States nationals occurring outside of the United States), 2332a (relating to use of weapons of mass destruction), 2332b (relating to acts of terrorism transcending national boundaries), 2339 (relating to harboring terrorists), 2339A (relating to providing material support to terrorists), 2339B (relating to providing material support to terrorist organizations), or 2340A (relating to torture) of this title;

'(ii) section 236 (relating to sabotage of nuclear facilities or fuel) of the Atomic Energy Act of 1954 (42 U.S.C. 2284); or

'(iii) section 46502 (relating to aircraft piracy), the second sentence of section 46504 (relating to assault on a flight crew with a dangerous weapon), section 46505(b)(3) or (c) (relating to explosive or incendiary devices, or endangerment of human life by means of weapons, on aircraft), section 46506 if homicide or attempted homicide is involved (relating to application of certain criminal laws to acts on aircraft), or section 60123(b) (relating to destruction of interstate gas or hazardous liquid pipeline facility) of title 49. ' .

SEC. 809. NO STATUTE OF LIMITATION FOR CERTAIN TERRORISM OFFENSES.

(a) IN GENERAL–Section 3286 of title 18, United States Code, is amended to read as follows:

'Sec. 3286. Extension of statute of limitation for certain terrorism offenses

'(a) EIGHT-YEAR LIMITATION–Notwithstanding section 3282, no person shall be prosecuted, tried, or punished for any noncapital offense involving a violation of any provision listed in section 2332b(g)(5)(B), or a violation of section 112, 351(e), 1361, or 1751(e) of this title, or section 46504, 46505, or 46506 of title 49, unless the indictment is found or the information is instituted within 8 years after the offense was committed. Notwithstanding the preceding sentence, offenses listed in section 3295 are subject to the statute of limitations set forth in that section.

'(b) NO LIMITATION–Notwithstanding any other law, an indictment may be found or an information instituted at any time without limitation for any offense listed in section 2332b(g)(5)(B), if the commission of such offense resulted in, or created a forseeable risk of, death or serious bodily injury to another person. ' .

(b) APPLICATION–The amendments made by this section shall apply to the prosecution of any offense committed before, on, or after the date of the enactment of this section.

'DISCLOSURE OF FOREIGN INTELLIGENCE ACQUIRED IN CRIMINAL INVESTIGATIONS; NOTICE OF CRIMINAL INVESTIGATIONS OF FOREIGN INTELLIGENCE SOURCES

'SEC. 105B. (a) DISCLOSURE OF FOREIGN INTELLIGENCE–(1) Except as otherwise provided by law and subject to paragraph (2), the Attorney General, or the head of any other department or agency of the Federal Government with law enforcement responsibilities, shall expeditiously disclose to the Director of Central Intelligence, pursuant to guidelines developed by the Attorney General in consultation with the Director, foreign intelligence acquired by an element of the Department of Justice or an element of such department or agency, as the case may be, in the course of a criminal investigation.

'(2) The Attorney General by regulation and in consultation with the Director of Central Intelligence may provide for exceptions to the applicability of paragraph (1) for one or more classes of foreign intelligence, or foreign intelligence with respect to one or more targets or matters, if the Attorney General determines that disclosure of such foreign intelligence under that paragraph would jeopardize an ongoing law enforcement investigation or impair other significant law enforcement interests.

'(b) PROCEDURES FOR NOTICE OF CRIMINAL INVESTIGATIONS–Not later than 180 days after the date of enactment of this section, the Attorney General, in consultation with the Director of Central Intelligence, shall develop guidelines to ensure that after receipt of a report from an element of the intelligence community of activity of a foreign intelligence source or potential foreign intelligence source that may warrant investigation as criminal activity, the Attorney General provides notice to the Director of Central Intelligence, within a reasonable period of time, of his intention to commence, or decline to commence, a criminal investigation of such activity.

'(c) PROCEDURES–The Attorney General shall develop procedures for the administration of this section, including the disclosure of foreign intelligence by elements of the Department of Justice, and elements of other departments and agencies of the Federal Government, under subsection (a) and the provision of notice with respect to criminal investigations under subsection (b). ' .

(b) CLERICAL AMENDMENT–The table of contents in the first section of that Act is amended by striking the item relating to section 105B and inserting the following new items:

'Sec. 105B. Disclosure of foreign intelligence acquired in criminal investigations; notice of criminal investigations of foreign intelligence sources.

'Sec. 105C. Protection of the operational files of the National Imagery and Mapping Agency. ' .

SEC. 906. FOREIGN TERRORIST ASSET TRACKING CENTER.

(a) REPORT ON RECONFIGURATION–Not later than February 1, 2002, the Attorney General, the Director of Central Intelligence, and the Secretary of the Treasury shall jointly submit to Congress a report on the feasibility and desirability of reconfiguring the Foreign Terrorist Asset Tracking Center and the Office of Foreign Assets Control of the Department of the Treasury in order to establish a capability to provide for the effective and efficient analysis and dissemination of foreign intelligence relating to the financial capabilities and resources of international terrorist organizations.

(b) REPORT REQUIREMENTS–(1) In preparing the report under subsection (a), the Attorney General, the Secretary, and the Director shall consider whether, and to what extent, the capacities and resources of the Financial Crimes Enforcement Center of the Department of the Treasury may be integrated into the capability contemplated by the report.

(2) If the Attorney General, Secretary, and the Director determine that it is feasible and desirable to undertake the reconfiguration described in subsection (a) in order to establish the capability described in that subsection, the Attorney General, the Secretary, and the Director shall include with the report under that subsection a detailed proposal for legislation to achieve the reconfiguration.

SEC. 907. NATIONAL VIRTUAL TRANSLATION CENTER.

(a) REPORT ON ESTABLISHMENT–(1) Not later than February 1, 2002, the Director of Central Intelligence shall, in consultation with the Director of the Federal Bureau of Investigation, submit to the appropriate committees of Congress a report on the establishment and maintenance within the intelligence community of an element for purposes of providing timely and accurate translations of foreign intelligence for all other elements of the intelligence community. In the report, the element shall be referred to as the 'National Virtual Translation Center'.

(2) The report on the element described in paragraph (1) shall discuss the use of state-of-the-art communications technology, the integration of existing translation capabilities in the intelligence community, and the utilization of remote-connection capacities so as to minimize the need for a central physical facility for the element.

(b) RESOURCES–The report on the element required by subsection (a) shall address the following:

(1) The assignment to the element of a staff of individuals possessing a broad range of linguistic and translation skills appropriate for the purposes of the element.

(2) The provision to the element of communications capabilities and systems that are commensurate with the most current and sophisticated communications capabilities and systems available to other elements of intelligence community.

(3) The assurance, to the maximum extent practicable, that the communications capabilities and systems provided to the element will be compatible with communications capabilities and systems utilized by the Federal Bureau of Investigation in securing timely and accurate translations of foreign language materials for law enforcement investigations.

(4) The development of a communications infrastructure to ensure the efficient and secure use of the translation capabilities of the element.

(c) SECURE COMMUNICATIONS–The report shall include a discussion of the creation of secure electronic communications between the element described by subsection (a) and the other elements of the intelligence community.

(d) DEFINITIONS–In this section:

(1) FOREIGN INTELLIGENCE–The term 'foreign intelligence' has the meaning given that term in section 3(2) of the National Security Act of 1947 (50 U.S.C. 401a(2)).

(2) ELEMENT OF THE INTELLIGENCE COMMUNITY–The term 'element of the intelligence community' means any element of the intelligence community specified or designated under section 3(4) of the National Security Act of 1947 (50 U.S.C. 401a(4)).

SEC. 908. TRAINING OF GOVERNMENT OFFICIALS REGARDING IDENTIFICATION AND USE OF FOREIGN INTELLIGENCE.

(a) PROGRAM REQUIRED–The Attorney General shall, in consultation with the Director of Central Intelligence, carry out a program to provide appropriate training to officials described in subsection (b) in order to assist such officials in—

(1) identifying foreign intelligence information in the course of their duties; and

(2) utilizing foreign intelligence information in the course of their duties, to the extent that the utilization of such information is appropriate for such duties.

(b) OFFICIALS–The officials provided training under subsection (a) are, at the discretion of the Attorney General and the Director, the following:

(1) Officials of the Federal Government who are not ordinarily engaged in the collection, dissemination, and use of foreign intelligence in the performance of their duties.

(2) Officials of State and local governments who encounter, or may encounter in the course of a terrorist event, foreign intelligence in the performance of their duties.

(c) AUTHORIZATION OF APPROPRIATIONS–There is hereby authorized to be appropriated for the Department of Justice such sums as may be necessary for purposes of carrying out the program required by subsection (a).

Glossary

311 system (p. 328) due to the many demands on the 911 emergency phone lines for reasons outside of the responsibility of the police, many municipalities have implemented 311 systems for all calls that do not require an emergency response.

911 system (p. 327) the implementation of 911 systems, in which citizens could call in incidents requiring immediate response, not only revolutionized citizen access to police service, but also created many conflicting demands.

actual damages (p. 103) in a civil lawsuit, actual damages refer to a verdict in which the plaintiff receives monetary compensation for the actual losses (e.g., wages, property damage, etc.) resulting from the defendant's actions.

actus reus (p. 99) an essential element in a criminal case, *actus reus* refers to the commission (or omission of duty) of the act that is prohibited by law.

administrative liability (p. 103) the legal responsibility of an organization or agency (e.g., police department) for the actions of its members. Examples of areas that can bring about administrative liability include inadequate training, unclear policies, etc.

administrative unit (p. 123) large police departments in the United States are typically divided into two parts: field services and administration. The administrative unit handles all the support functions for the smooth operation of the department. Examples of administrative functions include: human resources, training, research and planning, and internal affairs.

Advanced Generation of Interoperability for Law Enforcement (AGILE) (p. 345) AGILE is a prototype system designed to improve the communication across law enforcement and other criminal justice agencies within a jurisdiction.

affirmative action (pp. 256, 365) a policy of law enforcement or other agencies to correct a history of imbalances in the hiring of personnel through the creation of specific policies or quotas to guide future hiring. Affirmative action policies typically exist on the basis of race or gender, but can include other demographic concerns as well.

agent provocateur (p. 129) a law enforcement officer that has crossed the line between entrapment and encouragement in undercover operations, possibly planting the initial idea for the criminal action in the mind of the accused.

aggressive patrol (pp. 149, 247) similar to directed patrol, aggressive patrol involves the targeting of specific locations, times, and offenders. Aggressive patrol involves the zero tolerance enforcement of selected activities within the defined target area. Also referred to as **aggressive patrolling.**

alternative sanction (p. 29) within criminal justice, many alternative sanctions exist in lieu of the more traditional punishment. Alternative sanctions can include such punishments as community service, fines, or even diversion responses.

analysis (p. 308) the heart of the SARA problem-solving model, in analysis an examination of the underlying causes of a particular problem are examined prior to the selection of a response.

arraignment (p. 27) an early stage in the criminal justice process, in which the offender is brought before a judge for the first time, read the formal charges against him or her, and asked to submit a plea to the court. In some jurisdictions a first appearance before the court to hear the charges can occur prior to the arraignment, while in others the two are merged into one appearance.

arrest (p. 26, 179) the formal taking into custody of an individual upon the establishment of probable cause for the commission of a criminal act.

asocial offender (p. 203) often referred to as a schizoid or withdrawn personality type, according to the FBI's disorganized/organized typology for criminal profiling, this type of offender will often commit spontaneous acts with little regard for the amount of physical evidence left behind capable of incriminating him or her.

assessment (p. 309) the final stage of the SARA problem solving model, assessment is the evaluation of whether or not the selected response achieved the desired outcomes of reducing or eliminating the problem.

assigned shifts (p. 155) the permanent assignment of officers to a specific geographical area and time of day. Assigned shifts are much more common today, and considered an essential ingredient of community policing operations.

associative evidence (p. 200) all evidence used to demonstrate the linkages between offender, victim, and location necessary for the successful prosecution of a crime.

authoritarian (p. 223) a debate often heard within the policing research literature is related to the extent to which police officers have an authoritarian personality type involving higher levels of conservatism, cynicism, and need for power or control. Even among those researchers that believe in the existence of the authoritarian personality type in policing, there is significant debate as to whether or not officers enter the profession with these characteristics, or they are a product of the career socialization process.

automated fingerprint identification system (AFIS) (p. 207) automated computer systems that allow for the comparison of latent fingerprints found at a crime scene to a digitized database of stored fingerprints of known offenders. AFIS has revolutionized the speed and accuracy of fingerprint analysis from the days involving the manual matching of stored paper cards.

Automated Regional Information System (ARJIS) (p. 345) ARJIS is a database that facilitates the sharing of information among San Diego and neighboring criminal justice agencies.

automatic vehicle monitoring (AVM) (p. 347) created to enhance officer safety as well as accountability, AVM systems allow for the tracking of patrol vehicles in a jurisdiction, as well as such factors as whether or not a car door has been left open, etc.

bail (p. 96) allows for the release of a defendant from criminal justice custody while awaiting trial in order to be better able to prepare a defense and minimize interruption in the offender's life prior to the establishment of guilt. Bail can exist in many forms (e.g., ROR, credit, etc.) but is designed to ensure the reappearance of the defendant in court. According to the Supreme Court, the withholding of bail can be based on public safety concerns, but cannot be used as a form of punishment.

behavioral evidence (p. 200) the actions of an offender at the scene of the crime or during the post-crime period of interrogation and trial that can aid in the establishment of guilt. The observation of behavioral evidence is a key factor in criminal profiling.

beyond a reasonable doubt (p. 28) the standard of proof required for conviction in a criminal case involving the almost certainty of an individual's guilt based upon the evidence brought to trial.

bicycle patrol (p. 154) an alternative method of patrol involving officers conducting their patrol activities on bicycles. Bicycle patrol has the advantage of having officers closer to the community for interaction than is the case with automobile patrol, at the same time as it increases the mobility of officers to respond across distances than is the case with foot patrol.

Bill of Rights (p. 85) the first ten amendments of the United States Constitution that outline the civil rights and liberties guaranteed to all citizens of the country.

biometrics (p. 344) surveillance technology designed for the speedy identification of individuals on the basis of physical characteristics (e.g., fingerprints, facial structure, voice or retinal patterns, etc.).

blending (p. 128) potentially the most dangerous of undercover or covert operations, blending involves a law enforcement agent immersing him or herself completely in the criminal environment being investigated.

bobbies (p. 43) an early nickname for officers of the London Metropolitan Police (LMP) that still persists today, on the basis of their founder Sir Robert Peel.

booking (p. 26) the early stage of the criminal justice process, in which a suspect is formally entered into the system through fingerprinting, photographing, and the creation of a record.

boot camp (p. 28) considered an alternative to more severe criminal justice sanctions such as long prison sentences, boot camps are quasi-military in nature, designed to instill later compliance through strict adherence to discipline and structure. Boot camps are usually found with juvenile offender populations, although not exclusively.

Bow Street Runners (p. 41) under the guidance of Henry Fielding, the Bow Street Runners were a predecessor of the professional police detective function, charged with investigating larcenies and returning stolen property in a very high crime district of nineteenth century London.

broken windows theory (p. 297) the recognition that even low level misdemeanors or quality of life offenses can breed or foster more serious crimes in a community through their ability to attract more criminally-minded individuals and drive out more law-abiding residents or businesses.

brutality (p. 268) a form of police corruption, brutality involves the intent of an officer to cause harm to an individual beyond what is necessary to accomplish a legitimate law enforcement objective. Brutality can take both physical and verbal forms.

buffer zones (p. 334) a form of crime analysis using GIS that visually displays levels of risk around offending populations in a geographic area.

Bureau of Customs (p. 17) formerly a part of the Department of Treasury charged with controlling the continuous flow of goods across the nation's borders, the Bureau of Customs has recently been relocated into the newly formed Department of Homeland Security.

burnout (p. 371) a psychological state of despair, anxiety and/or withdrawal that is the result of excessive stress on the job and in other facets of life.

calls for service data (p. 330) with increasing technology, most major departments keep automated databases of calls for service within their jurisdictions. Such data can be a useful complement to formal arrests and incident reports because they reflect the level of concern or reporting within a jurisdiction. Given that calls-for-service data are by nature geographically based, it is able to be analyzed easily with GIS mapping technology.

canine (K9) units (p. 134) most major departments now have K9 units (or access to specially trained dogs) to support operations, particularly in the areas of drug interdiction and offender/victim tracking efforts.

case law (p. 85) the law that is the result of recorded cases and judicial decisions within a specific jurisdiction.

causation (pp. 100, 335) the proof that a particular act produced the resulting effect or harms that is an important ingredient in both criminal and civil law. Also referred to as **causation of harm.**

chain of evidence (p. 199) the careful documentation of the handling of evidence involved in an investigation from the point of the preliminary investigation (or arrival of the first law enforcement responder to the scene) all the way through to its ultimate presentation at trial.

chains of command (p. 114) the hierarchical lines of authority and communication illustrated in a formal organizational chart.

Chicago Alternative Policing Strategy (CAPS) (p. 341) considered by some experts to be a true example of a department-wide implementation of a community policing strategy, CAPS is the Chicago Police Department's innovative approach involving the fixed assignment of officers to a particular beat, the requirement that beat officers attend community beat meetings, and the training of both officers and residents in problem-solving approaches.

child pornography (p. 185) any visual depiction involving the use of a minor in a sexually explicit manner, whether it is an actual photograph or an image that has been modified or adapted to appear as a minor engaging in sexual conduct.

circadian rhythms (p. 156) the body's biological clock for sleep patterns; circadian rhythms can be seriously disrupted by rotating shift patterns previously common to many law enforcement agencies.

circle of investigation (p. 204) the pool of possible suspects in an investigation.

civil law (p. 83) the law dealing with private rights or wrongs against the individual, as opposed to the public matters embodied in criminal law. Rather than crimes, civil law involves torts.

civil liability (p. 103) liability dealt with under civil rather than criminal law, in which a government agency or individual is legally responsible for damages.

civil rights (p. 83) the rights guaranteed to all U.S. citizens under the Bill of Rights and other constitutional amendments such as the Fourteenth and Nineteenth.

Civil Rights Act (section 1983) (p. 101) a federal statute created to enforce the rights guaranteed by the Constitution; section 1983 holds that any law enforcement officer acting under the color of law that violates the civil rights of a citizen can be held civilly responsible for such action.

clear and present danger doctrine (p. 89) the doctrine that allows for the restriction of First Amendment freedom of speech where such speech can cause imminent and serious danger to the government or other citizens.

clearance rate (pp. 69, 195) the ratio of solved to reported crimes in a particular jurisdiction.

cleared crimes (p. 70) crimes in which an individual has been arrested and held responsible for his or her actions.

closed-circuit television (CCTV) (p. 342) a system of cameras recording actions in both private and public settings for the purpose of security; CCTV can be combined with biometrics, or facial recognition technologies.

Code of Hammurabi (p. 38) the first written legal codes of human history. Originating in Mesopotamia, the Code of Hammurabi is based upon the principle of *lex talionis*, or "an eye for an eye, a tooth for a tooth."

coercive force (p. 8) the use of force to physically stop an individual and/or take him or her into custody.

command (p. 114) at the lowest level of the use of force continuum, even an officer's mere **presence** or **voice** is viewed as offering a certain degree of authority.

commission (p. 271) an investigatory body on the federal, state, or local level that is created for the short-term objective of examining the existence or causes of a particular problem or issue (e.g., corruption, use of force, etc.).

Commission for the Accreditation of Law Enforcement Agencies (CALEA) (p. 66) a voluntary accreditation for law enforcement agencies based on a body of standards internationally accepted by the law enforcement community.

community (p. 294) a geographically distinct area that can encompass a number of dimensions, including socioeconomic composition, residential stability, racial/ethnic heterogeneity, local friendship relational networks, organizational participation, and supervisory capacity.

community mobilization (p. 313) techniques utilized by law enforcement to outreach to and involve various sectors of the community (i.e., residents, businesses, faiths, schools, media) in the maintenance of public security.

community ownership (p. 296) the degree to which a community feels responsible for maintaining public security in its area and has a sense of pride and responsibility with respect to its overall quality of life.

community policing (pp. 153, 300) the department-wide philosophy recognizing the need for partnership with the community and proactive problem-solving efforts in order to combat the conditions of crime more effectively. Community policing involves strategic, philosophical, and tactical elements, including the fixed assignment of officers to a particular shift/time, and the decentralization of decision-making within the department. The term **community-oriented policing (p. 305)** often is used to reflect the entirety of community policing dimensions.

community prosecution (p. 305) complementary to community policing approaches, community prosecution efforts involve the collaboration of prosecutors with other government agencies in the proactive targeting and resolution of the crime and quality of life concerns within a given area.

comprehensive plans (p. 315) in order to effectively combat crime and corruption, a full continuum of services and strategies are necessary, including suppression, intervention, and prevention efforts.

CompStat (p. 336) the strategic and organizational innovation first implemented by the New York City Police Department (NYPD) that includes the regular reporting of precinct commanders to agency top brass, the holding of commanders responsible for the crime in their precincts through timely and accurate information, and the use of GIS mapping to engage in problem-solving efforts for strategic planning.

computer-aided dispatch (CAD) (p. 327) automated systems aiding in the process of deploying officers to respond to citizen calls for service. Such technology also helps to record and make available calls for service data for analysis for research and strategic purposes.

concealed-carry handgun statutes (p. 92) statutes that allow citizens to apply for permits to carry concealed weapons, usually on the basis of some objective criteria (see also **shall issue statutes**).

concurrence (p. 99) the need to establish in criminal law that the act (*actus reus*) and the intent (*mens rea*) occurred at the same place and time.

constables (p. 40) originally designated to assist the shire-reeve in ensuring the law and order of a community during feudal England, after the Norman conquest constables often would supervise others whose responsibility it was to guard the gates of a community at night. Later the constables answered to the justice of the peace instead of the community itself. Constables would become a professional civilian body following the Metropolitan Police Act in 1829.

constitution (p. 84) the fundamental law of a country or state, organizing the division of powers as well as the balance between government powers and the individual.

constitutional law (p. 83) the body of law resulting from the interpretation of the U.S. Constitution by the Supreme Court, and the outlining of civil rights and liberties in the country.

contagion proposition (p. 297) as disorder increases and the quality of life decreases in a defined geographic area, more fear and crime is generated over time.

contaminants (p. 196) any element that can alter the quality or nature of evidence at a crime scene and thus impede the processes of association and reconstruction.

contempt of cop (COC) (p. 219) the term often used within the police culture to refer to the mistrust, attitude, and even hatred expressed by the community residents they are sworn to protect.

control beats (p. 150) within the Kansas City Preventive Patrol Experiment, these were the beats in which the same amount of patrol services were deployed as prior to the experiment. The control beats were included in the research design as a comparison to the results found in the proactive and reactive beats.

***corpus delicti* (p. 99)** literally means the "body of the crime," but in actuality refers to the elements of a crime that must be proven in order to establish guilt; while this refers mainly to the facts of an illegal act (*actus reus*),

ultimately the intent (*mens rea*) also must be established for most crimes.

correlations (p. 335) the statistical relationship between two variables in either a positive or negative direction. Correlation alone cannot be used to indicate that one variable causes another.

covert (undercover) operations (p. 127) investigative operations conducted generally in plainclothes that can take several forms: sting operations, buy-back, surveillance, and reverse sting.

crime analysis (pp. 310, 321) the proactive use of technology, research techniques, and triangulated data sources to analyze crime trends and patterns to develop strategy and make operational decisions.

crime control (p. 11) conceptualized as one of the two principal models of criminal justice by Herbert Packer, the crime control model emphasizes quantity and speed of arrests over due process considerations.

crime indices (p. 70) statistical calculations that allow crime trends to be comparable across jurisdictions of differing size and density (e.g., incidents per 100,000 population); a principal means for the reporting and comparison of FBI Uniform Crime Report (UCR) data.

crime mapping (p. 331) the visual display of crime data with a known geographic origin to facilitate pattern recognition and operational decisions. Although originally crime maps existed solely with pushpins on a map, geographic information systems (GIS) have drastically enhanced the ability of law enforcement agencies to engage in crime mapping.

crime prevention through environmental design (CPTED) (p. 302) the recognition that crime can be prevented or managed through the manipulation of guardianship, target vulnerability, and other locational dynamics.

crime scenes (p. 197) areas in which the crime actually took place (primary crime scene) and/or evidence relating to the crime is sound (secondary crime scene).

crime triangle (p. 309) used to facilitate crime analysis and problem solving, the crime triangle visually displays the three elements necessary in order for a crime to take place: victim, offender, and location.

crime-trend forecasting (p. 330) the use of crime analysis techniques to predict the nature and volume of crime in a specific area to aid deployment and strategy decisions.

criminal justice system (p. 23) the interconnected phases of the processing of a suspected individual from the point of arrest through to trial and ultimately the completion of his or her sentence (i.e., police, courts, and corrections).

criminal law (p. 82) the body of law defined in the penal code of a jurisdiction (e.g., federal, state, or local) that defines the actions or omissions that must be complied with by the public or face punishment by the state.

criminal liability (p. 103) being found criminally responsible for a given action.

criminal profiling (p. 201) the combined use of behavioral and physical evidence in order to develop a profile of the most likely offender type given a particular action or series of actions.

criminalistics (p. 200) the use of physical evidence to reconstruct a crime and associate offender, victim, and crime scene together for probative purposes.

critical incident stress debriefings (CISD) (p. 230) a staged system of therapy to help officers cope with the stress and trauma incurred during a crisis situation.

critical stage (p. 96) a stage in the processing of an offender through the criminal justice system in which the fair outcome of the case could be affected by the absence of legal representation, thereby triggering his or her Sixth Amendment right to counsel.

cross-cultural populations (p. 250) populations that are themselves distinct, and yet cross traditionally accepted racial and ethnic categories (e.g. lesbian gay and transgendered –LGBT, mentally ill, and deaf and hard of hearing).

cultural barriers (p. 248) difficulties in communication or interaction across groups that is caused by a lack of understanding or appreciation of another culture.

cultural cues (p. 201) nonverbal body language that can differ and carry significantly different meanings across cultures (e.g., eye contact, body space, hand gestures, etc.).

culture of lawfulness (p. 9) the acceptance of the majority of a particular society in the importance of rules and laws and a belief in the system of justice generally.

curtilage (p. 178) the part of a property adjoining a home (and usually, though not always, enclosed) that is generally protected from Fourth Amendment warrantless searches.

cyber crime (p. 184) any offense that occurs via the Internet as opposed to the real world. This is not the same as computer crime, which is any wrongful act occurring on or directed against a computer, though this can include cyber crime.

cyber sleuths (p. 184) individuals who regulate Internet use and enforce cyber laws, such as the possession and distribution of child pornography.

D.A.R.E (Drug Abuse Resistance Education) (p. 133) originally piloted by the Los Angeles Police Department (LAPD), DARE is a school-based program in which police officers teach students about the dangers of substance abuse. The program is now offered by police departments both nationally and internationally.

dark figure of crime (p. 72) the level of unreported crime in an area that is not known to the police or public.

deadly force (p. 269) the use of potentially lethal force by a police officer.

decentralization (pp. 117, 312) the localization of decision-making to a precinct or even neighborhood level.

decoy operation (p. 128) a type of undercover operation in which officers pose as potential victims, in order to apprehend offenders.

defenses (p. 100) the arguments made by the defense in trial to challenge the prosecution's case with regard to the commission of the act itself (alibis), the level of intent required (excuses), or the harm caused (justifications).

democratic accountability (p. 277) mechanisms to improve accountability of the police department to the community, such as an external review board.

Department of Homeland Security (p. 21) the result of the largest governmental reorganization in many years, the Department of Homeland Security includes the transfer of the Coast Guard, Customs Service, Border Patrol, Federal Emergency Management Agency, Secret Service, Transportation Security Administration, and border inspection component of the Animal and Plant Health Inspection service.

despecialization (p. 312) the process of restructuring an organization to include less specialized functions, and making line officers take on more of these responsibilities as generalists.

deviance (p. 7) the violation of both formal and informal rules, laws, or customs.

differential response (p. 148) an alternative form of dispatch in which callers in nonemergency situations are informed that an officer might not respond for several hours, the report is taken over the phone, or a non-sworn employee is sent to respond to the call. Differential response strategies are meant to free up line officer resources for more proactive operations or emergency situations.

directed patrol (p. 148) the deployment of patrol to a specific location and/or time on the basis of a review of crime patterns and trends in that area.

discovery crimes (p. 194) crimes that are discovered and/or reported long after the offense took place and the offender is gone. Home burglaries often are discovery crimes in which the resident returns home well after the incident actually occurred.

discretion (p. 9) the decision-making power of any criminal justice official.

dis-stress (p. 229) stress that outside of the normal range and very harmful over time.

division (p. 118) a group of police personnel that share responsibility for a particular policing function.

double jeopardy (p. 94) being prosecuted twice for virtually the same offense, circumstances, and evidence. The Fifth Amendment protects U.S citizens from double jeopardy.

Drug Enforcement Administration (DEA) (p. 17) within the Treasury Department, the primary responsibility of the DEA is to investigate and prepare evidence for the prosecution of major violators of controlled substances laws both domestically and internationally.

dual promotion lists (p. 373) separate promotional instruments for white male officers and all other officers. Such lists were found in many police departments throughout the 1980s to encourage the promotion of women and minorities.

due process (p. 11) the fair processing of an individual through the criminal justice system from the point of arrest through to sentencing. Protected by the Fifth, Sixth, and Fourteenth Amendments to the Constitution.

eight-hour shift structure (p. 155) a common shift structure in contemporary departments in which officers generally work five days a week for eight hours and then get two days off. Following an additional five days, the officer will receive four days off.

electronic surveillance (p. 93) mechanisms to monitor an offender's movements electronically, such as wiretapping, electronic bracelets and CCTV.

electronic warrant processes (p. 346) technological advances that allow the officer to electronically submit the affidavit for a warrant to the judge or magistrate in order to significantly speed up the time to issue.

empowerment (p. 300) the feeling of all parties in a partnership that they have equal input into decisions and the commitment of resources.

enhanced supervision partnerships (p. 306) seek to increase the odds of detecting offender violations of probation or parole by conducting joint supervision activities between police and probation, including random home visits.

entrapment (p. 129) a situation in which a law enforcement officer can be said to have "planted the seed" for an offense in the mind of the offender, in order to later prosecute him or her for said offense.

Environmental Systems Research Institute Inc. (ESRI) (p. 340) the leading developer of innovative and practical Geographic Information Systems (p. GIS) for both the public and private sectors.

equal protection clause (p. 97) a provision in the Fourteenth Amendment that requires the states to treat all people involved in similar circumstances equally under the law.

equity (p. 84) the principle of fairness under the law; the recognition that the law can be modified in accordance with the changing needs and dynamics of society.

essential criteria for crime analysis (p. 330) in order to have effective crime analysis capacities, departments should ensure that data collection processes are designed with timeliness, relevancy, and reliability concerns in mind.

establishment of religion clause (p. 88) in the First Amendment, this provision prohibits the government from creating or supporting a particular religion.

eustress (p. 229) stress that is normal and good, even providing on the job motivation.

exceptional clearance (p. 70) a category in the FBI's Uniform Crime Reporting procedures to account for those situations in which the law enforcement agency knows with certainty that a certain individual committed a particular crime, but for some reason cannot be brought to justice (e.g., death of the offender).

excessive force (p. 267) any amount of force by a law enforcement officer that is beyond that is necessary to achieve legitimate law enforcement objectives.

exclusionary rule (pp. 93, 171) the recognition that any evidence that is obtained illegally by law enforcement (or the fruits thereof) will not be admissible in court. Meant to deter illegal law enforcement conduct.

exigent circumstances (p. 174) an emergency or exceptional situation requiring immediate law enforcement action.

exonerated (p. 277) individuals that have been convicted of a crime that later are proven to be innocent on the basis of new evidence.

expressive purposes (p. 88) peaceable assemblies for religious, political, or social reasons, including protests. Protected under the First Amendment.

external authorizing environmental stakeholders (p. 146) any individual, group, or agency outside of the police department that can influence its policies or procedures.

external stressors (p. 229) problems or factors outside of the police department that can cause stress or disequilibrium for police management.

extra-legal factors (p. 10) variables outside of those directly pertaining to the circumstances of a particular incident, such as race or suspect demeanor, that nonetheless influence an officer's decision on how to handle the situation.

facial recognition software (p. 344) technology designed to recognize physical characteristics of an individual in order to enhance the utility of CCTV and related technology.

fatigue (p. 156) excessive tiredness while on the job.

Federal Bureau of Investigation (FBI) (p. 15) under the Department of Justice, the FBI is responsible for the investigation of all federal crimes, including an international presence related to counter-terrorism training and intelligence.

felony (p. 98) a serious offense that carries a potential sentence of more than a year of incarceration.

field interrogation (p. 170) a law enforcement officer's questioning of an individual that is not yet officially under police custody.

field training officers (FTO) (pp. 157, 370) once out of the academy, the FTO assists the police officer in applying.

fighting words (p. 89) a speech that is not necessarily protected by the First Amendment because it is capable of inciting violence.

flat organizations (p. 116) organizations in which many layers of bureaucracy have been reduced in order to facilitate rapid information sharing across ranks.

flattening (pp. 116, 312) the process of reducing layers of bureaucracy or ranks in an organization.

fleeing felony rule (p. 269) prior to the *Tennessee v. Garner* decision, it was acceptable practice in many jurisdictions to use deadly force when a felon fled from an officer regardless of the immediacy of threat involved in the situation.

force continuum (p. 265) used in the training of officers in most departments nationally, the force continuum demonstrates the increasing types of force allowable with the corresponding increase in offender resistance and threat.

formal social control (p. 8) the laws of a society, and the mechanisms for their enforcement.

free exercise of religion (p. 88) the recognition of the ability of individuals to practice whatever faith they so choose under the First Amendment, so long as such practice does not infringe on the rights of others or violate existing criminal law.

frisk (p. 170) a brief pat-down search of an individual that is restricted to the search for a weapon.

fruit of the poisoned tree (p. 172) the rule that any later evidence resulting from an illegal search or seizure will itself be held inadmissible under the exclusionary rule.

fugitive-apprehension partnerships (p. 306) partnerships formed between police and corrections to facilitate the capture of absconded felons in a particular jurisdiction.

functional structures (p. 118) a modification to traditional organizational structure to allow divisions with overlapping purpose (such as intelligence) to report to multiple divisions; functional structures are created to reduce the problem of linkage blindness.

fundamental attribution errors (p. 247) the tendency of some individuals to explain criminal behavior in terms of internal factors such as race or membership in a particular ethnic group, rather than by reference to external or situational factors, such as poverty or marginal social position.

furlough (p. 28) work release from a correctional institution.

generalists (p. 114) the tendency in some organizations to reduce specialization of functions and have officers readily able to respond to a variety of situations and operational needs. Generalist functions are much more common in rural jurisdictions by necessity.

geocoded (p. 333) the use of data with a geographic locator as a reference for the purpose of mapping relationships across indicators.

geographic information systems (GIS) (p. 331) software designed for the presentation of geographic data as maps to facilitate analysis possibilities.

geographic profiling (p. 340) the combined use of geography, psychology, and mathematics to identify the location of an offender; most commonly associated with tracking down serial killers, rapists, and arsonists.

global positioning systems (GPS) (p. 343) use satellite-based technologies for the purpose of tracking the movement of patrol cars, stolen vehicles, and in some cases even individuals.

good faith exception (p. 173) an exception to the exclusionary rule allowing evidence obtained from a search warrant later found to be invalid still to be admitted in court, if the officer(s) executing were acting under the belief that the warrant was legal. Also referred to as good faith immunity.

good time (p. 29) offenders who abide by the prison rules and receive only positive reports from correctional services can be released prior to their maximum sentence.

grass eaters (p. 271) one of two categories of corrupt police officers identified by the Knapp Commission's investigation into the corruption of the New York City Police Department, grass eaters refer to those officers who passively accept tips, bribes, or other corrupt activities.

halfway house (p. 28) a community-based correctional facility that houses offenders prior to their complete release into the community; meant to facilitate the process of reintegration.

hard of hearing (p. 251) a continuum of difficulty with auditory perception ranging from mild difficulties to complete deafness.

hierarchical accountability (p. 277) accountability to those structurally higher within the department.

hierarchy rule (p. 72) the UCR reporting guidelines that stipulate that only the most serious offense within a series of linked incidents is to be counted.

high-risk traffic stop (p. 159) a traffic stop in which the driver of the pursued vehicle is known to be a wanted felon or extremely dangerous in some known way.

J. Edgar Hoover (p. 53) former Director of the Federal Bureau of Investigation from 1935 until the 1970s, Hoover was responsible for many efforts to professionalize its agency policies, procedures, and methods.

horizontal differentiation (p. 117) the differentiation within the same layer of an organizational structure.

horse patrol (p. 154) patrol conducted on horse is most common in places that are inaccessible to automobiles or motorcycles, such as parks and wild terrain. Also used for increased visibility in urban settings during parades or demonstrations.

hostage-negotiation techniques (p. 132) techniques employed during a hostage situation to minimize the likelihood of having to resort to lethal force.

hot spots (p. 310) specific areas within a community that have the highest concentration of crime and other forms of disorder.

hue and cry (p. 40) in early England, the hue and cry was the constable's call for help; failure to heed the call by all men between the ages of fifteen and sixty was an offense.

hung jury (p. 28) a jury that is unable to reach a verdict with the acceptable majority.

immigrant communities (p. 249) concentrated areas within which reside a large number of foreign-born populations.

Immigration and Naturalization Service (INS) (p. 16) the agency responsible for determining the admissibility of all persons seeking entry into the country, and keeping detailed records on any person in the country who goes through the naturalization process. The INS also has been charged with patrolling the nation's borders and serving as checkpoints in all international airports. A part of the Department of Justice since 1940, many of its functions were split up and transferred to the newly formed Department of Homeland Security in 2002.

inchoate offenses (p. 99) a step is taken toward the commission of a crime that is not the complete offense itself, but deserving of punishment.

incident data (p. 330) data pertaining to the specifics of a particular criminal act.

incident to arrest (p. 175) once an officer has probable cause to arrest an individual, he or she is permitted under the Fourth Amendment to conduct a full-body search of the offender.

incident-driven policing (p. 148) is policing that is focused on responding to calls for service.

inevitable discovery (p. 173) when the prosecution can demonstrate that they would have found the evidence anyway, it may not be immediately dismissed under the exclusionary rule for being the fruit of an illegal source.

informal social control (p. 7) mechanisms for ensuring compliance with the formal and informal rules, laws, and customs of society that are outside the purview of the formal enforcement role of law enforcement, such as families, schools, peers, churches, media, and businesses.

Information Collection for Automated Mapping (ICAM) (p. 341) the Chicago Police Department's Web-based mapping system that allows both officers and residents to view crime trends in their areas.

information leakage (p. 22) information that gets lost between or within agencies due to problems in communication, territorial boundaries, technological inadequacies, or other issues.

information-sharing partnerships (p. 306) partnerships between police and corrections that are designed to foster enhanced sharing of needed intelligence and other information related to offenders in particular jurisdictions.

initial appearance (p. 26) the first appearance before a judge by a defendant to formally hear the charges being held against him or her.

Integrated Automated Fingerprint Identification System (IAFIS) (p. 345) an advanced automated fingerprint database kept by the FBI that allows a two-hour turnaround on electronically submitted criminal print searches from federal, state, and local agencies.

integrated patrol (p. 150) combining both automobile and foot patrol operations.

Intention (p. 99) holding the requisite mental capacity for the commission of a particular crime.

intentional wrong (p. 102) within civil law, wrongs to another or their property that is based on the knowing and purposeful deliberations of an individual.

interagency problem-solving partnerships (p. 306) police/corrections partnerships that are formed around the intention of engaging in problem-solving efforts with respect to a particular issue or type of offender population within a particular area.

interim order (p. 114) the distribution of a change to the formal policies of a department before it can be formally incorporated into the departmental guidelines.

internal affairs bureau (IAB) (pp. 125, 277) a division within large police departments staffed by sworn officers that serves to both investigate the complaints of citizens, as well as to initiate its own investigations.

Internal Revenue Service (IRS) (p. 17) the largest agency within the Treasury Department, the mission of the IRS is to regulate compliance with tax laws and to investigate tax evasion and fraud.

internal stressors (p. 229) factors within a department that can be a source of difficulty.

International Association of Chiefs of Police (IACP) (p. 65) a professional police organization that is committed to the production of materials and technical assistance efforts that can benefit the field both nationally and internationally.

International Association of Policewomen (IAP) (p. 66) a professional organization founded to serve the interests of policewomen, it has since disbanded as its own agency and been folded under the umbrella of IACP.

interrogation (p. 181) formally questioning a suspect under custody with the intention of eliciting a response related to the actions in question.

intervention services (p. 316) services provided to an offender after they have already committed an offense, usually with the intention of rehabilitation.

investigation (p. 26) police operations focused on the solution of previously committed crimes.

involvement crimes (p. 194) crimes in which the police respond to the scene and the offender is still present and/or the crime remains in progress.

Iron Law of Oligarchy (p. 216) suggests that the formal organization of bureaucracies inevitably leads to oligarchy, in which a small group of self-serving individuals seek to maintain their position of power.

jail (p. 28) incarceration on the municipal level for offenses serving time of less than a year. Also used to house offenders awaiting trial, awaiting transfer to prisons, probation or parole violators, etc.

Jim Crow laws (p. 46) the racist laws begun in the 1880s to enforce segregation between whites and blacks in schools, parks, restrooms, and other public facilities.

judicial review (p. 86) power given to the Supreme Court and the federal judiciary to "consider and overturn any congressional and state legislation or other official governmental action deemed inconsistent with the Constitution, Bill of Rights, or federal law."

jurisdiction (p. 12) local, state, and federal areas of responsibility under which contemporary law enforcement agencies operate.

justice of the peace (p. 14) a magistrate who presides in the justice's court and is of a lesser rank than those in higher courts.

justice's court (p. 14) courts on the county level that only maintain limited jurisdiction as described by statute in civil matters, such as the performance of marriages, and minor criminal offenses.

Kansas City Gun Experiment (p. 150) intensive patrols that targeted an 80-block high crime area, which revealed that aggressive patrol can significantly reduce gun crimes such as drive-by shootings and homicides without a measured displacement effect.

Kansas City Preventive Patrol Experiment (p. 150) study in 1972 using proactive, reactive, and controlled patrol beats that showed that random patrol on its own does not significantly affect in criminal activity.

Kansas City Response Time Study (p. 194) study showing that citizens take longer to report crimes to police than it takes police to respond.

kinesics (p. 200) body language.

law enforcement (p. 6) the role of the police in enforcing the existing legislation or rules of society.

Law Enforcement Assistance Administration (LEAA) (p. 357) organization that began emphasizing the need for police officers to attend college at this time as well, going as far as implementing a grant system for individuals who were or planned to be police officers upon graduation.

Law Enforcement Education Program (LEEP) (p. 61) established in 1964 to help provide the impetus for police-related training/courses in academic institutions across the country by offering financing for criminal justice professionals seeking post-secondary educational opportunities.

law of accelerating returns (p. 328) technological advancement is characterized by exponential growth, increasing doubly each year.

legalistic (p. 50) oriented toward the strict enforcement of the letter of the law.

legalistic style (p. 227) style of policing described by James Q. Wilson that emphasizes the importance of law enforcement and maintaining clear and impartial legal standards for both the police and public alike.

legitimate force (p. 265) the minimum amount of force necessary to control a situation.

less-than-lethal force (p. 266) minimal physical force that is not intended to be deadly, but rather to subdue the suspect so as to avoid harm to the officer or anyone in the surrounding area, including use of hands, pepper spray, mace, a taser, a baton, or rubber bullets.

lethal force (p. 266) force with a firearm.

lex taliones **(p. 38)** retributive principle that literally means an "eye for an eye."

line personnel (p. 114) the lowest in the chain of command, usually patrol officers.

linguistic barriers (p. 248) when ethnic minorities in the community do not have a working understanding of the English language, which can prevent minorities from gaining access to justice or taking advantage of important criminal justice services.

linkage analysis (p. 331) connecting a suspect to a series of incidents based on commonalities in *modus operandi* and suspect description, as well as known offenders that live close proximity to a given area.

linkage blindness (p. 5) the inability to analyze and link critical information across or within agencies.

Locard exchange principle (p. 199) states that it is impossible for anyone to enter a location without changing it in some way, either by bringing something to it or removing something from it, which is why offenders can be linked to a crime scene.

mandatory arrest policies (p. 214) elimination of officer discretion and requiring arrest in particular situations (e.g., domestic violence).

Massachusetts Bartley-Fox laws (p. 91) laws that mandate a one-year jail term for individuals caught carrying a handgun outside of the home without a permit.

matrix structures (p. 118) create a team problem-solving environment in which members of different divisions (i.e., detective bureau, patrol, vice/narcotic) are assigned to specific problem areas such as counterterrorism or organized crime.

max out (p. 29) when a prisoner serves his or her entire sentence in prison.

meat eaters (p. 271) when officers aggressively demand bribes in exchange for protection (or lack of) to the person from whom they are seeking the favor.

mediation (p. 282) alternative dispute resolution.

mens rea **(p. 99)** component of crime that literally means "a guilty mind."

Metropolitan Police Act (p. 42) provided funds for the establishment of a 1,000-officer police force in London governed by strict standards of conduct and discipline.

middle management (p. 114) officers such as captains and lieutenants who are not at the top of the command chain but have ranking power over some officer in the department.

Minneapolis Domestic Violence Experiment (p. 214) study testing the mandatory arrest policies for domestic violence, which showed that mandatory arrests might decrease the escalating violence of those males who could be adversely affected by criminal justice attention, such as the employed or political figures in a community.

Minnesota Multiphasic Personality Inventory (MMPI) (p. 362) most common psychological assessment tool in the screening of police applicants.

minority communities (p. 244) communities consisting largely of racial or ethnic minorities.

minority recruitment (p. 257) the seeking of minorities for positions in the police department.

***Miranda* rights (p. 181)** based on the case of *Miranda v Arizona*, police officers are required to explain to suspects prior to custodial interrogation that they have the right against self-incrimination and the right to counsel.

misdemeanor (p. 98) relatively minor crime subject to less than a year in a jail.

mission statement (p. 113) an expression of a police department's overall purpose and goals.

mobile digital communications (MDC) (p. 347) offer nonverbal means of communicating information between communication centers and patrol.

modus operandi (p. 202) how a crime is committed.

motive (p. 99) why a criminal act is committed.

motorcycle patrol (p. 154) type of patrol that is particularly useful in traffic enforcement activities given their ability to negotiate heavy traffic situations, such as in cases of high-profile police escorts and for parades.

moving violations (p. 158) enforcement of traffic regulations.

National Crime Information Center (NCIC) (p. 206) maintained by the FBI, NCIC makes information from jurisdictions nationally on wanted felons, stolen vehicles, missing children, and other important data available to the patrol officer in the field who can call into the department for a search.

National Crime Victimization Survey (NCVS) (p. 72) survey conducted by the Bureau of Justice Statistics that collects self-report data on all crimes against individuals or households, regardless of whether or not they were reported to the police.

National DNA Identification System (NDIS) (p. 207) maintained by the FBI, the NDIS contains automated DNA information for offenders convicted of certain offenses such as sexual crimes and other crimes of violence.

National Incident Based Reporting System (NIBRS) (p. 73) an incident-based crime reporting system implemented by FBI in 1989 as a means of improving existing statistical reporting and crime analysis standards nationally and eventually intended to replace the UCR.

National Institute of Justice (NIJ) (p. 62) created in 1960 as a research entity specifically targeting advanced study in the areas of policing and other areas of criminal justice reform

nearness principle (p. 340) offenders will remain within a limited range that is comfortable to them when committing their offenses.

needs assessment (p. 314) the identification of problems and sources of the problems in local communities in order to establish a proactive policing strategy.

negligent wrong (p. 102) the breach of a common law or statutory duty to act reasonably toward those who potentially may be harmed by an officer's conduct, for which the officer may be held civilly liable.

Newark Foot Patrol Experiment (p. 153) study showing that increased foot patrol did not appear to have a significant effect on overall crime levels in the community, though it did result in more positive attitudes toward the police as well as reductions in fear of crime.

***nolo contendere* (p. 101)** plea in a court of law that literally means "no contest," and in a criminal court is equivalent to a guilty plea.

nominal damages (p. 103) the Court acknowledges that the plaintiff proved his or her allegation but suffered no actual injury.

nonphysical force (p. 265) force conveyed through the use of body language, eye contact, presence, or even the mere significance of the uniform.

nonsocial offender (p. 203) an organized offender who is likely to meet the classification of a psychopath.

nonverbal cues (p. 200) changes in tone, pitch, or inflection that are important during interrogations.

objective reasonableness (p. 267) standard based on the circumstances of the case, usually in the use of force. The Court is required to judge whether the force used is legitimate based cvon the perspective of a "reasonable officer" on the scene who is required to make quick decisions on the amount of force that may be necessary to use to control a situation

ombudsman (p. 278) a neutral figure who reviews complaints against all public servants in an effort to combat organizational or systemic misconduct.

one-officer cars (p. 153) one patrol officer assigned per car.

operating stereotype (p. 247) preconceived ideas about groups of people—such as the belief that individuals from certain cultures are inherently less law-abiding—that can provide the basis for unwitting but serious discrimination on the grounds of race or ethnicity.

operational unit (p. 122) engaged in activities performed in direct assistance to the public, such as police patrol and traffic, and are typically staffed by sworn police officers.

order maintenance (p. 50) police duty that is not focused on crime-fighting but rather on preventing disorder in the community.

order of authority (p. 85) a hierarchy of legal authority that exists so that conflicts between different federal, state, and local laws could be resolved, with the U.S. Constitution having the highest authority.

organizational chart (p. 114) formal structure, in terms of both task and authority, that is required to "get a job done."

organized-disorganized typology (p. 202) explanation that helps to correlate crime scene elements with key personality characteristics, with the organized offender taking great care in the planning of his or her offense to ensure that there is little or no evidence remaining at the crime scene and the disorganized offender engaging in a chaotic, unplanned style of attack, in which substantial amounts of evidence are left behind at the crime scene.

parole (p. 29) early release from prison in which the offender is living in the community for the remainder of his or her sentence under supervision from a field agent.

Part I index crimes (p. 69) eight main crimes listed in the UCR, including four violent personal crimes—murder, rape, robbery, and aggravated assault—and four property crimes—burglary, larceny, motor vehicle theft, and arson.

Part II index crimes (p. 69) all crimes in the UCR that are not Part I offenses, including forgery, fraud, embezzlement, vandalism, weapons (carrying/possession), gambling, sex offenses (other than forcible rape, prostitution), drug abuse, and disorderly conduct.

participatory management model (p. 312) policing structure in which line officers are encouraged to be creative and resolve problems, rather than simply following directives.

partnership (p. 300) in which community residents and organizations becoming the "eyes and ears" of the police, and also includes working together on a common problem; identifying common goals; steady and consistent communication and information sharing; having a shared perception of problems and benchmarks for when problems are solved; and all parties contributing work toward accomplishing shared goals and objectives or solving the problem.

patrol deployment (p. 155) methods by which the police use officers for patrol, using various shift formats to best resolve crime related problems across diverse contexts.

pattern detection (p. 330) in tactical crime analysis, problem identification of multiple offenses over a short period of time that have common characteristics such as type of crime, *modus operandi*, and type of weapon used.

Pattern Identification Modules (PIMS) (p. 337) group comprised of housing, transit, patrol, detective, organized crime, and robbery squads implemented in each New York City borough to review daily index crime reports and thus identify crime clusters or patterns that need to be addressed for CompStat meetings.

Sir Robert Peel (p. 41) established the formal system of policing in London with the passing of the Metropolitan Police Act 1829.

Pendleton Act (p. 49) a federal bill aimed at eliminating the "spoils system" and the corruption endemic with the federal administration.

Peterloo Massacre of 1819 (p. 41) a political protest in England that turned riotous after the military was brought in to break it up, leaving 11 people dead and hundreds injured, leading up to the formation of a formal policing system.

philosophical dimension (p. 310) the recognition that community policing is best implemented as a department-wide philosophy rather than specialized function.

physical evidence (p. 199) tangible evidence linking a suspect to a crime scene, including type of forcible entry (in a property crime), blood, hair, fibers, fingerprints, and weapons, etc.

plain view (p. 93) immediately apparent.

plain view doctrine (p. 174) if a crime is committed in the immediate presence of an officer, he or she can take the person into custody without a warrant.

plea bargain (p. 28) negotiations of guilty pleas in exchange for reduced charges or lenient sentences.

police academy (p. 369) school where officers learn on-the-job techniques prior to receiving full police powers.

police corruption (p. 271) the misuse of authority by a police officer.

police personality (p. 223) certain core beliefs, values, and behavioral traits that are common to many police officers, and which help to explain how individual officers exercise their discretion, how they deal with members of the public, and how police organizations function.

Police Services Study (PSS) (p. 144) study of how police officers from 24 departments spent their time and their interactions with citizens in 60 residential neighborhoods, with findings that approximately two-thirds of an officer's shift was "unassigned."

police subculture (p. 224) can be the result of history and learned dispositions (socialization) such as cynicism, authoritarianism, and suspiciousness of the general public; these traits often can affect the way in which the police deal with particular groups, such as women and racial minorities.

policies (p. 113) a specific statement of principle that aims to guide individual decisions and ensure that those decisions reflect the overall objectives of the department.

policing goals (p. 112) an established set of objectives that aim to provide that department with a sense of purpose and direction.

police-minority tensions (p. 245) poor relationships between the police and the community, often resulting from a highly publicized case of police corruption or brutality in a particular neighborhood.

polygraph (p. 363) lie detector test used in the screening of police applicants.

Posse Comitatus Act (p. 41) Act signed in 1878 to separate military functions from local law enforcement in the United States.

posses (p. 40) group of villagers and other members of the community organized by the shire reeve to track down and apprehend offenders.

post-traumatic stress disorder (PTSD) (p. 230) disorder resulting from traumatic incidents, this is diagnosed when the person experiences a traumatic event that involved the actual or threatened death or injury to self or others; the traumatic event is persistently re-experienced through recurrent and intrusive recollections or dreams, acting or feeling as though the event were reoccurring; and intense psychological distress and physiological reactivity upon exposure to internal or external cues resembling an aspect of the traumatic event.

predisposition (p. 246) preformed opinions about groups of individuals that may lead to racist attitudes within the police.

preliminary investigation (p. 196) duties performed by first uniformed officer on arrival at a crime scene, which include determining whether the offender is at the scene or in the area, responding to the victim's needs, and ensuring the general safety of anyone in the immediate vicinity.

preponderance of the evidence (p. 100) the evidentiary standard for civil cases, meaning that the weight of the evidence must be in favor of the complainant.

presentence investigation (PSI) (p. 28) conducted by the office of probation to investigate the background of the offender, this helps the judge to determine what type of sentence is appropriate for an offender, within legislated parameters.

pretextual stops (p. 177) when an officer ostensibly stops a vehicle for some traffic violation (e.g., a broken taillight or speeding) and proceeds to use that stop to conduct a full-scale search of the car.

pretrial motions (p. 27) series of motions to be filed prior to the beginning of trial that can change the place of the trial, suppress evidence, and provide discovery.

prevalence (p. 310) the overall incidence of a problem in a geographical area.

primary scene (p. 198) the site of the original crime.

Principles of Policing (p. 43) basic rules and principles of the London Metropolitan police, as established by Sir Robert Peel.

prison (p. 29) a state or federal correctional facility that houses offenders serving sentences of one year or more.

proactive (pp. 75, 300) act before the problem occurs as a preventative measure.

proactive beats (p. 150) in which there is an increase in random patrol activity.

proactive patrol (p. 148) type of patrol, usually directed, that attempts to target problems rather than simply respond to them.

probable cause (pp. 26, 92, 169) evidentiary standard necessary for arrests and searches in which facts of a case lead a reasonable person to believe that an offense was committed and that the suspect committed that offense.

probation (p. 369) alternative sanction whereby the offender serves a sentence in the community in lieu of prison or jail; a trial period of one or two years during which the officer is evaluated .

problem solving (p. 300) the collaborative identification of problems and their underlying causes, rather than simply responding to incidents.

problem-oriented policing (p. 308) proactive policing strategies that focuses on the identification of underlying causes of problems, and the selection of solutions or remedies to prevent a problem from occurring again in the future.

problems (p. 301) in standard policing terminology, this means two or more incidents capable of causing harm, in which there is an expectation that the police and community can do something about it.

procedural due process (p. 94) protects individuals from arbitrary and unfair application of the laws.

procedural justice (p. 277) the outcome is less important than the procedure by which the outcome is produced.

procedural law (p. 98) specifies how the criminal justice system should deal with violations of the substantive laws in a manner that is both efficient and fundamentally fair.

profession (p. 61) occupation consisting of the following seven criteria: an organized body of theoretically grounded knowledge, advanced study, a code of ethics, prestige, standards of admission, a professional association, and a service ideal.

profoundly deaf (p. 251) incapable of any hearing.

programmatic dimension (p. 313) implementing a series of programs to gradually implement community policing into departmental operations.

Project Exile (p. 92) a coordinated approach to gun control that began in 1997 in which the U.S. Attorney's office works alongside an assistant commonwealth attorney to review cases involving felons with guns, drug users with guns, guns used in drug trafficking, and gun domestic violence referrals.

property crimes (p. 69) crimes relating to property rather than crimes against a person. The four main index property crimes in the UCR are burglary, larceny-theft, motor vehicle theft, and arson.

psychopath (p. 203) person with an anti-social personality disorder who is able to charm his victims on the one hand, but having a complete void of empathy that is often manifested in sadistic sexual pleasure.

public health model (p. 298) encourages law enforcement agencies to look at crime from a preventive standpoint, saying that just as people are responsible for their own health (through their diet, exercise) communities can take ownership of their neighborhoods and reject disorder and criminality.

public offense (p. 99) felony or misdemeanor committed in the presence of a police officer.

punitive damages (p. 103) the intent of the award is to punish or make an example of the wrongdoer, which often results in significant monetary awards.

pure speech (p. 88) words that are not accompanied by an action and are clearly protected by the U.S. Constitution.

quasi-military (p. 114) characterized by strict adherence to formal chains of command and the clear division of personnel into ranks.

quotas (p. 366) a specified number of jobs in which the police department was required to hire minorities.

race riots (p. 244) riots in the 1960s that began as an outcry to poor police practices in largely minority communities, including police brutality against minorities.

racism (p. 245) bias against racial minorities, resulting in their being treated more harshly than whites.

random patrol (p. 147) like routine patrol, when officers assigned to a specific area are asked to move around in an "unsystematic" way (usually by motor vehicle) in order to detect crimes in progress and deter crimes through presence.

reactive (p. 300) responding to an incident.

reactive beats (p. 150) when all random patrol activity is suspended and patrol officers only respond to situations.

reactive model (p. 69) model of policing that is incident-based rather than proactive.

reasonable expectations of privacy (p. 178) a person has a reasonable expectation of privacy if it is possible to show that he or she expected privacy, and that that expectation is reasonable.

reasonable suspicion (pp. 26, 93, 170) evidentiary standard, of a lesser degree than probable cause, necessary for frisks in which facts lend a person to reasonably believe that a person is carrying weapons.

recidivist (p. 29) repeat offender.

reconstruction (p. 196) when the police try to determine exactly what happened and by whom in a crime.

record management systems (RMS) (p. 341) databases for maintaining large amounts of data from the individual incident or offender level to larger organizational concerns.

relevancy (p. 330) when interpreting the meaning of information resulting from crime analysis, it is important to understand whether or not the data used in the analysis accurately reflect what is intended.

reliability (p. 330) when interpreting the meaning of information resulting from crime analysis, it is important to understand whether the same data, interpreted by different people at different times, would lead to the same conclusions.

repeat victimization (p. 310) when individuals are victims of multiple crimes, often property crimes such as burglary, since some locations are responsible for significant amounts of crime.

reported crime (p. 72) crime brought to the attention of the police.

resiliency theory (p. 315) the larger the number of risk factors influencing an individual at any given moment, the greater is the likelihood of criminal activity or other problem behavior.

response (p. 309) fourth component of the SARA model, in which strategy is selected based on what is actually causing the problem.

response time (p. 145) the time it takes an officer to respond to a citizen's call.

reverse discrimination (p. 366) hiring minorities at the expense of those in the majority.

reverse sting operations (p. 128) when officers pose as drug dealers and arrest those who buy drugs from them.

Rigel (p. 340) a computerized geographic profiling workstation that includes statistical analyses, GIS, and database management functions to aid in the process of offering calculated investigative suggestions.

risk factors (p. 314) predictor variables found to be associated with delinquent or criminal activity.

rotating shifts (p. 155) the rotation of officers across either different working hours or different divisions within the department.

routine activities theory (p. 317) in order for a crime to occur three elements must intersect at the same time and place: a motivated offender, the absence of capable guardianship, and a suitable target.

routine patrol (p. 147) in which officers assigned to a specific area are asked to move around in an "unsystematic" way (usually by motor vehicle) in order to detect crimes in progress and deter crimes through presence.

routine traffic stop (p. 159) traffic stop with no unusual circumstances or particularly high degree of risk.

rule of law (p. 10) Developed over many years through case law, statutes, and scholarly writings, this states that all people in society have the opportunity to participate in establishing the law, the rules apply to everyone, and the rule protect individuals as well as society.

S.W.A.T. (Special Weapons And Tactics) teams (p. 130) paramilitary units within many police departments that specialize in the use of force and aggressive policing techniques. They are responsible for handling high-risk law enforcement situations that are beyond the capabilities of ordinary patrol officers.

SARA (p. 308) term coined by Spelman and Eck related to the four separate components of the problem-solving process: scanning, analysis, response, and assessment.

saturation patrol (p. 150) placing extremely high levels of patrol within a narrowly defined geographic area.

scanning (p. 308) the first part of the SARA model, this is the clustering of incidents into meaningful problem units.

schizoid personality (p. 204) a person with a personality disorder characterized by being withdrawn from society.

school liaison officers (p. 133) officers who are permanently assigned to local high schools to investigate juvenile crime and serve as a resource to school staff and students.

search and seizure (p. 92) act that can be carried out by law enforcement officers in order to obtain illegal contraband. Citizens are protected from illegal searches and seizures by the Fourth Amendment, which protects citizens from unwarranted governmental intrusions.

search warrant (p. 173) formal court document obtained by an officer prior to a search specifying where the search will take place and what is to be the basis of the search.

secondary scene (p. 198) any subsequent scene of a crime after the primary crime scene.

Secret Service (p. 17) agency originally established to suppress counterfeit currency and whose duties now include protecting the President, the Vice-President, and the families of each.

seizure (p. 171) when a police officer confiscates illegal contraband in a search.

self-incrimination (p. 95) protected by the Fifth Amendment, a person does not have to say anything in a court of law that may implicate his or her guilt.

serious habituation offender criminal apprehension program (SHOCAP) (p. 309) study developed by the Office of Juvenile Justice and Delinquency Prevention that showed that 10 percent of offenders account for 55 percent of all crimes; 10 percent of victims account for 42 percent of all victimization; 10 percent of all locations account for 60 percent of the call load to the police.

service style (p. 227) style of policing described by James Q. Wilson where the police are primarily servants of the community, with particular emphasis placed on maintaining good police-public relations and on the use of informal policing methods aimed at keeping offenders out of the criminal justice system.

shall-issue statutes (p. 92) in which states create a list of objective criteria for obtaining a concealed weapon permit, and if the individual meets that criteria, the state is required to issue him or her a permit.

shire reeves (p. 40) precursor to the modern day sheriff in England.

shires (p. 40) geographic area in England similar to the American county that used to form the basis of an informal policing system.

signature (p. 202) what an offender needs or takes from a crime scene.

slave patrols (p. 45) first established in the South during the mid 1740s, officers on slave patrol were given broad powers to punish slaves who committed offenses or refused to submit to their masters.

social ecology of crime (p. 331) examination of the spatial trends of crime and delinquency by Shaw and McKay of the Chicago school.

socialization (pp. 7, 246, 370) the influences of parents, families, peers, and the community in training individuals about the norms, rules, and customs of a locality with an aim to compel conformity.

solvability factors (p. 197) anything that can potentially affect the probability of successfully concluding the case, such as the presence of witnesses and/or physical evidence.

Souillere's stages of technological advancement (p. 326) four stages of technological development in policing, consisting of introduction of mobile patrol and basic communications, technology for traffic violations, the development of response technology and an emergency hotline, and advanced technology such as imaging and GIS.

span of control (p. 116) number of people reporting to one commanding officer.

special relationship (p. 82) relationship between the police and a citizen in which litigation can arise if the police fail to protect the citizen.

specialized-enforcement partnerships (p. 306) police-corrections partnerships that are created to enforce and combat specially designated types of crimes, offenders, or problems.

Speech-plus conduct (p. 89) activities such as peaceful picketing, boycotts, and demonstrations that receive some First Amendment protection, though not to the same extent as pure speech.

spoils system (p. 48) system in the political era in which politicians appointed people to civil service jobs predominately based upon patronage, political affiliation, or in return for monetary payments.

stare decisis **(p. 98)** to follow the precedent from previous judicial decisions, this literally means "to stand on decided cases."

statutory law (p. 98) written law as passed by legislature.

stereotype (p. 246) preconceived opinion of a group of people that may be used by officers to discriminate between those citizens who are and those who are not regarded as generally law-abiding.

sting operations (p. 128) when undercover agents pose as buyers of illegal goods or services.

stop and frisk (p. 170) when the police stop a person and conduct pat-down search of the suspect on the outside of the clothing in order to determine whether the individual is carrying a weapon.

strategic crime analysis (p. 330) the collection and analysis of data spanning a long period of time.

structural changes (p. 311) a shift is the foundation of the departmental structure as the focus of the department changes from one goal (e.g., responding to incidents) to another (e.g., proactive crime prevention).

substantiated complaints (p. 280) when the officer is found guilty of the action alleged.

substantive due process (p. 94) protects against arbitrary or unfair laws.

substantive law (p. 98) defines the specific elements of the crime committed as well as the parameters available for punishment.

suppression-intervention-prevention (p. 316) strategy selection model based on the development of a needs assessment that involves targeting of specific offenders and locations, matching offenders to needed services in their community, and stopping a problem before future incidents can occur.

symbolic speech (p. 88) expression protected by the U.S. Constitution that takes place through tangible items such as signs, buttons, or flags.

systematic searches (p. 178) type of stop and search based on a systematic formula, such as roadblocks at sobriety checkpoints, allowed without probable cause.

tactical crime analysis (p. 330) data analysis using real-time data spanning several days.

tactics (p. 337) strategies used to address the patterns of crime data.

tall organizations (p. 116) organizations with many layers in the chain of command.

target area (p. 310) the particular neighborhood within the city in which the problem is occurring most often so that the police and community get a better idea of the underlying conditions that could inform strategy.

target profiling (p. 331) the use of data to determine the potential risks certain areas may have for criminal victimization based on known offense patterns in the area.

team policing model (p. 312) structure of policing consisting of assigned shift structures, increased officer discretion, team management, and despecialization.

teams (p. 312) having officers work together from different units (e.g., patrol, traffic, and the detective divisions) as a single unit to ensure that linkage blindness is minimized and needed resources are brought to bear on a problem.

telescoping (p. 73) phenomenon related to reporting of crimes in which serious incidents might be remembered as more recent to the victim than they really are leading to an over-reporting in the data.

thermal imaging (p. 175) a device used to determine the amount of heat emanating from premises.

thief catcher (p. 193) person in 18th century England who could be hired to aid in finding lost property.

thin blue line (p. 224) the belief that only the police hold off the dangers of chaos and disorder in society, and thus are themselves often tainted by their mission in society.

timeliness (p. 330) when interpreting the meaning of information resulting from crime analysis, it is important to understand whether the pattern or trend presented reflect a current problem or issue, or is it more representative of a previous situation.

tithings (p. 40) group of ten families within a shire, in which every citizen was tied to a particular tithe, and was jointly responsible with all other members of his or her group for the payment of taxes and the maintenance of order (informal policing system).

tokens (p. 367) officers that police departments were legally required to accept due to affirmative action policies.

torts (p. 100) noncriminal restrictions placed on the freedom of individuals that fall under the jurisdiction of civil law.

tour (p. 157) the sector assigned to police officers each shift at roll call.

township police departments (p. 13) police departments within the state that operate similarly to municipal police departments, though they can vary greatly according to level of law enforcement powers and authority.

traditional policing (p. 69) policing in the reform era that was based largely around patrol and incident response time.

truancy enforcement (p. 333) enforcement of school attendance.

twelve-hour plan (p. 156) shift plan in which officers work for three days at twelve hours before having the next four days off.

two-officer cars (p. 153) in which there are two patrol officers assigned per car.

Uniform Crime Reports (UCR) **(p. 69)** report on crime rates compiled by the FBI, based on crime statistics from local and state police departments, which is responsible for measuring and tracking crime trends.

unit (p. 120) within a division, staff may be organized into smaller groups, which deal with a specific aspect of the division's overall function.

U. S. Bureau of Alcohol, Tobacco and Firearms (ATF) (p. 18) an agency with the Department of Treasury, ATF originally had a taxation and licensing principal focus, but has since evolved to encompass many law enforcement operations both on its own and in collaboration with other law enforcement jurisdictions.

U.S. Marshal Service (USMS) (p. 15) U.S. agency responsible for the execution of warrants for the federal courts and the handling of federal suspects and prisoners.

U.S. Postal Service (p. 19) agency responsible for the enforcement of over 200 federal laws affecting the U.S. Mail and postal system.

us versus them (p. 268) attitude of police officers whereby they believe that non-police officers cannot understand the duties or dangers of their profession.

USA PATRIOT Act of 2001 (p. 4) rushed into implementation immediately following September 11, the PATRIOT Act grants law enforcement significantly increased investigative powers to combat terrorism, such as reductions on the probable cause requirements for certain types of warrants, expansions of the ability to gather internet usage activity, roving wiretaps, etc.

values (p. 113) the core beliefs and concerns of the department.

verbal force (p. 265) when the officer speaks to the persons against whom he or she is using force.

vertical differentiation (p. 116) the levels of formal power in an organization.

vigilante (p. 38) a person who takes the law into his or her own hands.

vigilante committees (p. 45) made up of area residents wishing to actively fight crime prior to the establishment of a formal policing system, they would take on all law enforcement duties, ranging from pursuing offenders to trying and punishing them.

vigiles **(p. 38)** first civilian police force in Rome established by the Emperor Augustus.

violation (p. 99) lesser wrong, such as not obeying a municipal ordinance, that is rarely considered to be part of the criminal law and usually results in fines.

Violent Crime Control and Law Enforcement Act (1994) (p. 157) provided funding for an additional 100,000 officers nationally to increase the availability of officers for foot patrol and other community policing functions.

Violent Criminal Apprehension Program (VICAP) (p. 206) was created by the FBI to help identify national homicide patterns. VICAP is a comprehensive database of solved and unsolved violent crimes that includes significant details related to the crime scene, victim characteristics, and offender characteristics.

violent personal crimes (p. 69) crimes against the person. The four main violent index crimes in the UCR are murder, rape, robbery, and assault.

virtual private networks (VPN) (p. 346) involve the use of encryption software to scramble the contents of communications so that even if the system becomes available to hackers, they are unable to read the information.

voiding (p. 27) when judges dismiss arrests prior to the adjudication process.

August Vollmer (p. 52) considered one of the pioneers of police reform and professionalization, Vollmer was the Chief of Police in Berkeley, California throughout the early twentieth century. Examples of some of his efforts to professionalize policing include the establishment of crime labs, enhancement of education and training standards, and significant utilization of motor vehicle patrol.

warrant (p. 92) formal court document that usually should be obtained before an arrest is made or a search is conducted.

watch systems (p. 45) consisting of volunteer citizens, these were based on the idea of community responsibility in which members of the community were required by local law enforcement officers to undertake patrols of their neighborhood under the guidance of local marshals or constables to watch for signs of criminal activity.

watchman style (p. 227) policing style described by James Q. Wilson, in which the approach places great emphasis on order maintenance and individual officer discretion.

water patrol (p. 155) types of patrol used by jurisdictions bordering on shorelines, beaches, and lakes given the tremendous amount of illegal activity that can begin on the water.

Wickersham Commission (p. 50) commission formed by Herbert Hoover in 1929 to address concerns with prohibition and the increasing crime rate, as well as problems with the juvenile justice and adult criminal justice processes.

O. W. Wilson (p. 52) protégé of August Vollmer who focused on use of science and technology in policing in the Reform Era, specifically in relation to response time and efficiency.

wiretapping (pp. 93, 179) electronic "search" of a phone or a computer in which words can be "seized."

working personality (p. 225) resulting from the solidarity within police culture, this is the idea that the police find it acceptable to lie to protect another officer, back up their fellow officers when dealing with the authorities, expect to be backed up in return, and do not support their fellow officers are regarded as "rats," who are not to be trusted and deserve to be excluded from the group.

writ (p. 28) a formal document requesting an appeal.

writ of certiorari (p. 28) a formal document requesting an appeal to have a case reviewed by the U.S. Supreme Court.

zero-tolerance policing (p. 217) when police officers are required to stop anyone they see committing such offenses, and have little or no discretion as to whether or not to arrest.

Index

Photo Credits